NINTH EDITION

THE POLICE
IN AMERICA

AN INTRODUCTION

SAMUEL WALKER
UNIVERSITY OF NEBRASKA AT OMAHA

CHARLES M. KATZ
ARIZONA STATE UNIVERSITY

Mc
Graw
Hill
Education

THE POLICE IN AMERICA: AN INTRODUCTION, NINTH EDITION

Published by McGraw-Hill Education, 2 Penn Plaza, New York, NY 10121. Copyright © 2018 by McGraw-Hill Education. All rights reserved. Printed in the United States of America. Previous editions © 2011, 2008, and 2005. No part of this publication may be reproduced or distributed in any form or by any means, or stored in a database or retrieval system, without the prior written consent of McGraw-Hill Education, including, but not limited to, in any network or other electronic storage or transmission, or broadcast for distance learning.

Some ancillaries, including electronic and print components, may not be available to customers outside the United States.

This book is printed on acid-free paper.

1 2 3 4 5 6 7 8 9 LCR 21 20 19 18 17

ISBN 978-1-259-14076-1
MHID 1-259-14076-8

Chief Product Officer, SVP Products & Markets: *G. Scott Virkler*
Vice President, General Manager, Products & Markets: *Michael Ryan*
Vice President, Content Design & Delivery: *Betsy Whalen*
Managing Director: *David Patterson*
Brand Manager: *Jamie Laferera*
Market Development Manager: *Meredith Leo*
Director, Content Design & Delivery: *Terri Schiesl*
Program Manager: *Deb Hash*
Content Project Managers: *Rick Hecker and Katie Klochan*
Buyer: *Sandy Ludovissey*
Design: *Jessica Serd*
Content Licensing Specialist: *Melisa Seegmiller*
Cover Image: *(c) Erica Simone Leeds; © McGraw-Hill Education; © Getty Images; © Shutterstock*
Compositor: *Aptara, Inc.*
Printer: *LSC Communications*

All credits appearing on page or at the end of the book are considered to be an extension of the copyright page.

Library of Congress Cataloging-in-Publication Data

Names: Walker, Samuel, 1942- author. | Katz, Charles M., author.
Title: The police in America : an introduction / Samuel Walker, University of
   Nebraska at Omaha, Charles M. Katz, Arizona State University.
Description: Ninth Edition. | Dubuque, IA : McGraw-Hill Education, [2017] |
   Revised edition of the authors' The police in America, c2013.
Identifiers: LCCN 2016053271| ISBN 9781259140761 (alk. paper) | ISBN
   1259140768 (alk. paper)
Subjects: LCSH: Police--United States. | Police administration--United States.
Classification: LCC HV8139 .W35 2017 | DDC 363.20973--dc23 LC record available at
   https://lccn.loc.gov/2016053271

The Internet addresses listed in the text were accurate at the time of publication. The inclusion of a website does not indicate an endorsement by the authors or McGraw-Hill Education, and McGraw-Hill Education does not guarantee the accuracy of the information presented at these sites.

mheducation.com/highered

About the Authors

Samuel Walker   Dr. Samuel Walker is Professor Emeritus at the University of Nebraska at Omaha, where he taught for 31 years before retiring in 2005. He is the author of 14 books on policing, criminal justice policy, and civil liberties. He continues to write and consult in the area of police accountability, with a special interest in police early intervention systems and federal litigation against police misconduct.

Charles Katz   Dr. Charles Katz is the Watts Family Director of the Center for Violence Prevention and Community Safety and is a Professor in the School of Criminology and Criminal Justice at Arizona State University. Dr. Katz earned his Ph.D. in Criminal Justice from the University of Nebraska at Omaha in 1997. He is coauthor of *Policing Gangs in America* (published by Cambridge University Press) and numerous articles on policing and gangs. He is currently working with several large metropolitan police agencies evaluating programs and practices.

Contents in Brief

Preface XVI

PART I Foundations 1

1 Police and Society 2
2 The History of the American Police 28
3 The Contemporary Law Enforcement Industry 70

PART II Officers and Organizations 101

4 Police Organizations 102
5 Police Officers I: Recruitment and Training for a Changing Society 130
6 Police Officers II: On the Job 166

PART III Police Work 211

7 Patrol: The Backbone of Policing 212
8 Peacekeeping and Order Maintenance 250
9 The Police and Crime 282
10 Advances in Police Strategy 324

PART IV Issues in Policing 367

11 Police Discretion 368
12 Legitimacy and Police—Community Relations 404
13 Police Corruption 454
14 Accountability of the Police 488

PART V Challenges for a New Century 543

15 The Future of Policing in America 544

Glossary 569 | Name Index 581 | Subject Index 584

Contents

Preface XVI

PART I Foundations 1

CHAPTER 1
Police and Society 2

The Goals of This Book 3

Why Do We Have Police? 3

A Framework for Understanding the Police and Policing 4

A Democratic Police 5

Democracy and Accountability 5

A Legitimate Police 6

Procedural Justice 7

Practices That Build Legitimacy 8

Legitimacy and Police—Public Interactions 8

Legitimacy, Trust, and Race Relations 9

An Open and Transparent Police 10

Practices That Create Openness and Transparency 11

An Accountable Police 12

Police Accountability: Goals and Methods 12

Accountability on Police Use of Force 12

Collecting and Analyzing Data on Use of Force 14

Accountability in Routine Police—Public Contacts 15

Training to Prevent Bias in Police Activities 15

Independent Investigations and Review of Critical Incidents 16

An Effective Police 17

The Complex Responsibilities of the Police 17

Ineffective Strategies for Controlling Crime and Disorder 18

Effective Strategies for Controlling Crime and Disorder 21

Partnerships with the Public 21

A Special Case: The Police and the Mentally Ill 22

A Special Case: The Police and Juveniles 23

Research and Policing: Evidence-Based Programs 23

Summary 24

Key Terms 25

For Discussion 25

Internet Exercises 25

CHAPTER 2
The History of the American Police 28

Flashback: Moments in American Police History 29

The First American Police Officer 29

Flash Forward: 1950 29

Why Study Police History? 29

The English Heritage 30

Creation of the Modern Police: London, 1829 31

Law Enforcement in Colonial America 32

The Quality of Colonial Law Enforcement 32

The First Modern American Police 33

The "Political Era" in American Policing, 1830s–1900 34

A Lack of Personnel Standards 35

Patrol Work in the Political Era 35

The Police and the Public 36

Corruption and Politics 37

Immigration, Discrimination, and Police Corruption 38

The Failure of Police Reform 39

The Impact of the Police on Crime and Disorder 40

The Professional Era, 1900—1960 40

The Police Professionalization Movement 41

The Reform Agenda 41

The Achievements of Professionalization 42

Other Impacts of Professionalization 43

Police and Race Relations 44

New Law Enforcement Agencies 44

Technology Revolutionizes Policing 45

New Directions in Police Administration, 1930—1960 47

The Wickersham Commission Bombshell 47

Professionalization Continues 47

Simmering Racial and Ethnic Relations 48

J. Edgar Hoover and the War on Crime 48

The Police Crises of the 1960s 49

The Police and the Supreme Court 49

The Police and Civil Rights 51

The Police in the National Spotlight 52

The Research Revolution 53

New Developments in Policing, 1970—2016 55

The Changing Police Officer 55

Administrative Rulemaking and the Control of Police Discretion 56

The Emergence of Police Unions 57

The Spread of Citizen Oversight of Police 57

Community Policing, Problem-Oriented Policing, and Other Innovations 58

Data-Driven Policing 60

Racial Profiling and Discrimination 60

Federal Investigations of Police Misconduct 61

Local Police and the War on Terrorism 62

The National Police Crisis, 2014—2016 63

CASE STUDY: De-escalating Police—Citizen Encounters 63

Summary 64

Key Terms 65

For Discussion 65

Internet Exercises 65

CHAPTER 3
The Contemporary Law Enforcement Industry 70

Basic Features of American Law Enforcement 71

An "Industry" Perspective 71

An International Perspective 72

Size and Scope of the Law Enforcement Industry 73

The Number of Law Enforcement Agencies 73

The Number of Law Enforcement Personnel 74

Understanding Law Enforcement Personnel Data 74

Civilianization 75

The Police—Population Ratio 75

The Cost of Police Protection 75

The Fragmentation Issue 76

Alternatives to Fragmentation 77

The Fragmentation Problem Reconsidered 79

Municipal Police 80

County Police 80

The County Sheriff 81

The Role of the Sheriff 81

Other Local Agencies 82

The Constable 82

The Coroner/Medical Examiner 82

Special District Police 83

Tribal Police 83

State Law Enforcement Agencies 85

Federal Law Enforcement Agencies 86

Federal Law Enforcement after September 11, 2001 86

The Private Security Industry 90

Minimum Standards: American Style 93

The Role of the Federal Government 93

The Role of State Governments 93

Accreditation 94

CASE STUDY: The Fraser/Winter Park (CO) Police Department 94

Summary 96

Key Terms 96

For Discussion 96

Internet Exercises 96

PART **II** Officers and Organizations 101

CHAPTER **4**
Police Organizations 102

The Quasi-Military Style of Police Organizations 103

Criticisms of the Quasi-Military Style 103

Police Departments as Organizations 105

The Dominant Style of American Police Organizations 105

Police Organizations as Bureaucracies 105

The Problems with Bureaucracy 108

The Positive Contributions of Bureaucracy in Policing 108

Informal Aspects of Police Organizations 108

Bureaucracy and Police Professionalism 110

Changing Police Organizations 110

Community Policing 110

Task Forces 112

COMPSTAT 113

Civil Service 115

Police Unions 116

Aspects of Police Unions 116

Collective Bargaining 117

Grievance Procedures 117

Impasse Settlement and Strikes 117

The Impact of Police Unions 120

Police Organizations and Their Environment 122

Contingency Theory 122

Institutional Theory 122

Resource Dependency Theory 123

CASE STUDY: COMPSTAT in Chicago 124

Summary 125

Key Terms 125

For Discussion 125

Internet Exercises 126

CHAPTER **5**
Police Officers I: Recruitment and Training for a Changing Society 130

The Changing American Police Officer 131

What Kind of Police Officer Do We Want? And for What Kind of Policing? 131

The Police Personnel Process 132

A Career Perspective 133

Beyond Stereotypes of Cops 133

The Personnel Process: A Shared Responsibility 134

Recruiting Police Officers 134

What Kind of Job? What Kind of Person? 135

Minimum Qualifications 135

The Recruitment Effort 139

Choosing Law Enforcement as a Career 139

Applicants' Motivations 139

Obstacles to Recruitment 140

Testing and Selecting Applicants 141

Selection Tests 141

Background Investigations 142

Predicting Police Officer Performance 142

Achieving Diversity in Police Employment 143

The Goals of Diversity 143

The Law of Equal Employment Opportunity 144

"Not Your Father's Police Department": Diversity in Policing 144

Women in Policing 146

Employment Discrimination Suits 147

The Impact of Increased Diversity 149

Police Training: Progress and New Challenges 149

New Thinking about Policing and Training 150

The Police Academy 150

Training on the Use of Force 152

Tactical Decision-Making 153

Scenario-Based Training 153

Fragmented and Inconsistent Training 154

The Consequences of Inadequate Training 154

Training on Unconscious Bias 155

Training on Procedural Justice 155

Field Training 155

In-Service Training 156

Training of Supervisors 157

The Probationary Period 157

CASE STUDY: Improving Training for Domestic Violence Incidents: A Problem-Oriented Approach 158

Summary 159

Key Terms 159

For Discussion 160

Internet Exercises 160

CHAPTER **6**
Police Officers II: On the Job 166

Reality Shock: Beginning Police Work 168

Encountering Citizens 168

Encountering the Criminal Justice System 169

Encountering the Department 169

Starting Out on the Job 170

Impact of the Seniority System 170

The Concept of a Unique Police Subculture 172

The Original Concept 172

The Capacity to Use Force as a Defining Feature of Policing 174

The Dangers of Policing: Potential versus Actual 175

Conflicting Work Demands 177

New Perspectives on a Complex and Changing Police Subculture 178

The Changing Rank and File: The Impact of Diversity 179

The Impact of Women Police Officers on the Police Subculture 179

Women Officers on Patrol Duty 181

Female versus Male Officers: Differences in Misconduct Issues 181

Sexual Harassment on the Job 182

African American Officers 182

African American Officers on the Job 183

Hispanic Officers 183

Gay and Lesbian Officers 184

The Intersection of Gender, Race, Ethnicity, and Sexual Identity 185

Does Diversifying a Department Change the Police Subculture? 186

Rising Levels of Police Officer Education 186

Cohort Effects on Performance 187

Organizational Effects on Attitudes and Performance 187

Attitudes toward Community Policing 188

The Relationship between Attitudes and Behavior 189

Styles of Police Work 189

Moving through Police Careers 190

Salaries and Benefits 190

Career Development 191

Promotion 191

Assignment to Special Units 192

Lateral Entry 193

Outside Employment 193

Performance Evaluations 194

Traditional Performance Evaluations 194

Problems with Performance Evaluations 195

Job Satisfaction and Job Stress 196

The Sources of Job Satisfaction 196

The Sources of Job Stress 197

Job Stress and Suicide 198

Community Policing and Job Satisfaction 199

Coping with Job Stress 200

The Rights of Police Officers 200

Turnover: Leaving Police Work 202

Decertification 203

Summary 203

Key Terms 204

For Discussion 204

Internet Exercise 204

PART III Police Work 211

CHAPTER 7
Patrol: The Backbone of Policing 212

The Central Role of Patrol 213

The Functions of Patrol 214

The Organization and Delivery of Patrol 214

Factors Affecting the Delivery of Patrol Services 214

Number of Sworn Officers 214

Assignment to Patrol 216

The Distribution of Patrol Officers 216

Assignment of Patrol Officers 218

"Hot Spots" 218

Types of Patrol 218

Foot Patrol 219

One-Officer versus Two-Officer Cars 219

Staffing Patrol Beats 220

Styles of Patrol 220

Individual Styles 220

Supervisors' Styles 221

Organizational Styles 221

Patrol Supervision: The Role of the Sergeant 222

The Communications Center 223

The Nerve Center of Policing 223

911 Systems 223

Processing Calls for Service 224

Operator—Citizen Interactions 226

The Systematic Study of Police Patrol 226

Standards for Systematic Social Observation 226

The Call Service Workload 228

The Volume of Calls 228

Types of Calls 228

Aspects of Patrol Work 230

Response Time 230

Officer Use of Patrol Time 231

Evading Duty 232

High-Speed Pursuits 232

The Effectiveness of Patrol 233

Initial Experiments 233

The Kansas City Preventive Patrol Experiment 234

Findings and Implications of the Kansas City Experiment 235

The Newark Foot Patrol Experiment 236

New Questions, New Approaches 237

Improving Traditional Patrol 237

Differential Response to Calls 237

Telephone Reporting Units 238

311 Nonemergency Numbers 238

Non-English 911 Call Services 239

Reverse 911 239

Computers and Video Cameras in Patrol Cars 239

Police Aides or Cadets 240

Directed Patrol and Hot Spots 241

Customer Feedback 242

Beyond Traditional Patrol 242

CASE STUDY: The Philadelphia Foot Patrol Experiment by Jerry Ratcliffe et al. 242

Summary 244

Key Terms 245

For Discussion 245

Internet Exercises 245

CHAPTER 8
Peacekeeping and Order Maintenance 250

The Police Role 251

Calling the Police 252

Public Expectations 252

Police Response 252

Traffic Enforcement 253

Drunk-Driving Crackdowns 255

Policing Domestic Disputes 256

Defining Our Terms 256

The Prevalence of Domestic Violence 257

Calling the Police 257

Police Response to Domestic Disturbances 258

Factors Influencing the Arrest Decision 259

A Revolution in Policy: Mandatory Arrest 260

The Impact of Arrest on Domestic Violence 260

Impact of Mandatory Arrest Laws and
Policies 262

Other Laws and Policies 262

The Future of Domestic Violence Policy 263

Policing Prostitution 263

Policing the Homeless 266

Policing the Mentally Ill 267

Police Response to the Mentally Ill 268

Old Problems/New Programs 269

Policing People with HIV 271

Policing Juveniles 272

Controversy over the Police Role 273

Specialized Juvenile Units 273

On-the-Street Encounters 274

The Issue of Race Discrimination 275

Crime Prevention Programs 275

**CASE STUDY: Responding to Chronically Inebriated
Individuals in Seattle, Washington 276**

Summary 276

Key Terms 277

For Discussion 277

Internet Exercises 277

CHAPTER **9**
The Police and Crime 282

The Police and Crime 283

Crime Control Strategies 283

Crime Control Assumptions 284

Measuring Effectiveness 285

Preventing Crime 285

Apprehending Criminals 286

Citizen Reporting of Crime 286

Reporting and Unfounding Crimes 288

Criminal Investigation 289

Myths about Detective Work 289

The Organization of Detective Work 290

The Investigation Process 291

The Preliminary Investigation 291

Arrest Discretion 291

Follow-Up Investigations 291

The Reality of Detective Work 292

Case Screening 292

**Measuring the Effectiveness of Criminal
Investigation 293**

The Clearance Rate 293

Defining an Arrest 294

Success and Failure in Solving Crimes 295

Case Structural Factors 295

Organizational Factors 296

Environmental Factors 297

Officer Productivity 297

The Problem of Case Attrition 298

**The Use of Eyewitness Identification,
Criminalistics, and DNA in
Investigations 298**

Eyewitness Identification 298

Criminalistics 299

DNA 299

Improving Criminal Investigations 300

Special Investigative Techniques 301

Undercover Police Work 301

Informants 302

Policing Drugs 303

Drug Enforcement Strategies 303

Minorities and the War on Drugs 304

The Special Case of Marijuana 305

Demand Reduction: The D.A.R.E. Program 306

Policing Gangs and Gang-Related Crime 306

Gang Suppression 307

Gang Prevention: The G.R.E.A.T. Program 308

Policing Career Criminals 308

Policing Guns and Gun Crimes 309

Gun Suppression 309

Policing Hate Crime 311

The Scope and Nature of Hate Crime 311

The Police Response to Hate Crime 312

Policing and Terrorism 313

The Scope and Nature of Terrorism 313

Domestic Terrorism 313

Foreign Terrorism 314

Responding to Terrorism 314

CASE STUDY: Untested Evidence in Law Enforcement Agencies 316

Summary 318

Key Terms 318

For Discussion 318

Internet Exercises 318

C H A P T E R **10**
Advances in Police Strategy 324

Impetus for Change in Policing 325

The Roots of Community Policing: The Broken Windows Hypothesis 326

Types of Disorder 327

Characteristics of Community Policing 327

Community Partnerships 329

The Effectiveness of Community Partnerships 332

Organizational Change 333

Evidence of Organizational Change 335

Problem Solving 336

Pulling It All Together: Implementing Community Policing at the Departmental Level 337

Chicago Alternative Policing Strategy (CAPS) Program 337

Community Policing: Problems and Prospects 342

A Legitimate Police Role? 342

A Political Police? 342

Decentralization and Accountability 343

Impact on Poor and Minority Communities 344

Conflicting Community Interests 344

But Does Community Policing Work? 344

The Roots of Problem-Oriented Policing 345

The Problem-Solving Process 347

Scanning 348

Analysis 349

Response 349

Assessment 349

Effectiveness of Problem-Oriented Policing 349

Problem-Oriented Policing in Newport News 349

Problem-Oriented Policing in San Diego 351

The Boston Gun Project: Operation Cease Fire 351

The Future of Problem-Oriented Policing 352

Characteristics of Zero-Tolerance Policing 353

The Effectiveness of Zero-Tolerance Policing 355

Zero-Tolerance Policing in New York City 355

Operation Restoration 357

Potential Problems with Zero-Tolerance Policing 357

But Does Zero Tolerance Policing Work? 359

CASE STUDY: Using Social Media as a Virtual Form of Neighborhood Watch in Sacramento, California 360

Summary 360

Key Terms 361

For Discussion 361

Internet Exercises 361

P A R T **IV** Issues in Policing **367**

C H A P T E R **11**
Police Discretion 368

Discretion in Police Work 369

A Definition of Discretion 370

New Perspectives on Police Discretion 370

A Short History of the Study of Police Discretion 370

A Richer Understanding of Police—Citizen Encounters 371

Potential Abuse of Discretion 372

Positive Uses of Discretion 373

Decision Points and Decision Makers 374

Patrol Officers' Decisions 374

Detectives' Decisions 375

Police Managers' Decisions 375

Underlying Sources of Police Discretion 375

The Nature of the Criminal Law 375

Conflicting Public Expectations 376

Social and Medical Issues 377

The Work Environment of Policing 377

Limited Police Resources 378

Factors Limiting Patrol Officer Discretion 379

Legal Factors 379

Administrative Factors 379

Organizational Culture Factors 380

Factors Influencing Discretionary Arrest Decisions 380

Situational Factors 380

Organizational Factors 384

Social and Political Factors 385

The Control of Discretion 385

The Need for Control 385

Abolish Discretion? 386

Enhancing Professional Judgment 387

Informal Bureaucratic Controls 387

Administrative Rulemaking: Controls through Written Policies 388

Examples of Administrative Rulemaking 388

Principles of Administrative Rulemaking 390

Contributions of Written Rules 390

The Impact of Administrative Rulemaking 392

Ensuring Compliance with Rules 392

Codifying Rules: The Standard Operation Procedure Manual 394

Systematic Rulemaking 395

Citizen Oversight and Policymaking 396

The Limits of Administrative Rulemaking 396

CASE STUDY: "Broken Windows" and Police Discretion 397

Summary 398

Key Terms 398

For Discussion 398

Internet Exercises 399

CHAPTER **12**
Legitimacy and Police—Community Relations 404

From Police—Community Relations to Legitimacy 405

The National Police Crisis, 2014—2016 405

Legitimacy and Procedural Justice 406

The Many Communities in Police-Community Relations 407

Understanding Race and Ethnicity 408

Official Data on Race and Ethnicity 408

The Major Racial and Ethnic Groups 409

Public Opinion about the Police 411

Factors that Affect Public Opinion about the Police 411

The Impact of Controversial Incidents 414

Additional Perspectives on the Police in American Society 415

The Police and American Society 415

The Police and Other Occupations 415

The American Police in International Perspective 416

Police Officer Perceptions of Citizens 417

Police—Citizen Interactions: Sources of Police—Community Relations Problems and Loss of Legitimacy 418

The Level of Neighborhood Police Protection 419

Delay in Responding to 911 Calls 420

Police Use of Deadly Force 420

Unconscious Bias and Police Use of Deadly Force 422

Use of Physical Force 423

Patterns in Officer Use of Force 424

Stops and Frisks 425

Arrests 426

Arrests and the War on Drugs 427

The Complex Interaction of Demeanor, Race, and Arrests 427

David Kennedy on the "Racial Divide" 428

Unconscious Bias, Stereotyping, and Arrests 429

Verbal Abuse and Racial and Ethnic Slurs 430

Traffic Enforcement and Racial Profiling 430

Building Legitimacy and Improving Police-Community Relations 436

The Different Dimensions of Trust and Confidence in the Police 436

Engaging the Community 438

Perspective: The Failure of the Police—Community Relations Unites in the 1960s 439

Ending Police Misconduct 440

Engaging Immigrant Communities 441

Immigration and Cultural Barriers in Policing 442

Language Barriers in Policing 442

A Representative Police Force 443

Citizen Oversight of the Police 444

Assign Officers on the Basis of Race or Ethnicity? 444

Do Citizens Care about the Ethnicity of the Officer? 445

Special Training over Race and Ethnicity 445

Summary 446

Key Terms 446

For Discussion 447

Internet Exercises 447

CHAPTER **13**
Police Corruption 454

A Definition of Police Corruption 455

The Costs of Police Corruption 456

Types of Corruption 458

Gratuities 458

Bribes 458

Theft and Burglary 460

Sexual Misconduct 461

Internal Corruption 463

Corruption and Brutality 463

Levels of Corruption 464

Pervasiveness of Corruption within a Police Organization 465

Theories of Police Corruption 466

Individual Officer Explanations 466

Social Structural Explanations 466

Neighborhood Explanations 468

The Nature of Police Work 468

The Police Organization 469

The Police Subculture 469

Becoming Corrupt 470

The Moral Careers of Individual Officers 470

Corrupting Organizations 471

Controlling Corruption 471

Internal Corruption Control Strategies 472

The Attitude of the Chief 472

Rules and Regulations 472

Managing Anticorruption Investigations 473

Investigative Tactics 474

Cracking the "Blue Curtain" 475

Proactive Integrity Tests 475

Effective Supervision 476

Rewarding the Good Officers 476

Personnel Recruitment 476

Field Training 478

External Corruption Control Approaches 479

Special Investigations 479

Criminal Prosecution 479

Mobilizing Public Opinion 482

Altering the External Environment 482

The Limits of Anticorruption Efforts 482

CASE STUDY: **Hurricane Katrina and the New Orleans Police Department 483**

Summary 483

Key Terms 484

For Discussion 484

Internet Exercises 484

CHAPTER **14**
Accountability of the Police 488

What Do We Mean by Police Accountability? 489

The Dilemmas of Policing in a Democracy 490

A Historical Perspective on Accountability 490

Accountability for *What* the Police Do 491

The Traditional Approach to Measuring Police Effectiveness 491

Alternative Measures and Their Limitations 492

COMPSTAT: A Neighborhood-Focused Approach 494

Accountability for *How* the Police Do Their Job 494

Internal Mechanisms of Accountability 495

Routine Supervision of Patrol Officers 495

Coaching, Mentoring, Leading, and Helping 498

Organizational Culture and Accountability 498

Command-Level Review of Force Incidents: The Emerging Standard 499

Corrective Action: Informal and Formal 500

Performance Evaluations 500

Internal Affairs/Professional Standards Units 501

The Discipline Process 502

Appropriate Levels of Discipline 503

Openness and Transparency for Disciplinary Actions 504

Standards for Investigating Citizen Complaints 504

Using Discipline Records in Personnel Decisions 505

The "Code of Silence" 505

Early Intervention Systems 506

Officers with Performance Problems 506

The Nature and Purpose of an EIS 507

Performance Indicators and Thresholds 507

Interventions for Officers 509

The Multiple Goals of an EIS 510

The Effectiveness of an EIS 511

Risk Management and Police Legal Advisors 511

Accreditation for Law Enforcement Agencies 512

The Nature of Accreditation 512

Pros and Cons of Accreditation 513

External Mechanisms of Accountability 513

Guiding the Police through the Political Process 513

The Courts and the Police 514

Federal "Pattern or Practice" Suits 518

The Collaborative Reform Approach: An Alternative to Litigation 522

Injunctions to Stop Patterns of Police Misconduct 423

Criminal Prosecution of Police Officers 523

Citizen Oversight of the Police 524

Blue-Ribbon Commissions 527

The Digital Revolution and Police Accountability 527

The News Media as a Police Accountability Mechanism 528

Public Interest Groups and Accountability 529

Accountability and Crime Control: A Trade-Off? 530

Conclusion: A Mixed Approach to Police Accountability 531

CASE STUDY: Policing Los Angeles under a Consent Decree: The Dynamics of Change at the LAPD: Executive Summary 532

Summary 533

Key Terms 534

Internet Exercises 534

PART **V** Challenges for a New Century 543

CHAPTER **15**
The Future of Policing in America 544

Police Technology 545

Major Technology Applications 545

The Use of Technology in the Field 548

The Future of Police Information Technology 552

Technologically Advanced Weapons 553

Crime Analysis 554

Types of Crime Analysis 554

Crime Mapping 555

The Outlook for Police Employment 556

Opportunities in Local, County, and State Law Enforcement 557

Local, County, and State Salaries 558

Opportunities in Federal Law Enforcement 558

Federal Salaries 558

The Future of Police Research 559

Does Research Do Any Good? 559

Politics and Research 560

Police Practitioner—Researcher Relationships 560

The Future of Federal Support for Research 561

Impact of the War on Terrorism 561

Role Expansion 562

Racial and Ethnic Profiling 562

Personnel Challenges 562

Role Change 563

CASE STUDY: Evaluating the Impact of Officer-Worn Body Cameras in Phoenix, Arizona, Project Focus 564

Summary 565

Key Terms 566

For Discussion 566

Internet Exercises 566

Glossary 569 | Name Index 581 | Subject Index 584

Preface

The Police in America: An Introduction provides a comprehensive introduction to the foundations of policing in the United States today. Descriptive and analytical, the text is designed to offer undergraduate students a balanced and up-to-date overview of who the police are and what they do, the problems they face, and the many reforms and innovations that have taken place in policing. The book is designed primarily for undergraduates enrolled in their first police or law enforcement course—such as an introduction to policing, police and society, or law enforcement systems.

Changes in the Ninth Edition

The ninth edition of *The Police in America: An Introduction* has undergone extensive revision. In response to reviewer feedback, we have not only updated all of the statistical information but also provided new examples of several important issues throughout the book. We have also included coverage of the latest research and practices in policing. Some of the most important changes we have made for the ninth edition are as follows:

- Chapter 1, "Police and Society" has been completely revised to use the President's Task Force on 21st Century Policing as a framework for understanding the police in America,.
- Chapter 2, "The History of the American Police," has been expanded to include discussion of the national police crisis of 2014–2016 and its impact.
- Chapter 3, "The Contemporary Law Enforcement Industry," has been revised and updated to include the most current data of law enforcement organizations.
- Chapter 4, "Police Organizations," has been revised to include the most important new research on law enforcement organizations.
- Chapter 5, "Recruitment and Training for a Changing Society," has been completely revised to incorporate the important new developments related to police training.
- Chapter 6, "Police Officers II: On the Job," includes a completely revised discussion of the police officer subculture and its impact on police officer behavior.
- Chapter 7, "Patrol: The Backbone of Policing," was revised to include the latest research on innovations in police patrol.
- Chapter 8, "Peacekeeping and Order Maintenance," has been expanded to include the latest research on policing traffic, domestic violence, and other social problems.
- Chapter 9, "The Police and Crime," has been extensively revised to include the latest research on policing gangs, drugs, and terrorism.

- Chapter 10, "Advances in Police Strategy" has been revised to include new perspectives on the goals and effectiveness of recent police innovations.
- Chapter 11, "Police Discretion," was revised to include new perspectives on the complexity of officer exercise of discretion.
- Chapter 12, "Legitimacy and Police-Community Relations," has been revised to incorporate the new interest in and reforms related to legitimacy because of the national police crisis, 2014–2016.
- Chapter 13, "Police Corruption," has been revised to incorporate new perspectives and research on police corruption.
- Chapter 14, "Accountability of the Police," has been extensively revised to include material and the full range of both internal and external accountability mechanisms.
- Chapter 15, "The Future of Policing in America," has been updated to include discussions of the latest developments related to technology, employment, police research and terrorism.

Overview of the Contents

Part I, "Foundations," provides students with an introduction to policing in America. It explains the role of the police in the United States, along with the realities of police work and the many factors that shape policing. It also traces the history of the police from the creation of the first modern police department through the many new developments that can be found in policing today. The section concludes with a discussion of the characteristics of the contemporary law enforcement industry, including a section on the Department of Homeland Security.

Part II, "Officers and Organizations," begins with an explanation of the characteristics of police organization, the role and influence of police unions, and a discussion of the theoretical rationales for why police organizations behave the way they do. It also includes an explanation of police recruitment, selection, and training practices, as well as a discussion of the characteristics of American police officers. The section covers the reality shock that officers encounter when beginning their job, the concept of police culture, and the relationship between the attitudes of the police and the behavior of the police.

Part III, "Police Work," includes explanations of what the police do and how they do it. Among the subjects covered are the functions of patrol, the delivery of services, and the effectiveness of traditional policing strategies. This section also discusses the various problems that the police face while on the job and the strategies they use to respond to these problems. The section closes with a discussion of advances in police strategy, such as community policing, problem-oriented policing, and zero-tolerance policing.

Part IV, "Issues in Policing," covers the various problems that police officers and police organizations encounter. The chapter on police discretion explains the nature of police discretion, sources of discretion, and how police organizations have attempted to control discretion. The section also includes a chapter on legitimacy and police–community relations. Attention is placed on citizen perceptions of the police, police perceptions of citizens, and sources of police–community relations problems.

Special emphasis is placed on race and ethnicity and its implications for policing in the United States. This section includes chapters on police corruption and police accountability, which discuss different types of police misbehavior and the strategies used to hold the police accountable.

Part V, "Challenges for a New Century," concludes the book with a chapter on the future of policing in America.

Pedagogy

A number of learning devices are included to make the text easier to teach and, for students, easier to learn, enlivening the material with practical, concrete examples and applications:

- Boxes called "Police in Focus" discuss a series of important issues in policing. This feature is designed to highlight particularly important points and can serve as the basis for class discussion. In each case, references are provided for students who want to pursue the issue further.
- Sidebars throughout the book expound on important concepts and feature contemporary issues related to the chapter.
- Cross-reference icons direct students to material elsewhere in the text that can further illuminate chapter topics.
- Chapter-opening outlines guide students through each chapter.
- Key terms are highlighted in the margins, boldfaced in the text, listed at the end of the chapter, and defined in a comprehensive glossary at the end of the book.
- End-of-chapter case studies—real-world examples that highlight major concepts or ideas from each chapter—enable students to begin to apply what they have learned.
- "Internet Exercises" at the end of each chapter can be used by students for further web-based study.
- "For Discussion" questions at the end of each chapter can be used to stimulate classroom discussion.

connect

The ninth edition of *The Police in America: An Introduction* is now available online with Connect, McGraw-Hill Education's integrated assignment and assessment platform. Connect also offers SmartBook for the new edition, which is the first adaptive reading experience proven to improve grades and help students study more effectively. All of the title's website and ancillary content is also available through Connect, including:

- An Instructor's Manual for each chapter.
- A full Test Bank of multiple choice questions that test students on central concepts and ideas in each chapter.
- Lecture Slides for instructor use in class.

©Getty Images/iStockphoto

McGraw-Hill Connect®
Learn Without Limits

Connect is a teaching and learning platform that is proven to deliver better results for students and instructors.

Connect empowers students by continually adapting to deliver precisely what they need, when they need it, and how they need it, so your class time is more engaging and effective.

Connect's Impact on Retention Rates, Pass Rates, and Average Exam Scores

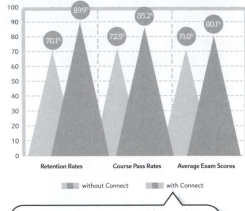

- without Connect
- with Connect

73% of instructors who use **Connect** require it; instructor satisfaction **increases** by 28% when **Connect** is required.

Using **Connect** improves retention rates by **19.8%**, passing rates by **12.7%**, and exam scores by **9.1%**.

Analytics

Connect Insight®

Connect Insight is Connect's new one-of-a-kind visual analytics dashboard—now available for both instructors and students—that provides at-a-glance information regarding student performance, which is immediately actionable. By presenting assignment, assessment, and topical performance results together with a time metric that is easily visible for aggregate or individual results, Connect Insight gives the user the ability to take a just-in-time approach to teaching and learning, which was never before available. Connect Insight presents data that empowers students and helps instructors improve class performance in a way that is efficient and effective.

Impact on Final Course Grade Distribution

without Connect		with Connect
22.9%	A	31.0%
27.4%	B	34.3%
22.9%	C	18.7%
11.5%	D	6.1%
15.4%	F	9.9%

Students can view their results for any **Connect** course.

Mobile

Connect's new, intuitive mobile interface gives students and instructors flexible and convenient, anytime–anywhere access to all components of the Connect platform.

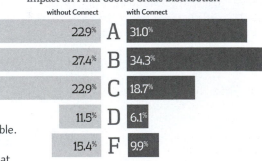

Adaptive

THE **ADAPTIVE READING EXPERIENCE** DESIGNED TO TRANSFORM THE WAY STUDENTS READ

More students earn **A's** and **B's** when they use McGraw-Hill Education **Adaptive** products.

SmartBook®

Proven to help students improve grades and study more efficiently, SmartBook contains the same content within the print book, but actively tailors that content to the needs of the individual. SmartBook's adaptive technology provides precise, personalized instruction on what the student should do next, guiding the student to master and remember key concepts, targeting gaps in knowledge and offering customized feedback, and driving the student toward comprehension and retention of the subject matter. Available on tablets, SmartBook puts learning at the student's fingertips—anywhere, anytime.

Over **8 billion questions** have been answered, making McGraw-Hill Education products more intelligent, reliable, and precise.

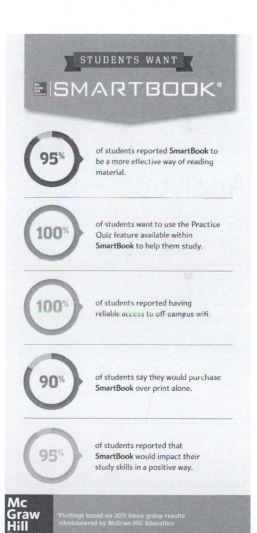

STUDENTS WANT

SMARTBOOK®

95% of students reported SmartBook to be a more effective way of reading material.

100% of students want to use the Practice Quiz feature available within SmartBook to help them study.

100% of students reported having reliable access to off-campus wifi.

90% of students say they would purchase SmartBook over print alone.

95% of students reported that SmartBook would impact their study skills in a positive way.

Mc Graw Hill Education

*Findings based on 2015 focus group results administered by McGraw-Hill Education

www.mheducation.com

Acknowledgments

Samuel Walker would like to thank his colleagues and friends in the world of policing and police accountability in particular. Special thanks go to former student and now friend and professional colleague Charles Katz for being a great coauthor. Charles did the bulk of the work on this, the ninth edition, and Sam is very appreciative of that.

Charles Katz would like to thank the many people who have contributed to the completion of this edition and to acknowledge his colleagues at Arizona State University, who have always been supportive and who have been willing to lend a helpful hand when asked. Special thanks, too, to four people in particular: to Charles's parents and his wife Keri, who have always been loving and supportive (this book, and his other work, is just as much a result of their dedication and efforts as his own), and to his coauthor Sam Walker. Sam has always been supportive, whether it be professionally or personally, and his insights continue to influence Charles today.

Samuel Walker
Charles M. Katz

PART I

Foundations

CHAPTER **1** Police and Society

CHAPTER **2** The History of the American Police

CHAPTER **3** The Contemporary Law Enforcement Industry

© David Frazier/Getty Images

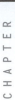

CHAPTER **1**

Police and Society

CHAPTER OUTLINE

The Goals of This Book

Why Do We Have Police?

A Framework for Understanding the Police and Policing

A Democratic Police

Democracy and Accountability

A Legitimate Police

Procedural Justice

Practices That Build Legitimacy

Legitimacy and Police—Public Interactions

Legitimacy, Trust, and Race Relations

An Open and Transparent Police

Practices That Create Openness and Transparency

An Accountable Police

Police Accountability: Goals and Methods

Accountability on Police Use of Force

Collecting and Analyzing Data on Use of Force

Accountability in Routine Police— Public Contacts

Training to Prevent Bias in Police Activities

Independent Investigations and Review of Critical Incidents

An Effective Police

The Complex Responsibilities of the Police

Ineffective Strategies for
  Controlling Crime and
  Disorder
Effective Strategies for
  Controlling Crime and Disorder
Partnerships with the Public

A Special Case: The Police and the
  Mentally Ill
A Special Case: The Police and
  Juveniles
Research and Policing: Evidence-
  Based Programs

Summary
Key Terms
For Discussion
Internet Exercises

The Goals of This Book

The Police in America provides a comprehensive picture of policing in the America. It describes what police do (see Chapter 7); the different problems that arise; the decisions that officers make; and who those officers are, including who applies to be police officers and how they are selected. It also covers important issues in day-to-day policing, such as police patrol and how it has changed over the years (Chapter 7), police officer exercise of discretion (Chapter 11), and legitimacy and community relations (Chapter 12). Police personnel issues include how police officers are selected, the demographic profile of police officers today (Chapter 5), the factors that shape officer behavior (Chapter 6), and how police organizations operate (Chapter 4). Chapter 2 examines the history of policing in America and how traditions that were created many decades ago continue to influence policing today.

Before we begin, in this chapter we provide a framework for understanding the police in America. The framework that follows is adapted from the *Final Report of the President's Task Force on 21st Century Policing*. The Task Force was the first-ever presidential commission or task force devoted exclusively to the police. The *Final Report* brought together all the best current thinking about the police in America today.

Why Do We Have Police?

Why do we have police? What purpose do they serve? What do we want them to do? What do they do that other government agencies do not do? How do we want them to do these things? How do we make sure they do what we want? What do we do if they engage in misconduct?

These are all basic questions related to the role of police in society. Most Americans think they know what the police are: They are the officers who patrol the street where they live. Why do we have them? Most people would answer that they are there to fight crime and protect us.

Unfortunately, the answers most people give are too vague and simplistic. Policing is extremely complex.[1] The police have multiple responsibilities involving controlling crime, maintaining order, and providing miscellaneous services to the public. Even the idea of "fighting crime" is complex. Which crimes? There is an old cliché that says, "if the police enforced all the laws on the books, we would all be in jail."

The police solve this dilemma by using their discretion not to enforce all the laws all the time. People stopped by an officer while driving are often let go with a warning, even though they were speeding. But do the police make good decisions when not enforcing the law? There are no easy answers to this question. We examine police discretion in detail in Chapter 11.

We examine the police and crime in detail in Chapter 9.

The task of maintaining order is just as complex. What exactly do we mean by "order"? One person's idea of disorder is their neighbor's idea of a fun party. One group's idea of an offensive protest march is another group's idea of freedom of speech and assembly, protected by the First Amendment. When does a protest cross the line? When it blocks the entrance to a building? Day-in and day-out, the police make difficult decisions about these problems. We discuss order maintenance in detail in Chapter 8.

What do we want the police to do to accomplish their tasks? When asked, most people say they want more police patrols in their neighborhood. But is that the most effective way to control crime? As we will learn in this book, adding more police patrols to what already exists does not reduce crime.[2] There are other alternatives, innovations that have developed in recent years that are effective and represent "smart policing."

What should we do when police officers do things that are improper? What is the proper remedy to a fatal officer-involved shooting that appears unjustified? Many people think we should leave the investigation and discipline of such incidents to the police. After all, don't they know best? Many other people disagree strongly with that view. They don't believe the police are capable of fairly investigating themselves, and they want independent external review of officer conduct. As we will learn in this book, this is a bitterly contested political issue, and the debate over it continues today. We cover police accountability in detail in Chapter 14.

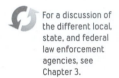

For a discussion of the different local, state, and federal law enforcement agencies, see Chapter 3.

Finally, it is difficult to define the kind of organization that a police department or law enforcement agency represents. The answer may seem obvious, but it is not. There are literally thousands of police departments in the United States, including 15,388 local departments.[3] City police and county sheriff's departments have different roles and responsibilities, and significant differences exist in the responsibilities of county sheriff's departments. State law enforcement agencies, meanwhile, also vary in many important respects. Some are limited entirely to highway patrol. Others have general law enforcement responsibilities. Some are independent state agencies, while some others are branches of the state attorney general's office. Federal agencies all have very specific missions, defined by federal law. The Federal Bureau of Investigation (FBI) is the principal federal law enforcement agency, but the Drug Enforcement Agency (DEA) and Immigration and Customs Enforcement (ICE) have specific responsibilities, as well.

A Framework for Understanding the Police and Policing

The issues surrounding policing are extremely complex. To make sense of them, we use the 2015 report of the **President's Task Force on 21st Century Policing** as a useful framework for understanding the basic principles of good policing. In a series of public hearings around the country, the Task Force learned about all the best new ideas in policing and incorporated them into its final report.[4]

President's Task Force on 21st Century Policing

The Task Force's framework addressed the following issues: a democratic police, a legitimate police, an open and transparent police, an accountable police, and an effective police. These key principles are closely linked and reinforce each other.

A Democratic Police

The United States is a democracy, which means that the people ultimately control the agencies of government. This includes the police. In totalitarian societies, the people have no control over law enforcement agencies. If they are not happy with what the police are doing, there is nothing they can do about it. Police in totalitarian societies are also not governed by the rule of law; they only follow the dictates of the supreme ruler. **Democracy and the police** means that the police are both answerable to the people and accountable to the rule of law.

In the United States, mayors appoint police chiefs, and city councils provide the budget. Governors appoint the head of state police agencies, and state legislators appropriate their budgets. The president of the United States appoints the directors of federal law enforcement agencies: the directors of the FBI and the DEA, and all the other federal agencies. Congress appropriates their budgets.

The political control of the police, while an essential part of democracy, raises a number of difficult problems. For many years in history, elected officials used the police for personal or political benefit, appointing their friends as police officers and using the police to protect illegal drinking and gambling (see Chapter 2). We call that "politics."[5] Making sure that the police are responsive to the public but are not used for improper purposes is a major challenge for the American police.

The President's Task Force made a number of recommendations to ensure that the police are responsive to the people they serve. These recommendations include holding regular public meetings with residents of the community (Recommendation 4.5.1); conducting surveys of the public they serve (Recommendation 1.7); making official policies and procedures publicly available, on their websites; and establishing some form of civilian (citizen) oversight of the police (Recommendation 2.8).

Democracy and Accountability

Public control of the police has its dangers, however, and there have been many instances in our history when those dangers became tragic realities. The worst case involves policing in the southeastern United States, during both the slave era and Reconstruction, when the police and the entire criminal justice system were used to maintain a racial caste system, put in place by duly elected white majorities.[6] That system was formally dismantled during the civil rights era, through a combination of court rulings upholding the Fourteenth Amendment's guarantee of Equal Protection of the Law and federal civil rights laws.

In the rest of the country, local majorities supported "get tough on crime" practices by the police that violated standards of due process. The Supreme Court curtailed these practices with decisions affirming constitutional guarantees against unreasonable searches and seizures (*Mapp v. Ohio*) and the right to an attorney during police investigations (*Miranda v. Arizona*). In the wake of the events in Ferguson, Missouri, in 2014, a federal investigation found that elected city officials were using the police to generate revenue to support the city's budget.[7] The result was a pattern of heavy-handed law enforcement, particularly with regard to traffic tickets, that violated the Fourteenth Amendment and created a serious problem with police–community relations, which erupted in riots in August 2014.

democracy and the police

For a discussion of the history of politics and the police, see Chapter 2.

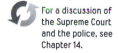
For a discussion of the Supreme Court and the police, see Chapter 14.

POLICE *in* FOCUS | Justice Department Investigations of Local Police Departments

Since 1997, the Civil Rights Division of the U.S. Justice Department has investigated and reached settlements with about 25 local police departments. The settlements are in the form of a "consent decree" or a "settlement agreement." There has been great controversy over this program. Community activists argue that it is a necessary and effective means of correcting systemic police misconduct. Critics charge that the federal government is overstepping its authority. Others argue that the resulting consent decrees or settlement agreements are too expensive. Finally, the police and local authorities argue that there were no systemic patterns of police abuse in the first place.

Let's take a look at the Justice Department program. Both the initial investigations and the resulting settlements are available on the website of the Special Litigation Section (visit http://www.justice.gov/crt/conduct-law-enforcement-agencies; scroll down and click on "Cases and Matters"; look for the state and then the case name or police department). Some of the important settlements involve Seattle, New Orleans, Cleveland, and Ferguson, Missouri. Let's examine these documents in terms of the following issues:

- What legal authority does the Justice Department have to investigate a local police department? The rationale is always stated in the first pages of the investigation letter or the settlement agreement. Does the Justice Department have the authority to investigate a police department because it has failed to control crime? To put it another way, is incompetence and mismanagement a violation of federal law?
- What policies or practices by a police department constitute violation of federal civil rights law? What kind of police conduct constitutes a "pattern or practice" of the

violation of the rights of local residents? Pick one or more settlements and review the document quickly. Does the Justice Department make a persuasive case that a *pattern or practice* of police misconduct exists?

- What kinds of reforms do the settlements or consent decrees require? What reforms are intended in terms of how a police department controls its officers' use of force? Are there any changes in the responsibilities for sergeants? If so, what are they now supposed to do?
- What aspects of the consent decrees or settlements are consistent with the elements of the framework discussed in this chapter? Is there anything that is likely to promote legitimacy? Or achieve greater openness and transparency? What reforms are likely to enhance the accountability of officers?
- Many of the settlements require police departments to establish an early intervention system (EIS). What exactly is an EIS? How is it supposed to hold police officers accountable for their actions?
- What kinds of changes to a police department's training program are required by settlements or consent decrees?
- How long does a consent decree or settlement last? In your opinion, is this too long, and unfair to the local department, or is it not long enough to accomplish the necessary reforms?
- In your opinion, are the reforms required by federal consent decrees or settlement agreements likely to increase the department's effectiveness in responding to crime and disorder? Or are they likely to interfere with effective crime-fighting and the control of disorder? Explain.

A Legitimate Police

legitimacy

The police in a democracy need to be legitimate.[8] **Legitimacy** means more than just the police following the rule of law. It means that the people they serve have trust and confidence in them: trust that comes from respectful treatment; trust that the police are conducting themselves in a lawful manner; and confidence that they are controlling crime and disorder effectively. The President's Task Force recommended that *"[l]aw enforcement culture should embrace a guardian mindset to build public trust and legitimacy. Toward that end, police and sheriff's departments should adopt procedural justice as the guiding principle for internal and external policies and practices to guide their interactions with citizens they serve"* (Recommendation 1.1).

The "guardian" mindset is the opposite of the "warrior" mindset, in which police officers see their work as combat and too often view members of the public as the "enemy." When the police view people as the enemy, they are less likely to be responsive to their needs and more likely to use force when it is not necessary. Sue Rahr, a member of the President's Task Force, explained that in 2012 her staff at the Washington State Criminal Justice Training Commission "began asking the question, 'Why are we training police officers like soldiers?'" Even though police officers wear uniforms and are authorized to use firearms, they have very different roles. Rahr further explained that "[t]he soldier's mission is that of a warrior: to conquer. The rules of engagement are decided before the battle. The police officer's mission is that of a guardian: to protect. The rules of engagement evolve as the incident unfolds. Soldiers must follow orders. Police officers must make independent decisions. Soldiers come into communities as an outside, occupying force. Guardians are members of the community, protecting from within."[9]

Rahr's observation touches on all of the issues we discuss in this chapter. A guardian mindset involves cultivating trust and legitimacy in the police, being open and transparent about police activities, holding both the organization and individual officers accountable, and, finally, adopting the recognized best practices from around the country in order to be effective in controlling crime and maintaining order.

Procedural Justice

Procedural justice is now recognized as an essential guiding principle for good policing. The theory of procedural justice developed out of the field of social psychology. It holds that, for example, in dealing with an organization, people are concerned not just with what happens to them but also with how they are treated. In policing, this means the difference between getting a traffic ticket (the substantive outcome) and how the officer acted: for example, being rude, being polite, not answering the person's questions, explaining the reason for the stop, and so on. Research consistently finds that people notice how they are treated by police officers and that it makes a difference to them. In Chicago, Wesley Skogan found that 80 percent of whites expressed a "favorable" attitude about whether the police "clearly explained why they wanted to talk with them," but only 48 percent of African Americans and 63 percent of English-speaking Hispanics expressed a similar attitude.[10] Not only do people notice and remember how the police treat them, but there are large racial and ethnic gaps in those perceptions. We examine the legitimacy of the police further in Chapter 12.

Tom Tyler's research has found that when people have a sense of procedural justice, they are more likely to obey the law.[11] Consequently, the President's Task Force concluded that *"[d]ecades of research and practice support the premise that people are more likely to obey the law when they believe that those who are enforcing it have authority that is perceived as legitimate by those subject to the authority.*

procedural justice

The public confers legitimacy only on those whom they believe are acting in procedurally just ways. In addition, law enforcement cannot build community trust if it is seen as an occupying force coming in from outside to impose control on the community."[12]

What procedural justice teaches us, then, is not only that the police have the responsibility for controlling crime but also that their activities, when done properly, can have the effect of promoting law-abiding behavior. The police don't just keep the peace; they build the peace in our communities.

Practices That Build Legitimacy

There are many ways in which the police can build trust and legitimacy. These steps, moreover, do not interfere with crime control efforts, and in fact, as we will explain, they can help to enhance effective crime control.

For a discussion of the role of legitimacy and police–community relations, see Chapter 12.

The President's Task Force recommended that *"[i]n order to achieve external legitimacy, law enforcement agencies should involve the community in the process of developing and evaluating policies and procedures"* (Action Item 1.5.1). When community residents understand a police department's policies on the handling of domestic violence incidents, the treatment of homeless people, and the use of officer body-worn cameras, they will feel more confident that the police are handling each of these situations properly, and this will help to build greater trust in the police. As we will see shortly, many steps designed to build trust and legitimacy include the department's taking steps to provide greater openness and transparency regarding its operations.

If people do not feel that their police departments have a sound policy for handling domestic violence incidents, for example, there should be opportunities for them to voice their concerns to the department. To this end, the President's Task Force recommended that *"[l]aw enforcement agencies should schedule regular public forums and meetings where all community members can interact with police and help influence programs and policy"* (Recommendation 4.5.1). Such public events give community members a chance to express their concerns and have a constructive dialogue with high-ranking police officials, which helps to build trust and legitimacy.

The effectiveness of community meetings, of course, depends on how they are conducted. If they are completely controlled by police officials in charge of the meeting, with only limited opportunity for members of the public to voice their concerns, then they will likely be counterproductive. In their study of the Chicago community policing effort CAPS (Chicago Alternative Policing Strategy), which had an extensive program of neighborhood meetings with local residents, Wesley Skogan and Susan Hartnett observed that "[m]aking [police] beat meetings work was hard." The four most commonly discussed issues were drug dealing, "youth problems," traffic enforcement, and "police disregard for citizens." In the end, the meetings "created important opportunities for participation" by neighborhood residents.[13]

Legitimacy and Police–Public Interactions

Trust in the police and legitimacy depend very much on how police officers interact with people in routine encounters: traffic stops, 911 disturbance calls, neighborhood problems, and so on. Procedural justice research has found that it is important for officers to treat people with respect, regardless of who they are or their condition.

Respectful policing includes the police introducing themselves, explaining the reason they are there (the reason for a traffic stop, for example), listening to people, and answering their questions.

It is extremely important that police officers speak respectfully to people. There has been a long and unfortunate tradition of rude and offensive language by police officers, including offensive racial and ethnic epithets. Almost 40 years ago, the Kerner Commission, which had been appointed to study the urban riots of the 1960s, found that "verbal discourtesy" occurred in 15 percent of all encounters between officers and community residents.[14] The problem continues today. To address this problem, the President's Task Force recommended that *"[b]ecause offensive or harsh language can escalate a minor situation, law enforcement agencies should underscore the importance of language used and adopt policies directing officers to speak to individuals with respect"* (Recommendation 4.4.1).

As we will explain shortly, prohibiting offensive language is also an important accountability measure, a means of holding officers to a high standard of performance when dealing with people in the community. We discuss this subject again in the section on accountability, where we emphasize the point that *all* procedures designed to enhance accountability by controlling officer misconduct have a direct impact on legitimacy.

One police practice that offends the public and undermines trust and legitimacy involves formal or informal department quotas that require officers to write a certain number of traffic tickets or make a certain number of arrests each month or year. Quotas are also wrong in principle since they require officers to write tickets or make arrests they would not otherwise make. The President's Task Force recommended that the police *"should refrain from practices requiring officers to issue a predetermined number of tickets, citations, arrests or summons, or to initiate investigative contacts with citizens for reasons not directly related to improving public safety, such as generating revenue"* (Recommendation 2.8).

The most serious case of the abuse of quotas was exposed in the 2015 Justice Department report on Ferguson, Missouri, site of the August 2014 shooting of Michael Brown, an unarmed African American, by a white police officer.[15] The city of Ferguson was using the police department as a source of revenue to meet the annual budget, pressuring the department to write traffic tickets, for example, to generate fines. As a result, the massive enforcement of minor offenses had the effect of creating a sense of oppression among African Americans in the community.

Legitimacy, Trust, and Race Relations

Building trust and legitimacy requires that a police department have a workforce that is representative of the community, in terms of race, ethnicity, and gender. The President's Task Force recommended that *"[l]aw enforcement agencies should strive to create a workforce that contains a broad range of diversity including race, gender, language, life experience, and cultural background to improve understanding and effectiveness in dealing with all communities"* (Recommendation 1.8). In the 1960s, the lack of African American officers in major city departments undermined trust and was a contributing factor to the riots of the period. The city of Cleveland, for example, was 34 percent African American, but only 7 percent of the officers were African American.[16]

For a discussion of diversity and the employment of police officers, see Chapter 5.

Maintaining a representative police force is a continuing challenge. The U.S. population continues to change, and many cities experience significant changes in their population composition over relatively short periods of time. Immigration continues to transform our communities, in big cities and small communities, just as it did 100 years ago.

The arrival of new community members for whom English is not their native language has created significant communication problems. People need to be able to communicate with 911 operators if they want to report a crime. (Some departments have contracts with agencies that provide immediate interpreter services.) Officers need to be able to communicate with all the people present at a domestic violence incident or when responding to a street-corner situation that might escalate into a disturbance. (Many departments provide incentive pay for offices who are bilingual, especially those who speak Spanish in communities with large Spanish-speaking populations.) The President's Task Force recommended that *"[l]aw enforcement agencies should ensure reasonable and equitable language access for all persons who have encounters with police or who enter the criminal justice system"* (Action Item 1.9.2).

We examine past and current police–community relations problems in detail in Chapter 12.

Another issue that undermines trust and confidence in the police is that, historically, police departments have refused to admit that they make mistakes. This is especially true in the case of controversial officer-involved shooting incidents or excessive-force cases. This issue has long been a factor in aggravating race relations. Racism and discrimination have been a part of U.S. history (see Chapter 2), and the history of policing has been no exception.

As a consequence, the President's Task Force recommended that *"[l]aw enforcement agencies should acknowledge the role of policing in past and present injustice and discrimination and how it is a hurdle to the promotion of community trust"* (Recommendation 1.2). This recommendation is a part of being open and transparent, but it obviously has significant impact on building legitimacy as well.

For a discussion of use-of-force reporting, see Chapter 11.

The Police Executive Research Forum pointed out in a 2015 report that "a great deal of damage can be done to police–community relationships if [departments] fail to comment or to act following a questionable incident" involving the use of force. It cited a case in which the chief of police in Houston, Texas, in response to a serious excessive-force incident that had been recorded, quickly contacted community leaders and called a press conference at which he said that the officers involved had been relieved of duty because of their actions.[17] In short, admitting mistakes and explaining what actions a department is taking can pay dividends in terms of legitimacy.

An Open and Transparent Police

openness and transparency

One of the most important ways police departments can build trust and legitimacy is to be open and transparent about their operations. **Openness and transparency** involves the police explaining to the public what they do and how they handle certain critical situations, such as domestic violence incidents. One way to accomplish this is for police departments to make their policies available to the public. Historically, American police departments have been closed bureaucracies, unwilling the share any information about their operations with the public (see Chapter 2).[18]

Practices That Create Openness and Transparency

Making department policies available contributes to public understanding of the police and helps to build legitimacy. Involving members of the community in the development of new policies and the revision of existing policies also enhances public understanding, provides an opportunity for the revised policies to address community concerns, and gives the community a sense of ownership in the resulting policies.

The President's Task Force recommended that *"[t]o embrace a culture of transparency, law enforcement agencies should make all department policies available for public review and regularly post on the department's website information about stops, summonses, arrests, reported crime, and other law enforcement data aggregated by demographics"* (Action Item 1.3.1). Along the same lines, the Task Force recommended that departments *"should collaborate with community members to develop policies and strategies in communities and neighborhoods disproportionately affected by crime . . ."* (Recommendation 2.1).

As already mentioned, to address community concerns about police practices, the Task Force recommended that departments *"should schedule regular forums and meetings where all community members can interact with police and help influence programs and policies"* (Recommendation 4.5.1). Public forums provide an opportunity for people to express their concerns and for the police department to answer their questions.

Openness and transparency are also enhanced if departments *"engage community members"* in officer training programs (Recommendation 5.2). This should include both preservice police academy training and regular in-service training. Particularly valuable insights can be contributed by community experts on such issues as race relations, homelessness, juvenile justice, and domestic violence. Community experts can explain their views of current problems and needs, along with best practices in their areas.

Community members are concerned about the composition of police departments, and whether officers represent the community in terms of race, ethnicity, and gender. To address these concerns, the President's Task Force recommended that police departments should also *"report and make available to the public census data regarding the composition of their departments including race, gender, age, and other relevant demographic data"* (Recommendation 2.5).

For a discussion of police–community relations, see Chapter 12.

The composition of a police force is extremely relevant to trust and legitimacy. If, for example, Hispanics are significantly underrepresented, the Hispanic community is less likely to feel that the police understands and serves them. The lack of officers with Spanish-language skills, moreover, is likely to inhibit the ability of the department to respond effectively to 911 calls, disorder incidents, and traffic stops.

Making data available about the composition of the police force is also an accountability issue. If the data show that African American, Hispanic, or female officers are significantly underrepresented in a particular department, that information can become the basis for corrective action. The department can then work in partnership with relevant community groups to develop recruitment strategies that will help to establish a more representative police force.

Finally, as a means of building and maintaining open relationships with the community, the President's Task Force recommended that police departments require their officers *"to identify themselves by their full name, rank, and command . . . and provide that information in writing to individuals they have stopped . . ."* (Recommendation 2.11). Enabling people to identify by name the officer they encountered, whether it was a positive or negative experience, puts a name to a face and communicates the message that the department is not trying to hide what it is doing and who is doing it. Historically, police–community relations have not been positive when people have felt the police are strangers, or even an occupying army.

An Accountable Police

Police Accountability: Goals and Methods

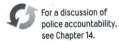

accountability

The police should be accountable to both the public and to the law for their operations. **Accountability** is one of the basic elements of a democratic police. As we explained at the beginning of this chapter, the elected representatives of the people give law enforcement agencies direction and provide their budgets. Mayors and city council members should have good information on what their police departments are doing so that they can make informed decisions about a new chief, the police department's budget, or any problems with police activities.

For a discussion of police accountability, see Chapter 14.

Law enforcement agencies are also accountable to the law. They should not be doing anything illegal. The law takes many forms: criminal law, criminal procedures, court decisions, and internal police policies. Holding the police accountable to the law is one way to guard against improper political influence on the police that involves favoritism and arbitrary or discriminatory law enforcement. Accountability to the law requires good internal accountability procedures. Officers are far less likely to be involved in questionable shooting incidents if the department has a use-of-force policy that represents current best practices, has academy and in-service training programs that reinforce that policy, and requires sergeants on the street to closely monitor and supervise the officers under their command. James J. Fyfe's research found that a good policy on the use of deadly force, based on the defense-of-life principle, significantly reduced the number of shootings in the New York City Police Department (NYPD).[19]

There is no single way of achieving police accountability. As we will learn in this book, much controversy exists over the best means of accountability. Police departments should have policies governing officer use of force. But what is the best use-of-force policy? How strict or permissive should it be? This is a major controversy today. Who should review incidents to determine whether an officer violated either the law or departmental policy? Should police departments be allowed to police themselves exclusively? Or should there be external agencies to investigate and police the police? Is citizen oversight a necessary and proper approach to policing the police? If so, what authority should a citizen oversight agency have? These are complex, difficult, but very important questions. We discuss these and other questions in Chapter 14.

Accountability on Police Use of Force

The use of force by police officers is a critically important issue with regard to accountability. First, the police have extraordinary powers: the power to stop and detain people on the street; the power to conduct a frisk or a search; the power to arrest; and, finally, the ultimate power to take someone's life. In one of the most important

POLICE *in* FOCUS | The Role of Local Police in Homeland Security

Since September 11, 2001, many local police agencies have become involved in matters related to homeland security. Maguire and King note that since 9/11 the police are "developing new areas of investigative experience, cooperating much more with federal law enforcement and intelligence agencies, working more closely with the military, increasing their levels of surveillance over their communities, and paying more attention to the safety of critical infrastructure." The first municipal police agency to expend a significant amount of resources on homeland security was the NYPD. In 2002, then–Police Commissioner Raymond W. Kelly established a Counterterrorism Bureau. As a result, New York City police officers are stationed in such cities as London, Tel Aviv, and Hamburg, working on a variety of issues involving counterterrorism.

Some critics believe that this kind of attention to homeland security diverts attention and resources away from more traditional policing responsibilities. Regardless, the day-to-day activities of most general service law enforcement agencies, and most police officers, do not involve addressing issues related to

homeland security. This is because police agencies typically focus on issues of local concern and center their officers' attention on small subsections of communities called *beats* and *precincts*. Unless a suspected terrorist is believed to be in the agency's jurisdiction, most local police departments do not expend a substantial amount of resources on searches for terrorists. However, some local police agencies have become more involved with protecting particular places from potential terrorist activity. This effort has largely involved developing emergency response plans and providing preventive patrols in locations where the risks of terrorism are higher, such as stadiums, parks, and other locations that host large public gatherings. Therefore, although some local police agencies participate in homeland security efforts, homeland security plays a small role in most police organizations.

Source: Edward Maguire and William King, "Trends in the Policing Industry," *Annals of the American Academy of Political and Social Sciences* 593 (2004): 15–41; David Thacher, "The Local Role in Homeland Security," *Law & Society Review* 39 (2005): 635–676.

essays on policing, Egon Bittner argues that the capacity to use coercive force is the defining feature of the police.[20] No other profession has powers comparable to those of the police. This makes it all the more urgent for police departments to have good policies on all types of use of force.

To control police use of force, the President's Task Force recommended that *"[l]aw enforcement agencies should have comprehensive policies on the use of force that include training, investigations, prosecutions, data collection, and information sharing. These policies must be clear, concise, and openly available for public inspection"* (Recommendation 2.2). In short, police department **policies on the use of force** need to cover when and in what circumstances officers are authorized to use force, including both deadly force and physical force; training that ensures all officers know their department's use-of-force policy; procedures for thoroughly and fairly investigating use-of-force incidents to determine whether an officer acted according to the department's policy; and mandatory use-of-force reports to facilitate investigations and to permit the department to identify problems that need to be corrected.

policies on the use of force

In recent years, the idea of officers de-escalating encounters with people has gained wide acceptance.[21] Police leaders recognize that many officer use-of-force incidents could have been avoided if the officer had de-escalated the encounter, using verbal techniques when appropriate. Too often, officers respond to what they perceive as disrespect by escalating the encounter with verbal disrespect or use of force. Accordingly, the President's Task Force recommended that *"[l]aw enforcement agency policies for training on use of force should emphasize de-escalation and alternatives to arrest or summons in situations where appropriate"* (Recommendation 2.2.1).

de-escalation

De-escalation does not involve a permissive or overly lenient style of policing. It is a technique that should be used when appropriate (and certainly not when there is a clear threat of a physical attack on an officer) and as an alternative to the officer's escalating an incident and using unnecessary force. The respected Police Executive Research Forum recommended that officers learn both the tactics and the value of "tactical disengagement."[22] Not every situation requires a formal police action. De-escalation avoids unnecessary use-of-force incidents, which have a damaging impact on community relations and trust and confidence in the police. And if a department decides to adopt a formal de-escalation policy, it should follow the President's Task Force recommendation to engage community members in the development of that policy (Action Item 1.5.1) and then to make the policy public, by putting it on its website (Action Item 1.3.1).

Collecting and Analyzing Data on Use of Force

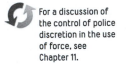

For a discussion of the control of police discretion in the use of force, see Chapter 11.

A basic strategy for holding individual officers and departments accountable for their use of force is the collection and analysis of data on use-of-force incidents. It is today a standard best practice for police departments to require that officers complete a use-of-force report any time they use force. The reporting officer's sergeant should critically review the reports, requiring more detail and explanation if the initial report is inadequate, and then forward the report up the chain of command.

At a higher level of command in the department, a review team should analyze all the force reports over time to identify recurring problems that need to be corrected by changes in policy, training, or supervision, and to identify officers who are involved in significantly more force incidents than other officers. In many departments this team is known as the Use of Force Review Board. It is important, for example, to know whether there are racial or ethnic disparities in persons against whom force is being used, or whether use of force appears to be problematic in certain situations, such as in encounters with people having a mental health crisis.[23]

With respect to data on other activities, the President's Task Force recommended that law enforcement agencies *"should be encouraged to collect, maintain, and analyze demographic data on all detentions (stops, searches, summons, and arrests)"* (Recommendation 2.0). The analysis of traffic stop data, for example, can determine whether a pattern of racial profiling exists. In this way a police department can identify and correct a problem before more people are victimized and the issue becomes a public controversy.

The President's Task Force also recommended that departments have a policy on the release of information about individual force incidents, and stated that publicly released information should include *"a summary statement regarding the circumstances of the incident by the department as soon as possible and within 24 hours."*[24] The failure of departments to release information about what happened in a controversial force incident is a major grievance for community groups. The prompt release of information would represent openness and transparency on the part of the department and help to build trust and legitimacy.

The state of Texas in 2015 went even further than the President's Task Force, with all law enforcement agencies making details of all shooting incidents available on their websites. This includes the police departments in the cities of Houston, Dallas, and Austin.[25]

As we discussed in the section on legitimacy, the use of quotas on the number of arrests or traffic tickets is an issue of great concern to the public. It is also an important accountability issue, since quotas result in tickets or arrests that would not otherwise be made. The President's Task Force made a strong recommendation against quotas (Recommendation 2.9).

Accountability in Routine Police–Public Contacts

Building legitimacy and trust in the police requires that officers conduct themselves in a professional manner in routine contacts with people. To this end, the President's Task Force recommended that police training programs *"should ensure that basic officer training includes lessons to improve social interaction as well as tactical skills"* (Recommendation 5.7). As mentioned earlier, procedural justice involves officers introducing themselves in encounters (and providing their identifying information in writing), explaining why they have intervened, listening to what people say, and answering their questions.

A far more serious issue involves patterns of **systematic bias** in routine police law enforcement activities. Systematically stopping, searching, and arresting African Americans has been labeled *racial profiling*. Racial profiling has several adverse consequences. First, stops, searches, and arrests based on race or ethnicity are a violation of the equal protection clause of the Fourteenth Amendment. Second, patterns of biased policing damage police–community relations and seriously damage the legitimacy of the police. The President's Task Force strongly recommended that all law enforcement agencies adopt policies prohibiting all forms of discrimination in police activities, and urged them to *"adopt and enforce policies prohibiting profiling based on race, ethnicity, national origin, religion, age, gender, gender identity/ expression, sexual orientation, immigration status, disability, housing status, occupation, or language fluency"* (Recommendation 2.13).

systematic bias

Searches of persons is another police activity that needs to be controlled. Under the law, when someone has been arrested, an officer can conduct a search "incident to the arrest." Searches when there is no arrest are far more problematic, however. Officers can request consent to search. Many people give consent because they are intimidated by police authority and are afraid of what might happen if they refuse. The President's Task Force recommended that departments should have a policy requiring officers to *"state the reason for the search if one is conducted"* (Recommendation 2.11).

Training to Prevent Bias in Police Activities

Training is essential if officers are to comply with a department's policy on bias-free policing. The President's Task Force recommended that departments *"should ensure both basic recruit and in-service training incorporates content around recognizing and confronting implicit bias and cultural responsiveness"* (Recommendation 5.9). Most people who are not familiar with the details of policing focus on preserve

For a discussion of the problem of bias and police– community relations, see Chapter 12.

police academy training. At least as important, and in many respects more important, is regular in-service training. It is easy for officers to either forget their academy training or fall into bad habits under the pressure of the job. Consequently, annual in-service refresher training on such critical issues as communication skills and use of force is extremely important. Almost every state requires a certain number of hours of in-service training each year.

Bias, particularly with regard to race and ethnicity, can be unconscious as well as conscious and deliberate. It is unlikely that many officers say to themselves, "I am going to stop that driver because he is black." Research, however, has found that **unconscious bias** plays an important role in policing. This involves officers acting on the basis of deeply embedded stereotypes about racial or ethnic groups, involvement in crime, or the perceived "dangerousness" of certain people. One study, using simulated encounters between officers and citizens, found that "[o]fficers with negative attitudes toward Black suspects and negative beliefs regarding the criminality of Black people tended to shoot unarmed Black suspects more often in the simulation than officers with more positive attitudes and beliefs toward Blacks."

unconscious bias

 For a discussion of all aspects of police training, see Chapter 5.

The President's Task Force recommended that, with respect to training, police departments should ensure that *"both basic recruit and in-service training incorporates content around recognizing and confronting implicit bias and cultural responsiveness"* (Recommendation 5.9). The project on Fair and Impartial Policing explains that "[i]mplicit bias might lead [an] officer to automatically perceive crime in the making when she observes two young Hispanic males driving in an all-Caucasian neighborhood or lead an officer to be 'under-vigilant' with a female subject because he associates crime and violence with males."[26] Whether conscious or unconscious, bias in police actions has a negative impact on trust and legitimacy and needs to be eliminated.

An important part of new officer training involves post-academy field training, where a new officer is partnered with a field training officer who provides close monitoring and instruction. The President's Task Force recommends that *"[t]he U.S. Department of Justice should support the development and implementation of improved Field Training Officer programs"* (Recommendation 5.13).

Independent Investigations and Review of Critical Incidents

One frequent criticism of the police, especially in the case of officer-involved shootings, is that departmental internal investigations are not independent, thorough, and free of bias in favor of the officer being investigated. In response to this issue, the President's Task Force recommended that there should be *"mandate[d] external and independent criminal investigations in cases of police use of force resulting in death, officer-involved shootings resulting in injury or death, or in-custody deaths"* (Action Item 2.2.2). Additionally, in those cases where there is probable cause to believe that the officer committed a crime, the Task Force recommended *"the use of independent prosecutors in cases of police use of force resulting in death, officer-involved shootings resulting in injury or death, or in-custody deaths"* (Recommendation 2.2.3).

The handling of citizen complaints by police internal affairs units has been a long controversy. Civil rights groups have alleged that these units are biased in favor of officers and as a result do not conduct thorough and bias-free investigations.

Research has found, for example, that internal affairs investigators sometimes ask hostile questions to complainants and leading questions to officers under investigation, helping them to explain their actions.[27] To provide independent complaint investigations, civil rights groups have long demanded citizen review of the police, meaning that complaints would be investigated by a separate agency, independent of the police department, which would make recommendations to the police chief.

The President's Task Force recommended that *"[s]ome form of civilian oversight of law enforcement is important in order to strengthen trust with the community"* (Recommendation 2.8), and that local communities should determine for themselves which form of oversight is appropriate. According to the National Association for Civilian Oversight of the Police (NACOLE), there are now over 100 citizen oversight agencies across the country.[28]

For a discussion of citizen oversight, see Chapter 14.

There are two basic forms of **citizen oversight** of the police.[29] Complaint review boards investigate individual citizen complaints, determine the disposition of the complaint (sustained, not sustained, or unfounded), and make a recommendation to the police chief for action. Police auditors or inspectors general, by contrast, do not investigate complaints but instead are designed to investigate the policies and practices of the police department for the purpose of identifying problems that exist and recommending improvement. In 2015, for example, the inspector general for the NYPD examined the reporting of use-of-force incidents by department officers and found many systemic problems. The department's use-of-force policy was "vague and imprecise, providing little guidance" to officers; the process for "documenting and reporting force incidents [was] fragmented;" and the patrol guide did not "properly instruct officers to de-escalate encounters with the public."[30]

citizen oversight

Auditors and inspectors general have, for example, investigated patterns in the use of force, the deployment of canines, the quality of use-of-force investigations, data on civil suits against police departments, and many other issues. Auditors and inspectors general issue public reports that represent an important element of openness and transparency for the departments for which they are responsible. To the extent that their recommendations result in the reform of police practices, they contribute to accountability.

An Effective Police

The Complex Responsibilities of the Police

We want the police to be effective in fulfilling their three major responsibilities: controlling crime, maintaining order, and providing services to the public. First, however, we need to have a good understanding of the **complex responsibilities of the police,** and the nature and complexities of each to the three major areas. The development of effective policing is inhibited by the many myths and stereotypes about police work. The most enduring myth is that the police are primarily crime fighters, devoting most of their efforts to patrolling neighborhoods to deter crime, investigating crimes, and arresting criminals. The reality of police, however, is very different from that.[31]

complex responsibilities of the police

The myth of the crime fighter endures for several reasons. The entertainment media, in movies and television police programs, feature crime-related stories

For a discussion of police crime-fighting, see Chapter 9.

because they offer drama, fast-paced action, and violence. Think for a moment about the latest Hollywood cop movie: How many car chases were there? How many shootouts? The news media also overemphasize crime and the police. A study of crime and the news media concluded that "crime stories are frequently presented and prominently displayed," and the number of these stories is "large in comparison with other topics."[32] An old cliché of television news is that "if it bleeds, it leads." A violent crime has a human element: a victim who engages our sympathies, and a dangerous perpetrator. There is often an element of drama: Will the police catch the offender?

crime-fighter image

The police perpetuate the **crime-fighter image** themselves. They present themselves to the community as the protectors of public safety. Crime fighting is a way for the police to tell the public they are doing something and doing something important. And as we discussed earlier, the crime-fighting image encourages the police to adopt a "warrior" mindset, which too easily can involve practices that harm community relations and undermine legitimacy.[33] This mindset can cause officers, for example, to resort to use of force in situations where alternative tactics, such as de-escalation, are more appropriate.

Most important, the crime-fighter image does not represent an accurate picture of the reality of police work. Studies of 911 calls and direct observations of police patrol work have established that the vast majority of police work involves order maintenance and peacekeeping (Exhibit 1–1). Reporting data from a major study of police services shows that crime-related calls represent only 19 percent of all 911 calls for service.[34] The emphasis on crime fighting prevents us from intelligently evaluating the full scope of police activities. It also creates unrealistic public expectations about the ability of the police to prevent crime and catch criminals. Movies and TV shows, for example, give the impression that the police are highly successful in solving crimes, when in fact only 20 percent of all reported Index crimes are solved. The police themselves suffer from the emphasis on crime fighting. Particularly important, this emphasis devalues the tasks of settling disputes to maintain order and providing services to people who have an emergency and need assistance.

Responding to crime and disorder is a difficult challenge. It is far more than simply patrolling the streets. In the sections that follow, we look at some of the strategies for addressing both crime and disorder.

Ineffective Strategies for Controlling Crime and Disorder

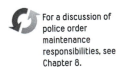

For a discussion of police order maintenance responsibilities, see Chapter 8.

The first principle in effective crime control is that the police must *not* engage in tactics and behavior that are either illegal, or damage their relations with the public, or are simply ineffective. For this reason, the President's Task Force recommended that *"[l]aw enforcement agencies should consider the potential damage to public trust when implementing crime fighting strategies"* (Recommendation 1.6). Almost 50 years ago, the Kerner Commission argued that "aggressive preventive patrol," which in some cases involved "roving task force[s] moving from neighborhood to neighborhood," damaged community relations.[35] In today's terms, we would say that it undermines legitimacy. Saturation patrols of high-crime neighborhoods, for example, create the impression among many community residents of a military occupation. "Sweep" arrests, where the police arrest large numbers of gang members, have been used in the past and found to be both illegal and ineffective in controlling gangs

EXHIBIT 1–1

Citizen Calls for Police Services, by General Problem Types and Subcategories

Type of Problem	Number of Calls	Percent of Total	Percent of Category
Violent Crimes	**642**	**2**	
1. Homicide	9		1
2. Sexual attack	26		4
3. Robbery	118		18
4. Aggravated assault	74		12
5. Simple assault	351		55
6. Child abuse	38		6
7. Kidnapping	26		4
Nonviolent Crimes	**4,489**	**17**	
1. Burglary and break-ins	1,544		34
2. Theft	1,389		31
3. Motor vehicle theft	284		6
4. Vandalism, arson	866		19
5. Problems with money/credit/documents	209		5
6. Crimes against the family	29		1
7. Leaving the scene	168		4
Interpersonal Conflict	**1,763**	**7**	
1. Domestic conflict	694		39
2. Nondomestic arguments	335		19
3. Nondomestic threats	277		16
4. Nondomestic fights	457		26
Medical Assistance	**810**	**3**	
1. Medical assistance	274		34
2. Death	38		5
3. Suicide	34		4
4. Emergency transport	203		25
5. Personal injury, traffic accident	261		32
Traffic Problems	**2,467**	**9**	
1. Property damage, traffic accident	1,141		46
2. Vehicle violation	543		22
3. Traffic-flow problem	322		13
4. Moving violation	292		12
5. Abandoned vehicle	169		7
Dependent Persons	**774**	**3**	
1. Drunk	146		19
2. Missing persons	318		41
3. Juvenile runaway	121		16
4. Subject of police concern	134		17
5. Mentally disordered	55		7
Public Nuisances	**3,002**	**11**	
1. Annoyance, harassment	980		33
2. Noise disturbance	984		33
3. Trespassing, unwanted entry	302		10
4. Alcohol, drug violations	130		4
5. Public morals	124		4

(continued)

EXHIBIT 1–1   *(continued)*

Type of Problem	Number of Calls	Percent of Total	Percent of Category
6. Juvenile problem	439		15
7. Ordinance violations	43		1
Suspicious Circumstances	**1,248**	5	
1. Suspicious person	674		54
2. Suspicious property condition	475		38
3. Dangerous person or situation	99		8
Assistance	**3,039**	12	
1. Animal problem	755		25
2. Property check	616		20
3. Escorts and transports	86		3
4. Utility problem	438		14
5. Property discovery	240		8
6. Assistance to motorist	154		5
7. Fires, alarms	112		4
8. Crank calls	114		4
9. Unspecified requests	425		14
10. Other requests	99		3
Citizen Wants Information	**5,558**	21	
1. Information, unspecified	248		4
2. Information, police-related	1,262		23
3. Information about specific case	1,865		34
4. Information, nonpolice-related	577		10
5. Road directions	189		3
6. Directions, nontraffic	55		1
7. Requests for specific unit	1,362		25
Citizen Wants to Give Information	**1,993**	8	
1. General information	1,090		55
2. Return of property	156		8
3. False alarm	176		9
4. Complaint against specific officer	105		5
5. Complaint against police in general	350		18
6. Compliments for police	20		1
7. Hospital report to police	96		5
Internal Operations	**633**	2	
1. Internal legal procedures	63		10
2. Internal assistance request	134		21
3. Officer wants to give information	298		47
4. Officer wants information	132		21
5. Other internal procedures	6		1
Total Calls	**26,418**	100	

Source: Eric J. Scott, *Calls for Service: Citizen Demand and Initial Police Response* (Washington, DC: U.S. Government Printing Office, 1981), 28–30.

and crime. Today, there are more sophisticated and effective strategies for addressing gangs and gang-related crimes, many of which are labeled *focused-deterrence programs*. For example, the Cincinnati Initiative to Reduce Violence (CIRV), which employed focused deterrence, was effective in reducing gang-related homicides.[36]

Between 2000 and 2013, the NYPD conducted a massive stop and frisk program, reaching a peak of 685,724 stops of people in 2011 (up from 97,296 in 2002). Community groups protested, charging that the program discriminated against African Americans (52.9 percent of all stops) and Hispanics (33.7 percent). Slightly more than half (55.7 percent) of those stopped were frisked, but frisks were extremely unproductive. Only 1.9 percent of frisks found a gun. In short, the stop and frisk program damaged community relations and was ineffective in controlling crime.[37] In 2013, a federal district court ruled that the NYPD's stop and frisk program as practiced was unconstitutional, in violation of the Fourth Amendment protection against unreasonable searches and seizures and also of the Fourteenth Amendment guarantee of equal protection of the law.[38]

Effective Strategies for Controlling Crime and Disorder

A number of effective strategies for controlling crime and disorder have emerged in recent years. Most are based on the best research and knowledge about crime and disorder and about what it is possible for the police to accomplish.[39]

Problem-oriented policing (POP) is a widely used program that has been effective in responding to both crime and disorder. Information about POP programs is available on the website of the Center for Problem-Oriented Policing.[40] As developed by Herman Goldstein, POP involves disaggregating the police workload into specific problems (for example, household burglaries, drunk driving, graffiti), identifying recurring problems, developing working partnerships with community groups, and together developing strategies to reduce or eliminate a specific problem.[41] POP represents a proactive approach, which is very different from the reactive approach of simply responding to 911 calls. The category of disorder, for example, can be disaggregated into separate problems: domestic disturbances, juvenile rowdiness, and chronic alcoholism on the street. A different strategy would be developed for each problem.

problem-oriented policing

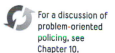 For a discussion of problem-oriented policing, see Chapter 10.

Partnerships with the Public

Problem-oriented policing involves a new role for the police. Officers function as community organizers, working with community groups, discussing community problems and developing possible responses, and in many cases negotiating with local government service agencies, such as the sanitation department or the parks and recreation department, to obtain better services for the neighborhood. The principle of working partnerships with community groups is now recognized as an important element of effective strategies for controlling crime and disorder. The President's Task Force strongly recommended "*working with neighborhood residents to coproduce public safety. Law enforcement agencies should work with community residents to identify problems and collaborate on implementing solutions that produce meaningful results for the community*" (Recommendation 4.5).

Partnerships with community groups contrast sharply with traditional police practice in which the police presented themselves as the professional experts on crime fighting, who had nothing to learn from ordinary citizens. The police generally told community people what they should do (install secure locks on doors, report suspicious activity, and the like) but did not seek their opinion about crime conditions or how best to respond to them. As already mentioned, CAPS, the Chicago community policing experiment, involved regular neighborhood meetings between the police and area residents.[42]

Involving community groups as partners pays several dividends. First, neighborhood residents know a lot about conditions in the area. Most important, they know about the issues that concern them the most: drug sales in an abandoned house, a neighborhood park that is not a safe place, and so on. Second, community partnerships give neighborhood residents a sense of ownership in the strategy that is chosen, and a commitment to help make it work. Third, this approach greatly enhances the legitimacy of the police, which pays dividends in many other ways.

Since the 1980s, police experts have recognized that effective policing requires a police department to have the cooperation of members of the public. Community residents play a vital role in (a) reporting crimes to the police; (b) notifying the police about neighborhood problems (for example, open drug-dealing on certain street corners or in certain houses, graffiti on certain blocks); (c) being witnesses in criminal cases; and (d) participating in police-sponsored anticrime programs. Police experts define these activities as "co-producing" police services.[43]

A Special Case: The Police and the Mentally Ill

Responding to incidents in which a person is having a mental health crisis has become an increasing part of routine police work.[44] Such incidents present major challenges for police officers in terms of choosing the right course of action. In many incidents, the person has a gun, a knife, or another dangerous object. As a starting point, police departments should have clear policies on how to respond to such incidents. The policy should be reinforced with both academy training and regular in-service training for all officers. Local mental health professionals should be involved in all training programs.

For a discussion of police handling of mental-health-related cases, see Chapter 8.

One of the most popular approaches to responding to mental-health-related incidents is with crisis intervention team (CIT) training. CIT programs can take one of two forms. One approach is to have a certain number of officers with specialized CIT training who are available to respond to mental health crisis incidents. An alternative approach is for all officers in the department to receive CIT training. The training involves giving officers background on mental health issues so that they can recognize certain symptoms and assess potential dangers. Also, officers are trained in how to talk to people having a mental health crisis in order to de-escalate situations. Finally, training includes guidelines on the proper use of force when it becomes necessary. The President's Task Force recommended that police departments "*should make Crisis Intervention Training (CIT) a part of both basic recruit and in-service officer training*" (Recommendation 5.6).

CIT International explains the crisis intervention approach that is consistent with many of the principles we have been discussing.[45] The first core element involves a working partnership among law enforcement, community activists, and mental health professions. The second involves community "ownership" of the program, which includes a major role in planning, implementation of the program, and networking among the various stakeholders. The third core element involves clear and consistent policies and procedures on the proper handling of different kinds of mental-health-related incidents and relationships with social service agencies. A CIT program can be seen as a form of problem-oriented policing, because it involves identifying a recurring situation in routine police work, working with community partners (in this case, mental health professionals), and developing specific guidelines for assessing and effectively responding to different types of incidents.

A Special Case: The Police and Juveniles

Problems involving juveniles are another recurring part of day-to-day police work. It is generally accepted that preventing juveniles from engaging in minor delinquency is one of the most effective ways of keeping them from becoming adult criminals. The President's Task Force recommended that police departments *"should adopt policies and programs that address the needs of children and youth most at risk for crime and violence . . ."* (Recommendation 4.6).

Additionally, departments should *"reduce aggressive law enforcement tactics that stigmatize youth and marginalize their participation in schools and communities"* (Recommendation 4.6). In short, just as aggressive law enforcement police tactics can undermine community trust in the police, so can overly aggressive law enforcement strategies against juveniles undermine their participation in school and community activities that are likely to help them refrain from committing more serious delinquent acts and serious crime. Many people argue that excessive use of suspensions and expulsions from school puts many young people into a "school to prison pipeline." To guard against that, the President's Task Force recommended that, to keep young people in school, police departments *"should work with schools to encourage the creation of alternatives to student suspensions and expulsion through restorative justice, diversion, counseling, and family interventions"* (Action Item 4.6.2).

For a discussion of police handling of juveniles, see Chapter 8.

Working with schools is an excellent example of partnerships with community organizations. An effective working relationship with local schools, moreover, can help to build legitimacy for the police.

Research and Policing: Evidence-Based Programs

Effective police programs should be based on evidence of their effectiveness. Evidence-based policymaking is now used in many areas of life, including medical treatment. The President's Task Force recommended that police departments adopt *"scientifically supported practices"* (Recommendation 2.4). Many people believe that having more police patrols in their neighborhood will prevent crime. But, as we will see in Chapter 7, the Kansas City Preventive Patrol Experiment found more than 40 years ago that simply adding more patrols has no impact on the crime rate.[46] As a result, the police have developed a number of programs to control crime and disorder that are based on empirical evidence and are often described as "smart" policing, including, for example, focused deterrence and hot-spots policing. The Center for Evidence-Based Crime Policy explains that "a series of rigorous evaluations have suggested that police can be effective in addressing crime and disorder when they focus in on small units of geography with high rates of crime."[47]

To help develop evidence-based programs and policies, the President's Task Force recommended that police departments *"establish partnerships with academic institutions to develop rigorous training practices, evaluation, and the development of curricula based on evidence-based practices"* (Action Item 5.1.2). Over the past half-century, social science research has had a profound impact on police policy. The 1972–1973 Kansas City Preventive Patrol Experiment found that simply increasing or reducing the amount of routine police patrol had no impact on crime.[48] This finding challenged the basic assumption about patrol that had guided the police since Robert Peel created the first modern police department in 1829. The findings from the Kansas City experiment stimulated the rethinking of police responses to crime and spurred the development of innovative programs such as community policing and problem-oriented policing.

Another study that had a major impact on police policy was James J. Fyfe's study of a new policy regulating officer use of deadly force in the NYPD. Fyfe found that a restrictive policy (known as the defense-of-life policy) effectively reduced the overall number of firearms discharges, reduced the number of fatal shootings by police, and had no adverse effect on either the crime rate or officer safety.[49] The basic strategy of the new deadly force policy—of having a written policy to control discretion, requiring a written report of each firearms discharge, and having a mandatory review of each shooting—was subsequently applied to other critical incidents: high-speed vehicle pursuits, domestic violence incidents, the deployment of canines, and many more.

SUMMARY: PUTTING THE PIECES TOGETHER

Now that we have examined the main features of our framework for understanding the police, it is important to put all the pieces together. Throughout the chapter we have explained how the elements of the framework relate to each other. To put it all together, it is helpful to begin with the last part of our discussion. We want an *effective* police. As we pointed out, to be effective in fighting crime, the police need community cooperation. That cooperation, however, does not come automatically. People are more likely to cooperate if they regard the police as *legitimate*. People, moreover, are more likely to regard

the police as legitimate if the police department is *open and transparent*. They are also more likely to regard the police as legitimate if the police are *accountable*, with respect to controlling the use of force and disciplining officers who violate the law or department policies.

The framework discussed in this chapter is a comprehensive approach to policing. The police cannot have one of these elements of the framework without the others. And each element depends on the others. We will discuss each of these framework elements throughout *The Police in America*.

KEY TERMS

President's Task Force on
    21st Century Policing, 4
democracy and the police, 5
legitimacy, 6
procedural justice, 7
respectful policing, 9

openness and transparency, 10
accountability, 12
policies on the use of force, 13
de-escalation, 14
systematic bias, 15
unconscious bias, 16

citizen oversight, 17
complex responsibilities of the
    police, 17
crime-fighter image, 18
problem-oriented policing, 21

FOR DISCUSSION

1. Divide into groups, with each group assigned to discuss one of the key issues in the framework for understanding the police and policing (for example, legitimacy, openness and transparency, accountability, and police effectiveness). Each group should discuss its topic *critically*. Questions for discussion include the following: Is this issue clearly explained? Does it make sense for American policing? What are the possible negative consequences? What are the possible positive consequences?

2. Discuss how a problem-oriented policing approach might apply to a topic such as homeless people, graffiti, a pattern of residential burglaries, an abandoned house that is the center for drug dealing, or another related topic.

3. Discuss how the legitimacy of the police and effective crime-fighting are related.

4. Discuss whether it is a good or possibly bad idea for the police to make data on officer-involved shooting incidents publicly available.

INTERNET EXERCISES

Exercise 1 Visit the Center for Problem-Oriented Policing website at http://www.popcenter.org/. Click on the tab "POP Guides." Find a guide that covers an issue in which you are interested. Review the guide quickly. Do the recommendations in the guide make sense to you? If so, why? If not, why not?

Exercise 2 Many police departments have adopted de-escalation policies. Search for five police departments on the Internet, and first find if they place their policy manuals on their websites (often

found under "About Us" or "Reports"). If they do, see if they have a de-escalation policy. Most such policies are included under the topic "Use of Force," but some may have them listed separately under "De-escalation." Rate the five departments in terms of openness and transparency on three points: (a) the policy manual is/is not on the website; (b) the department does/does not have a de-escalation policy; and (c) the department's website is/is not easy to use.

NOTES

1. Herman Goldstein, *Policing a Free Society* (Philadelphia: Ballinger, 1977); President's Commission on Law Enforcement and Administration of Justice, *Task Force Report: The Police* (Washington, DC: U.S. Government Printing Office, 1967), ch. 1; see also the discussion in

American Bar Association, *Standards Relating to the Urban Police Function*, 2nd ed. (Boston: Little, Brown, 1980), 1–31 to 1–32.

2. George L. Kelling et al., *The Kansas City Preventive Patrol Experiment: A Summary Report* (Washington, DC: The Police Foundation, 1974).

3. Brian A. Reaves, *Local Police Departments, 2013: Personnel, Policies, and Practices* (Washington, DC: U.S. Department of Justice, 2015), table 1.

4. President's Task Force on 21st Century Policing, *Final Report* (Washington, DC: U.S. Department of Justice, 2015), http://www.cops.usdoj.gov/pdf/taskforce/taskforce_finalreport.pdf.

5. Samuel Walker, *A Critical History of Police Reform* (Lexington, MA: Lexington Books, 1977).

6. Samuel Walker, *Popular Justice: A History of American Criminal Justice*, 2nd ed. (New York: Oxford University Press, 1998).

7. U.S. Department of Justice, Civil Rights Division, *Investigation of the Ferguson Police Department* (2015), http://www.justice.gov/sites/default/files/crt/legacy/2015/03/04/ferguson_findings_3-4-15.pdf.

8. Nicole Haas, Maarten Van Craen, Wesley G. Skogan, et al., "Explaining Officer Compliance: The Importance of Procedural Justice and Trust Inside a Police Organization, *Criminology and Criminal Justice* (January 2015): 1–22.

9. Sue Rahr and Stephen K. Rice, *From Warriors to Guardians: Recommitting American Police Culture to Democratic Ideals* (Cambridge: Harvard University, 2015), http://www.hks.harvard.edu/programs/criminaljustice/research-publications/executive-sessions/executive-session-on-policing-and-public-safety-2008-2014/publications/from-warriors-to-guardians-recommitting-american-police-culture-to-democratic-ideals.

10. Wesley G. Skogan, "Citizen Satisfaction with Police Encounters," *Police Quarterly* 8 (September 2005): 313, table 2.

11. Tom Tyler, *Why People Obey the Law* (New Haven: Yale University Press, 1990).

12. President's Task Force on 21st Century Policing, *Final Report*, 1.

13. Wesley G. Skogan and Susan M. Hartnett, *Community Policing, Chicago Style* (New York: Oxford University Press, 1997), 110–160.

14. National Advisory Commission on Civil Disorders, *Report* (New York: Bantam Books, 1968), 302–303.

15. U.S. Department of Justice, Civil Rights Division, *Investigation of the Ferguson Police Department*.

16. National Advisory Commission on Civil Disorders, *Report*, 312.

17. Police Executive Research Forum, *Re-engineering Training on Police Use of Force* (Washington, DC: Author, 215), 33–35.

18. Samuel Walker, *Popular Justice*, 2nd ed. rev. (New York: Oxford University Press, 1998), 150–151, 199–201.

19. James J. Fyfe, "Administrative Interventions on Police Shooting Discretion: An Empirical Examination," *Journal of Criminal Justice* 7 (Winter 1979): 309–323.

20. See the pioneering discussion in Egon Bittner, "The Capacity to Use Force as the Core of the Police Role," in Bittner, *Aspects of Police Work* (Boston: Northeastern University Press, 1990), 120–136.

21. Police Executive Research Forum, *An Integrated Approach to De-Escalation and Minimizing Use of Force* (Washington, DC: Author, 2012).

22. Ibid., iv.

23. Samuel Walker and Carole A. Archbold, *The New World of Police Accountability*, 2nd ed. (Newbury Park, CA: Sage, 2014), 178–208.

24. President's Task Force on 21st Century Policing, *Final Report*, 22.

25. See, for example, the data on officer-involved shootings on the Dallas, Texas, police department website at http://www.dallaspolice.net/ois/ois.html.

26. See the Fair and Impartial Policing website at http://www.fairimpartialpolicing.com/.

27. Samuel Walker, *Police Accountability: The Role of Citizen Oversight* (Belmont, CA: Wadsworth, 2001).

28. See the National Association for Civilian Oversight of Law Enforcement website at www.nacole.org.

29. Walker, *Police Accountability*.

30. Office of the Inspector General for the NYPD, *Police Use of Force in New York City: Findings and Recommendations on NYPD's Policies and Practices* (New York: Office of the Inspector General, 2015), http://www.nyc.gov/html/oignypd/assets/downloads/pdf/oig_nypd_use_of_force_report_-_oct_1_2015.pdf.

31. Goldstein, *Policing a Free Society*, 29–31.

32. Steven M. Chermak, *Victims in the News: Crime and the American News Media* (Boulder, CO: Westview Press, 1995), 47.

33. Rahr and Rice, *From Warriors to Guardians*.

34. Eric J. Scott, *Calls for Service: Citizen Demand and Initial Police Response* (Washington, DC: U.S. Government Printing Office, 1981); Albert J. Reiss, *The Police and the Public* (New Haven: Yale University Press, 1971).

35. National Commission on Civil Disorders, *Report*, 304.

36. Robin S. Engel et al., "Using Focused Deterrence to Reduce Gang Violence: Evaluating the Cincinnati Initiative to Reduce Violence (CIRV)," *Justice Quarterly* 30, no. 3 (2013): 403–439.

37. Data on the *Floyd* stop and frisk case are available at the website for the Center for Constitutional Rights at http://ccrjustice.org/home/what-we-do/our-cases/floyd-et-al-v-city-new-york-et-al.

38. New York Civil Liberties Union, *Stop and Frisk 2011* (New York: Author, 2012); *Floyd, at al., v. City of New York*, (2013). Information about the case is available at http://ccrjustice.org/home/what-we-do/our-cases/floyd-et-al-v-city-new-york-et-al.

39. Wesley G. Skogan and Kathleen G. Frydl, *Fairness and Effectiveness in Policing: The Evidence* (Washington, DC: National Academies Press, 2004).

40. See the Center for Problem-Oriented Policing website at http://www.popcenter.org.

41. Herman Goldstein, "Improving Policing: A Problem-Oriented Approach," *Crime and Delinquency* 25 (April 1979): 236–258; Herman Goldstein, *Problem-Oriented Policing* (New York: McGraw-Hill, 1990).

42. Skogan and Hartnett, *Community Policing, Chicago Style*.

43. Wesley G. Skogan and George E. Antunes, "Information, Apprehension, and Deterrence: Exploring the Limits of Police Productivity," *Journal of Criminal Justice* 7 (Fall 1979): 217–241.

44. See Gary Cordner, *People with Mental Illness. Guide No. 40* (Phoenix: Center on Problem-Oriented Policing, 2006), http://www.popcenter.org/problems/mental_illness/.

45. See the CIT International website at http://www.citinternational.org/.

46. Kelling et al., *The Kansas City Preventive Patrol Experiment*.

47. Center for Evidence-Based Crime Policy, "Hot Spots Policing," http://cebcp.org/evidence-based-policing/what-works-in-policing/research-evidence-review/hot-spots-policing/.

48. Kelling et al., *The Kansas City Preventive Patrol Experiment*.

49. Fyfe, "Administrative Interventions on Police Shooting Discretion."

© Bettmann/Getty Images

2

The History of the American Police

CHAPTER OUTLINE

Flashback: Moments in American Police History
The First American Police Officer
Flash Forward: 1950
Why Study Police History?
The English Heritage
Creation of the Modern Police: London, 1829
Law Enforcement in Colonial America
The Quality of Colonial Law Enforcement
The First Modern American Police
The "Political Era" in American Policing, 1830s–1900
A Lack of Personnel Standards
Patrol Work in the Political Era
The Police and the Public

Corruption and Politics
Immigration, Discrimination, and Police Corruption
The Failure of Police Reform
The Impact of the Police on Crime and Disorder
The Professional Era, 1900–1960
The Police Professionalization Movement
The Reform Agenda
The Achievements of Professionalization
Other Impacts of Professionalization
Police and Race Relations
New Law Enforcement Agencies
Technology Revolutionizes Policing

New Directions in Police Administration, 1930–1960

The Wickersham Commission Bombshell

Professionalization Continues

Simmering Racial and Ethnic Relations

J. Edgar Hoover and the War on Crime

The Police Crises of the 1960s

The Police and the Supreme Court

The Police and Civil Rights

The Police in the National Spotlight

The Research Revolution

New Developments in Policing, 1970–2016

The Changing Police Officer

Administrative Rulemaking and the Control of Police Discretion

The Emergence of Police Unions

The Spread of Citizen Oversight of Police

Community Policing, Problem-Oriented Policing, and Other Innovations

Data-Driven Policing

Racial Profiling and Discrimination

Federal Investigations of Police Misconduct

Local Police and the War on Terrorism

The National Police Crisis, 2014–2016

CASE STUDY

Summary

Key Terms

For Discussion

Internet Exercises

Flashback: Moments in American Police History

The First American Police Officer

The day the first American police officer went out on patrol in 1838, he had received no training, patrolled on foot, had no two-way radio, could not be dispatched through a 911 system, and carried no weapon. Moreover, he had little education, received no formal preservice training, and had no manual of policies or procedures. Policing in the late 1830s, in short, was completely different from what it is today.

Flash Forward: 1950

The police officer in 1950 worked in a very different situation. He probably had a high school education; was definitely male, because there were no women on patrol for another 16 years; and had only a few African American or Hispanic colleagues, if any. In only some departments did he receive any police academy training before going out on the street, but never any in-service training. The department gave him a very short police manual, but it contained no policies on when to use deadly force, how to handle domestic violence incidents, or when to do a high-speed pursuit. He did not have to worry about any Supreme Court rulings on search and seizure, or interrogating criminal suspects. And he did not worry too much about being disciplined if he beat up someone with his billy club. Policing had changed a lot since the 1830s, but it was still a long way from where it is today.

The police today are the product of their history. This chapter examines the history of the American police, from its roots in England and colonial America to present-day issues related to use of force, procedural justice, community policing, racial profiling, and other matters.

Why Study Police History?

Why study police history? Because it can help us understand policing today. Many people believe the police do not change. That is a myth. In fact, policing has changed tremendously, even in the past several years. David Bayley argued in 1994 that "the

The Relevance of History

The study of police history can do the following:

1. Highlight the fact of change.
2. Put current problems into perspective.
3. Help us understand which reforms have worked.
4. Alert us to the unintended consequences of reforms.

last decade of the twentieth century may be the most creative period in policing since the modern police officer was put onto the streets of London in 1829."[1] The changes he described have continued, possibly at an even faster pace since he made that comment, with the development of officer-worn body cameras, early intervention systems, concerns about legitimacy and procedural justice, and more.

Studying this history can help us understand how and why important changes occur. Racial profiling, for example, is nothing new; it just did not have a name. The problem of police–community relations has a long history. It is useful to understand why this problem continues despite many reforms intended to eliminate discrimination. The patrol car revolutionized police work, and it is important to understand both its positive contributions and its negative effects.

The English Heritage

English heritage

American policing is a product of its **English heritage.** The English colonists brought with them a criminal justice system as part of their political and cultural baggage. This heritage included the English common law, the high value placed on individual rights, the court systems and forms of punishment, and different law enforcement agencies.[2]

The English heritage contributed three enduring features to American policing. The first is a tradition of limited police authority. The Anglo American legal tradition places a high value on individual liberty and on limited government authority.[3] In the United States, these limits are embodied in the Bill of Rights. Continental European countries, by contrast, give their law enforcement agencies much broader powers. German citizens today, for example, are required to carry either an identity card or a passport, and produce it upon request.

The second feature is a tradition of local control of law enforcement agencies. Almost every other country in the world has a centralized system of policing, with a single national police force, or possibly three national forces with distinct responsibilities. England has 43 separate police forces.

The third feature, which is a consequence of local control, is a highly decentralized and fragmented system of law enforcement. The United States in 2013 had 15,388 separate local law enforcement agencies (and that does not include state, federal, and "special district" agencies), subject only to minimal coordination and little national control or regulation.[4]

Formal law enforcement agencies emerged in England in the thirteenth century and over the years evolved in an unsystematic fashion. Responsibility for law enforcement and keeping the peace was shared by the constable, the sheriff, and the justice of the peace. Private citizens, however, retained much of the responsibility for law enforcement, pursuing offenders on their own and initiating criminal cases. This approach was brought to America and persisted into the nineteenth century.[5]

Creation of the Modern Police: London, 1829

On September 29, 1829, the first officers with the new London Metropolitan Police stepped out on the streets of London, England, and modern policing was born. **Robert Peel** is the "father" of modern policing. An important political leader in England, he saw a serious decline in public order and fought for more than 30 years to improve law enforcement. By the early 1800s, the old system of law enforcement collapsed under the impact of urbanization and industrialization. London suffered from poverty, disorder, ethnic conflict, and crime. The 1780 Gordon Riots, a clash between Irish immigrants and English citizens, triggered a 50-year debate over how to provide better public safety. Peel finally persuaded Parliament to create the **London Metropolitan Police** in 1829. It is recognized as the first modern police force, and officers are still known as "Bobbies" in honor of Peel.[6]

Robert Peel

London Metropolitan Police

What exactly is "modern" about the type of policing created by Peel? The three core elements involve the mission, strategy, and organizational structure of the police.

The great innovation of Peel's new police was its mission of **crime prevention.** This reflected the utilitarian idea that it is better to prevent crime than to respond after the fact. Before the London police, all law enforcement was reactive, responding to crimes that had been committed.

crime prevention

The strategy for achieving crime prevention was preventive patrol. Peel introduced the idea of officers patrolling fixed "beats" on a continuous basis, to maintain a visible police presence throughout the community that would deter crime. The deterrent effect of patrol remained the core of policing until it was tested in the 1972 to 1973 Kansas City Preventive Patrol Experiment, one of the most important research efforts in the entire history of policing.

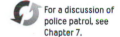

For a discussion of police patrol, see Chapter 7.

To organize police operations, Peel borrowed from the military. This included a hierarchical organization, uniforms, rank designations, and an authoritarian system of command and discipline. This "quasi-military" style still exists in certain respects in American police administration, but as we will see, American police departments have always been very "unmilitary" in important respects. Police officers on the street, for example, were long subject to few controls over such critical issues as use of force, with chiefs exercising little effective control over their conduct.

The mission of the modern police represented a new concept in social control. Allan Silver argues that a continuous presence of police reflected a growing "demand for order" in urban industrial society.[7] David Bayley, meanwhile, argues that to accomplish this the modern police are "public, specialized, and professional."[8] They are professional in the sense that they are full-time, paid employees. Bayley cautions that these characteristics did not appear all at once. Although 1829 is traditionally cited as the birth of the London police, in reality all the new features did not appear for many decades. The American police, in particular, were slow to become fully "modern."

Law Enforcement in Colonial America

When the first English colonists in America created their own law enforcement agencies, they borrowed from their English heritage (Sidebar 2–2). The three important institutions were the sheriff, the constable, and the watch. In the new environment of America, however, these institutions acquired distinctive American features (see Exhibit 2–1).[9]

The sheriff was the most important law enforcement official in America. Appointed by the colonial governor, the sheriff had a broad role that included law enforcement, collecting taxes, supervising elections, maintaining bridges and roads, and other miscellaneous duties.[10]

The constable also had responsibility for enforcing the law and carrying out certain legal duties. Initially an elected position, the constable gradually evolved into a semiprofessional appointed office. In Boston and several other cities, the office of constable became a desirable and often lucrative position.[11]

the watch

The watch most closely resembled the modern-day police. Watchmen patrolled the city to guard against fires, crime, and disorder. At first there was only a night watch. As towns grew larger, they added a day watch. Boston created its first watch in 1634. Following the English tradition, all adult males were expected to serve as watchmen as part of their civic duty. Many men tried to avoid this duty, either by outright evasion or by paying others to serve in their place. Eventually, the watch evolved into a paid professional force.[12]

For a discussion of the issues of race and police–community relations in today's society, see Chapter 12.

Policing in the southeastern states where slavery existed had a distinctive institution: the slave patrol. Because the white majority was so concerned about slave revolts (of which there were many), and runaway slaves, they created this new form of law enforcement. The slave patrols, in fact, were the first modern police forces in the United States. The Charleston, South Carolina, slave patrol, for example, had about 100 officers in 1837 and was far larger than any northern city police force at that time.[13]

The Quality of Colonial Law Enforcement

Colonial law enforcement was inefficient, corrupt, and affected by political interference. Contrary to popular myth, there was never a "golden age" of efficiency, effectiveness, and integrity in American policing.

For a discussion of police crime-fighting strategies today, see Chapter 9.

With respect to crime, the sheriff, the constable, and the watch had little capacity to prevent crime or apprehend offenders. Sheriffs and the constables were reactive agencies, responding to complaints citizens brought to them. Watchmen patrolled, but they were too few in number to really prevent crime. None of the three agencies had enough personnel to investigate more than just a few crimes. Crime victims could not easily report crimes. There was no telephone in those days, and a victim had to seek

---

SIDEBAR 2–2

Contributions of the English Heritage to American Policing

1. Tradition of limited police authority.
2. Tradition of local control.
3. Decentralized and fragmented police system.

EXHIBIT 2-1

Law Enforcement Institutions in Colonial America
Sheriff
Constable
Watch
Night watch
Day watch
Slave patrol

---

out the sheriff. Finally, the sheriff and the watchmen were paid by fees for particular services. As a result, they had greater incentive to work on their civil responsibilities, which offered more certain payment, than on criminal law enforcement.[14]

Colonial agencies were also ill-equipped to maintain order. With few watchmen on duty, there was little they could do in response to crime or disorder. Cities were in fact very disorderly in those years, with much public drunkenness, clashes between different ethnic groups, and periodic riots. The three law enforcement agencies of the time, moreover, had no capacity to provide routine and emergency services to the public.

In practice, ordinary citizens played a major role in maintaining order through informal social control: a comment, a warning, or a stern rebuke to friends, neighbors, or strangers. People suspected of adultery or drunkenness were often "tried" by their church congregations. The severest penalty, expulsion from the congregation, was an extreme one in small, homogeneous communities. There was much face-to-face contact, and people shared the same basic values. This system of informal social control broke down as communities grew into larger towns and cities where the population was constantly changing and moving, and people often did not know their neighbors.[15]

If policing was ineffective in cities and towns, it was almost nonexistent on the frontier. Organized government did not appear in many areas for decades. As a result, settlers relied on their own resources, simply taking the law into their own hands. The result was a tradition of vigilantism that left a terrible legacy that lasted into the twentieth century. Mobs drove out of town or even killed people whom they did not like. The lynching of African Americans was used to maintain the system of racial segregation in the South.[16]

Corruption appeared early in American policing. The criminal law was even more moralistic than today, with many restrictions on drinking, gambling, and sexual practices. As a result, people bribed law enforcement officials to overlook violation of the law.

The First Modern American Police

The **first modern American police** forces were established in the United States in the 1830s and 1840s. As in England, the old system of law enforcement broke down under the impact of urbanization, industrialization, and immigration. In the 1830s, a wave of riots struck American cities. Boston had major riots in 1834, 1835, and 1837. Philadelphia, New York, Cincinnati, Detroit, and other cities all had major disturbances. Abraham Lincoln, as a member of the Illinois state legislature in 1838, warned of the "increasing disregard for law which pervades the country."[17]

first modern American police

Many riots were clashes between different ethnic groups: Irish or German immigrants versus native-born English Protestants, or Irish versus German immigrants. Other riots were economic in nature: angry depositors vandalized failed banks, for example. Moral issues also produced violence. People objecting to medical research on cadavers attacked hospitals; and residents of Detroit staged several "whorehouse riots," attempting to close down houses of prostitution. Finally, pro-slavery whites attacked abolitionists and free black citizens in northern cities.[18]

Despite the breakdown in law and order, Americans moved slowly in creating modern police forces. New York City did not create a new police force until 1845, 11 years after the first serious riots. Philadelphia could not make up its mind, creating and abolishing several different law enforcement agencies between 1834 and 1854, before finally creating a consolidated, citywide police force on the London model.[19]

Americans were uncertain about modern police forces for several reasons. The idea of a continual law enforcement presence on the streets brought back memories of the hated British colonial army. Many people, meanwhile, were afraid their political opponents would control the police and use them to their advantage. Finally, police departments are expensive and taxpayers simply did not want to pay for a public police force.

Many of the first American police departments were basically expanded versions of the existing watch system. The Boston police department had only nine officers in 1838. The first American police officers did not wear uniforms, or carry weapons, and they were identified only by a distinctive hat and badge. Weapons did not become standard police equipment until the late nineteenth century, in response to rising levels of crime and violence.

Americans borrowed most of the features of modern policing from London: the mission of crime prevention, the strategy of visible patrol over fixed beats, and the quasi-military organizational structure. The structure of political control of the police, however, was very different. The United States was a far more democratic country than Britain. American voters—only white males with property, until the latter part of the nineteenth century—exercised direct control over all government agencies. London residents, by contrast, had no direct control over their police. As a result, American police departments were immediately immersed in local politics, a situation that led to many serious problems. The commissioners of the London police, freed from political influence, were able to maintain high personnel standards.[20]

The "Political Era" in American Policing, 1830s–1900

"political era"

Politics influenced every aspect of American policing in the nineteenth century, and the period from the 1830s to 1900 is often called the **"political era"** (see Exhibit 2–2). Historian Robert Fogelson called police departments in this era "adjuncts of the [political] machine." Inefficiency, corruption, and lack of professionalism were the result.[21]

E X H I B I T   2–2

Three Eras of American Policing

  I. The political era: 1830s—1900
 II. The professional era: 1900—1960s
III. The era of conflicting pressures: 1960s—present

A Lack of Personnel Standards

Police departments in the political era had no personnel standards as we understand them today. Officers were selected entirely on the basis of their political connections. Men with no formal education, those in bad health, and those with criminal records were hired. There were a few female matrons for the jail, but no female sworn officers until the early twentieth century. In New York City, a $300 payment to the Tammany Hall political machine was the only requirement for a job on the police force.[22]

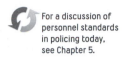

For a discussion of personnel standards in policing today, see Chapter 5.

In most departments, recruits received no formal preservice training. They were handed a badge, a baton, and a copy of the department rules (if one even existed), and then sent out on patrol duty. Cincinnati created one of the first police academies in 1888, but it lasted only a few years. New York City established a School of Pistol Practice in 1895 but offered no training in any other aspect of policing until 1909. Even then, a 1913 investigation found it gave no tests and all recruits were automatically passed.[23]

Police officers had no job security and could be fired at will. In some cases, almost all the officers were fired after an election. In 1886, after elections brought a different political party into power in Cincinnati, 238 of the 289 patrol officers were immediately fired and replaced by political favorites.[24] Nonetheless, it was an attractive job because salaries were generally higher than those for most blue-collar jobs. In 1880, officers in most big cities earned $900 a year, compared with $450 for factory workers.

Jobs on the police force were a major form of **patronage,** which local politicians used to reward their friends. Consequently, the composition of departments reflected the ethnic and religious makeup of the cities. When Irish Americans began to win political power, they appointed their friends as police officers. When Barney McGinniskin became the first Irish-born police officer in Boston on November 3, 1851, it provoked major protests from the English and Protestant establishment in the city.[25] Many German Americans served as police officers in Cleveland, Cincinnati, Milwaukee, and St. Louis, where German immigration was heavy. After the Civil War, some African Americans were appointed police officers in northern cities where the Republicans, the party of Abraham Lincoln, were in power.

patronage

Patrol Work in the Political Era

Routine police patrol in the political era was hopelessly inefficient. Officers patrolled on foot and were spread very thin. In Chicago, beats were three or four miles long. In many cities, entire areas were not patrolled at all. The telephone did not exist, and so it was impossible for citizens to call about crime and disorder. And with no patrol cars, officers could not have responded quickly, if at all, anyway. As a result, supervision was weak or nonexistent. Sergeants also patrolled on foot and could not keep track of the officers under their command. Many reports from those years indicate that officers easily evaded duty and spent much of their time in saloons and barbershops, where they could also escape from bad weather—rain, snow, and extremely hot weather.[26] The first primitive communications systems involved a network of call boxes that allowed patrol officers to call precinct stations. Officers soon learned to sabotage them, however: leaving receivers off the hook (which took the early systems out of operation), or lying about where they actually were. The lack of an effective communications system made it difficult, if not impossible, for citizens

---

The Diary of a Police Officer: Boston, 1895

We know very little about what police officers did on patrol in the early years. Most of the evidence comes from reformers or journalists seeking to expose corruption and inefficiency. Their reports are inherently biased. An 1895 diary of Boston police officer Stillman S. Wakeman provides a rare glimpse into actual police work 100 years ago.

Officer Wakeman was "an officer of the neighborhood." He spent most of his time on patrol responding to little problems that neighborhood residents brought to him: disputes, minor property crimes, and so on. He spent relatively little time on major offenses: murder, rape, robbery. He resolved most of the problems informally, acting as a neighborhood magistrate. His role was remarkably similar to that of contemporary patrol officers. He was reactive and a problem solver. The major difference was the absence of modern police technology: the patrol car and the 911 telephone system.

Source: Alexander von Hoffman, "An Officer of the Neighborhood: A Boston Patrolman on the Beat in 1895," *Journal of Social History* 26 (Winter 1992): 309–330.

---

to contact the police. In the event of a crime or disturbance, a citizen had to go out into the street and find an officer. (See Sidebar 2–3.)

The Police and the Public

For a discussion of legitimacy and police–community relations, see Chapter 12.

There was never a "golden age" of American policing in which the police were friendly, knowledgeable about their neighborhoods, and enjoyed good relations with the public. There were so few police officers that they could not possibly have known many people on their beats. The turnover rate among officers was high, and the population was even more mobile than today. Many reports, moreover, indicate that many police officers drank on duty and frequently used excessive physical force. When Theodore Roosevelt, a newly appointed police commissioner in New York City (and future president of the United States), walked the streets at night to observe officers at work, he often had trouble finding even one.[27] As a result, citizens were often disrespectful to the officers they encountered. Juvenile gangs, for example, made a sport of throwing rocks at the police or taunting them. People who were arrested often fought back, causing officers to use excessive force.[28]

Historian Christopher Thale, analyzing the records of officer assignments in New York City in the nineteenth century, convincingly argues that it was "not mathematically plausible" for officers to know many people on their beats. First, the composition of neighborhoods changed continually under the pressure of massive immigration. Second, officer assignments were not stable. When the New York City Police Department (NYPD) was established, officers were required to live in their precincts. This policy was often ignored, however, and then abolished in 1857. The pressure of providing police services forced the department to assign officers where they were needed, particularly in new and growing neighborhoods. Thale concludes that citizens "experienced not 'the' cop on the beat, but 'the cops'."[29]

Police-citizen relations were characterized by ethnic and religious tensions. The NYPD became largely Irish Catholic, and officers were often hostile to or even brutal toward the new Italian and Jewish immigrants. In short, long before the introduction of the police car in the twentieth century, American urban policing was highly imper-sonal and marked by police-citizen conflict. The idea of the friendly "neighborhood cop" is pure myth.

What went wrong with American policing? In a provocative comparative study, Wilbur Miller argues that the London police became highly professional, while the American police were completely unprofessional. The difference was that the com-missioners of the London Metropolitan Police were free from political interference and able to maintain high personnel standards. As a result, London Bobbies eventu-ally won public respect. By contrast, the lack of adequate supervision in America meant that police misconduct was tolerated, resulting in public disrespect. From the very start, in short, police in the two countries went in different directions.[30]

American police officers eventually began to carry firearms in response to increasing citizen violence. As late as 1880, the police in Brooklyn (then an indepen-dent city of 500,000 people) were unarmed. In some cities, weapons were optional or carried at the discretion of a sergeant. As crime and violence increased in the late 1800s, however, officers began to carry firearms as standard equipment.

The role of the police was very different in the political era from what it is today. The police were a major social welfare institution. Precinct stations provided lodging to the homeless. The Philadelphia police gave shelter to more than 100,000 people a year during the 1880s. This began to change around 1900. The police pro-fessionalized, concentrating on crime, and care for the poor became the responsibil-ity of what were then newly-created professional social work agencies.[31]

Corruption and Politics

George W. Plunkitt represented everything that was wrong with American policing in the nineteenth century. A district leader for Tammany Hall, the social club that con-trolled New York City politics for several generations, he is a famous historical figure because he explained in writing exactly how corruption worked: Tammany Hall "always stood for rewardin' the men that won the victory." Jobs in the police department were one of the major rewards he and other political leaders had to offer. Tammany Hall re-ceived bribes from saloon-keepers, gamblers and prostitutes. Why did police corruption last so long? Plunkitt explained that the people "knew just what they were doin'." They liked the rewards they received and were not offended by the illegal activity.[32]

Police **corruption** was epidemic in the nineteenth century. Historian Mark Haller argues that corruption was not a form of deviant behavior but was one of the main functions of local government, and the police were a major part of it.[33] The police took payoffs for not enforcing laws on drinking, gambling, and prostitution. The money was then divided among officers at all ranks. Corruption extended to personnel decisions. Officers often had to pay bribes for promotion. In New York City, an officer seeking promotion to sergeant had to pay a bribe of $16,000.[34] The cost of obtaining a promotion was compensated for by the greater opportunities for graft. The New York City police commissioner, forced to resign in 1894, admitted that he had amassed a personal fortune of more than $350,000 (equivalent to millions in today's dollars).[35]

Corruption served important social and political ends. Consider the case of drinking. Protestant Americans saw sobriety as a badge of respectability and

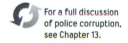
For a full discussion of police corruption, see Chapter 13.

corruption

self-discipline. They sought to impose their morality on working-class immigrant groups, especially the Irish and Germans, by limiting or outlawing drinking. For blue-collar immigrants, the neighborhood saloon was not only a place to relax (remember: people in those days did not have homes with recreation rooms), but also the base of operations for political machines. Thus, the attack on drinking was also an attack on working-class social life and political power. Working-class immigrants fought back by gaining political control of the police, and simply not enforcing the laws on drinking.[36]

Immigration, Discrimination, and Police Corruption

On December 3, 1882, the New York City police arrested 137 people for violating the "Sunday Closing Law." The crackdown was a dramatic reversal of traditional practice. Laws requiring businesses to close on Sunday had been on the books since the colonial period but were usually ignored. The new enforcement effort, and the controversy that lasted for many years afterward, illustrates the connection among immigration, ethnic and religious discrimination, and police corruption.[37]

SIDEBAR 2–4

The Saga of Barney McGinniskin, First Irish-Born Police Officer in Boston

When Barney McGinniskin went out on duty on November 5, 1851, he was the first-ever Irish-born police officer in the city of Boston. The saga of McGinniskin's appointment and career with the Boston police illuminates the conflicts over immigration, prejudice, and politics that engulfed all police departments in the nineteenth century.

McGinniskin's appointment was part of an ongoing political struggle for control of the Boston police in the 1850s. Elections in the state broke the political power of the established Whig Party (a predecessor of the Republican Party), which was dominated by the descendants of the original Protestant settlers of Massachusetts Bay Colony. With different groups vying for control of Boston, the idea of appointing an Irish-born police officer developed as a strategy for appealing to Irish Democrats.

McGinniskin was 42 years old and had lived in the U.S. for 22 years. Opposition arose quickly, however, and one political leader declared that it was "a dangerous precedent to appoint a foreigner to stations of such trust." The opposition focused on the dire poverty that afflicted recent immigrants from Ireland, and the crime and disorder that existed in their neighborhoods. Protestants, who generally strictly limited their consumption of alcohol, stereotyped the Irish as heavy drinkers. Irish-born individuals had held other political offices, but the police department was regarded as a special case. McGinniskin was attacked as a "common cabman," from the notorious Ann Street area; and he had been convicted of participating in a riot 10 years earlier. In the end, McGinniskin was appointed a police officer.

In the political turmoil that ensued, the mayor of Boston fired the entire night police force, leaving the city protected only by the old night watch. Similar mass firings for political reasons occurred in many cities during this period. Within just a few years, however, McGinniskin was fired (for reasons that are not clear). In 1861, 10 years after he had been appointed, there were no Irish-born officers on the police force. Political fortunes changed, however, and by 1886 there were more than 40.

Source: Roger Lane, *Policing the City: Boston 1822–1885* (Cambridge: Harvard University Press, 1967), 75–78.

Almost all of those arrested that Sunday in 1882 were Jewish small business-men: butchers, barbers, bakers, and so forth. They worked on Sunday because their religious beliefs required them to close on Saturday to observe the Jewish Sabbath. Complying with the state law meant they would be closed two days a week, while their non-Jewish competitors only had to close for one day.

As the battle over enforcement of the Sunday Closing Law continued for many years, several patterns emerged, according to cultural historian Batya Miller. "Reform" mayors, who were generally Protestant, were the most vigorous in enforcing the laws. Future U.S. president Theodore Roosevelt, who served as New York police commissioner from 1895 to 1897, advocated strict enforcement, for example. The Tammany Hall political machine, dominated by Irish Catholics, by contrast, generally ignored the law when it was in power. This did not mean that Jewish business-men were free from discrimination, however. Tammany Hall politicians extorted a $5 fee from street peddlers to avoid being arrested. In fact, police officers marked the peddlers' street carts of those who did not pay with chalk, indicating to other officers that they were fair game for arrest. At the same time, police brutality against Jews by Irish Catholic officers was "not uncommon," according to Miller.

In short, cultural conflict over religious holidays was at the heart of arbitrary enforcement of the laws, corruption, police brutality, and deeper ethnic and religious conflict in city politics. This was no "golden age" of good law enforcement.

The Failure of Police Reform

On the night of February 14, 1892, Rev. Charles H. Parkhurst, minister of the Madison Square Presbyterian Church in New York City, stood before 800 of his parishioners and delivered a searing indictment of the corruption that pervaded the city and its police department. He called the mayor and all the police captains a "lying, perjured, rum-soaked and libidinous lot." Gambling, illegal liquor sales, and prostitution were everywhere, protected by a system of payoffs that, in effect, licensed crime.[38]

Parkhurst's call to action launched yet another attempt to root out corruption and to reform the police in New York City. Similar events occurred in other cities. Reformers came, made much noise, and then they went away, leaving no significant changes in policing in their wake. In many cases, they concentrated on changing the formal structure of control of police departments, usually by creating a board of police commissioners appointed by the governor or the legislature. This struggle for control reflected divisions along the lines of political parties, ethnic groups, and urban and rural perspectives. New York created the first state-controlled police commission in 1857. In many cities, the battle for control of the police was endless. Cincinnati underwent ten major changes in the form of police control between 1859 and 1910.[39]

Reformers failed to improve the quality of policing because they had no vision of how a police department might be better organized and managed. They primarily sought to replace "bad" people (their political opponents) with "good" people (their own supporters). They did not have any new ideas about police administration, and they did not make any lasting changes in recruitment standards, training, or supervision. They gave no attention to use of excessive force or race discrimination—two issues that are of paramount concern today.

For a full discussion of current police accountability measures and their impact, see Chapter 14.

Theodore Roosevelt

Theodore Roosevelt, who was later president of the United States (1901–1909), was a brief beneficiary of Rev. Parkhurst's reform campaign in New York City. He was appointed one of the four commissioners of the police in 1895, and for two years he conducted a flamboyant campaign to clean up the police department. With the famous crusading journalist Jacob Riis at his side, he walked the streets at night, searching for police officers, often in vain. The ones he found were usually either sleeping in one of their favorite "coops" (secluded hiding places) or standing in front of saloons. Like other reformers, he saw reform as a personal crusade, not an effort in organizational change. He resigned in 1897, having accomplished nothing. Roosevelt was elected vice president of the United States the next year, and in 1901 after President William McKinley was assassinated, he was suddenly president.[40]

The Impact of the Police on Crime and Disorder

Did the early American police departments reduce crime and disorder? Did a young man in the slums of Cincinnati or Baltimore refrain from committing a burglary or robbery because he was afraid of being caught? Probably not. As already indicated, there were too few officers on patrol and patrolling on foot they were unable to cover much territory or respond quickly to crimes. Nor was there any way for crime victims to efficiently contact the police.

impact of the police on crime

Historians debate the **impact of the police on crime** and society. Cities did become more orderly as the nineteenth century progressed. Historians argue that the growth of order was primarily a result of a natural adaptation to urban life. The daily routine of urban life—reporting to work every day at the same hour—cultivated habits of self-discipline and order. The police, according to this view, played a supporting role at best.[41]

For a discussion of contemporary police crime-fighting strategies, see Chapter 9.

The police were often used to suppress labor unions or union-organizing efforts, from the nineteenth century through the mid-1930s when the Wagner Act guaranteed workers the right to organize unions "of their own choosing." The police were used to harass labor unions and break strikes. American labor relations during these years were extremely violent. Management fought unions, and many strikes led to violence. In some communities, particularly those with coal and steel industries, strikes were like a civil war. In some cities, however, the police were friendly to organized labor, mainly because they came from the same blue-collar communities, and refused to serve the interests of businessmen.[42]

In the end, although the modern police were created to deal with the problems of crime and disorder, their impact on crime was minimal at best. In fact, the police became a social and political problem themselves, with political influence and rampant corruption. Particularly serious, the roots of today's police problems were firmly planted in the nineteenth century. There were no controls over police officer conduct, and discrimination and brutality went unchecked. The next century of American police history was devoted to ending these problems.

The Professional Era, 1900–1960

American policing underwent a dramatic change in the first half of the twentieth century. The two principal forces for change were an organized movement for police professionalism, followed by the introduction of modern technology, particularly the telephone and the patrol car.

The Police Professionalization Movement

If Robert Peel was the father of the modern police, **August Vollmer** was the father of American police professionalism. Vollmer served as chief of police in Berkeley, California, from 1905 to 1932 and, more than any other person, defined the reform agenda that continues to influence policing today. He is most famous for advocating higher education for police officers, hiring college graduates in Berkeley and organizing the first college-level police science courses at the University of California in 1916. In that respect, he is also the father of modern criminal justice education. Vollmer also served as a consultant to many local police departments and national commissions. In 1923, he took a year's leave from Berkeley to serve as chief of the Los Angeles Police Department. He also wrote the 1931 Wickersham Commission *Report on Police,* which summarized the reform agenda of modern management for police departments, including higher recruitment standards for officers. A number of his students went on to become reform-minded police chiefs in California and other states.[43]

August Vollmer

Vollmer was part of a new generation of leaders at the turn of the century who launched an organized effort to professionalize the police. Police reform was part of a much broader political movement known as progressivism between 1900 and 1917. Progressive reformers sought to regulate big business, eliminate child labor, improve social welfare services, and reform local government, as well as professionalize the police.[44]

The Reform Agenda

The **professionalization movement** developed a specific agenda of reform (see Exhibit 2–3). First, the reformers defined policing as a profession. This meant that the police should be public servants with a professional obligation to serve the entire community on a nonpartisan basis. Second, reformers sought to eliminate the influence of politics on policing. Third, they argued for hiring qualified chief executives to head police departments, people who had proven ability to manage a large organization. Arthur Woods, a prominent lawyer, served as police commissioner in New York City from 1914 to 1917, while Philadelphia hired Marine Corps General Smedley Butler to head its police department from 1911 to 1915.[45]

professionalization movement

Fourth, the reformers tried to raise personnel standards for rank-and-file officers. This included establishing minimum recruitment requirements of intelligence, health, and moral character. New York City created the first permanent police training academy in 1895. In most cities the process of reform was painfully slow. Some cities did not offer any meaningful training until the 1950s.

EXHIBIT 2–3

The Reform Agenda of the Professionalization Movement

1. Define policing as a profession.
2. Eliminate political influence from policing.
3. Appoint qualified chief executives.
4. Raise personnel standards.
5. Introduce principles of modern management.
6. Create specialized units.

Fifth, professionalism meant applying modern management principles to police departments. This involved centralizing command and control and making efficient use of personnel. Until then, police chiefs had exercised little real control; captains in neighborhood precincts and their political friends had the real power. Reformers closed precinct stations and used the new communications technology to control both middle management personnel and officers on the street.

Sixth, reformers created the first specialized units devoted to traffic, juveniles, and vice. Previously, police departments had only patrol and detective units. Specialization, however, increased the size and complexity of the police bureaucracy, increasing the challenge of managing departments. Juvenile units led to a historic innovation: the first female sworn officers. Until then, policing had been an all-male occupation. The Portland (Oregon) police hired the first policewoman, Lola Baldwin, as a juvenile specialist in 1905.

Alice Stebbins Wells became the leader of the policewomen's movement. She joined the Los Angeles Police Department in 1910, and was soon active at the national level. She organized the International Association of Policewomen in 1915 and gave many talks around the country about the role of policewomen. By 1919, more than 60 police departments employed female officers. Wells shared the dominant values of her time regarding women, however, which limited their role in policing.[46]

The first policewomen did not perform regular patrol duty, usually did not wear uniforms, did not carry weapons, and had only limited arrest powers. Policewomen advocates argued that women were specially qualified to work with children and that they should not handle regular police duties. Female officers did not work on regular patrol duty until 1968.

Alice Stebbins Wells

 For a discussion of women in policing, see Chapter 5.

The Achievements of Professionalization

Professionalization progressed slowly but did achieve a number of important gains in terms of the quality of policing. By 1920, police departments in Milwaukee, Cincinnati, and Berkeley had emerged as leaders in the field, with reputations for new standards of police management and personnel standards. Unfortunately, progress in most departments was slow, with corruption and inefficiency the norm. August Vollmer spent 1923 and 1924 trying to reform the Los Angeles police but gave up and returned to Berkeley in despair over his inability to make any significant changes. Chicago seemed to resist all efforts at reform. In some cities, the police made notable steps forward, only to slide backward a few years later. Philadelphia, for example, implemented many reforms between 1911 and 1915, only to have all progress wiped out when the city's old political machine regained control.[47] Milwaukee had one of the best departments in the 1920s, but by the 1960s it had deteriorated and experienced serious conflict with the African American community, including a riot in 1967.[48]

The greatest failure of progressivism was its complete inattention to controlling officer conduct on the street. There was no discussion in any of the reform literature of police use of force, both deadly force and physical force; discrimination against African Americans or Hispanics; or abusive treatment of the unemployed or radical political groups. Even the fourth edition of O. W. Wilson's extremely influential book on *Police Administration,* published in 1977, contained no discussion of police discretion, or how the lack of controls on its exercise could result in the abuse of police authority.[49] (The first serious discussion of police discretion did not even begin until the mid-1960s, and the first book on the subject was not published until 1975).[50] The failure of police reformers in this regard was symptomatic of American law and politics in general during the first five decades of the twentieth century. The civil rights and civil liberties revolutions in the law did not begin to gain momentum until the mid-1950s.

Despite these failures, the professionalization movement reformers achieved some important successes. The idea of professionalism was established as the goal for modern policing. Reformed departments also became models for other cities.

Other Impacts of Professionalization

Professionalization had other impacts that proved to be problematic for the future. As part of the new management style of professionalization, reformers enhanced the military ethos of police departments. In the nineteenth century, police departments had some military-style elements—uniforms and rank designations—but in practice they were extremely undisciplined, with politicians rather than the chief making important decisions. Professional-oriented reformers added parades, close-order drills, military-style commendations, and a new emphasis on police firearms.[51] These changes left an unfortunate legacy for the future. The command system became far more centralized and authoritarian than it had been in the old days.

Another unfortunate consequence of professionalization was that rank-and-file police officers became the forgotten people. Reformers placed all their hopes on strong police chiefs and regarded the rank and file as clay that had to be remolded through better training and discipline. As a result, officers retreated into an isolated and alienated police subculture that opposed most reforms.

The most dramatic expression of the new police subculture was the emergence of police unions. As policing became a profession and officers thought in terms of the job as a career, they demanded better salaries and a voice in decisions affecting their jobs. The problem reached crisis proportions during World War I, when increases in the cost of living eroded the value of police salaries. This set the stage for the 1919 **Boston police strike,** one of the most famous events in police history. Salaries for Boston police officers had not been raised in nearly 20 years. When their demand for a 20 percent raise was rejected, they voted to form a union. Police Commissioner Edwin U. Curtis then suspended the union leaders, and 1,117 officers went out on strike, leaving only 427 on duty. Violence and disorder erupted throughout the city. Massachusetts governor Calvin Coolidge called out the state militia and won national fame (and eventually became U.S. president) for his comment, "There is no right to strike against the public safety by anybody, anywhere, at any time." The strike collapsed quickly, and all the strikers were fired.[52]

The violence in Boston produced a national backlash against police unions, and unionization efforts in other cities evaporated quickly. Police unionism did not revive until the 1960s, but the problem of an alienated rank and file remained.

Professionalism also created new problems in police administration. As departments grew in size and created new specialized units, they became increasingly complex bureaucracies, which required increasingly sophisticated management. Managing police organizations continued to be a major challenge into the twenty-first century.

For a discussion of the control of police discretion, see Chapter 11.

Boston police strike

Police and Race Relations

On July 2, 1917, in East St. Louis, Illinois (just across the river from St. Louis, Missouri), a car filled with white males drove through the African American neighborhood and fired guns into a group on a street corner. When the next car appeared, African Americans fired at it, killing a police officer. Soon, the entire city was engulfed in one of the worst race riots in the early twentieth century.[53]

For a discussion of contemporary problems in police–community relations, see Chapter 12.

The early years of the police professionalization movement coincided with major conflict between the police and African American communities across the country. In addition to East St. Louis, riots erupted in Washington, D.C.; Chicago; Omaha; and other cities in the hot summer of 1919. All of the riots involved bands of whites attacking African Americans. The underlying cause of the East St. Louis riot was tensions arising from major employers hiring African Americans to replace striking white workers. The Chicago riot erupted when a young African American crossed a boundary line that racially segregated the beach on Lake Michigan. In all the riots, police officers stood by, not arresting marauding whites. In some cases, police officers joined in the racist violence themselves.[54]

The Chicago Riot Commission recommended several steps to improve police–community relations, but nothing was done to either hire more African American officers or eliminate race discrimination in police work. Even when some departments outside the South hired a few African American officers, they usually assigned them to the black community. Most southern police departments, meanwhile, hired no African American officers at all, while some put them in a second-class category, assigning them only to the black community and not allowing them to arrest whites. Conflict between the police and the African American community remained a serious problem in all parts of the country, but it did not receive any serious attention until the riots of the 1960s.[55]

New Law Enforcement Agencies

In the years before World War I, two important new law enforcement agencies appeared in the United States: the **state police** and the Bureau of Investigation.

state police

Several states had created state-level law enforcement agencies in the nineteenth century, but they remained relatively unimportant. The Texas Rangers were established in 1835. The Pennsylvania State Constabulary, created in 1905, was the first modern state police force. It was not typical of most of the other state agencies, however. It was a highly centralized and very militaristic agency that concentrated on controlling strikes. Business leaders felt that local police and the militia were unreliable during strikes. Organized labor bitterly attacked the Constabulary, denouncing its officers as "cossacks."[56]

For a discussion of state and federal law enforcement agencies, see Chapter 3.

Among the other new state police, about half were highway patrols, limited to traffic enforcement, and the other half were general law enforcement agencies. Although business interests wanted Pennsylvania-style agencies, organized labor in several states was able to limit their powers or block their creation altogether.[57]

The Bureau of Investigation was established in 1908 by executive order of President Theodore Roosevelt. (It was renamed the Federal Bureau of Investigation in 1935.) Until then, the federal government had no full-time criminal investigation agency. Private detective agencies were sometimes used under contract on an as-needed basis. The new Bureau of Investigation was immediately involved in scandal, however, when some agents were caught opening the mail of a U.S. senator who had opposed creating the bureau. Even greater abuses occurred in 1919 and 1920, in the Palmer Raids, in which bureau agents conducted massive roundups of thousands of alleged political radicals. The raids involved gross violations of due process, as people arrested were held without bail in overcrowded jails, unable to contact family or lawyers. Many of those who were immigrants were soon deported. More scandals followed in the 1920s, as the bureau hired people with political connections as "dollar a year" men.[58]

The bureau was finally cleaned up and put on a professional basis when J. Edgar Hoover was appointed director in 1924. Hoover kept a low profile for about a decade, shrinking the bureau in size and raising personnel standards. But in the early 1930s, however, he changed abruptly, launching a "war on crime," that was accompanied by an aggressive public relations campaign that exaggerated the image of the FBI, and at the same time reinstituted political spying that had been ended in 1924.

Technology Revolutionizes Policing

Today, people routinely pick up the telephone to call the police when a crime, neighborhood disorder, or some other problem occurs. They expect the police to arrive quickly and often complain when it takes 20 minutes for an officer to get there. It was not always this way. There was a time when people could not just call the police, and there was no way for the police to get to the scene of a crime or disorder quickly.

Technology revolutionized policing as a result of the introduction of the patrol car, the two-way radio, and the telephone. The result was a complete transformation of routine patrol work, the dynamics of police-citizen contacts, public expectations about the police, and the supervision of officers (see Exhibit 2–4).[59]

The patrol car first appeared just before World War I and by the 1920s was in widespread use across the country. The police adopted it in part because they had to keep up with citizens and criminals who were now driving cars. Even more important, police chiefs believed the patrol car would make possible efficient and effective patrol coverage. Patrolling by car would allow officers to cover their beats more intensively, passing any point more than once during a shift. Following the principles of Robert Peel, chiefs were convinced this would deter crime more effectively than

the patrol car

EXHIBIT 2–4

The Technological Revolution in Policing

New Technology	Impact
Telephone	Citizens can easily call the police.
Two-way radio	Police are dispatched to calls quickly.
	Patrol officers are under constant supervision.
Patrol car	Police respond quickly to citizen calls.
	Patrol coverage is efficient.
	Patrol officers are isolated.

foot patrol. Also, patrol officers would be able to respond quickly to crimes and arrest more criminals as a result. American police departments steadily converted from foot to motor patrol, and by the 1960s only a few major cities still relied heavily on foot patrol.

The patrol car had important unintended consequences, however, that created new problems. It removed the officer from the street and reduced informal contact with law-abiding citizens. The police became isolated from the public, and in the 1960s African Americans in particular saw the police as an occupying army.

The two-way radio developed slowly as a result of improvements in radio technology, finally becoming widespread in the late 1930s. This technology had two important consequences for routine policing. First, it allowed departments to dispatch officers in response to citizen calls for service. Second, it revolutionized police supervision by allowing the department to maintain continuous contact with patrol officers.

The telephone was invented in 1877, but it did not have a great impact on policing until it was linked with the patrol car and the two-way radio in the mid-twentieth century. Together, the three pieces of technology completed a new communications link between citizens and the police. Citizens could now easily call the police, the two-way radio enabled the department to dispatch a patrol car immediately, and the patrol car allowed the officer to reach the scene quickly.

Police departments encouraged people to call, promising an immediate response. Gradually, citizens became socialized into the habit of "calling the cops" to handle even the smallest problems. Over time, Americans developed higher expectations about the quality of life because they could now call someone to deal with all sorts of problems. As a result, the call workload increased steadily. When the rising number of calls overloaded the police, departments responded by adding more officers, more patrol cars, and more sophisticated communications systems. These added resources, however, only encouraged more calls, and the process repeated itself. Police departments found themselves the prisoners of 911 calls, with an ever-increasing workload. Finally, in the 1980s, with the emergence of the idea of community policing, experts questioned the value of responding to each and every call for service.[60]

Telephone-generated calls for service altered the nature of police-citizen contacts. Previously, police officers rarely entered private dwellings. Patrolling on foot, they had no way of learning about problems in private areas. Nor did citizens have any way of summoning the police. The new technology made it possible for citizens to invite the police into their homes. The result was a complex and contradictory change in police-citizen contacts. Whereas the patrol car isolated the police from people on the streets, the telephone brought police officers into people's living rooms, kitchens, and bedrooms. There, officers became involved in the most intimate domestic problems: domestic disputes, alcohol abuse, parent-child conflicts, and other social problems.[61]

Finally, as the technological revolution made it possible for people to easily call the police, it altered public expectations about the quality of life in their communities. Beforehand, if there was any kind of disorder—a fight out on the street, or a domestic disturbance in the apartment upstairs—there was no way they could summon the police to restore order. As a result, they simply tolerated such nuisances and possible threats. But when calling the police became possible, people came to expect peace and quiet in their neighborhood, in the house next door, or in their apartment building. This expectation is a routine part of American life today, but the unforeseen consequence was an enormous workload for the police.[62]

New Directions in Police Administration, 1930–1960

The Wickersham Commission Bombshell

In 1931, the **Wickersham Commission** report *Lawlessness in Law Enforcement* created a national sensation with its blunt conclusion that "the third degree—the inflicting of pain, physical or mental, to extract confessions or statements . . . is extensively practiced." Police officers routinely beat suspects, threatened them with worse punishment, and held them illegally for protracted questioning. The report cited examples of a suspect who was held by the ankles from a third-story window and another who was forced to stand in the morgue with his hand on the body of a murder victim. The chief of police in Buffalo, New York, openly declared that he would violate the Constitution if he felt he had to, in order to get a confession.[63]

Wickersham Commission

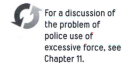

For a discussion of the problem of police use of excessive force, see Chapter 11.

The Wickersham Commission had been created by President Herbert Hoover in 1929 to study a wide range of issues in the American criminal justice system, and the report on police lawlessness was one of its 14 reports in 1931. The report had an enormous long-term impact on policing. It inspired a new generation of police administrators, which included many protégés of August Vollmer, who made new efforts to professionalize the police.

Professionalization Continues

Influenced by August Vollmer, California police departments took the lead in professionalization from the 1920s through the 1960s. Vollmer's protégés became police chiefs throughout the state, spreading the reform agenda. The first undergraduate law enforcement program was established at San Jose State College in 1931. California also developed a system of regional training for police officers in the late 1930s.[64]

O. W. Wilson, Vollmer's most famous protégé, emerged as the leader of police reform from the late 1930s through the early 1960s. He served as chief of police in Wichita, Kansas, from 1928 to 1939, Dean of the University of California School of Criminology from 1950 to 1960, and Superintendent of the Chicago police from 1960 to 1967.[65]

O. W. Wilson

Wilson made his greatest impact through his two textbooks on police management: the International City Manager's Association's *Municipal Police Administration* and his own *Police Administration* (1950). The latter book became the informal "bible" of police administration, influencing a generation of police chiefs.[66] But as mentioned earlier, Wilson's influential book contained no discussion of police discretion, police use of both deadly and physical force, or patterns of discrimination in arrest (as relates, for example, to racial discrimination or police handling of domestic violence incidents).

Wilson's major contribution to police management involved the efficient management of personnel, particularly patrol officers. In 1941, he developed a formula for assigning patrol officers on the basis of a workload formula that reflected reported crime and calls for service in each area of the city. This formula, refined and updated through modern management information systems, is still used by police departments today. Unfortunately, however, Wilson's preoccupation with patrol allocation, which influenced the entire police profession, drew attention away from issues of officer conduct on the street and how to control both discretion and misconduct.

Simmering Racial and Ethnic Relations

Despite the progress in professionalization, the reformers did almost nothing to improve relations with racial and ethnic minority communities. They completely ignored the recommendations of the report on the 1919 Chicago race riot. In 1943, another wave of racial violence swept the country, with serious disturbances in Detroit, New York City, and Los Angeles. The Detroit riot was serious, disrupting production of tanks and other vehicles needed in World War II. As was the case in the riots of the 1917–1919 period, police officers failed to stop or arrest marauding whites who were attacking African Americans. Thurgood Marshall, the NAACP's chief lawyer (and future Supreme Court justice) denounced the Detroit police as a "gestapo," in a blunt reference to Nazi Germany.[67]

Zoot Suit Riot

The 1943 Los Angeles riot brought attention to growing conflict between the police and the Latino community. Often referred to as the **Zoot Suit Riot,** the violence was the product of many factors. The population of Los Angeles was changing, with an increase in immigrants from Mexico. In addition to discrimination in employment and housing, the Latino community experienced brutality and discrimination at the hands of the police. World War II added another volatile element, because many U.S. Navy personnel were usually on leave in the city. The news media encouraged the idea that young Mexican Americans were responsible for an increase in crime and juvenile delinquency. And because many Latino youth wore the so-called zoot suit, it became both a stereotype and a symbol of the violence that erupted in 1943. The riot broke out on June 3, 1943, and lasted for a week. Although recommendations were made to improve police–community relations, little was done in the years that followed.[68]

The riots of the 1940s gave birth to the modern police–community relations movements. A number of departments created special police–community relations units and offered the first training programs on race relations. The most significant progress occurred in California, under the leadership of Governor Earl Warren (who later became Chief Justice of the U.S. Supreme Court). Michigan State University began sponsoring a series of annual conferences on police–community relations in cooperation with the National Conference of Christians and Jews.[69]

Despite these efforts, however, relatively little progress was made in improving relations between the police and the African American community. Departments in major cities hired relatively few African American officers, even though African American communities continued to grow, largely because of migration from the South. Departments also did little to control police officer use of force, including deadly force, and allegations of "police brutality" grew. These problems finally erupted in a series of riots in the 1960s.

J. Edgar Hoover and the War on Crime

J. Edgar Hoover

The most important new figure in American law enforcement in the 1930s was the director of the Bureau of Investigation, **J. Edgar Hoover.** He cleaned up the scandal-ridden bureau after being appointed in 1924, but in the early 1930s underwent a dramatic transformation. Capitalizing on public fears about a national crime wave, he promoted himself as the nation's "top cop" and changed the name of the bureau to the Federal Bureau of Investigation (FBI) in 1935. In 1930, he won control of the new Uniform Crime Reporting (UCR) system, and a set of new federal laws 1934 gave the FBI authority over bank robberies and the power to arrest criminals who crossed state lines in order to avoid prosecution. The following year, the FBI opened its National Academy, which trained bureau agents and, by invitation, some local police officers.[70]

Hoover developed a mastery of public relations, and skillfully manipulated the media to project an image of the FBI agent as the paragon of professionalism: dedicated, honest, well-trained, and relentlessly efficient. He exaggerated the FBI's role in several famous cases—John Dillinger and Pretty Boy Floyd, for example—and manipulated crime data to create an exaggerated impression of the bureau's effectiveness. He concentrated on small-time bank robbers, while ignoring organized crime, white-collar crime, and violations of federal civil rights laws.[71] Some of Hoover's reputation was deserved. FBI agents were far better educated and trained than local police officers.

Hoover's FBI had a powerful impact on local police. The emphasis on education and training established a new model for personnel standards. The introduction of the UCR, the development of the Ten Most Wanted list, and the creation of the FBI crime lab all served to emphasize the crime-fighting role of the police, at the expense of order maintenance and service to the public. Hoover was also hostile to civil rights, however, and this reinforced the failure of city police departments to address the growing police–community relations problem in America.

There was also an ugly political underside to Hoover's expanded role for the FBI. Beginning in 1935, at the request of President Franklin D. Roosevelt, he resumed political spying by the bureau, compiling secret files on individuals and political groups he disliked.[72] This included all radicals and left-wing groups, many liberals, and civil rights leaders and groups. The result was the longest-running violation of the civil liberties of Americans in U.S. history. The most notorious case involved his secret attempt to destroy Martin Luther King Jr. as a civil rights leader. Hoover's misuse of power did not become known until after his death in 1972, and it was not fully exposed until the investigations of the Senate Church Committee in 1975–1976.[73]

The Police Crises of the 1960s

In the 1960s, the United States experienced a series of upheavals—a series of Supreme Court decisions expanding the scope of individual rights; a new militancy on the part of the civil rights movement; urban riots between 1964 and 1968; student protests against the Vietnam War; and the emergence of a "youth subculture" that challenged established standards about freedom of expression, sexuality, and drugs. All of these dramatic changes directly affected the police (see Exhibit 2–5).

The Police and the Supreme Court

Ernesto Miranda was just an ordinary career criminal. Between the ages of 14 and 18, he had been arrested six times and imprisoned four times. On the evening of March 2, 1963, he raped a young woman in Phoenix, Arizona. His arrest eleven days

---

EXHIBIT 2–5

Conflicting Pressures on the Police, 1960 to Present

Supreme Court rulings on search and seizures, interrogations

High crime rates; fear of crime; political reaction

Civil rights protests, riots, police—community relations crisis

Research and innovation

Traditional professionalization (recruitment standards, patrol management)

Affirmative action (race and gender)

Administrative control of discretion on deadly force, domestic violence, pursuits

Community policing and problem-oriented policing

Citizen oversight of the police

Police unions

The national police crisis

---

later set the stage for one of the most famous Supreme Court decisions in American history. In *Miranda v. Arizona* (1966), the Court overturned his conviction and ruled that police officers had to advise suspects of their right to remain silent and their right to an attorney before being interrogated.[74]

Miranda **decision**

    The ***Miranda* decision** was only one of several famous cases in which the Supreme Court established constitutional standards for the police and for other parts of the criminal justice system. In *Mapp v. Ohio* (1961), the Court held that evidence gathered in an illegal search and seizure could not be used against the defendant. These decisions provoked an enormous political controversy. Civil libertarians hailed these and related decisions as long-overdue affirmations of the constitutional rights of Americans. The police and their supporters, however, claimed that the Court had "handcuffed" them in the fight against crime. Conservative politicians accused the Court of favoring the rights of criminals over the rights of victims and law-abiding citizens.[75]

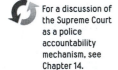 For a discussion of the Supreme Court as a police accountability mechanism, see Chapter 14.

    The Supreme Court's decisions related to the police had an enormous impact on searches and seizures and interrogations. Most important, they provoked police departments to develop new training and supervision procedures for officers, to ensure that they complied with the law and would not lose criminal cases. Departments also began raising the entry-level requirements for becoming a police officer.[76] Additionally, the Court's decisions prompted law enforcement leaders to develop a system of accreditation for agencies, similar to accreditation procedures in law, medicine, education, social work, and virtually every other profession. The Commission on Accreditation for Law Enforcement Agencies (CALEA) published its first set of Standards for Law Enforcement Agencies in 1983.[77] Finally, police departments began the process of developing written policies to guide officers in the exercise of discretion. Administrative rulemaking, as it is called, first addressed police use of deadly force and then was extended to cover the handling of domestic violence incidents, high-speed pursuits, the use of physical force, and more areas of routine police work (see "New Developments in Policing, 1970–2016" section, later in this chapter).[78]

The Police and Civil Rights

The civil rights movement entered a new militant phase in on February 1, 1960, when four African American college students conducted a sit-in at a lunch counter in Greensboro, North Carolina, challenging discrimination in public accommodations. That now-famous event sparked similar direct action challenges to racial segregation in other aspects of American life. Inevitably, civil rights groups challenged racially discriminatory practices by the police.[79]

As civil rights protests rose, the white police officer in the black ghetto became a symbol of white power and authority. Studies of deadly force found that police officers shot and killed African American citizens about eight times as often as white citizens. Because of employment discrimination, meanwhile, African Americans were seriously underrepresented as police officers.

On the night of July 16, 1964, James Powell, an African American, was shot and killed by a white off-duty New York City police officer. The shooting sparked six days of protests that included looting and violence in Harlem, the center of the African American community in New York City. The ensuing riot was the first of many over the next four years—in what became known as the **"long hot summers."**[80]

Tensions between the police and the African American community escalated in the early 1960s, as civil rights groups protested unjustified shootings by police officers, use of excessive force, inadequate police protection in their neighborhoods, the lack of effective citizen complaint procedures, and racial discrimination in the hiring of police officers. The rising tensions finally exploded in a nationwide wave of riots between 1964 and 1968. Many riots were sparked by an incident involving the police, as was the case in New York City in 1964. The 1965 riot in the Watts district of Los Angeles was sparked by a simple traffic stop. After devastating riots in Detroit and Newark in the summer of 1967, many Americans feared a complete collapse of law and order in the big cities. President Lyndon Johnson responded by appointing the **Kerner Commission** to study the riots and make recommendations for reform. The commission counted more than 200 violent disorders in 1967 alone.[81]

In response to the crisis, police departments established special police–community relations (PCR) units. PCR programs included speaking to community groups and schools, "ride-along" programs that allowed citizens to view police work from the perspective of the police officer, and neighborhood storefront offices to facilitate communication with citizens. A Justice Department report, however, found that these programs had little impact on day-to-day police work and did little to improve police–community relations.[82]

Civil rights leaders demanded the creation of citizen review boards to investigate citizen complaints of excessive force. At first, the demand for civilian review was unsuccessful. The Philadelphia Police Advisory Board, created in 1958, was abolished in 1967 as a result of pressure from the police union. In New York City, the police union in 1966 succeeded in abolishing a citizen-dominated Civilian Complaint Review Board for the police department. (In a series of changes in the 1980s and 1990s, it was again given a citizen majority.) By the end of the 1960s, even though the riots had stopped, relations between the police and minority communities remained tense.[83]

"long hot summers"

For a discussion of race relations, see Chapter 12.

Kerner Commission

The Police in the National Spotlight

The crime rate in America increased sharply around 1963, and the combination of crime and riots provoked an unprecedented reexamination of the police. The American Bar Foundation had conducted the first-ever field observations of police work in 1955–1957. The observations found many things about policing that are now taken for granted: that police officers exercised broad discretion and that most police work involved noncriminal activity.[84]

President's Crime Commission

The President's Commission on Law Enforcement and Administration of Justice (known as the **President's Crime Commission**) (1965–1967) conducted a comprehensive study of the entire criminal justice system, including the police, and sponsored some important police research. The commission's *Task Force Report: The Police* (1967) included a thoughtful analysis of the complexity of the police role and the fact that only a relatively small part of police work was devoted to criminal law enforcement. The commission sponsored Albert Reiss and Donald Black's quantitative study of police patrol work, which produced important findings on police discretion and the use of force. The main commission report, *The Challenge of Crime in a Free Society* (1967), endorsed much of the traditional agenda of professionalization: higher recruitment standards, more training, and better management and supervision. In an important departure, it also called for controls over police discretion through administrative rulemaking.[85]

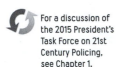 For a discussion of the 2015 President's Task Force on 21st Century Policing, see Chapter 1.

The Kerner Commission report in 1968 found "deep hostility between police and ghetto communities as a primary cause of the disorders." It recommended that routine police operations be changed "to ensure proper individual conduct and to eliminate abrasive practices," that more African American police officers be hired, and that police departments improve their procedures for handling citizen complaints.[86] Both the Kerner Commission and the President's Crime Commission found that procedures for handling citizen complaints were completely inadequate. Many departments had no formal process for receiving and investigating complaints. In many instances, people seeking to file complaints were turned away, or even threatened with arrest.

The Kerner Commission questioned some of the traditional assumptions about police professionalization. It noted that "many of the serious disturbances took place in cities whose police are among the best led, best organized, best trained, and most professional in the country." It pointed out that the patrol car removed the officer from the street and isolated the police from ordinary citizens.[87] In short, traditional "tough" law enforcement practices did great damage to community relations, especially with regard to the African American community. This insight set in motion a rethinking about the police role that eventually culminated in the development of community policing in the 1980s. The President's Crime Commission and the Kerner Commission both expressed concern about the low personnel standards for officers that existed. A 1965 police chief's survey found that 85 percent of all officers received no preservice police academy training.

Chief William Parker of the Los Angeles Police Department (LAPD) illustrated the commission's point about how aggressive crime-fighting aggravated police–community relations. Parker was nationally recognized for turning the LAPD into what was then widely regarded as the most professional department in the country. Parker took command of a notoriously corrupt LAPD in 1950 and quickly asserted strict control over it. He instituted high personnel standards, modern management principles, and an aggressive anticrime approach to policing. Like J. Edgar Hoover, Parker was a master of public relations. Working closely with Jack Webb, he helped the television program *Dragnet* become one of the top-rated programs, and it projected an image of the LAPD as flawlessly professional and efficient.[88]

Parker's style of policing came at a price, however. The aggressive law enforcement tactics aggravated conflict with minority communities, and the LAPD's famous disciplinary system overlooked officer use of excessive force. Historian Martin Schiesl argues that LAPD officers "under the direction of strong-willed chiefs, confused professional obligations with the unrestrained use of power and undermined the civil liberties of racial minorities and politically active groups."[89] Civil rights groups protested, but Parker tolerated no criticism and accused the National Association for the Advancement of Colored People (NAACP) and the American Civil Liberties Union (ACLU) of supporting the criminal element. Parker's legacy lived on in the LAPD long after he retired. The LAPD generated national controversy as a result of the 1991 beating of Rodney King and again in 1999 with the Rampart scandal involving an anti-gang unit. In both cases, the LAPD was accused of tolerating excessive use of force, particularly against racial and ethnic minorities, and of failing to discipline its officers.[90]

In 1973, the American Bar Association published its *Standards Relating to the Urban Police Function*. Most important, the *Standards* recommended administrative rulemaking involving policy guidelines to control the exercise of police discretion. Rulemaking by police departments caught on, and in the years ahead departments developed written policies over use of deadly force, high-speed pursuits, and the handling of domestic violence incidents (discussed in more depth later in this chapter).[91]

The Research Revolution

The crises of the 1960s also spurred rapid expansion of research on the police. This led to the growth of criminal justice/criminology as a significant academic discipline. The **research revolution** produced a substantial body of knowledge about all aspects of policing: patrol work, the exercise of discretion, officer use of force, criminal investigation, police officer attitudes, and more (see Sidebar 2–5). Over the

research revolution

SIDEBAR 2–5

The Research Revolution: An Assessment

The research revolution on policing that began in the 1960s challenged many basic assumptions about policing. The Kansas City Preventive Patrol Experiment, for example, found that simply adding more patrol officers does not reduce crime. By undermining the basic assumption about police patrol that went all the way back to Robert Peel and the first modern police department in 1829, it forced police experts to think about what the police can do to control crime. The resulting crisis over police effectiveness sparked a series of innovations, including community policing, problem-oriented policing, "hot spots" policing, focused deterrence, and others, that have been among the most important developments in policing over the past 30 years.

years, this research had a profound impact on policy, providing a basis for community policing, hot-spots policing, focused deterrence, and other innovations.

The federal government funded much of the new police research, through the Law Enforcement Assistance Administration (LEAA) (1968–1976) and later through the National Institute of Justice. In 1970, the Ford Foundation established the Police Foundation with a grant of $30 million. The foundation sponsored some of the most important police research, including the Kansas City Preventive Patrol Experiment. Later, the Police Executive Research Forum, a professional association of big-city police managers, emerged as the leader in research and innovation in policing.[92]

Kansas City Preventive Patrol Experiment

Some of the most important research undermined traditional assumptions about policing. The **Kansas City Preventive Patrol Experiment** (1972–1973), perhaps the most important experiment in the history of policing, tested the effect of different levels of patrol on crime. The researchers found that increased patrol did not reduce crime and that reduced patrol did not lead to an increase in crime or public fear of crime. These findings had a profound effect on thinking about the police and laid the foundation for the development of community policing a few years later.[93]

 For a detailed discussion of the Kansas City Preventive Patrol Experiment, see Chapter 7.

Other studies, meanwhile, questioned the value of rapid police response to crimes, finding that it did not result in more arrests. Few crime calls involve crimes in progress, and many crime victims do not call the police immediately. In these situations, no offender is present when the police arrive.[94] The Rand Corporation study of criminal investigation, meanwhile, shattered traditional myths about detective work. Most crimes are solved through information obtained by the first officer on the scene, using information from victims or witnesses. Follow-up detective work, of the kind portrayed in the movies and on television, is relatively unproductive and involves routine paperwork.[95]

With respect to police officers' attitudes and behavior, William Westley identified a distinct police subculture, characterized by hostility toward the public, group solidarity, and secrecy. Jerome Skolnick followed up on this insight and found that policing has a distinct working environment, dominated by danger and the exercise of authority. The pressure to achieve results in the form of arrests and convictions, moreover, encourages officers to violate legal procedures. Subsequent studies significantly altered the original view of the police subculture. Police officers' attitudes are shaped by the organizational culture of the police department (and they do vary from department to department), and the introduction of more women, African Americans, Hispanics, and lesbian and gay people has made the police workforce far more diverse than ever before. These changes brought new ideas and perspectives about policing into police departments.[96]

Finally, James J. Fyfe's pioneering study of police use of deadly force in New York City found that a restrictive shooting policy that clearly specifies when an officer can and cannot shoot effectively reduces the number of shootings.[97] The research revolution in policing continues today, with a significant impact on innovations in policing. The most notable research-based policies, which are discussed in later chapters, include community policing and problem-oriented policing (Chapter 10), COMPSTAT (Chapter 14), and focused deterrence (Chapter 10).

New Developments in Policing, 1970–2016

Dramatic changes in policing continued to accelerate from the 1970s to the present. The principal changes include the changing demographic profile of police officers; changes in the definition of the police role and how departments should address crime and disorder; and stricter standards about how officers should exercise their powers of arrest, stops, and use of force. Finally, relations between the police and the African American community have continued to be filled with conflict, exploding into a national crisis in 2014–2016.

The Changing Police Officer

The profile of the American police officer changed significantly beginning in the 1970s. Law professor David Sklansky described policing as "not your father's police department."[98] The employment of African American and Hispanic officers increased significantly. Underrepresentation of African American officers on big-city police departments was one of the major complaints raised by civil rights groups in the 1960s. For example, the Kerner Commission found that, in 1967, African Americans represented 34 percent of the population of Cleveland but only 7 percent of the police officers; in Oakland, they were 31 percent of the population but only 4 percent of the officers.[99] As a result of improved minority hiring efforts, the percentage of African American officers across the country increased to 12 percent in 2007 but did not increase over the next six years.[100] By the 1990s, African American officers were a majority in Detroit, Washington, and Atlanta. Charles Ramsey, an African American, served as chief of the Washington, D.C., police department from 1998 to 2007 and then as commissioner of the Philadelphia police from 2008 to 2016. In 2014 he was named co-chair of the President's Task Force on 21st Century Policing.[101]

 For a discussion of the recruitment of police officers and the issue of diversity, Chapter 5.

The percentage of **Hispanic police officers** across the country also increased, from 6.4 percent in 1989 to 11.6 percent in 2013.[102] In 2006, 48 percent the police officers in San Antonio, Texas, were non-Hispanic white, 46 percent were Hispanic, and 6 percent were African American. Art Acevedo, a Hispanic and former commander with the California Highway Patrol, became chief of police in Austin, Texas, in 2007.

Hispanic police officers

Felicia Shpritzer made history in breaking down the barriers against women in policing. She joined the New York City police department in 1942 and, following the model established by Alice Stebbins Wells and the other pioneer policewomen, served almost 20 years in the juvenile unit. In 1961, she and five other female officers applied for promotion to sergeant. Their applications were rejected, and in fact they were not even allowed to take the promotional exam. They sued, and in 1963 the courts declared the NYPD policy illegal and ordered the department to allow them to take the exam. The following year, 126 policewomen took the exam; Shpritzer and one other woman passed. The other woman, Gertrude Schimmel, became the first female captain in the NYPD in 1971 and was deputy chief when she retired in 1981. Shpritzer had retired as a lieutenant in 1976.[103]

Traditional barriers to **women in policing** collapsed under the impact of the 1964 Civil Rights Act, which barred discrimination on the basis of sex, and the women's movement. By the mid-1990s, about 13 percent of officers in most big-city departments were women. Additionally, departments eliminated requirements (such as minimum height or special strength tests) that had discriminated against female

women in policing

applicants. In an important breakthrough, female officers were assigned to routine patrol duty for the first time in 1968. Evaluations of female officers on patrol in Washington, D.C., and New York City found their performance to be as effective as that of comparable groups of male officers.[104]

Penny Harrington broke another barrier in 1985 when she was appointed chief of the Portland, Oregon, police department. She was the first woman to head a large police department. (There had been several female chiefs since 1919, but all involved small agencies, according to historian Dorothy Schulz.) Harrington was followed by Elizabeth Watson, appointed chief of the Houston, Texas, police department in 1990. Since then, a number of women have served as chiefs of large city and state law enforcement agencies.[105]

Police departments also began to recruit college students. In the early 1960s, the typical officer had only a high school education. The federal government, meanwhile, encouraged the development of college criminal justice programs. Whereas only 20 percent of all sworn officers had any college education in 1960, the figure had risen to 65 percent by 1988.[106]

Preservice training improved dramatically. The length of training increased from an average of about 300 hours in the 1960s to more than 1,000 hours in many departments by the 1990s. Departments also added field training programs, in which a new officer would be partnered with a veteran officer, designated a field training officer for a number of weeks.[107] Police academy curricula added units on race relations, domestic violence, and ethics. New York and California introduced mandatory training for all police officers in 1959, and eventually every state had a training and certification requirement. Previously, many small police and sheriff's departments offered no preservice training whatsoever. In all but a few states today, state law mandates a certain number of hours of annual in-service training for all officers.

Despite these changes, police training remained inadequate in some important respects. A 2015 report by the Police Executive Research Forum found that police training across the country had serious deficiencies. Police academies spent an average of 58 hours on firearms training, compared with only 40 hours on legal issues (for example, search and seizure), and a mere ten hours on communication skills.[108]

An increasing number of states, meanwhile, adopted procedures for decertifying officers who had been found guilty of misconduct. Decertification meant that the person was not eligible to work as a sworn officer in the state (although this did not prevent him or her from working as a sworn officer in another state, if the hiring department did not bother to do a thorough background check).[109]

Administrative Rulemaking and the Control of Police Discretion

Progress in the control of police discretion continued from the 1970s to the present. The control of deadly force was one of the most important reforms. James Fyfe's research, discussed earlier, found that a written policy restricting the use of firearms, and also requiring a report of each weapons discharge, effectively reduced the overall number of weapons discharges and the number of people shot by the police.[110] Within just a few years, other departments adopted similar policies. As a result, the number of citizens shot and killed by the police nationwide dropped substantially between 1970 and the mid-1980s.[111]

The **administrative rulemaking** model for controlling police discretion, which was the basis for the new rules on the use of deadly force, was soon applied to other aspects of policing. The model called for a written policy providing clear guidance on when to shoot or not shoot, and the factors officers should take into account when exercising their discretion. Equally important, the model requires officers to complete a use of force report after each incident, and for all reports to be carefully reviewed by high-ranking command officers.[112]

Rising public concern about domestic violence led to a revolution in police policy in that area as well. Women's groups sued the police in New York City, Oakland, and other cities for failing to arrest men who had committed domestic assault. These suits produced departmental policies prescribing mandatory arrest in cases where there was a felonious assault. Soon, other departments across the country adopted similar policies.[113] Departments also adopted written policies regarding high-speed vehicle pursuits, limiting pursuits involving people suspected of only minor crimes, limiting the number of police cars in any pursuit, and directing officers to take into account the risks to bystanders caused by the presence of pedestrians or unsafe road conditions due to bad weather.[114]

administrative rulemaking

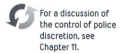

For a discussion of the control of police discretion, see Chapter 11.

The Emergence of Police Unions

Police unions spread rapidly in the 1960s and by the 1970s were a powerful force in American policing. Officers were angry and alienated over Supreme Court rulings, criticisms by civil rights groups, poor salaries and benefits, and arbitrary disciplinary practices by police chiefs.[115] Associations of officers had existed for many decades (for example, an association of Irish American officers). A police union, however, involves a legally recognized collective bargaining agent that has the authority to negotiate a binding contract with the city over wage and working conditions.

police unions

Unions had a dramatic impact on police administration. They won significant improvements in salaries, fringe benefits, and pensions for officers, along with grievance procedures that allowed an officer to challenge unfair treatment. Far more controversial were contract provisions that related to departmental investigations of alleged officer misconduct and disciplinary procedures. In a number of cities, the police union contract provided that an officer involved in a shooting incident, for example, could not be questioned by supervisors for 48 hours. Some union contracts require or permit the purging of officer disciplinary records after a specified number of years.[116] Critics of the police charged that such provisions protected officer misconduct. Finally, police unions exercised considerable political power. Police unions consistently opposed citizen oversight of the police and other reforms designed to improve police–community relations. In a highly publicized incident in late 2014, the New York City Patrolmen's Benevolent Association attacked the mayor of New York City, Bill de Blasio, accusing him of not supporting the police and blaming him for the recent fatal shooting of two officers.[117]

The Spread of Citizen Oversight of Police

Citizen oversight of the police spread beginning in the 1980s, and by 2015, it was estimated that there were between 100 and 200 oversight agencies. By 1995, there were enough agencies that a professional association was established, the National Association for Civilian Oversight of Law Enforcement (NACOLE).[118]

In the 1990s, a new form of citizen oversight appeared: the police auditor or inspector general. Unlike civilian review boards, which reviewed individual citizen complaints, police auditors examined police department policies and procedures, and then recommended changes that would help improve the quality of policing and reduce citizen complaints. The Special Counsel to the Los Angeles Sheriff's Department, created in 1993 (but abolished in 2014), issued semiannual reports that covered virtually every aspect of policing: use-of-force trends, civil suits against the department, foot pursuits, the deployment of canine, training, and many others.[119]

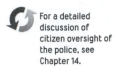 For a detailed discussion of citizen oversight of the police, see Chapter 14.

In 2013, New York City created an inspector general for the NYPD. Based on the auditor model of oversight, the inspector general had the authority to investigate any issue within the NYPD. In 2015, for example, it issued a report that found serious problems with how officers reported use-of-force incidents and made a set of recommendations for improvement.[120]

Community Policing, Problem-Oriented Policing, and Other Innovations

The most important new development in policing in the 1980s and 1990s was the advent of community policing (COP) and problem-oriented policing (POP). Both represented a new vision of the role of the police in addressing crime and disorder. Advocates of **community policing** hailed it as a new era in policing. As early as 1988, Kelling argued that "a quiet revolution is reshaping American policing."[121] The U.S. Justice Department encouraged the growth of community policing through the Office of Community Oriented Policing Services (known as the COPS Office), which distributed the money to hire 100,000 new officers.

community policing

In the seminal article "Broken Windows," James Q. Wilson and George L. Kelling summed up the recent research on policing: patrol had only limited deterrent effect on crime, faster response times did not increase arrests, and the capacity of detectives to solve crimes was limited. This research suggested two important points: that the police could not fight crime by themselves, but were dependent on citizens, and that the police could reduce fear of crime by concentrating on less serious quality-of-life problems (for example, "broken windows").[122]

Community policing challenged the norms of traditional police professionalization, arguing that police departments had become centralized bureaucracies that were isolated from the communities they served. In addition, community policing advocates argued that police departments had focused too much on crime control and neglected the broad range of disorder issues. Several developments spurred the idea of community policing. The civil rights crisis of the 1960s indicated that the police had a serious problem in relation to the African American community. The research revolution also had a major impact. The Kansas City Preventive Patrol Experiment found that simply adding more patrol officers did not reduce crime. The Newark Foot Patrol Experiment, meanwhile, found that adding foot patrols also did not reduce crime.[123]

 For a detailed discussion of community policing and problem-oriented policing, see Chapter 10.

To develop more effective strategies to address crime and disorder, community policing involved decentralizing policymaking to the neighborhood level and developing partnerships with neighborhood residents. Problem-oriented policing, meanwhile, emphasized focusing on particular crime or disorder problems in different neighborhoods and developing specific strategies for each one.

POLICE in FOCUS | Charles Ramsey: Reform Police Executive

Charles Ramsey began his career in law enforcement with the Chicago Police Department. He rose to the position of deputy superintendent and played a major role in developing community policing in Chicago, in a program known as CAPS (Chicago Alternative Policing Strategy).

He left Chicago in 1998 to become commissioner of the Washington, D.C., police department, which at the time had serious problems with its organization and with excessive use of force. As commissioner, he encouraged the U.S. Department of Justice to investigate the department. The result was a Memorandum of Agreement (MOA), which mandated a set of major reforms involving officer use of force, the investigation of force incidents, an early intervention system, and improvements in officer training. After several years, the court-appointed monitor of the MOA concluded that the Washington, D.C., police department was substantially improved as a result of the reforms.

In 2008, Ramsey became the commissioner of the Philadelphia Police Department, which also had a long history of problems related to officer-involved shootings and the use of excessive force. To address these problems, Ramsey invited the Critical Response Team of the Justice Department's COPS Office to investigate the policies and practices regarding use of force in Philadelphia. The investigation concluded with a report that identified the underlying problems related to the department's use-of-force policies and also its practices regarding the investigation of force incidents.

While still commissioner of the Philadelphia Police Department, Ramsey was named co-chair of the President's Task Force on 21st Century Policing. The final report of the task force, released in April 2015 and which is covered in detail in Chapter 1 of this book, brought together all the best thinking in American policing, including legitimacy and public trust, procedural justice, and greater openness and transparency on the part of police departments.

In early 2016, shortly after Ramsey retired as commissioner of the Philadelphia Police Department, he became a consultant to the Chicago Police Department, which was engulfed in a major scandal involving the fatal shooting in the back of an African American male.

Departments all across the country adopted community policing. A 2015 report by the Bureau of Justice Statistics found that about 90 percent of all police departments in large cities had a community policing mission statement.[124] The most ambitious community policing program was CAPS. It was a citywide effort that included regular neighborhood meetings between police and residents for the purpose of identifying neighborhood problems and developing solutions. An evaluation of CAPS found that it resulted in greater citizen involvement with the police, improved cooperation between the police and other government agencies (for example, sanitation) over neighborhood problems, a decline in neighborhood problems, and improved public perceptions of the police department.[125] Unfortunately, the CAPS program was cut back sharply because of political pressures over a rise in violent crime. At the national level, meanwhile, community policing programs also faded away. Wesley Skogan told the President's Task Force on 21st Century Policing in 2015 that the status of community policing programs was very uncertain.[126]

The concept of **problem-oriented policing** (POP) was developed by Herman Goldstein. It holds that instead of thinking in terms of global concepts such as "crime" and "disorder," the police should address particular problems and develop creative responses to each one. Instead of crime fighters, officers should be problem solvers, planners, and community organizers.[127] In the first POP experiment, officers in Newport News, Virginia, attacked crime in a deteriorated housing project by

problem-oriented policing

helping the residents organize to improve conditions in the project itself. This included working with both government agencies and private companies to fulfill their responsibilities regarding building conditions and sanitation.

The evidence on the success of community policing programs, however, is mixed. Many police departments received federal funds for additional officers and established community policing programs, without adopting the core elements of community policing. Many programs vanished when the federal funds ended. The Chicago CAPS program, as mentioned earlier, was cut back sharply. Problem-oriented policing remains viable, however. The Center for Problem-Oriented Policing publishes an extensive series of guides on how to address different problems and organizes an annual conference where the best POP programs are recognized as winners of the Herman Goldstein Award.[128]

Data-Driven Policing

By the 1990s, police departments had become increasingly data-driven, with computer technology facilitating the analysis of large datasets on crime, disorder, and officer conduct. The capacity to analyze large datasets led to a series of innovations in police strategy that are often labeled "smart policing."

COMPSTAT, pioneered by the NYPD, is a computerized data system with timely data on criminal activity by precinct or sector. The major focus of COMPSTAT is to hold police managers (typically captains) accountable for crime and disorder in their areas of command. At regular COMPSTAT meetings, crime patterns in managers' respective areas are reviewed, and they are expected to explain what they are doing to address the crime problems that exist. The response may include variations of problem-oriented policing, hot-spots policing, or other innovative approaches.[129]

Hot-spots policing developed out of research indicating that particular crimes are typically concentrated in certain areas. The hot-spots phenomenon was first identified by Lawrence Sherman's analysis of 911 calls in Minneapolis in the 1980s. After the hot spots are identified, police managers can develop strategies to reduce crime in those areas. Those strategies might include intensive patrol or problem-oriented policing.[130]

early intervention system   An **early intervention system** is a computer-based system for police accountability. An EIS contains anywhere from five to more than 20 indicators of police officer performance. They include all uses of force, all citizen complaints, disciplinary histories, use of sick leave and overtime, and other indicators. Some departments include arrests and traffic stops in their EISs, whereas others do not. Analysis of the data identifies those officers with a higher than average number of problematic indicators (for example, uses of force). Some of those identified are then referred for intervention designed to help officers improve their performance. An EIS does not involve discipline. Interventions may include counseling by the officer's immediate supervisor; retraining on police actions identified by the EIS data; or referral to professional counseling for substance abuse, anger management, or other issues. Following intervention, officers are tracked to determine whether their performance has improved.[131]

Racial Profiling and Discrimination

On the morning of May 8, 1992, Robert Wilkins was driving on Interstate 95 in Maryland with three members of his family. They were returning to Washington,

D.C., from the funeral of a family member in Chicago. They were stopped by an officer of the Maryland State Police who told them to get out of the car and then asked for permission to search the car. Wilkins, an attorney and a graduate of Harvard Law School, informed the officer that without an arrest of the driver, a search would be illegal. The officer ignored this advice and made the four family members stand in the rain while they waited for the agency's drug dog to arrive. The dog eventually found no trace of drugs, and Wilkins was finally given a $105 speeding ticket. Wilkins believed not only that the traffic stop was illegal but that he was stopped only because he is African American. This traffic stop eventually led to a major lawsuit (*Wilkins v. Maryland*) that sparked national controversy over the practice of **racial profiling,** or what some people called "driving while black."[132]

 For a discussion of racial profiling and other forms of police discretion, see Chapter 12.

racial profiling

    Civil rights leaders charged that the police stopped African American drivers solely on the basis of their race and not on the basis of any suspected criminal activity. Data presented as part of an ACLU lawsuit against the Maryland State Police indicated that although African Americans represented only 17 percent of all drivers on Interstate 95 and 18 percent of all observed traffic law violators, they represented 72.9 percent of all drivers stopped by the state police. Additionally, among those drivers stopped, 81.3 percent of those searched after being stopped were African American. Many observers argued that racial profiling, particularly on interstate highways, was a result of the national "war on drugs" and that police officers stereotyped both African Americans and Hispanics as drug dealers.[133]

    Several strategies were developed to combat racial profiling. Civil rights groups advocated the collection of data on traffic stops for the purpose of documenting police practices. Some states passed laws requiring all law enforcement agencies to collect data. The San Jose Police Department was one of the first departments to begin collecting data voluntarily and then issuing reports on the data. A number of states, meanwhile, passed laws requiring all police departments in the state to collect data on traffic stops.

    The most common effort to curb racial profiling is through administrative rulemaking and the adoption of a department policy on when race or ethnicity can and cannot be used in police actions (for example, stops, frisks, arrests). A 2001 report by the Police Executive Research Forum presented a model policy on the use of race or ethnicity. The model policy prohibits the use of race or ethnicity when it is the *sole* basis for a police action. Race or ethnicity may be used as one factor in combination with specific and credible evidence about a criminal suspect. In short, the police cannot stop someone simply because he or she is African American. But they can stop a suspect on the basis of a detailed description, based on credible sources, that includes height, weight, apparent age, dress (baseball cap or no hat), grooming (beard or no beard), and also race or ethnicity.[134]

Federal Investigations of Police Misconduct

A race riot erupted in Cincinnati, Ohio, in April 2001 after the 15th fatal shooting of an African American male in five years. In response, the U.S. Justice Department brought a "pattern or practice" suit against the Cincinnati Police Department. The authority of the Justice Department to investigate is based on Section 14141 of the 1994 Violent Crime Control Act, which authorizes the department to investigate law enforcement agencies when there is a pattern or practice of violations of civil rights (for example, a pattern of excessive force or racial profiling). As mentioned in Chapter 1, where violations are found to exist, Justice Department investigations are settled through a consent decree, an MOA, or a settlement agreement, which requires the department to make certain reforms designed to end the civil rights violations. The purpose of DOJ suits is not to bring criminal charges against individual officers but to require reforms that will bring about organizational change.[135]

The first Justice Department case involved the Pittsburgh Police Bureau in 1997. Other cases have involved the New Jersey State Police; the Los Angeles Police Department; and police departments in Cincinnati, New Orleans, and Seattle. The required reforms have included developing a new, state-of-the-art use-of-force policy, including a procedure for investigating force incidents, an EIS, an improved citizen complaint process, and training related to all of these matters. Settlements also include a court-appointed monitor to oversee implementation of the required reforms.

The federal investigations and consent decrees have been controversial. Critics charge that they are an unjustified intrusion of the federal government into local police affairs, and are an expensive burden on local communities. Walker and Macdonald, by contrast, argue that they are an effective remedy for police departments with systemic abuse problems and that seem incapable of reforming themselves.[136] The monitor for the Cincinnati Police Department, in recommending an end to the consent decree, concluded in late 2008 that "[t]he City of Cincinnati is now in a very different situation than it was in 2002." The department "has improved its training, its policies and procedures, its investigations of uses of force and citizen complaints, its risk management and its accountability." An evaluation of the Los Angeles consent decree experience, meanwhile, concluded that the LAPD was "much changed" and that "both the quantity and the quality of enforcement [activities] have risen substantially." In short, LAPD officers were not just working harder, but they were working smarter.[137]

Local Police and the War on Terrorism

The terrorist attacks on the two towers of the World Trade Center in New York City and the Pentagon in Washington, D.C., on September 11, 2001, had a profound effect on American policing. They introduced a new concern about homeland security terrorism (see "Police in Focus" in Chapter 1). One consequence was to divert police attention and resources away from traditional police priorities and recent community policing experiments. Departments undertook special training for terrorist-related disasters (such as bomb threats) in cooperation with other law enforcement agencies in the area. The wars in Afghanistan and Iraq, meanwhile, caused the mobilization of both military reserve units and National Guard units, which included some police officers, and caused the temporary loss of officers for police departments. Finally, many departments took advantage of the federal government's 1033 program, which made available military equipment at no cost. Over $5 billion in equipment had been transferred by 2014. Critics charged that much of the equipment, especially Mine Resistant Ambush Protected (MRAP, or "em-wrap") vehicles, was unnecessary and inappropriate for domestic police, and shifted the focus of policing away from its traditional responsibilities.[138]

The National Police Crisis, 2014–2016

On August 9, 2014, Officer Darren Wilson of the Ferguson, Missouri, police department shot and killed Michel Brown, an unarmed 18-year-old African American. The shooting touched off angry protests, which were met with a heavy military-style response by the police and then escalated into violence and looting. National cable news channels broadcast almost nonstop coverage of the events.

The tragic developments in Ferguson touched off two years of police-related events that created a **national crisis over policing** and race relations, to a degree not seen since the urban riots of the 1960s. Earlier, on July 17, 2014, New York City police officers arrested Eric Garner, an African American, on Long Island for selling illegal cigarettes. Officers sat on him to hold him down and did not respond to Garner's repeated cries, "I can't breathe!" Garner died and the incident was recorded on cell phone video and broadcast repeatedly over national television. In April 2015, in North Charleston, South Carolina, Walter Scott, an African American, was shot in the back and killed by a white officer as Scott was running away. The shooting was captured on cell phone video and clearly showed the lack of any justification for the shooting. On April 19, 2015, Freddie Gray, a 25-year-old African American died after being arrested by Baltimore, Maryland, police a week earlier and then given a "rough ride" in a police van where he sustained serious neck injuries. Gray's death touched off protests and then violence, arson, and looting.

The sequence of events has provoked several national responses. Civil rights activists protesting deaths at the hands of the police organized around the slogan "Black Lives Matter." President Barack Obama in December 2014 appointed a President's Task Force on 21st Century Policing. It was the first-ever presidential commission or task force devoted exclusively to the police. After a series of hearings around the country, the commission delivered its final report, with a broad set of recommendations for improving policing and addressing the police–race relations crisis.[139] The shootings exposed the fact that the United States did not have a reliable database on the number of people shot and killed by the police each year. The official FBI figure for 2014 was 444. The *Washington Post* began compiling its own records and discovered that the actual number of persons shot and killed by the police was twice the FBI figure for preceding years: 986 people in 2015, for example.[140]

national crisis over policing

CASE STUDY

De-escalating Police–Citizen Encounters

Although police administrators may take steps to attempt to eliminate misconduct by individual police officers, many departments have adopted patrol practices that, in the words of one commenter, have "replaced harassment by individual patrolmen with harassment by entire departments."

These practices, sometimes known as *"aggressive preventative patrol,"* take a number of forms, but invariably they involve a large number of police–citizen contacts initiated by police rather than in response to a call for help or service. *One such practice utilizes a roving task force,* which moves into high crime districts without prior notice and conducts intensive, often indiscriminate, street stops and searches. A number of persons who might legitimately be described as suspicious are stopped. But so also are persons who are respected members of the community. Such tasks forces are often deliberately moved from place to place, making it impossible for its members to know the people with whom they come in contact.

In some cities aggressive patrol is not limited to special task forces. The beat patrolman himself is expected to participate and to file a minimum number of stop-and-frisk or field interrogation reports for each tour of duty. This pressure to produce, or a lack of familiarity with the neighborhood and its people, may lead to widespread use of these techniques without adequate differentiation between genuinely suspicious behavior and behavior that is suspicious to a particular officer merely because it is unfamiliar. *Police administrators, pressed by public concern about crime, have instituted such patrol practices often without weighing their tension-creating effects* and the resulting relationship to civil disorder.

Motorization of police is another aspect of patrol that has affected law enforcement in the ghetto. The patrolman comes to see the city through a windshield and hear about it over a police radio. To him, the area increasingly comes to consist only of lawbreakers. To the ghetto resident, the policeman comes increasingly to be only an enforcer.

Loss of contact between the police officer and the community he serves adversely affects law enforcement. If an officer has never met, does not know, and cannot understand the language and habits of the people in the area he patrols, he cannot do an effective police job. His ability to detect truly suspicious behavior is impaired. He deprives himself of important sources of information. *He fails to know those persons with an "equity" in the community*—homeowners, small businessmen, professional men, persons who are anxious to support proper law enforcement—and thus sacrifices the contributions they can make to maintaining community order.

Source: Excerpt from the Kerner Commission Report, 1968, pp. 304–305. Emphasis added.

SUMMARY: FROM PAST TO PRESENT

The *Final Report of the President's Task Force on 21st Century Policing*, released in April 2015, dramatized the main themes in the history of the American police. It brought together the best thinking about policing, highlighting the creativity of current police practices and thinking. At the same time, however, it highlighted how serious the police-community problem is and how much needs to be done to establish fully professional and accountable policing, particularly with regard to race relations.

The President's Task Force report minced no words about the problems facing policing. It bluntly began by stating, "Trust between law enforcement agencies and the people they protect and serve is essential in a democracy. It is key to the stability of our communities, the integrity of our criminal justice system, and the safe and effective delivery of policing services." The recommendations for change highlighted many problems that needed to be fixed: the need for greater openness and transparency on the part of the police; the need for better data collection on police use of force and other activities; the need for citizen oversight of the police; the need to work more closely with schools to help young people maintain law-abiding lives; and so on.

The report embodied many important new ideas in policing, which reflected well on an openness to criticism of traditional approaches and a willingness to innovate. These ideas included the importance of establishing the legitimacy of the police; how procedural justice strategies can contribute to that end; the need to discard the traditional "warrior" mindset of policing and replace it with a community-focused "guardian" mindset; and many others.

KEY TERMS

English heritage, 30
Robert Peel, 31
London Metropolitan
    Police, 31
crime prevention, 31
the watch, 32
first modern American
    police, 33
"political era", 34
patronage, 35
corruption, 37
Theodore Roosevelt, 40
impact of the police on crime, 40
August Vollmer, 41

professionalization
    movement, 41
Alice Stebbins Wells, 42
Boston police strike, 43
state police, 44
the patrol car, 45
Wickersham
    Commission, 47
O. W. Wilson, 47
Zoot Suit Riot, 48
J. Edgar Hoover, 48
Miranda decision, 50
"long hot summers," 51
Kerner Commission, 51

President's Crime
    Commission, 52
research revolution, 53
Kansas City Preventive Patrol
    Experiment, 54
Hispanic police officers, 55
women in policing, 55
administrative rulemaking, 57
police unions, 57
community policing, 58
problem-oriented policing, 59
early intervention systems, 60
racial profiling, 61
national crisis over policing, 63

FOR DISCUSSION

The 1968 Kerner Commission report on the urban riots of the 1960s identified a number of police practices that created problems with racial and ethnic minority communities. Has anything changed in the nearly 50 years since then? Discuss this issue with reference to Chapter 1 of this book and the developments discussed in this chapter. Specifically, consider the following questions:

1. Has anything changed with regard to aggressive anticrime patrol activities?
2. How has technology, particularly computers, assisted in the development of "smart policing" strategies to address crime and disorder? What new programs have been developed?
3. Has the composition of police departments changed with regard to race, ethnicity, and gender? Do you think this has helped improve policing?
4. Citizen oversight of the police has grown since 1968. Do you believe this has helped to improve policing and police–community relations?

INTERNET EXERCISES

Many police departments include material on the history of their departments in their annual reports or on their websites.

Exercise 1 Select several police departments from your region, or from different parts of the county and check their websites for discussions of their history. How many agencies share their history? What issues are emphasized? What issues are not mentioned?

Exercise 2 Visit the website of the Los Angeles Police Museum at http://laphs.org/. Take a look at both the Media Gallery and the History of the

LAPD (buttons on the left side of the home page). What issues are emphasized? Based on what you have learned in this chapter, what important issues are not covered? What image of policing emerges from this museum's web page?

Exercise 3 Visit www.popcenter.org/learning/goldstein_interview/ and view Dr. Samuel Walker's interviews with Herman Goldstein on his work on the President's Crime Commission, the American Bar Association Survey, and the origins of problem-oriented policing. As a class, discuss Goldstein's influence on American policing.

NOTES

1. David Bayley, *Police for the Future* (New York: Oxford University Press, 1994), 126.
2. Samuel Walker, *Popular Justice: A History of American Criminal Justice*, 2nd ed. (New York: Oxford University Press, 1998), ch. 1.
3. T. A. Critchley, *A History of Police in England and Wales*, 2nd ed. (Montclair, NJ: Patterson Smith, 1972).
4. Brian A. Reaves, *Local Police Departments, 2013: Personnel, Policies, and Practices* (Washington, DC: Department of Justice, 2015), table 1.
5. Allen Steinberg, *The Transformation of Criminal Justice, Philadelphia, 1800–1880* (Chapel Hill: University of North Carolina Press, 1989).
6. Critchley, *A History of Police in England and Wales*, ch. 2.
7. Allan Silver, "The Demand for Order in Civil Society: A Review of Some Themes in the History of Urban Crime, Police, and Riot," in David J. Bordua, ed., *The Police: Six Sociological Essays* (New York: John Wiley, 1967), 12–13.
8. David Bayley, *Patterns of Policing: A Comparative International Analysis* (New Brunswick, NJ: Rutgers University Press, 1985), 23.
9. Walker, *Popular Justice*, ch. 1.
10. Julian P. Boyd, "The Sheriff in Colonial North Carolina," *North Carolina Historical Review* 5 (1928): 151–181.
11. Roger Lane, *Policing the City* (New York: Atheneum, 1971), ch. 1.
12. Ibid.
13. Sally E. Hadden, *Slave Patrols: Law and Violence in Virginia and the Carolinas* (Cambridge, MA: Harvard University Press, 2001).
14. Douglas Greenberg, *Crime and Law Enforcement in the Colony of New York, 1691–1776* (Ithaca, NY: Cornell University Press, 1976).
15. Walker, *Popular Justice*, ch. 1.
16. Richard Maxwell Brown, *Strain of Violence: Historical Studies of American Violence and Vigilantism* (New York: Oxford University Press, 1975).
17. Richard Hofstadter and Michael V. Wallace, eds., *American Violence: A Documentary History* (New York: Vintage Books, 1971).
18. Ibid.
19. Steinberg, *The Transformation of Criminal Justice*, 119–149.
20. Wilbur R. Miller, *Cops and Bobbies: Police Authority in New York and London, 1830–1870* (Chicago: University of Chicago Press, 1977).
21. Samuel Walker, *A Critical History of Police Reform* (Lexington: Lexington Books, 1977); Robert Fogelson, *Big City Police* (Cambridge, MA: Harvard University Press, 1977).
22. Richard Zacks, *Island of Vice: Theodore Roosevelt's Quest to Clean Up Sin-Loving New York* (New York: Anchor Books, 2012); Jay Stuart Berman, *Police Administration and Progressive Reform: Theodore Roosevelt as Police Commissioner of New York* (New York: Greenwood Press, 1987).
23. Walker, *A Critical History of Police Reform*, 71–72.
24. Ibid., 9.
25. Lane, *Policing the City*, 75–78.
26. Walker, *A Critical History of Police Reform*, 14–19; Miller, *Cops and Bobbies*.
27. Zacks, *Island of Vice;* Berman, *Police Administration and Progressive Reform*.
28. Walker, *A Critical History of Police Reform*, 14–19.
29. Christopher Thale, "Assigned to Patrol: Neighborhoods, Police, and Changing Deployment Practices in New York City Before 1930," *Journal of Social History* 37, no. 4 (2004): 1037–1064.
30. Miller, *Cops and Bobbies*.
31. Walker, *A Critical History of Police Reform*, 18–19.
32. William L. Riordan, ed., *Plunkitt of Tammany Hall* (New York: Dutton, 1963).
33. Mark Haller, "Historical Roots of Police Behavior: Chicago, 1890–1925," *Law and Society Review* 10 (Winter 1976): 303–324.
34. Fogelson, *Big City Police*.
35. Berman, *Police Administration and Progressive Reform*, 51.
36. Walker, *A Critical History of Police Reform*, 25–28.
37. Batya Miller, "Enforcement of the Sunday Closing Law on the Lower East Side, 1882–1903," *American Jewish History* 91 (June 2003): 269–286.
38. Zacks, *Island of Vice*, 7–8.
39. James F. Richardson, *The New York Police: Colonial Times to 1901* (New York: Oxford University Press, 1970); Walker, *A Critical History of Police Reform*.
40. Zacks, *Island of Vice;* Berman, *Police Administration and Progressive Reform*.
41. Roger Lane, *Violent Death in the City* (Cambridge, MA: Harvard University Press: 1979); Walker, *Popular Justice*, 66–69.
42. Sidney L. Harring, *Policing a Class Society: The Experience of American Cities, 1865–1915* (New Brunswick, NJ: Rutgers University Press, 1983). Walker, *A Critical History of Police Reform*, 28–31.

43. Gene E. Carte and Elaine H. Carte, *Police Reform in the United States: The Era of August Vollmer* (Berkeley: University of California Press, 1975).

44. Walker, *A Critical History of Police Reform*, 53–78.

45. Ibid.

46. Ibid., 84–94.

47. Ibid., 61–66.

48. Patrick Jones, *The Selma of the North: Civil Rights Insurgency in Milwaukee* (Cambridge, MA: Harvard University Press, 2009).

49. O. W. Wilson and Roy C. McLaren, *Police Administration*, 4th ed. (New York: McGraw-Hill, 1977).

50. Kenneth C. Davis, *Police Discretion* (St. Paul, MN: West Publishing, 1975).

51. Walker, *A Critical History of Police Reform*, 66–67.

52. Francis Russell, *A City in Terror: 1919—The Boston Police Strike* (New York: Viking Press, 1975).

53. Elliott M. Rudwick, *Race Riot at East St. Louis, July 2, 1917* (Carbondale: University of Southern Illinois Press, 1963); William M. Tuttle, *Race Riot; Chicago in the Red Summer of 1919* (New York: Atheneum, 1970).

54. Walker, *Popular Justice*, 148–151.

55. Chicago Commission on Race Relations, *The Negro in Chicago* (Chicago: University of Chicago Press, 1922).

56. Walker, *Popular Justice*, 140.

57. H. Kenneth Bechtel, *State Police in the United States: A Socio-Historical Analysis* (Westport, CT: Greenwood, 1995).

58. Kenneth D. Ackerman, *Young J. Edgar: Hoover, The Red Scare, and the Assault on Civil Liberties* (New York: Da Capo Press, 2008); Curt Gentry, *J. Edgar Hoover: The Man and the Secrets* (New York: Norton, 1991).

59. Samuel Walker, "'Broken Windows' and Fractured History: The Use and Misuse of History in Recent Police Patrol Analysis," *Justice Quarterly* I (March 1984): 77–90.

60. Malcolm K. Sparrow, Mark H. Moore, and David M. Kennedy, *Beyond 911: A New Era for Policing* (New York: Basic Books, 1990).

61. Walker, "'Broken Windows' and Fractured History."

62. Ibid.

63. National Commission on Law Observance and Enforcement, *Lawlessness in Law Enforcement* (Washington, DC: U.S. Government Printing Office, 1931; reprinted: New York: Arno Press, 1971).

64. Carte and Carte, *Police Reform in the United States*.

65. William J. Bopp, *O. W.: O. W. Wilson and the Search for a Police Profession* (Port Washington, NY: Kennikat Press, 1977).

66. O. W. Wilson, *Police Administration* (New York: McGraw-Hill, 1950).

67. Alfred McClung Lee and Norman D. Humphry, *Race Riot* (New York: Dryden Press, 1943).

68. Mauricio Mazon, *The Zoot-Suit Riots: The Psychology of Symbolic Annihilation* (Austin: University of Texas Press, 1984); Edward J. Escobar, *Race, Police, and the Making of a Political Identity: Mexican Americans and the Los Angeles Police Department, 1900–1945* (Berkeley: University of California Press, 1999).

69. Walker, *Popular Justice*, 170–172.

70. Ackerman, *Young J. Edgar*; Gentry, *J. Edgar Hoover*.

71. Richard Gid Powers, *G-Men: Hoover's FBI in American Popular Culture* (Carbondale: Southern Illinois University Press, 1983).

72. Samuel Walker, *President's and Civil Liberties: From Wilson to Obama* (New York: Cambridge University Press, 2012), 98–100.

73. Athan G. Theoharis and John Stuart Cox, The Boss: *J. Edgar Hoover and the Great American Inquisition* (Philadelphia: Temple University Press, 1988); Gentry, *J. Edgar Hoover*.

74. *Miranda v. Arizona,* 384 U.S. 436 (1966); Liva Baker, *Miranda: Crime, Law, and Politics* (New York: Atheneum, 1983).

75. *Mapp v. Ohio,* 367-643 (1961); Carolyn Long, *Mapp v. Ohio: Guarding Against Unreasonable Searches and Seizures* (Lawrence: University Press of Kansas, 2006).

76. Walker, *Popular Justice*, 181–193.

77. See Commission on Accreditation for Law Enforcement website at http://www.calea.org/.

78. Samuel Walker and Carol Archbold, *The New World of Police Accountability*, 2nd ed (Newbury Park, CA: Sage, 2014), 66–103.

79. Walker, *Popular Justice,* 193–199.

80. National Advisory Commission on Civil Disorders, *Report* (New York: Bantam Books, 1968).

81. Ibid., 315–316, 321–322.

82. Department of Justice, *Improving Police/Community Relations* (Washington, DC: U.S. Government Printing Office, 1973).

83. Samuel Walker, *Police Accountability: The Role of Citizen Oversight* (Belmont, CA: Wadsworth, 2001), ch. 2.

84. Samuel Walker, "Origins of the Contemporary Criminal Justice Paradigm: The American Bar

Foundation Survey, 1953–1969," *Justice Quarterly* 9 (March 1992): 47–76.

85. President's Commission on Law Enforcement and Administration of Justice, *The Challenge of Crime in a Free Society* (Washington, DC: U.S. Government Printing Office, 1967); President's Commission on Law Enforcement and Administration of Justice, *Task Force Report: The Police* (Washington, DC: U.S. Government Printing Office, 1967).

86. National Advisory Commission on Civil Disorders, *Report*.

87. Ibid., 301.

88. Lou Cannon, *Official Negligence: How Rodney King and the Riots Changed Los Angeles and the LAPD* (New York: Times Books, 1997), ch. 3.

89. Martin Schiesl, "Behind the Shield: Social Discontent and the Los Angeles Police Since 1950," in Martin Schiesl and Mark Morrall Dodge, eds., *City of Promise: Race and Historical Change in Los Angeles* (Claremont: Regina Books, 2006), 166.

90. Christopher Commission, *Report of the Independent Commission on the Los Angeles Police Department* (Los Angeles: The Christopher Commission, 1991); Cannon, *Official Negligence*.

91. American Bar Association, *Standards Relating to the Urban Police Function*, 2nd ed. (Boston: Little, Brown, 1980).

92. Wesley G. Skogan and Kathleen Frydl, *Fairness and Effectiveness in Policing: The Evidence* (Washington, DC: National Academies Press, 2004).

93. George L. Kelling et al., *The Kansas City Preventive Patrol Experiment: A Summary Report* (Washington, DC: The Police Foundation, 1974).

94. U.S. Department of Justice, *Response Time Analysis* (Washington, DC: U.S. Government Printing Office, 1978).

95. Peter Greenwood, *The Criminal Investigation Process* (Santa Monica, CA: Rand, 1975).

96. William A. Westley, *Violence and the Police* (Cambridge, MA: MIT Press, 1970); Jerome Skolnick, *Justice without Trial: Law Enforcement in a Democratic Society*, 3rd ed. (New York: Macmillan, 1994).

97. James J. Fyfe, "Administrative Interventions on Police Shooting Discretion: An Empirical Analysis," *Journal of Criminal Justice* 7 (Winter 1979): 309–323.

98. David Alan Sklansky, "Not Your Father's Police Department: Making Sense of the New Demographics of Law Enforcement," *Journal of Criminal Law and Criminology* 96 (Spring 2006): 1209–1213.

99. National Advisory Commission on Civil Disorder, *Report*, 321–322.

100. Reaves, *Local Police Departments, 2013: Personnel, Policies, and Practices*, table 5.

101. President's Task Force on 21st Century Policing, *Final Report* (Washington, DC: U.S. Department of Justice, 2015).

102. Reaves, *Local Police Departments, 2013,* table 5.

103. "Felicia Shpritzer Dies at 87; Broke Police Gender Barrier," *New York Times*, December 31, 2000; "Gertrude Schimmel, First Female New York Police Chief, Dies at 96," *New York Times,* May 12, 2015.

104. Susan E. Martin, *Women on the Move: The Status of Women in Policing* (Washington, DC: The Police Foundation, 1990); Peter B. Bloch and Deborah Anderson, *Policewomen on Patrol: Final Report* (Washington, DC: The Police Foundation, 1974).

105. Dorothy Moses Schulz, "Women Police Chiefs: A Statistical Profile," *Police Quarterly* 6 (September 2003): 330–345.

106. David L. Carter et al., *The State of Police Education* (Washington, DC: Police Executive Research Forum, 1989).

107. Michael S. Campbell, *Field Training for Police Officers: State of the Art* (Washington, DC: U.S. Department of Justice, 1986).

108. Police Executive Research Forum, *Re-Engineering Training on Police Use of Force* (Washington, DC: Author, 2015).

109. Roger L. Goldman, "A Model Decertification Law," *Saint Louis University Public Law Review* XXXII (2012): 147–157.

110. Fyfe, "Administrative Interventions on Police Shooting Discretion."

111. William A. Geller and Michael S. Scott, *Deadly Force: What We Know* (Washington, DC: Police Executive Research Forum, 1992).

112. Samuel Walker, "Historical Roots of the Legal Control of Police Behavior," in David Weisburd and Craig Uchida, eds., *Police Innovation and the Rule of Law* (New York: Springer, 1991), 32–55; Samuel Walker, *Taming the System: The Control of Discretion in Criminal Justice, 1950–1990* (New York: Oxford University Press, 1993), 21–53.

113. Lawrence W. Sherman, *Policing Domestic Violence* (New York: Free Press, 1992).

114. Geoffrey P. Alpert and Cynthia M. Lum, *Police Pursuit Driving: Policy and Research* (New York: Springer, 2014).

115. Hervey A. Juris and Peter Feuille, *Police Unionism* (Lexington, MA: Lexington Books, 1973).

116. See Campaign Zero website at http://www.joincampaignzero.org/#vision.

117. John Nichols, "Bill de Blasio is Not the First New York City Mayor to Clash with Police Unions, *The Nation* (December 28, 2014).

118. Walker, *Police Accountability*.

119. Walker and Archbold, *The New World of Police Accountability*, 185–189.

120. Office of the Inspector General for the NYPD, *Police Use of Force in New York City: Findings and Recommendations on NYPD's Policies and Practices* (New York: Author, 2015), http://www.nyc.gov/html/oignypd/pages/news/news-reports.shtml.

121. George L. Kelling, *Police and Communities: The Quiet Revolution*, Perspectives on Policing (Washington, DC: U.S. Government Printing Office, 1988).

122. James Q. Wilson and George L. Kelling, "Broken Windows: The Police and Neighborhood Safety," *Atlantic Monthly* 249 (March 1982): 29–38.

123. Kelling et al., *The Kansas City Preventive Patrol Experiment;* The Police Foundation, *The Newark Foot Patrol Experiment* (Washington, DC: Author, 1981).

124. Reaves, *Local Police Departments, 2013,* table 8.

125. Wesley G. Skogan and Susan M. Hartnett, *Community Policing, Chicago Style* (New York: Oxford University Press, 1997).

126. Wesley G. Skogan, "What Happened to Community Policing, Testimony, President's Task Force on 21st Century Policing, February 13, 2015.

127. Michael S. Scott, *Problem-Oriented Policing: Reflections on the First Twenty Years* (Washington, DC: U.S. Department of Justice, 2000).

128. See the Center for Problem-Oriented Policing website at http://www.popcenter.org/.

129. James J. Willis, Stephen D. Mastrofski, and David Weisburd, "Compstat and Bureaucracy: A Case Study of Challenges and Opportunities for Change," *Justice Quarterly* 21 (September 2004): 463–496.

130. Lawrence W. Sherman and David Weisburd, "General Deterrent Effects of Police Patrol in Crime 'Hot Spots': A Randomized Controlled Trial," *Justice Quarterly* 12 (December 1995): 625–648.

131. Samuel Walker, *Early Intervention Systems for Law Enforcement Agencies: A Planning and Management Guide* (Washington, DC: U.S. Department of Justice, 2003).

132. Details of the case are in David Harris, "'Driving While Black' and All Other Traffic Offenses: The Supreme Court and Pretextual Traffic Stops," *Journal of Criminal Law and Criminology* 87, no. 2 (1997): 563–564; David A. Harris, *Profiles in Injustice: Why Racial Profiling Cannot Work* (New York: The New Press, 2002).

133. ACLU, *Driving While Black* (New York: Author, 1999).

134. Lorie Fridell, *Racially Biased Policing: A Principled Response* (Washington, DC: Police Executive Research Forum, 2001).

135. Samuel Walker and Morgan Macdonald, "An Alternative Remedy for Police Misconduct: A Model State 'Pattern or Practice' Statute," *George Mason Civil Rights Law Journal* 19 (2009): 479–552.

136. Ibid.

137. Christopher Stone, *Policing Los Angeles Under a Consent Decree: The Dynamics of Change at the LAPD* (Cambridge, MA: Harvard University, 2009), p. i.; City of Cincinnati, Independent Monitor's Final Report (December 2008), p. 1.

138. ACLU, *War Comes Home: The Excessive Militarization of American Police* (New York: Author, 2014).

139. President's Task Force on 21st Century Policing, *Final Report*.

140. Federal Bureau of Investigation, *Uniform Crime Reports*, Expanded Homicide Data, (Washington, DC: U.S. Department of Justice, 2015), table 14; "Final Tally: Police Shot and Killed 986 People in 2015," *Washington Post,* January 6, 2016.

© Derik Holtman/The News-Democrat/AP Images

The Contemporary Law Enforcement Industry

CHAPTER OUTLINE

Basic Features of American Law Enforcement
An "Industry" Perspective
An International Perspective

Size and Scope of the Law Enforcement Industry
The Number of Law Enforcement Agencies
The Number of Law Enforcement Personnel
Understanding Law Enforcement Personnel Data
Civilianization
The Police–Population Ratio
The Cost of Police Protection

The Fragmentation Issue
Alternatives to Fragmentation
The Fragmentation Problem Reconsidered

Municipal Police
County Police

The County Sheriff
The Role of the Sheriff

Other Local Agencies
The Constable
The Coroner/Medical Examiner
Special District Police
Tribal Police
State Law Enforcement Agencies

Federal Law Enforcement Agencies
    Federal Law Enforcement after September 11, 2001
The Private Security Industry

Minimum Standards: American Style
    The Role of the Federal Government
    The Role of State Governments
    Accreditation

CASE STUDY

Summary
Key Terms
For Discussion
Internet Exercises

Basic Features of American Law Enforcement

Law enforcement in the United States is a large and extremely complex enterprise. There are almost 18,000 federal, state, and local agencies, along with a private security industry that employs more than a million additional people.

Several basic features characterize the law enforcement industry. Most important is the tradition of **local political control.** The primary responsibility for police protection rests with local governments: cities and counties. This tradition was inherited from England during the colonial period.

local political control

As a result, American policing is highly fragmented.[1] There is no formal, centralized system for coordinating or regulating all the different agencies. There are some mechanisms for federal and state regulation of local police. They are discussed later in this chapter.

For further reading on the history of the police, see Chapter 2.

Fragmentation produces tremendous variety. Police services are provided by four different levels of government: city, county, state, and federal. Agencies at each level have different roles and responsibilities. Within each category, moreover, there is tremendous variety. The six largest police departments—New York City, Chicago, Los Angeles, Philadelphia, Houston, and Washington (DC) Metropolitan Police—differ significantly from the 9,240 police departments with fewer than 25 officers.[2]

As a result of this variety, it is difficult to generalize about American policing. All police departments have some characteristics in common, but most generalizations about the "typical" police department are extremely risky. Writing about the county sheriff, David N. Falcone and L. Edward Wells reject the common assumption that "policing is policing" and argue that the sheriff "represents a historically different mode of policing that needs to be distinguished more clearly from municipal policing."[3]

An "Industry" Perspective

Because of its fragmentation and variety, it is useful to take an industry perspective on American law enforcement. This approach provides a comprehensive picture of all the different producers of police services in a particular area.[4]

The industry approach also provides a consumer's perspective on policing. On a typical day, the average citizen receives police services from several different agencies. Consider the case of Mr. and Mrs. Smith. The small local police department patrols their suburban neighborhood. Mrs. Smith works downtown, where she is served by the big-city police department. Mr. Smith is a sales representative and drives through small towns and areas patrolled by the county sheriff. The office building where Mrs. Smith works hires private security guards. On her way home,

Mrs. Smith drives on the interstate highway, which is patrolled by the state patrol. Meanwhile, the Federal Bureau of Investigation (FBI), the Drug Enforcement Agency (DEA), and other federal agencies are at work investigating various violations of federal law.

Exhibit 3–1 indicates the various components of the law enforcement industry.

An International Perspective

A quick look at law enforcement in other countries provides a useful perspective on the decentralization and **fragmentation** of American law enforcement.

fragmentation

EXHIBIT 3–1

Components of the American Law Enforcement Industry

Government Agencies

Local
  Municipal police
  County police
  County sheriffs

State
  State police
  Bureaus of criminal investigation

Federal
  Federal law enforcement agencies
  Military law enforcement

Special district police
  Public schools
  Transit police
  College and university police

Native American tribal police

Private Security
  Private security firms
  Security personnel

England, with a population one-fourth that of the United States, has 43 police departments: 41 provincial departments and 2 police forces in London. This is half the number of law enforcement agencies in the state of Nebraska (total of 93). All 43 agencies are administered by the home secretary, who is one of the top officials in the national government (and, in some respects, the equivalent of the attorney general in the United States). Each provincial department also answers to a local police commission. The home secretary has the power to issue administrative regulations on personnel and police operations. Additionally, each of the 43 police departments receives 51 percent of its annual budget from the home secretary's office, giving it the power to enforce regulations.[5]

The Japanese police system also balances central coordination with local control. The National Police Agency is responsible for coordinating the operations of the 47 prefectural police. Each prefecture is officially independent, but the National Police Agency can recommend operational standards and, as in England, provides a significant part of each local agency's budget.[6]

Size and Scope of the Law Enforcement Industry

The Number of Law Enforcement Agencies

There are about 18,000 law enforcement agencies in the United States. This includes about 12,500 local police departments, about 3,000 sheriff's departments, 50 state police agencies, about 1,700 special police agencies, and 73 federal agencies (Exhibit 3–2).[7]

The Myth of 40,000 Agencies

For many years there was great controversy over exactly how many law enforcement agencies exist in the United States. In 1967, the President's Crime Commission incorrectly reported that there were 40,000 agencies, repeating an unconfirmed figure that had been used for years.[8] The correct figure is about 18,000 state and local agencies.

EXHIBIT 3–2

General purpose state and local law enforcement agencies

| Type of agency | Number of agencies | Number of Employees | | | | | |
| | | Full-Time | | | Part-Time | | |
		Total	Sworn	Civilian	Total	Sworn	Civilian
Total	17,759	1,139,653	785,122	335,882	98,711	43,965	54,746
Local police[a]	12,326	604,959	477,317	127,642	57,317	26,745	30,572
Sheriff[a]	3,012	351,904	188,952	162,952	25,179	12,356	12,823
State police[a]	50	88,497	58,421	30,076	1,003	0	1,003
Special jurisdiction[b]	1,733	90,262	56,968	33,294	14,681	4,451	10,230
Constable/marshal[b]	638	4,031	3,464	567	531	413	118

Source: [a]Reaves, Brian, Local Police Departments, 2013: Personnel, Policies, and Practices, 2015;
[b]Reaves, Brian, Census of State and Local Law Enforcement Agencies, 2008.

EXHIBIT 3–3

Local Police and Sheriffs Departments, by Number of Sworn Personnel

Number of Sworn Personnel*	Agencies		Full-Time Sworn Personnel	
	Number	Percentage	Number	Percentage
All sizes	15,338	100	666,269	100
1,000 or more	65	0.4	199,365	29.9
500—999	91	0.6	62,872	9.4
250—499	183	1.2	62,764	9.4
100—249	676	4.4	98,786	14.8
50—99	1187	7.7	79,118	11.9
25—49	2353	15.3	79,469	11.9
10—24	4259	27.8	59,595	8.9
5—9	3448	22.5	18,258	2.7
2—4	2464	16.1	5535	0.8
0—1	611	4.0	505	0.1

*Detail may not add to total because of rounding.

Source: Figures above calculated through data obtained from Reaves, Brian, Local Police Departments, 2013: Personnel, Policies, and Practices, 2015; Andrea Burch, Sheriffs' Office Personnel, 1993–2013, (Washington, DC: U.S. Government Printing Office, 2016).

The typical local police department is very small. As Exhibit 3–3 indicates, about forty percent of all local law enforcement agencies have nine or fewer sworn officers. The 156 largest departments, which represent 1 percent of the departments, employ about 40 percent of all full-time sworn officers.[9]

The Number of Law Enforcement Personnel

Today, there are about 785,000 full-time sworn law enforcement officers employed by local and state law enforcement agencies (Exhibit 3–2). In addition, there were 105,000 federal law enforcement officers authorized to carry firearms and make arrests (this figure, however, does not include military law enforcement personnel).[10] The number of state and local law enforcement personnel has grown significantly since 1992. There are about 35 percent more full-time sworn officers today than there were in 1987.[11]

Understanding Law Enforcement Personnel Data

There is often much confusion about law enforcement personnel data. The important question is: How much police protection does a community receive? The *total number of employees* includes clerical staff and civilian specialists in computers, criminalistics, and so on. The *number of sworn officers* refers to those employees who are legally recognized as police officers, with full arrest power and the like.

authorized strength   It is also important to distinguish between an agency's **authorized strength** and the number of sworn officers *currently employed*. Because of retirements, resignations, and terminations, most departments are below their authorized strength. The annual average attrition rate is about 11 percent.[12] Hiring is often delayed as a way of allowing the city or county to cope with a budget shortfall.[13]

Thus, if you want to know the level of police protection in Los Angeles, for example, you need to determine the number of full-time sworn officers currently employed.

Civilianization

Civilianization is the process of replacing sworn officers with nonsworn personnel for certain positions. Today, about 30 percent of all local police department employees are civilians. This represents an increase from 11.1 percent in 1960 and 18.4 percent in 1980. Nonsworn personnel have been increasingly used as dispatchers, research and planning specialists, crime-data analysts, and computer technicians.[14]

There are several reasons for utilizing **civilians** in police work. First, they free up sworn officers for critical police work that requires a trained and experienced officer. Second, they possess needed expertise in such areas as computers or data analysis. Third, in many cases they are less expensive than sworn officers, thereby representing a cost saving.[15] For these reasons, a number of experts use the proportion of civilian employees within a police agency as an indicator of departmental professionalism.[16]

civilians

The Police–Population Ratio

The standard measure for the level of police protection in a community is the **police–population ratio.** This is usually expressed as the number of sworn officers per thousand residents. The national average for local agencies is 2.1 sworn officers per thousand. The ratio for large cities with populations of 250,000 or more is 2.3. Small cities (population 50,000 to 99,999) have the lowest ratio (1.6 per thousand).

police–population ratio

Police–population ratios vary tremendously among big cities. Washington, D.C., has a ratio of 6.1 per thousand residents, compared with 3.6 in Detroit and 1.4 in San Diego.[17] There is no clear relationship between the police–population ratio and the crime rate. In many respects, instead of higher levels of police protection producing lower crime rates, higher crime rates lead to the employment of more police.[18] The relationship of the police–population ratio to the crime rate is discussed in detail in Chapter 7.

The Cost of Police Protection

Law enforcement is an extremely expensive enterprise. Each year local government agencies spend a total of $64.1 billion on police services. This costs each and every resident in the United States, on average, about $279 every year. The police represent about 46 percent of all criminal justice system expenditures. These figures do not, however, include the cost of private security.[19]

Law enforcement is a labor-intensive industry. On average, full-time sworn officers cost their communities about $131,273 per officer, per year.[20] Personnel costs, including salaries and fringe benefits, consume about 85 to 90 percent of an agency's budget. For this reason, the efficiency of a police department depends heavily on how well it manages its personnel and what percentage of officers it places in patrol and investigative units (see Chapter 7).

The Fragmentation Issue

In 1967, the President's Crime Commission concluded that "a fundamental problem confronting law enforcement today is that of fragmented crime repression efforts resulting from the large number of uncoordinated local governments and law enforcement agencies."[21] As an illustration of this conclusion, the commission published a map of the Detroit metropolitan area indicating the 85 agencies in the area. As Exhibit 3–4 illustrates, almost half of these agencies had 20 or fewer officers.

The major problem, according to critics, is a lack of coordination between agencies in the same geographic area. Criminals do not respect political boundaries. In a large metropolitan area, a burglar may commit crimes in several different communities, each with its own police force. Auto-theft rings are often multistate operations. Detectives in one police department may have information that would help solve a series of crimes in a neighboring jurisdiction. In many instances, however, agencies compete rather than cooperate with one another.

Second, fragmentation of responsibility can also lead to crime displacement, especially with respect to vice crimes. One community may adopt a policy of strict enforcement of laws against gambling or prostitution. This often has the effect of driving vice activities to a neighboring jurisdiction, where different community standards exist.

Third, many experts believe there is a serious problem of duplication of services, with the resulting increase in costs. A city police department and the local sheriff's department may both operate their own 911 telephone systems and their own training academies. Several agencies in the same area may operate their own crime laboratories.

Fourth, fragmentation leads to inconsistent standards. Law enforcement agencies in the same area may have very different recruitment standards, training programs, and salary scales. In countries with a single national police force, uniform standards are established at the national level. In England, which has a tradition of local control of the police, minimum national standards are achieved through a process of inspection and financial incentives. The Home Office inspects each of the 43 local police constabularies annually.

SIDEBAR 3–2

Exercise: Studying the Fragmentation Problem in Your Area

1. Prepare a map and accompanying table indicating the number of law enforcement agencies in your metropolitan area, the names of these agencies, and the number of sworn officers in each.

2. Research the nature of any contract or collaborative arrangements between these agencies (e.g., shared communications systems, jail services).

EXHIBIT 3-4

Detroit Metropolitan Area

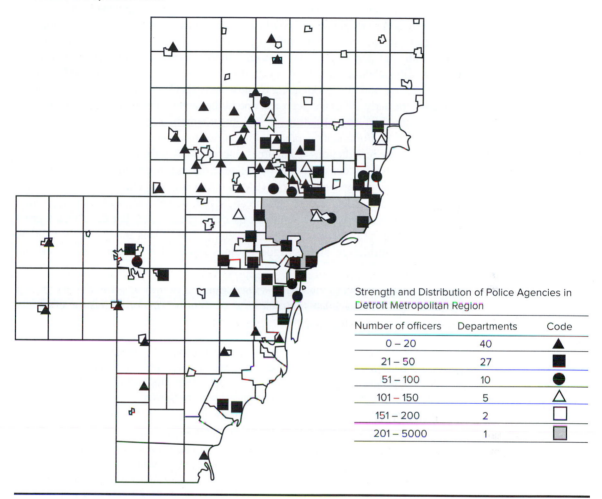

Strength and Distribution of Police Agencies in Detroit Metropolitan Region

Number of officers	Departments	Code
0 – 20	40	▲
21 – 50	27	■
51 – 100	10	●
101 – 150	5	△
151 – 200	2	□
201 – 5000	1	▨

Alternatives to Fragmentation

The fragmentation problem is not easily solved. The independence of local governments is deeply rooted in American history. The principle of local control, not just of police but of schools and other government services, is deeply rooted in American political culture. There has always been a strong fear of a national police force and suspicion of federal control of schools and police. The major remedies for fragmentation include consolidation and contracting, discussed in the sections that follow.

Consolidation

Some experts argue that small agencies should be consolidated into larger ones. The National Advisory Commission on Criminal Justice Standards and Goals recommended the consolidation of all agencies with 10 or fewer sworn officers (or about half of the current police agencies today).[22] In 2005, the towns of Fraser and Winter Park, Colorado, consolidated police services through the creation of a new police department after complaints that the county sheriff's department was not providing what both towns believed were necessary police services. In 2012, in Pennsylvania, the Lewisburg Borough Police Department and the East Buffalo Township Police consolidated into the Buffalo Valley Police Department to cut costs and improve services.[23] In a few larger urban areas, the city police and the sheriff's department have also been merged. The Charlotte, North Carolina, and the Mecklenburg County Sheriff's Departments, for instance, were merged in the early 1990s and represent one of the larger consolidations in policing.

public safety consolidation

Rather than consolidation of law enforcement services between multiple towns, cities, and/or counties, other communities have opted to consolidate services within the same jurisdiction—sometimes referred to as **public safety consolidation.** This can involve the consolidation of police, fire, and other public safety agencies such as emergency medical services (EMS) into a single agency.[24] The most recent example of public safety consolidation can be found in Rockford, Michigan, with a population of 6,000 residents. Analysis by the city revealed that there was a great amount of duplication between police, fire, and EMS services and that costs could be cut. The consolidation process took about 10 years to complete, given all the

---

SIDEBAR 3–3

Types of Consolidation

Many of today's police agencies are facing a financial crisis. As a means of addressing their financial problems, A number of police agencies have examined the possibility of police consolidation. A planning document by the International Association of Chiefs of Police (IACP) outlines the seven types of police consolidation that are possible:

1. Functional: Two or more agencies combine certain functional units, such as emergency communications, dispatch, or records.

2. Cross deputization/mutual enforcement zones/overlapping jurisdictions: Agencies authorize each other's officers to pool resources and improve regional coverage—for example, permitting a city police officer to make arrests in the county and a sheriff's deputy to make arrests in the city.

3. Public safety: City or county governments may unite all police, fire, and emergency medical services agencies under one umbrella.

4. Local merger: Two separate police agencies form a single new entity. The agencies may be in small communities or metropolitan areas.

5. Regional: A number of agencies combine to police a geographic area rather than a jurisdictional one.

6. Metropolitan: Two or more agencies serving overlapping jurisdictions join forces to become one agency serving an entire metropolitan area.

7. Government: A city and adjoining county consolidate their entire governments, creating a "metro" form of government for all citizens.

Source: Adapted from *Consolidating Police Services: An IACP Planning Approach* (St. Alexandria, VA: International Association of Chiefs of Police, 2003), 1–2.

complexities associated with different entrance requirements, salary schedules, and various certification requirements.

Contracting

Another alternative to fragmentation is for small agencies to contract with larger agencies for specific services. About half of all cities and counties contract with other government units for various services. These contracts cover everything from sewage disposal to tax assessment and water supply. The most common criminal justice services include jails and detention facilities and police–fire communications systems.[25] In many cases, the county sheriff maintains the 911 service for small towns in the area. In other cases, small towns contract with the sheriff for all police services. The Los Angeles County Sheriff's Department, for example, contracts with 43 separate towns. These contract law enforcement programs account for more than $550 million in revenue each year.[26]

One of the most sophisticated studies examining the efficacy of contracting for police services was conducted in California, where about 30 percent of all cities in the state contract with their sheriff's departments for law enforcement services. The study reported that those cities that contract for police services are characterized as being "newer" and less densely populated, with less taxable business activity, higher median household income, and lower rates of crime. It also reported that cities that contract for police services "spend far less per capita on police services than those cities that operate their own police departments." The study found that while contract cities spent less on police services, the quality of services remained more or less the same. For example, the study pointed out that clearance rates in contract cities were higher for violent crime and about the same for property crime.[27]

The Fragmentation Problem Reconsidered

Some experts believe the fragmentation problem may not be as serious as others have argued. The Police Services Study (PSS) undertook the first systematic research on the issue in the 1970s, examining the activities of 1,827 law enforcement agencies in 80 medium-sized metropolitan areas. Contrary to the traditional image of fragmentation, the study found that "informal interagency assistance is common," and "strict duplication of services is almost nonexistent in the production of direct police services."[28]

With respect to patrol, for example, informal arrangements involving coordination, sharing, or alternating responsibility were common. No areas were left completely unpatrolled; nor were areas being patrolled by two or more agencies. With respect to auxiliary services, small police departments routinely had access to crime laboratories, training academies, communications systems, and other services provided by larger agencies.

Even more important, the PSS concluded that small police departments were not necessarily less efficient than large departments. Small departments put a higher percentage of their officers on the street, performing direct police services. Larger departments did not necessarily achieve any advantages of scale.[29] Larger agencies had more complex bureaucratic structures, with the result that a smaller percentage of officers were available for direct police services. Gary Cordner found that among Maryland agencies, the complexity of the community social structure, not the size of the agency, was most important in determining the effectiveness of criminal investigation: the less complex the community, the more effective the police.[30]

Finally, the emphasis on decentralized policing under community policing suggests that small local law enforcement agencies might be preferable to large consolidated agencies.[31]

Municipal Police

Municipal or city police are the most important component of American law enforcement. They represent 70 percent of all law enforcement agencies and employ 60 percent of all sworn officers.[32]

municipal police

Even more important, **municipal police** play a more complex role than any other type of law enforcement agency. The external environment heavily influences all agencies.[33] Cities, and big cities in particular, represent the most complex environments, particularly in terms of the diversity of the population. City police departments have the heaviest responsibility for dealing with serious crime, which is disproportionately concentrated in cities. They are also responsible for difficult order maintenance problems and are asked to provide a wide range of emergency services.[34]

Among all municipal police departments, a few very large departments play a disproportionately important role. A Police Foundation report on the big six police departments—New York, Los Angeles, Chicago, Houston, Philadelphia, Detroit—found that they are responsible for 7.5 percent of the U.S. population but face 23 percent of all violent crime, including 34 percent of all robberies.[35] Although these six represent a tiny fraction of all departments, they employ almost 13 percent of all sworn officers. The New York City police department towers over all others, with 34,454 sworn officers. Chicago is second with about 12,042 officers.[36]

The big departments dominate public thinking about the police. Events in New York or Los Angeles—the Rampart scandal, mentioned earlier, for example—are reported by the national news media. Moreover, a disproportionate amount of the research on policing has been conducted in New York, Chicago, Los Angeles, Philadelphia, Boston, and Washington. Much less is known about medium-sized police departments, and almost no research has been done on small departments, even though they are more representative of policing in America.

The typical municipal police department is in a small town. About half (49.5 percent) employ fewer than 10 sworn officers.[37] Small-town and rural police operate in a very different context than big-city police. There is less serious crime than in urban areas. The majority of calls for police service involve noncriminal events and minor disturbances.[38] In one study, traffic problems accounted for 25 percent of all calls, public disturbances accounted for 19 percent, family disturbances represented 18 percent, and stray dogs another 11 percent. (The remaining 27 percent were miscellaneous calls.)[39]

County Police

county police

A few areas are served by **county police** departments. They are essentially municipal police that operate on a countywide basis but do not have any of the non-law-enforcement roles of the county sheriff (see Exhibit 3–5). Less than 1 percent of all local departments are county police. The largest are New York State's Suffolk County police (2,396 sworn officers) and Nassau County police (2,243 sworn officers).[40]

EXHIBIT 3–5

Responsibilities of Sheriff's Departments

Function	Percentage of Agencies
Routine patrol	98%
Crime investigation	92
Enforcement of traffic laws	90
Process serving	99
Court security	94
Jail operations	76
Search and rescue	56

Source: Adapted from Debra Hoffmaster, Gerard Marphy, Shannon McFadden, and Molly Griswold, *Policing and Immigration: How Chiefs Are Leading Their Communities through the Challenges* (Washington, DC: Police Executive Research Forum, 2010).

The County Sheriff

There are 3,012 sheriff's departments in the United States.[41] The county sheriff's office is unique among American law enforcement agencies, in terms of both its legal status and its role.[42]

The legal status of the **sheriff** is unique because in 37 states it is a constitutional office, whose responsibilities are defined in the state constitution. Also, sheriffs are elected in all but two states. In Rhode Island, they are appointed by the governor; in Hawaii, they are appointed by the chief justice of the state supreme court. As elected officials, sheriffs are directly involved in partisan politics in ways that municipal police chiefs are not. Historically, in rural areas the sheriff was the most powerful politician in the county.[43]

sheriff

The Role of the Sheriff

Sheriffs have a unique role in that they serve all three components of the criminal justice system: law enforcement, courts, and corrections. As Exhibit 3–5 indicates, almost all sheriff's departments perform the basic law enforcement functions of patrolling and investigating crimes. Almost all serve the courts by process serving (subpoenas, etc.) and providing security for the courts. In many urban areas, sheriffs spend more time on civil court duties than on criminal law enforcement. Furthermore, 76 percent of all sheriff's departments maintain the county jail. In most big cities, the jail is operated by a separate department of corrections.[44]

Lee Brown identified four different models of sheriff's departments, according to their responsibilities: (1) full-service model sheriff's departments carry out law enforcement, judicial, and correctional duties; (2) law enforcement model agencies carry out only law enforcement duties, with other responsibilities assumed by separate agencies; (3) civil-judicial model agencies handle only court-related duties (e.g., counties in Connecticut and Rhode Island); and (4) correctional-judicial model agencies (e.g., San Francisco County) handle all responsibilities except law enforcement.[45]

The distribution of sheriff's departments resembles that of the municipal police. There are a few very large departments and many small ones. The largest is the Los Angeles County Sheriff's Department (9,461 sworn officers). About 29 percent of all sheriff's departments, however, have fewer than 10 sworn officers.[46]

Other Local Agencies

The American law enforcement picture is complicated by the existence of other local agencies that have some law enforcement responsibilities.

The Constable

constable

Like the sheriff, the **constable** is an office whose roots can be traced back to colonial America. Urbanization and the consequent growth of city departments have stripped the constable's office of most of its functions. The U.S. Advisory Commission on Intergovernmental Relations found it to be "of minor importance" and recommended its abolition.[47]

For a full discussion of policing in colonial America, see Chapter 2.

There are few constables left in the United States today. Depending on the state, constables can be elected or appointed, and their role and function is defined by the state constitution. Modern constables typically work within the county court system. They are responsible for serving warrants and subpoenas, transporting prisoners, and providing security for district judges. They also work with county commissioners to post delinquent tax notices and assist attorneys in serving divorce papers.[48]

The Coroner/Medical Examiner

coroner

The office of the **coroner,** or medical examiner, is often considered a law enforcement agency because it has the responsibility to investigate crimes. Medical examiners and coroners' offices are responsible for a wide range of activities, including investigating death scenes, conducting autopsies, and determining the cause of violent or unexpected deaths. A Bureau of Justice Statistics special report found a total of 1,998 coroners or medical examiners in the United States.[49]

Coroners and medical examiners are usually employed by a state, county, or city agency. The type of "death investigator" used by a jurisdiction is typically mandated by law. The Bureau of Justice Statistics reported that "16 states had a centralized statewide medical examiner system, 14 states had a county coroner system, 7 had a county medical examiner system, and 13 had a mixed county medical examiner and coroner system."[50]

There are a number of important distinctions between coroners and medical examiners. First, coroners are not typically trained as physicians and have received little, if any, medical training; whereas medical examiners are physicians and often have received special training in death investigation. Second, coroners are typically elected to their positions; medical examiners are usually appointed by an elected official. Third, although both are responsible for the investigation of deaths, medical examiners are expected to rely heavily on their medical expertise to understand the cause of death.[51]

The Centers for Disease Control and Prevention (CDC) reports that about 20 percent of deaths in the United States are investigated by a coroner or medical examiner. Although guidelines vary on which deaths are required to be investigated, most jurisdictions require that the following types of deaths be investigated:

- Deaths due to homicide, suicide, or accidental causes such as car crashes, falls, burns, or the ingestion of drugs.
- Sudden or suspicious deaths, deaths from sudden infant death syndrome (SIDS), and unattended deaths.
- Deaths caused by an agent or disease constituting a threat to public health.
- Deaths that occur at a workplace.
- Deaths of people who were in custody or confinement, or who were institutionalized.
- Deaths of people to be cremated.[52]

Special District Police

Special district police agencies serve particular government agencies or special geographic boundaries. Many airports and parks, for example, have their own police forces. Some urban transit systems maintain separate law enforcement agencies. The Metro Transit Police Department in the Washington, D.C., subway system overlaps three different political jurisdictions: the District of Columbia, Virginia, and Maryland.[53]

special district police

College and university campus police are an important example of special district police.[54] About 68 percent of four-year colleges and universities with 2,500 or more students use sworn officers to provide police services to their campuses. Their officers have general arrest powers, often carry firearms, are certified by the state, and participate in the FBI's Uniform Crime Reporting (UCR) system. Today, the nation's 861 law enforcement agencies that serve universities with 2,500 or more students employ about 32,000 full-time employees. These employees include about 15,000 sworn officers, 11,000 security officers, 5,000 civilians, and 1,000 student employees.[55] Other colleges and universities use private security or their own non-sworn security officers.

Tribal Police

A unique aspect of the criminal justice in the United States is that many Native American tribes maintain their own separate criminal justice systems, including **tribal police** departments, on their reservations. Native American tribes are separate nations that signed treaties with the U.S. government and retain a significant degree of legal autonomy. In a number of important respects, tribes and reservations are not subject to federal or state law (see Exhibit 3–6).[56]

tribal police

About 200 police agencies in the United States have primary responsibility for providing police services to the roughly 330 reservations in Indian country. The Bureau of Indian Affairs (BIA) provides police services to more than one reservation and many tribes are not entitled to their own police departments. Historically, policing Indian country has been the responsibility of the BIA, which is located in the U.S. Department of the Interior. Today, however, a number of different administrative arrangements are used to police Indian nations.[57]

Getting to Know Your Campus Police

1. Is your campus police agency a certified law enforcement agency?

2. If so, what state-mandated training do officers receive? How many hours of training? What is the content of the curriculum? Who provides the training?

3. If it is not, what are the recruitment standards? What kind of training do officers receive? Who provides the training?

4. If your campus police agency is a certified law enforcement agency, does it file the required UCR report?

5. If not, does it file an annual crime report anyway?

6. Are your campus police officers armed? What kind of training in firearms use do they receive? What kind of retraining or recertification are the officers required to receive?

7. Does your campus police agency have a written deadly force policy? What does that policy say? (See Chapter 14 on deadly force policies.)

The most common administrative arrangement is for the tribe's police agency to be created under the Indian Self-Determination and Education Assistance Act of 1975. This act, also known as Public Law 93-638, gives Indian nations the right to establish their own organizational framework and to establish their own performance standards for their police departments. Although officers and civilians in these agencies are considered tribal employees, they are typically funded with federal monies. The majority of Indian police departments are configured in this way.[58]

The second most common administrative arrangement in Indian country is for the BIA to assume policing responsibilities. About 64 Indian nations still rely on the BIA for policing. Under this model, all staff are federal employees and work under the authority of the BIA. Many Indian nations that are policed by the BIA are assigned a local BIA superintendent who assumes many of the responsibilities granted to chiefs of police in municipal police departments. BIA superintendents

Types of Indian Police Departments and Their Characteristics

Type of Law Enforcement Program	Public Law 93-638	BIA	Self-Governance	Tribal Funded
Administered by	Tribe	Federal government	Tribe	Tribe
Officers are employees of	Tribe	Federal government	Tribe	Tribe
Funding	Federal (often with tribal contribution)	Federal government	Tribe	Tribe

of small tribes are often administratively responsible for more than one tribe.[59] About 37 police agencies are operated by the BIA.[60]

A less popular administrative arrangement is self-governance. Under this model, Indian nations contract with the BIA for policing services. Because the BIA is paid through block grants, the Indian nation is afforded a higher degree of organizational freedom. The least used administrative arrangement is the tribally funded Indian police department. Although this model affords Indian nations complete control over their police services, most Indian nations do not have the financial resources for such an agency.[61]

Most tribally operated police agencies are small. Only seven tribal police agencies have 50 or more full-time sworn officers, and about one-third have fewer than five officers. These agencies are also typically responsible for policing relatively small populations that are dispersed over large land areas, making officers' jobs difficult to manage.[62]

State Law Enforcement Agencies

State law enforcement agencies fall into three categories: state police, highway patrols, and state investigative agencies. This book focuses on the first two because they are regarded as general service law enforcement agencies.[63]

State police (sometimes called Departments of Public Safety) are defined as agencies "having statewide police powers for both traffic regulation and criminal investigations." **Highway patrols** are defined as agencies having "statewide authority to enforce traffic regulations and arrest non-traffic violators under their jurisdiction."[64]

state police

highway patrol

There are 50 general-service state law enforcement agencies in the United States, with each state having its own. In the latest report by the Bureau of Justice Statistics, the 50 primary state law enforcement agencies had just over 93,148 sworn and civilian personnel. Most state law enforcement agencies are large by local law enforcement standards. For example, 20 of the 50 primary state law enforcement agencies have 1,000 or more sworn officers, and another 15 state law enforcement agencies have at least 500 sworn officers. Only five of these state agencies have fewer than 500 sworn officers. The largest state law enforcement agency is the California Highway Patrol, with 7,202 sworn officers, followed by the New York State Police (4,847), the Pennsylvania State Police (4,458), and the Texas Department of Public Safety (3,529).[65]

Several states have more than one state law enforcement agency. California, for example, maintains both the California Highway Patrol and the California Division of Law Enforcement; in Ohio there is both the Ohio Highway Patrol and the Ohio Bureau of Criminal Identification and Investigation. However, many of these agencies are not regarded as general-service law enforcement agencies. The roles and missions of state law enforcement agencies are defined by state law; hence, they vary widely from state to state.

There is considerable variation in the administrative structure of state law enforcement agencies. One report found that "almost every possibility" exists. Several states have an umbrella agency containing a number of different departments responsible for various services. The New Jersey Department of Public Safety includes eight divisions: Division of Law, State Police, Division of Motor Vehicles, Division of Alcoholic Beverage Control, Division of Criminal Justice, Division of Consumer Affairs, Police Training Commission, and State Athletic Commissioner.

Roles and Responsibilities

State police and highway patrol provide a variety of law enforcement services. In terms of patrol, state police have concurrent or shared responsibility with local police agencies. In about half of the states, the state police or highway patrol agency has the primary responsibility for enforcing traffic laws on the main highways.[66]

State laws vary regarding responsibility for criminal investigation. In some states, the state police have general responsibility; in others, the investigative powers are limited. About half of all state agencies provide crime lab services (ballistics, drug testing) for local police departments. Finally, 77.6 percent of state police agencies operate a training academy. In some states, they are responsible for training recruits from local police departments.[67]

Federal Law Enforcement Agencies

The federal component of the law enforcement industry is relatively small but more complex than generally recognized. It is estimated that there are 120,000 full-time federal law enforcement employees. This figure includes all personnel "authorized to carry firearms and make arrests." It does not include military police, however.[68]

Because many federal agencies have enforcement or regulatory powers, there is no agreement about the exact size of federal law enforcement activities. Most of these agencies are not general-service agencies, as defined earlier. They do not provide the basic services of protection and criminal investigation.

Twenty four federal law enforcement agencies employ 250 or more sworn officers. U.S. Customs and Border Protection is the largest with 36,863 full-time sworn officers, followed by the FBI with 12,760 officers. The DEA employs 4,308 sworn officers. The complexity and variety of federal law enforcement activities is indicated by the fact that the largest agencies include the U.S. Fish and Wildlife Service (598 officers) and the U.S. Forest Service (644 officers).[69]

The role of each federal agency is specified by federal statute. In important respects, federal agencies have a far less complex role than that of municipal agencies. Federal agents do not have the ambiguous and difficult responsibility for order maintenance, do not maintain 911 emergency telephone services, and are not asked to handle vague "disturbance" calls.

We discuss the role of the largest federal law enforcement agencies in the United States in the next section.

Federal Law Enforcement after September 11, 2001

After September 11, 2001, President George W. Bush led a substantial movement to alter the organizational structure of federal law enforcement in the United States. He restructured federal law enforcement roles and responsibilities into two departments: the Department of Homeland Security and the Department of Justice (see Exhibit 3–7).

EXHIBIT 3–7

Largest Federal Law Enforcement Employers and Their Departments

Department of Homeland Security	Department of Justice
Bureau of Customs and Border Protection	Drug Enforcement Administration
Bureau of Immigration and Customs Enforcement	Federal Bureau of Investigation
Federal Emergency Management Agency	Bureau of Alcohol, Tobacco,
Transportation Security Administration	Firearms, and Explosives
U.S. Coast Guard	U.S. Marshals Service
U.S. Secret Service	

The Department of Homeland Security

On November 25, 2002, the Homeland Security Act was passed, creating the Department of Homeland Security (DHS), a new cabinet-level department that is responsible for activities pertaining to homeland security. This act launched the largest government reorganization since 1947.[70] Twenty-two agencies, and about 170,000 employees, all with functions related to homeland security, were organizationally moved to DHS. The six largest federal law enforcement employers with DHS are:

- Customs and Border Protection (CBP)
- Immigration and Customs Enforcement (ICE)
- Federal Emergency Management Agency (FEMA)
- Transportation Security Administration (TSA)
- U.S. Coast Guard
- U.S. Secret Service

Customs and Border Protection. Many of the functions formerly carried out by the U.S. Customs Service, the Immigration and Naturalization Service (INS), Inspection Service, the Border Patrol, and the Agricultural Quarantine Inspection program were combined into Customs and Border Protection (CBP). CBP is responsible for ensuring that persons and cargo enter the United States legally and safely through official ports of entry. The agency works to prevent illegal immigration and the smuggling of controlled substances, weapons of mass destruction (WMD), and illegal and diseased plants and animals into the country.[71]

Immigration and Customs Enforcement. Immigration and Customs Enforcement (ICE) is DHS's largest investigative bureau. It conducts many of the functions formerly carried out by the U.S. Customs Service and INS. ICE is comprised of two operational divisions: (1) Enforcement and Removal Operations (ERO), which is responsible for enforcing immigration laws, identifying and apprehending removable aliens, and detaining and removing illegal aliens from the United States; and 2) Homeland Security Investigations (HSI), which investigates cross-border criminal activity such as cybercrimes, transnational gangs, human trafficking, and gun and drug smuggling.[72]

Federal Emergency Management Agency. The Federal Emergency Management Agency (FEMA) was established in 1979 and became part of DHS on March 1, 2003. It currently employs about 15,000 employees. FEMA is responsible for preparing for, preventing, and responding to natural and human-made disasters. FEMA typically does not work alone, but instead coordinates and partners with government, private, and nonprofit organizations to manage emergency preparedness and response efforts.[73]

Transportation Security Administration. The Transportation Security Administration (TSA) was created on November 19, 2001, in direct response to the terrorist attacks on September 11, 2001. TSA is responsible for protecting the nation's transportation system. Although many people are aware of its responsibility for maintaining security at airports, it is also responsible for other transportation systems, including roads, railways, seaports, bridges, and pipelines.[74] TSA is the largest employer within DHS, employing about 60,000 persons.[75]

U.S. Coast Guard. The U.S. Coast Guard was established by Alexander Hamilton in 1790 as the Revenue Cutter Service, under the Department of Transportation. Although the U.S. Coast Guard has been administratively housed in many government agencies over the years, it was transferred to the Department of Transportation in 1967 and moved to DHS on March 1, 2003. The U.S. Coast Guard is a multifunctional, multimission service that has missions that are both security and nonsecurity related.[76] For example, it is responsible for security missions such as port, waterway, and coastal security; drug interdiction; migrant interdiction; and defense readiness. It is also responsible for conducting nonsecurity missions such as maritime safety, search and rescue, protecting the environment and living marine resources. As such, the U.S. Coast Guard is unique in that it has been granted authority and responsibilities that are similar to both the military and the police.

U.S. Secret Service. The U.S. Secret Service was established in 1865 for the purpose of investigating the counterfeiting of U.S. currency. Today, it has a wide array of investigative responsibilities and is responsible for the protection of current and former U.S. presidents, vice presidents, and their immediate family members. Many of their investigative responsibilities were changed with the advent of more sophisticated forms of communication.[77] The U.S. Secret Service is currently responsible for investigating "crimes that involve financial institution fraud, computer and telecommunication fraud, false identification documents, access device fraud, advance fee fraud, electronic funds transfer, and money laundering."[78]

The Department of Justice

In 1870, Congress established the Department of Justice with the attorney general as its administrative head. Congress made the Department of Justice responsible for enforcing and prosecuting all federal laws.[79] Although the structure of the Department of Justice has changed, its fundamental mission has remained the same. The five largest Department of Justice agencies are

- Drug Enforcement Administration (DEA)
- Federal Bureau of Investigation (FBI)

- Bureau of Alcohol, Tobacco, Firearms, and Explosives (ATF)
- U.S. Marshals Service

Drug Enforcement Administration. The mission of the DEA is to enforce federal laws and regulations pertaining to controlled substances. The primary focus of its law enforcement efforts is on those individuals and organizations that grow, manufacture, and distribute illegal drugs. Therefore, its mission is primarily dedicated to reducing the supply of illegal drugs to residents in the United States. For example, DEA agents investigate individuals involved in high-level drug trafficking within the United States and individuals who traffic major amounts of illegal drugs into the United States. They also work with local police agencies to reduce the availability of illegal drugs at the street level and with foreign governments to eradicate crops associated with illegal drugs.[80] The DEA is staffed with about 4,300 special agents.[81]

Federal Bureau of Investigation. The role of the FBI has historically been shaped by administrative and political factors. Under J. Edgar Hoover (1924–1972), the FBI concentrated its efforts on investigating alleged "subversives" and apprehending bank robbers and stolen cars. Critics charged that the FBI ignored white-collar crime, organized crime, and violations of the civil rights of minorities. After Hoover's death it was discovered that, under his direction, the FBI had committed many violations of citizens' rights: It was guilty of spying on individuals and groups because of their political beliefs, conducting illegal wiretaps, and even burglarizing the offices of groups it was spying on.[82] However, since Hoover's death, subsequent FBI directors reoriented the bureau's mission, placing more emphasis on white-collar crime, organized crime, and political corruption.

In 2002, after the terrorist attacks on the World Trade Center and the Pentagon, the FBI announced that it was going to make a fundamental change in its mission, which would focus first on preventing future terrorist attacks. In particular, the FBI crafted a new mandate that focused on 10 priorities:

1. Protect the United States from terrorist attack.
2. Protect the United States against foreign intelligence operations and espionage.
3. Protect the United States against cyber-based attacks and high-technology crimes.
4. Combat public corruption at all levels.
5. Protect civil rights.
6. Combat transnational and national criminal organizations and enterprises.
7. Combat major white-collar crime.
8. Combat significant violent crime.
9. Support federal, state, local, and international partners.
10. Upgrade technology to successfully perform the FBI's mission.[83]

Bureau of Alcohol, Tobacco, Firearms, and Explosives. In 2003, under the Homeland Security Act, the law enforcement functions of the U.S. Bureau of Alcohol, Tobacco, Firearms, and Explosives (ATF) were transferred from the U.S. Treasury Department to the Department of Justice. First, ATF is responsible for enforcing federal firearms laws. It investigates firearms trafficking and identifies and arrests armed career criminals. Second, it is responsible for regulating the explosives-related industry to prevent terrorists and criminals from coming into possession of explosives and to ensure that those in possession of explosives are properly licensed. It also provides training to federal, state, and local officials for the detection, handling, and destruction of explosives. Finally, ATF is responsible for enforcing federal laws as they pertain to the collection of federal taxes on alcohol and tobacco products.[84]

U.S. Marshals Service. The U.S. Marshals Service, established in 1789, is the nation's oldest federal law enforcement agency. The U.S. Marshals Service is responsible for providing security to the federal courts, housing federal detainees, and conducting fugitive investigations. Each year U.S. marshals arrest more than 33,000 persons wanted by federal law enforcement agencies, such as the FBI, DEA, and ATF, and house more than 55,000 detainees through cooperative agreements with local, state, and private jails. The U.S. Marshals Service is also responsible for administering the nation's witness protection program. Since 1971, it has provided new identities and relocated 8,500 witnesses and about 10,000 of their family members.[85]

The Private Security Industry

Private security is an important part of American law enforcement. Its exact size is difficult to determine because it involves many small, private agencies; part-time employees; and security personnel that are employed by private businesses. It is estimated that there are as many as 90,000 private security organizations that employ more than 2 million people.[86] Elizabeth Joh reports that this amounts to roughly three private security officers for every one public police officer in America. She further points to the fact that it is estimated the United States spends twice as much money on private policing as it does on public policing.[87] These estimates include the following categories of jobs: private detectives and investigators, patrol services, security guards, loss prevention specialists, gaming officers and investigators, and armored car services. According to the Service Employees International Union (SEIU), a very small number of corporations control the private security market in the United States. The largest firm, Securitas, employs about 100,000 private security officers. The six largest security firms—Securitas, G4S, Universal Protection Services, U.S. Security Associates, Guardsmark, and ABM Security Services—control about half of the private security market in the United States.[88] Brian Forst points out that Sears, Roebuck employs about 6,000 security guards, which is significantly more personnel than almost any metropolitan police department.[89]

Today, private security firms are responsible for patrolling and providing protection at public and private housing complexes, gated communities, business parks, malls, office complexes, power plants, and airports.[90] They have also begun to play a major role in traffic regulation through the operation of cameras that detect red-light running and automated radar stations for administering speeding tickets. According to a news story that illustrated the extent of private security in American life: "There are certain areas in Florida—home of Wackenhut [now G4S] HQ—where your housing estate is policed by Wackenhut, you get on the train to go to work and that's

Looking for a Job with the FBI?

A lot of students are curious about the qualifications needed for a job with the FBI. Here are many of the frequently asked questions about employment with the FBI and the answers to them.

What are the preliminary standards for the Special Agent position?

To be considered for the Special Agent position, you must be a U.S. citizen, be 23 to 36-½ years old, possess a bachelor's degree, have 3 years of full-time work experience, meet residency requirements, possess a valid driver's license, and be completely available for assignment anywhere in the FBI's jurisdiction.

How does the background investigation process work?

Due to the sensitive nature of the FBI's missions, all FBI positions require a Top Secret security clearance. Before employees can start work with the FBI, they must undergo an intensive background investigation that includes a polygraph; a test for illegal drugs; credit and records checks; and extensive interviews with former and current colleagues, neighbors, friends, professors, and the like, at least 10 years back.

Are there any automatic disqualifiers?

Applicants with a felony and/or domestic violence misdemeanor conviction; who have engaged in acts designed to overthrow the U.S. government; who have failed to pay court-ordered child support or alimony payments; who currently have a federally funded student loan in default; who failed to file federal, state, or local income tax returns; or who are found in violation of the FBI's drug policy will be immediately discontinued and ineligible for future FBI employment.

Do certain degrees provide a more desirable educational background for the Special Agent position?

The FBI seeks applicants with a broad range of backgrounds to support its diverse and complex caseload. The FBI does not recommend particular courses, schools, or degrees (although your college or university must be U.S. Department of Education accredited). Study a field you enjoy and obtain experiences that will demonstrate your ability to master the Special Agent core competencies, specifically:

Leadership

Oral communication

Initiative and motivation

Adaptability and flexibility

Organizing, planning, and prioritizing

Interpersonal skills

Evaluating information and making decisions

Writing

I want to be an FBI "Profiler." Where do I begin the application process?

The FBI does not have a job called "Profiler." Supervisory Special Agents assigned to the National Center for the Analysis of Violent Crime (NCAVC) at Quantico, Virginia, perform the tasks commonly associated with "profiling." Despite popular depictions, these FBI Special Agents do not get "vibes" or experience "psychic flashes" while walking around fresh crime scenes. In reality, it is an exciting world of investigation and research—a world of inductive and deductive reasoning; crime-solving experience; and knowledge of criminal behavior, facts, and statistical probabilities.

How do I apply to become a Special Agent?

After carefully reading the preliminary standards and ensuring you meet them, the next step toward becoming an FBI Special Agent is to complete the online application. Your processing field office is determined by the ZIP code you provide when you apply via fbijobs.gov. You must process your application through the FBI office nearest your current residence, place of education, or place of employment.

Source: Information was adapted from https://www.fbijobs.gov/information-center/faqs/special-agent-faqs#background-investigation.

policed by Wackenhut, and you get to work and the corporate office is policed by Wackenhut. And if you do something wrong, you end up in a Wackenhut prison."[91]

Private police organizations display four characteristics that differentiate them from the public police. First, private police organizations focus on more than crime. They also concern themselves with broader issues such as property, personal assets, and general consumer satisfaction. Second, private police organizations have many more alternatives at their disposal for addressing problems. For example, they can have employees fired, ban persons from establishments, fine those who do not follow policies and guidelines, and pursue prosecution in the criminal courts. As such, private police have much more discretion in how they resolve problems. Third, private police organizations place significantly more emphasis on the prevention of problems. Public police organizations have traditionally emphasized reacting to problems after they occur, whereas private police invest more of their resources in problem prevention. Fourth, private police concern themselves primarily with matters occurring on, or with, private property. For instance, private police are typically associated with large privately held spaces such as malls, housing developments, and business complexes.[92]

The size of the private security industry raises a number of important issues. The first is the quality of private security personnel. Requirements for employment are minimal, and in many cases training is nonexistent. In fact only about half of all states require security personnel to undergo any training. Similarly, 9 states do not have any state laws regulating who can serve as a private security officer, and 14 states do not require a criminal background check for hiring.[93] The result is that in many states, private security is often the last resort for people unable to find other jobs.

Second, there are few federal, state, or local laws that guide private police conduct. The courts have repeatedly articulated that the laws that guide the behavior of public police officers are not applicable to private security. For example, the Supreme Court has ruled that decisions such as *Miranda* and *Mapp* apply only to public police, and private security officers are not bound by these decisions. Likewise, few states have sought to enact legislation to guide private security conduct and instead have chosen to hold private security officers accountable in the same way as they do private citizens.

Third, there are problems related to cooperation between public and private police. In large part, this appears to be a consequence of the attitudes and beliefs held by each group about the other. Research indicates that private police officers believe that public police officers do not respect them, are more concerned with making arrests and less concerned about crime prevention, and are generally unwilling to share information with them. Similar studies examining public police reveal that they perceive private police to be unprofessional, too client-oriented, and often unwilling to prosecute.[94]

This last problem has become particularly pronounced since the terrorist attacks on September 11, 2001. The 9/11 Commission noted that 85 percent of the nation's critical infrastructures are protected by private security organizations[95] and roughly 5 percent of all private police are responsible for guarding and protecting a critical infrastructure or asset.[96] For example, private police are responsible for protecting nuclear power plants, major financial institutions, chemical facilities, and water plants. Advisors to Congress have begun to publicly question the wisdom of placing the nation's most valuable assets in the hands of those who are so poorly trained and who earn less than half the average salary of the police.[97]

Minimum Standards: American Style

Unlike most other countries, the United States does not have a national police system. There is no federal agency responsible for supervising local agencies or ensuring minimum standards. In England, each local department receives half of its budget from the national government and undergoes a regular inspection as part of the process.[98] Nonetheless, federal and state governments require some minimum standards for law enforcement agencies in the United States. The process for developing and enforcing these standards, however, is not systematic.

The Role of the Federal Government

The most important set of national standards are the decisions of the U.S. Supreme Court related to police procedures. Decisions such as *Mapp v. Ohio, Miranda v. Arizona,* and *Tennessee v. Garner* set minimum national standards based on provisions of the U.S. Constitution. Beginning in the 1960s, these and other Supreme Court decisions were a major instrument of reform, forcing departments to significantly improve personnel standards and management and supervision.[99]

For a full discussion of these court decisions, see Chapters 2, 11, and 14.

Relying on the Supreme Court to define minimum standards for police has serious limitations, however. First, most aspects of policing do not raise issues of constitutional law—for example, the length of police academy training or the content of that training. Second, enforcing Supreme Court decisions is extremely difficult. A police department may systematically violate the *Miranda* requirement; it is enforced only when someone is convicted and then appeals that conviction on the basis of the *Miranda* decision.[100]

Congress has passed a number of laws that directly apply to state and local law enforcement agencies. Most important is the 1964 Civil Rights Act, which prohibits discrimination on the basis of race, color, national origin, religion, or sex. Local and state agencies are forbidden to discriminate in recruitment, promotion, or assignment of officers.[101] The law, however, does not cover many police personnel issues. It does not, for example, establish minimum standards for recruitment or training. No federal law specifies a minimum level of education for police recruits. Nor does any law require a minimum police–population ratio or set standards for patrol operations.

The U.S. Department of Justice also uses grants to encourage changes in policing. In 2009, for example, the SMART Policing Initiative (SPI), sponsored by the Bureau of Justice Assistance (BJA), sought to encourage local police to focus their resources on places and people that most responsible for crime and violence. Under a national competitive solicitation, BJA has selectively awarded SPI grants to approximately 30 law enforcement agencies throughout the United States.[102]

The Role of State Governments

State governments also set minimum standards for police in a number of areas. State supreme courts rule on issues under their state constitutions. State codes of criminal procedure also define what police must do and what they may not do.

The most important role of state governments has been to require the licensing or certification of all sworn officers. In particular, this includes mandatory preservice training. New York and California were pioneers in this area in 1959, and by the 1970s every state had some kind of certification requirement. Prior to this time, it was not uncommon in small departments for officers to have no preservice training whatsoever.[103]

In a further development of this approach, most states have adopted procedures for delicensing or decertifying police officers. In Florida, for example, when an officer's license is revoked by the state, that person is not eligible to be employed by any other law enforcement agency in the state.[104] In some states, however, it is still possible for an officer to be fired by one police department and then hired by another.

Accreditation

accreditation

A final approach to establishing minimum national standards in policing is through **accreditation**.[105] Accreditation is a process of professional self-regulation, similar to those processes that exist in medicine, law, education, and other occupations. The Commission on Accreditation of Law Enforcement Agencies (CALEA) was established in 1979. The fifth edition of its *Standards for Law Enforcement* includes separate standards. Some standards are mandatory, whereas others are only recommended.[106]

The major weakness with accreditation is that it is a voluntary process. There is no penalty for a police department's not being accredited. By comparison, a nonaccredited educational institution is not eligible for certain federal funds, and graduates from nonaccredited institutions find that their credits are not accepted by other schools.[107]

The process of becoming accredited is expensive, in terms of both the formal CALEA fees and the staff time required to meet the various standards.[108] Today, however, about 1,037 agencies have been accredited by the CALEA.[109]

Critics question the impact of accreditation on police work. Mastrofski suggests that accreditation standards "add[s] to the proliferation of rules in already rule-suffused bureaucracies, without appreciably affecting patterns of police behavior."[110] Others, however, have found that accreditation has a positive impact on police organizations. For example, McCabe and Fajardo reported that accredited agencies, when compared to nonaccredited agencies, are more likely to require more training, are more likely to have higher minimum educational requirements for new officers, and are twice as likely to require drug testing for sworn officers. Agencies that are accredited were also found to be more likely to have specialized units to respond to child abuse and to enforce drug laws.[111]

In short, American law enforcement agencies must meet *some* minimum standards. These standards cover only a limited range of issues, and there is no system for developing and implementing a comprehensive set of standards.

CASE STUDY

The Fraser/Winter Park (CO) Police Department

Fraser, Colorado, was established in 1905 in anticipation of the arrival of the Moffat Tunnel, which provided Denver with its first link west through the Continental Divide. The town was incorporated in 1953 and today has a population of about 1,200. The town of Winter Park was first settled as a construction camp for the Moffat Tunnel. A flood of winter sports enthusiasts to the area in the late 1930s led to its development as a winter sports center, with a ski area opening in 1940. The town was incorporated in 1978 and today has a population of about 1,000.

Prior to 2004, the Grand County Sheriff provided law enforcement services in Winter Park and Fraser. In Colorado, county sheriffs are obligated to provide law enforcement services to towns in their counties, but the level of service is usually quite modest. To enhance service, both Fraser and Winter Park contracted with the sheriff for additional services. Even though contract deputies were assigned to the two communities, these officers had other assignments and the communities thought they were not receiving coverage commensurate with their contract fees. As a result, both communities asked the sheriff to dedicate resources more specifically to Winter Park and Fraser. The towns and the sheriff failed to reconcile these differences, and the sheriff announced his intention to end the contract in 90 days.

In response, the towns formed the Fraser/Winter Park Police Department in early 2005. The agency was formed in about four months. The department plan called for all members to be employees of the town of Winter Park, but the chief would report to both town managers.

All of the new employees from the department came from the Grand County Sheriff's Office, including the chief, who had been undersheriff and had previously served in a suburban Denver police department. The initial staffing was six officers, including the chief. The department purchased police vehicles from the sheriff.

This strategy of hiring former sheriff's employees eased implementation in several ways. The members of the new department knew one another and were familiar with both communities. The department also adopted policies and procedures used in the sheriff's office and by other county agencies.

Although such a transition might appear relatively seamless, in fact the new department had several issues to resolve. One of the biggest problems the new chief faced was that, even though the officers had worked in the towns, the residents did not know them well. There was also concern that some of the ill-will directed toward the sheriff would be transferred to the new department and its members who were former sheriff's employees. To build good will, the chief reached out to elected officials and community leaders in both communities. He also sought to strengthen the relationship between the officers and the citizens.

As noted, the chief reports to both town managers. Although the towns are similar in size and character, and both communities use the same district court for misdemeanor and felony crimes, they do have some different ordinances and priorities for law enforcement. For example, Fraser places a stronger emphasis on parking enforcement. The chief works to keep open lines of communication with both town managers and ensures that officers are sensitive to the unique issues in each town.

Reporting to two managers of towns with differing priorities might appear to pose a dilemma for the chief, but he indicates that it does not. The chief suggests that it is not unlike working in a larger community with differing area or neighborhood issues. Similarly, the officers hired by the department understand that they are serving two communities, and this appears to pose no problems for them.

The department operates under an intergovernmental agreement in which Fraser pays Winter Park an annual fee based on the proportion of calls in each community. Currently, Fraser contributes 35 percent to Winter Park's $1,200,000 public safety budget.

Source: Adapted from Jeremy M. Wilson, Alexander Weiss, and Clifford Grammich, *Pathways to Consolidation: Taking Stock of Transitions to Alternative Models of Police Service* (Washington, DC: Office of Community Oriented Policing Services, 2015).

SUMMARY

Law enforcement is an extremely complex activity in the United States. The delivery of police services is fragmented among thousands of city, county, state, special district, federal, and private security agencies. There are tremendous differences in the size, role, and activities of these agencies. Consequently, it is extremely difficult to generalize about the police in America.

KEY TERMS

local political control, 71
fragmentation, 72
authorized strength, 74
civilians, 75
police–population
    ratio, 75

public safety consolidation, 78
municipal police, 80
county police, 80
sheriff, 81
constable, 82
coroner, 82

special district police, 83
tribal police, 83
state police, 85
highway patrol, 85
accreditation, 94

FOR DISCUSSION

1. Visit your campus law enforcement agency's headquarters and request a copy of last year's campus crime statistics. Ask the desk attendant how many full-time employees work for the agency. Ask how many are sworn officers and how many are nonsworn officers. As a class, discuss whether you think there are too many or too few personnel working for your campus law enforcement agency in light of the campus's reported crime problems.

2. What are some of the advantages and disadvantages of civilianization?

3. What are the strengths and weaknesses of leaving the primary responsibility for police protection to local governments versus the federal or state government?

INTERNET EXERCISES

Exercise 1 Visit www.nij.gov/multimedia/presenter/presenter-sherman/ and watch a presentation by Professor Lawrence Sherman. He explains why he believes that reallocating funding spent on prisons to the police will prevent more crime.

Exercise 2 Visit the website of an agency in your region and find out (a) the total number of employees who are authorized to work for the agency, (b) the total number of sworn officers authorized to work for the agency, and (c) the total number of employees who are currently employed by the agency.

Exercise 3 Visit the website www.calea.org. Examine the process that a police department must go through to become accredited by the CALEA.

Exercise 4 Visit the websites of your local police and sheriff's departments and find out what services are duplicated by the two agencies.

NOTES

1. Elinor Ostrom, Roger Parks, and Gordon P. Whitaker, *Patterns of Metropolitan Policing* (Cambridge, MA: Ballinger, 1978).

2. Bureau of Justice Statistics, *Local Law Enforcement Agencies, 2013: Personnel, Policies, and Practices* (Washington, DC: U.S. Government Printing Office, 2015).

3. David N. Falcone and L. Edward Wells, "The County Sheriff as a Distinctive Policing Modality," *American Journal of Police* XIV, no. 3/4 (1995): 123–124.

4. Ostrom, Parks, and Whitaker, *Patterns of Metropolitan Policing.*

5. Richard J. Terrill, *World Criminal Justice Systems: A Survey,* 3rd ed. (Cincinnati, OH: Anderson, 1997), 12–13.

6. Ibid., 246–248.

7. Reaves, Brian, Local Police Departments, 2013: Personnel, Policies, and Practices, 2015; Bureau of Justice Statistics, *Federal Law Enforcement Officers, 2004* (Washington, DC: U.S. Government Printing Office, 2006).

8. President's Commission on Law Enforcement and Administration of Justice, *The Challenge of Crime in a Free Society* (Washington, DC: U.S. Government Printing Office, 1967).

9. Figures above calculated through data obtained from Reaves, Brian, Local Police Departments, 2013: Personnel, Policies, and Practices, 2015; Andrea Burch, Sheriffs' Office Personnel, 1993–2013, (Washington, DC: U.S. Government Printing Office, 2016).

10. Ibid.; Bureau of Justice Statistics, *Federal Law Enforcement Officers, 2004.*

11. Bureau of Justice Statistics, *Local Law Enforcement Agencies, 2013: Personnel, Policies, and Practices* (Washington, DC: U.S. Government Printing Office, 2015).

12. Wareham, Jennifer, Brad W. Smith, and Eric G. Lambert. "Rates and Patterns of Law Enforcement Turnover: A Research Note," *Criminal Justice Policy Review* (2013).

13. James J. Fyfe, "Police Personnel Practices, 1986," *Municipal Yearbook 1987* (Washington, DC: ICMA, 1987), table 3/2, p. 17.

14. Bruce L. Heininger and Janine Urbanek, "Civilization of the American Police: 1970–1980," *Journal of Police Science and Administration* 11 (1983): 200–205; William King

and Edward Maguire, "Police Civilianization, 1950–2000: Change or Continuity?" presented at the American Society of Criminology (November 2000); Bureau of Justice Statistics, *Local Law Enforcement Agencies, 2013.*

15. David Bayley, *Police for the Future* (New York: Oxford University Press, 1994).

16. Edward Maguire, *Organizational Structure in American Police Agencies* (Albany, NY: SUNY Press, 2003).

17. Bureau of Justice Statistics, *Local Law Enforcement Agencies, 2013*; Bureau of Justice Statistics, *Census of State and Local Law Enforcement Agencies, 2008;* Bureau of Justice Statistics, *Local Police Departments, 2007* (Washington, DC: U.S. Government Printing Office, 2011).

18. Thomas B. Marvell and Carlisle E. Moody, "Specification Problems, Police Levels, and Crime Rates," *Criminology* 34 (November 1996): 609–646.

19. Bureau of Justice Statistics, *Local Law Enforcement Agencies, 2013.*

20. Ibid.

21. President's Commission on Law Enforcement and Administration of Justice, *Task Force Report: The Police* (Washington, DC: U.S. Government Printing Office, 1967), 68.

22. National Advisory Commission on Criminal Justice Standards and Goals, *Police* (Washington, DC: U.S. Government Printing Office, 1973), 73–76.

23. Jeremy Wilson, Alexander Weiss, and Clifford Grammich, *Pathways to Consolidation: Taking Stock of Transitions to Alternative Models of Police Service* (Washington DC: Office of Community Oriented Policing Services, 2015).

24. Ibid.

25. International City Management Association, "Intergovernmental Service Arrangements and the Transfer of Functions," *Baseline Data Report* 16 (June 1984).

26. Contract Law Enforcement Services, revised 2009, http://www.sheriffs.org/sites/default/files/uploads/CLESDocument.pdf.

27. Peter Nelligan and William Bourns, "Municipal Contracting with County Sheriffs for Police Services in California: Comparison of Cost and Effectiveness," *Police Quarterly* 14 (2011): 70–95.

28. Ostrom, Parks, and Whitaker, *Patterns of Metropolitan Policing.*

29. Ibid., xxi, 101.

30. Gary W. Cordner, "Police Agency Size and Investigative Effectiveness," *Journal of Criminal Justice* 17, no. 1 (1989): 153.

31. Ralph A. Weisheit, David N. Falcone, and L. Edward Wells, *Crime and Policing in Rural and Small-Town America: An Overview of the Issues* (Washington, DC: U.S. Government Printing Office, 1995), 69–73.

32. Bureau of Justice Statistics, *Census of State and Local Law Enforcement Agencies, 2004* (Washington, DC: U.S. Government Printing Office, 2007).

33. John P. Crank and Robert Langworthy, "An Institutional Perspective on Policing," *Journal of Criminal Law and Criminology* 83, no. 2 (1992): 341–346.

34. Herman Goldstein, *Policing a Free Society* (Cambridge, MA: Ballinger, 1977).

35. Anthony Pate and Edwin E. Hamilton, *The Big Six: Policing America's Largest Cities* (Washington, DC: Police Foundation, 1991).

36. Bureau of Justice Statistics, *Local Law Enforcement Agencies, 2013.*

37. Bureau of Justice Statistics, *Local Police Departments, 2003.*

38. Weisheit, Falcone, and Wells, *Crime and Policing in Rural and Small-Town America.*

39. John F. Galliher et al., "Small-Town Police: Troubles, Tasks, and Publics," *Journal of Police Science and Administration* 3 (March 1975): 19–28.

40. Bureau of Justice Statistics, *Census of State and Local Law Enforcement Agencies, 2004;* Bureau of Justice Statistics, *Local Law Enforcement Agencies, 2013.*

41. Bureau of Justice Statistics, *Local Law Enforcement Agencies, 2013.*

42. Falcone and Wells, "The County Sheriff as a Distinctive Policing Modality."

43. National Sheriffs' Association, *County Law Enforcement: Assessment of Capabilities and Needs* (Washington, DC: Author, 1976).

44. Bureau of Justice Statistics, *Law Enforcement Management and Administrative Statistics, 1999 (Washington, DC: U.S. Government Printing Office, 2000).*

45. Lee P. Brown, "The Role of the Sheriff," in Alvin W. Cohn, ed., *The Future of Policing* (Beverly Hills, CA: Sage, 1978), 227–228.

46. Bureau of Justice Statistics, *Census of State and Local Law Enforcement Agencies, 2008.*

47. U.S. Advisory Commission on Intergovernmental Relations, *State and Local Relations in the Criminal Justice System* (Washington, DC: U.S. Government Printing Office, 1971), 28.

48. National Constable Association, *Who Is and What Is a Constable?* www.angelfire.com/la/nationalconstable/.

49. Bureau of Justice Statistics, *Medical Examiners' and Coroners' Offices, 2004* (Washington, DC: U.S. Government Printing Office, 2007).

50. Ibid., 1.

51. Ibid.; National Association of Medical Examiners, *So You Want to Be a Medical Detective,* www.thename.org/medical_detective.htm.

52. CDC, Division of Public Health Surveillance and Informatics, *About MECISP,* www.cdc.gov/epo/dphsi/mecisp/about.htm.

53. Martin Hannon, "The Metro Transit Police Force: America's First Tri-State, Multi-Jurisdictional Police Force," *FBI Law Enforcement Bulletin* 47 (November 1978): 16–22.

54. John J. Sloan, "The Modern Campus Police: An Analysis of Their Evolution, Structure, and Function," *American Journal of Police* XI, no. 2 (1992): 85–104.

55. Bureau of Justice Statistics, *Campus Law Enforcement, 2011–12* (Washington, DC: U.S. Government Printing Office, 2015).

56. Ken Peak, "Criminal Justice, Law, and Policy in Indian Country: A Historical Perspective," *Journal of Criminal Justice* 17, no. 5 (1989): 393–407.

57. Stewart Wakeling, Miriam Jorgensen, Susan Michaelson, and Manley Begay, *Policing on American Indian Reservations* (Washington, DC: National Institute of Justice, 2001).

58. Ibid.

59. Ibid.

60. Bureau of Justice Statistics, *Tribal Law Enforcement* (Washington, DC: U.S. Government Printing Office, 2002).

61. Wakeling, Jorgensen, Michaelson, and Begay, *Policing on American Indian Reservations.*

62. Bureau of Justice Statistics, *Tribal Law Enforcement.*

63. Donald A. Torres, *Handbook of State Police, Highway Patrols, and Investigative Agencies* (New York: Greenwood Press, 1987).

64. Ibid., 12.

65. Bureau of Justice Statistics, *Census of State and Local Law Enforcement Agencies, 2008.*

66. Department of Justice, *Profile of State and Local Law Enforcement Agencies, 1987* (Washington, DC: U.S. Government Printing Office, 1989).

67. Ibid.

68. Bureau of Justice Statistics, *Federal Law Enforcement Officers, 2008.*

69. Ibid.

70. Bureau of Justice Statistics, *Federal Law Enforcement Officers, 2002* (Washington, DC: U.S. Government Printing Office, 2003).

71. U.S. Customs and Border Protection, About CBP, https://www.cbp.gov/about.

72. ICE Who we are. www.ice.gov/about

73. FEMA, About FEMA, http://fema.gov/about/index.shtm.

74. Transportation Security Administration. https://www.tsa.gov/about/tsa-leadership

75. TRACREPORTS, *Department of Homeland Security Employment Levels by Organizational Component, March 2003*, http://trac.syr.edu/tracreports/tracdhs/030825/dhs_org.html.

76. About the Coast Guard, http://www.gocoastguard.com/about-the-coast-guard

77. U.S. Secret Service, Protection, www.secretservice.gov/protection.shtml.

78. U.S. Secret Service, Investigations, www.secretservice.gov/investigations.shtml.

79. Department of Justice, About DOJ, www.usdoj.gov/02organizations/.

80. DEA Mission Statement, www.dea.gov/agency/mission.htm.

81. Bureau of Justice Statistics, *Federal Law Enforcement Officers, 2008.*

82. Curt Gentry, *J. Edgar Hoover: The Man and the Secrets* (New York: Norton, 1991).

83. Department of Justice, *FBI Reorganization Fact Sheet* (Washington, DC: U.S. Government Printing Office, 2002).

84. ATF 2003 Performance and Accountability Report, www.atf.gov/pub/gen_pub/2003annrpt/discussionandanalysis.pdf.

85. U.S. Department of Justice, *United States Marshals Service Fact Sheet, Facts and Figures 2015* (Washington, DC: U.S. Government Printing Office, 2015).

86. U.S. Department of Justice, *National Policy Summit: Building Private Security/Public Policing Partnerships to Prevent and Respond to Terrorism and Public Disorder* (Washington, DC:

International Association of Chiefs of Police, 2005).

87. Elizabeth Joh, "The Paradox of Private Policing," *The Journal of Criminal Law & Criminology* 95no. 1 (2004): 49–131.

88. Found at http://www.securitymagazine.com/articles/86806-th-annual-top-guarding-firms-listing

89. Brian Forst, "The Privatization and Civilianization of Policing," in Charles Friel, ed., *Criminal Justice,* 2 (2000): 19–79.

90. Bud Hazelkorn, "Making Crime Pay," *San Francisco Chronicle,* August 17, 2003, 1.

91. Ibid.

92. Joh, "The Paradox of Private Policing"; Clifford Shearing, "Private Security: Implications for Social Control," in K. R. E. McCormick and L. A. Visano, eds., *Understanding Policing* (Toronto: Canadian Scholars Press, 1992), 521.

93. Michael Klein and Craig Hemmens, "Public Regulation of Private Security: A Statutory Analysis of State Regulation of Security Guards," *Criminal Justice Policy Review*. In press.

94. Don Hummer and Mahesh Nalla, "Modeling Future Relations between the Private and Public Sectors of Law Enforcement," *Criminal Justice Studies* 16, no. 2 (2003): 87–96.

95. The 9/11 Commission Report, *Executive Summary*, www.9-11commission.gov.

96. Paul Parfomak, *Guarding America: Security Guards and U.S. Critical Infrastructure Protection* (Washington, DC: Congressional Research Service, 2004).

97. Ibid.

98. Terrill, *World Criminal Justice Systems,* 9–25.

99. Samuel Walker, "Historical Roots of the Legal Control of Police Behavior," in David Weisburd and Craig Uchida, eds., *Police Innovation and Control of the Police* (New York: Springer, 1993), 32–55.

100. Anthony Amsterdam, "Perspectives on the Fourth Amendment," *Minnesota Law Review* 58 (1974): 428.

101. Susan E. Martin, *On the Move: The Status of Women in Policing* (Washington, DC: Police Foundation, 1990), 11–24.

102. Found at www.smartpolicinginitiative.com/.

103. International Association of Directors of Law Enforcement Standards and Training, *Sourcebook of Standards and Training Information* (Charlotte: University of North Carolina at Charlotte, 1993).

104. Roger Goldman and Stephen Puro, "Decertification of Police: An Alternative to Traditional Remedies for Police Misconduct," *Hastings Constitutional Law Quarterly* 15 (Fall 1987): 45–80.

105. Jack Pearson, "National Accreditation: A Valuable Management Tool," in James J. Fyfe, ed., *Police Management Today: Issues and Case Studies* (Washington, DC: ICMA, 1985), 45–48.

106. See www.calea.org. Commission on Accreditation for Law Enforcement Agencies, *Standards for Law Enforcement Agencies,* 5th ed. (Fairfax, VA: CALEA, July 20, 2012).

107. Stephen D. Mastrofski, "Police Agency Accreditation: The Prospects of Reform," *American Journal of Police* VI, no. 2 (1986): 45–81.

108. W. E. Eastman, "National Accreditation: A Costly, Unneeded Make-Work Scheme," in James J. Fyfe, ed., *Police Management Today: Issues and Case Studies* (Washington, DC: ICMA, 1985), 49–54.

109. CALEA, *4-Year Status,* http://www.calea.org/content/calea-client-database.pdf.

110. Mastrofski, "The Prospects of Change in Police Patrol," 25.

111. Kimberly McCabe and Robin Fajardo, "Law Enforcement Accreditation: A National Comparison of Accredited vs. Nonaccredited Agencies," *Journal of Criminal Justice* 29 (2001): 127–131.

© Richard Mei/AP Images

Officers and Organizations

CHAPTER **4** Police Organizations

CHAPTER **5** Police Officers I: Recruitment and Training for a Changing Society

CHAPTER **6** Police Officers II: On the Job

PART II

© Richard Mei/AP Images

4 Police Organizations

CHAPTER OUTLINE

The Quasi-Military Style of Police Organizations

Criticisms of the Quasi-Military Style

Police Departments as Organizations

The Dominant Style of American Police Organizations

Police Organizations as Bureaucracies

The Problems with Bureaucracy

The Positive Contributions of Bureaucracy in Policing

Informal Aspects of Police Organizations

Bureaucracy and Police Professionalism

Changing Police Organizations

Community Policing

Task Forces

COMPSTAT

Civil Service

Police Unions

Aspects of Police Unions

Collective Bargaining

Grievance Procedures

Impasse Settlement and Strikes

The Impact of Police Unions

Police Organizations and Their Environment
  Contingency Theory
  Institutional Theory
  Resource Dependency Theory

CASE STUDY
  Summary
  Key Terms

For Discussion
Internet Exercises

P olice services are delivered to the public through organizations. The quality of policing depends on how well a department is organized and managed. Some critics argue that the nature of police organizations is a major problem in policing: that the departments are isolated from the public, resist change, and do not make good use of their personnel.

This chapter examines the dominant features of American law enforcement organizations. Some of those features are unique to police organizations, whereas others are common to all large bureaucracies. This chapter identifies the major strengths and weaknesses of the prevailing style of organization and discusses alternative ways of organizing police work. It also discusses the impact of both civil service and police unions on police organizations. The chapter concludes with a discussion of organizational theory and its application to understanding police organizations.

The Quasi-Military Style of Police Organizations

American law enforcement agencies are organized along quasi-military lines.[1] That is, they resemble the military in some but not all respects. This style of organization originated with Robert Peel's plan for the London Metropolitan Police in 1829 and was adopted by American police departments.

The police resemble the military in the following respects. First, police officers wear uniforms. Second, police departments use military-style rank designations such as sergeant, lieutenant, and captain. Third, the command structure is hierarchical, with commands flowing from the top. Fourth, the organizational style is authoritarian, with penalties for failing to obey orders. Fifth, police officers carry weapons and have the legal authority to use deadly force, physical force, and to deprive people of their liberty through arrest.

For a full discussion of Robert Peel and the London Metropolitan Police, see Chapter 2.

At the same time, however, the police are different from the military in several important respects. The police serve a citizen population rather than fight a foreign enemy. The police also provide services designed to help people, and these services are often requested by individual citizens. Additionally, the police are constrained by laws protecting the rights of citizens, and they routinely exercise individual discretion, whereas military personnel are not constrained by civilian laws and are trained and expected to operate as members of military units.[2]

For a full discussion of police discretion, see Chapter 11.

Criticisms of the Quasi-Military Style

Many experts believe that the **quasi-military style** is inappropriate for the police. They argue that, first, the military ethos cultivates an "us versus them" attitude that is used to justify mistreatment of citizens. Second, it encourages the idea of a "war on crime" that is inappropriate for serving a citizen population.[3] Third, the authoritarian command style is contrary to democratic principles of participation. Fourth,

quasi-military style

103

SIDEBAR 4-1

The Myth of the Military Model

For years the police organizational structure has been said to be modeled after the military. An essay by Thomas Cowper, a former Marine and 17-year veteran of the New York State Police, argues that this perception is the result of several "wrong" assumptions. In particular, he states that the military and policing professions differ in terms of organizational characteristics and operational activities. With respect to organizational characteristics, he argues that the military is founded on the idea of teamwork and leadership, whereas the police profession emphasizes individuality, monitoring (from a variety of distances), and supervision. Cowper believes that military leaders are schooled in the art of war to more effectively perform their jobs and innately have the ability to promote esprit and heighten morale; whereas police leaders, he argues, are not highly trained on matters of concern to their profession and monitor the activities of their subordinates only to ensure that they follow policies. Similarly, he adds that although police officers act as a "lone ranger" on patrol, rarely working with others in their departments, soldiers work closely as a team, producing a more effective result. With regard to operational strategy, Cowper points out that the military has one mission—to wage war—whereas the police have several missions: crime fighting, order maintenance, and service. Additionally, he argues that the military engages in proactive operations, whereas police work is primarily reactive in nature.

1. Discuss whether or not you think that Cowper is correct in his characterization of the military and police professions.
2. As a class, discuss other differences between the military and the police.
3. As a class, discuss similarities between the military and the police.

Source: Adapted from Thomas Cowper, "The Myth of the Military Model of Leadership in Law Enforcement," *Police Quarterly* 3, no. 3 (2000): pp. 228–246.

---

the authoritarian style produces low morale, and the rigid rank structure fails to provide sufficient job satisfaction for police officers.

In the 1960s and early 1970s, some critics argued that the police should deemphasize their military image, primarily to improve police–community relations. They suggested using civilian-style blazers rather than military-style uniforms. A few small police departments experimented with using blazers. For example, the Menlo Park (California) Police Department found that the wearing of blazers created no serious problems, but when the Lakewood (Colorado) Police Department adopted blazers, and did not use the traditional rank designations, problems arose because the public image of the police was so closely associated with military-style uniforms that it was difficult for the department to depart from the norm.[4]

In recent years, some scholars have noted a shift back toward the militarization of the police. Peter Kraska points out that since the end of the cold war, a militaristic culture has begun to sweep back through police organizations. He contends that this phenomenon is seen most clearly in the rise in the number of police paramilitary units created throughout the United States in recent years. Police paramilitary units, which are often regarded as the most elite in a police agency, employ a strict military command structure, train similarly to elite military units, and handle high-risk situations (their sole purpose) that are in progress and that call for use-of-force specialists. Kraska further notes that officers in these units typically wear battle dress uniforms (BDUs), combat boots, and Kevlar helmets and carry specialized weapons such as machine guns, sniper rifles, CS gas, and surveillance equipment.[5]

Campbell and Campbell note, however, that prior discussions of the matter are a bit one sided, pointing out that not only are the police becoming more similar to the military but the military are becoming more similar to the police. They posit that since 9/11, the military and the police face similar pressures. Both are becoming more involved in fighting terrorism and global crime and in responding to ethnic conflict, and both are increasingly engaging in joint missions and operations to achieve similar goals. These converging environmental pressures, they argue, are resulting in the police and the military increasingly imitating one another.[6]

Police Departments as Organizations

The quasi-military aspect is only one feature of American police departments. To understand how police departments operate, and how they deliver services to the public, it is necessary to understand them as *organizations*. Many of the problems in policing are related to organizational features. It is important to also understand why these features exist and what positive contributions they make.

The Dominant Style of American Police Organizations

American police departments are remarkably similar in terms of organizational structure and administrative style. The typical police department is a complex **bureaucracy,** with a hierarchical structure and an authoritarian management style. The only exceptions to this rule are found in very small departments, which have simple organizational structures and more informal management styles. At the same time, all but the smallest agencies are governed by some form of civil service rules that regulate personnel policies. Finally, most of the large police departments are legally bound by collective bargaining contracts with unions representing rank-and-file officers.

bureaucracy

Police Organizations as Bureaucracies

The modern police department is a bureaucratic organization, as are other large organizations in modern society: private corporations, universities, religious organizations, government agencies, and so on. Police departments share similar characteristics of bureaucracy with these other organizations.[7]

The bureaucratic form of organization exists because it is the most efficient means developed for organizing and directing many different activities in the pursuit of a common goal. This does not mean that the bureaucratic form is completely efficient, only that no other organizational form has been found that is better able to carry out multiple tasks simultaneously in the pursuit of a common goal.

The modern bureaucracy has the following characteristics:[8]

1. It is a complex organization performing many different tasks in pursuit of a common goal.
2. The different tasks are grouped into separate divisions, or "bureaus" (hence, the term *bureaucracy*).
3. The organizational structure is hierarchical or pyramidal, with a clear division of labor between workers, first-line supervisors, and chief executives.
4. Responsibility for specific tasks is delegated to lower-ranking employees.
5. There is a clear chain of command, which indicates who is responsible for each task and who is responsible for supervising each employee.

6. There is a clear unity of command, so that each employee answers to one and only one supervisor.
7. Written rules and regulations are designed to ensure uniformity and consistency.
8. Information flows up and down through the organization according to the chain of command.
9. There are clear career paths by which personnel move upward through the organization in an orderly fashion.

The modern police bureaucracy began to emerge in the early twentieth century, as a part of the professionalization movement.[9] With the creation of new specialized units (for example, traffic, juvenile, vice, training), departments became more complex organizations. The new field of police management developed to help cope with this new complexity. Experts borrowed modern management principles from business administration and applied them to police administration. The leaders of this movement were **August Vollmer, Bruce Smith,** and **O. W. Wilson.** Wilson's textbook, *Police Administration,* became the unofficial bible on the subject by the 1950s.[10]

**August Vollmer
Bruce Smith
O. W. Wilson**

For example, see Exhibit 4–1, which is the organizational chart of the Phoenix Police Department. It is representative of other big-city police departments and illustrates the main features of the modern police bureaucracy.

As is evident in the chart, the Phoenix Police Department's organizational structure is pyramidal, reflecting a hierarchical management style. The organization is structured to be able to perform many different tasks simultaneously: patrol, traffic, criminal investigation, records, training, planning and research, and so on. The Phoenix Police Department has also grouped together related tasks in a logical fashion: patrol and related functions are organizationally located in a patrol division, criminal investigation is in another division, professional standards in another, and so on.

Additionally, the lines of authority in the Phoenix Police Department are clear, with responsibility for supervision flowing from the chief of police down through the organization. It is possible to identify who is responsible for particular tasks. This approach reflects the principle of unity of supervision: each person reports to one supervisor. Under the principle of span of control, each supervisor is responsible for a limited number of people. In the patrol units, the ideal span of control involves a sergeant supervising between 8 and 12 patrol officers.

The degree of specialization in a police department depends on the size of the community, the nature of its problems, and the size of the department itself.[11] The police department in a medium-sized city with relatively little serious crime does not need a separate homicide unit. The police department in a big city with many murders does need, and can afford to create, a homicide unit. Small and medium-sized departments cannot afford to maintain their own training academies. These tasks can be performed more efficiently for them by a state agency that serves many departments.

For a full discussion of the use of written policies and administrative rulemaking, see Chapters 11 and 14.

What is not evident from the organizational chart is the set of rules governing employee behavior. Police departments rely on written rules and collect them in a standard operating procedure (SOP) manual or policy manual. Also, the career paths for officers will be indicated in its civil service procedures.

EXHIBIT 4–1

Phoenix Police Department Organizational Chart

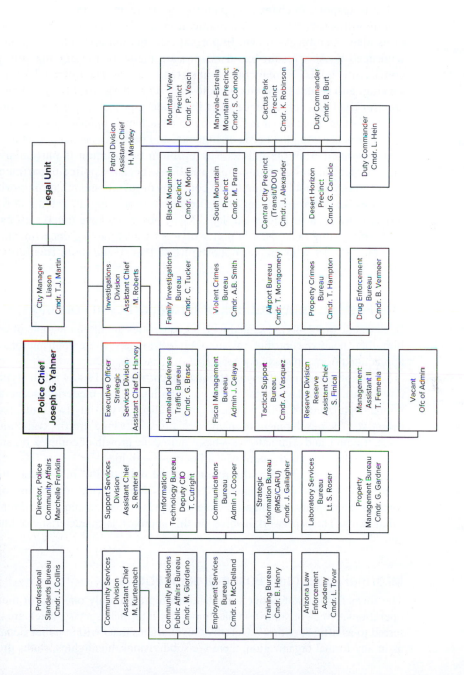

The Problems with Bureaucracy

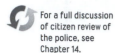 For a full discussion of the relationship between the police and ethnic communities, see Chapter 12.

There are several major criticisms of the bureaucratic form of organization, all of which apply to police organizations.[12] Bureaucracies are often rigid, inflexible, and unable to adapt to external changes. Thus, for example, many business administration experts argue that American corporations have failed to adapt to changing markets and the new global economy. Police departments have often failed to respond to changes in patterns of crime and in the composition of the communities they serve.[13] Communication within large bureaucratic organizations also often breaks down. Important information does not reach the people who need it. As a result, bad decisions are made, or the organization pursues conflicting goals. Bureaucracies also tend to become inward looking, self-serving, and isolated from the people they serve. Organizational self-protection and survival take precedence over the basic goals of the organization. Thus, businesses are accused of not catering to customer demands, universities are accused of not serving the needs of students, and police departments are accused of being isolated from the public. The problem of isolation is particularly acute with respect to police–community relations, because police departments have been accused of not listening to the concerns of racial- and ethnic-minority communities. Last, bureaucracies are criticized for not using the talents of their employees and even stifling creativity.[14] Many observers have found serious morale problems among rank-and-file police officers and argue that departments need to provide officers with greater opportunities at work and more flexibility to perform their duties.

For a full discussion of citizen review of the police, see Chapter 14.

For a full discussion of the control of police discretion and police misconduct through bureaucratization, see Chapters 11 and 13.

The Positive Contributions of Bureaucracy in Policing

Because the problems associated with bureaucracies are often the topic of conversation, their positive contributions are often overlooked. These contributions are best appreciated from a historical perspective.

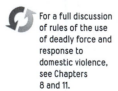 For a full discussion of the impact of written rules on police discretion, see Chapter 11.

A comparison of the typical police department in 1900 with the typical big-city department today illustrates the contributions of the modern bureaucracy. The police department of 1900 was very unspecialized, with only two units, patrol and detective. The development of many specialties—juvenile, traffic, community relations, training, and criminalistics—has required the growth of complex organizations that have the capacity to coordinate all of these activities.[15]

The control of police discretion and the reduction of misconduct have also been achieved through bureaucratic principles. Written rules on the use of deadly force or the response to domestic violence represent the technique of administrative rulemaking. The paperwork involved in this approach is characteristic of bureaucracies.[16]

For a full discussion of rules of the use of deadly force and response to domestic violence, see Chapters 8 and 11.

Informal Aspects of Police Organizations

The formal aspects of police organizations represent only one part of their actual operations. Every organization has important informal aspects, which are often referred to as office politics.[17] Dorothy Guyot argues that "within police departments, as in any formal organization, there are subdivisions, hierarchies, status groupings, and other formal arrangements. There are also informal relationships, cliques, friendship patterns, and temporary collaborations."[18]

For example, information does not always flow up and down the organization in the manner prescribed by the organizational chart. Sensitive and potentially embarrassing information is often withheld. Rank-and-file officers cover up each other's mistakes. Sergeants cover up mistakes by officers under their command because it would reflect poorly on their own performance. In some important respects, chief executives do not want to know about certain things. This allows them to publicly deny that such things exist when questioned by the news media or members of the public.

At the same time, however, information does flow to friends in the organization, outside of the prescribed channels. Such information is often referred to as gossip. Gossip falls into two general categories: true and false information. Gossip that is false is created and circulated to discredit someone. Gossip that is true is often useful. It may be important to know, for example, that someone is planning to retire or leave the organization or that a person is in serious trouble because of mistakes on the job.

John Crank argues that within almost all police departments there are "cliques," or informal networks of officers. These cliques, Crank explains, are formed to protect officers from "administrative bullshit." There are two types of protective cliques: vertical and horizontal. **Vertical cliques** are formed between lower and higher ranking officers. These cliques oftentimes have a shared understanding of situations and problems and work together to address them in an agreeable manner. **Horizontal cliques** are formed between similarly ranked officers. Most horizontal cliques are created to protect line officers from supervisory oversight and accountability.[19]

vertical cliques

horizontal cliques

Cliques in a police department are often based on work groups. Officers who work together day in and day out, on patrol or as detectives, tend to develop close personal ties. They see things from the perspective of their unit and, when a conflict arises, defend their colleagues, even if they know their colleagues are wrong.

One dysfunctional result of this process is rivalry among different units. Patrol officers often resent the higher status that detectives enjoy. There are also rivalries among patrol officers assigned to different shifts. To a certain extent, the seniority system aggravates these tensions, because the evening shift gets the younger officers while the day shift has the older officers.

At the same time, there are cliques throughout the organization based on personal friendships. Often these cliques originated in shared experiences as members of the same recruit class or members of the same patrol crew. The folklore of policing includes the belief that some police officers develop closer relationships with their partners than with their spouses. A partner is someone who can understand the unpleasant aspects of policing that an officer would not want to discuss at home.

Friendship patterns become important in the management of a police department. Westley found that a police chief needs both information about what is going on in the organization and information about the people in order to perform sensitive tasks. As a result the chief relies on "a group of favorites within the department whom he can depend on to handle delicate assignments."[20] A chief maintains this network of friends by handing out rewards in the form of favorable assignments and by punishing real or imagined enemies by giving them low-status assignments.

Bureaucracy and Police Professionalism

The bureaucratic aspects of policing conflict in many ways with the professionalism as understood in other occupations. In law, medicine, and education, a professional is someone with special expertise, resulting from extensive training and experience, who exercises independent judgment about critical events. The doctor, for example, makes critical decisions about diagnosis and treatment of patients. The professional is not expected to follow a rigid set of rules.[21]

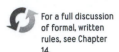 For a full discussion of formal, written rules, see Chapter 14.

The bureaucratic aspects of policing represent a different approach to the control of behavior. The quasi-military nature of police organizations, for example, has emphasized hierarchical command and control rather than collegial decision making. Police organizations also attempt to control police officer behavior through formal, written rules.

police professionalism

Because of the history of the American police, **police professionalism** acquired a special meaning. Professionalism meant the same thing as bureaucratization. Thus, the professional departments were the ones that adopted O. W. Wilson's principles of police administration: specialization, hierarchy, clear lines of authority, written rules and policies, and so on. Professional departments were the ones in which officers did their jobs "by the book," meaning that they followed written departmental rules.[22]

To a certain extent, however, the professional autonomy of the traditional professions is disappearing. Doctors increasingly work in large hospitals or medical facilities. Like other bureaucracies, these organizations impose formal controls over doctors' behavior. Lawyers increasingly work in large law firms or corporations, which also seek to control the lawyers' behavior by monitoring the number of hours billed.

Changing Police Organizations

 For a full discussion of police discretion, see Chapter 11.

There is much dissatisfaction with the current state of police organizations. There are two schools of thought on how to improve them. The dominant school of thought accepts the basic principles of bureaucratic organization and seeks to apply them more effectively. Advocates of this approach, for example, support greater control of discretion through written rules.[23] The other school of thought seeks to use alternative decision-making procedures that operate within the existing formal structure.

Community Policing

Community policing represents an alternative to the traditional form of police organizations. Traditional police organizations are extremely bureaucratic structures, which are said to necessarily limit the effectiveness and efficiency of the police because of the many impersonal rules, the lack of discretion officers are permitted to use, and the hierarchical nature of the organizational structure. Accordingly, community policing attempts to modify the police organization through debureaucratization. Specifically, it attempts to **decentralize** decision making both territorially and administratively. This requires the police to place greater responsibility on rank-and-file officers at the neighborhood level and to become more responsive to neighborhood residents. It also requires the police to **deformalize,** eliminating many

decentralize

deformalize

of the rules and policies that often stifle creativity and do not encourage problem solving. Under community policing, organizations are also encouraged to **despecialize** functions. This means replacing specialized units with neighborhood officers, who are more knowledgeable about the problems that face their neighborhood. Finally, community policing attempts to **delayerize,** decreasing the amount of social and administrative distance between the beat officer and the chief of police. This, reformers argue, will increase the speed at which decisions are made and will empower beat officers. In this respect, community policing responds to the standard criticisms of bureaucracies discussed earlier.[24]

Whether or not organizations have been able to accomplish these goals is still a matter of debate. The most definitive study to date was conducted by Edward Maguire, who examined 353 large municipal police departments across the United States. Maguire found some support for the view that the community policing movement was having an impact on the organizational structure of police agencies. In particular, he found that large police departments across the country have become less centralized and less bureaucratic and are increasingly relying on civilians to perform police work. But he also found that police departments have not decreased the amount of social or administrative distance between line officers and the chief of police, and they have not reduced their reliance on specialized units.[25]

despecialize

delayerize

SIDEBAR 4–2

Toward a Life-Course Perspective of Police Organizations

William King recently proposed a new and innovative strategy for understanding police organizations and police organizational change. He argues that all police organizations, like people, go through stages of development that have significant impact on their structure and behavior. King stipulates that police organizations go through several stages or events. Two of these events are inevitable: organizational birth and death; the other four stages—all of which may or may not be experienced by a police organization—include early founding effects, growth, decline, and crisis.

Organizational Birth. All police organizations had to have been created at some point. King points out that, depending on the time and place, history has shown that several factors have led to the creation of police organizations, such as increases in crime, riots, public drunkenness, and class conflict. He further points out that a number of local police agencies have been created in the United States over the past 20 years, but that scholars do not have a strong understanding of why they were created.

Early Founding Effects. Soon after creation, the police organization develops routines, structures, and behaviors that are "imprinted" into the organization. King calls these early founding effects. He maintains that the founders of the organization, and other like police organizations, set the template for how the police organization will be structured and managed and how it will behave. As a consequence, King posits that early decisions made by the police organization have a substantial impact on its trajectory for a long period of time.

Growth. King states that some police organizations go through periods of substantial growth. If an organization goes through a period of growth, this growth not only is accompanied

(continued)

SIDEBAR 4-2

(continued)

by increased hiring and training but also provides substantial amounts of opportunity for existing employees. For example, as a police organization grows, there is increased potential for promotion, increased opportunity for the creation of specialized units, and increased potential for rewards. Organizations that are growing are also typically viewed as successful, which often results in increases in resources that are available to the organization.

Decline. *By contrast, King maintains that some organizations experience periods of decline. This occurs when there is a reduction in the number of employees in the police organization. This is often viewed as a sign that the organization is failing. Promotions are more difficult to obtain, employees are asked to serve in multiple roles, and they are expected to do more with a reduction in resources.*

Crisis. *Many police organizations endure crises. King explains that crises can occur inside or outside of the police organization. An externally generated crisis might include increased crime rates or a reduction in budget. Internally generated crises might include police corruption, excessive use of force, or a labor dispute. How a police organization adapts to crises has the potential to have a significant impact on whether it experiences a period of growth or decline.*

The Disbanding of Police Organizations. *King notes that most people are familiar with a business failing or going bankrupt, but few are familiar with the disbanding of a police organization. However, he points out that it is more common than many believe. For example, over the past three decades, 117 local police agencies in Ohio were disbanded. Most of these agencies were relatively small and served small communities. He also points out that some of the largest police organizations in the country have been disbanded. These include the New York City school, transit, and housing police agencies, and the Compton, California, and Lauderdale, Florida, police departments. King argues that the life-course perspective calls on policymakers and scholars to better understand why a police organization might disband and what existing police organizations might learn from those that do.*

1. Discuss whether you think that King is correct in his characterization of police organizations having a life course.

2. As a class, discuss the characteristics of a declining police organization and the impact that it could have on police productivity.

Source: Adapted from William R. King, "Toward a Life-Course Perspective of Police Organizations," *Journal of Research in Crime and Delinquency* 46 (2009): 213–244.

Task Forces

An alternative to changing the structure of police organizations is to develop decision-making procedures that operate within the existing formal structure. One example is the use of **task forces** consisting of officers from different ranks within the same agency. A task force on drug enforcement, for example, might include a captain, a lieutenant, two sergeants, and three police officers. An interagency task force allows the police chief to select particular officers from different ranks, based on their talents rather than just their rank.

task forces

The interagency task force approach addresses several problems related to the traditional police organizational structure. It recognizes the fact that many officers at the lowest rank are competent to make intelligent decisions about police policy.

Involving these officers offers them greater job satisfaction, prepares them for supervisory responsibilities later in their careers, and increases the likelihood that innovations will be accepted within the organization.

The success of interagency task forces has led a number of law enforcement organizations to adopt multiagency task forces. Multiagency task forces operate as special law enforcement organizations, usually with multijurisdictional authority, created through formal agreements between several government agencies for the purpose of more effectively and efficiently combating specific crime problems.[26] It is estimated that between 900 and 1,100 multiagency task forces are funded by the federal government alone.[27]

Multiagency task forces typically consist of two or more sworn officers from several participating agencies, with each agency donating personnel and equipment. Often one of the participating agencies is selected as the lead agency to coordinate law enforcement efforts. Arizona's Gang and Immigration Intelligence Team Enforcement Mission (GIITEM) task force is a statewide multiagency task force consisting of officers from many of the state's municipal and county police agencies as well as agents from federal law enforcement agencies. It is led by the state's department of public safety and is responsible for policing gangs and illegal immigrants—specialized functions that are too expensive and time intensive for many of the police agencies in the state.

Phillips notes that there are five major advantages to using multiagency task forces: (1) They eliminate the duplication of services in surrounding communities, (2) they afford smaller agencies services that they otherwise might not be able to afford, (3) they result in the benefit of shared resource management, (4) they allow officers to work in jurisdictions where they might not otherwise have authority, and (5) they increase the amount of information that officers have at their disposal.[28]

COMPSTAT

Over the past two decades, police organizations have been increasing the amount of technology they employ to more effectively and efficiently make use of their resources. However, it was not until 1994, when the New York City Police Department (NYPD), led by Commissioner William Bratton, implemented **COMPSTAT** (short for "compare stats"), that technology was used as an organizational tool to achieve crime control through accountability. In the NYPD, the COMPSTAT model attempts to blend timely intelligence, effective tactics, rapid deployment of personnel, and relentless follow-up and assessment.[29] Under COMPSTAT, the police department continuously collects arrest, calls for service, and complaint data from each precinct or beat within the agency and analyzes those data for reporting purposes at that level. This organizational model of management in New York City places the responsibility for crime control on precinct commanders. At weekly meetings, crime trends are examined, and precinct commanders are "grilled" about the strategies they have used to control crime in their precincts. Commanders who are not successful in reducing crime are reassigned to less prestigious and demanding positions.[30]

COMPSTAT

Weisburd and his associates performed an exhaustive study examining the adoption of COMPSTAT across the country and the primary goals associated with the strategy. They found six key elements or features associated with COMPSTAT:[31]

1. COMPSTAT clarifies the department's mission, goals, and values.
2. COMPSTAT holds managers within the organization accountable.
3. Organizational power and authority are transferred to commanders who are responsible for geographic areas.
4. Resources are transferred to commanders who are responsible for geographic areas.
5. Data are used to identify problems and to evaluate success and failure.
6. Middle managers are expected to use innovative problem-solving tactics.

Since its implementation in New York City, COMPSTAT has been hailed as one of the most important organizational innovations in American policing. This is in large part because a number of policymakers and police officials claimed that COMP-STAT was responsible for the dramatic drop in crime in New York City. Following the implementation of COMPSTAT, index crimes in New York City decreased by 55 percent, compared with 24 percent in other large cities. Similarly, during the same period, homicides in New York City decreased by 66 percent, compared with a decrease of 24 percent in other cities. As a result, the model has been implemented in a number of police departments throughout the United States.[32] A recent survey of police agencies across the country showed that about 79 percent of them use COMPSTAT and 6 percent were planning on implementing it in the near future.[33]

A number of critics, however, have pointed out that the decrease in crime came at the expense of due process and morale. Citizen complaints escalated dramatically as commanders were required to use more aggressive policing strategies. For example, complaints against the police for conducting illegal searches increased 135 percent in the first two years. Likewise, many police managers in the NYPD complained that COMPSTAT was no more than a numbers game that was used to foster fear among management. Those managers who did not increase arrests and decrease crime in the areas they commanded were subject to public embarrassment by police executives who scolded them in COMPSTAT meetings.[34]

There have been a handful of evaluations of COMPSTAT. One was conducted in Fort Worth, Texas. The researchers examined monthly crime trends prior to and after the implementation of COMPSTAT. They reported that although the implementation of COMPSTAT resulted in significantly less property and total index crimes, it did not have an impact on violent crime.[35] Another evaluation was conducted in a large southeastern police department. Dabney reported that most line-level officers misunderstood the purpose of COMPSTAT and that sergeants did not follow through to identify and provide oversight of COMPSTAT processes. Dabney also found that COMPSTAT increased competition among units, resulting in less information sharing and cooperation.[36] Most recently, a randomized field experiment was conducted in Lowell, Massachusetts, to compare the effectiveness of COMP-STAT with problem-oriented policing, which has been found to be an effective crime control strategy (discussed in Chapter 10). The authors reported that problem-solving processes resulted in more innovative responses and led to greater reductions in crime, compared to processes associated with COMPSTAT.[37]

Civil Service

Civil service procedures are a major feature of American police organizations. Civil service represents a set of formal and legally binding procedures governing personnel decisions. Civil service is nearly universal. With the exception of some of the smallest departments, police departments in the United States operate under some form of civil service. The purpose of civil service is to ensure that personnel decisions are based on objective criteria and not on favoritism, bias, or political influence.

　　State law or local ordinance establishes civil service systems. In most cities, ultimate authority over personnel procedures rests with a board or commission consisting of three to five persons. The mayor or a city manager government unit typically appoints board members for a specified term. The board sets basic policy and hires a personnel director to administer policy on a day-to-day basis.[38]

　　The civil service agency and the police department share responsibility for personnel policies. Civil service agencies are responsible for developing job descriptions and pay scales, developing recruitment procedures, developing and administering recruitment tests, certifying qualified applicants, developing promotional criteria, developing and administering promotional tests, developing disciplinary procedures, and hearing appeals of disciplinary actions. Police departments provide input on job descriptions, participate in recruiting, conduct some of the recruitment tests, and select recruits from certified lists.

　　Civil service systems reinforce the hierarchical structure of police departments. William King points out that there are four formal hierarchies (typically outlined under civil service systems) that stratify organizational members.[39] First, there is a **rewards hierarchy.** This hierarchy typically corresponds with an officer's rank and seniority within the department. It does not, however, typically correspond with individual skill or performance.

　　Second, officers are differentiated on the basis of a **seniority hierarchy.** Officers with more years of service are typically paid more and are given advantage over which shifts and jobs they are assigned.

　　Third, officers are differentiated on the basis of a **status hierarchy**—their assigned status within the police department. Officers who are assigned to a specialized unit, such as detective, or who occupy a particular job in the department, such as special assistant to the chief, typically have greater authority and responsibility in particular situations. In these cases, an officer who occupies an assigned status can have command and control over those who outrank him or her. However, an officer carries the title and authority only while assigned or appointed to a particular job; if reassigned, the person loses both the title and the authority.

　　Fourth, officers are differentiated on the basis of a **rank hierarchy.** An officer carries his or her rank permanently, until promoted (demotions are extremely rare under civil service). For example, an officer holding the rank of sergeant is restricted to those jobs designated for sergeants by civil service job descriptions.

　　Civil service creates a number of problems for police organizations. It limits the power of police chiefs, for instance, in making personnel decisions. A chief cannot hire, fire, or promote personnel at will. Nor can a chief change existing personnel standards at will (for example, imposing a college education requirement for all new recruits).

civil service

rewards hierarchy

seniority hierarchy

status hierarchy

rank hierarchy

It also limits the opportunities and incentives for individual officers. Officers cannot earn financial bonuses or receive rapid promotions for exceptional performance.

Additionally, many critics argue that the provisions for discipline make it extremely difficult for chiefs to terminate bad officers or even to discipline officers for poor performance.

Police Unions

Police unions are another structural feature of police organizations. A **police union** is an organization legally authorized to represent police officers in collective bargaining with the employer. Under American labor law, employers are required to recognize and negotiate with democratically chosen unions. Police unions are extremely powerful, and union contracts are an important feature of police organizations.

Aspects of Police Unions

The majority of sworn police officers in the United States today are members of police unions. According to the Law Enforcement Management and Administrative Statistics (LEMAS) survey, officers are represented by unions in 73 percent of all municipal police departments and 43 percent of all sheriff's departments.[40] Almost all of the big and medium-sized cities have police unions, whereas small city and county departments (10 sworn officers or fewer) do not. Although union membership has been declining in the private sector of the economy, it has been growing in the public sector. The police are not the most heavily unionized group of public employees. A higher percentage of firefighters and public school teachers are members of unions.[41]

Unlike in other parts of the economy, there is no single national union that represents all police officers. The United Automobile Workers, for example, represents all employees in the automobile industry; the International Brotherhood of Teamsters represents all truck drivers; and so on. Police unions are fragmented among several different national federations. Today, there are three major police unions:

1. *Fraternal Order of Police:* The Fraternal Order of Police (FOP) is the oldest and largest police organization. It represents about 50 percent of law enforcement officers in the nation. Today, it is reported that the FOP has 330,000 members.[42]

2. *International Union of Police Associations:* The International Union of Police Associations (IUPA) is one of 89 chartered unions affiliated with the AFL-CIO. However, in recent years the AFL-CIO has not provided the IUPA with much assistance. It is estimated that the IUPA has 35,000 members.[43]

3. *Teamsters Law Enforcement League:* The Teamsters Law Enforcement League, which is a division of the International Brotherhood of Teamsters, is perhaps the most controversial police union, given its historical involvement with organized crime. Like the IUPA, the Teamsters Law Enforcement League is affiliated with the AFL-CIO. The Teamsters mostly represents officers in suburban and rural law enforcement agencies. Today, it is estimated that the Teamsters represents about 15,000 officers in 225 police organizations.[44]

Collective Bargaining

Collective bargaining is defined as "the method of determining conditions of employment through bilateral negotiations." The basic principles of collective bargaining are that (1) employees have a legal right to form unions of their own choosing, (2) employers must recognize employee unions, (3) employees have a right to participate in negotiations over working conditions, and (4) employers are required to negotiate with the union's designated representatives. The process is designed to provide a structured framework for settling differences between employers and employees.[45]

collective bargaining

In some departments, the union represents all of the officers except the chief. In others, it represents all of the officers from the rank of captain on down; deputy chiefs are excluded on the grounds that they are part of management. In some large departments, there are separate unions for different ranks: one for police officers, one for sergeants, and so on. In these cases, the chief must negotiate with two or, in some cases, three unions. There may also be a separate union for the civilian employees.

The 1935 National Labor Relations Act defined the scope of collective bargaining as "wages, hours, and other conditions of employment." The scope of conditions of employment is ambiguous and subject to negotiations. It generally excludes management rights issues, such as the right to recruit, assign, transfer, or promote employees. In some cities, however, the union has won the right to control such issues as patrol staffing.[46]

Grievance Procedures

One of the most important conditions of work involves disciplinary procedures. Almost all police unions have formal grievance procedures designed to protect officers against unfair discipline. Grievance procedures provide due process for employees.

The typical grievance procedure (see Exhibit 4–2) requires that an officer be notified (usually in writing) about a disciplinary action and that the officer has the right to a hearing, the right to an attorney, and the right to appeal any disciplinary action. In some instances, these procedures are referred to as the police officers' bill of rights (see Exhibit 4–3).

The chief, for example, might announce a plan to add a fourth patrol shift. The union might argue that this represents a change in working conditions, because the officers involved will have to work different hours. The chief will reply that his or her power to create a fourth shift is a management right. The two sides will try to settle this disagreement informally. If they cannot, the union may file a grievance under the contract. Contracts typically contain a formal grievance procedure to settle these conflicts.

Impasse Settlement and Strikes

When the union and the city or county cannot agree on a contract, an impasse exists. In the private sector, the union often goes out on strike, or the employer conducts a lockout of the employees. Police strikes are illegal in many states, and other

EXHIBIT 4–2

Article 8: Grievance Procedure

Step 1   An employee or Union who has a grievance shall present the same, in writing, to the Police Chief, or his designated representative, within ten (10) working days from the date on which the employee or Union became aware of the grievance. The written grievance must set forth the sections and articles of this Agreement upon which the matter of interpretation or application is involved. The Chief, or his designated representative, will respond to the grievant in writing within ten (10) working days from the date on which the written grievance was received.

Step 2   If satisfactory settlement is not reached under Step 1 hereof, then the aggrieved employee or Union may, within ten (10) working days of receipt of the Chief's response to Step 1 hereof appeal the Chief's decision to the Department Head, or his designated representative, who shall have ten (10) working days in which to respond, in writing, to the employee.

Step 3   In the event the employee or Union is still dissatisfied with the response of the Department Head, or his designated representative, then the employee or Union may, within ten (10) working days from the date of the response given by the Department Head or his designated representative, appeal said decision, in writing to the Labor Relations Director, or his designated representative. The Labor Relations Director or his designated representative shall respond to the grievant, in writing, within ten (10) working days from the date on which the grievance appeal was received. An extension on the time period may be granted when mutually agreed to by the Labor Relations Director and the Union.

Step 4   If satisfactory settlement is not reached under Step 3 hereof, either the aggrieved employee, the Union, or the City of Omaha by and through the Labor Relations Director, or his representative shall, within twenty (20) working days from the expiration of the limits as set forth in Step 3 or any extension thereof as set forth in Section 3, by written notice to the other party, request arbitration. The City shall furnish the Union with a copy of any such notice sent or received requesting arbitration.

The arbitration proceeding shall be conducted by an arbitrator to be mutually selected by the parties within thirty (30) calendar days after the submission of written demand for arbitration. The UNION shall at its discretion become a party for the purpose of selecting an arbitrator. The UNION and the grievant shall together be considered one party. If the parties are unable to mutually agree as to the selection of an arbitrator within such time limit and either party continues to demand arbitration, the parties shall jointly request the Federal Mediation and Conciliation Service to provide a list of five (5) arbitrators. Each party shall have the right to strike two (2) names from the list of arbitrators as submitted. The party requesting arbitration shall have the right to strike the first name and the other party shall then strike one name with the same process being repeated so that the person remaining on the list shall be the arbitrator.

Source: Omaha Police Department, "Union Contract," *Standard Operating Procedure Manual,* pp. 12–13.

impasse settlement procedures exist, such as mandatory mediation, fact finding, or arbitration.

Strikes are the most controversial aspect of police unionism. Many people argue that the police have absolutely no right to strike—that it is unprofessional and that it creates a serious danger to the public. Police unions reply that they should have the same right to strike as other unions. Withholding one's labor is the ultimate weapon that working people have to force the employer to reach an agreement. Most

EXHIBIT 4–3

Florida Police Officers' Bill of Rights

112.532 Law Enforcement Officers' and Correctional Officers' Rights

All law enforcement officers and correctional officers employed by or appointed to a law enforcement agency or a correctional agency shall have the following rights and privileges:

1. **Rights of Law Enforcement Officers and Correctional Officers While under Investigation.** Whenever a law enforcement officer or correctional officer is under investigation and subject to interrogation by members of his or her agency for any reason that could lead to disciplinary action, suspension, demotion, or dismissal, the interrogation must be conducted under the following conditions:

   a. The interrogation shall be conducted at a reasonable hour, preferably at a time when the law enforcement officer or correctional officer is on duty, unless the seriousness of the investigation is of such a degree that immediate action is required.

   b. The interrogation shall take place either at the office of the command of the investigating officer or at the office of the local precinct, police unit, or correctional unit in which the incident allegedly occurred, as designated by the investigating officer or agency.

   c. The law enforcement officer or correctional officer under investigation shall be informed of the rank, name, and command of the officer in charge of the investigation, the interrogating officer, and all persons present during the interrogation. All questions directed to the officer under interrogation shall be asked by or through one interrogator during any one investigative interrogation, unless specifically waived by the officer under investigation.

   d. The law enforcement officer or correctional officer under investigation must be informed of the nature of the investigation before any interrogation begins and he or she must be informed of the names of all complainants. All identifiable witnesses shall be interviewed, whenever possible, prior to the beginning of the investigative interview of the accused officer. The complaint, all witness statements, including all other existing subject officer statements, and all other existing evidence, including, but not limited to, incident reports, GPS locator information, and audio or video recordings relating to the incident under investigation, must be provided to each officer who is the subject of the complaint before the beginning of any investigative interview of that officer. An officer, after being informed of the right to review witness statements, may voluntarily waive the provisions of this paragraph and provide a voluntary statement at any time.

   e. Interrogating sessions shall be for reasonable periods and shall be timed to allow for such personal necessities and rest periods as are reasonably necessary.

   f. The law enforcement officer or correctional officer under interrogation may not be subjected to offensive language or be threatened with transfer, dismissal, or disciplinary action. A promise or reward may not be made as an inducement to answer any questions.

   g. The formal interrogation of a law enforcement officer or correctional officer, including all recess periods, must be recorded on audio tape, or otherwise preserved in such a manner as to allow a transcript to be prepared, and there shall be no unrecorded questions or statements. Upon the request of the interrogated officer, a copy of any recording of the interrogation session must be made available to the interrogated officer no later than 72 hours, excluding holidays and weekends, following said interrogation.

   h. If the law enforcement officer or correctional officer under interrogation is under arrest, or is likely to be placed under arrest as a result of the interrogation, he or she

(continued)

EXHIBIT 4–3

(continued)

shall be completely informed of all his or her rights before commencing the interrogation.

i. At the request of any law enforcement officer or correctional officer under investigation, he or she has the right to be represented by counsel or any other representative of his or her choice, who shall be present at all times during the interrogation whenever the interrogation relates to the officer's continued fitness for law enforcement or correctional service.

j. Notwithstanding the rights and privileges provided by this part, this part does not limit the right of an agency to discipline or to pursue criminal charges against an officer.

Source: Florida Statutes, Sec. 112.532.

---

union leaders, however, are opposed to strikes either because they are illegal in that state or because of the negative public reaction.[47]

Instead of actual strikes, police officers occasionally engage in job actions, defined as a deliberate disruption of normally assigned duties. One example is the "blue flu," where many officers do not go to work, claiming they are sick.[48] In some cases, such as in San Francisco in 1975, police officers tried to exert pressure on the city by refusing to write any traffic tickets or writing massive numbers of tickets.[49] A police strike is a major crisis for the community. Police strikes in Baltimore (1974), San Francisco (1975), and New Orleans (1979) resulted in violence and disorder. In many strikes, some officers remain on duty, feeling a sense of obligation to the community.

Police strikes are rare, and there have been few since the 1970s. Public school teachers strike far more often than police officers do. Even in the private sector, the number of strikes has declined substantially since the 1970s.[50]

The Impact of Police Unions

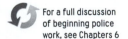

For a full discussion of beginning police work, see Chapters 6 and 15.

Police unions have had a powerful impact on American policing. Most important, they have produced significant improvements in police officer salaries and benefits. In the mid-1960s, many police departments were having great difficulty recruiting and holding qualified officers. By the late 1980s, the picture had changed dramatically. Police departments generally had many applicants for each opening and were able to recruit people with at least some college education. In other words, jobs with the police department were competitive with other jobs that a person with some college education might consider.

Jobs in law enforcement became more competitive in part because of the increase in pay police officers received as a consequence of unionization. One study conducted in Florida found that after the enactment of legislation that allowed sheriffs' departments to unionize, the annual entry-level salary for sheriff's deputies increased significantly, by almost $5,000, compared to their nonunion counterparts.[51] Jihong Zhao and Nicholas Lovrich performed one of the few nationwide studies examining the impact of collective bargaining on police compensation. They reported that about 70 percent of today's large police agencies engage in collective bargaining. Agencies that do not engage in collective bargaining were found to be less likely to receive hazardous duty pay, shift differential pay, and education incentive pay. The researchers' findings led them to conclude that collective bargaining is a successful strategy for "the advocacy of policies promoting the well-being of police personnel."[52]

Samuel Walker notes that unions have affected law enforcement in at least four other ways. First, they have radically altered the process of police management, reducing the power of chiefs and introducing a process of shared governance. Unions give officers a voice in some, but not all, decisions about the operation of the department. Prior to the late 1960s, chiefs had an almost completely free hand in managing their departments. Second, unions have had an impact on discipline and accountability by introducing due process into discipline procedures, limiting the power of police chiefs to arbitrarily or unfairly discipline officers, and opposing citizen oversight of the police. Third, they have negatively influenced police–community relations by aggressively defending police officers accused of misconduct, opposing policies that would improve police–community relations, and opposing affirmative action hiring plans. Fourth, police unions have substantial financial and political resources. This allows them to endorse and sponsor political candidates, and ballot initiatives, as well as influence local government budgeting.[53]

As a consequence, it should not be surprising that several scholars and police executives claim that police unions are a serious obstacle to positive change in police organizations. They claim, for example, that in many cities unions have fought the implementation of lateral entry, changes in department policies, disciplinary procedures, and promotion procedures. They also claim that unions have been associated with restricting management's ability to efficiently run a police department by opposing policies associated with staffing allocations, the implementation of a fourth shift, and changes in overtime procedures.[54]

SIDEBAR 4-3

Should Police Unions Be Able to Advocate for State Legislation?

In 2010, the Phoenix Law Enforcement Association, the primary union for officers in the Phoenix Police Department, became actively involved in advocacy for a state anti-immigration bill known as Senate Bill 1070. The bill would grant local police more authority to stop and question suspected illegal immigrants. The union filed numerous motions with federal and state courts supporting the bill. When the Phoenix Police Department's police chief (Jack Harris) voiced opposition to the bill, the Phoenix police union requested local and state officials to look into whether the chief violated any rules or policies. As a consequence of the disagreement over the legislation, a heated dispute between the union and the chief of police ensued. The union lost about 10 percent of its membership over the matter. Additionally, shortly after the dispute, the chief of police retired. Local politicians speculated that the chief retired because of the political fallout from the dispute.

Source: Mike Sunnucks, "Police Union Irked by Phoenix Chief's Opposition to Immigration Law," *Phoenix Business Journal,* July 12, 2010, www.bizjournals.com/phoenix/stories/2010/07/12/daily37.html; Michael Ferraresi and Lynh Bui, "Phoenix Police Union Loses Members over Dissension," *Arizona Republic,* January 7, 2011, www.azcentral.com/news/articles/2011/01/07/20110107phoenix-police-union-dispute.html; William Hermann and Lynh Bui, *Arizona Republic,* April 16, 2011, www.azcentral.com/community/phoenix/articles/2011/04/15/20110415phoenix-police-chief-harris-resigned-brk.html.

Police Organizations and Their Environment

Researchers have used three primary theories to understand police organizational structures and operational strategies: contingency theory, institutional theory, and resource dependency theory. Each of these models emphasizes the importance of understanding the environment in which the police operate and how that environment impacts police organizations.

Contingency Theory

contingency theory

Contingency theory has emerged as the dominant theoretical framework for understanding the structures and practices of police organizations. The underlying premise of contingency theory is the belief that organizations are created and structured to achieve specific goals, such as crime control. According to contingency theory, organizations are rational entities, adopting organizational structures and operational activities that are most effective and efficient in achieving specific goals. It is argued that organizations that fail to make the appropriate adjustments to the environmental contingencies they face will not prosper and, in some cases, will not survive.[55]

Solomon Zhao, a leading police organizational theorist, contends that contingency theory, therefore, makes two primary assumptions about police organizations. The first is that police organizations "must adapt themselves to the external environment when their existing goals are affected by changes in their operating conditions." The second is that police organizations must be dynamic so that they maintain "fit" between themselves and their environment over time. A good fit between a police organization and its environment results in higher performance. Zhao points out that these two underlying assumptions make contingency theory well suited for helping students of police organizations understand why law enforcement agencies change their organizational arrangements and operational strategies.[56]

Researchers and policymakers have often used contingency theory to understand police innovation. For example, Inglewood, California, faced a growing gang problem in the early 1970s. In response to the proliferation of gangs and gang-related problems, the police department established a police gang unit to enhance the success of departmental crime control efforts. Similarly, many researchers and policymakers have argued that community-oriented policing has been adopted because past attempts by the police to control crime have failed.[57]

Institutional Theory

institutional theory

Institutional theory holds that police organizations are social institutions that operate in relation to their external social and political environment. The central premise of institutional theory, as applied to the police, is a belief that the organization and activities of the police must be understood in the context of their institutional environment. Institutional environment, here, refers to powerful actors, called *sovereigns,* who have the capacity to influence the policies and decisions of police organizations.[58] Sovereigns in a given community might include the mayor, the city council, special interest groups, citizens, and other criminal justice agencies.

Within the institutional perspective, it is argued that the organization and activities performed by the police do not necessarily reflect rationality. That is, police departments do not create organizational structures or engage in operational activities simply because they are more efficient and/or more effective. Instead, police departments create organizational structures and engage in operational activities because they reflect the ideas and values that are shared by their institutional environment.[59] Therefore, institutional theory holds that for police departments to establish legitimacy, their organizational structures and operational activities must be performed in accordance with the ideas and beliefs held by various powerful actors within their environment.[60] Those police organizations that conform to the ideas and beliefs that are prescribed to them by their external environment are more likely to obtain "cultural support" and, henceforth, improve their chances for organizational survival.[61] Conversely, those organizations that do not conform to the ideas and beliefs that are held by their institutional environment are at risk of being perceived as useless or unimportant and may lose any legitimacy that their institutional environment previously granted them.[62]

Charles Katz examined the utility of institutional theory in his ethnographic study of the establishment of one police gang unit. Katz found that the institutional pressures placed on the police department had a significant impact on the creation of the gang unit. Observations and internal documents showed that the city had only a minor gang problem that did not substantiate the need for a specialized gang unit. However, the gang unit was created because of external pressures exerted on the chief of police by powerful local political, business, and community stakeholders; and once the unit was created, its strategic response was driven largely by its need to incorporate the ideas and beliefs of sovereigns in its environment. As such, Katz reported that attempting to measure and account for key elements of the environment in which police organizations operate can be important for understanding existing organizational arrangements and operational activities.[63]

Resource Dependency Theory

Resource dependency theory suggests that organizations must obtain resources to survive and that to obtain these resources they must engage in exchanges with other organizations in their environment. This, resource dependency theorists argue, requires organizations to alter their organizational structure and/or operational strategy so that it accommodates others in their environment who have the capacity to provide much-needed resources. As a consequence, the argument continues, those in an organization's environment who have the capacity to provide resources necessarily have indirect or direct power through resource exchanges. At the same time, proponents of resource dependency theory hold that organizations are not simply passive organisms at the mercy of others in their environment but that they also have the capacity to influence their environment to ensure the flow of resources.[64] Organizations actively scan their environment for opportunities that may provide access to valuable resources.[65] Adherents of resource dependency theory maintain that, although environmental factors influence the structure and activities of organizations, organizations also have the ability to influence the environment in which they operate to ensure the flow of resources.[66] Thus, at the core of resource dependency theory is the belief that organizational structures and practices are adopted to meet resource needs, rather than to increase the efficiency or effectiveness of the police organization.[67]

resource dependency theory

Only a few studies to date have used resource dependency theory to understand police organizations. Katz, Maguire, and Roncek, who examined 285 police agencies across the country, found that even when controlling for the amount of gang-related crime, departments that received external funding for gang-control functions were about 4.8 times more likely to have established a specialized gang unit than were agencies that had not received funding. They argued that gang units might have been created because of the plentiful resources that were available for crime control efforts aimed at gangs rather than because there was a real and growing gang problem.[68] Similarly, Maguire, Zhao, and Lovrich argue that one of the reasons so many police agencies have implemented community-oriented policing is to obtain their share of the $8.8 billion to be distributed by the Department of Justice to facilitate community policing.[69]

CASE STUDY

COMPSTAT in Chicago

After he was named Superintendent of Police in 2011, Garry McCarthy used COMPSTAT as a way to bring his message and strategy to the Chicago Police Department. "I'm doing a lot of coaching, actually," he said. "I can't see managing a large organization without COMPSTAT. It allows you to implement crime strategies and evaluate commanders. How could you maintain organizational change without a performance management vehicle like COMPSTAT?"

Chief Robert Tracy, who runs Chicago's COMPSTAT program and spent the first part of his career at NYPD, said he saw "a metamorphosis" take place within NYPD due to COMPSTAT. "We went from reactive to proactive, and now in Chicago we are trying to replicate the success of New York City while also modifying COMPSTAT to respond to Chicago's unique challenges," he said.

Chicago police leaders decided that for COMPSTAT to be successful in Chicago, they had to modify the organizational structure of the department. Chief Tracy said, "In the past, we had a lot of city-wide units. District commanders were dependent on those city-wide units to help them fight crime, but they couldn't control the city-wide units. It wouldn't be fair to hold district commanders accountable for crime under that type of model." To ensure district commanders could control the resources they needed to reduce crime, leaders moved many officers from city-wide units into patrol districts. With the department's new structure, Chief Tracy said district commanders have "the authority, resources, and accountability" necessary for success. In addition to giving district commanders more resources, Chief Tracy said it is important to create a culture where district commanders know "they don't need to ask permission to take action. They need to work within the constraints of department policies, but within those boundaries they should take the initiative to solve problems."

Another challenge for the department was making sure that the appropriate intelligence was available for the COMPSTAT process in a timely manner. "Our reports were taking too long, so we couldn't identify crime patterns fast enough," said Chief Tracy.

The COMPSTAT process has helped the department identify several problems. For instance, Chief Tracy said, "We found that the times when the most crime took place were also the times when we had the least police coverage. This is an obvious problem. The cops have to be working when the bad guys are working, so that was a quick fix. COMPSTAT is helping us become a whole new department. It ensures commanders have a plan to reduce crime, and they are accountable to their peers and the department's executives. It makes our talent shine and exposes those who might need more coaching or don't have their heart in it anymore." Finally, Chief Tracy emphasized that "it is not a sin for a district commander to experience a crime increase in their area. The sin is if they do not know about the crime increase, or do not have a plan to address it."

Source: Excerpt from Police Executive Research Forum, *COMPSTAT: Its Origins, Evolution, and Future in Law Enforcement Agencies* (Washington, DC: Author, 2013), 12.

SUMMARY

Police organizations are a critical element in policing. They are the instruments through which police services are organized and delivered to the public. Many police problems are associated with the problems of bureaucracy. Past attempts to restructure police departments, such as team policing, have not been successful. More recent attempts, such as community policing and COMPSTAT, represent efforts to revitalize police organizations by making them more open and responsive to the communities they serve and to changing social conditions.

KEY TERMS

quasi-military style, 103
bureaucracy, 105
August Vollmer, 106
Bruce Smith, 106
O. W. Wilson, 106
vertical cliques, 109
horizontal cliques, 109
police professionalism, 110

decentralize, 110
deformalize, 110
despecialize, 111
delayerize, 111
task forces, 112
COMPSTAT, 113
civil service, 115
rewards hierarchy, 115

seniority hierarchy, 115
status hierarchy, 115
rank hierarchy, 115
police union, 116
collective bargaining, 117
contingency theory, 122
institutional theory, 122
resource dependency theory, 123

FOR DISCUSSION

1. If you were a police chief, how would you organize your department? For example, would it have many specialized units? Would it have many or few rules?
2. How has police professionalism been enhanced in the past 20 years?
3. Explain the difference between a centralized organization and a decentralized one. What are the advantages and disadvantages of each?
4. Explain how police unions affect police departments today.
5. What are some of the advantages and disadvantages of specialization?

INTERNET EXERCISES

Exercise 1 Many police departments include their organizational charts on their websites. Find the organizational charts for several of each department size: very large (3,000 sworn officers), large (700-plus sworn officers), medium-sized (200 to 700 sworn officers), and small (less than 100 sworn officers). What are the obvious differences? How do they compare in terms of degree of specialization?

Exercise 2 Visit www.iupa.org to learn about the International Union of Police Associations. After reading about the union, discuss the benefits and limitations of police unions.

NOTES

1. Egon Bittner, *Aspects of Police Work* (Boston: Northeastern University Press, 1990), 136–147.
2. Ibid.
3. Ibid., 132–136.
4. James H. Tenzel, Lowell Storms, and Harvey Sweatwood, "Symbols and Behavior: An Experiment in Altering the Police Role," *Journal of Police Science and Administration* 4, no. 1 (1976): 21–28.
5. Peter Kraska and Louis Cubellis, "Militarizing Mayberry and Beyond: Making Sense of American Paramilitary Policing," *Justice Quarterly* 14, no. 4 (1997): 607–630.
6. Donald Campbell and Kathleen Campbell, "Police/Military Convergence in the USA as Organizational Mimicry," *Policing and Society* 26, no. 3 (2016): 332–353.
7. William R. King, "Bending Granite Revisited: The Command Rank Structure of American Police Organizations," *Policing* 26, no. 2 (2003): 208–230.
8. Charles Perrow, *Complex Organizations: A Critical Essay* (New York: Random House, 1986).
9. Samuel Walker, *A Critical History of Police Reform* (Lexington, MA: Lexington Books, 1977).
10. James Fyfe, Jack Greene, William Walsh, O. W. Wilson, and Roy C. McLaren, *Police Administration,* 5th ed. (New York; McGraw-Hill, 1997).
11. Charles M. Katz, Edward Maguire, and Dennis Roncek, "The Creation of Specialized Police Gang Units: A Macro-Level Analysis of Contingency, Social Threat, and Resource Dependency Explanations," *Policing* 25, no. 3 (2002): 472–506.
12. James Q. Wilson, *Bureaucracy* (New York: Basic Books, 1989).
13. Henry I. DeGeneste and John P. Sullivan, *Policing a Multicultural Community* (Washington, DC: PERF, 1997).
14. Perrow, *Complex Organizations*.
15. Walker, *A Critical History of Police Reform*.
16. Samuel Walker, "Legal Control of Police Behavior," in D. Weisburd and C. Uchida, eds., *Police Innovation and Control of the Police* (New York: Springer-Verlag, 1993), 32–55.
17. John Crank, *Understanding Police Culture,* 2nd ed. (Cincinnati: Anderson Publishing, 2004).
18. Guyot, Dorothy. (1991). Policing as though people matter. Philadephia: Temple University Press.
19. John P. Crank, "The Influence of Environmental and Organizational Factors on Police Style in Urban and Rural Environments," *Journal of Research in Crime & Delinquency* 27 (May 1990): 166–190.
20. William A. Westley, *Violence and the Police* (Cambridge, MA: MIT Press, 1970), 23.
21. Steven Brint, *In an Age of Experts: The Changing Role of Professionals in Politics and Public Life* (Princeton, NJ: Princeton University Press, 1994).
22. Jihong Zhao, *Why Police Organizations Change* (Washington, DC: Police Executive Research Forum, 1996).
23. Samuel Walker, *Taming the System* (New York: Oxford University Press, 1994).
24. Edward Maguire, "Structural Change in Large Municipal Police Organizations during the Community Policing Era," *Justice Quarterly* 14, no. 3 (1997): 547–676; Stephen Mastrofski and Richard Ritti, "Making Sense of Community Policing: A Theory-Based Analysis," presented at the annual meeting of the American Society of Criminology, Boston (1995).
25. Edward Maguire and Yeunhee Shin, "Structural Change in Large Police Agencies during the 1990s," *Policing* 26, no. 2 (2003): 251–275.
26. Jihong (Solomon) Zhao, *Evaluation on the Implementation of Total Quality Management in*

the Omaha Police Department: An Interim Report
(Omaha, NE: 1998).

27. Peter W. Phillips, "De Facto Police Consolidation: The Multi-Jurisdictional Task Force," *Police Forum* 9, no. 3 (1999): 1–5; G. Orvis, "The Evolution of the Crime Task Force and Its Use in the Twenty-First Century," presented at the annual meeting of the Academy of Criminal Justice Sciences, Orlando (1999).

28. Phillips, "De Facto Police Consolidation."

29. Phillips, "De Facto Police Consolidation."

30. David H. Bayley, *Police for the Future* (New York: Oxford University Press, 1994), 101.

31. U.S. Department of Justice, *Mapping Out Crime* (Washington, DC: National Partnership for Reinventing Government, 1999).

32. John Eck and Edward Maguire, "Have Changes in Policing Reduced Violent Crime? An Assessment of the Evidence," in Alfred Blumstein and Joel Wallman, eds., *The Crime Drop in America* (Cambridge, U.K.: Cambridge University Press, 2000), 207–265.

33. Police Executive Research Forum, *COMPSTAT: Its Origins, Evolution, and Future in Law Enforcement Agencies* (Washington, DC: Author, 2013).

34. Robert Davis and Pedro Mateu-Gelabert, *Respectful and Effective Policing: Two Examples in the South Bronx* (New York: Vera Institute of Justice, March 1999).

35. Hyunseok Jang, Larry Hoover, and Hee-Jong Joo, "An Evaluation of Compstat's Effect on Crime: The Fort Worth Experience," *Police Quarterly* 13, no. 4 (2010): 387–412.

36. Dean Dabney, "Observations Regarding Key Operational Realities in a COMPSTAT Model of Policing," *Justice Quarterly* 27, no. 1 (2010), 28–51.

37. Brenda J. Bond and Anthony A. Braga, "Rethinking the COMPSTAT Process to Enhance Problem-Solving Responses: Insights from a Randomized Field Experiment," *Police Practice and Research* 16, no. 1 (2015): 22–35.

38. George W. Griesinger, Jeffrey S. Slovak, and Joseph J. Molkup, *Civil Service Systems: Their Impact on Police Administration* (Washington, DC: U.S. Government Printing Office, 1979).

39. William R. King, "The Hierarchical Nature of Police Organizations: Conception and Measurement," unpublished paper (Bowling Green, OH: Bowling Green University, 2003).

40. Bureau of Justice Statistics, *Law Enforcement Management and Administrative Statistics, 1997*

(Washington, DC: U.S. Government Printing Office, 1999), xiv.

41. Bureau of the Census, *Statistical Abstract of the United States, 1997* (Washington, DC: U.S. Government Printing Office, 1997), 438–442.

42. John Burpo, Ron DeLord, and Michael Shannon, *Police Association Power, Politics, and Confrontation* (Springfield, Ill.: Charles C. Thomas Publisher, 1997); "About the Fraternal Order of Police," www.fop.net/CmsPage.aspx?id=223.

43. John Burpo, Ron DeLord, and Michael Shannon, *Police Association Power, Politics, and Confrontation* (Springfield, Ill.: Charles C. Thomas Publisher, 1997).

44. Ibid.

45. International Association of Chiefs of Police, *Guidelines and Papers from the National Symposium on Police Labor Relations* (Washington, DC: Author, 1974).

46. Michael T. Leibig and Robert B. Kliesmet, *Police Unions and the Law: A Handbook for Police Organizers* (Washington, DC: Institute for Police Research, 1988).

47. Jack Steiber, *Public Employee Unionism: Structure and Growth* (Washington, DC: The Brookings Institution, 1973), 159–192.

48. Margaret Levi, *Bureaucratic Insurgency* (Lexington, MA: Lexington Books, 1977), 91–130.

49. William J. Bopp, "The San Francisco Police Strike of 1975: A Case Study," *Journal of Police Science and Administration* 5, no. 1 (1977): 32–42.

50. Bureau of the Census, *Statistical Abstract of the United States, 1997*, 439.

51. William M. Doerner and William G. Doerner, "Collective Bargaining and Jobs Benefits: The Case of Florida Deputy Sheriffs," *Police Quarterly* 13, 4 (2010): 367–386.

52. Jihong Zhao and Nicolas Lovrich, "Collective Bargaining and the Police," *Policing* 20, 3 (1997): 508–518.

53. Samuel Walker, "The Neglect of Police Unions: Exploring One of the Most Important Areas of American Policing," *Police Practice and Research* 9 (2008): 95–112.

54. Colleen Kadleck, "Police Employee Organizations," *Policing* 26, no. 2 (2003): 341–350.

55. Lex Donaldson, *American Anti-Management Theories of Organization* (Cambridge, U.K.: Cambridge University Press, 1995); Katz, Maguire, and Roncek, "The Creation of Specialized Police

Gang Units"; Stephen Mastrofski, "Community Policing and Police Organizational Structure," in Jean-Paul Brodeur, ed., *How to Recognize Good Policing* (Thousand Oaks, CA: Sage, 1998), 161–189.

56. Jihong "Solomon" Zhao, Ni He, and Nicholas Lovrich, "Community Policing: Did It Change the Basic Functions of Policing in the 1990?" *Justice Quarterly* 20, no. 4 (2003): pp. 697–724.

57. Katz, Maguire, and Roncek, "The Creation of Specialized Police Gang Units."

58. John Crank and Robert Langworthy, "An Institutional Perspective of Policing," *The Journal of Criminal Law and Criminology* 83 (1992): 338–363; Paul Di Maggio and Walter Powell, "The Iron Cage Revisited: Institutional Isomorphism and Collective Rationality in Organizational Fields," in Walter Powell and Paul Di Maggio, eds., *The New Institutionalism in Organizational Analysis* (Chicago: University of Chicago Press, 1991); John Meyer and Brian Rowan, "Institutionalized Organizations: Formal Structure as Myth and Ceremony," *American Journal of Sociology* 83 (1977): 340–348.

59. Meyer and Rowan, "Institutionalized Organizations."

60. Ibid.; Crank and Langworthy, "An Institutional Perspective of Policing"; John Crank, "Watchman and Community: Myth and Institutionalization in Policing," *Law and Society Review* 28, no. 2 (1994): 325–352.

61. Meyer and Rowan, "Institutionalized Organizations."

62. John Crank and Robert Langworthy, "An Institutional Perspective of Policing," *The Journal of Criminal Law and Criminology* 83 (1992): pp. 338–363.

63. Charles Katz, "The Establishment of a Police Gang Unit: An Examination of Organizational and Environmental Factors," *Criminology* 39 (2001): 37–75.

64. Donaldson, *American Anti-Management Theories of Organization.*

65. Ibid.; Katz, Maguire, and Roncek, "The Creation of Specialized Police Gang Units."

66. William Scott, "Introduction," in J. M. Meyer and W. R. Scott, eds., *Organizational Environments* (London: Sage Publications, 1992).

67. Donaldson, *American Anti-Management Theories of Organization;* R. H. Hall, *Organizations: Structures, Processes, and Outcome* (Upper Saddle River, NJ: Prentice Hall, 1999); P. S. Tolbert and L. G. Zucker, "The Institutionalization of Institutional Theory," in S. R. Clegg, C. Hardy, and W. R. Nord, eds., *The Handbook of Organizational Studies* (Thousand Oaks, CA: Sage, 1997).

68. Katz, Maguire, and Roncek, "The Creation of Specialized Gang Units."

69. Ed Maguire, Jihong Zhao, and Nicholas Lovrich, "Dimensions of Community Policing," unpublished manuscript (Omaha, Nebraska).

© James Poulson/Daily Sitka Sentinel/AP Images

5 Police Officers I: Recruitment and Training for a Changing Society

CHAPTER OUTLINE

The Changing American Police Officer

What Kind of Police Officers Do We Want? And for What Kind of Policing?

The Police Personnel Process

A Career Perspective

Beyond Stereotypes of Cops

The Personnel Process: A Shared Responsibility

Recruiting Police Officers

What Kind of Job? What Kind of Person?

Minimum Qualifications

The Recruitment Effort

Choosing Law Enforcement as a Career

Applicants' Motivations

Obstacles to Recruitment

Testing and Selecting Applicants

Selection Tests

Background Investigations

Predicting Police Officer Performance

Achieving Diversity in Police Employment

The Goals of Diversity

The Law of Equal Employment Opportunity

"Not Your Father's Police
  Department": Diversity in
  Policing
Women in Policing
Employment Discrimination Suits
The Impact of Increased Diversity
**Police Training: Progress and New
  Challenges**
New Thinking about Policing and
  Training
The Police Academy
Training on the Use of Force

Tactical Decision-Making
Scenario-Based Training
Fragmented and Inconsistent
  Training
The Consequences of Inadequate
  Training
Training on Unconscious Bias
Training on Procedural Justice
Field Training
In-Service Training
Training of Supervisors
The Probationary Period

CASE STUDY

Summary
Key Terms
For Discussion
Internet Exercises

The Changing American Police Officer

What Kind of Police Officers Do We Want?
And for What Kind of Policing?

What kind of police officers do we want? And for what kind of policing? Who should we recruit for police jobs? And how should we train them?

The answers to these questions will have a major impact on the quality of police services that Americans receive. By 2014–2016, there was considerable ferment among leaders of the police profession over these questions, and about police training in particular. Many traditional assumptions and practices about police training were being questioned. The President's Task Force on 21st Century Policing (see Chapter 1) endorsed new ideas about police training designed to increase public trust and confidence in local police departments.[1]

In a highly influential article, Sue Rahr and Stephen K. Rice defined the new thinking about policing in terms of **warriors versus guardians.**[2] The warrior mentality, which they argue dominates much policing and police training, embodies a military-style approach to policing, in which officers define their relationship between themselves and the community as "us versus them." This approach sees hostility and danger everywhere in routine policing, with the result that the police are "detached and separated from the community." The warrior culture is instilled in police academy training, which operates like a military "boot camp." Training officers yell at recruits, are often verbally abusive, and train officers to follow orders and not question higher authority.

Rahr and Rice argue that the boot camp culture of police academies "has little to do with the daily reality of policing." Day-to-day police work, as we will learn in Chapters 7, 8, 9, and others, involves working with people, in difficult, often uncertain, and challenging situations. There is usually no supervisor present to tell the officer what to do. Officers have to assess each situation, including its potential for danger, and choose the best way to resolve the situation. Although danger is often possible, traditional police training has placed too much emphasis on "physical control tactics and weapons" and too little on "communication and de-escalation skills." A 2015 report by the Police Executive Research Forum (PERF) confirmed this point

warriors versus guardians

POLICE *in* FOCUS | "Making Good Cops in the Twenty-First Century"

In a review of police recruitment and training, Michael D. White and Gipsy Escobar identified seven concerns that need to be addressed for "Making Good Cops in the Twenty-First Century":

1. The need for police departments to become more proactive in recruitment in order to overcome personnel shortages and to achieve diverse and representative officer work forces.
2. The need to recruit officers with higher education in order to address the complexities of the police role, the increasing use of computers and data-driven strategies, and increasingly sophisticated police strategies to deal with crime and disorder.
3. The need to develop training programs that are scenario-based and realistic about police work (what others call reality-based training, or RBT). Traditional lecture-based training programs are no longer adequate for today's world.

4. The need to develop training programs that prepare officers for problem-solving strategies that are a part of community policing and problem-oriented policing.
5. The need to prepare police recruits to work in an increasingly diverse society in terms of race, ethnicity, and culture.
6. The need to recruit and train officers who can deal with the technological revolution in policing, which includes data-driven strategies to address crime and disorder, such as COMPSTAT, and accountability systems such as early intervention systems.
7. The need to incorporate homeland security programs and strategies into training programs.

Source: Adapted from Michael D. White and Gipsy Escobar, "Making Good Cops in the Twenty-First Century: Emerging Issues for the Effective Recruitment, Selection, and Training of Police in the United States and Abroad," *International Review of Law, Computers & Technology* 22 (March–July 2008): 119–134.

with a survey finding that police academies devote an average of 58 hours to firearms training but only 10 hours to communication skills (see Exhibit 5–7, later in this chapter).[3]

The guardian mentality, Rahr and Rice continue, involves the police developing and maintaining close relations with the communities they serve. Officers need to be trained and become experienced in finding peaceful ways to resolve difficult encounters with people. This can be done by instructing recruits that peaceful resolution is their primary goal and that use of force is the last resort (except when force is immediately necessary). Officers need to be trained in the tactics of de-escalation. Officers also need to be trained to use their judgment in assessing situations, to consider all the possible alternatives, and to choose the best option. Recruits who have been yelled at and trained only to follow orders will not become the best police officers in today's complex society. Officers trained to think and use good judgment in difficult situations, and to use force only when absolutely necessary, will be more likely to gain voluntary cooperation from members of the community.

The Police Personnel Process

As we learned in Chapter 2, before about 100 years ago, there were no formal requirements for becoming a police officer, except for having the right political connections, and recruits received no training before they stepped out on the streets to begin policing. Today, it is impossible to imagine a police officer with no formal education, a history of heavy drinking or a record of arrests, no training on the law of arrest and search and seizure, or no instruction on when to use force. Police recruitment and training procedures improved dramatically from what existed 100 years ago. But in today's highly complex world, many more improvements are needed.

In this chapter, we take a comprehensive look at police recruitment and training. It is not a simple matter of just hiring some people and then sending them to the police academy. The personnel process involves several stages, each of which is highly complex.

A Career Perspective

Working for a law enforcement agency is more than a job; it is both a profession and a career. It begins with recruitment and continues through to retirement. For some officers, it continues after retirement, as many retired officers have second careers in other police departments or in jobs in which they use their police experience.

A **career perspective** promotes understanding of how police officers interact with law enforcement organizations. Far too much attention is given to the recruitment stage—the entry requirements, the testing and hiring, and so on. Maintaining high-quality police services requires departments to hire *and retain* the best officers. It is necessary to pay close attention to all the stages of officer careers. A police department can do a good job at one stage of the personnel process, but then undermine that effort by failing at one or more other stages. For example, a department can make the following mistakes:

career perspective

- Hire good recruits, but not train them properly
- Train their officers well, but not supervise them adequately
- Fail to have a good personnel evaluation system that recognizes good performance
- Fail to discipline officers whose performance is unprofessional
- Fail to provide career opportunities that promote good morale and help retain good officers
- Fail to promote the best officers

Beyond Stereotypes of Cops

How many times have you heard someone say something like, "All cops are _____"? How many jokes have you heard about police officers spending all their time at donut shops? How often have you heard someone say that people become cops because they like to use force? Or, how many times have you heard someone say that police officers have difficult and dangerous jobs and therefore should not be criticized if they sometimes use too much force?

Statements and jokes of this sort reflect stereotypes about police officers. **Stereotypes about cops** heavily influence the public image of who police are, what they believe, and how they act. These stereotypes fall into two categories. On one

stereotypes about cops

For more discussion of the relationship of police officer attitudes to behavior, see Chapter 6.

For more discussion of the realities of police work, see Chapter 1.

civil service system

side, a negative stereotype views officers as poorly educated, untrained, prejudiced, brutal, and corrupt. On the other side, a positive stereotype views them as heroic saints, risking their lives in the face of hostility from the public, the media, and the courts. Arthur Niederhoffer characterizes the police officer as "a 'Rorschach' in uniform. . . . To people in trouble the police officer is a savior," but to others the officer is "a fierce ogre."[4] Neither stereotype is accurate.

Inaccurate stereotypes about policing affect the recruitment of new officers. The National Center for Women and Policing argues that stereotypes emphasizing officer use of force and the need for physical size and strength discourage women from considering careers in policing.[5] In reality, most police work is uneventful, and police–citizen encounters primarily require communication skills. Finally, inaccurate stereotypes affect police officers' self-image and how they do police work. As Rahr and Rice argue, the warrior self-image of the police contributes to increased conflict with the community rather than better cooperation.

The Personnel Process: A Shared Responsibility

Police chiefs do not completely control the recruitment and selection of new officers. Personnel decisions in policing are a shared responsibility. Police departments control some of the decisions, but other government agencies, such as the **civil service system** and/or the city personnel department, control the others. A police chief, for example, cannot unilaterally change personnel standards or procedures by raising the minimum educational requirement or simply promoting an officer he or she likes. These procedures are governed by the civil service and/or city personnel department, and a number of issues are influenced by the collective bargaining agreement with the police officers' union.

Civil service developed as a great reform, to eliminate the politics that dominated policing in the nineteenth century. In Chapter 2, we learned about the episode following the 1886 elections in Cincinnati, in which the new mayor fired 238 of the 289 patrol officers.[6] Formal recruitment and other personnel standards are designed to make personnel decisions as objective as possible, without political interference.

Typically, the civil service agency has the responsibility for developing job descriptions; establishing the minimum standards required for each position; developing tests for each position; announcing job openings; conducting some, but not all, of the tests; and certifying a list of persons eligible to be hired or promoted. Police departments, meanwhile, generally advise the civil service agency on job descriptions, requirements, and tests; conduct much of the actual recruitment of applicants; and administer some of the recruitment tests.[7] Exhibit 5–1 outlines the application process for the Los Angeles Police Department (LAPD) in 2016.

Recruiting Police Officers

To hire good officers, a department must first attract a pool of good applicants. The recruitment process includes four separate elements: (a) establishing the minimum qualifications for the job; (b) the recruitment effort; (c) the applicant's decision to apply for a position; and (d) the screening of applicants and selection of new recruits.

EXHIBIT 5-1

Seven Steps in the Application Process for the Los Angeles Police Department (LAPD)

Step 1:   *Preliminary Background Application (PBA) and Job Preview Questionnaire*
Completed online by applicants, who bring the results to the application test site.

Step 2:   *Personal Qualifications Essay (PQA)*
An "essay with questions related to judgment, decision making and behavioral flexibility."

Step 3:   *Background Investigation and Polygraph Examination*
Includes a Personal History Statement, followed by an interview, and then a background investigation.

Step 4:   *Physical Abilities Test (PA)*
The first part measures "strength, agility, and endurance." The second measures "aerobic capacity."

Step 5:   *Department Interview*
An interview before a panel to assess "job motivation, instrumentality, interpersonal skills, continuous learning capacity, and oral communication skills."

Step 6:   *Medical Evaluation and Psychological Evaluation*
Physical examination, written psychological test, and interview with psychologist.

Step 7:   *Certification and Appointment*

The first two elements are discussed in this section, and the other two elements are discussed in later sections of this chapter.

What Kind of Job? What Kind of Person?

We have already discussed the new thinking in police training that emphasizes officers using critical thinking in difficult situations. In the LAPD, according to a 2016 report, there is a new effort "to enhance officers' critical thinking skills." The basic goal is to place "greater responsibility onto officers in determining what tactics they should use in a given operational scenario." This includes having officers "constantly assess based on the fluidity of the situation," and to use "critical thinking" about the appropriate response.[8]

On its website, the San Diego Police Department lists its "Job Dimensions for Police Officers" (Exhibit 5–2). The top categories are integrity, interest in people, interpersonal sensitivity, communication skills, and problem-solving ability. These are not the qualities associated with the old stereotypes about policing, with its military-style culture and the belief that officers needed to be big and strong (and male) so that they would have a commanding presence in dealing with people.

Minimum Qualifications

Age

Is an 18-year-old mature enough to be a police officer? Does an 18-year-old have sufficient work experience and emotional maturity to be able to handle the stress and complex demands of police work? Virtually all experts believe not, and most law enforcement agencies today require all applicants to be at least 21 years old.

EXHIBIT 5–2

San Diego Police Department: Job Dimensions for Police Officers, 2016

Integrity	Observational skills
Interest in people	Learning ability
Interpersonal sensitivity	Appearance
Communication skills	Dependability
Problem-solving ability	Physical ability
Judgment under pressure	Desire for self-improvement
Willingness to confront problems	Operation of a motor vehicle
Credibility as a witness	

Source: City of San Diego, "Police: Join Us," https://www.sandiego.gov/police/recruiting.

Height and Weight

height requirement

Can you be too short to be a police officer? Forty years ago, nearly all police departments required officers to be at least 5 feet 8 inches tall.[9] The **height requirement** reflected the old stereotype that officers needed to be physically imposing in order to gain compliance from citizens. As we discuss in later chapters, however, physical confrontations are fairly rare. Officers use force in only about 1 to 2 percent of all encounters with citizens. Citizens generally comply with officers' requests that they stop doing something or leave the premises, and communication skills and good judgment are considered more important for police work than physical strength.[10]

The old height requirements were challenged in lawsuits arguing that they discriminated against women, Hispanic Americans, and Asian Americans. Only a handful of big-city departments still had minimum height requirements by 1994.[11] Departments today require that *weight be proportional to height*. But as everyone can see, many police officers are overweight. In some cases, they are seriously overweight relative to their height. Why are they still on the force? Traditionally, law enforcement agencies have not enforced fitness standards throughout officers' careers.

Education

Virtually every police department today requires only a high school diploma for new police officers. This fact is misleading, however, because most departments hire people with some college education. In 2013, only 1 percent of all local police departments required a four-year college degree, and 14 percent required at least some college. Those data, however, include the thousands of very small departments (with five or fewer officers) across the country. The picture for big-city departments is quite different. In cities with populations between 250,000 and 999,999 residents, 30 percent require some college (and between 4 and 7 percent of the total require a four-year college degree). College requirements have been rising, with the most dramatic change being the increase from about 5 to 23 percent of all departments requiring a two-year college degree.[12]

Minimum entry requirements, as we mentioned, do not reflect who is actually hired. Departments typically hire applicants with more than the required minimum level of education. The average recruit in the San Diego Police Department in the late 1980s had two years of college, even though there was no formal college education requirement. By 2016, 71 percent of all new recruits had a four-year college degree. The department also has a typing skill requirement of at least 30 words per minute.[13] Keyboard skills are important in today's police departments. Policing today is a sophisticated enterprise involving computers; cell phones; and large databases for programs such as COMPSTAT (see Chapter 4), hot-spots policing (Chapter 7), early intervention systems (Chapter 14), and others.

SIDEBAR 5–1

Issue for Debate: Should Police Departments Require a College Degree?

For many years, some experts have argued that all police recruits should be required to have a four-year college degree. The argument is based on several assumptions. First, it is assumed that higher education will shape the values of students and make them better able to understand the complex role of the police in a diverse and democratic society. The more educated officer will be better able to understand and comply with complex rules of criminal procedure and department policies on use of force and other critical matters. Second, it is assumed that higher levels of education will result in better on-the-street performance by giving officers the capacity to make better judgments in dealing with people of races and ethnicity different than their own, with people having mental health crises, and with people in domestic violence incidents. Third, the achievement of a college degree indicates a person's character, including a desire for self-improvement and a capacity for hard work and task completion. Fourth, today's police departments are part of the digital world, in which mastery of computers and cell phones, and the capacity to use large databases, are important parts of police work.[14]

Finally, it is important for the police to keep pace with the rising levels of education in American society. In 1960, 41 percent of Americans had a high school diploma. By 2015, that proportion had risen to 88.4 percent (although significant variations by race and ethnicity exist). The proportion of the population with a four-year degree had risen from 7.7 percent in 1960 to 32.5 percent in 2015.[15]

All of the issues discussed above have merit, but there are also other considerations. The main argument against requiring a college degree for all police recruits is that it would limit the pool of applicants and, in particular, have a disparate impact on African Americans and Hispanics who have historically been the victims of inferior schooling. In 2015, for example, only 22.5 percent of African Americans and 15 percent of Hispanics had college degrees, compared with 36.2 percent of non-Hispanic whites.[16]

In 1985, however, federal courts upheld a requirement by the Dallas Police Department that recruits have at least 45 hours of college education with a minimum grade point average of 2.0. A 1991 PERF discussion paper concluded that "there appears to be an adequate pool of both minority and majority college-educated men and women interested in police employment" to justify a college requirement.[17]

The direct impact of education on police officer performance, however, is not known. The National Academy of Sciences report on policing concluded that the evidence "does not permit conclusions regarding the impact of education on officer decision making." Studies have typically used the number of hours of college credit officers have earned, without taking into account "the content of the education."[18] Having a four-year degree by itself says nothing about the courses taken, their quality, or their possible impact on police work. In the United States today, what would be more relevant to police work: a course on police report writing, or a course on Hispanic American culture and history? Interestingly, Michael D. White's study found that an officer's reading level (regardless of major or courses taken) was the most powerful predictor of performance.[19]

Criminal Record

criminal record

Should someone with an arrest record be eligible to work as a police officer? Some experts argue that a **criminal record** of any sort should automatically disqualify an applicant on the grounds that it indicates a lack of ethical standards.[20] Others argue in favor of a flexible standard that takes into account the nature of the offense (felony or misdemeanor, adult or juvenile), the number of arrests versus convictions, and how recently the last offense was committed.[21] The Dallas Police Department in 2016, for example, disqualifies any applicant who has been "convicted, plead guilty or nolo contendere, placed on probation or deferred application for any felony," or for a Class A misdemeanor, or for a Class B misdemeanor offense "within the last 10 years or since the [person's] 17 birthday," or who has been convicted of a family violence offense, public lewdness, indecent exposure, or prostitution.[22]

Drug offenses pose the most difficult questions. An officer with a drug trafficking charge is more likely to become corrupt, but drug use is extremely prevalent in today's society. The National Survey on Drug Use and Health found that, in 2014, 44.2 percent of all Americans ages 12 years and older had used marijuana (and/or hashish) in their lifetime. Among those ages 18 to 25, who are the people most likely to seek or soon seek police jobs, 52.6 percent had used marijuana in their lifetime, and 31.9 percent had in the past year.[23] Automatically excluding all of these people from consideration would severely limit the applicant pool for police jobs. The 2013 ACLU report on marijuana arrests, meanwhile, found that African American males are almost four times more likely to be arrested for possession than whites. The arrests create a record that disqualifies people from being hired by many police departments.[24]

The dominant approach nationwide with regard to a criminal record is a flexible one. An applicant with a felony record is barred by virtually all police departments. Misdemeanor records are assessed by the circumstances. How recent was the last arrest or conviction? Are there any arrests or convictions for violent offences, which most departments regard as a disqualifier? Are there multiple arrests and/or convictions? Is there any evidence of a lawful and positive lifestyle since the last conviction?

Residency Requirements

residency requirements

Should police officers be required to live in the city they police? Does being a resident make officers more committed to the quality of life in that that city than officers who live outside the city? **Residency requirements** are intended to heighten officers' familiarity with the community and their commitment to its well-being. The American Civil Liberties Union (ACLU) of Southern California argues that it does make a difference. They reported that 83 percent of all Los Angeles police officers lived outside the city of Los Angeles. The ACLU argued that police officers must be "a true part of the community they patrol" and not appear to be "an outside hired force."[25] The President's Task Force on 21st Century Policing endorsed residency requirements.[26]

Opponents of residency requirements argue that it infringes on the freedom of officers to choose where they live. Others argue that residency does not affect a person's behavior as a police officer.

In 2014, about 15 of the largest police departments had strict residency requirements (but as the largest departments, they represent a disproportionate number of all police officers in the country). They included Boston, Philadelphia, Kansas

For coverage of alternative strategies for getting officers to be more involved in the communities they police, see Chapter 10.

City, and New Orleans.[27] There is no empirical evidence, however, to support residency requirements. There is no research on how an officer's place of residence affects his or her performance as an officer.

The Recruitment Effort

The best possible candidates for a career in policing do not automatically walk in the door to apply. The size and quality of the applicant pool depend on a department's recruitment effort. An active effort will produce a larger pool, yielding more candidates who are likely to be highly qualified. If a department wants to increase the representation of college-educated, African American, Hispanic, Asian, or female officers, it needs to direct recruitment efforts toward those groups. To recruit more Hispanic or African American applicants, for example, the department needs to meet with groups and leaders in those communities. College campuses are an obvious place to recruit people with at least some college education.

Historically, police departments did not actively recruit. This practice gave people with political or family ties to the police department an advantage, because they were most likely to hear about hiring opportunities. Open recruitment efforts, including public advertising of opportunities, are required by law today. A 2010 RAND report on recruitment, selection, and retaining standards found that 80 percent of all departments had a special recruitment strategy for people of color; slightly less (74 percent) had a special strategy for recruiting women, and about 66 percent actively sought veterans and college graduates. About 50 percent had a special program for recruiting people with prior police experience and foreign language speakers.[28]

Choosing Law Enforcement as a Career

Applicants' Motivations

A police department cannot hire someone who does not apply and does not want to become a police officer. The recruitment effort depends greatly on individuals' career plans. Why do people want to become police officers? Some erroneous stereotypes surround this question. Many people believe that a lot of recruits want to become cops because they want to exercise authority over people, including using force. Research on the motivations of police recruits, however, does not support this view.

Surveys of recruits and new police officers consistently find that they choose law enforcement for two main reasons: the nature of police work and the material benefits of the job. In a survey of male and female officers in two midwestern police departments, respondents listed the top five reasons for choosing policing as a career in the following rank order: "help people," "job security," "fight crime," "excitement of the job," and "prestige of the job." There were no significant differences between male and female officers. Contrary to the negative stereotypes about police, recruits appear to be relatively idealistic, perhaps even slightly more so than the average person, in seeking to help people and the community. Significantly, both male and female officers ranked "authority/power" ninth out of a total of 11 items. In short, applicants are not motivated primarily by a desire to enforce the law or to use force against other people.[29]

Research has consistently found that people of color are motivated by the same factors as white applicants: a combination of the nature of the work and the material benefits of the job. In a study of African American officers in New York City, Nicholas Alex concludes that "the motives of the white policeman for choosing police work seem little different from those of the black policeman."[30]

The state of the economy affects people's decisions to seek law enforcement careers. When the economy is good, and jobs are plentiful, people with good qualifications have more options. When the economy is weak, law enforcement jobs are more attractive, particularly because of the **job security** they offer. In the recession that struck in 2008, for example, police officer jobs were very attractive.

job security

Fringe benefits and job security are a major attractions for police recruits. Police unions have succeeded in negotiating fringe benefits—sick leave, vacation days, health care, and pensions, for example—that are generally among the best in the American economy. Union contracts (and in some cases local or state civil service laws) also provide elaborate due process provisions regarding the investigation of alleged misconduct, including the fatal shooting of people. As a consequence, it is difficult to fire officers for misconduct. Some critics argue that certain police union contract provisions, such as 48-hour waiting periods before an officer can be questioned about misconduct are excessive, are not found in other employment situations, and impede accountability.[31] After the probationary period, officers can be fired only for a specific cause, and any officer who is terminated has the right to appeal. Job security is a particularly appealing factor for individuals whose family experience included periodic unemployment.

Family connection has traditionally been a factor in choosing law enforcement as a career. Some applicants have a parent, a brother or sister, or some other relative who is a police officer. In the 1960s, for example, more than half of all sergeants in the Chicago Police Department had a relative on the force. Because of past discrimination, African Americans, Hispanics, and women are less likely to have a family member to provide a role model or encouragement for choosing law enforcement as a career.[32]

Some applicants who apply and are accepted do not have clearly defined life goals when they apply, however. They "drift" into police work, often after trying several other jobs.[33] Among those with clear goals, meanwhile, career expectations are often not fulfilled. Persons expecting an exciting job discover that patrol work is often very boring. Others, expecting good opportunities for advancement, are disappointed by the limited opportunities in police organizations.

Obstacles to Recruitment

With respect to African Americans, Hispanics, and women, informal barriers inhibit their interest in becoming police officers. The long history of police–community relations problems, reinforced by current controversies over police shootings and use of excessive force, has created a distrust of the police among young African Americans. Police reform expert David Kennedy, in his book *Don't Shoot,* vividly describes that deep racial gulf in which both young African American men and police officers each bring their "narratives" of distrust to encounters on the street.[34] Robert Kaminski, for example, found that African Americans were significantly less likely to accept a job with the Albany, New York, police department if it were offered to them.[35] The racial disparities in the war on drugs, meanwhile, has resulted in many young African American men with marijuana arrest records that exclude them as possible police recruits.[36]

Many women do not apply because they see policing as a traditionally male occupation. The traditional warrior culture of policing has a heavily masculine tone, emphasizing aggressiveness, psychological toughness, and physical strength.[37] The need for great physical strength, however, is a myth. For instance, it is low on the San Diego Police Department's list of job dimensions (see Exhibit 5–2). And see the discussion of "myths" about women and policing by the Charlotte-Mecklenburg, North Carolina, police department in the "Police in Focus" feature on p. 147.

Testing and Selecting Applicants

Selection Tests

Once a police department has a pool of applicants, a series of tests is used to select a group of new recruits. These tests include written and medical exams, a background check, and interviews of finalists. About 26 percent of departments use a polygraph or lie detector.[38] Exhibit 5–1 outlined the steps in the application and selection process for the LAPD. Notable are the stages in the process that examine an applicant's "judgment, decision making and behavioral flexibility," along with "job motivation, instrumentality, interpersonal skills, continuous learning capacity, and oral communication skills." These qualities are consistent with the new emphasis on critical thinking and tactical decision-making in handling the difficult situations police officers encounter.

Long delays between the time a person files an application for a police job and the decision about who is accepted is a major problem. In some cases, delays last many months, leading some applicants to drop out because they either find other jobs or lose interest. Many of the best applicants are likely the ones who have other job opportunities. A study in New York City found that delay accounted for a significant degree of attrition among minority applicants. Nearly 60 percent of the African American applicants who passed the initial written and physical examinations dropped out before the background investigation phase, compared with an overall dropout rate of 18 percent.[39]

Almost all police departments use **oral interviews** of applicant finalists. Interviews typically last about 45 minutes and involve two or three interviewers. Interviews can detect attitudes that might be incompatible with good police work (for example, arrogance, inability to listen, extreme passivity, racial bias). Interviews explore positive qualities such as common sense, verbal communication skills, motivation, appearance, quick thinking, compassion, sexism, and patience. Exhibit 5–1 summarized the personal skills that the LAPD looks for in its oral interviews. Interviews are time consuming and expensive, however, and they open the door to possible bias on the part of the interviewers. To ensure consistency and eliminate potential bias, most departments use a standardized interview format, have a structured marking sheet, and train their interviewers.[40]

oral interviews

Can a 45-minute interview really determine who will be a good police officer? Can an interview determine how a person will perform as a police officer? William G. Doerner correlated oral interview scores in the Florida State Law Enforcement Training Academy with subsequent performance records. He found a "persistent inability of this selection technique to isolate suitable candidates" for law enforcement.[41] Policing is a complex and difficult profession, and as yet we still do not have testing and screening techniques that are reasonably certain to select the best possible police officers.

Background Investigations

The **background investigation** of applicants is perhaps the most important part of the selection process. A thorough investigation can identify factors related to future job performance as a police officer: for example, a good work record in previous jobs, the ability to get along with people, and the absence of disciplinary problems in school or jobs. It can also identify a criminal record, prior involvement with drugs, or behavior problems in school or on jobs.

Applicants to the San Diego Police Department must complete a 342-question Pre-Investigation Questionnaire, covering education and employment history as well as any history of acts of racism, sexual harassment, or viewing of restricted information on the Internet. Recruits also must complete a Personal History Statement. Background investigations in San Diego also include researching the applicant's "publicly available social media accounts." The background investigation in San Diego is not just a process of "ruling out applicants" but also of looking for "competitive" candidates, "by applying a 'whole person' view" that takes into account intangible qualities of the ability to get along with people, particularly people from different cultures, and an evident capacity to learn and grow.[42]

Poorly conducted background investigations open the door to subjective judgments and bias. In 1972, Anthony Bouza, deputy chief inspector of the New York City Police Department (NYPD), argued that character investigations traditionally reflected the "biases of the investigating sergeant." This was especially true for African American and Hispanic applicants being interviewed and assessed by white sergeants. The NYPD adopted standardized procedures in an effort to eliminate bias.[43]

Failure to conduct good background investigations can result in serious problems later on. For example, in the early 1990s, the Washington, D.C., police department, under pressure from Congress to quickly hire an additional 2,000 officers, abandoned its standard background investigations. As a result, a large number of applicants submitted false references and work histories that were never checked. Some applicants even had serious criminal histories. Consequently, a number of those hired became corrupt officers involved in drug activity. The department paid a terrible price in terms of negative publicity, loss of public respect, damage to department morale, and dollar costs related to firing those officers and hiring new ones.[44] More recently, an investigation of the Los Angeles Sheriff's Department found that the department had hired "dozens" of officers for whom the background investigations had found "serious misconduct on or off duty." Twenty-nine had previously been fired or pressured to resign from other law enforcement agencies because of alleged misconduct. About 100 people hired had given evidence of dishonesty.[45]

Predicting Police Officer Performance

Can we predict who will become a good police officer? Are there any specific factors that help to predict which applicants are likely to be the best possible officers and which ones should not be hired at all?

Some studies have attempted to correlate background characteristics with subsequent performance records. Bernard Cohen and Jan Chaiken studied 1,608 New York City police officers hired in 1957. They examined 33 background characteristics, including race, age, IQ, father's occupation, previous occupational history (last job, number of jobs, and so on), military record, marital status, education, and criminal record. The only factor that correlated with good on-the-job performance (as indicated by performance records), however, was the recruit training score. The study concluded that it is not possible to predict which individuals will become good officers on the basis of background characteristics.[46]

In a review of selection procedures commonly used by police departments, J. Douglas Grant and Joan Grant conclude that "efforts to improve the quality of police officer performance by screening out those recruits who will not make good police officers have generally been unsuccessful." They argue that existing pre-employment psychological tests, such as the widely used Minnesota Multiphasic Personality Inventory (MMPI), do not successfully predict future behavior as a police officer.[47] And as discussed earlier, there is no conclusive evidence that an applicant's level of educational attainment predicts performance as a police officer.

A study of Tallahassee, Florida, police recruits found that neither pre-employment psychological test scores (the MMPI and the California Psychological Inventory were used) nor a clinical assessment by a psychologist correlated with recruits' performance ratings during field training.[48] The 1991 Christopher Commission, reviewing psychological evaluations given to LAPD applicants, concluded that "this initial screening can identify obvious social misfits in the grossest sense, but cannot test for more subtle abnormalities which may make an individual ill-suited to be a police officer, such as poor impulse control and the proclivity toward violence."[49]

Achieving Diversity in Police Employment

The Goals of Diversity

Almost without exception, all police experts argue that police departments should reflect the communities they serve, and engage in active efforts to ensure diversity among their officers with respect to race, ethnicity, and gender. The recommendation was made by the Kerner Commission in 1968 and reiterated 47 years later by the President's Task Force on 21st Century Policing. In between, the Commission on Accreditation for Law Enforcement Agencies (CALEA) adopted Standard 31.2.1, stating that departments should have "a ratio of minority group employees in approximate proportion to the makeup of the agency's law enforcement service community."[50]

Diversity in the employment of police officers has several goals. First, police departments, and all employers, are obligated to comply with federal and state laws of equal employment opportunity. Second, many people believe that officers from different backgrounds will be better able to relate to segments of the community. (We examine the evidence on this issue in Chapter 6.) Third, many experts argue that departments that reflect the communities they serve enjoy a better public image and improved police–community relations. Fourth, many people argue that employing officers of diverse backgrounds will bring different perspectives to the department and have a positive impact on the police officer subculture (we discuss the police subculture in Chapter 6).

The Law of Equal Employment Opportunity

Title VII of the 1964 Civil Rights Act

The underrepresentation of African Americans, Hispanics, and women in policing was a historic problem in American policing, and it continues to be an issue today. **Title VII of the 1964 Civil Rights Act** makes it unlawful for an employer "to fail or refuse to hire or to discharge any individual, or otherwise to discriminate against any individual . . . because of such individual's race, color, religion, sex, or national origin" (see Exhibit 5–3). The 1972 Equal Employment Opportunity Act extended the coverage of the 1964 law to state and local governments, which include police and sheriff's departments. State and local civil rights laws also prohibit employment discrimination. Virtually all cover discrimination on the basis of race, religion, age, and national origin, and some state laws have prohibited discrimination on the basis of sexual orientation.

The 1990 Americans with Disabilities Act, meanwhile, prohibits discrimination against disabled persons. This raises special issues in terms of law enforcement jobs. Is a handicapped person qualified for a job as a police officer? It is easy to answer this question about a paraplegic person who cannot walk a patrol beat, chase a suspect, or subdue a person who is physically resisting arrest. But what about a person who suffers only from some limited use of one hand? What about the person with a moderate speech impediment?[51]

bona fide occupational qualifications (BFOQs)

These questions have been resolved in terms of the **bona fide occupational qualifications (BFOQs)** standard. A BFOQ is any requirement that is "reasonably necessary to the normal operation of that particular business."[52] A few examples illustrate how BFOQs apply to policing. Because driving a patrol car is one of the basic tasks of a police officer, a department can legitimately refuse to hire someone who cannot drive a car because of a certain disability. By contrast, the old height requirements are not job related because it has not been demonstrated that people shorter than 5 feet 8 inches cannot effectively perform police work. In *Davis v. City of Dallas,* the Fifth Circuit Court of Appeals ruled that a requirement of 45 hours of college credits did not discriminate against people who lacked that level of education because it was reasonably related to the job of a police officer, which includes the capacity to exercise judgment in complex and difficult situations.[53]

"Not Your Father's Police Department": Diversity in Policing

Law professor David Sklansky argues that, because of the dramatic changes in police employment in recent decades, it's "Not Your Father's Police Department" any more.

EXHIBIT 5–3

Title VII, 1964 Civil Rights Act

SEC. 703. (a) It shall be an unlawful employment practice for an employer—

1. to fail or refuse to hire or to discharge any individual, or otherwise to discriminate against any individual with respect to his compensation, terms, conditions, or privileges of employment, because of such individual's race, color, religion, sex, or national origin; or
2. to limit, segregate, or classify his employees in any way which would deprive or tend to deprive any individual of employment opportunities or otherwise adversely affect his status as an employee, because of such individual's race, color, religion, sex, or national origin.

EXHIBIT 5–4

Race, Ethnicity, and Gender, Local Police Departments, 2007–2013 (as a percentage of all officers)

	2007	2013
White, non-Hispanic	74.7%	72.8%
African American	11.9	12.2
Hispanic	10.3	11.6
Asian, Native Hawaiian, Pacific Islander	2.0	2.4
American Indian, Alaska Native	0.7	0.6
Two or more races	0.3	0.5
Women	11.9	12.2

Source: Bureau of Justice Statistics, *Local Police Departments, 2007* (Washington, DC: U.S. Department of Justice, 2010); Bureau of Justice Statistics, *Local Police Departments, 2013: Personnel, Policies,* and *Practices* (Washington, DC: U.S. Department of Justice, 2015).

African Americans, Hispanics, women, and homosexuals have entered policing (see Exhibit 5–4). Police departments look different than they did in the past, and one result is that the traditional police subculture (which we discuss in Chapter 6) is a thing of the past.[54]

In the mid-1960s, African Americans represented only 3.6 percent of all sworn police officers in the country. The figure rose to 6 percent in 1973, 7.6 percent in 1982, and 11.9 percent by 2007. Between 2007 and 2013, however, the percentage remained virtually unchanged, rising slightly to 12.2 percent. Hispanics represented 11.6 percent of all officers in 2013, rising from 6.2 percent in 1993 and 10.3 percent in 2007.[55] Long-term data on Hispanic employment are difficult, if not impossible, to obtain because early surveys did not ask for data on Hispanic officers.

National data on the employment of officers of color are misleading, however, because different racial and ethnic groups are not evenly distributed across the country. African Americans are concentrated in the South and many big cities (but not all). Hispanic Americans are concentrated in particular cities in the Southwest, on the East Coast, and in the South. The best way to determine whether a department complies with the recommendation that departments reflect the diversity of the communities they serve is with the **equal employment opportunity (EEO) index,** which compares a police department's workforce with the racial and ethnic composition of the community it serves. If a community is 30 percent Hispanic and the police department is 15 percent Hispanic, for example, the EEO index is 0.50.[56] Data from San Jose, California, illustrate how the EEO index works (see Exhibit 5–5).

Special considerations relate to the employment of Hispanic officers. Because the ability to communicate with people is the most important aspect of police work, it is crucial that police departments take active steps to ensure that they are able to communicate with Spanish-speaking people.[57] Selecting recruits who speak Spanish (even if they are non-Hispanic whites) addresses that issue. In Washington State, the ability to speak Spanish is by law a BFOQ for 911 operators (although the law does not mention police officers).[58]

equal employment opportunity (EEO) index

EXHIBIT 5–5

The EEO Index Applied to the San Jose Police Department, 2014

	San Jose Population	Police Officers	EEO Index
Hispanic	33%	23%	0.70
Asian American	32	15	0.47
White, non-Hispanic	29	54	1.86
African American	3	4	1.33

Source: San Jose Independent Police Auditor, *2014 Annual Report*, Appendix I (San Jose: Author, 2015), 116.

Women in Policing

Lucie Duvall, one of the first female officers in Cleveland, Ohio, had a difficult and often humiliating experience as a rookie officer. The department's precinct stations did not have separate locker rooms or restrooms for women. Some of the male officers, who resented women's presence on the force, deliberately changed clothes in front of them, as a form of subtle harassment.[59]

As more women entered policing in the 1970s, and began working as patrol officers for the first time in history, police departments had to change many male-centered policies. The entry of women also challenged many aspects of the male-dominated police subculture. Old rules on hair falling below the collar were not consistent with common women's hairstyles. Police departments had to develop policies for pregnant officers. The federal Pregnancy Discrimination Act prohibits employment discrimination on the basis of pregnancy, childbirth, or any pregnancy-related medical condition.[60]

Prior to the late 1960s, police departments hired only a few women, restricted to a separate job category of "policewoman"; excluded them from many assignments, including patrol; and, in some departments, barred them from promotion above a certain rank (see Chapter 2).[61] Everything began to change after the 1964 Civil Rights Act outlawed employment discrimination and female officers were assigned to patrol duty on an equal basis with men. Nonetheless, many forms of covert discrimination continue to exist. As a result, women are still underrepresented in police departments relative to their presence in the workforce. The percentage of all sworn officers who are women increased from 2 percent in 1972, to 12 percent in 2013 (but about 17 percent in big-city departments). The percentage of female officers is generally higher in large police departments, but it reaches 20 percent in only a few departments. Yet today, women make up about 46 percent of the adult labor force.[62]

A report by the National Center for Women and Policing found a number of current barriers to the employment of women. Entrance examinations that emphasize upper-body physical strength favor men. There is no evidence, however, that great physical strength (as opposed to good health) affects an officer's ability to perform well. On-the-job discrimination, particularly sexual harassment and discriminatory assignments, either discourages women from applying or encourages them to resign their jobs. Many police departments, meanwhile, recruit heavily from the military, which is a male-dominated work environment. Finally, some police departments embrace an old-fashioned model of policing, emphasizing aggressiveness and authoritarianism, which is unappealing to many potential women applicants.[63]

POLICE *in* FOCUS | Women in the Charlotte-Mecklenburg (North Carolina) Police Department

The Charlotte-Mecklenburg, North Carolina, police department had current female officers describe their careers in the department. Another section debunks some myths about women and policing. Three of those myths are as follows:

"Myth: Police work requires people who are physically imposing."

Fact: Police work is not all about size and muscles." Physical encounters are statistically rare in police work. Communication skills are most important in routine police-citizen encounters.

"Myth: Women police are faced with a lot more situations where they must use a gun."

Fact: Research has found that female offices do not encountere more situations where they are more likely to use a firearm. And they do not fire their weapons more often than male officers. Officers receive over 120 hours of training specifically in firearms, shoot-don't-shoot scenarios, use of force, and legal training which helps prepare them for this type of situation. Statistically, though, the majority of men and women police officers retire from law enforcement without ever having to use deadly force.

"Myth: Police officers aren't supposed to get scared."

Fact: Dangerous situations do occur, and fear is a normal reaction.

Source: Charlotte-Mecklenburg Police Department.

Employment Discrimination Suits

Much of the initial progress in the hiring of more African Americans, Hispanics, and women was a result of employment discrimination suits under Title VII of the 1964 Civil Rights Act. Successful suits produce a number of different results. First, they can result in direct benefit to the plaintiffs, including financial damages for being discriminated against. Second, they often result in a court order eliminating discriminatory tests or procedures (for example, height requirements that discriminated against women and Hispanics). Third, there may be a court-ordered affirmative action plan with specific goals and timetables for future recruiting.

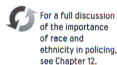

For a full discussion of the importance of race and ethnicity in policing, see Chapter 12.

The LAPD in 1980, for example, signed a consent decree with the U.S. Justice Department awarding $2 million in back pay and agreeing that 45 percent of all new recruits would be African American or Hispanic and 20 percent of all new recruits would be women. By 1990, the department had met its target of having 10.9 percent African American officers out of the total force, but it was still short of its goal on Hispanic officers (20 percent, versus the 24.6 percent target) and women (12 percent, versus the 20 percent target).[64]

The most controversial issue in police employment is **affirmative action.** The concept of affirmative action means that an employer must take positive steps (hence, *affirmative* action) to remedy past discrimination. Affirmative action originated in 1965, with presidential Executive Order 11246, which required all federal contractors to develop written affirmative action programs. Today, all private employers and government agencies receiving federal funds are required to have affirmative action plans. The basic premise of affirmative action is that simply ending discrimination (as required by the 1964 Civil Rights Act) does not automatically correct for the legacy of past discrimination. An affirmative action plan consists of several elements. The employer must (a) conduct a census of current employees,

affirmative action

(b) identify underutilization or concentration of minorities and women, and (c) develop a recruiting plan to correct any underutilization. The U.S. Equal Employment Opportunity Commission defines *underutilization* as "having fewer minorities or women in a particular job category than would reasonably be expected by their presence in the relevant labor market."[65]

reverse discrimination

An affirmative action plan can be voluntary on the part of the employer, with clear goals and timetables. It does not, however, automatically involve the use of racial, ethnic, or gender quotas in hiring. Opponents of quotas argue that they involve an illegal form of **reverse discrimination,** in which white or male applicants claim they were not hired because quotas required the hiring of African American or Hispanic applicants who had weaker credentials. Opponents of affirmative action also argue that it lowers personnel standards by forcing employers to hire people with lower qualifications. There is no evidence to support this belief, however, at least with properly conducted affirmative action plans. There have been cases were departments chose to lower their recruitment standards, but the fault was with the department and not the affirmative action plan. A PERF study, however, found a steady rise in the levels of education among police officers from the 1960s through the late 1980s, a

---

SIDEBAR 5–2

Hiring Quotas: Fair or Unfair?

A number of employment discrimination lawsuits have been settled through consent decrees that include a hiring quota for women, African Americans, or Hispanics. A typical example would be the requirement that 40 percent of all new recruits be female until a specified target is reached.

Are quotas fair or unfair? Consider the following example: Assume that a department is operating under a 40 percent quota for women. It plans to hire 50 new officers; therefore, 20 must be women and 30 will be men. When all the test scores are compiled, the 20th-highest-scoring female applicant has a combined score of 82 out of 100. She is hired. A male applicant who has a combined score of 83 ranked 31st on the men's list. He is not hired. Is this system fair? Consider the following questions:

1. Is it fair to the male applicant who had a higher score but was not hired? Is it fair to women as a group, who have historically been denied employment with the police?

2. How significant is the difference between a score of 83 and a score of 82? Do those numbers really predict who will be the better police officer? How reliable are the tests that contributed to that composite score? If the department used a general intelligence test, does it really identify who will be an effective police officer? Does a difference of a few points on a standard psychological test indicate that the person with the slightly higher score will be the better police officer? (Point of fact: The department set a combined score of 70 as the minimum for employment. Anyone with a score of 69 or lower could not be hired.)

3. The courts have upheld quota systems as a remedy for past discrimination. If you feel this system is unfair, what strategy would you recommend for remedying past discrimination?

period that included affirmative action programs. The educational levels of white, African American, and Hispanic officers in 1988, moreover, were nearly comparable. The study found that 62.2 percent of whites had some college credits, compared with 67.5 percent of Hispanics and 63.2 percent of African Americans.[66]

The question of whether affirmative action results in lower personnel standards depends on how a police department implements its affirmative action plan. If, for example, an agency hires people who do not meet the normal minimum standards, then it is lowering its standards. The intent of affirmative action is to prod employers to recruit more aggressively to expand its pool of applicants in order to find qualified employees. If an agency cannot meet a quota, then the proper course of action is to suspend the hiring process and conduct a more vigorous recruitment effort in order to increase the size of the applicant pool.

Some critics of affirmative action cite the earlier-mentioned example of the Washington, D.C., police department, which conducted a major hiring campaign in the early 1990s and in the process failed to conduct the standard background investigations of applicants. As a result, many unqualified officers were hired, some of whom had criminal records and eventually became corrupt officers. But as we noted earlier, the recruitment standards were lowered because of political pressure to hire more officers because of high crime rates, not because of affirmative action considerations.[67]

Do affirmative action programs achieve their goals? There is conflicting evidence on this question. Susan Martin's research on women in policing found that departments with affirmative action plans did, in fact, have a higher percentage of women in their applicant pools. And partly as a result, they hired more women as police recruits.[68] With respect to the employment of African American officers, however, a national survey of 281 police departments found that the presence of an affirmative action plan had only modest impact. The most important explanation for the employment of African American officers was the size of the African American population in the local community.[69]

The constitutionality of affirmative action programs is still somewhat uncertain, even after many decisions following the 1978 *Bakke* decision, in which it upheld the principle of affirmative action but ruled that quotas were unconstitutional. In 2016, in *Fisher v. Texas,* the Supreme Court ruled that is was constitutional for the University of Texas to use race as one of many factors in making undergraduate admission decisions. How this decision affects police hiring, however, is not clear at this point.[70]

The Impact of Increased Diversity

The increase in the numbers of African American and Hispanic officers, together with the assignment of women officers to patrol duty in the 1970s, and more recently the presence of openly gay and lesbian officers, has had a significant although complex impact on policing. These changes have challenged the traditional white male subculture of policing. We examine this issue in detail in Chapter 6.

Police Training: Progress and New Challenges

In 2015, PERF issued a blistering report on the state of police training. Chief Michael Chitwood of the Daytona Beach, Florida, police department summed it up by saying, "What we did 20 years ago is not good enough."[71] Standard police academy programs, the report argued, gave far too much emphasis to firearms training and not enough to communication skills and techniques for avoiding the unnecessary use of force. Enormous progress had been made in police training in recent decades, but much more needs to be done. The national police crisis of 2014–2016 (see Chapter 2) dramatized the urgent need for major improvements in officer use of force, communication skills, tactical decision-making, and other key aspects of policing.

One problem hindering our understanding of police training, however, is that although there are many descriptions of training programs, "[t]here has been little systematic research on police training," as Wesley Skogan and colleagues argue.[72] We do not really know what works and which training methods are more effective than others.

An important theme of this chapter is that police training is not a one-time event. Too many people focus only on preservice police academy training. To ensure the highest quality of police service to the public, training needs to be an ongoing process, including supervised field training, regular roll-call training, and annual in-service training. There are also special training moments, such as refresher training for officers involved in an officer-involved shooting (OIS) incident, or individualized training as part of the intervention component of an early intervention system (see Chapter 14).

New Thinking about Policing and Training

As we learned in Chapter 2, the national police crisis of 2014–2016 stimulated a broad rethinking of the police role in society, what strategies police departments should adopt to deal with crime and disorder, and what police officers should do in their interactions with community residents. The new thinking has important implications for police training. As we pointed out at the beginning of this chapter, the President's Task Force on 21st Century Policing strongly recommended replacing the warrior mindset of policing, with its "us versus them" attitude toward the community, with a guardian mindset, in which the police protect and serve.[73] As discussed earlier, Rahr and Rice argue that traditional police academy training reinforces the warrior mindset.[74]

The new approach to recruit training seeks to develop officers who are *problem-solvers* who know how to assess a potentially dangerous situation, choose the appropriate response, and reassess the situation as it changes and change tactics accordingly. The training director from the LAPD explained that in the past they "told recruits to sit down, shut up, and listen for six months." Today, they want "to create officers who are self-motivated, interdependent, community-motivated critical thinkers and problem-solvers."[75]

The major elements of the new approach to police training include de-escalation, tactical decision-making, communication skills, and procedural justice (see Exhibit 5–6). They also include new styles of teaching, including fewer lectures, more scenario-based teaching, and a shift toward training officers to think and use their judgement in difficult situations rather than simply to follow orders. We discuss all of these elements in this chapter.[76]

The Police Academy

police academy

Police training begins with the **police academy,** where new recruits receive their introduction to policing and to the department. Large police departments today

EXHIBIT 5–6

Innovations in Police Training

De-escalation and alternatives to use of force

Tactical decision-making

Scenario-based training

Training on unconscious bias

Training in procedural justice

maintain their own academies. Smaller departments send their officers to a state police training academy or to state-certified regional academies. The average length of **preservice training** programs quadrupled between the 1950s and 2000, increasing from about 300 to more than 1,400 hours, including both classroom and field training. Many new subjects were added to the curriculum as part of this expansion: human relations, domestic violence, responding to mental health crises, and others.[77] One of the most important changes in police training in the past 50 years has been the development of state laws requiring preservice training for all officers. California and New York were the first states to adopt this requirement in 1959. In 1965, 85 percent of all officers received no preservice training.[78] By the early 1980s, every state had some form of state-mandated training. Academy classroom training is followed by field training, where officers are on the street under the supervision of a field training officer.

preservice training

The police academy experience has several different formal and informal effects. The basic function is to provide basic training on the law; department policies on use of force, arrest and booking procedures, and other subjects; along with the proper handling of domestic violence incidents and other special situations. The academy is also an opportunity for weeding out recruits whose performance is unsatisfactory. An average of about 14 percent of all recruits fail the police academy training program.[79]

The academy is also a rite of passage that socializes recruits into the world of policing, where officers develop an identification with the department and the prevailing police subculture. As already mentioned, a number of critics today argue that the military-style boot camp atmosphere, in which officers are trained to follow orders and not ask questions, develops the wrong set of values.

A 2015 report on the use of deadly force in the Philadelphia Police Department identified some of the major shortcomings of police academy training at that time, along with the major new ideas. Academy training in the Philadelphia Police Department in 2015 involved 32 weeks and 1,214 hours, 777 of which were devoted to subjects mandated by the state Municipal Police Officers' Education & Training Commission.[80] The training staff, however, were certified as trainers in their subject areas only once in their career, and they were never required to be recertified. In short, there was no guarantee that trainers were knowledgeable about the latest developments in policing. Additionally, too much training involved "little more than lectures and observations." Large class sizes limited recruit participation in scenario-based training, which is now regarded as a more effective approach. When surveyed,

EXHIBIT 5–7

Average Number of Hours of Police Academy Training, by Subject, 2015

Subject	Hours of Training
Firearms	58
Defensive Tactics	49
Communication Skills	10
De-escalation	8
Crisis intervention	8

Source: Police Executive Research Forum, *Re-Engineering Training on Police Use of Force* (Washington, DC: Author, 2015), 11.

recruits expressed a desire for more scenario-based training, which they were not receiving.[81] Additionally, the report found that most of the training sessions on uses of force "end with the officer having to use force." There were too few scenarios in which officers "peacefully resolve a situation by using proper verbal skills." The department took the findings of the report seriously, and by 2016 had already made a number of significant changes to its training programs.[82]

Training on the Use of Force

A comment by Chief Matthew Pontillo of the NYPD at the 2015 PERF conference on re-engineering training highlighted how new thinking has challenged old police ways. He explained that "we were teaching take-down techniques," until we asked the question, "Why are we putting everybody on the ground?" Take-downs had always been assumed to be important, but the best new thinking in policing emphasizes reducing the use of force, particularly through de-escalation.[83]

Police training has put too much emphasis on the use of force, without adequate consideration of alternative ways of resolving an incident. As Exhibit 5–7 indicates, the PERF survey of police training curricula found that an average of 58 hours were devoted to firearms training (the highest ranked subject), and only 10 hours to communication skills and 8 hours each to de-escalation and crisis intervention.[84]

de-escalation

The most important alternative to an officer using physical force is **de-escalation.** The Seattle Police Department policy on use of force (adopted in late 2013 as a result of a federal consent decree), begins by stating that "when time, circumstances, and safety permit, officers will seek to gain compliance and de-escalate conflict without using physical force."[85] The President's Task Force strongly recommended that "Law Enforcement policies for training on use of force should emphasize de-escalation and alternatives to arrest and summons in situations where appropriate."[86]

De-escalation is particularly important when someone expresses disrespect or does something the officer perceives as disrespectful. The police have a long history of responding to such situations with force and/or arrest, to show the person who is in charge. Christy Lopez defines such incidents as arrest for "contempt of cop."[87] At the PERF conference, a New York police training officer said that they now teach recruits not to take apparent disrespect personally: "You have to be a professional. . . .

[R]espect begets respect, and disrespect begets disrespect. . . . We tell officers that they do not always need to 'stand their ground.' . . . This is not giving up."[88]

Tactical Decision-Making

Traditional police training has been very directive and rule-bound, essentially telling recruits (and veteran officers during in-service training), "This is our policy; do it this way." The new thinking about police training, however, has moved in the direction of preparing officers to assess each situation and make tactical decisions about the best way to handle it. In short, it seeks to prepare officers to *think*.

A 2016 report on changes in training in the LAPD explained that "there has been a move away from the provision of specific guidance to officers, toward an emphasis on concepts," designed "to enhance officers' critical thinking skills." The basic goal is to place "greater responsibility onto officers in determining what tactics they should use in a given operational scenario." This includes having officers "constantly assess based on the fluidity of the situation" and use "critical thinking" about the appropriate response. "This change in philosophy places greater emphasis and responsibility on officers to think about when and why they might use the force option, rather than simply how to apply an option."[89]

Tactical decision-making challenges the traditional stereotype of the "split-second decision" in policing, where a threat appears suddenly and the officer feels he or she has no choice about what to do. In fact, however, most police–citizen encounters develop over time, some are as short as a few minutes, but others last as long as 20 or 30 minutes, or even longer. In these time periods, officers have an opportunity to make tactical decisions that can shape subsequent events and the final outcome. Consider the case of a person with a knife who is having a mental health crisis. If the officer moves in close, it increases the chances that the person will lunge and create the necessity of using deadly force. Stepping back and creating space, by contrast, reduces the possibility of having to use any kind of force and also creates the opportunity for resolving the situation peacefully.

tactical decision-making

Cathy Lanier, chief of the Washington, D.C., police department, told the PERF conference that "the decisions leading up to the moment when you fired a shot ultimately determine whether you had to or not." A commander from the LAPD explained the formula for tactical decision-making: "distance plus cover equals time." Time means gaining the ability to "communicate with the suspect," to "make a tactical plan," and to "get resources to the scene."[90]

Scenario-Based Training

An LAPD training commander said that the department's training in the 1980s was "an academy of lecture" and that they were "boring officers to death with lecture-based training."[91] One of the most important recent advances in training has been the move away from lectures and toward the use of scenario-based training. Some scenario-based training units, particularly with regard to deadly force and high-speed pursuits, involve computerized simulations. But they can also take the form of person-to-person role-playing.

The value of scenario-based training lies in its ability to have "officers interact with unfolding video scenarios and have to make judgments." Because it engages officers in real-world simulations, it is a far more effective teaching method than lectures. Officers in Philadelphia in 2015 intuitively understood this and expressed "a strong desire for more reality-based training (RBT) throughout the department."[92] Deputy Chief Danielle Outlaw of the Oakland, California, police department told the 2015 PERF conference that the change to scenario-based training represented a "huge paradigm shift" for the department, and cited declines in officer uses of force and citizen complaints as evidence of the impact on policing.[93]

The NYPD greatly expanded the use of scenarios in its recruit classes, under a 2013 court-ordered mandate to improve training because of a law suit that successfully challenged its stop and frisk law practices. The changes included using mock environments in the academy (for example, subway stations and street scenes) and also taking recruits out of the classroom for two-week sessions in local police precincts for hands-on experience in a real-world context.[94]

Fragmented and Inconsistent Training

The 2015 PERF report found that police academy training programs were often fragmented, covering the topics in a disorganized fashion and often providing conflicting training on the same issue.[95] An investigation of the use of force by the Las Vegas Metropolitan Police, meanwhile, found that inconsistency in training was "a common theme" among discussions with police officers.[96] The 2015 report on the use of deadly force in Philadelphia found that "training staff provides inconsistent or contradictory instruction to recruits. . . . Academy instruction materials on the use of force policy and use of force continuum," for example, were "inconsistent."[97] The PERF report on re-engineering police training saw a great need for "organized, systematic thinking" about designing training programs.

Training that gives police recruits incomplete, erroneous, or mixed messages about the proper way to handle certain situations is poor training, leaving the recruits liable to make serious mistakes once they are on the street as officers.

The Consequences of Inadequate Training

The lack of effective training has important legal implications. In the case of *City of Canton, Ohio v. Harris,* the Supreme Court held in 1989 that police departments could be liable for a "failure to train." "In light of the duties assigned to specific officers or employees," the Court held, "the need for more or different training is so obvious, and the inadequacy so likely to result in the violation of constitutional rights, that the policymakers of the city can reasonably be said to have been deliberately indifferent to the need." Thus, "the failure to provide proper training may fairly be said to represent a policy for which the city is responsible, and for which the city may be held liable if it actually causes injury."[98]

There have been instances in which some police training has been simply erroneous on important points. In New York City, a U.S. District Court found that the NYPD's aggressive stop and frisk program violated both the Fourth Amendment on searches and seizures and the Fourteenth Amendment on equal protection of the law. One serious problem with the department's policy was with its training program. The judge concluded that the training "flaws effectively encourage officer to commit constitutional violations." Officers, for example, were trained that they could make a stop and frisk based on "furtive behavior" on the part of a person. The training defined "furtive behavior" as "strange, suspicious, or evasive behavior," without specifying any behavior that created a reasonable suspicion that a person was committing or was about to commit a crime (which is the prevailing legal standard). As a result, 42 percent of officer stop reports cited "furtive behavior" as justification for the stop.[99]

Training on Unconscious Bias

Bias on the basis of race, ethnicity, sexual orientation, immigrant status, homelessness, lifestyle, or any other factor that does not involve criminal activity is contrary to the law of equal protection and to principles of good, professional policing. It is now understood that much bias is unconscious, reflecting deeply held stereotypes about certain categories of people. This is true among all Americans, and police officers are no exception.

Elimination of bias in policing requires addressing **unconscious or implicit bias** in police training. Lorie Fridell, director of the Fair and Impartial Policing (FIP) project, points out that "people may not be aware of their *implicit* biases." Stopping and questioning a young man *because* he is an African American is a clear-cut case of bias. But many police actions are also based on unconscious assumptions that associate African American men with criminal activity and "dangerousness." In Fridell's FIP training program involving role-playing scenarios, police recruits "are consistently under-vigilant with women—not finding the gun in the small of the back." That is, they do not associate women with dangerousness and a threat to their safety.[100]

unconscious or implicit bias

Training on Procedural Justice

The President's Task Force on 21st Century Policing strongly endorsed **procedural justice** as a way for the police to enhance public confidence and trust in the police (see Chapter 1).[101] The core elements of procedural justice involve a police officer engaged in an encounter with a citizen introducing himself or herself, explaining the reason for the stop, listening to what the citizen has to say, and answering any questions. Research on procedural justice has found that people in any involvement with an organization (an employee, a student, or a citizen in a police encounter) is as much concerned with the process (how he or she was treated) as with the result (the grade, the traffic ticket).[102]

procedural justice

Field Training

To supplement classroom academy training, most departments also operate field training programs. These involve practical experience in police work under the supervision of an experienced **field training officer (FTO).** Today, about a third of all departments require field training.[103] The original San Jose field training program in the 1970s that set the model for today's programs consisted of 16 weeks of classroom training, followed by 14 weeks of field training. During field training by this model, the recruit is assigned to three different FTOs for four-week periods each, followed by a final two weeks with the original FTO. Each FTO makes daily reports on the recruit's performance, and supervisors complete weekly evaluation reports.[104]

field training officer (FTO)

POLICE *in* FOCUS | San Jose Police Department Field Training Program

The San Jose Police Department Field Training Program, implemented in the early 1970s, was cited as a model program by the International Association of Chiefs of Police. The California legislature, meanwhile, established the San Jose program as the model for its statewide Peace Officer Standards and Training (POST) requirements.

In 2016, the program consisted of 17–20 weeks of training in the field, with daily performance evaluations completed by a field training officer. New officers are required to meet "specific performance standards in 30 performance categories" before they can be certified to work alone as patrol officers. Near the end of the field training program, a "formal oral board examination" reviews each officer's performance.

The objectives of the program include the following:

- Training and evaluating all recruit officers to prepare them for solo patrol duty
- Achieving a 90 percent success rate for all recruits
- Training newly appointed field training officers and sergeants for their new responsibilities
- Providing information and training to other law enforcement agencies

Source: San Jose Police Department, "Field Training Officer (FTO) Program," http://www.sjpd.org/BFO/FieldTraining/.

Even though police departments have been doing field training since the 1970s, some departments did not keep up with this important aspect of training. Philadelphia, for example, had no field training program as recently as 2015.[105]

Field training programs also vary in quality. A sex discrimination suit by female officers in one department exposed serious problems with the existing informal post-academy field training program. The officers alleged that the FTOs were biased against them. The suit found that the field training program had no curriculum, no performance evaluation system based on actual tasks, and no training for the FTOs. The suit resulted in a new and improved field training program.[106] This particular case illustrates the way in which employment discrimination suits often result in general reforms of police department policies and practices.

In-Service Training

in-service training

Regular **in-service training** is as important as preservice academy training. Recruits have difficulty completely absorbing all they are taught during the intensive academy experience, and it is even more difficult to recall everything as the next few years roll by. In-service training is designed to provide a refresher on basic issues such as the use-of-force policy and also to introduce new issues, such as new state legislation or important court decisions that affect police procedures.

The California POST system, in fact, has a special set of training it labels "Perishable Skills," which every officer is required to take. Once every two years, all peace officers in the state must complete at least 12 hours of in-service training, with 4 hours in each of three areas: arrest and control, driver training/awareness or driving simulator, and tactical firearm or force options simulator.[107] The idea of perishable skills is important. It recognizes that even the best officers can easily forget their training and, under the pressure of difficult situations, do things that are not consistent with department policies. Regular in-service training brings their skills back to the highest level.

The Las Vegas Metropolitan Police Department added an Advanced Officer Skills Training (AOST) in-service training program, which is a mandatory nine-hour course for all patrol officers that involves both classroom and scenario-based training. The curriculum consists of one hour of firearms qualification, two hours of electronic-conducted recertification, two hours of use-of-force training, and four hours of reality-based decision-making scenario training.[108]

An important innovation in in-service training is return-to-duty training for any officer involved in an officer-involved shooting incident. The LAPD used to postpone the training until all the issues surrounding the incident had been adjudicated. Recognizing that the delay was a "big mistake," the LAPD now requires involved officers to receive a "general training update" within 90 days of an OIS incident. The NYPD sends every OIS-involved officer for a one-day "tactics refresher." Additionally, each OIS is reviewed by command officers "to determine the immediate lessons learned" from the incident, and the lessons learned are incorporated into the regular training curriculum very quickly."[109]

Training of Supervisors

Training of officers newly promoted to a supervisory rank was long neglected in American policing. Today, it is mandatory in most departments. Being a sergeant involves responsibilities that are very different from those of a patrol officer, and training is essential.

The Oakland, California, police department, as part of a long and difficult consent decree process, substantially improved its training of supervisors in 2013–2015. In particular, it "raised the bar for use-of-force investigations." One commander explained that "[i]t used to be that sergeants would take what officers said at face value" and "push it up the chain." Sergeants are now expected to critically examine officers' reports and, if necessary, demand more detailed information about the incident. A Seattle commander also said that improved training on supervisors' responsibilities was "one of the most significant areas of improvement" in accountability. In 2014, for example, the department provided supervisors with 24 hours of training.[110]

In most states, small departments send their new officers to a state training academy or state-certified program. Some programs are operated through community colleges. The separate police academies run by the large police departments are similarly certified by the state. The minimum state training requirements are usually lower, in terms of the number of hours of training, than the programs operated by big-city police academies. Officers who complete state training are then certified or licensed as peace officers in the state.

The Probationary Period

Upon completing preservice training, a recruit is sworn in and assigned to regular duty. The officer is on probationary status for a period that may range from six months to two years, depending on the department (some departments count the time in training as part of this period).[111]

probationary period

During the **probationary period,** an officer can be dismissed without cause. After the probationary period is completed, dismissal must be based on cause under rules established by the local civil service regulations and/or police union contract.

An average of about 7 percent of all recruits are rejected during their probationary period.[112] Susan Martin found significant differences in how departments used the probationary period, however. In Phoenix, 47 percent of all officers who left the department were in their probationary period at the time. This included 26 percent of all female recruits and 14 percent of all male recruits. In Washington, D.C., however, only 15 percent of those leaving the department were in the probationary period (representing 5 percent of both males and females).[113]

Many experts argue that a longer probationary period permits more time for observing performance and an opportunity to dismiss those whose performance is unsatisfactory. A 1986 report on the Philadelphia Police Department found that the six-month probationary period included 19 weeks of academy training, leaving only a very short period for on-the-street experience. The report concluded that this was "insufficient to allow supervisors to determine whether a particular candidate is qualified to be a police officer" and recommended at least a six-month probationary period following completion of academy training.[114]

CASE STUDY

Improving Training for Domestic Violence Incidents: A Problem-Oriented Approach

Virtually all police departments today cover domestic violence in their police academy training programs. A review of the subject by Eigenberg, Kappler, and McGuffee, however, found that a number of myths and uncritical assumptions pervade police thinking about domestic violence and inhibit the development of effective training programs.

One myth is that there is only one kind of domestic violence and that all incidents are essentially the same. One study identified three different types of domestic violence. *Intimate terrorism* involves the aggressor's use of violence as only one tactic to control the partner's behavior. Other control tactics include financial control, emotional abuse, manipulation, and others. *Violent resistance* involves one party resorting to violence in response to intimate terrorism. *Situational couple violence* occurs when there is "mutual" violence with no clear primary aggressor.

Effective police training needs to acknowledge the different types of domestic violence, train officers how to recognize each type, and train officers on the appropriate response to each one.

A second myth is that domestic violence is the same as other crimes. Domestic violence is a very frequent incident for the police, and the volume of cases makes a difference. The nature of the power relations between couples involved in intimate terrorism creates difficult issues that are not found in most other violent crimes.

Effective police training needs to address the special factors involved in each of the different forms of domestic violence.

A third myth is that domestic violence incidents are particularly dangerous for police officers. Criminologists who have examined this myth found that it originated with problems with FBI crime data and a misinterpretation of that data. The FBI data lumped together all disturbances, including genuine domestic disturbances, bar fights, and other general neighborhood disturbances. The myth had the effect of developing a mindset among police officers that their safety is always at risk when responding to a domestic violence call.

Effective training needs to present a realistic, evidence-based picture of domestic violence, and the prevalence of assaults on police officers.

In short, police training on domestic violence needs to be "problem-oriented," with an evidence-based picture of the different types of domestic violence, the risks associated with each one, and the proper response to the different types of incidents.

Source: Adapted from Helen M. Eigenberg, Victor E. Kappler, and Karen McGuffee, "Confronting the Complexities of Domestic Violence: A Social Prescription for Rethinking Police Training," *Journal of Police Crisis Negotiations* 12 (2012): 122–145.

SUMMARY

The recruitment and training of American police officers have changed significantly since the 1970s. There are now more African American, Hispanic, female, and college-educated officers than ever before. Many old personnel practices have been eliminated because they discriminated against particular groups. Training of officers is today in the midst of a dramatic change, with a new emphasis on procedural justice and de-escalation designed to reduce officer use of force and improve public trust and confidence in the police. New methods of training, especially scenario-based training, have replaced the traditional emphasis on lectures. There is also increased emphasis on in-service training to ensure that experienced officers maintain their knowledge and skills at the highest levels.

KEY TERMS

warriors versus guardians, 131
career perspective, 133
stereotypes about cops, 133
civil service system, 134
height requirement, 136
criminal record, 138
residency requirements, 138
job security, 140
oral interviews, 141

background investigation, 142
Title VII of the 1964 Civil
    Rights Act, 144
bona fide occupational
    qualifications (BFOQs), 144
equal employment opportunity
    (EEO) index, 145
affirmative action, 147
reverse discrimination, 148

police academy, 150
preservice training, 151
de-escalation, 152
tactical decision-making, 153
unconscious or implicit bias, 155
procedural justice, 155
field training officer (FTO), 155
in-service training, 156
probationary period, 158

FOR DISCUSSION

This chapter has described several important new innovations regarding police training. Discuss the following issues raised by these innovations:

1. How exactly is the guardian mentality likely to improve the quality of policing? Are there any dangers involved in this approach?
2. Discuss why scenario-based training is likely to be more effective even than good, detailed lectures, where recruits have an opportunity to ask questions about situations and tactics?
3. There is a lot of emphasis today on de-escalation. Is it appropriate for all encounters with people? Describe situations where it is not appropriate, and situations where it is most appropriate. Out there, on the street, how is an officer to determine which situations are appropriate and which ones are not?

INTERNET EXERCISES

Exercise 1 How do the recruitment standards for the law enforcement agencies in your area compare with those in other parts of the country? First, create a list of agencies in your area. Choose either the agencies in your immediate metropolitan area (which would include the major city police department and suburban departments) or the state, or, for example, a multistate region if applicable (say, for example, the Kansas City area, which would include two states and a combination of city and suburban departments). Second, use the web to identify the minimum qualifications for each agency. Most (but not all) agencies post employment criteria on their websites. Information may also be available on a city's personnel department or human relations department web site. Third, compile the data in a table that is easily readable. Are there any significant differences in employment standards by size of agency or other factors? Does any particular agency appear to have relatively low standards?

Exercise 2 Some police departments have special hiring provisions for applicants who are bilingual. This represents an effort to increase the number of officers who can speak Spanish, or Vietnamese, or some other language. Often, the special provision involves granting extra points in the application process. First, identify cities with large Hispanic and/or Asian populations. Data from the 2010 U.S. Census are available on the web https://www.census.gov/quickfacts/). The websites of the police departments you have chosen often have data on their personnel, including race, ethnicity, and gender. Do any police departments make special efforts to hire bilingual officers? How prevalent are such efforts? What special provisions do these efforts involve?

NOTES

1. President's Task Force 21st Century Policing, *Final Report* (Washington, DC: U.S. Department of Justice, 2015), http://www.cops.usdoj.gov/pdf/taskforce/taskforce_finalreport.pdf.
2. Sue Rahr and Stephen K. Rice, *From Warriors to Guardians: Recommitting American Police Culture to Democratic Ideals* (Cambridge, MA: Harvard Kennedy School, 2015), https://www.ncjrs.gov/pdffiles1/nij/248654.pdf.
3. Police Executive Research Forum, *Re-Engineering Training on Police Use of Force* (Washington, DC: Police Executive Research Forum, 2015), http://www.policeforum.org/assets/reengineeringtraining1.pdf.
4. Arthur Niederhoffer, *Behind the Shield: The Police in Urban Society* (Garden City, NY: Anchor Books, 1967), 1.
5. National Center for Women and Policing, *Recruiting and Retaining Women: A Self-Assessment Guide for Law Enforcement* (Los Angeles: National Center for Women and Policing, 2001), 43, www.womenandpolicing.org.

6. Samuel Walker, *A Critical History of Police Reform* (Lexington, MA: Lexington Books, 1977), 9.

7. George W. Griesinger, Jeffrey S. Slovak, and Joseph J. Molkup, *Civil Service Systems: Their Impact on Police Administration* (Washington, DC: U.S. Government Printing Office, 1979).

8. Los Angeles Police Commission, Office of the Inspector General, *Ten Year Overview of Categorical Use of Force Investigations, Policy, and Training* (Los Angeles: Office of the Inspector General, March 10, 2016), http://media.wix.com/ugd/b2dd23_3139a5342cc34ce2860af75368 87f149.pdf.

9. President's Commission on Law Enforcement and Administration of Justice, *Task Force Report: The Police* (Washington, DC: U.S. Government Printing Office, 1967), 130.

10. Geoffrey P. Alpert and Roger G. Dunham, *Understanding Police Use of Force: Officers, Suspects, and Reciprocity* (New York: Cambridge University Press, 2004).

11. Robert Langworthy, Thomas Hughes, and Beth Sanders, *Law Enforcement Recruitment, Selection and Training* (Highland Heights, KY: Academy of Criminal Justice Sciences, 1995), 24.

12. Bureau of Justice Statistics, *Local Police Departments, 2013: Personnel, Policies, and Practices* (Washington, DC: U.S. Department of Justice, 2015), http://www.bjs.gov/content/pub/pdf/lpd13ppp.pdf.

13. David L. Carter, Allen D. Sapp, and Darrell W. Stephens, *The State of Police Education* (Washington, DC: Police Executive Research Forum, 1989), 84; Police Executive Research Forum, *Police Accountability—Findings and Implications of an Assessment of the San Diego Police Department* (Washington, DC: U.S. Department of Justice, 2015), 24–26, https://www.sandiego.gov/sites/default/files/legacy/police/pdf/perfrpt.pdf.

14. See the argument, based on the U.K. experience, for mandating higher education for police recruits: Steve Christopher, *Policing: A Journal of Policy and Practice* 9 (December 2015): 388–404; Michael Heidingsfield, "Six Reasons to Require College Education for Police Officers," *Subject to Debate* 9 (December 1995): 5–7.

15. U.S. Census Bureau, *Educational Attainment in the United States, 2015: Population Characteristics* (Washington, DC: U.S. Bureau of the Census, 2016), table 1, https://www.census.gov/content/dam/Census/library/publications/2016/demo/p20-578.pdf.

16. Ibid.

17. David L. Carter, Allen D. Sapp, and Darrel W. Stephens, "Higher Education as a Bona Fide Occupational Qualification (BFOQ) for Police: A Blueprint," *American Journal of Police* 7 (Fall 1988): 1–27; *Davis v. City of Dallas*, 777 F.2d 205 (5th Cir. 1985); David L. Carter and Allen D. Sapp, *Police Education and Minority Recruitment: The Impact of a College Requirement* (Washington, DC: PERF, 1991), 27.

18. Wesley G. Skogan and Kathleen Frydl, *Fairness and Effectiveness in Policing: The Evidence* (Washington, DC: National Academies Press, 2004), 139.

19. Michael D. White, "Identifying Good Cops Early: Predicting Recruit Performance in the Academy," *Police Quarterly* (2008): 27–49.

20. Griesinger et al., *Civil Service Systems*, 102.

21. Victor E. Kappler, "'Can You Become a Police Officer with a History of Drug Use?,'" *Police Studies Online* (January 15, 2013), http://plsonline.eku.edu/insidelook/can-you-become-police-officer-history-drug-use.

22. Dallas Police Department, "Disqualifying Factors," http://www.dallaspolice.net/joindpd/Pages/Disqualifying-Factors.aspx.

23. National Institute on Drug Abuse, *National Survey of Drug Use and Health: Trends in Prevalence of Various Drugs* (Washington, DC: Author, 2015), https://www.drugabuse.gov/national-survey-drug-use-health.

24. ACLU, *The War on Marijuana in Black and White* (New York: ACLU, 2013,

25. American Civil Liberties Union of Southern California, *From the Outside In: Residency Patterns within the Los Angeles Police Department* (Los Angeles: ACLU-Southern California, 1994), i.

26. President's Task Force on 21st Century Policing, *Final Report*, Recommendation 1.5.2., p. 10.

27. Batya Ungar-Srgon and Andrew Flowers, "Re-Examining Residency Requirements for Police Officers," http://fivethirtyeight.com/features/reexamining-residency-requirements-for-police-officers/.

28. Jeremy Wilson, Bernard Rostker, and Cha-Chi Fan, *Recruiting and Retaining America's Finest* (Santa Monica, CA: RAND Corporation, 2010).

29. M. Steven Meagher and Nancy Yentes, "Choosing a Career in Policing: A Comparison of Male and

Female Perceptions," *Journal of Police Science and Administration* 14, no. 4 (1986): 320–327; Virginia B. Ermer, "Recruitment of Female Police Officers in New York City," *Journal of Criminal Justice* 6, no. 3 (Fall 1978): 233–246.

30. Nicholas Alex, *New York Cops Talk Back* (New York: John Wiley, 1976), 9.

31. Griesinger et al., *Civil Service Systems*; Samuel Walker, *Police Union Contract "Waiting Periods" for Misconduct Investigations Not Supported by Scientific Evidence* (July 1, 2015), http://samuelwalker.net/wp-content/uploads/2015/06/48HourSciencepdf.pdf; Campaign Zero, *We Can End Police Violence in America* (2015), http://www.joincampaignzero.org/#vision.

32. Ermer, "Recruitment of Female Police Officers"; James Q. Wilson, "Generational and Ethnic Differences among Career Police Officers," *American Journal of Sociology* 69 (March 1964): 526.

33. David H. Bayley and Harold Mendelsohn, *Minorities and the Police*: Confrontation in America (New York: Free Press, 1969), 30.

34. David M. Kennedy, *Don't Shoot: One Man, A Street Fellowship, and the End of Violence in Inner-City America* (New York: Bloomsbury, 2011), "Across the Race Divide," 124–155.

35. Robert J. Kaminski, "Police Minority Recruitment: Predicting Who Will Say Yes to an Offer for a Job as a Cop," *Journal of Criminal Justice* 21 (1993): 395–409.

36. American Civil Liberties Union, *The War on Marijuana in Black and White* (New York: ACLU, 2013). https://www.aclu.org/sites/default/files/field_document/1114413-mj-report-rfs-rel1.pdf.

37. Susan E. Martin, *On the Move: The Status of Women in Policing* (Washington, DC: Police Foundation, 1990).

38. Bureau of Justice Statistics, *Local Police Departments, 2007* (Washington, DC: U.S. Government Printing Office, 2010).

39. Bernard Cohen, "Minority Retention in the New York City Police Department: A Policy Study," *Criminology* 11 (November 1973): 287–306.

40. Langworthy, Hughes, and Sanders, *Law Enforcement Recruitment, Selection and Training*, 27.

41. William G. Doerner, "The Utility of the Oral Interview Board in Selecting Police Academy Admissions," *Policing* 20, no. 4 (1997): 784.

42. Police Executive Research Forum, *Police Accountability—Findings and National*

Implications of an Assessment of the San Diego Police Department (Washington, DC: U.S. Department of Justice, 2013), 27–29.

43. Anthony V. Bouza, "The Policeman's Character Investigation: Lowered Standards or Changing Times?" *Journal of Criminal Law, Criminology, and Police Science* 63 (March 1972): 120–124.

44. "D.C. Police Force Still Paying for Two-Year Hiring Spree," *Washington Post*, August 28, 1994.

45. Robert Faturechi and Ben Poston, "Sheriff's Department Hired Officers with Histories of Misconduct," *Los Angeles Times*, December 1, 2013, http://graphics.latimes.com/behind-the-badge/.

46. Bernard Cohen and Jan M. Chaiken, *Police Background Characteristics and Performance* (Lexington, MA: Lexington Books, 1973), 87, 90–91.

47. J. Douglas Grant and Joan Grant, "Officer Selection and the Prevention of Abuse of Force," in W. A. Geller and H. Toch, eds., *And Justice for All* (Washington, DC: Police Executive Research Forum, 1995), 161–162.

48. Benjamin S. Wright, William G. Doerner, and John C. Speir, "Pre-employment Psychological Testing as a Predictor of Police Performance during an FTO Program," *American Journal of Police* IX, no. 4 (1990): 65–84.

49. Christopher Commission, *Report of the Independent Commission on the Los Angeles Police Department* (Los Angeles: The Christopher Commission, 2001), 110.

50. National Advisory Commission on Civil Disorders, *Report* (New York: Bantam Books, 1968), 315–317; President's Task Force on 21st Century Policing, *Final Report*, Recommendation 1.8; Commission on Accreditation of Law Enforcement Agencies, *Standards for Law Enforcement Agencies*, 4th ed. (Fairfax, VA: Author, 1998), Standard 31.2.1, www.calea.org.

51. Paula N. Rubin, *The Americans with Disabilities Act and Criminal Justice: An Overview* (Washington, DC: U.S. Government Printing Office, 1993), https://www.ncjrs.gov/txtfiles/adae.txt.

52. Ibid., 102.

53. *Davis v. City of Dallas*, 777 F.2d 205 (1985).

54. David Alan Sklansky, "Not Your Father's Police Department: Making Sense of the New Demographics of Law Enforcement," *Journal of Criminal Law and Criminology* 96 (Spring 2006): 1209–1213.

55. Bureau of Justice Statistics, *Local Police Departments, 2013*, table 5; Bureau of Justice Statistics, *Police Departments in Large Cities, 1990–2000* (Washington, DC: U.S. Department of Justice, 2002).

56. William G. Lewis, "Toward a Representative Bureaucracy," *Public Administration Review* 49 (May–June 1989): 257–267.

57. Leigh Herbst and Samuel Walker, "Language Barriers in the Delivery of Police Services," *Journal of Criminal Justice* 29 (July 2001): 1–12.

58. State of Washington, WAC 162-16-240, http://apps.leg.wa.gov/WAC/default.aspx?cite=162-16-240.

59. Tamar Hosansky and Pat Sparling, *Working Vice: The True Story of Lt. Lucie Duvall—America's First Woman Vice Squad Chief* (New York: Harper Paperbacks, 1993).

60. National Center for Women and Policing, *Equality Denied: The Status of Women in Policing* (Los Angeles: National Center for Women and Policing, 1998), www.womenandpolicing.org.

61. Walker, *A Critical History of Police Reform,* 84–94; Samuel Walker, *Popular Justice: A History of American Criminal Justice,* 2nd ed. (New York: Oxford University Press, 1998), 135–137, 170–174.

62. Bureau of Justice Statistics, *Local Police Departments, 2013*, table 4.

63. National Center on Women and Policing, *Equality Denied.*

64. James R. Lasley, James Larson, Chandrika Kelso, and Gregory Chris Brown, "Assessing the Long-term Effects of Officer Race on Police Attitudes towards the Community: A Case for Representative Bureaucracy Theory," *Police Practice and Research* 12 (December 2011): 474–491.

65. U.S. Equal Employment Opportunity Commission, *Affirmative Action and Equal Employment*, vol. 1 (Washington, DC: U.S. Government Printing Office, 1974), 23.

66. David L. Carter, Allen D. Sapp, and Darrel W. Stephens, *The State of Police Education* (Washington, DC: Police Executive Research Forum, 1988).

67. "D.C. Police Force Paying for Two-Year Hiring Spree," *Washington Post,* August 18, 1994; follow-up story: "District Police Are Still Paying for Forced Hiring Binge," *Washington Post,* December 20, 2013, https://www.washingtonpost.com/local/district-police-are-still-paying-for-forced-hiring-binge/2013/12/20/7e313a4e-69c4-11e3-ae56-22de072140a2_story.html.

68. Martin, *On the Move*, 39.

69. Jihong Zhao and Nicholas Lovrich, "Determinants of Minority Employment in American Municipal Police Agencies: The Representation of African American Officers," *Journal of Criminal Justice* 26, no. 4 (1998): 267–278.

70. *Fisher v. University of Texas at Austin*, ___ U.S. ___ (2016).

71. Police Executive Research Forum, *Re-Engineering Training on Police Use of Force*, 10, 53.

72. Wesley G. Maarten Skogan, Maarten Van Craen, and Cari Hennesey, "Training Police for Procedural Justice, *Journal of Experimental Criminology* (September 2015): 319–334.

73. President's Task Force on 21st Century Policing, *Final Report*, 11–12; Rahr and Rice, *From Warriors to Guardians.*

74. Rahr and Rice, *From Warriors to Guardians*, 8.

75. Police Executive Research Forum, *Re-Engineering Training of Police Use of Forc*e, 59.

76. The new thinking about training is best summed up in Police Executive Research Forum, *Re-Engineering Training on Police Use of Force.*

77. Thomas M. Frost and Magnus J. Seng, "Police Entry-Level Curriculum: A Thirty Year Perspective," *Journal of Police Science and Administration* 12 (March 1984): 66–73.

78. President's Commission on Law Enforcement and the Administration of Justice, *Task Force Report: The Police* (Washington, DC: U.S. Government Printing Office, 1967).

79. Bureau of Justice Statistics, *State and Local Law Enforcement Training Academies, 2006* (Washington, DC: U.S. Department of Justice, 2009), table 15, http://www.bjs.gov/content/pub/pdf/slleta06.pdf.

80. George Fachner and Steven Carter, *An Assessment of Deadly Force in the Philadelphia Police Department* (Washington, DC: U.S. Department of Justice, 2015).

81. Fachner and Carter, *An Assessment of Deadly Force in the Philadelphia Police Department,* 57–60, 67–69.

82. Ibid., Finding 19, p. 73. Philadelphia Police Department, Reform Implementation Matrix (no date). Accessed October 12, 2016. https://www.phillypolice.com/assets/directives/CNAPTFnocostpdf.pdf,

83. Police Executive Research Forum, *Re-Engineering Training on Police Use of Force*, 51.

84. Ibid., 11.

85. Seattle Police Department, Policy Manual, Policy 8.000, Use of Force, http://www.seattle.gov/police/compliance/finished_policy/Use_of_Force_Policy_11_27_2013.pdf.

86. President's Task Force on 21st Century Policing, *Final Report*, Action Item 2.2.1.

87. Christy Lopez, *Disorderly (Mis)Conduct: The Problem with "Contempt of Cop" Arrests* (Washington, DC: American Constitution Society, 1910), https://www.acslaw.org/sites/default/files/Lopez_Contempt_of_Cop.pdf.

88. Pontillo, quoted in Police Executive Research Forum, *Re-Engineering Training of Police Use of Force,* 51.

89. Los Angeles Police Commission, Office of the Inspector General, *Ten Year Overview of Categorical Use of Force Investigations, Policy, and Training* (Los Angeles: Office of the Inspector General, March 10, 2016), 1, 13–14, http://media.wix.com/ugd/b2dd23_3139a5342cc34ce2860af7536887f149.pdf.

90. Police Executive Research Forum, *Re-Engineering Training on Police Use of Force,* 17 (Lanier); 52–53 (LAPD).

91. Police Executive Research Forum, *Re-Engineering Training on Police Use of Force*, 53.

92. Fachner and Carter, *An Assessment of Deadly Force in the Philadelphia Police Department*, 5.

93. Police Executive Research Forum, *Re-Engineering Training on Police Use of Force*, 38, 54–55.

94. New York City Police Department, *Second Report of the Independent Monitor* [re: *Floyd v. City of New York*] (February 16, 2016), 39, http://nypdmonitor.org/wp-content/uploads/2016/02/2016-02-16FloydvCityofNY-MonitorsSecondStatusReport.pdf.

95. Police Executive Research Forum, *Re-Engineering Training on Police Use of Force*, 4.

96. James K. Stewart, et al., *A Review of Officer-Involved Shootings in the Las Vegas Metropolitan Police Department* (Washington, DC: U.S. Department of Justice, 2012), 72.

97. Fachner and Carter, *An Assessment of Deadly Force in the Philadelphia Police Department*, 68, 73.

98. *City of Canton, Ohio v. Harris,* 489 U.S. 378 (1989).

99. *Floyd, et al., v. City of New York*, Opinion and Order, p. 100.

100. Police Executive Research Forum, *Re-Engineering Training of Police Use of Force*, 37–38; Fair and Impartial Policing Project website at http://www.fairimpartialpolicing.com/.

101. President's Task Force on 21st Century Policing, *Final Report,* 9.

102. Tom Tyler, *Why People Obey the Law* (New Haven: Yale University Press, 1990).

103. Bureau of Justice Statistics, *State and Local Law Enforcement Training Academies*, 2006, table 10.

104. Michael S. Campbell, *Field Training for Police Officers: State of the Art* (Washington DC: U.S. Government Printing Office, 1986).

105. Fachner and Carter, *An Assessment of Deadly Force in the Philadelphia Police Department*, 5, 80–81.

106. William G. Doerner and E. Britt Patterson, "The Influence of Race and Gender upon Rookie Evaluations of Their Field Training Officers," *American Journal of Police* XI, no. 2 (1992): 23–36.

107. CA.gov, Commission on Peace Officer Standards and Training, "Perishable Skills Program," https://post.ca.gov/perishable-skills-program.aspx.

108. Stewart et al., *A Review of Officer-Involved Shootings*, 28, 68.

109. Police Executive Research Forum, *Re-Engineering Training of Police Use of Force*, 52–53.

110. Ibid., 55–57.

111. Langworthy, Hughes, and Sanders, *Law Enforcement Recruitment, Selection, and Training*, 39.

112. Bureau of Justice Statistics, *Local Police Departments, 2013*, table 8.

113. Martin, *On the Move*, 131–132.

114. Philadelphia Police Study Task Force, *Philadelphia and Its Police: Toward a New Partnership* (Philadelphia: City of Philadelphia, 1986), 94.

© Hill Street Studios/Blend Images LLC

6

Police Officers II: On the Job

CHAPTER OUTLINE

Introduction

Reality Shock: Beginning Police Work

Encountering Citizens

Encountering the Criminal Justice System

Encountering the Department

Starting Out on the Job

Impact of the Seniority System

The Concept of a Unique Police Subculture

The Original Concept

The Capacity to Use Force as a Defining Feature of Policing

The Dangers of Policing: Potential versus Actual

Conflicting Work Demands

New Perspectives on a Complex and Changing Police Subculture

The Changing Rank and File: The Impact of Diversity

The Impact of Women Police Officers on the Police Subculture

Women Officers on Patrol Duty

Female versus Male Officers: Differences in Misconduct Issues?

Sexual Harassment on the Job

African American Officers

African American Officers on the Job

Hispanic Officers

Gay and Lesbian Officers

The Intersection of Gender, Race, Ethnicity, and Sexual Identity

Does Diversifying a Department Change the Police Subculture?

Rising Levels of Police Officer Education

Cohort Effects on Performance

Organizational Effects on Attitudes and Performance

Attitudes toward Community Policing

The Relationship between Attitudes and Behavior

Styles of Police Work

Moving through Police Careers

Salaries and Benefits

Career Development

Promotion

Assignment to Special Units

Lateral Entry

Outside Employment

Performance Evaluations

Traditional Performance Evaluations

Problems with Performance Evaluations

Job Satisfaction and Job Stress

The Sources of Job Satisfaction

The Sources of Job Stress

Job Stress and Suicide

Community Policing and Job Satisfaction

Coping with Job Stress

The Rights of Police Officers

Turnover: Leaving Police Work

Decertification

Summary

Key Terms

For Discussion

Internet Exercise

Introduction

After completing the probationary period, a police officer becomes a full-fledged sworn officer and begins a career. Many factors influence the course of an officer's career. Some officers are promoted, whereas others remain at the rank of police officer for their entire careers. Some quit, and some are fired. Officers' attitudes about the job, the profession, the department, and citizens often change over time. Exhibit 6–1 indicates some of the major events in the life course of a hypothetical police officer. This chapter examines the experience of being on the job as a police officer.

EXHIBIT 6–1

Hypothetical Life Course Events in the Career of a Police Officer

Moving from civilian to recruit

Moving from recruit to officer

Changing patrol shift and area

Moving from patrol to detective

Promotion to sergeant, patrol

Assignment to internal affairs as sergeant

Promotion to lieutenant, patrol

Assignment to public information office

Outside employment in private security

Retirement

Second job in private security

Source: Adapted, with modifications, from Dennis P. Rosenbaum, Arnie M. Schuck, and Gary Cordner, *The National Police Research Platform: The Life Course of New Officers.* (n.d.), https://www.hsdl.org/?view&did=687727.

Reality Shock: Beginning Police Work

reality shock

The first weeks and months on the job for a new police officer are often a rude awakening. In his classic study of the police subculture, William Westley calls the experience **reality shock.**[1] The new officer quickly encounters the unpleasant aspects of dealing with the public, the criminal justice system, and the department.

Encountering Citizens

Police officer attitudes toward the public change significantly during the first weeks and months on the job. McNamara found that the percentage of officers agreeing with the statement "Patrolmen almost never receive the cooperation from the public that is needed to handle police work properly" rose from 35 percent at the beginning of police academy training to 50 percent after two years on the job.[2] A later study found similar changes in attitudes occurred among new Detroit police officers. After four months on the job, officers gave substantially lower ranking to the importance of "listening attentively when the victim expresses feelings or emotions."[3] Changes

hostility from citizens

in officers' attitudes are partly the result of encountering **hostility from citizens.** As we learned in Chapter 5, most officers enter law enforcement because they want to work with people and help the community, so it is a shock to find that some people do not want their services. Even though encountering citizen hostility is statistically an infrequent event, officers tend to remember the unpleasant experiences. Research consistently finds that officers use force in only about 1 to 2 percent of all encounters with people.[4] But they are difficult, stressful, and dangerous events that stay in the officer's mind. Police officers are no different from other people in this regard. Recalling unpleasant or traumatic experiences is a phenomenon common to all people.[5]

Officers particularly resent official complaints filed by citizens, which are then investigated by the department's internal affairs unit or an external citizen oversight agency. A citizen complaint questions an officer's conduct, alleging that he or she did something improper. The investigation of complaints often compounds officers' feelings of resentment. A study by the Denver Office of the Independent Monitor (OIM) found that officers resent the process of complaint investigations: being accused of misconduct and having their statements challenged by the investigators, who are fellow officers. After the OIM instituted reforms in the investigation process, officer satisfaction with the process rose from 12 to 34 percent. Even more dramatically, the percentage of officers reporting that the information they provided to investigators was taken seriously rose from 24 to 78 percent.[6]

Officers also react to being stereotyped by people who react to their uniform, badge, and gun, rather than to them as individuals. As is the case with racial stereotyping, people find it unpleasant to be treated as a category rather than as an individual. Additionally, many citizens feel uncomfortable around a person with arrest powers. To avoid these reactions, police officers tend to socialize primarily with other officers, thereby increasing their isolation from the public.[7]

Police officer attitudes also change because they perform society's "dirty work," handling unpleasant tasks that no one else wants to perform or is able to handle. The police see humanity at its worst. They are the first people to find the murder victim or the victim of rape, domestic violence, or child abuse. In one study, for example, officers ranked dealing with an abused child as the most stressful kind of situation they encounter.[8] These experiences accumulate over time and eventually give officers a very cynical view of humanity, thinking that many if not most people are capable of doing terrible things.

When police officers refer to "the public," they refer not just to people they encounter on the job but also to the news media and elected officials. Officers are generally unhappy with the news media, seeing it emphasizing the negative aspects of policing and ignoring the positive aspects. The media focus on dramatic "news-worthy" events: the officer-involved shooting, the excessive force allegation, and so on. The routine disorder call—a bar fight, a minor domestic violence incident—where the officer successfully restores order is not "news."

Police officers also believe that elected officials ("politicians") do not adequately support them. Mayors and city councils, they believe, do not provide adequate budgets for salaries and new equipment. In most cities, they see certain officials try to gain political advantage by criticizing the police for failing to control crime or for incidents of officer use of excessive force.

Encountering the Criminal Justice System

A second shock for new officers involves learning about the criminal justice system. Police officers are **criminal justice system insiders,** who see firsthand how the system works. They see arrest charges dismissed or serious crimes plea-bargained to lesser offenses. They see incompetent prosecutors, defense attorneys, and judges. As a result, many become cynical about the ability of the system to be fair and effective. Generally, police officers believe that the courts are too lenient.[9] A survey of officers in Washington, D.C., found that only 27 percent expressed trust in the courts, compared with 63 percent who expressed trust in their department commanders.[10]

Officers also often feel that lawyers and judges do not respect them. When they testify in court, defense attorneys challenge the quality of their work, particularly with regard to how evidence or confessions were obtained. When judges exclude evidence or confessions they have obtained, officers tend to take it personally.[11]

criminal justice system insiders

Encountering the Department

When researchers asked New York City police officers what they disliked about being a cop, most cited aspects of their own departments, not hostility from citizens. The most frequently mentioned problem was that the leadership of their department "doesn't care" about them, followed by "precinct-level supervisors." "Lack of respect from the public" was third in this survey.[12] When the National Police Research Platform asked new officers who had been on the job for five months to indicate the sources of stress they experienced, danger on the streets ranked first, not surprisingly, but department-related factors ranked second and third (work schedule, report writing) and then sixth and seventh (supervisors, department rules) (see Exhibit 6–2). Feelings of alienation or even anger at top officials among low-ranking employees is common in virtually all organizations. It is particularly strong in police organizations, however, and is one of the main reasons why officers organized police unions.

Reasons for officer dissatisfaction with how they are treated by their own departments include the following: not feeling that their work is appreciated; not being

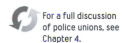

For a full discussion of police unions, see Chapter 4.

E X H I B I T   6–2

Sources of Police Officer Stress

Score: 0 (no stress) to 100 (high stress)

Danger on the streets	49.3
Work schedule	40.9
Report writing	36.7
Balancing act	34.8
Interacting with citizens	26.5
Supervisors	26.0
Department rules	23.7
Coworkers	22.6

Source: Peter Finn and Julie Esselman Tonz, *Developing a Law Enforcement Stress Program for Officers and Their Families* (Washington, DC: Department of Justice, 1997).

consulted on matters of police policy; feeling that assignments are arbitrary or based on personal favoritism; feeling that some assignments are punitive or discriminatory; and feeling that internal affairs investigations are often "head-hunting" operations, in which investigators are out to get them. Conflicts exist between the rank and file and management in all organizations. A study of Washington, D.C., police officers found that although 82 percent were satisfied with their jobs and 87 percent expressed trust in their fellow officers, only 63 percent trusted their commanders and 51 percent expressed trust in the chief of police.[13]

In response to this problem, the President's Task Force on 21st Century Policing recommended that police departments apply the principles of procedural justice to internal police management issues. In routine police work, procedural justice involves treating people on the street with respect, for example, by explaining why they have been stopped, allowing them to ask questions, and then answering those questions. To promote internal procedural justice, the President's Task Force recommended that departments "should involve employees in the process of developing policies and procedures."[14]

Does internal procedural justice work, or is it just a nice-sounding theory? Procedural justice is still a new idea, but a study among officers in the Buenos Aires Metropolitan Police (which has a different history and culture from police departments in the United States) found that internal procedural justice enhances officer compliance with department rules and regulations. The "perceptions of fair treatment by supervisors and trust in supervisors," the study found, "are positively associated with compliance with department rules."[15]

Starting Out on the Job

Impact of the Seniority System

When new officers first take to the streets, they are typically assigned to patrol duty, usually in high-crime areas and on the evening shift. Assignments in most police departments are governed by union contract provisions that use a **seniority system.**

seniority system

Officers with greater seniority who do not get a preferred special assignment (for example, criminal investigation, traffic) typically request day-shift patrol in a low-crime precinct. This generalization does not apply to all officers, however. Some officers with seniority seek out higher crime neighborhoods because they enjoy the activity and excitement of "busy" shifts and areas. For the most part, however, new officers are given the least desirable assignments. Many experts argue that it is unwise to assign the least experienced officers to areas with the highest crime rates where use of force, including deadly force, is far more likely to occur.[16]

The different shifts have significant effects on officers' personal lives. The evening shift (shifts have a variety of names in different departments: "A," "B," "C," or "Morning," "Day," "Evening"), typically 4 P.M. to midnight, is the most disruptive to family life, since an officer is not home when his or her children are home from school. It is also the busiest shift in terms of crime and disorder. The early or morning shift, typically midnight to 8 A.M., by contrast, allows an officer to be home with family in the afternoons and evening. It is also a mixed period in terms of workload. Calls for service remain relatively high until about 2 or 3 A.M. before dropping significantly. Day shift, typically 8 A.M. to 4 P.M., resembles the standard work day for most people. It also has fewer violent crimes and serious disorders than does the 4 P.M. to midnight shift.

The seniority principle has both good and bad points. On the positive side, it eliminates favoritism and discrimination. In the 1960s, for example, a study for the President's Crime Commission found that "slum precinct stations, not unlike slum schools, collect the rejects" among police officers.[17] On the negative side, it means that the least experienced officers get the most difficult assignments: patrolling the highest-crime neighborhoods on the busiest shift with the most crime and calls for service. A related consequence is that in departments that have significantly improved their personnel standards, the younger officers are likely to be better qualified and better trained for such work than the older officers. At the same time, in departments that have recently hired significant numbers of officers of color and female officers, those officers will be disproportionately represented in the least desirable assignments.[18]

A number of departments now use 10-hour or 12-hour shifts. Common sense suggests that if an 8-hour shift is stressful for police officers, a longer shift would only aggravate the problem. Fatigue in the additional hours could result in faulty judgment in driving, firing a weapon, or maintaining composure during a high-stress

SIDEBAR 6–1

Issue for Discussion: The Impact of the Seniority System

The seniority system means that rookie officers will generally be assigned to patrol in the highest-crime neighborhoods during the busiest shift (usually 4 P.M. to midnight) when most of the serious crime occurs.

1. Is this a good system for assigning officers? Does it result in the best police service in those times and places that demand the most skill?

2. Discuss the major drawbacks to this system. Can you devise an alternative system?

911 call. An evaluation of different length shifts, however, found no fatigue or judgment problems with 10-hour shifts, but there were some with 12-hour shifts, particularly increased levels of sleepiness and lower levels of alertness.[19]

The Concept of a Unique Police Subculture

Is there a unique police subculture? Is there a set of attitudes and behaviors among police officers that is significantly different from those in other occupations? This section reviews the original concept of a police subculture and then examines recent criticisms of that concept.

The Original Concept

police subculture

William Westley tells a poignant and revealing story about his pioneering research on the **police subculture.** When his interviews in the Gary, Indiana, police department began to touch on a particularly sensitive subject, the officers stopped talking to him. Eventually, he explained to a sergeant that his academic career would be ruined if he could not complete his research. The sergeant then "gave the officers hell" for not helping him, and immediately afterward they were extremely cooperative. Westley's experience illuminates two aspects of the police subculture: on the one hand, an attitude of secrecy toward outsiders studying the department, and on the other hand, a genuine eagerness to help someone having difficulty with an assignment.[20]

For a full discussion of the warriors versus guardians issue, see Chapter 5.

    Westley's study approached the police from the perspective of occupational sociology, seeking "to isolate and identify the major social norms governing police conduct, and to describe the way in which they influence police action in specific situations."[21] He concluded that a distinct subculture exists among police officers, emphasizing secrecy, solidarity, and violence. In his view, police officers view the public as the "enemy" and believe that they are justified in lying to protect other officers from criticism by citizens, and also in using force against citizens. Sue Rahr and Stephen K. Rice's influential 2015 article on warriors versus guardians argues that the "us versus them" mentality continues today in the warrior mentality.[22]

    Selective contact with the public, Westley argues, is a major influence on the police subculture. Police officers do society's dirty work, handling the unpleasant, difficult, and sometimes dangerous tasks that other agencies cannot handle. Officers do not often meet the average person in a routine setting. Instead, they deal with people with problems: crime victims, criminal offenders, the drunk and disorderly, people in domestic violence incidents, drivers in traffic stops, and so on. Many of these people resent the police officer's presence. A small percentage resist the officer, and the officer needs to use force.[23] In short, officers get a heavy dose of unpleasant encounters with people, and they begin to stereotype people and to see hostility where it does not exist. In this context, Westley continues, officers believe they can rely only on their fellow officers in times of crisis. Among the officers he interviewed, 73 percent thought citizens were hostile to the police.[24] That figure does not reflect actual behavior toward the police, however. Research found that people voluntarily comply with police requests (to stop what they are doing; to leave the premises, for example) in 78 percent of all encounters.[25] In short, police officer perceptions are not in accord with the reality of citizen attitudes and behavior.

Hostility to the public encourages a strong sense of **group solidarity.** As an officer in Washington, D.C., explains, "I've been working with my partner now for two and one-half years. I think I know more about him than his wife does. . . . He knows everything about me: I think you get a certain relationship when you work together with a partner."[26] Group solidarity, of course, exists in all professions and workplaces. Policing is somewhat different, however. The very nature of police work—working closely together, often spending long hours together in a patrol car, facing the same uncertainties and danger—fosters a very strong sense of group solidarity.

group solidarity

Secrecy, Westley continues, serves "as a shield against the attacks of the outside world." Secrecy, in turn, justifies lying. Westley asked officers if they would report a fellow officer who took money from a person arrested for drunkenness. A total of 73 percent said they would not. Westley concluded that most officers believed that "illegal action is preferable to breaking the secrecy of the group."[27] A national study by the Police Foundation found that over half (52.4 percent) of all officers agreed with the statement that "it is not unusual for a police officer to turn a blind eye to improper conduct by other officers."[28]

Secrecy is maintained by the **code of silence,** which involves not testifying against other officers accused of misconduct, for example, in a citizen complaint. The Christopher Commission, created after the highly publicized 1991 beating of Rodney King in Los Angeles, reported a Los Angeles police officer saying, "It is basically a non-written rule that you do not roll over, tell on your partner, your companion."[29] In the Police Foundation study, almost 17 percent believed that the "code of silence is an essential part" of good policing.[30] The 2016 report of the mayor's task force on police problems in Chicago found that the code of silence is a major obstacle to accountability, and that it is "not just an unwritten rule, or an unfortunate element of police culture past and present." It is reinforced by both police department rules and reinforced by police union contracts.[31] The code of silence is perhaps the most serious obstacle to police accountability and the reduction of both corruption and police use of excessive force (see Chapter 14).

code of silence

Westley also found that public hostility and group solidarity are used to justify violence against citizens. Officers feel a need to use force to maintain respect in encounters with citizens. More than a third of the officers (39 percent) surveyed by Westley thought that they were justified in using force when faced with citizen disrespect. Two-thirds of the officers (66 percent) gave some rationalization for the illegal use of force.[32] In the Police Foundation survey, about one-quarter (24.5 percent) of all officers agreed that "it is sometimes acceptable to use more force than is legally allowable to control someone who physically assaults an officer."[33]

Jerome Skolnick expands on Westley's concept of a police subculture in his classic study, *Justice Without Trial*. He found that police officers develop a "working personality" shaped by two aspects of the police role: danger and authority. Because the potential for danger is an ever-present feature of police work, officers become routinely suspicious of all people. Officers develop a "perceptual shorthand" of visual cues associated with people who they believe are criminals or are potentially dangerous. These visual cues include race, ethnicity, gender, age, apparent income level, and styles of clothing. The cues become a form of stereotyping involving young low-income people of color.[34]

S I D E B A R   6–2

The Code of Silence in Operation

The pervasiveness of the code of silence is itself alarming. But what we found particularly troubling is that it often appears to be strongest where corruption is most frequent. This is because the loyalty ethic is particularly powerful in crime-ridden precincts where officers must depend upon each other for their safety each day—and where fear and alienation from the community are most rampant. Thus, the code of silence influences honest officers in the very precincts where their assistance is needed most.

The pervasiveness of the code of silence is bolstered by the grave consequences for violating it: Officers who report misconduct are ostracized and harassed, become targets of complaints and even physical threats, and are made to fear that they will be left alone on the streets in a time of crisis. This draconian enforcement of the code of silence fuels corruption because it makes corrupt cops feel protected and invulnerable. As former police officer Bernard Cawley testified at the public hearings:

Question: Were you ever afraid that one of your fellow officers might turn you in?
Answer: Never.
Question: Why not?
Answer: Because it was the Blue Wall of Silence. Cops don't tell on cops. And if they did tell on them, just say if a cop decided to tell on me, his career's ruined. He's going to be labeled as a rat. So if he's got fifteen more years to go on the job, he's going to be miserable because it follows you wherever you go.

Source: Excerpt from Mollen Commission, *Report of the Commission to Investigate Allegations of Police Corruption and the Anti-Corruption Procedures of the Police Department* (New York: Author, 1994). Available at www.parc.info.

The perceptual shorthand of young men of color, of course, is the basis for racial profiling, in which people are stopped by the police on the basis of their age, gender, and race or ethnicity, which officers believe fits the profile of criminal suspects, rather than on the basis of reasonable suspicion of criminal activity. There are several remedies for racial profiling and other improper uses of race or ethnicity in policing. The Police Executive Research Forum (PERF) issued a model policy, which says that the race or ethnicity of a person can be used only in combination with credible evidence (for example, height, weight, dress, grooming) that links a particular person to a specific crime.[35] The Fair and Impartial Policing project, meanwhile, provides training on unconscious bias, which seeks to help officers recognize deeply rooted cultural stereotypes that associate certain groups with criminal behavior.[36]

The Capacity to Use Force as a Defining Feature of Policing

The police are different from other professions. No other profession has the legal authority to use force against people, including both physical and deadly force. It is an awesome power, and it plays a major role in defining the police subculture. Egon Bittner, in a classic essay, argues that the **capacity to use force** is the defining feature of the police, distinguishing them from other occupations.[37] The power to arrest, to deprive people of their liberty, is also a form of coercive force. These powers are inherent in the police role and apply to every sworn officer. The uniform, the badge, and an officer's weapon are the convenient symbols of these unique powers.

capacity to use force

POLICE in FOCUS | The Brass Ceiling: Penny Harrington's Road to Police Chief

Penny Harrington made history in January 1985 when she was appointed chief of the Portland, Oregon, police department. There had been women chiefs of small-town departments before, but she was the first female chief of a big-city department. Portland had 940 sworn officers in 1985.

Harrington's career illuminated some important milestones in the history of women and policing. When she joined the Portland Police Bureau in 1964, she was assigned to the women's protective division, the only assignment open to female officers. Female recruits were required to have a college degree (Harrington graduated from Michigan State University), whereas males needed only a high school diploma. They were paid less than male officers and not issued regular uniforms. Protective division officers investigated only sex offenses and juvenile cases. In 1971, Portland finally eliminated the categories of "policewoman" and "policeman," creating a gender-neutral "police officer" category. Harrington was promoted to sergeant in 1972, and in 1975 she became the first female sergeant to supervise male patrol officers.

Source: Lynn Langton, *Women in Law Enforcement, 1987–2008* (Washington, DC: Bureau of Justice Statistics, 2010).

People are very much aware of the power of the police to use force. When an officer arrives at the scene of a disorder, for example, everyone there knows that he or she has the power to make an arrest or use physical force. An officer does not have to say anything to remind people of these powers. The uniform and the badge communicate the message. People respond to these symbols of the power to use force in different ways. Most people comply with an officer's suggestion or order to stop what they are doing or to leave the premises, in part because of their understanding that the officer has the power to use force or make an arrest. Some people, by contrast, react negatively to the symbols of power and challenge or resist the police officer. As police reform expert David Kennedy argues in his book *Don't Shoot,* a deep racial divide exists in African American neighborhoods because many people on the street bring to an encounter the community "narrative" about the history of police misconduct and bad police–community relations. They often react to an officer not as an individual or based on what he or she has done, but as a symbol of the inequalities in American society. The power of the police officer to use force is a symbol of the broader power of injustice in American society.[38]

The Dangers of Policing: Potential versus Actual

Police work is a dangerous occupation. The risk of being injured or killed in the line of duty is always present. Perhaps most important, the dangers of police work are fundamentally different from the risks in other occupations. In construction, coal mining, and firefighting, three dangerous occupations, injuries and deaths are the result of *accidents*. In policing, a large percentage of deaths and injuries are the result of *felonious assaults*.

Danger plays out in complex ways in the minds of police officers. Skolnick argues that the *potential* for danger, especially attacks by citizens, shapes the police subculture, shaping attitudes toward the public. In what Rahr and Rice have labeled the warrior mentality of policing, officers exaggerate the real risk of danger and

EXHIBIT 6–3

Officers Feloniously Killed in the Line of Duty, by Type of Incident, 2014

Type of Incident	Number of Deaths
Disturbance call	11
(bar fight, person with firearm, etc.)	(10)
(domestic disturbance)	(1)
Arrest situation	4
Investigation suspicious person/circumstance	7
Ambush	7
Investigative activity	5
Person with mental illness	3
Traffic pursuit/stop	9
Tactical situation (barricade, hostage, etc.)	4
Unprovoked attack	1
Total	51

Source: Federal Bureau of Investigation, *Law Enforcement Officers Killed or Assaulted, 2014* (Washington, DC: Author), table 21.

develop the habit of seeing it in many encounters where it does not exist. They further argue that the warrior mentality and the sense of omnipresent danger are exaggerated in traditional police academy training.[39] Occupational safety data show that police work is not the most dangerous occupation. In fact, measured in terms of felonious killings of police officers, police work has become much safer in the past several decades and is far safer than it was in the 1920s and 1930s. The number of felonious deaths fell from 134 in 1973 to 51 in 2014 (see Exhibit 6–3).[40]

Among the 51 officers feloniously killed in 2014 in the United States, 27 were employed by city police departments. All were male, with an average age of 39 and 13 years of law enforcement service. Forty-seven were white, and 2 were African American (given the FBI's data systems, it is likely that any Hispanic officers killed were classified as white). Disturbance calls accounted for the largest number of deaths, but only one was in a domestic disturbance. Nine were killed in traffic stops or pursuits. Various law enforcement activities (for example, investigating suspicious circumstances or persons, conducting surveillance or other investigations) accounted for a total of 23 deaths.[41]

Despite the inherent dangers of police work, policing is not the most dangerous job in terms of on-the-job deaths. Data from the Occupational Safety and Health Administration indicate that the death rates per 100,000 full-time equivalent (FTE) workers per industry are 116 for fishing-related industries, 91.9 for logging, 70.6 for aircraft pilots and flight engineers, 41.4 for farmers and ranchers, 32.4 for roofers, and only 18 for police and sheriff's patrol officers. Thus, on-the-job deaths for police officers are higher than the national average for all occupations (3.5 per 100,000) but considerably lower than for many other jobs. Deaths are only one part of the dangers of policing. There are also numerous assaults and injuries to officers. In 2014, 48,315 police officers were assaulted on the job and 13,654 (or 28.3 percent) of them were injured, according to the FBI.[42]

Historical Data on Officer Deaths

Policing is much safer than it was in the past, and the death rate (per 100,000) has fallen even further. There are no national data on the total number of police officers in the United States before the 1970s, so it is impossible to compute the death rates for earlier decades. For a class exercise, discuss the possible reasons for the decline in officer deaths.

Total Number of Officers Killed, All Causes (Including Accidental Deaths but Excluding Suicides), Selected Years

Year	Number of Officers
1925	246
1935	221
1945	113
1955	121
1965	138
1975	239
1985	176
1995	194
2005	163
2015	123

Source: National Law Enforcement Officers Memorial Fund, *Officer Deaths by Year* (April 2016), http://www.nleomf.org/facts/officer-fatalities-data/year.html.

Conflicting Work Demands

Police officers also face difficult conflicting demands regarding law and order. Skolnick, in *Justice Without Trial,* argues that officers are under pressure to "produce," meaning getting results through arrests and convictions. The law, however, limits police powers in order to protect the constitutional rights of individual citizens. Police officers cannot legally stop someone on the street without reasonable suspicion that the individual is committing or is about to commit a crime, and they cannot legally arrest someone without probable cause. The Fourth Amendment prohibits unreasonable searches and seizures. The Supreme Court in *Terry v. Ohio* has allowed frisks, a pat down of a person who has been stopped, but only to locate weapons so as to protect officer safety.[43] In fact, however, officers often violate these legal requirements. In Chapter 14 we will discuss the different accountability measures designed to end these abuses.

The result of this conflict is that officers feel pressured to evade or bend the rules to obtain physical evidence or confessions. The Police Foundation found that almost half (42.9 percent) of all officers agree that "always following the rules is not compatible with getting the job done." In his classic study, Herbert Packer defines the tension between the demand for results and the rule of law as a conflict between "crime control" values and "due process" values.[44] Historically, some departments, or some precinct commanders, have required officers to meet quotas in stops and/or arrests. In the highly publicized New York City stop and frisk controversy, there was evidence that officers were expected to meet certain quotas of stops.[45]

Quotas are a serious problem because they put pressure on police officers to stop or arrest people they otherwise would not. Understandably, officers deeply resent quotas because stops made without reasonable suspicion are illegal. New York state enacted a law prohibiting quotas, and the President's Task Force on 21st Century Policing recommended that both law enforcement agencies and local governments should "refrain from practices that require officers to issue a predetermined number of tickets, citations, arrests or summonses."[46]

New Perspectives on a Complex and Changing Police Subculture

The traditional concept of the police subculture as developed by Westley and Skolnick has come under serious criticism in recent years, and few experts believe that it adequately explains the complex world of police officers today. There are two main criticisms. First, some scholars argue that the traditional concept greatly oversimplified the work experience of police officers, giving too much emphasis to certain features and ignoring other important ones. Second, because of the entry of more African American, Hispanic, and female officers, and more recently, gay and lesbian officers, today's police departments are far more diverse than ever before. Officers now have a wider range of backgrounds and perspectives. Law professor David Sklansky argues that, as a result of these dramatic changes, "[p]olice officers are far less unified today and far less likely to have an us–them view of civilians."[47]

The most comprehensive critique of the traditional concept of a police subculture concept is Steve Herbert's ethnographic study of Los Angeles officers. He identified six factors that shape and help to explain police officer behavior:

1. *The law*: Even though officers exercise broad discretion (see Chapter 11), the law defines the boundaries of permissible actions.
2. *Bureaucratic control*: Officers do not act completely alone. They are subject to control by other members of the department and the criminal justice system bureaucracy: supervisors, defense attorneys, prosecutors, and judges.
3. *A culture of "adventure/machismo":* Herbert found that, in Los Angeles, officers put a high premium on active and aggressive police work. They respect other officers who have this style of work and do not respect more passive officers.
4. *Safety*: A concern for personal safety shapes how officers behave in different situations. This point is close to Skolnick's argument about how danger shapes the police subculture.
5. *Competence*: Officers take pride in their own competence and respect other officers they believe are competent. Having to call in officers from other units to help with calls (referred to as "dropping calls") is a sign of lack of competence.
6. *Morality*: Officers make moral judgments about people, and they regard some people as "good" and others as "bad." "Good" people (law-abiding crime victims, for example) deserve more respect and better treatment than "bad" people (drug dealers or prostitutes, for example).[48]

In short, police officers are subject to many different influences. Officers are people, and like people in other occupational settings, they respond differently to the same influences. On Herbert's point #2, for example, some officers will follow the rules more diligently than others. On point #3, some will be more adventuresome and active than others. And on point #6, officers differ on their moral judgment of drunk drivers, prostitutes, drug users, and so on. As a result, we should be skeptical of sweeping generalizations about the attitudes and behavior of police officers.

Herbert's main argument is that the traditional concept of the police subculture fails to take into account the complexity of the many different formal limits, informal influences, and pressures on police officers. Equally important, the traditional concept painted a negative image of policing (emphasizing secrecy, lying, and violence). The factors identified by Herbert are neutral and as a group represent a far more balanced view of the police (emphasizing competence and morality).

This is not to say that Westley and Skolnick were wrong about their basic points. A high degree of group solidarity exists among officers, along with a strong element of secrecy. Officers do lie, to the extent that there is even a term for it: "testilying."[49] The 2016 mayor's task force on police problems in Chicago concluded that officers involved in the highly controversial fatal shooting of Laquan McDonald, an unarmed African American, gave "remarkably similar reports" of the incident and also did so in other shooting incidents.[50] Herbert's view of the police subculture, however, is simply more balanced.

The Changing Rank and File: The Impact of Diversity

The original concept of a police subculture developed at a time in police history when rank-and-file officers were almost all white and male, and typically had only a high school education.[51] As we learned in Chapter 5, there has been significant progress in the employment of African American, Hispanic, and female officers. And as discussed shortly, the addition of openly gay and lesbian officers has added an additional element of diversity. We now look at the impact of this change on the police subculture. Robin Haarr argues that "the initial concept of a single, unified occupational culture is now being replaced by an alternative conceptualization of diversity, variation, and contrast within the police organization and occupation."[52]

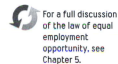 For a full discussion of the law of equal employment opportunity, see Chapter 5.

The Impact of Women Police Officers on the Police Subculture

Although women have made considerable progress in employment as police officers (see Chapter 5), they are still underrepresented in police departments relative to their presence in the workforce. The percentage of all sworn officers who are women increased from 2 percent in 1972, to 10.6 percent in 2000, to 12 percent in 2013 (but about 17 percent in big-city departments). The percentage of female officers is generally higher in large police departments, but it reaches 20 percent in only a few departments. Yet today women make up about 46 percent of the adult labor force.[53]

A report by the National Center for Women and Policing found a number of current barriers to the employment of women. Entrance examinations that emphasize upper-body physical strength favor men. There is no evidence, however, that great physical strength (as opposed to good health) affects an officer's ability to perform well, and experts today emphasize the importance of communication skills and social interaction skills in good policing. On-the-job discrimination, particularly sexual harassment and discriminatory assignments, either discourages women from applying or encourages them to resign their jobs. Many police departments, meanwhile, recruit heavily from the military, which is a male-dominated work environment. Finally, some police departments embrace an old-fashioned warrior culture of policing, emphasizing aggressiveness and authoritarianism, which is unappealing to many potential women applicants.[54]

Susan Martin found that the introduction of women into policing broke up the traditional solidarity of the work group. Women officers, for example, do not share the same outside interests as male officers: hunting, fishing, and cars. She also argues that policewomen "alter the rules of the game" of how to act as a police officer. Traditional masculine characteristics of not expressing emotion publicly and of settling disputes physically are no longer appropriate. (This aspect of police culture has begun to change. See the material on the open discussion of officer suicides later in this chapter.) Expressions of friendship, which were acceptable between two male officers, are problematic between officers of different sexes.[55]

Martin also found significant differences among the male officers, especially in terms of their attitudes toward women officers. The traditionals were committed to the image of policing as dangerous work involving aggressive action and requiring physical strength. The **moderns,** by contrast, accepted policewomen relatively easily, recognizing that police work rarely calls for physical strength and accepting the idea that job opportunities should be open to everyone on the basis of individual merit. The moderates were somewhere in between, with many accepting the idea of policewomen in principle but unhappy about women on patrol duty.[56] Martin's research highlighted the point that the original research on the police subculture failed to take into account important differences in attitudes among white male officers.

moderns

Women today have become more integrated into policing, but in recent years, however, the number of women in policing appears to be "stuck on a plateau," as Gary Cordner and AnnMarie Cordner put it in their study of Pennsylvania police departments. (Others refer to the persistent barrier to women in employment as the "glass ceiling.") They found that a relatively low number of women apply for police jobs, in part because of the perceived male-dominated culture of policing, and that recruitment standards have a disparate impact on women applicants, especially requirements requiring certain levels of strength.[57]

A number of women have served as chiefs of big-city police departments, and many serve in top command positions. Susan Ehrlich Martin and Nancy Jurik report that "the resistance faced by the first women on patrol was blatant, malicious, widespread, organized, and sometimes life-threatening." With the passage of time, the hostility has become less blatant and more subtle.[58]

Sexism continues to exist in many police departments. Carol Archbold and Dorothy Moses Schulz found that most (79 percent) of the female officers in one department felt they had to work harder than male officers. Most felt they had been treated differently and at some point had been treated like tokens. Nonetheless, the same percentage indicated they did not feel isolated on their jobs, and most

(64 percent) would recommend law enforcement as a career to other women. The remaining 36 percent said it would depend on the women involved. None of the female officers would *not* recommend law enforcement as a career.[59]

Women Officers on Patrol Duty

The major change in policing in the 1970s was the assignment of women officers to patrol duty. Previously, women had been confined to juvenile and vice units. Did the assignment of women to patrol make a difference in policing? Do female officers behave differently from male officers?

The Police Foundation conducted the first systematic study of female officers on routine patrol duty. Comparing 86 male and 86 female new officers, the study found that male and female officers performed in a generally similar manner. There were some slight differences in performance (for example, in arrest activity), but they were not significant. Female officers were less likely to engage in conduct unbecoming an officer. Most important, there were no observed incidents that cast doubt on the capacity of female officers to handle patrol duty.[60]

A similar study of patrol officers in New York City compared 41 male and 41 female new officers in 1975 and 1976. The female officers' style of police work was "almost indistinguishable" from that of male officers. Both used different verbal and nonverbal techniques to control situations at virtually identical rates. Particularly important, female officers used force at exactly the same rate as male officers. Although the female officers were "slightly less active" than the male officers, "civilians rated the female officers more competent, pleasant, and respectful."[61]

Female versus Male Officers: Differences in Misconduct Issues?

The National Center for Women in Policing made the bold claim that police departments should hire more women officers because "female officers are less likely to use excessive force."[62] Is this true? Does the evidence support this claim?

The NCWP argument was based on data from the Los Angeles Police Department (LAPD) indicating that male officers were much more likely to be "problem" officers. They cost the city $63.4 million in damage awards between 1990 and 1999, compared with only $2.8 million for female officers. Females represented 18 percent of the LAPD officers but were responsible for only 4.4 percent of the total damage awards. Kathy Spillar, then head of the Feminist Majority, cosponsor of the study, argues that "the single most fundamental reform that the LAPD could make would be to gender balance its police force."[63] The data used in this study, however, need to be interpreted with caution. From other cities there have been media reports on the "worst" officers, usually measured in terms of damage awards in civil suits. In virtually all cases, the officers involved were male. But this is a small and exclusive group. Studies of officer performance in a broad range of categories has not found significant differences in performance between male and female officers.

In the end, the data indicate that in terms of routine policing—day-to-day patrol, crime fighting, and order maintenance—there are no substantial differences between the performance of male and female officers. In this respect, the introduction of female officers has made some changes in the police subculture, but has not fundamentally changed policing on the street.

Sexual Harassment on the Job

The introduction of significant numbers of women police officers accentuated the problem of sexual harassment in police departments. **Sexual harassment** is defined as unwanted sexual advances; offensive, sexually related behavior such as suggesting a sexual affair or commenting on a female officer's body; or discrimination in assignments or promotion.

A 2011 report by the International Association of Chiefs of Police (IACP) titled *Addressing Sexual Offenses and Misconduct by Law Enforcement* covered both sexual offenses by officers against citizens (male officers using police authority to coerce sexual favors from women) and sexual harassment on the job among officers. The report grew out of a 2007 session at the IACP annual meeting in which it became clear that a number of police chiefs regarded these problems as serious. The report contained a set of recommendations to control sexual harassment. Recommendations included the following: (a) having a clear policy prohibiting sexual harassment; (b) training on ethical issues related to policing (including the full range of ethical issues such as corruption and lying); (c) implementing performance review systems, such as early intervention systems (see Chapter 14) to identify patterns of misconduct among officers; and (d) thorough investigations of misconduct.[64]

How do female officers respond to sexual harassment incidents? In interviews with 117 female officers, Somvadee Chaiyavej and Merry Morash found that only 19 percent reported the incidents to an authority. The most common responses were "hinting dissatisfaction" (mentioned by 61 percent), deflecting the offensive behavior (57 percent), or directly protesting to the offending person (52 percent) (Respondents could answer more than one response, so the totals do not add up to 100 percent).[65]

One reason victims of sexual harassment typically do not file complaints is that many female officers believe that departments would not take them seriously and, therefore, fail to investigate complaints and discipline guilty officers. In response to a series of sexual harassment lawsuits, the Los Angeles Sheriff's Department revised its policies and practices. A subsequent investigation found that, as a result, the department was responding more quickly to allegations, conducting speedier and more thorough investigations, and had ended its practice of imposing only lenient discipline on officers found guilty of harassment.[66]

To develop more systematic national data on the prevalence of sexual harassment, the President's Task Force on 21st Century Policing recommended that the Bureau of Justice Statistics Police-Public Contact Survey include questions on sexual harassment by law enforcement officers, and also that the Centers for Disease Control and Prevention add similar questions to its National Intimate Partner and Sexual Violence Survey.[67]

African American Officers

In a remarkable break with the norm of group solidarity in the traditional police subculture, the National Black Police Association (NBPA) published a pamphlet on police brutality, urging officers to report misconduct by other officers. An officer who witnesses brutality, it argued, should "report the incident to your supervisor, whether or not he/she is supportive." No other police officer organization had ever urged its officers to report misconduct.[68] A Police Foundation study of officer attitudes about police abuse of authority found a striking difference between the perceptions of white and African American officers, with African Americans far more likely to see patterns of misconduct in their departments.[69] In this respect, the increased number of African American officers has changed the police subculture by bringing in different perspectives and ideas about policing and good police–community relations.

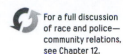 For a full discussion of race and police—community relations, see Chapter 12.

In many, if not most, of the larger police departments, there are separate organizations of the African American officers. They are social groups and are separate from the police union (where one exists), which is the recognized collective bargaining agent for all officers. In addition to the NBPA, there is also the National Organization of Black Law Enforcement Executives (NOBLE), representing African American chiefs and command-level officers.[70]

African American Officers on the Job

Are there significant differences in the behavior of African American officers and white officers? Civil rights leaders have always urged police departments to hire more African American and Hispanic officers as a way to improve police–community relations. They argue that these officers will have more rapport with the African American community and will not discriminate in arrests or other police actions.[71] Does the evidence support this argument? Do racial and ethnic minority officers police differently from white officers?

In terms of performance on the street, there appears to be no significant difference between African American and other police officers. Albert Reiss found no significant differences in the use of force by white and African American officers.[72] Similarly, official data on citizen complaints in New York City and San Jose indicate that white, African American, and Hispanic officers receive complaints in proportion to their presence in a police department.[73] On the critical issue of deadly force, James J. Fyfe found that, after controlling for place of assignment, white and African American officers fired their weapons at the same rates. The most powerful predictor of use of deadly force was the nature of the precinct where officers were assigned. Not surprisingly, officers assigned to high-crime precincts in New York City used deadly force more frequently than those assigned to low-crime precincts. Within each type of precinct, white and black officers used deadly force at essentially the same rates.[74]

Hispanic Officers

The employment of Hispanic Americans in policing has been increasing significantly in recent years. The Hispanic community in America is diverse, in terms of length of residency in the United States (some families have been in the United States for many generations), immigration, country of origin, and self-identity. These same differences are found among Hispanic police officers. Dawn Irlbeck interviewed all of the Hispanic officers in one midwestern police department and found complex patterns of identity. A few identified themselves entirely as police officers, whereas many had dual identities as both police officers and members of the Hispanic community. None, however, identified completely with the Hispanic community. Those who had dual identities used their identification with and knowledge about the Hispanic community as a guide and resource in their police work. This did not involve leniency toward Hispanic offenders, however.[75]

In a number of departments today, Hispanic officers are the majority, as is the case with African American officers in some departments. Unfortunately, no studies have systematically compared the behavior of Hispanic police officers with white and African American officers with respect to arrest patterns and use of force. As already noted, in New York City and San Jose, Hispanic officers receive citizen complaints in direct proportion to their representation in the department.

Gay and Lesbian Officers

Sergeant Charles Cochrane Jr. of the New York City Police Department (NYPD) took a bold step in 1982, announcing that he was gay and that he planned to form an organization of gay officers in the NYPD. As a staff psychologist with the NYPD later explained, the words *gay* and *police* "did not fit together comfortably in American society [at that time] let alone in the NYPD." Four years earlier, the mayor of New York City had banned employment discrimination against homosexuals in all city agencies. The head of the police union angrily denounced the policy, arguing that it would "do more harm than good." In his view, police officers form very close working relationships with their colleagues, and the employment of homosexual officers would undermine cohesion among the rank and file.[76]

A number of police officers today are lesbian or gay. In some departments, they are open about their sexual orientation and have formed their own organizations. The Gay Officers Action League (GOAL) in New York City began publishing a newsletter in 1982. By 1992, at least 10 police departments openly recruited lesbian and gay officers. Some of these departments are in states where antidiscrimination laws cover sexual orientation. Others are in cities with large lesbian and gay communities, and these communities have officers designated as liaisons to them.[77] Some departments today actively recruit gay and lesbian officers. An increasing number of state and local governments prohibit discrimination on the basis of sexual orientation. In cities with large gay and lesbian populations, police departments have made special efforts to better serve that segment of the community. Having officers who are gay or lesbian who can serve as liaisons helps to advance a police department's mission.

Even so, strong barriers to the hiring of gay and lesbian officers continue to exist. Lesbian and gay officers represent a clear challenge to the traditional warrior stereotype of policing as a tough, macho, male occupation. Susan Miller and colleagues interviewed 17 gay and lesbian police officers in a small midwestern city to investigate how they coped with the organization and other officers. Their sample consisted of eight gay officers and nine lesbians, with a mix of race and ethnicity in both groups. All had disclosed their sexual identity to other gay and lesbian officers, but only some were "out" to the department as a whole. All felt that they are "constantly scrutinized" by people around them in the department, and all had either heard or had been the target of homophobic remarks. Some of the lesbian officers felt a bond with heterosexual women officers with respect to their common experience of sexism. Most felt that the traditional male culture of policing prevailed, and that "proving masculinity" was a significant issue.[78]

A survey of gay and lesbian officers found that they chose law enforcement as a career for the same reasons other people have traditionally chosen it: 41 percent cited job security, career opportunity, and civic duty as the three top reasons they chose policing. Many, however, experienced discrimination on the job. Two-thirds (67 percent) reported hearing homophobic talk on the job, and 51 percent reported being treated like an outsider. Nearly a quarter (22 percent) cited barriers to promotion, and 17 percent saw barriers in assignment because of their sexual orientation.[79] There are, however, no studies of the performance of gay and lesbian officers.[80] In the end, with little open conflict, gay and lesbian police officers have become integrated into the departments in which they work.

The Intersection of Gender, Race, Ethnicity, and Sexual Identity

A comment by an African American female supervisor interviewed by Susan Martin illustrates the complex relationships resulting from increased diversity within police departments. This supervisor had problems with a white male officer under her command. After he transferred, however, he had similar problems with his new male supervisor. She concluded that "it wasn't a female thing . . . but at the time I couldn't be sure . . . I felt he was rebelling against me because I was a female lieutenant and a black lieutenant."[81] In short, relationships among officers of different genders, races, and ethnicities are extremely complex, and it is often difficult to determine which is the primary factor in any given situation.

In many departments, some tension and conflict exist among racial, ethnic, and gender groups. Robin Haarr found that white officers believed they were being discriminated against because promotions and preferred assignments were being given to African American officers who were less qualified.[82] In this respect, police departments are no different from other places of work. The increase in the number of female officers has generated conflict in a number of different areas of the workplace.

As is the case in much of American society, a pattern of self-segregation exists in police departments. In a midwestern police department, Haarr found limited day-to-day interaction between officers of different races or genders. She measured interaction in terms of daily "meets" between officers, including handling calls together, backing each other up, eating meals together, and gossiping or joking. White male officers largely interacted with other white male officers. Most (75 percent) of the African American male officers indicated they mainly interacted with other male officers (either African American or white). The three African American female officers interacted primarily with other African American officers, either male or female. White female officers interacted mainly with other female officers, rather than with partners or former partners. Finally, at roll call, officers "separated themselves spatially by race and gender as to where they sat and whom they interacted with."[83]

Divisions along racial, ethnic, and gender lines are reflected in the fact that groups form separate social and fraternal associations representing African American, Hispanic, and female officers. There are also national associations of African American, Hispanic, and female officers. In many departments, the recognized police union reflects the views of the white officers.

Does Diversifying a Department Change the Police Subculture?

Does changing the racial, ethnic, or gender composition of a police department make a difference? How does it affect the traditional police subculture? Does it affect the attitudes of white officers? Does it improve police–community relations? After reviewing all the available research, the National Academy of Sciences concluded that "there is no credible evidence that officers of different racial or ethnic backgrounds perform differently during interactions with citizens *simply because of race or ethnicity*" (emphasis added).[84] Consequently, merely increasing the number of African American or Hispanic officers will not *by itself* change the quality of a department's policing on the street.

An increased number of officers of color can, however, change the public image of a department and improve police–community relations. There is some evidence that it can also serve to change the officer subculture in terms of attitudes. A longitudinal study in Los Angeles found significant changes in the attitudes of officers over the course of 15 years as a result of a more diverse workforce. A consent decree required the LAPD to hire more officers of color and more women officers. The study surveyed officers in two waves, 1992 and 2007, asking them whether, in their opinion, "closer personal contact between police and the community will improve citizen's opinions of police officers," "make people more willing to help police stop crime," and make officers "more sensitive" to the community. It also asked three questions regarding possible negative effects (for example, whether it would "give citizens too much control over officers").[85]

In the initial 1992 survey, African American and Hispanic officers were more positive about the effect of police–community contact than were whites. By the 2007 survey, however, the attitudes of all officers had become more favorable. Perhaps most important, the attitudes of white officers improved more than did those of African American and Hispanic officers. The study's authors argued that this "unexpected finding" suggests that the introduction of more African American and Hispanic officers into a department "served to 'unfreeze' and change many of the pre-existing, less community-oriented attitudes" held by white officers. In short, diversifying the workforce can help to change the internal culture of a police department.

Rising Levels of Police Officer Education

The profile of the American police officer has been changing because of rising educational levels. In the 1960s, 80 percent of all sworn officers had only a high school education. By 1988, that figure had fallen to 34.8 percent. The percentage of officers with a four-year college degree rose from 2.7 to 22.6 percent in the same period.[86] In many departments, there is an **education generation gap** between the younger, better-educated officers and the veteran officers with less education.

education generation gap

Does education change the police subculture? Does more education make a difference in police performance? Is a police officer with a college education more effective than an officer with only a high school diploma? There is no strong evidence that officers with a college education behave on the street differently from officers with less education.[87] One study, however, did find that college-educated officers tended to receive fewer complaints, and another study found that they were less likely to use force than officers with less education.[88]

The research on the relationship between education and performance has been weak. The National Academy of Sciences identified three problems with the research on this subject.[89] First, studies have not used good measures of police officer behavior and performance. This highlights the much larger problem of how to measure officer performance. The number of arrests is not a good measure because some officers have more opportunity to make arrests, and the total number does not reflect the quality of the arrests (measured by convictions). A low number of citizen complaints or use-of-force incidents, meanwhile, may indicate only that an officer has not initiated much activity.

Second, studies have not taken into account the content of educational programs. The number of college credit hours does not reflect either what courses were taken or the quality of the instruction. Finally, studies have not controlled for the effects of other factors that influence officer behavior and performance. Individuals with a strong commitment to self-improvement are also likely to have continued their education. The factors that cause them to seek more education also shape their performance as officers.

Cohort Effects on Performance

Throughout society there are generation gaps: conflicts between young people and old people, between children and their parents. These conflicts involve clothes, hairstyles, music, lifestyle, and issues of morality. In the 1960s, there were deep conflicts between generations over the Vietnam War. Then and now, there are conflicts over sexual morality. Similar conflicts exist within police departments. Social scientists refer to these as **cohort effects.** That is, the officers hired in one decade will have different ideas and lifestyles from officers hired in later decades.

cohort effects

As new groups of officers enter policing, they accept as standard practice things that older officers had earlier reacted to with hostility. Skolnick's study in the 1960s found that officers were hostile to Supreme Court decisions placing limits on searches and seizures and interrogations. From their perspective, the rulings were something *new* that changed the rules of policing.[90] Fifty years later, a new generation of officers takes the exclusionary rule and the *Miranda* warning as established parts of policing. A study of narcotics officers in Chicago in the 1980s similarly found a high degree of support for the exclusionary rule. On the whole, officers did not regard it as a barrier to effective police work, and many officers felt that it played an important role in deterring police misconduct.[91]

Along the same lines, Elizabeth Reuss-Ianni found two cultures among police officers in the department she studied. One group identified with the old **street cop culture** that values street experience and a tough, personalized way of dealing with people on the street. The other group identified with the new bureaucratic style of written rules and formal procedures for dealing with both police work on the street and departmental governance. This latter group is more accepting of, for example, Supreme Court rules on police practices, along with other formal procedures designed to control discretion and ensure police accountability.[92]

street cop culture

Organizational Effects on Attitudes and Performance

The officer subculture also varies in important ways from department to department because of organizational factors. Some departments have reputations for professionalism and a commitment to innovation regarding programs to address crime and disorder. Others have reputations for high levels of misconduct and a failure to embrace innovation and change. (We should, of course, be very careful about relying on reputations that are unverified by independent research.) These differences reflect the attitudes and behavior of officers on the street, but they are generally a product of the leadership and policies and practices in the organization.

About 25 state and local law enforcement agencies since 1997 have been investigated by the Civil Rights Division of the U.S. Department of Justice and have entered into consent decrees or settlements mandating sweeping reforms of department procedures on officer use of force, racial profiling, and other problems. Those departments include Cincinnati, Ohio; Los Angeles, California; Cleveland, Ohio; and Seattle, Washington. The settlements typically require improved policies to control officer use of force and to investigate use-of-force incidents.[93] The departments that have been investigated by the Justice Department, by definition, allowed a police subculture to develop that tolerated abusive and illegal conduct. Reform can make a difference. An evaluation of the Los Angeles consent decree found that officer use of force decreased as a result of the consent decree and that crime rates in the city also declined. In short, a significant change in department policies and practices reshaped officer conduct on the street in a positive direction.[94]

Organizations make a difference. Leadership is extremely important. Does the department have state-of-the-art policies on key issues such as use of force? Does the department investigate allegations of misconduct seriously? Are officers found guilty of misconduct given meaningful discipline? Police departments with good leadership and policies have different—and better—police subcultures than departments that do not.

Attitudes toward Community Policing

"Can we affect crime?" asked a Chicago police officer. "Not really," he said, answering his own question. "We can't control the social fabric. It can't be done." These comments reflect the negative attitude toward community policing held by many tradition-bound officers. Other Chicago officers, however, were more favorable toward community policing, agreeing with the idea that "police officers should work with citizens to try and solve problems in their beat."[95]

The community policing program in Chicago (Chicago Alternative Policing Strategy, or CAPS) made a special effort in "winning the hearts and minds" of the rank and file. Skogan and Hartnett's evaluation of CAPS found significant differences of opinion among Chicago officers regarding community policing. Older officers and African American officers were consistently more supportive of community policing. African American officers were "ready for change," while white officers were satisfied with the status quo and most pessimistic about the likely success of CAPS.[96]

In a review of evaluations of community policing in 12 different cities, Arthur Lurigio and Dennis Rosenbaum found that involvement in community policing had a somewhat positive effect on officer attitudes (and on citizen perceptions of the police). Officers were generally more likely to have increased job satisfaction and motivation, as well as improved relationships with both citizens and coworkers. Lurigio and Rosenbaum cautioned against being overly optimistic about the impact of community policing on officer attitudes, but there is some evidence that changes in the police organization can affect officer attitudes.[97]

The Relationship between Attitudes and Behavior

The graduate students observing police work in Boston, Chicago, and Washington, D.C., in Reiss's pioneering study for the President's Crime Commission observed more than 75 percent of the officers making racially prejudiced statements. They did not, however, observe a pattern of systematic mistreatment of African Americans, in terms of either use of force or discriminatory arrests.[98] The contradictions in this study illustrate the complex relationship between the attitudes and behavior of police officers.

Common sense suggests a direct relationship between attitudes and behavior: that people who express prejudicial *attitudes* about race, ethnicity, or gender will automatically *behave* in a discriminatory manner. In practice, this is not necessarily true. The National Academy of Sciences reviewed the literature and found only "weak relationships between specific officer attitudes and behavior."[99]

Several factors mediate the effect of attitudes on officer behavior. First, police officers are constrained by the police bureaucracy and the criminal justice system. An arrest comes to the attention of other officials: the officer's sergeant, the prosecutor and defense attorney, and a judge. All review the officer's performance and have the power to correct any gross abuse of power. The prosecutor can reject the charges, and a judge can exclude evidence or confessions that were obtained improperly. These factors illustrate Herbert's point about the impact of the criminal justice bureaucracy on the police subculture. The result is that an officer is not free to act solely on the basis of his or her personal prejudices.[100]

A second constraint is the possibility of a citizen complaint or a lawsuit. Either one could affect an officer's career. Third, in a professional department with high standards of conduct, supervisors will be more likely to advise officers that both prejudicial statements and discriminatory actions are contrary to the values of the department and could result in disciplinary action.

Styles of Police Work

Conducting a series of ride-alongs with patrol sergeants in the Wilshire Division of the LAPD in 1993 and 1994, criminologist Steve Herbert observed that officers had labels to describe the different work styles of their fellow officers. Some were called "hard chargers": active, often aggressive officers who would volunteer to handle potentially dangerous situations, and enjoyed the excitement of high-speed pursuits. Some others, meanwhile, were labeled "station queens" because they were seen as initiating little activity and avoiding danger.[101]

Individual officers have different work styles; some work very hard, some do as little as possible. The same is true in every organization. **Active officers** initiate more contacts with citizens (field interrogations, traffic stops, building checks); back up officers on other calls, even when not dispatched to those calls; assert control of situations with citizens; and make more arrests. Passive officers, by contrast, initiate few contacts with citizens; respond only to calls to which they are dispatched; and

active officers

EXHIBIT 6-4

Active versus Passive Police Officer Work Styles

Active	Passive
Taking charge of the situation	Standing by, observing
Right: Assertive but not belligerent	
Wrong: Aggressive, accusatory	
Asking questions to determine what is happening	Not asking questions
Right: Neutral questions	
Wrong: Accusatory questions	
Answering peoples' questions	Not responding to questions
Right: Firm but polite answers	
Wrong: Insulting answers	
Responding to hostility	No response (possibly inviting escalation)
Right: Firm but low-key response	Finally resorting to use of force
Wrong: Escalating the conflict	
Right: Explaining possible consequences	
Wrong: Finally using hostile language, threats	
Right: De-escalation techniques	
Wrong: Escalating the conflict	
Exit	
Explaining action	No explanation
(arrest/no arrest, warning)	

---

make few traffic stops, field interrogations, and arrests. Data on arrests, traffic stops, and field interrogations consistently indicate that a few officers are very productive, while some other officers engage in little activity.[102]

For a full discussion of police discretion in handling complex situations, see Chapter 11.

David Bayley and James Garofalo observed officers responding to specific situations and found that active officers were more likely to take charge of the situation by asking probing questions, requesting that citizens explain themselves, and giving direction or advice to the people involved. Passive officers, by contrast, were more likely to just observe a situation, take notes, and leave without taking any specific action.[103]

An active officer is not necessarily a good officer, however. Some active officers may be overly aggressive in dealing with people: giving orders instead of listening first, not explaining why the police have been called, and so on. The new standards of procedural justice emphasize officers introducing themselves, actively asking questions to determine what the situation is and who may be at fault, listening to people and answering their questions, and so on. Exhibit 6–4 outlines the differences between active and passive officers, and the right and wrong ways of being an active officer.

Moving through Police Careers

Salaries and Benefits

The salaries and fringe benefits offered to police officers in most departments are generally one of the most attractive aspects of jobs in law enforcement. They are one of the main reasons people choose law enforcement as a career. Salaries are rigidly structured by civil service procedures and/or union contracts, however. Pay is tied to an officer's rank. Typically, there are several pay steps at the rank of police officer, which an officer gains through seniority or special assignment.

Job security has always been important in policing. Because of civil service rules and police union contracts, it is extremely difficult to fire an officer, except for criminal conduct. It is almost impossible to fire an officer simply for doing little work.

The only way to achieve a significant pay increase in police departments is through promotion. Unlike employees in the private sector, a police chief cannot reward an outstanding officer through a bonus or discretionary pay increase. Thus, there are no immediate financial rewards for outstanding performance. Most departments offer additional pay for certain assignments or qualifications. Analysis of 2007 Justice Department data indicates that 45 percent of all municipal departments offer incentive pay for college education, 14 percent offer hazardous duty pay for certain assignments, and 33 percent provide shift differential pay. Another 30 percent offer various forms of merit pay increases.[104]

The major source of additional pay is overtime. Certain assignments, particularly those that involve frequent court appearances, such as criminal investigation and traffic enforcement, offer the greatest opportunities for overtime pay. As a result, assignment to these units is highly desired among most officers.

Career Development

The lack of opportunities for career development is recognized as a problem in American police departments. **Career development** involves opportunities to use one's talents and develop expertise in a particular area. In a two-wave survey of Detroit police officers, more than half in both 1978 (53 percent) and 1988 (54 percent) indicated low satisfaction with the opportunity for career advancement. Few (10 percent in 1978 and 16 percent in 1988) expressed high satisfaction with the advancement opportunities. Traditionally, the two main career opportunities are promotion to higher rank and assignment to a preferred unit such as criminal investigation or traffic.[105]

career development

To promote career development, many departments have educational incentive programs through which officers receive additional pay based on their level of education. The Cincinnati Police Department went even further in 2008, creating a Chief's Scholars Program. The department assigned three officers to attend the University of Cincinnati to obtain a master's degree in criminal justice as part of their regular duty assignment. As part of its strategic plan, meanwhile, the department also developed a succession planning program to prepare officers for vacancies created by anticipated retirements. The Lincoln, Nebraska, police department developed a similar program to mentor younger officers to prepare them for future command responsibilities.[106]

Promotion

Opportunities for **promotion** are typically limited in policing. First, civil service regulations usually require an officer to serve a certain number of years in rank before being eligible to apply for promotion. Time-in-rank requirements typically range from two to five years.[107]

promotion

SIDEBAR 6-4

Studying Your Own Community

What are the requirements for in-service training among the law enforcement agencies in your community? Is there a state requirement? If so, how many hours and in what subjects? Do local agencies have their own requirements? Do they go beyond what is required by state law? What subjects are required to be covered every year beyond firearms recertification?

Second, there are only a few openings at higher rank. Additionally, promotions are often affected by the city or county's financial condition. In a time of financial crisis, postponing hiring and promotions is an easy way to save money. The national financial crisis of 2008–2009 forced many law enforcement agencies to either cancel or postpone recruit classes and/or postpone or cancel promotions.

Third, promotions are based on a formal testing process, typically involving a written examination and an oral interview. Supervisory positions require different skills than on-the-street police work: directing other people, writing **performance evaluations,** dealing with performance problems, and so forth. It is not clear that the testing procedures select people who have the proper skills. Interviews are generally conducted by the chief of police, a committee of high-ranking officers, and often members of the local civil service agency group.[108] Some departments use the assessment center technique, which presents the applicant with hypothetical situations and evaluates the quality of his or her proposed resoponses.

Several studies have found that a glass ceiling exists with regard to female officers, and women are underrepresented in higher ranks. Interestingly, Archbold and Schulz found that even though more than half the female officers in their study felt that promotional opportunities were "very good" or "good" in their departments, many were reluctant to test for sergeant because of a perception they would be promoted only because they were female. Almost half (43 percent) could mention a potential male "sponsor" to help them with promotion.[109]

performance evaluations

Assignment to Special Units

An important career opportunity involves assignment to a special unit: criminal investigation, the gang unit, traffic enforcement, training, juvenile, and so on. These assignments are typically at the discretion of the chief. Traditionally, giving these assignments to friends or allies was one of the ways a chief maintained control over a department.

Assignments must be within the officer's rank. A lieutenant, for example, cannot be assigned as commander of a unit if that position is designated as a captain's position. The rigidity of these personnel classification systems limits both the career opportunities for individual officers and the management flexibility of the chief executive.[110] Special assignments play an important role in promotional opportunities. Serving in a number of special units gives an officer broad experience, an opportunity to become known to other officers, and the chance to establish a reputation for ability.

In all law enforcement agencies, rank-and-file officers regard certain assignments as highly desirable. These are sometimes referred to as **"coveted" assignments.** Officers prefer these assignments for two reasons. First, they are usually challenging assignments that are more interesting than basic patrol. Second, experience in these assignments often helps gain promotion to higher rank.

"coveted" assignments

A report on the Los Angeles Sheriff's Department identified the following coveted assignments: Special Enforcement Bureau, Narcotics Bureau, and station detectives. All three involve specialized crime-fighting activities. In most departments, detective and crime-related assignments are the most desired. At the same time, the study identified "high-profile" assignments that tend to bring the officer "to the attention of persons in a position to notice and promote him or her." The three most significant high-profile assignments for Los Angeles sheriff's deputies are operations deputy, Recruitment Training Bureau, and field training officer.[111]

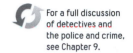

For a full discussion of detectives and the police and crime, see Chapter 9.

Exclusion of certain groups from coveted positions has been an important form of employment discrimination. The Los Angeles Sheriff's Department study, for example, found that female officers were less than 2 percent of all Special Enforcement Bureau deputies and less than 3 percent of all field training officers. Exclusion from such assignments creates barriers to promotion.

Lateral Entry

The opportunity to move to other police departments was traditionally limited in American departments. Someone transferring from another department lost all seniority and had to start as a rookie officer. This was a serious impediment to career development. In other professions, someone can move to a different organization without losing seniority and often to a higher position with better pay.

Some experts regard lateral entry as a potential means of enhancing police professionalism. They argue that it would create greater career opportunities for talented and ambitious officers and would allow departments to bring in fresh blood and new ideas. **Lateral entry** is opposed because officers jealously guard the few promotional opportunities that do arise in a department and resent the idea of outsiders getting these jobs.[112]

lateral entry

Personnel policies have been changing, and many departments now offer lateral entry programs. The LAPD has had a lateral entry program that admits people with state POST certification and prior experience with another agency. They are required to take an abbreviated four-week training course and, on the salary schedule, are given one year of credit for every two years of previous experience (up to a maximum of six years). They can also advance one step for 60 hours of college credits (2.0 GPA required) and two steps for an undergraduate degree.[113]

Outside Employment

A significant number of police officers supplement their incomes with **outside employment.** In addition, officers who are frustrated by the lack of career opportunities look for challenges and rewards outside the department. Many of those jobs are in private security, where the officer wears his or her police uniform. A 1988 Justice Department study found that half of all officers in some departments work off duty and in uniform.[114]

outside employment

Outside employment creates a number of potential problems. First, it may diminish an officer's commitment to his or her job with the police department. A study of arrest productivity among New York City police officers found that those officers who held outside jobs made significantly fewer arrests than officers who did not. Apparently, officers were deterred from making arrests out of fear that the resulting court appearances would interfere with their outside work.[115]

Second, off-duty work in uniform creates potential conflicts of interest. An off-duty officer working in a bar, for example, may be caught between the duty to enforce the law and the interests of the bar owner. Finally, outside work in uniform may lower the dignity of the department.[116]

The San Jose independent police auditor exposed another conflict of interest by pointing out that some officers working off duty were hiring their supervisors as employees on those jobs. This practice potentially undermines discipline in the department, because a supervisor might be afraid to discipline an officer under his or her command out of fear of being fired from the off-duty job.[117]

Performance Evaluations

In any professionally managed organization, employee performance evaluations are extremely important. Regular evaluations serve to identify good performance that can be rewarded and poor performance that needs to be corrected.

Traditional Performance Evaluations

New York City police officer Michael Dowd received outstanding performance evaluations. His 1987 evaluation concluded that he had "excellent street knowledge" and could "easily become a role model for others to emulate."[118] Unfortunately, the Mollen Commission investigating corruption in the NYPD found that he was one of the most brutal and corrupt officers in the police department. Something was clearly wrong with the performance evaluation system in the NYPD.

Effective performance evaluations are a critical part of a police department's personnel system. An effective system should identify and reward good performance, establish a basis for which officers deserve promotion, identify inadequate performance, and provide a basis for correcting those performance problems. The CALEA accreditation standards state that "a written directive requires that a performance evaluation of each employee be conducted and documented at least annually."[119]

Performance evaluations do not always reflect an officer's actual performance. The Christopher Commission, for example, found that some of the Los Angeles officers with the highest number of citizen complaints had received excellent performance evaluations.[120] One of the most damning indictments of police personnel evaluation procedures was made by the LAPD about its own system. In the wake of the Rampart corruption scandal in 2000, the department undertook a full-scale board of inquiry investigation that resulted in a 350-page report. The report concluded that the department's "personnel evaluations have little or no credibility at any level in the organization . . ." and recommended major changes "so that [evaluations] can be relied upon as a true measure of performance."[121]

Some departments, in fact, only recently began to conduct regular performance evaluations. The Pittsburgh Police Bureau, for example, did not conduct regular performance evaluations prior to a 1997 consent decree with the U.S. Justice Department to settle a suit over officer use of excessive force.[122]

Problems with Performance Evaluations

Traditional police performance evaluation systems have been heavily criticized. A 1977 Police Foundation report concluded that "the current status of performance appraisal systems is discouragingly low."[123] Changes over the next 20 years resulted in only marginal improvements. A 1997 report by the Community Policing Consortium concluded that "most performance evaluations currently used by police agencies do not reflect the work officers do."[124] This is a strong indictment of police personnel evaluations.

There are a number of problems with traditional performance evaluations. First, the definitions are often not clear. They do not explain, for example, how effective police work is to be measured. When an officer successfully resolves a domestic dispute, for example, how do we measure it? What data would be used? What documentation is there indicating that the resolution was a success? Second, because of the "halo effect," officers rated high on one factor are likely to be rated high on all others. An officer who arrests a known major offender often gets a good reputation that affects his or her ratings on all areas of performance. Third, because of the "central tendency" phenomenon, the ratings of all officers tend to cluster around one numerical level. Finally, through "grade inflation," there is a tendency to rate everyone highly.[125] Additionally, supervisors have consistently failed to consult available departmental data on citizen complaints, uses of force, and civil suits against officers, which provide valuable information about officers' performance.

An officer may be skilled at defusing conflicts among people (for example, in a domestic situation or a bar fight). Doing that successfully provides an important service to the public. It prevents possible harm to people, keeps the neighborhood quiet, and avoids arrest and the potential use of force. Yet, traditional personnel evaluation systems are not good at identifying and rewarding this skill.

Performance evaluations may also reflect patterns of racial, ethnic, or gender bias within a department. There is some indication that African American and Hispanic officers are more likely to be cited for departmental violations. Martin and Jurik argue that traditional performance criteria such as aggressiveness are male oriented and inevitably biased against female officers.[126]

A major problem with police personnel systems is that they have traditionally focused on punishing misconduct rather than rewarding good behavior. Critics have called police organizations "punishment-centered bureaucracies."[127] There are elaborate rules in the department policy and procedure manual that can be used, often selectively, to catch and punish officers, but few methods are available for positively rewarding officers. An independent report sponsored by the police union in Los Angeles following the Rampart scandal concluded that supervisors often harassed officers by citing them for minor violations of department policy while ignoring major forms of misconduct such as use of excessive force.[128]

A more positive view of police personnel evaluation emerged from Bayley and Garofalo's study of New York City police officers. Officers in three precincts were asked in confidence to identify three other officers they thought were "particularly skilled at handling conflict situations." The officers receiving the highest scores were then matched with comparison groups in the same precincts. An analysis of 467 police–citizen encounters involving potential violence found that officers rated highly by their peers handled situations differently from the members of the comparison groups. They were more likely to take charge of situations, less likely to simply stand by and observe, more likely to probe with questions and ask citizens to explain themselves, more likely to verbally defuse situations, less likely to threaten the use of physical force, more likely to ask people to disperse, and less likely to order people to do so.[129]

Bayley and Garofalo found that the peer evaluations corresponded with the differences in officer behavior they observed in their study. More important, the officers who were rated more highly by their peers and who performed better on the job also received higher ratings in official departmental evaluations. They received higher ratings in such categories as appearance, community relations skills, impartiality, decision making, ethics, and street knowledge.[130]

Regular performance evaluations are completed by an officer's immediate supervisor. For a patrol officer, that is the patrol sergeant. The recommended "span of control" (the number of employees one supervisor is responsible for) is about eight officers per sergeant. When the span of control is higher than that, the sergeant does not have sufficient time to stay in contact with and properly supervise all of the officers. Sergeants are expected to respond to serious incidents and in some cases take control of the situation. It is through these contacts that sergeants get to know their officers and how they perform. Increasingly, sergeants are required to respond to all officer-involved shooting incidents and serious use-of-force incidents, to critically review the officers' force reports, to demand revisions of reports that lack the proper detail or contain inconsistencies, and then to complete their own report of the incident.

Job Satisfaction and Job Stress

The Sources of Job Satisfaction

What do police officers like about their jobs? What factors cause them stress on the job? Several studies have found that, contrary to what many people think, officers are more stressed out by what their own department does than by what citizens on the street do. A survey of community policing officers in New York City found that in response to the question "What do you dislike about being a cop?" the most frequently cited response was "department/headquarters doesn't care" (mentioned by 58.2 percent of the officers). Another 22.4 percent mentioned "precinct level-supervisors." Meanwhile, "lack of respect from the public" ranked third and was mentioned by only 16.4 percent of the officers.[131]

The factors associated with job satisfaction in policing fall into five general categories:[132]

1. *The nature of police work,* including working with people, serving the community, and the excitement of the work. This finding is consistent with the research discussed in Chapter 5 about the reasons people choose to become police officers.

2. *Organizational factors,* including recognition for good performance, opportunities for advancement, and support from organization leaders.
3. *Relations with the community,* including cooperation from citizens in encounters, the presence or absence of overt conflict with citizens, and positive feedback for good performance.
4. *Relations with the media and political leaders,* including positive or negative coverage in the news media, positive support from political leaders, and the presence or absence of direct political interference from political leaders.
5. *Personal or family factors,* including a family environment that understands police work, the presence or absence of conflict between job and family responsibilities, and the presence or absence of family problems (divorce, problems with children, and so on).

As we have already learned, however, these factors do not always provide the satisfaction that officers seek. Officers often see the public as hostile to them. The management of the department is often a source of great dissatisfaction. Officers often see the public as not cooperative (for example, in not being willing to come forward as witnesses to a crime). Media coverage of controversial incidents is a deep source of complaints for many officers. In short, being a police officer is a complex and difficult job, with some factors being sources of both satisfaction and dissatisfaction.

A majority of police officers are generally satisfied with their jobs. In Washington, D.C., 82 percent indicated that they were satisfied or very satisfied. A study of Detroit police officers found that, in 1988, 61 percent expressed medium satisfaction and 8 percent expressed high satisfaction. This represented lower levels of satisfaction than 10 years earlier, when 53 percent expressed medium and 28 percent expressed high satisfaction with their jobs. About three-quarters (78 percent) said they would choose law enforcement again as a career, but 64 percent also said that the work is stressful. Few of the Detroit officers indicated that they felt low satisfaction in terms of job fulfillment (3 percent in 1978 and 8 percent in 1988), defined in terms of freedom to make decisions and overall feelings of accomplishment.[133]

Continued stress can lead to "burn-out," which is a problem in all jobs. Burn-out can manifest itself in mood changes, increases in alcohol use, inability to sleep, and illnesses. On the job, significant mood changes and loss of sleep can lead to lack of attention to detail (which might put an officer in a dangerous situation) or a short temper when dealing with a difficult 911 call (which can lead to conflict and unnecessary use of force). At the extreme, burn-out can lead to suicide, which is a significant problem in policing (discussed later in this chapter).[134]

The Sources of Job Stress

Policing is a stressful occupation. There is the constant potential for danger. Disturbance calls can escalate into conflict. Patrol work can involve long periods with no calls, punctuated by a sudden conflict situation. Calls that involve finding a suicide victim or a serious case of child abuse are extremely difficult to handle and cause a high level of emotional stress.

There is some disagreement over whether policing is more stressful than other demanding occupations. Some studies have reported higher rates of suicide, alcoholism, heart attack, and divorce among police officers, compared with the general population. A study of suicides in New York City between 1964 and 1973 found a rate of 17.2 per 100,000 among police officers, compared with 8.3 per 100,000 for the city as a whole and 11 per 100,000 for males in the city. Similar findings are reported today. For example, the Centers for Disease Control and Prevention recently reported that nationwide the suicide rate for police officers is 18 per 100,000 compared to 14.6 per 100,000 for persons aged 25 to 50, and 11.1 per 100,000 for the whole U.S. population.[135]

Some studies in the past claimed to find divorce rates as high as 30 percent in some police departments and suggested that police officers were more likely to be divorced because of job-related stress.[136] Today, however, national data indicate that police officers actually have lower divorce rates than the general public, even after controlling for socioeconomic and work-related characteristics.[137]

job stress

The threat of danger is a basic element of police work that creates **job stress.** Nevertheless, threatening incidents, such as physical assaults in the form of being attacked with a weapon, are statistically infrequent. Similarly, as mentioned earlier, the number of police officers feloniously killed in the line of duty is low, and the on-the-job fatality rate is lower than in many other industries.

Citizen disrespect and challenges to police authority are another source of job stress. Even though such incidents are statistically infrequent, they loom large in an officer's consciousness. Equally important is the problem of boredom. Routine patrol work often involves long periods of inactivity. Shifting suddenly from inactivity to a high state of readiness is also a source of stress. Another major cause of stress in policing involves dealing with extreme human suffering. Officers regularly handle calls involving people who have been killed or seriously injured, or who are in a state of extreme psychological disorder.

The police department itself is a major source of stress. For many officers, the department is a more serious source of stress than are problems arising from dealing with the public. Officers often feel that command officers do not support them adequately, that incompetent officers are given preferred assignments because of personal friendships, and that the department changes policies in reaction to criticism from the media or politicians.[138]

Female police officers experience special gender-related forms of stress, such as sexual harassment or lack of acceptance by male police officers.[139] Additionally, female officers often have greater child care responsibilities than male officers and take more sick leave in order to handle them. African American and Hispanic officers also experience discrimination within their departments, often in terms of exclusion from preferred assignments.

Job Stress and Suicide

suicide

Job stress in policing can lead officers to kill themselves. More officers die from **suicide** than are shot and killed in the line of duty: 51 in the first half of 2015, 126 in 2012, and 143 in 2009. One expert labeled the problem "silent suffering," because officers rarely talk about the stress they are under and that they are thinking about taking their own lives. Refusal to talk about personal problems and seek help is one aspect of the traditional warrior culture of policing, in which officers feel they have to prove they are "tough enough" to take the pressures of the job.[140] Police departments and police professional associations have also not addressed the problem directly and openly. A recent IACP report called suicides the "dirty little secret" in policing involving, "topics very few want to address or acknowledge."[141]

The National Institute for Occupational Safety and Health reports that police and firefighters (referred to jointly as "protective services" occupations) have the highest suicide rate among all occupational groups: 5.3 per one million workers, three times the national workplace suicide rate. The typical police suicide victim is male (91 percent, indicating that even some women officers embrace the police subculture of "toughness"), between the ages of 40 and 44, and with 15 to 19 years on the job. Interestingly, 63 percent were single, suggesting that marriage or a stable intimate relationship has a positive mental health effect. About two-thirds (64 percent) of the suicides were regarded as a "surprise" by people around them, which confirms the point that most police who kill themselves do not talk about their problems beforehand.[142]

The IACP report, *Breaking the Silence on Law Enforcement Suicides,* declared that "[n]ow is the time to remove the stigma attached to mental health issues" and to "openly address the reality" of the problem. The report began by arguing for a "culture change" within policing in which the police would move away from the traditional attitude that "the mere presence of an emotional problem indicates a weakness on the officer's part." Interestingly, on this point the IACP's thinking is closely in line with Rahr and Rice's argument that the police need to move from away from the warrior mindset and toward a guardian view of policing. The IACP recommended that departments adopt "policies and practices to adequately address mental wellness and suicide prevention"; properly train officers on the policies; adopt mental wellness programs and services for officers; train officers to recognize warning signs of stress and mental illness in themselves and other officers; develop intervention methods for supervisors when they suspect an officer is at risk for suicide; and encourage officers to "police themselves for mental health issues and to look out for the mental well-being" of other officers.[143]

Community Policing and Job Satisfaction

Many advocates of community-oriented policing (COP) argue that it leads to greater job satisfaction for officers than traditional policing does. According to this view, under COP, officers will be less isolated from the communities they serve, will have greater autonomy in their work, will not be subject to as many rigid rules, will have the opportunity for greater personal development, and will be able to see the results of their work.

In an innovative approach to the study of police officer job satisfaction, David Brody and colleagues surveyed both police officers and non-police employees in 12 governments in Washington State. Also, they compared police officers in terms of the level of COP implementation by the police department. Departments were classified as having high, medium, or low COP implementation. Finally, the study used 11 measures of job satisfaction.[144]

The adoption of COP raised the level of job satisfaction among police officers and reduced the gap in levels of satisfaction between police and non-police employees.

The positive effects were confined, however, to departments with a high commitment to COP. In departments with only a medium COP commitment, levels of job satisfaction in some arenas were actually lower than in departments with a low COP commitment. The authors of the study speculate that an incomplete commitment to COP may cause confusion and frustration among officers. This finding has important implications for reform and organizational change. It suggests that a half-hearted and incomplete change effort may be worse than not attempting any organizational change at all.

Coping with Job Stress

Until recently, few police departments tried to help officers in coping with job stress. They either ignored the problem or assigned an officer with obvious problems to an easier job. For their part, troubled officers either relied on the support of their fellow officers or internalized their problems—a response that often led to alcohol abuse, mental illness, or even suicide.[145]

The National Police Research Platform asked officers how they cope with job stress. The good news is that unhealthy responses were the least cited. Drinking was cited by only 2.5 percent of officers, and "criticizing myself" by only 9.8 percent. The most common response was looking for something good in their current situation (85.4 percent), followed by seeking emotional support (78 percent) and praying (58.5 percent).[146]

Today, many police departments maintain programs to help officers cope with the pressures of the job and/or other personal problems. These programs take several different forms. Some use mental health professionals, while others rely on peer support. Mental health professionals are employed either on a contract/referral basis or as full-time staff members of an employee assistance program (EAP). EAPs are typically run by the city or county and serve all city or county employees. Many experts regard peer counseling as particularly valuable, because the officer can relate well to the counselor as a fellow police officer. Also, some peer counselors can provide a role model of having dealt, for example, with an alcohol abuse problem.[147] The President's Task Force on 21st Century Policing recommended more programs and services to help officers deal with mental health issues.[148]

One of the key issues in EAPs is confidentiality. Officers seek assistance when they are assured that the fact that they sought assistance will not become public or be used against them in a disciplinary action.[149] Many officers refuse to seek professional help when they are having problems because of the traditional macho image of police officers as tough individuals who can handle any problem.

The Rights of Police Officers

Police officers enjoy the same civil and constitutional rights as other citizens, subject only to certain limitations related to the special circumstances of law enforcement. These include the constitutional rights of freedom of speech and association, due process of law, and privacy. Specific **rights of police officers** are enumerated in two aspects of the law: law enforcement officer's bill of rights (LEOBR) laws, and police union contracts. There is much controversy over whether some provisions of LEOBRs and union contracts are excessive and pose unreasonable barriers to the

rights of police officers

effective investigation of alleged officer misconduct and the discipline of officers found guilty of misconduct.

About 17 states have enacted LEOBR laws (although in some states, civil service laws also cover police officers). LEOBRs provide both First Amendment and due process protections for officers. Officers have the First Amendment free speech right to speak publicly, including about police-related issues, which could involve criticizing their own departments. (Some speech, however, may not be protected if it discloses confidential information about persons or the department.) As private individuals, but not as police officers, they have the right to support political candidates or ballot issues. Officers under investigation for alleged misconduct have due process rights to fair investigations. This includes a right to notice of the allegations against them and interviews at reasonable times of day and for reasonable periods of time, including time for rest room breaks. Officers sought these provisions in LEOBRs because, through the 1960s, officers were at times subjected to completely unreasonable investigations and interrogations. Officers also have the right to legal representation when being investigated. A national study of the state LEOBRs found only two (Maryland and Rhode Island) that have provisions that inhibit the investigation of misconduct.[150]

Police union contracts have a broad range of protections covering salaries, benefits, and provisions governing the investigation of alleged misconduct and the discipline of officers. Except for very small departments, most police departments have collective bargaining agreements with their rank-and-file officers.[151] (A few departments also have separate unions for supervisory officers, but they are the exception.) Most of the provisions of union contracts are reasonable protections of First Amendment and due process rights.

For a discussion of the rights of police officers and police accountability, see Chapter 14.

The controversial union contract provisions related to investigations and discipline include waiting periods, in which an officer in a use-of-force incident, for example, cannot be interviewed by the department for 48 hours. The Chicago contract provides for a delay of a "reasonable" period of time. The Baltimore contract and the Maryland state LEOBR provided for a 10-day waiting period, until it was cut to five days in 2016. Police unions argue that a 48-hour waiting period is justified because an officer-involved shooting or serious use-of-force case causes stress that affects memory and that an officer needs two "sleep cycles" (48 hours) for memory to recover fully. An examination of the psychological research on stress and memory found that the evidence is mixed and does not support a 48-hour waiting period.[152] Civil right advocates, meanwhile, argue that a 48-hour waiting period impedes the thorough investigation of force incidents. The 2016 Chicago mayor's task force on police accountability argued that a waiting period "provides officers time to protect themselves by agreeing on a false story" they can give to investigators. Another argument is that waiting periods allow the officer involved time to create a justification for the use of force. The emerging standard on force investigations, moreover, which is found in Justice Department consent decrees with troubled police departments, requires that officers complete a use-of-force report at the scene of the incident or before the end of the shift, and answer any questions his or her immediate supervisor might have. Finally, critics say, waiting periods create a culture of impunity among officers, which contradicts the principle of accountability. The 2016 report of the mayor's task force on the Chicago police found additional ways in which the police union contract inhibited thorough investigations.[153]

Two other issues involving the rights of police officers deserve mention. First, the U.S. Supreme Court in the 1966 *Garrity* case ruled that police officers have a Fifth Amendment right not to be compelled to testify against themselves if their conduct involves possible criminal action. The Court held that "policemen [sic], like teachers and lawyers, are not relegated to a watered-down version of constitutional rights." Officers can, however, be compelled to give possibly incriminating statements, but such statements cannot then be used against them in a criminal trial.[154] Second, the federal Employee Polygraph Protection Act prohibits employers from using lie detectors in recruitment. Law enforcement agencies, however, are exempted and may administer polygraph tests to job applicants.

Turnover: Leaving Police Work

turnover

Every year, about 5 percent of all police officers leave their jobs. This **turnover,** or attrition, rate appears to have been steady since the 1960s. Officers leave police work because of retirement, death, dismissal, voluntary resignation, or layoffs resulting from financial constraints.[155]

Martin found that women leave policing at a slightly higher rate than men (6.3 percent annually, compared with 4.6 percent), but for reasons other than retirement. Women are more likely to resign voluntarily (4.3 percent versus 3.0 percent) and to be terminated involuntarily (1.2 percent versus 0.6 percent). As discussed earlier, some women officers experience a hostile work environment because they are women. Women, especially single parents, have greater difficulty combining work with family responsibilities. Inadequate pregnancy leave policies make it difficult or impossible for women to have children and continue to work.[156]

William Doerner found significantly higher attrition rates for female officers, both African American and white, compared with male officers in the Tallahassee Police Department. He suggests that this pattern raises an issue of concern for affirmative action programs for women, which focus almost exclusively on recruitment and ignore long-term employment patterns.[157]

Relatively little research has examined the reasons for voluntary resignation. A study of Memphis police officers who resigned found that dissatisfaction with opportunities for promotion and with department policies was more important than inadequate pay and benefits or the feeling that their efforts were not being appreciated. Not all officers who are unhappy choose to resign, however. The Memphis study concluded that "dissatisfaction is a necessary but not a sufficient condition to cause resignation." As is the case with employees in all occupations, the decision is made in the context of many different personal, familial, and economic factors, including perceived career alternatives. The Memphis study identified several key "turning points" leading to the decision to resign. These include, in order of importance, (1) the feeling that one's career had stagnated (for example, "I just can't see any future in being a police officer"); (2) a particularly intense experience that brought accumulated frustrations to a head; (3) lack of a sense of fulfillment on the job; (4) family considerations; (5) the conduct of coworkers; (6) a particular department policy or policies; and (7) new employment opportunities.[158]

Decertification

As we learned in Chapter 5, all states today require preservice training and certification of job candidates before they can become police officers. Forty-three states also have provisions for **decertification**—that is, revoking the license of officers for misconduct.

decertification

Decertification has both strengths and weaknesses. The major reason for decertification is that it prevents someone who has committed serious misconduct as an officer from getting a job with another law enforcement agency in the state. An officer who has been found guilty of a crime (drunk driving, domestic violence, shoplifting, for example) has demonstrated a lack of ethics, which disqualifies him or her from the position of public trust that a police officer holds. Unfortunately, decertification applies only to the state in which the officer was certified. There is nothing to prevent the individual from going to another state to find a new job in policing. Some departments do not do thorough background checks and as a result hire people with bad records from their old departments.

One major problem with decertification laws involves the offenses they cover. Some states can decertify an officer only for a criminal conviction. A number of other states can decertify an officer for a criminal conviction or a hearing before an administrative law judge that he or she engaged in conduct prohibited by law. Some states can decertify someone who was terminated as a police officer or resigned voluntarily rather than be terminated. There are problems with each of these approaches. Limiting decertification to criminal convictions is far too restrictive. Few officers are ever convicted of crimes, and there are many forms of misconduct (including use of excessive force) that disqualifies a person from being a police officer. In terms of voluntary resignation instead of termination, Roger Goldman, the leading expert on the subject, points out that some chiefs may "plea bargain" with the officer and promise not to report the resignation to the state agency if the officer agrees to resign.[159]

Although decertification is a necessary and proper response to misconduct, existing programs have had only limited effect. Florida has the most active program, having decertified almost 6,000 officers over the years, according to Goldman. But most states decertify few officers. A National Decertification Index exists, but the public does not have access to it, and many police departments do not consult it when hiring.

SUMMARY

Careers in law enforcement are subject to many influences. Most popular stereotypes about police officer attitudes and behavior are not supported by the evidence. There is no evidence that a particular type of person is attracted to law enforcement or that this explains police behavior. The evidence does suggest, however, that certain aspects of police work have a powerful influence on both attitudes and behavior. At the same time, it is evident that recent changes in police employment patterns have brought a new diversity to the rank and file. Racial and ethnic minorities and women bring different expectations to policing. Law enforcement careers are heavily influenced by factors associated with police departments, particularly the opportunities for career advancement. The nature of police organizations is explored in more detail in Chapter 4.

KEY TERMS

reality shock, 168
hostility from citizens, 168
criminal justice system
 insiders, 169
seniority system, 170
police subculture, 172
group solidarity, 173
code of silence, 173
capacity to use force, 174

moderns, 180
sexual harassment, 182
education generation gap, 186
cohort effects, 187
street cop culture, 187
active officers, 189
career development, 191
promotion, 191
performance evaluations, 192

"coveted" assignments, 193
lateral entry, 193
outside employment, 193
job stress, 198
suicide, 198
rights of police officers, 200
turnover, 202
decertification, 203

FOR DISCUSSION

1. As a class, discuss why you might or might not be interested in a career in law enforcement. How do those reasons compare to the ones discussed in this chapter?
2. Police officers across the country supplement their income with outside employment. Often times, this outside work is related to performing security work in their uniform.

Discuss the potential benefits and problems that can arise from outside employment.
3. Although some aspects of police culture are universal, each law enforcement agency is distinctive in how police culture plays out within it. Discuss how the introduction of women and minorities has shaped police culture and how it might vary by agency.

INTERNET EXERCISE

Many organizations representing different groups of police officers maintain their own websites. Check out the websites for groups such as the Hispanic American Police Command Association, the International Association of Women Police, the

Emerald Society of the Boston Police, and others. Whom do these organizations represent? Do they provide their membership figures? What do they do? What activities do they sponsor? Do they offer any reports or other literature?

NOTES

1. William A. Westley, *Violence and the Police* (Cambridge, MA: MIT Press, 1970), 159–160.
2. John H. McNamara, "Uncertainties in Police Work: The Relevance of Police Recruits' Backgrounds and Training," in David J. Bordua, ed., *The Police, Six Sociological Essays* (New York: Wiley, 1967), 163–252.
3. Arthur J. Luirgio and Dennis P. Rosenbaum, "The Travails of the Detroit Police-Victims Experiment: Assumptions and Important Lessons," *American Journal of Police* XI, no. 3 (1992): 24.
4. Geoffrey P. Alpert and Roger M. Dunham, *Understanding Police Use of Force: Officers, Suspects, and Reciprocity* (New York: Cambridge University Press, 2004).
5. Albert Reiss, *The Police and the Public* (New Haven: Yale University Press, 1971), 51; John A. Groger, *Memory and Remembering: Everyday Memory in Context* (New York: Longman, 1997), 189–197.
6. Joseph De Angelis, *Assessing the Impact of the Office of the Independent Monitor on Complainant and Officer Satisfaction* (Denver: Office of the Independent Monitor, 2008). www.denvergov.org/OIM/.
7. John P. Clark, "Isolation of the Police: A Comparison of the British and American Situations," *Journal of Criminal Law, Criminology, and Police Science* 56 (September 1965): 307–319.

8. Westley, *Violence and the Police*, 18–19; Stephen B. Perrott and Donald M. Taylor, "Crime Fighting, Law Enforcement and Service Provider Role Orientations in Community-Based Police Officers," *American Journal of Police* XIV, no. 3/4 (1995): 182.

9. Westley, *Violence and the Police*.

10. Richard Seltzer, Sucre Aone, and Gwendolyn Howard, "Police Satisfaction with Their Jobs: Arresting Officers in the District of Columbia," *Police Studies* 19, no. 4 (1996): 33.

11. Westley, *Violence and the Police*, 76–82.

12. Jerome E. McElroy, Colleen A. Consgrove, and Susan Sadd, *Community Policing: The CPOP* in New York (Newbury Park, CA: Sage, 1993), 27.

13. Seltzer, Aone, and Howard, "Police Satisfaction with Their Jobs," 33.

14. President's Task Force on 21st Century Policing, *Final Report*, Action Item 1.4.1, 14, http://www.cops.usdoj.gov/pdf/taskforce/taskforce_finalreport.pdf.

15. Nicole E. Haas, Maarten Van Craen, Wesley G. Skogan, and Diego M. Fleitas, "Explaining Officer Compliance: The Importance of Procedural Justice and Trust Inside a Police Organization," *Criminology and Criminal Justice* 15 (September 2015): 442–463.

16. George W. Griesinger, Jeffrey S. Slovak, and Joseph J. Molkup, *Civil Service Systems: Their Impact on Police Administration* (Washington, DC: U.S. Government Printing Office, 1979); James L. O'Neill and Michael A. Cushing, *The Impact of Shift Work on Police Officers* (Washington, DC: PERF, 1991).

17. Albert J. Reiss, *The Police and the Public* (New Haven: Yale University Press, 1971), 168; see also President's Commission on Law Enforcement and Administration of Justice, *Task Force Report: The Police* (Washington, DC: U.S. Government Printing Office, 1967), 165.

18. James J. Fyfe, "Who Shoots? A Look at Officer Race and Police Shooting," *Journal of Police Science and Administration* 9 (December 1981): 373.

19. Karen Amendola, et al., *The Shift Length Experiment: What We Know About 8-, 10-, and 12-hour Shifts in Policing* (Washington, DC: The Police Foundation, 2011), http://www.policefoundation.org/publication/shift-length-experiment/.

20. Westley, *Violence and the Police*, viii.

21. Ibid., 11.

22. Sue Rahr and Stephen K. Rice, *From Warriors to Guardians: Recommitting American Police Culture to Democratic Ideals* (Cambridge, MA: Harvard Kennedy School, 2015), https://www.hks.harvard.edu/content/download/76023/1708385/version/1/file/WarriorstoGuardians.pdf.

23. Westley, *Violence and the Police.*, 76–82.

24. Ibid.

25. Stephen D. Mastrofksi, Jeffrey B. Snipes, and Anne E. Supina, "Compliance on Demand: The Public's Response to Specific Requests," *Journal of Research in Crime and Delinquency* 33 (August 1996): 296–305.

26. Susan Martin, *Breaking and Entering: Police Women on Patrol* (Berkeley: University of California Press, 1980), 97.

27. Ibid., 113.

28. David Weisburd and Rosann Greenspan, with Edwin E. Hamilton, Hubert Williams, and Kellie Bryant, *Police Attitudes Toward Abuse of Authority: Findings from a National Study* (Washington, DC: Department of Justice, 2000), http://www.policefoundation.org/wp-content/uploads/2015/06/Weisburd-et-al.-2001-The-Abuse-of-Police-Authority.pdf.

29. Christopher Commission, *Report of the Independent Commission to Investigate the Los Angeles Police Department* (Los Angeles: City of Los Angeles, 1991), 168–171, www.parc.info.

30. Weisburd et al., *Police Attitudes Toward Abuse of Authority.*

31. Police Accountability Task Force, *Recommendations for Reform: Restoring Trust between the Chicago Police and the Communities They Serve* (Chicago: Author, April 2016), 69–70.

32. Westley, *Violence and the Police*, 121–122.

33. Weisburd et al., *Police Attitudes Toward Abuse of Authority.*

34. Jerome H. Skolnick, *Justice without Trial: Law Enforcement in Democratic Society*, 3rd ed. (New York: Macmillan, 1994), 44–47.

35. Police Executive Research Forum, *Racially Biased Policing: A Principled Response* (Washington, DC: Author, 2001), http://www.policeforum.org/assets/docs/Free_Online_Documents/Racially-Biased_Policing/racially%20biased%20policing%20-%20a%20principled%20response%202001.pdf.

36. Fair and Impartial Policing Project website at http://www.fairimpartialpolicing.com/.

37. Egon Bittner, "The Functions of the Police in Modern Society," in Egon Bittner, ed., *Aspects of Police Work* (Boston: Northeastern University Press, 1990), 120–132.

38. David M. Kennedy, *Don't Shoot: One Man, A Street Fellowship, and the End of Violence in Inner-City America* (New York: Bloomsbury, 2011).

39. Skolnick, *Justice without Trial*; Rahr and Rice, *From Warriors to Guardians*.

40. Bureau of Justice Statistics, *Policing and Homicide, 1976–98: Justifiable Homicide by Police, Police Officers Murdered by Felons* (Washington, DC: U.S. Department of Justice, 2000).

41. Federal Bureau of Investigation, *Law Enforcement Officers Killed or Assaulted, 2014* (Washington, DC: Department of Justice, 2015), https://www.fbi.gov/about-us/cjis/ucr/leoka/2014/officers-feloniously-killed/main.

42. Ibid., tables 71, 76.

43. Skolnick, *Justice without Trial*; *Terry v. Ohio,* 392 U.S. 1 (1968).

44. Skolnick, *Justice Without Trial*, 1–21, 199–223; Herbert Packer, *The Limits of the Criminal Sanction* (Stanford: Stanford University Press, 1968), ch. 8.

45. *Floyd v. City of New York* (2013).

46. Nathaniel Bronstein, "Police Management and Quotas: Governance in the Compstat Era," *Columbia Journal of Law and Social Problems* 48, no. 4 (2015): 544–581; President's Task Force on 21st Century Policing, *Final Report*, Recommendation 2.9, 26.

47. David Sklansky, "Not Your Father's Police Department: Making Sense of the New Demographics of Law Enforcement," *Journal of Criminal Law and Criminology* 96 (Spring 2006): 1209–1248.

48. Steve Herbert, "Police Subculture Reconsidered," *Criminology* 36, no. 2 (1998): 343–368.

49. Christopher Slobogin, "Testilying: Police Perjury and What to Do about It," *University of Colorado Law Review* 67 (Fall 1996): 1037–1059.

50. Police Accountability Task Force, *Recommendations for Reform*, 71.

51. Samuel Walker, "Racial-Minority and Female Employment in Policing: The Implications of 'Glacial Change'," *Crime and Delinquency* 31 (October 1985): 555–572.

52. Robin N. Haarr, "Patterns of Interaction in a Police Patrol Bureau: Race and Gender Barriers to Integration," *Justice Quarterly* 14 (March 1997): 53.

53. Bureau of Justice Statistics, *Local Police Departments, 2013: Personnel, Policies, and Practices* (Washington, DC: U.S. Department of Justice, 2015), http://www.bjs.gov/content/pub/pdf/lpd13ppp.pdf.

54. National Center for Women and Policing, *Equality Denied. The Status of Women in Policing 2000* (Los Angeles: Author, 2001).

55. Martin, *Breaking and Entering*, 79–108.

56. Ibid., 102–107.

57. Gary Cordner and AnnMarie Cordner, "Stuck on a Plateau? Obstacles to Recruitment," Selection and Retention of Women Police, *Police Quarterly* 14, no. 3 (2011): 207–226; Bureau of Justice Statistics, *Local Police Departments, 2013*, table 4.

58. Susan Ehrlich Martin and Nancy Jurik, *Doing Justice, Doing Gender: Women in Law and Criminal Justice Occupations* (Thousand Oaks, CA: Sage, 1996), 68; Susan E. Martin, *On the Move: The Status of Women in Policing* (Washington, DC: The Police Foundation, 1990).

59. Carol A. Archbold and Dorothy Moses Schulz, "Making Rank: The Lingering Effects of Tokenism on Female Police Officers' Promotion Aspirations," *Police Quarterly* 11 (March 2008): 50–73.

60. Peter B. Bloch and Deborah Anderson, *Policewomen on Patrol: Final Report* (Washington, DC: The Police Foundation, 1974). The various studies are summarized in Martin and Jurik, *Doing Justice, Doing Gender,* chs. 3 and 4. For a critique of these studies, however, see Merry Morash and Jack R. Greene, "Evaluating Women on Patrol: A Critique of Contemporary Wisdom," *Evaluation Review* 10 (April 1986): 230–255.

61. Joyce L. Sichel, Lucy N. Friedman, Janice C. Quint, and Michael E. Smith, *Women on Patrol: A Pilot Study of Police Performance in New York City* (Washington, DC: U.S. Government Printing Office, 1978).

62. National Center for Women and Policing, *Men, Women, and Police Excessive Force: A Tale of Two Genders* (Los Angeles: Author, 2002); Kimberly A. Lonsway, *Hiring and Retaining More Women: The Advantages to Law Enforcement Agencies* (Los Angeles: National Center for Women and Policing, 2000).

63. National Center for Women and Policing, *Men, Women, and Police Excessive Force.*

64. International Association of Chiefs of Police, *Addressing Sexual Offenses and Misconduct by Law Enforcement: Executive Guide* (Alexandria, VA: Author, 2011), http://www.nccpsafety.org/assets/files/library/Addressing_Sexual_Offenses_and_Misconduct_by_LE.pdf.

65. Somvadee Chaiyavej and Merry Morash, "Reasons for Policewomen's Assertive and Passive Reactions to Sexual Harassment," *Police Quarterly* 12 (2009): 63–85.

66. Merrick Bobb, *13th Semiannual Report of the Special Counsel to the Los Angeles Sheriff's Department* (Los Angeles: PARC, December 2000), 57–74, www.parc.info.

67. President's Task Force on 21st Century Policing, *Final Report*, Action Item 2.13.1 and Action Item 2.13.2.

68. National Black Police Officers Association, *Police Brutality: How to Stop the Violence* (Washington, DC: NBPOA, n.d.), http://www.blackpolice.org/.

69. Weisburd et al., *Police Attitudes toward Abuse of Authority*.

70. National Black Police Officers Association website at http://www.blackpolice.org/ and NOBLE website at http://www.noblenational.org/home.aspx.

71. President's Commission on Law Enforcement and Administration of Justice, *The Challenge of Crime in a Free Society* (Washington, DC: U.S. Government Printing Office, 1967), 101–102.

72. Albert Reiss, "Police Brutality—Answers to Key Questions," *Transaction* 5 (July–August 1968): 10–19.

73. New York City, Civilian Complaint Review Board, *Status Report, January–December 2007*, table 9; San Jose Independent Police Auditor, *Annual Report, 2007* (San Jose: Author, 2008), 50.

74. James J. Fyfe, "Who Shoots? A Look at Officer Race and Police Shooting," *Journal of Police Science & Administration* 9 (December 1981): 367–382.

75. Dawn Irlbeck, "Latino Police Officers: Patterns of Ethnic Self-Identity and Latino Community Attachment," *Police Quarterly* 11 (December 2008): 468–495.

76. Patrick Suraci, "The Beginning of GOAL," www.goalny.org.

77. Stephen Leinen, *Gay Cops* (New Brunswick, NJ: Rutgers University Press, 1993).

78. Susan L. Miller, Kay B. Forest, and Nancy Jurik, "Diversity in Blue: Lesbian and Gay Police Officers in a Masculine Occupation," *Men and Masculinities* 5 (April 2003): 355–385.

79. Roddrick Colvin, "Shared Perceptions among Lesbian and Gay Police Officers: Barriers and Opportunities in the Law Enforcement Work Environment," *Police Quarterly* 12 (2009): 86–101.

80. Ibid.

81. Susan E. Martin, "Outsider within the Station House: The Impact of Race and Gender on Black Women Police," *Social Problems* 41 (August 1994): 393.

82. Haarr, "Patterns of Interaction in a Police Patrol Bureau," 65.

83. Ibid.

84. Wesley G. Skogan and Kathleen Frydl, *Fairness and Effectiveness in Policing: The Evidence* (Washington, DC: National Academies Press, 2004), 148.

85. James R. Lasley, James Larson, Chandrika Kelso, Gregory Chris Brown, "Assessing the Long-Term Effects of Officer Race on Police Attitudes towards the Community: A Case for Representative Bureaucracy Theory," *Police Practice and Research* 12 (December 2011): 474–491.

86. David L. Carter, Allen D. Sapp, and Darrel W. Stephens, *The State of Police Education* (Washington, DC: Police Executive Research Forum, 1989), 38.

87. Lawrence W. Sherman, *The Quality of Police Education* (San Francisco: Jossey-Bass, 1978).

88. Victor E. Kappeler, David Carter, and Allen Sapp, "Police Officer Higher Education, Citizen Complaints, and Departmental Rule Violation," *American Journal of Police* 11, no. 2 (1992): 37–54; Jason Rydberg and William Terrill, "The Effect of Higher Education on Police Behavior," *Police Quarterly* 13, no 1 (2010): 92–120.

89. Wesley G. Skogan and Kathleen Frydl, *Fairness and Effectiveness in Policing: The Evidence*, (Washington, DC: National Academies Press, 2004), 141–147.

90. Skolnick, *Justice without Trial*, 199–223.

91. Myron Orfield, "The Exclusionary Rule and Deterrence: An Empirical Study of Chicago Narcotics Officers," *University of Chicago Law Review* 54 (Summer 1987): 1016–1055.

92. Elizabeth Reuss-Ianni, *The Two Cultures of Policing* (New Brunswick, NJ: Transaction Books, 1983).

93. Samuel Walker and Morgan Macdonald, "An Alternative Remedy for Police Misconduct: A Model State 'Pattern or Practice' Statute," *George Mason University Civil Rights Law Journal* 19, no. 3 (2009): 479–552; Stephen Rushin, "Federal Enforcement of Police Reform," *Fordham Law Review* 82 (2014), 3189–3247.

94. Christopher Stone, Todd Foglesong, and Christina M. Cole, *Policing Los Angeles under a Consent Decree: The Dynamics of Change at the LAPD* (Cambridge, MA: Harvard Kennedy School, 2009).

95. Wesley G. Skogan and Susan M. Hartnett, *Community Policing, Chicago Style* (New York: Oxford University Press, 1997), 80, 83.

96. Ibid.

97. Arthur J. Lurigio and Dennis P. Rosenbaum, "The Impact of Community Policing on Police Personnel," in Dennis P. Rosenbaum, ed., *The Challenge of Community Policing* (Thousand Oaks, CA: Sage, 1994), 147–163.

98. Albert J. Reiss Jr., *The Police and the Public* (New Haven: Yale University Press, 1971), 147.

99. Wesley G. Skogan and Kathleen Frydl, *Fairness and Effectiveness in Policing: The Evidence*, 135.

100. Robert Friedrich, "Racial Prejudice and Police Treatment of Blacks," in Ralph Baker and Fred A. Meyer Jr., eds., *Evaluating Alternative Law Enforcement Policies* (Lexington, MA: Lexington Books, 1979).

101. Steve Herbert, "Police Subculture Reconsidered," *Criminology* 36, no. 2 (1998): 355–356.

102. Joan R. Petersilia, Allan Abrahamse, and James Q. Wilson, *Police Performance and Case Attrition* (Santa Monica, CA: RAND, 1987).

103. David H. Bayley and James Garofalo, "The Management of Violence by Police Patrol Officers," *Criminology* 27 (February 1989): 1–25.

104. Bureau of Justice Statistics, *Law Enforcement Management and Administrative Statistics, 2007* (Washington, DC: U.S. Department of Justice, 2010).

105. Eve Buzawa, Thomas Austin, and James Bannon, "The Role of Sociodemographic and Job-Specific Variables in Predicting Patrol Officer Job Satisfaction, *American Journal of Police* 13, no. 2 (1994): 68.

106. "Chief's Scholars Program at UC to Aid City Cops," Cincinnati.com, December 28, 2008; Cincinnati Police Department, *Strategic Plan* (May 2007), 15; Lincoln Police Department, *Five Year Strategic Plan, 2007–2012* (Lincoln, NE: Lincoln Police Department, 2007).

107. Police Executive Research Forum, *Survey of Police Operational and Administrative Practices–1981* (Washington, DC: Author, 1981), 378–382.

108. Ibid., 342–346.

109. Carol A. Archbold and Dorothy Moses Schulz, "Making Rank: The Lingering Effects of Tokenism on Female Police Officers' Promotion Aspirations," *Police Quarterly* 11 (March 2008): 50–73.

110. Dorothy Guyot, "Bending Granite: Attempts to Change the Rank Structure of American Police Departments," *Journal of Police Science and Administration* 7, no. 3 (1979): 253–284.

111. Merrick Bobb, *6th Semiannual Report* (Los Angeles: Los Angeles Sheriff's Department, 1996), 50–61, www.parc.info.

112. Minneapolis Police Department website at www.ci.minneapolis.mn.us/police; Herman Goldstein, *Policing a Free Society* (Cambridge, MA: Ballinger, 1977), 241–243.

113. See the Los Angeles Police Department website at www.lapdonline.org.

114. Albert J. Reiss, *Private Employment of Public Police* (Washington, DC: U.S. Department of Justice, 1988).

115. William F. Walsh, "Patrol Officer Arrest Rates: A Study of the Social Organization of Police Work," *Justice Quarterly* 3 (September 1986): 276.

116. Reiss, *Private Employment of Public Police.*

117. San Jose Independent Police Auditor, *1998 Annual Report*, www.cityofsanjose.gov/ipa/.

118. Mollen Commission, *Commission Report* (New York: City of New York: 1994), 81.

119. Standard 35.1.2, Commission on Accreditation for Law Enforcement Agencies, *Standards for Law Enforcement Agencies*, 4th ed. (Fairfax, VA: CALEA, 1999).

120. Christopher Commission, *Report of the Independent Commission on the Los Angeles Police Department* (Los Angeles: Author, 1991).

121. Los Angeles Police Department, *Rampart Area Corruption Incident: Public Report* (Los Angeles: Los Angeles Police Department, 2000), "Executive Summary," 7.

122. Walker and Macdonald, "An Alternative Remedy for Police Misconduct: A Model State 'Pattern or Practice' Statute."

123. Frank J. Landy, *Performance Appraisal in Police Departments* (Washington, DC: The Police Foundation, 1977), 1.

124. Timothy N. Oettmeier and Mary Ann Wycoff, *Personnel Performance Evaluation in the Community Policing Context* (Washington, DC: Community Policing Consortium, 1997), 5.

125. Landy, *Performance Appraisal in Police Departments.*

126. Martin and Jurik, *Doing Justice, Doing Gender*, 86–87.

127. McNamara, "Uncertainties in Police Work," 177–178.

128. Los Angeles, *Rampart Area Corruption Incident.*

129. Bayley and Garofalo, "The Management of Violence by Police Patrol Officers."

130. Ibid.

131. Jerome E. McElroy, Colleen A. Cosgrove, and Susan Sadd, *Community Policing: The CPOP in New York* (Newbury Park, CA: Sage, 1993), 27.

132. See the categories used in Jack R. Greene, "Police Officer Job Satisfaction and Community Perceptions: Implications for Community-Oriented Policing," *Journal of Research in Crime and Delinquency* 26 (May 1984): 168–183.

133. Buzawa, Austin, and Bannon, "The Role of Selected Sociodemographic and Job-Specific Variables in Predicting Patrol Officer Job Satisfaction."

134. William P. McCarty, Arnie Schuck, Wesley Skogan, and Dennis Rosenbaum, *Stress, Burnout, and Health* (National Police Research Platform, n.d.), http://static1.1.sqspcdn.com/static/f/733761/10444483/1296183365827/Stress+Burnout++and+Health+FINAL.pdf?token=eNtnpmo72jP4eR5ytHEWgV4hWr8%3D.

135. John Ritter, "Suicide Rates Jolt Police Culture," *USA Today,* February 8, 2007, www.usatoday.com/news/nation/2007-02-08-police-suicides_x.htm.

136. Arthur Niederhoffer, *The Police Family* (Lexington, MA: Lexington Books, 1978).

137. Shawn P. McCoy and Michael G. Aamodt, "A Comparison of Law Enforcement Divorce Rates with Those of Other Occupations," *Journal of Police and Criminal Psychology* 25, no. 1 (2010): 1–16.

138. O'Neill and Cushing, *The Impact of Shift Work.*

139. Martin and Jurik, *Doing Justice, Doing Gender*, 95.

140. *The Badge of Life: A Study of Police Suicide 2008–2015,* http://www.policesuicidestudy.com; Mark Bond, "Silent Suffering: Warning Signs and Steps to Prevent Police Suicide," Inpublicsafety.com (March 17, 2014), http://inpublicsafety.com/2014/03/silent-suffering-warning-signs-and-steps-to-prevent-police-suicide/.

141. International Association Chiefs of Police, *Breaking the Silence on Law Enforcement Suicides* (Arlington, VA: Author, 2014), iii.

142. "NIOSH: Police Officers, Firefighters Have the Highest Rate of Suicide," *Safety and Health Magazine* (April 18, 2016), http://www.safetyandhealthmagazine.com/articles/12084-niosh-police-officers-firefighters-have-highest-rate-of-suicide; *Badge of Life: A Study of Police Suicide 2008–2015.*

143. International Association of Chiefs of Police, *Breaking the Silence on Law Enforcement Suicides.*

144. David C. Brody, Christianne DeMarco, and Nicholas P. Lovrich, "Community Policing and Job Satisfaction: Suggestive Evidence of Positive Workforce Effects from a Multijurisdictional Comparison in Washington State," *Police Quarterly* 5, no. 2 (2002): 181–205.

145. Gail A. Goolkasian, *Coping with Police Stress* (Washington, DC: U.S. Government Printing Office, 1985), 11–12.

146. Dennis P. Rosenbaum, Arnie Schuck, and Gary Cordner, *The National Police Research Platform: The Life Course of New Officers* (n.d.), http://

static1.1.sqspcdn.com/static/f/733761/10618445/1297062716553/Recruits+Life+Course.pdf?token=QbYZVZXu5MtKOgiho24VJfFD3O8%3D.

147. Peter Finn and Julie Esselman Tomz, *Developing a Law Enforcement Stress Program for Officers and Their Families* (Washington, DC: U.S. Government Printing Office, 1997).

148. President's Task Force on 21st Century Policing, *Final Report*, Action Item 6.1.2.

149. Ibid., 79–88.

150. Kevin Keenan and Samuel Walker, "An Impediment to Police Accountability? An Analysis of Statutory Law Enforcement Officers Bill of Rights," *Boston University Public Interest Law Journal* 14 (Spring 2005): 185–244.

151. Bureau of Justice Statistics, *Local Police Departments, 2013: Personnel, Policies, and Practices,* appendix table 3. The data in the table are ambiguous, as a large number of departments are cited as having "Expired" collective bargaining agreements. This could mean that at the time of the survey no agreement had been reached on a new contract.

152. Samuel Walker, *Police Union Contract "Waiting Periods" For Misconduct Investigations Not Supported by Scientific Evidence* (July 1, 2015), http://samuelwalker.net/wp-content/uploads/2015/06/48HourSciencepdf.pdf.

153. Police Accountability Task Force, *Recommendations for Reform.*

154. *Garrity v. New Jersey*, 385 U.S. 493 (1966).

155. President's Commission on Law Enforcement and Administration of Justice, *Task Force Report: The Police*, 9.

156. Martin, *On the Move.*

157. William G. Doerner, "Officer Retention Patterns: An Affirmative Action Concern for Police Agencies," *American Journal of Police* XIV, no. 3/4 (1995), 197–210.

158. Jerry Sparger and David Giacopassi, "Swearing In and Swearing Off: A Comparison of Cops' and Ex-Cops' Attitudes toward the Workplace," in Daniel B. Kennedy and Robert J. Homer, eds. *Police and Law Enforcement* (New York: AMS, 1987), 35–54.

159. Roger L. Goldman, "A Model Decertification Law," *St. Louis University Public Law Review* XXXII (2012): 147–156.

© Lon C. Ciehl/PhotoEdit

PART III

Police Work

CHAPTER **7**   Patrol: The Backbone of Policing

CHAPTER **8**   Peacekeeping and Order Maintenance

CHAPTER **9**   The Police and Crime

CHAPTER **10**   Advances in Police Strategy

© Lon C. Ciehl/PhotoEdit

7

Patrol: The Backbone of Policing

CHAPTER OUTLINE

The Central Role of Patrol

The Functions of Patrol

The Organization and Delivery of Patrol

Factors Affecting the Delivery of Patrol Services

Number of Sworn Officers

Assignment to Patrol

The Distribution of Patrol Officers

Assignment of Patrol Officers

"Hot Spots"

Types of Patrol

Foot Patrol

One-Officer versus Two-Officer Cars

Staffing Patrol Beats

Styles of Patrol

Individual Styles

Supervisors' Styles

Organizational Styles

Patrol Supervision: The Role of the Sergeant

The Communications Center

The Nerve Center of Policing

911 Systems

Processing Calls for Service

Operator—Citizen Interactions

The Systematic Study of Police Patrol

Standards for Systematic Social Observation

The Call Service Workload

The Volume of Calls

Types of Calls

Aspects of Patrol Work
    Response Time
    Officer Use of Patrol Time
    Evading Duty
    High-Speed Pursuits
The Effectiveness of Patrol
    Initial Experiments
    The Kansas City Preventive Patrol
    Experiment
    Findings and Implications of the
    Kansas City Experiment

The Newark Foot Patrol Experiment
New Questions, New Approaches
Improving Traditional Patrol
    Differential Response to Calls
    Telephone Reporting Units
    311 Nonemergency Numbers
    Non-English 911 Call Services
    Reverse 911
    Computers and Video Cameras in
    Patrol Cars
    Police Aides or Cadets

Directed Patrol and Hot Spots
Customer Feedback
Beyond Traditional Patrol
CASE STUDY

Summary
Key Terms
For Discussion
Internet Exercise

Patrol is the **backbone of policing,** the central feature of police operations. This chapter examines the nature of patrol work in contemporary American policing: how patrol is organized and delivered, the nature of citizen calls for service, the effectiveness of patrol in deterring crime, and programs designed to improve patrol services.

backbone of policing

The Central Role of Patrol

The cop on the beat is both the symbol of American policing and the center of police activity. First, the majority of police officers are assigned to patrol, and in that capacity, they deliver the bulk of police services to the public.

Second, the marked patrol car and the uniformed patrol officer are the visible symbols of the police. They are a lightning rod for public attitudes about the role of the police in society.

Third, patrol officers are the most important decision makers in policing and the gatekeepers of the entire criminal justice system. James Q. Wilson points out that police departments are unique in that discretion increases as one moves *down* the organizational hierarchy. In deciding whether or not to make an arrest, or how to handle a domestic disturbance, patrol officers are the real policymakers in policing. Making decisions that affect people's lives, they are "street-level bureaucrats."[1]

Fourth, experience on patrol is a formative part of a police officer's career. In virtually all American police departments, assignments are based on seniority. New officers start out on patrol duty, usually on the evening shift and in the highest-crime neighborhoods. This street experience becomes an important part of the police officer subculture, forging a bond of common experience among officers.

Despite its central role, patrol duty has generally been considered the least desirable assignment, and career advancement usually means promotion or assignment to something more desirable, especially detective work. The National Advisory Commission on Criminal Justice Standards and Goals comments that "the patrolman is usually the lowest-paid, least-consulted, most taken-for-granted member of the force. His duty is looked on as routine and boring." Community policing seeks to

For more discussion of community policing, see Chapter 10.

correct this long-standing problem by giving patrol officers more decision-making authority as problem solvers who respond to neighborhood problems.[2]

The Functions of Patrol

functions of patrol

Robert Peel, creator of the modern police, defined the functions of police patrol.[3] The three basic **functions of patrol** are as follows:

1. To deter crime.
2. To enhance feelings of public safety.
3. To make officers available for service.

For a full discussion of Robert Peel and the creation of the modern police, see Chapter 2.

O. W. Wilson, for decades the leading expert on police management, explained that patrol seeks to deter crime by creating "an impression of omnipresence" that will eliminate "the actual opportunity (or the belief that the opportunity exists) for successful misconduct."[4]

The second function of patrol is to maintain feelings of public safety. The visible presence of patrol officers seeks to assure law-abiding citizens that they are being protected against crime. Most people believe that patrol deters crime, and when asked to suggest improvements in policing, they want more police and/or more patrol in their neighborhoods.[5]

The third function of patrol is to make officers available for service by dispersing officers throughout the community. Albert Reiss observes that "no other professional operates in a comparable setting."[6] The clients of other professionals—doctors, lawyers, and dentists—must go to the professionals' offices. The police may be the last profession to make house calls.

The Organization and Delivery of Patrol

Visit different police departments and you will find that patrol is carried out in different ways. New York City uses a lot of foot patrol: 39 percent of all patrol units, according to Law Enforcement Management and Administrative Statistics (LEMAS) data. The San Jose, California, police department, meanwhile, uses no foot-patrol units. In Florida, one-third of all patrol units in St. Petersburg involve officers on motorcycles, compared with only 5 percent in Miami.[7]

Factors Affecting the Delivery of Patrol Services

When people say they want more police protection, they generally mean more *patrol* officers, and usually more *patrol* officers *in their neighborhoods*. Not all police departments are efficient in organizing and delivering patrol to the public. Efficiency depends on the following factors: the number of sworn officers, the percentage of officers assigned to patrol, the distribution of patrol officers by time of day and area, the type of patrol used (automobile versus foot), one-officer versus two-officer patrols, and the work styles of patrol officers.

Number of Sworn Officers

police–population ratio

How many officers should a police department have? The traditional measure of the level of police protection in a community is the **police–population ratio.** Some cities have a lot of police officers, whereas others have relatively few. In Washington, D.C.,

POLICE in FOCUS | The Best Kept Secret

David Bayley notes that one of the best kept secrets in policing is that to add just 1 officer on the street, an agency must hire an additional 10 officers. He explains that, on average, about 60 to 70 percent of officers perform visible street patrol. Of these officers, only about 17 percent are on the street at any given time because they work different shifts or days of the week. Next, 17 percent of these officers do not work because of sick days, required training, and other personal or professional activities.

Source: David Bayley, *Police for the Future* (New York: Oxford University Press, 1994).

there were 6.1 sworn officers for every 1,000 people in 2013. In San Diego, California, by contrast, there were only 1.4 per 1,000. The national average for larger municipal departments in 2013 was 2.3 officers per 1,000 population.[8] (See Exhibit 7–1.)

Does a higher police–population ratio mean that a city receives better police protection? Although the ratio is widely used as a measure of the amount of police service, cities with more police per population do not necessarily have lower crime rates. The reverse is often true: Cities with high crime rates often have more police officers, because high crime rates produce public demand for more police.[9]

Washington, D.C., with the highest police–population ratio in the nation, does not have a correspondingly low crime rate. Failure to utilize patrol officers efficiently results in fewer officers being available on the street to respond to calls for service. Exhibit 7–2 compares two hypothetical police departments in cities of the same size. The department in City A has 50 percent more officers than City B does and a higher police–population ratio: 1.8 per 1,000 versus 1.2 per 1,000. Because it utilizes its officers in a more efficient manner, City B has more officers on patrol during the high-crime period between 4 P.M. and midnight. How does this happen? First, City B assigns a higher percentage of its officers to patrol. Then it assigns a higher percentage of its patrol officers to the busy 4 P.M. to midnight shift, when more officers are needed. Finally, it puts most of its patrol officers in one-officer patrol cars (with some two-officer patrols for the very high crime areas).

EXHIBIT 7–1

Police–Population Ratios, Selected Cities, 2013

City	Sworn Officers per 1,000 Residents
Washington, D.C.	6.1
New York City	4.1
Detroit	3.6
Baltimore	4.7
San Diego	1.4
San Antonio	1.6
San Jose	1.0

Source: Bureau of Justice Statistics, *Local Police Departments, 2013* (Washington, DC: U.S. Department of Justice, 2015), appendix table 2.

EXHIBIT 7–2

Deployment of Patrol Officers in Two Hypothetical Cities

	City A	City B
Population	500,000	500,000
Sworn officers	900	600
Percentage of officers assigned to patrol	50%	70%
Officers assigned to patrol	450	420
Percentage of patrol officers assigned to 4 P.M. to midnight shift	33%	50%
Patrol officers, 4 P.M. TO midnight shift	148	210
One-officer patrols	20	190
Two-officer patrols	64	10
Total patrols, 4 P.M. to midnight	84	200

The result of efficient management? City B spends less on police services but gets more actual police protection on the street. This analysis also demonstrates why the official police–population ratio is not a good measure of the level of police services.

Assignment to Patrol

As a first step, a certain percentage of officers must be assigned to patrol duty. Surprisingly, this percentage varies widely from department to department. Some departments place as many as 80 percent of all their officers on patrol (including traffic units), whereas others are able to place only 50 or 65 percent. Many of those departments have sworn officers in assignments that other departments give to civilian employees.

The Distribution of Patrol Officers

Officers assigned to patrol need to be allocated to shifts and areas, based on a workload formula, involving citizen calls for service and reported crimes.[10]

Most serious crimes occur at night, as do the majority of disturbances (family disputes, bar fights, and so on). Exhibit 7–3 indicates the distribution of 911 calls for service and the assignment of officers by shift in Omaha, Nebraska.[11] The data indicate that the assignment of officers is reasonably related to the workload. All police departments do not operate in a rational manner, however. An investigation of the Philadelphia police found that "the same number of officers are on the street at all times—during the early morning, when there is practically no activity, and on weekend evenings, when the calls for service are heaviest."[12]

Some departments use a fourth patrol shift, beginning in the late afternoon and ending in the early morning (for example, 6 P.M. to 2 A.M.).[13] This approach provides additional officers on the evening shift, when the number of calls is highest, and avoids overstaffing in the early morning hours, when the number of calls is at its lowest.

Crime and disorder are not evenly distributed throughout the community. In his study of deadly force by New York City police officers, James J. Fyfe found that the police department gave precincts different experience ratings. The A precincts were classified as high-experience assignments because they were high-crime areas,

EXHIBIT 7–3

Distribution of 911 Calls, Omaha, Nebraska

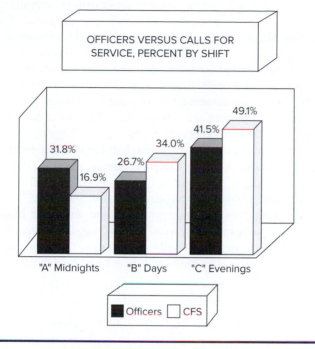

OFFICERS VERSUS CALLS FOR
SERVICE, PERCENT BY SHIFT

49.1%

41.5%

34.0%

31.8%

26.7%

16.9%

"A" Midnights   "B" Days   "C" Evenings

■ Officers □ CFS

B precincts were medium-experience assignments, and C precincts were low-experience. Fyfe described C precincts as "residential 'country clubs' that place comparatively few demands on their police."[14]

Crime is more prevalent in poorer neighborhoods, and low-income people are the heaviest users of police services for order maintenance and general assistance. The National Crime Victimization Survey (NCVS) reports that the violent crime rate for the poorest households (income of $15,000 or less) was 40.6 per 1,000, compared with 18.1 per 1,000 for households with incomes over $75,000.[15]

Low-income people are also the heaviest users of police services for noncrime events: medical emergencies and other types of situations requiring assistance. And because a disproportionate number of racial and ethnic minorities live in low-income neighborhoods, more police are generally assigned to minority neighborhoods.

Some departments fail to redraw beat boundaries regularly to adjust for social change. Neighborhoods grow or decline in population. Some deteriorate economically; as a neighborhood shifts from middle income to low income, crime and calls for service generally increase. The report on Philadelphia found that the department had not redrawn its boundaries in 16 years. Partly as a result, officers in the Thirty-Fifth District handled an average of 494 calls, while officers in the Fifth District handled only 225. The disparity in workload was even greater in terms of serious crime: Officers in the Thirty-Fifth District handled an average of 38 major offenses per year, compared with only 8 major offenses for officers in the Fifth District.[16]

Assignment of Patrol Officers

Police departments use a variety of methods for assigning patrol officers to particular shifts and patrol areas. Some assign officers on the basis of a strict seniority system and permit bidding for new assignments every six months or annually.

The issue of how often to change patrol officers' assignments involves conflicting principles. Many experts favor keeping officers in the same assignment for long periods of time. This allows patrol officers to get to know the people and the problems of their area. Some community policing programs are based on this principle. At the same time, however, it may cause officers to become bored and frustrated at the lack of new opportunities. As an anticorruption measure, some experts recommend frequent assignment changes to keep officers from developing too close relations with potentially corrupting influences.

Some departments rotate officers through different shifts every month, or on an even shorter time frame. A Police Executive Research Forum (PERF) report concludes that frequent changes in shift are "deleterious to the physical and psychological health of the individual and to the well-being of the organization."[17]

Problems include loss of sleep, cardiovascular and other health problems, on-the-job accidents, disrupted family lives, and low morale. The report recommends steady shift assignments, based primarily on seniority, but with some managerial discretion in assignment based on performance and workload needs.

"Hot Spots"

Patrol Beat 144 in Kansas City was one of the most dangerous areas in the nation. In 1991, the homicide rate was 177 per 100,000, about 20 times the national rate. Partly for this reason, the beat was chosen as the site for the Kansas City Gun Experiment, an innovative program to remove guns from the streets.[18]

hot spot

Beat 144 is a classic example of a **hot spot:** an area that receives a disproportionate number of calls for police service and/or has a very high crime rate. A study of calls for service to the Minneapolis Police Department found that only 5 percent of the addresses in the city accounted for 64 percent of all calls. Meanwhile, 60 percent of the addresses never called the police for any reason. Reviewing this body of literature, John Eck and Emily Eck reported that hot spots remain hot over long periods of time—for years or even several decades.[19] For example, Anthony Braga and colleagues reported that, in Boston, gun crime and robbery were highly concentrated in a small number of the same places from 1980 through 2008.[20]

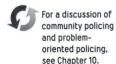 For a discussion of community policing and problem-oriented policing, see Chapter 10.

Routine police work is heavily skewed: A relatively small number of citizens in a community are extremely high consumers of police services.[21] Focusing police activities on hot spots is one of the most important innovations in policing, particularly in community policing and problem-oriented policing programs.

Types of Patrol

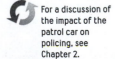 For a discussion of the impact of the patrol car on policing, see Chapter 2.

Most (84 percent) police patrol in the United States today involves automobile patrol. Only 4 percent of all patrol is done on foot, 5 percent is done on motorcycle, and another 5 percent on bicycles.[22] Automobile patrol provides more efficient coverage than foot patrol. A patrol car can cover more area, pass each point more often, return to particular spots in an unpredictable manner if necessary, and respond quickly to calls for service. The efficiency of the patrol car in this regard is the reason police departments converted from foot patrol to car patrol between the 1920s and the 1950s.

Efficiency comes at a price, however. An officer in a patrol car loses direct contact with most citizens, especially law-abiding people. As a result, some people begin to see the police as an occupying army. William A. Westley was probably the first expert to notice this effect of automobile patrol. In his 1950 study of Gary, Indiana, he noted that "in contrast to the man on the beat, the man in the car is isolated from the community."[23] A decade and a half later, when riots were erupting across the country, no one could ignore the problem. The President's Crime Commission observed in 1967 that "the most significant weakness in American motor patrol operations today is the general lack of contact with citizens except when an officer has responded to a call. Forced to stay near the car's radio, awaiting an assignment, most patrol officers have few opportunities to develop closer relationships with persons living in the district."[24]

Foot Patrol

Foot patrol involves a difficult trade-off between efficiency and community relations. An officer on foot cannot cover as much territory as an officer in a patrol car. This inefficiency is offset, however, by positive gains in community relations. They can have more personal contact with neighborhood residents, and this can help build trust. The Newark Foot Patrol Experiment, meanwhile, found that an increase in the number of foot-patrol officers in an area resulted in people having less fear of crime and more positive attitudes toward the police.

For this reason, many community policing programs include a foot-patrol element. But because of their limited mobility, it is not possible for a department to put all its patrol officers on foot patrol. Only about 4 percent of all patrol officers in the United States today patrol on foot.[25]

Striking the proper balance between efficiency and better community relations is a difficult issue. The Santa Barbara, California, police department utilizes both bicycle and foot patrol as part of its Tactical Patrol Force. These patrols are deployed on a regular basis in the central business district and the beach area; they are also used for special events such as parades or athletic events. The department regards them as an effective approach to both community relations and the police operations.[26]

foot patrol

The Newark Foot Patrol Experiment is described in more detail later in this chapter.

One-Officer versus Two-Officer Cars

A 1996 proposal in New York City to convert from two-officer to one-officer patrols in low-crime districts caused a predictable outcry. One critic angrily accused the mayor of "jeopardizing the lives of cops."[27] Many rank-and-file officers have opposed one-officer patrol assignments on the grounds that this approach endangers their safety.

Most patrol units—89 percent of all patrols in municipal police departments—involve single police officers. One-officer patrols are more efficient than two-officer patrols: two one-officer cars can patrol twice as much area and be available for twice as many calls as one two-officer car. Some police departments, however, still rely primarily on two-officer patrols in some neighborhoods and following some critical incidents.[28]

Although some rank-and-file officers favor two-officer cars, believing that they are safer, a Police Foundation study of patrol staffing in San Diego found that officers in one-officer units were assaulted less often and were less involved in resisting arrest incidents than those in two-officer units. The one-officer patrol units, moreover, made more arrests and wrote more crime reports than two-officer units. Police officer concern about safety appears to be exaggerated. In 56.5 percent of the incidents in which backup officers were dispatched in San Diego, it was later determined that they were not needed. Meanwhile, only 2.8 percent of the incidents were underdispatched, in the sense that the officers responding to the call had to request backup after they had arrived at the scene.[29]

Some police departments were slow to convert to one-officer patrols. At 6:00 A.M. on July 16, 2003, the Buffalo Police Department converted from two-officer to one-officer patrol cars. Buffalo was one of the last cities in the United States to rely exclusively on two-officer patrols. The mayor of Buffalo said, "This is an exciting time in the history of our city." The police commissioner estimated that the change would result in a 25 percent increase in the number of cars patrolling the city. The plan would allow the city to reduce the size of the police department and save an estimated $10 to $12 million per year for the financially strapped city.[30]

Staffing Patrol Beats

Robert Peel's original ideal called for a patrol officer (or more than one) on every beat. The reality of policing is very different. On any given night, no officer is available for many patrol beats. When investigators for a mayor's task force in Philadelphia went out on a randomly selected Saturday night, they were shocked at the level of police patrol. Less than half (47 percent of all patrol sectors: 190 out of 450) were fully staffed with the assigned number of patrol officers.[31]

Police patrol is an extremely expensive, labor-intensive enterprise. Staffing a single patrol beat around the clock, seven days a week, requires almost five (4.8) officers. In addition to the three officers assigned to each shift, almost two others are needed because of days off, vacations, illness, and injuries. In practice, police departments are often shorthanded and have a difficult time fully staffing patrol beats.

Styles of Patrol

Individual Styles

How much work do patrol officers do? A New York City police officer explained that "it depends on what [you] want to make of it. . . . You can make it as easy or difficult as you want. If it's done the way it's probably supposed to be done, it's probably not easy at all. But, it's the type of assignment you can also 'skate' in."[32]

officer-initiated activity   In short, the amount of police work done by patrol officers depends on their work styles. Some officers initiate more activity than others. **Officer-initiated activity** includes stopping, questioning, and frisking suspicious citizens; making informal contacts with law-abiding citizens; stopping vehicles for possible violations;

EXHIBIT 7–4

Ratio of Dispatch-Initiated to Self-Initiated Contacts with Citizens, Six Departments

Department	Ratio
A	3.8 : 1
B	3.6 : 1
C	1.5 : 1
D	1.2 : 1
E	1.1 : 1
F	1.0 : 1

Source: Stephen D. Mastrofski, Roger B. Parks, Albert J. Reiss Jr., Robert E. Worden, Christina DeJong, Jeffrey Snipes, and William Terrill, *Systematic Observation of Public Police* (Washington, DC: U.S. Department of Justice, 1998), exhibit 6.

writing traffic tickets; checking suspicious events; and making arrests. The amount of officer-initiated contact with citizens varies considerably from department to department. Exhibit 7–4 indicates the ratio of dispatch-initiated to officer-initiated contacts with citizens in six police departments. The 1:1 ratio for Department F means that half of all citizen contacts are officer-initiated. In Departments A and B, only about 20 percent of all contacts are officer-initiated.

In citizen-initiated calls for service, some officers initiate more activity than others. David Bayley and James Garofalo found that some officers were likely to simply observe the situation and leave, whereas others took control over the situation, asked probing questions, and had citizens explain themselves.[33] The NCVS found that in 20 percent of all reported property crimes, police officers only "looked around." They took a report in only about half of all property crimes.[34]

Supervisors' Styles

The level of an officer's activity can also be shaped by his or her supervisor's style. This issue is discussed in detail in the next section. (See also Sidebar 7–1.)

Organizational Styles

Patrol officer activity is also affected by different departmental styles of policing. James Q. Wilson identified three distinct organizational styles. The **watchman style** emphasizes peacekeeping, without aggressive law enforcement and with few controls over rank-and-file officers. The **legalistic style** emphasizes aggressive crime fighting and attempts to control officer behavior through a rule-bound, by-the-book administrative approach. The **service style** emphasizes responsiveness to community expectations and is generally found in suburban police departments where there is relatively little crime.[35] The Los Angeles Police Department has traditionally had an organizational culture that emphasizes aggressive police work, including high rates of officer-initiated contacts with citizens and high arrest rates.[36]

Some departments attempt to influence the work activity of patrol officers through quotas for traffic tickets, arrests, or field interrogations. Most experts, however, believe that numerical quotas are not related to the quality of police work.[37]

watchman style

legalistic style

service style

> ### SIDEBAR 7-1
>
> ## Supervisors' Styles of Work
>
> ### Traditional Supervisors
> *Traditional supervisors expect aggressive enforcement from subordinates rather than engagement in community-oriented activities or policing of minor disorders. They are more likely than other types of supervisors to make decisions because they tend to take over encounters with citizens or tell officers how to handle those incidents.*
>
> *Traditional sergeants and lieutenants are highly task oriented and expect subordinates to produce measurable outcomes—particularly arrests and citations—along with paperwork and documentation. Traditional supervisors give more instruction to subordinates and are less likely to reward and more likely to punish patrol officers. The traditional supervisor's ultimate concern is to control subordinate behavior.*
>
> ### Innovative Supervisors
> *Innovative supervisors are characterized by a tendency to form relationships (i.e., they consider more officers to be friends), a low level of task orientation, and more positive views of subordinates. These supervisors are considered innovative because they generally encourage their officers to embrace new philosophies and methods of policing.*
>
> ### Supportive Supervisors
> *These supervisors support subordinates by protecting them from discipline or punishment perceived as "unfair" and by providing inspirational motivation. They often serve as a buffer between officers and management to protect officers from criticism and discipline. They believe this gives their officers space to perform duties without constant worry of disciplinary action for honest mistakes.*
>
> ### Active Supervisors
> *Active supervisors embrace a philosophy of leading by example. Their goal is to be heavily involved in the field alongside subordinates while controlling patrol officer behavior, thus performing the dual function of street officer and supervisor. They take a relatively positive view of subordinates. Active supervisors also give importance to engaging in patrol work themselves.*
>
> Source: Excerpt from Robin Shepard Engel, *How Police Supervisory Styles Influence Patrol Officer Behavior* (Washington, DC: U.S. Justice Department, 2003).

Patrol Supervision: The Role of the Sergeant

Standard police management texts call for close supervision of patrol officers by their sergeants. Community policing (see Chapter 10), by contrast, generally involves less direct supervision and more discretion and control over time for officers on the street. Some New York City police officers preferred the department's community policing program because you "have more freedom . . . [you] aren't monitored by the radio and have only one sergeant who spends most of his time doing administrative work."[38]

The style of supervision affects the amount of work performed by patrol officers. The basic unit of police patrol consists of a sergeant and a crew of patrol officers. The principle of the *span of control* holds that a supervisor can effectively manage only a limited number of people. In policing, the general standard is a span of control of one sergeant to eight patrol officers.[39]

An improper span of control can have a tremendous impact on the quality of police work. A sergeant cannot keep in touch regularly with his or her officers and, most important, cannot respond to critical incidents. The special counsel to the Los Angeles Sheriff's Department found that a high rate of shootings by officers assigned to the Century Station was due in part to the span of control in that station being at times as high as 20 or 25 officers per sergeant, far in excess of the department's own recommended standard of 8 to 1.[40]

The Communications Center

The Nerve Center of Policing

Peter Manning's visit to a police **911 communications center** was a powerful experience: "My impressions of the communications center remain vivid and powerful. It was a smelly, smoky, poorly lit room reeling under the glare of harsh flickering fluorescent lights. Windowless, stuffy, with restricted exit and entry, few amenities. Nervous anxiety and worry was the prevalent tone. . . . I have rarely endured such an unpleasant field work experience."[41]

911 communications center

The communications center is the real nerve center of the modern police department. Patrol work, in fact, is dominated by modern communications technology: the telephone, the two-way radio, and the patrol car. Contemporary 911-driven police work is citizen dominated, reactive, and incident based. Critics call this system "dial a cop" and argue that the 911 system runs the police department, preventing any rational planning and proactive police response to problems.[42]

The communications center receives incoming calls from citizens, makes a series of discretionary decisions about how to handle those calls, and in many but not all cases dispatches police cars to the scene of the incident. The decisions by communications center personnel play a major role in shaping police work.[43] George Antunes and Eric Scott argue that the operator is "the key decision maker in the police bureaucracy."[44]

Exhibit 7–5 offers a schematic diagram of a police communications center. In most large police departments today, the communications system is staffed by civilians rather than sworn officers. In many departments, these personnel are not employed by the police department itself. Some states have only recently considered legislation to require training and licensing of communications center personnel.[45]

911 Systems

The 911 emergency number was introduced by the American Telephone and Telegraph (AT&T) Company in 1968. The first system went into operation in Haleyville, Alabama. Today, almost all police departments participate in a 911 system.[46]

Because of their convenience, and because police departments advertise the number, 911 systems have contributed to the great increase in calls for service. Some departments experienced increases of more than 50 percent in the first 12 months after the 911 system was installed. To manage the overload, departments assigned priorities to incoming calls based on the seriousness of the problem and the need for an immediate response. Aided by the call-stacking capabilities of computer-aided dispatch, police were able to more efficiently manage delayed responses to certain nonemergency calls.[47]

EXHIBIT 7–5

911 Communications Center

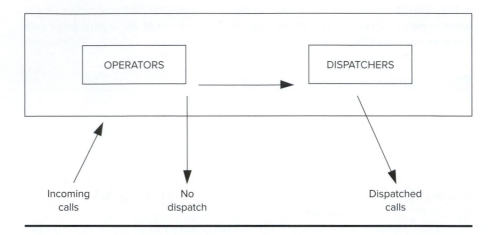

Processing Calls for Service

Processing Calls for Service

communications center operators

The 911 system is an information processing system. The **communications center operators,** dispatchers, and patrol officers are "information brokers" who receive citizen calls and translate them into official bureaucratic responses.[48] The operator obtains information from the caller and then makes a decision about the appropriate response. If he or she decides that the call requires a police response, the call is communicated to the dispatcher. The dispatcher then communicates information about the call to a patrol officer.

Operators exercise tremendous discretion, just as police officers do. Manning illustrates the processing of calls with a description of a call reporting an alleged kidnapping. The operator has available four different kidnapping-related codes, but "there are no rules given to determine selection among these options." The operators have a 300-page procedure manual, but it "is virtually never used" because it is too large and there is no room for it on the operators' consoles.[49]

The 911 call workload has certain peak periods. To cope with this, the Communications Section in Seattle has two extra shifts of operators. In addition to the three basic shifts—First Watch (11:45 P.M.–7:45 A.M.), Second Watch (7:45 A.M.–3:45 P.M.), and Third Watch (3:45 P.M.–11:45 P.M.)—there are two overlapping watches—Fourth Watch (7:45 P.M.–3:45 A.M.) and Fifth Watch (11:45 A.M.–7:45 P.M.) during peak hours.[50]

Only about half of all calls received by 911 communications centers result in the dispatch of a police officer. The Police Services Study found that 17 percent of all calls are referred to another agency. The operator takes information from the citizen in 16 percent of all calls and gives information to the citizen in 9 percent. In the remaining 14 percent of the calls, the citizen is told that the police cannot handle the call, the call is transferred, or some other response is given.[51]

Obtaining information from citizen callers is often difficult. Callers frequently provide vague, incomplete, or inaccurate information. Many are confused or frightened. Some are intoxicated or mentally disturbed. A situation that a caller describes as a "disturbance" could range from a party with only loud noise to an armed or mentally disordered person. The information is often incorrect. Bayley and Garofalo, for example, found that a weapon was actually present in only 25 percent of the reported "weapon present" calls.[52]

James Gilsinan observed 911 operators in a large midwestern city handling 265 calls over one 24-hour period. He found that operators interpret incoming information from callers and translate it into a category that fits an established bureaucratic response. Operators interact with callers in a problem-solving process, especially asking for more details, to reach the final determination.[53]

The dispatcher also exercises tremendous discretion in making important decisions. The basic decision involves which patrol unit to dispatch. The unit assigned to a particular beat is often not available: either "out of service" handling another call or not on duty at all that day. Consequently, officers are routinely assigned to calls outside their beat.[54] The most critical decision is whether the situation is an emergency and requires an expedited patrol response. Exhibit 7–6 indicates the processing of calls for service to the Los Angeles Police Department in 2010. More than 3.5 million calls were received at the department's communications center. Only about 21 percent resulted in the dispatch of a police unit. About half of the dispatches were either "emergency" or "urgent" status; 49 percent were dispatched as routine incidents.

Patrol officers process the information they receive from dispatchers, which is limited and often inaccurate. Thus, patrol officers respond to calls in the context of great uncertainty. They are dependent on the information as given by the caller, interpreted by the operator, communicated to the dispatcher, communicated to the patrol officer, and interpreted by the patrol officer. In most departments, patrol officers are not required to provide detailed records of how they handle calls. Reports are often limited to "service rendered" or "no police action required."[55]

A discussion of 911 services for callers who do not speak English is covered later in this chapter.

EXHIBIT 7–6

Calls for Service and Police Units Dispatched, Los Angeles Police Department, 2010

Total Calls for Service	3,557,626
Police Units Dispatched	732,257
Percentage of calls for service	20.6%

Dispatch Status		Percentage of Total Dispatches
Emergency	117,088	16%
Urgent	253,175	35
Routine	361,994	49

Source: Los Angeles Police Department, *Statistical Digest, 2010,* www.lapdonline.org.

Operator–Citizen Interactions

Obtaining information from a caller is one of the most important aspects of the 911 communications system. The system needs to provide a dispatched police officer with as much accurate information as possible. The process of asking questions of a caller can create problems, however. A study of 911 calls in "Citywest" analyzed operator–citizen interactions in terms of "face," defined as the desire of people to maintain a desirable public image and not experience humiliation or embarrassment (that is, to "save face").[56] The study found that many interactions are lengthy, involving many questions. Operators are trained to engage in "persistent repetition" when they cannot obtain clear or consistent information from a caller. This created problems in some calls, however.

Some questions can be perceived as threats to a caller's trustworthiness. In one call, for example, the caller finally asked, "Why are you asking [about what clothes he was wearing]?" The operator explained that the responding officers needed to be able to identify who had requested help. Some questions can be perceived as threats to a caller's intelligence. In one call, for example, the operator asked, "What do you mean . . . ?" This could be interpreted as meaning that the caller did not make any sense.

Some questions can be perceived as threats to a caller's personal character. In one call, the operator asked the caller, "You don't know your own sister's name?" implying a dysfunctional family relationship. Some questions can be perceived as questioning the caller's judgment. Operators are trained to determine whether or not an emergency actually exists. Some callers believe they know that an emergency exists and object to what they see as unnecessary questions.

In short, questions do more than elicit information. They can communicate—or appear to communicate—messages that affect the person being asked in a negative way. The study found that the different roles of the operator (call-taker) and dispatcher can conflict. Dispatchers want as much information as possible, but having operators ask many questions can alienate callers.

The Systematic Study of Police Patrol

Patrol work is the most important aspect of policing. It is the point of most police–citizen interactions. Because of the decentralized nature of the job, with officers dispersed throughout the community, studying patrol systematically is extremely difficult and expensive.[57]

There have been four major observational studies of police patrol since the mid-1950s. Sidebar 7–2 indicates the title, year, methodology, principal findings, and major publications from each one.

Standards for Systematic Social Observation

Police patrol is an extremely complex activity. Relying on single incidents or impressions will not produce an accurate picture. The process of *systematic social observation* is designed to provide an accurate, representative picture.[58]

Systematic social observation of police patrol work is accomplished by trained observers who accompany police officers at work in their cars, on foot, or even on bicycles. The expectation is that an observer accompanies the assigned officer everywhere that officer goes. Officers are told that they may direct their

```
S I D E B A R   7 – 2
```

Studies of Police Patrol

American Bar Foundation Survey, 1956–1957

Methodology: direct observation, qualitative

Sites: Kansas, Michigan, Wisconsin

Major findings: pervasive exercise of discretion; complexity of police role; use of criminal law for purposes other than prosecution

Publications: Wayne Lafave, *Arrest* (Boston: Little Brown, 1966); Donald Newman, *Conviction* (Boston: Little Brown, 1966).

President's Crime Commission, 1965–1967

Methodology: direct observation, quantitative

Sites: Boston, Chicago, Washington, D.C.

Major findings: quantitative analysis of patrol activities and exercise of discretion; situational factors in the exercise of discretion; officer use of force

Publications: Albert J. Reiss, *The Police and the Public* (New Haven, CT: Yale University Press, 1971); Donald J. Black, *The Manners and Customs of the Police* (New York: Academic Press, 1980).

Police Services Study, 1977

Methodology: direct observation, quantitative

Sites: metropolitan areas in St. Louis, Missouri; Rochester, New York; St. Petersburg, Florida

Major findings: 911 call workload; race and gender in the exercise of discretion

Publications: Christy A. Visher, "Gender, Police, Arrest Decisions, and Notions of Chivalry," *Criminology* 21 (February 1983): 5–28; Douglas A. Smith, Christy A. Visher, and Laura A. Davidson, "Equity and Discretionary Justice: The Influence of Race on Police Arrest Decisions," *Journal of Criminal Law and Criminology* 75, no. 1 (1984).

Project on Policing Neighborhoods, 1996–1997

Methodology: direct observation, quantitative

Sites: Indianapolis, Indiana; St. Petersburg, Florida

Major findings: activities of community-policing versus non-community-policing officers; citizen compliance with officer requests

Publications: Steven Mastrofski et al., *Systematic Observation of Public Police* (Washington, DC: U.S. Department of Justice, 1998); Stephen D. Mastrofski, Michael Reisig, and John D. McCluskey, "Police Disrespect toward the Public: An Encounter-Based Analysis," *Criminology* 40 (March 2006): 519–552.

---

observer not to accompany them if they believe that safety is at issue. In our experiences, such instances occur rarely and officers quickly acclimate to the observer's presence throughout the shift.

While accompanying their assigned officer, observers may make field notes to help them reconstruct what they observe. These are written on a small notepad that is easily carried in a pocket or purse. Observers quickly develop their own shorthand for recording information that will assist their recall of the who-when-where-how of what happened. Officers are allowed, even encouraged, to read the notes made by their observer, but these notes may not be shown to or discussed with those outside the research team. Because the observed officer may ask to read the observer's notes at any time, observers are careful not to record anything the officer may find objectionable. Some people might think that observer note taking is too obtrusive, perhaps making officers nervous or self-conscious; others find that when done judiciously it can enhance rapport. Observers simply explain it as a part of their job, likening it to the reports that officers are required to complete. Most officers readily understand and accept this.

The Call Service Workload

The Volume of Calls

They are called the "Twin Cities," but Minneapolis and St. Paul represent very different 911 workloads for patrol officers. Minneapolis patrol officers handle twice as many calls per year as St. Paul officers: 550 versus 221. The Chicago police, meanwhile, handle 282 calls per year per officer, compared with 489 in the San Francisco police department.[59] In short, even though the basic technology of 911 systems is the same, the resulting workloads vary tremendously.

Types of Calls

"When you're in [patrol] you handle all kinds of jobs—maybe ones that just happened," explained a New York City patrol officer. Also, "you don't get to stay at a job for very long . . . the job is over in 15 minutes."[60]

Routine patrol work involves handling "anything and everything" that comes in over the 911 system. Each call is an isolated incident that the officer handles as quickly as possible before moving on. Studies of the 911 call workload give us a comprehensive picture of routine police patrol work. The most important finding is that only 20 to 30 percent of all calls for service involve criminal law enforcement. Most calls are **order maintenance calls** or **service calls.** Exhibit 7–7 presents the Police Services Study data on calls for service to 24 police departments in three metropolitan areas. Other studies of 911 calls have found a similar distribution of calls.

Several basic points emerge from these data. First, criminal law enforcement represents a minority of all calls for service. The police are not primarily crime fighters but are peacekeepers and problem solvers.

Second, the vast majority of crime-related calls involve property crimes. Only 3 percent of all calls in Exhibit 7–7 involve a violent crime. Thus, the media image of policing that emphasizes the crime-fighting role, with a particular emphasis on violent crime and dangerous criminals, is a distortion of routine police work.

Third, most police work involves order maintenance, or conflict management, and service. For this reason, policing is best characterized as peacekeeping (see Chapter 1). Elain Cumming and colleagues characterize the police officer as "a philosopher, guide, and friend."[61]

order maintenance calls
service calls

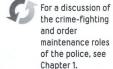

For a discussion of the crime-fighting and order maintenance roles of the police, see Chapter 1.

EXHIBIT 7–7

Crime and Noncrime Incidents and Their Distribution in the Police Services Study

	Percentage of All Encounters
Crime incidents	
Violent crimes	
Murder, robbery, assault, kidnapping, rape, child abuse	3.0%
Nonviolent crimes	
Theft, selling or receiving stolen goods, breaking and entering, burglary, vandalism, arson, fraud, leaving the scene, false report, nonsupport	15.0
Morals crimes	
Drug violations, gambling, prostitution, obscene behavior, pornography	1.3
Suspicious circumstances	
Reports or observations of prowlers, gunshots, screams, suspicious persons or conditions	9.8
Total	29.1%
Noncrime incidents	
Traffic (regulation and enforcement)	
Violation of traffic laws, traffic-flow problem, accidents, abandoned vehicles	24.1%
Disputes	
Fights, arguments, disturbances involving interpersonal conflict	8.6
Nuisances	
Annoyance, harassment, noise disturbance, trespassing, minor juvenile problem, ordinance violation	10.7
Dependent persons	
Drunks, missing persons, juvenile runaway, mentally disordered, other person unable to care for self	3.4
Medical	
Injured accident victims, suicide and attempts, deaths, others needing medical attention	1.9
Information request	
Road directions, referral, police or government procedures, miscellaneous requests where no additional police action mentioned	4.0
Information offer	
Return property, missing or stolen property, false alarm report, complaint or compliment about police, general information provision	2.8
General assistance	
Animal problem, lost or damaged property, utility problem, fire or other disaster, assist motorist, lockouts, companionship, irrational or crank call, house check, escort, transportation	9.2
Miscellaneous	
Internal legal procedures, assistance request, officer wants to give information, officer wants information, officer assists, courier	4.4
Gone on arrival	
Dispatched calls where parties to the problem are not at the scene	1.8
Total	70.9%

Source: Stephen Mastrofski, "The Police and Noncrime Services," in G. Whitaker and C. Phillips, eds., *Evaluating the Performance of Criminal Justice Agencies* (Beverly Hills, CA: Sage, 1983), 40.

For a discussion of police discretion, see Chapter 11.

Fourth, many situations are ambiguous and require the officers to exercise discretion. It is not clear what the best response should be to situations classified as interpersonal conflict or public nuisance. Many calls that citizens characterize as crime related do not necessarily involve an actual criminal incident. The caller may believe a crime has been committed, but there may not be sufficient evidence to support that belief. Reiss found that citizens defined 58 percent of all incidents as a criminal matter, but responding police officers recorded only 17 percent as crime related. Reiss argues that "many citizens have only a vague understanding of the difference between civil, private, and criminal matters."[62] Officers need to use their judgment based on the particular circumstances of each situation.

Fifth, many of the order maintenance and service calls involve family problems that occur in private homes. The 911 system allows people to invite the police into their homes, which the police would normally not have a legal right to enter.[63] As a result, the police encounter, firsthand, the most intimate human problems: family disputes, mental illness, alcoholism, and so on.

Sixth, calls for service do not come from a representative sample of the community. Some people are very heavy users of police services; others rarely, if ever, call the police. Low-income people are the heaviest users of police services.[64] A study of calls for service in Minneapolis during one 12-month period found that 5 percent of the addresses accounted for 64 percent of all the calls. These areas are now referred to as hot spots, as discussed earlier. Some individuals or households have chronic problems and call the police repeatedly within a period of a few months. Meanwhile, 60 percent of the addresses in the Minneapolis study never called the police.[65]

Aspects of Patrol Work

Response Time

response time

Getting to the scene of a crime quickly has traditionally been a top police priority. Quick **response time** to calls is a part of the folk wisdom of policing. Both police and citizens believe that it will (1) increase the probability of an arrest and (2) increase public satisfaction. The standard model emphasized the fastest possible response to all calls for service.

Unfortunately, research has not supported the folk wisdom about rapid response time. Several studies have found that response time has little effect on making an arrest (i.e., clearance rates).[66] The total amount of time between the commission of a crime and the moment a police officer arrives on the scene includes separate parts:

1. *Discovery time:* The interval between the commission of the crime and its discovery.
2. *Reporting time:* The interval between discovery and when the citizen calls the police.
3. *Processing time:* The interval between the call and the dispatch of a patrol car.
4. *Travel time:* The length of time it takes patrol officers to reach the scene.

A Police Foundation study found that processing time took an average of 2 minutes and 50 seconds, while travel time averaged 5 minutes and 34 seconds.

Gary Cordner and colleagues found similar times in a study of calls to the Pontiac, Michigan, police department.[67]

The police cannot control **discovery time,** reporting time, or processing time (items 1, 2, and 3). A PERF study found that 75 percent of all reported crimes are discovery or cold crimes, and only 25 percent are involvement crimes (for example, a confrontation between the victim and the offender). Most burglaries, for example, are not discovered until hours after they occurred. Cordner and colleagues found that the discovery delay, the interval between the time the crime occurred or was discovered and reported, was measured in hours for property crimes and about 30 minutes for personal crimes of violence. In this context, the police travel time (item 4) is largely irrelevant in terms of catching the offender on the premises.[68]

discovery time

In involvement crimes, the PERF study found that victims took an average of 4.0 to 5.5 minutes to call the police. Of these involvement crimes, 13 percent were reported while the crime was in progress and 14 percent were reported within the first minute after it was committed. Victim delay in calling the police undermines any potential gain by a faster police travel time. The study concluded that between 80 and 90 percent of serious crimes were reported to the police "too slowly for a response-related arrest to be made, even if the police response time was zero."[69]

Citizens delay calling the police for several different reasons:

- To verify that a crime has actually occurred (e.g., whether anything was stolen).
- To regain their composure.
- To call a friend or family member first.
- To decide whether they want to involve the police.
- Because a telephone is not immediately available (as in a street robbery).

Citizen satisfaction with police service is affected by response time. Frank Furstenburg and Charles Wellford found that citizens who had to wait more than 15 minutes for the police to arrive were significantly less satisfied than those who obtained a faster response. For both black and white citizens, satisfaction dropped steadily as response time increased from 5 to more than 15 minutes.[70]

Satisfaction is a function of citizen *expectations* about how soon the police will arrive. Citizens are most likely to be dissatisfied when they expect a quick response but do not receive it. Experiments with differential response to calls (discussed later) found that citizens were satisfied if they were informed that the police would not be there immediately.[71]

There have been no studies of the impact of the effect of faster response time on the crime rate. The National Academy of Sciences speculated that there might be some marginal impact on crime if the average offender noticed quicker response times and perceived an increased risk of arrest. The Academy report noted, however, that this is a "remote possibility," because offenders generally have "limited or sometimes even invalid information on police activity."[72]

Officer Use of Patrol Time

One of the traditional negative stereotypes about police officers involves the donut shop: that officers spend all their time eating donuts instead of patrolling and doing police work. This stereotype raises the crucial question of how patrol officers use their time. What does a typical patrol officer do during a typical eight-hour shift? How much "real" police work does he or she do? Another stereotype about policing is that the job is highly stressful and that officers are continually rushing from one call to another. Is that stereotype valid?

How officers spend their time is also important from a cost standpoint. Personnel costs consume 80 to 90 percent of a police department's budget. Maximizing the productivity of a police department requires getting patrol officers to do as much work as possible.

The Project on Policing Neighborhoods is the most thorough study to date of routine police work. It found that regular patrol officers spend only about 20 percent of their time in encounters with citizens. That translates into about an hour and a half per shift. They spend an average of slightly more than 20 percent of their time per shift on "general patrol" and about 15 percent traveling to locations. As expected, community policing officers spent less time in general patrol, but, surprisingly, they also spent less time than regular patrol officers in encounters with citizens.[73]

In Baltimore, patrol officers handled an average of about five calls per shift, with calls averaging 20 minutes each. This left about six and a half hours per shift of unassigned time. The authors concluded that patrol officers "have an inordinate amount of discretionary time." The study also found that only about 6 percent of unassigned time activities were directed by supervisors, dispatchers, other officers, or citizens. Also, when patrol officers were directed by supervisors to engage in an activity, the directives were very vague and generally did not involve problem solving or other proactive strategies.[74]

Arrests have a major impact on patrol officers' use of time. An arrest can take one and a half to two hours to process. Many arrests require two or more officers, depending on a department's standard operating procedures.[75] Each arrest removes the patrol officer from the street, thereby reducing the amount of time available for preventive patrol and for responding to calls.

Evading Duty

Despite the fact that the two-way radio allows direct communication with patrol officers, officers are still able to avoid work. The easiest way is to delay reporting the completion of a call. A dispatcher assumes that an officer is still busy with the call (committed) until he or she reports that the call has been completed. Officers can create free time for themselves by simply delaying that call.[76]

High-Speed Pursuits

High-speed pursuits are a major problem in police patrol. A pursuit is defined as a situation in which a police officer attempts to stop a vehicle and the suspect knowingly flees at a high rate of speed. Pursuits are fairly common and pose serious risks to police officers, the persons being pursued, and other drivers and bystanders.[77]

Geoffrey Alpert and Roger Dunham's study of pursuits by the Metro-Dade, Florida, police found that 33 percent resulted in accidents and 17 percent resulted in injuries. Slightly less than 1 percent resulted in the death of the suspect. Other studies have found even higher accident rates (44 percent in one study, but 18 percent in another). Studies have found injury rates that range from a high of 24 percent to a low of 5 percent of all pursuits.[78]

Studying and attempting to control high-speed pursuits is made difficult because all pursuits may not be reported by officers. In most departments, officers are required to complete an official report on every pursuit. Yet, many pursuits are of very short duration, and it is possible that officers do not report some of these. Officers may also not report pursuits when they know they have violated the department's pursuit policy (for example, pursuing when road conditions are hazardous).

Until recently, patrol officers had complete discretion to initiate a pursuit. Most police departments today, however, attempt to control pursuits through written policies. These policies fall into three general categories. About 60 percent of all departments have *restrictive* policies limiting discretion by specifying the conditions under which pursuits may or may not be initiated. Another 7 percent have *discouraging* policies that advise officers against pursuits in certain situations but are not as limiting as restrictive policies. Finally, 23 percent of all departments have *discretionary* or *judgmental* policies that give officers broad discretion about whether to engage in pursuits.[79]

 For a complete discussion of police discretion, see Chapter 11.

The Miami-Dade Police Department policy prohibits pursuits when less serious crimes are involved: traffic offenses, misdemeanors, and nonviolent felonies where the identity of the violator is known.[80] Many experts argue that the potential risks are not justified in the case of minor offenses. Other departments restrict pursuits when bad weather creates unsafe driving conditions or when pedestrians are present.

The Effectiveness of Patrol

Since the time of Robert Peel, the basic assumption of policing has been that a visible police presence deters crime. A related assumption is that increasing the number of officers on patrol will increase the deterrent effect. Until the early 1970s, however, no scientific experiments had tested these assumptions.

Initial Experiments

Initial experiments designed to test the effectiveness of patrol in the 1950s and 1960s did not meet contemporary standards of scientific research. In Operation 25, the New York City Police Department doubled the number of patrol officers in the Twenty-Fifth Precinct for four months during 1954. The department claimed that the increased patrol reduced muggings (street robberies) by 90 percent over the same period a year before, and that auto thefts declined by two-thirds.[81]

The Operation 25 experiment was methodologically flawed, however. It was not independently evaluated, raising the possibility that department officials manipulated the Uniform Crime Reporting (UCR) figures on reported crime to achieve the desired results. The research design did not control for the possible displacement of crime to other areas or for other variables that might have affected criminal activity.

In another New York City experiment, the city more than doubled the number of police officers on the subways (from 1,200 to 3,100) between 8 P.M. and 4 A.M. After a short-term decline, crime began to increase rapidly. By 1970, there were six times as many subway robberies as in 1965, before the additional police were

POLICE in FOCUS | The Deadly Consequences of Police Pursuits

USA *Today* conducted a review of deaths resulting from police pursuits between 1979 and 2013. During this period, 11,506 people had died as a consequence of a police chase, of which 139 were police officers, 6,301 were fleeing drivers, and 5,066 were nonviolators (of which at least 2,456 to 2,750 were bystanders). The table details results for the top counties.

Top Counties for Police-Pursuit-Related Deaths, 1979–2013

County	Total Dead	Police	Fleeing Drivers	Nonviolators
Los Angeles	412	0	190	222
Cook (Chicago)	211	2	85	124
Wayne (Detroit)	188	5	83	100
Harris (Houston)	150	1	75	74
San Diego	144	1	72	71

Source: Thomas Frank, "High-Speed Police Chases Have Killed Thousands of Innocent Bystanders," *USA Today,* July 30, 2015, http://www.usatoday.com/story/news/2015/07/30/police-pursuits-fatal-injuries/30187827/.

deployed. Moreover, it was later discovered that the transit police deliberately manipulated the crime reports to lower the number of reported crimes during the experimental period.[82]

The Kansas City Preventive Patrol Experiment

In 1972, Kansas City Police Chief Clarence M. Kelley decided to take a dangerous gamble. No chief had ever been willing to experiment with different levels of police patrol over a long period of time. And most dangerously, from a political standpoint, no chief had ever been willing to endorse an experiment in which some patrol beats would receive *less* than the normal amount of patrol. There was always the possibility of a public backlash that could cost the chief his job. The experiment was also professionally risky. What if the experiment found that routine police patrol made no difference in the crime rate? Kelley was willing to take the risks, however. He was a strong chief who had brought many reforms to the Kansas City Police Department. In recognition of his leadership qualities, he was appointed director of the FBI in 1973, before the patrol experiment was completed.

Kansas City Preventive Patrol Experiment

The **Kansas City Preventive Patrol Experiment** (1972–1973) was a landmark event in American policing. It was the first experiment testing the effectiveness of patrol that met minimum standards of scientific research. The Police Foundation, a private and independent organization, funded the experiment, provided the expertise in research design, and ensured that the evaluation was independent and objective.[83]

The research design involved 15 of the 24 beats in the South Patrol Division (9 were eliminated as unrepresentative of the area). They were matched on the basis of crime data, number of calls for service, ethnic composition, median income, and transiency of population; and separated into five groups of three each. Beats were assigned one of three levels of patrol: (1) reactive beats received "no preventive patrol" as such, police vehicles assigned to these beats entered them only in response to calls for service, and noncommitted time was spent patrolling other beats; (2) proactive beats received two or three times the normal level of patrol; (3) control beats were assigned the normal level of patrol (one car per beat).

The experiment investigated the following questions:

- Would citizens notice changes in the level of police patrol?
- Would different levels of police patrol affect the level of crime, as measured by UCR data or victimization surveys?
- Would different levels of patrol affect citizen fear of crime, and if so, would there be any changes in behavior or lifestyle?
- Would different levels of patrol affect citizen satisfaction with the police?

The experiment measured the impact of different levels of patrol on (1) criminal activity, (2) community perceptions and attitudes, and (3) police officer behavior and police department practices. Criminal activity was measured through official UCR data on reported crime and arrest and through a victimization survey. This was one of the first important applications of the relatively new victimization survey technique. The victimization survey was used to measure criminal victimization, citizen fear of crime, protective measures taken by citizens, protective measures taken by businesses, and citizen attitudes toward the police. Data were also gathered on police response time, arrest practices, police officer use of time, and officer attitudes. No previous police experiment had investigated such a wide range of issues, used such a variety of data sources, or relied on data independent of official departmental records. The experiment began in July 1972 but was suspended within a month when it was discovered that the experimental conditions were not being maintained. After being reorganized, the study resumed in October 1972 and ran for 12 months.

Findings and Implications of the Kansas City Experiment

The experiment's findings were extremely important and had enormous implications for police policy. The major findings were as follows:

- *Variations in the level of patrol had no significant impact on crime.*
- *Variations in the level of patrol had no significant impact on citizen feelings of safety.*
- *There were no significant changes in behavior or lifestyle because of perceived changes in police protection.*
- *Variations in the level of patrol did not affect attitudes toward the police.*

The findings challenged traditional assumptions about routine patrol. More patrol did not reduce crime, and lower levels of patrol did not lead to an increase in crime. Nor did citizens notice the different levels of police patrol. Because there was never any area that had absolutely no police presence, the experiment *did not prove that routine patrol has no effect on crime.* Patrol cars entered the reactive beats in response to calls, and marked police cars from other units also entered these areas.

Why did different levels of patrol have no impact on either crime or public perceptions? There are several reasons. First, as Lawrence Sherman and David

Weisburd point out, patrol is spread so thin under normal conditions that doubling it is not likely to have any measurable impact.[84] Second, many crimes are not likely to be deterred by patrol because they occur indoors and are often impulsive acts. NCVS data indicate that 33.7 percent of all sexual assaults occur at home, while another 21.3 percent occur at, in, or near someone else's house. More assaults occur inside a home, restaurant, or commercial building than occur on the street.[85]

About 60 percent of all murders, meanwhile, involve people who know each other. Crimes that occur indoors are not likely to be suppressed by the level of patrol on the street. Moreover, many of the offenders in these crimes do not rationally calculate the risk of arrest and punishment and, in particular, do not assess the level of police patrol in the area. In short, the traditional approach to police patrol has grossly exaggerated the extent to which many crimes are suppressible, or capable of being deterred by patrol.[86]

residual deterrence

Third, people did not perceive the different levels of patrol coverage in Kansas City in part because of the "phantom effect," or what criminologists call **residual deterrence.**[87] Most people believe the police are present even when there is no patrol in the area. They have seen the police at some other time or place (for example, the day before or in another area) and assume that the police are patrolling their area at the present moment. The initial perception has a residual effect, carrying over to other times and places.

Fourth, the Kansas City experiment tested only the *level* of police patrol. It did not study what patrol officers actually *do*—what activities they engage in. Community policing and problem-oriented policing (see Chapter 10) are important innovations primarily because they emphasize police activities that are different from traditional patrol. Critics found some flaws in the Kansas City experiment. Richard Larson points out that police vehicles from other specialized units (which were not part of the experiment) operated in the reactive beats, thus adding to a visible police presence. Officers in the reactive beats engaged in more self-initiated activities (such as vehicle stops) and used their sirens and lights more often in responding to calls. There was also a higher incidence of two or more cars responding to a call for service in those beats. All of these actions may have created the perception of a greater police presence than actually existed.[88]

One of the most important implications of the data was that officers' uncommitted time (about 60 percent of their time on duty) might be used more effectively. Anthony Pate argues that because reduced patrol levels do not result in increased crime, "patrol can be removed, at least temporarily, without incurring negative consequences" and officers can be redeployed to other areas for specific purposes.[89]

The Newark Foot Patrol Experiment

The Kansas City experiment involved officers patrolling in cars. The findings quickly stimulated questions about whether or not foot patrol might have a different effect on crime and public attitudes. These questions led to the **Newark Foot Patrol Experiment** (1978–1979). The design of the experiment was similar to the Kansas City experiment. Some beats received additional foot patrol, others received less foot patrol, and others served as control beats. The experiment tested the effect of different levels of foot patrol on crime, arrest rates, and community attitudes.[90]

Newark Foot Patrol
Experiment

The Newark Foot Patrol Experiment found that additional foot patrol did not reduce serious crime: "Generally, crime levels . . . are not affected by foot patrol for residents or commercial respondents at a significant level." Different levels of foot patrol did, however, have a significant effect on citizen attitudes. Citizens were "acutely aware" of the different levels of foot patrol, and residents in beats with added foot patrol consistently saw "the severity of crime problems diminishing in their neighborhoods at levels greater than other areas studied."[91]

Increased foot patrol had other positive effects. Reduced fear of crime was also associated with more positive attitudes toward the police, including other police activities unrelated to foot patrol. At the same time, foot-patrol officers reported more positive attitudes about citizens, believing them to be more supportive of the police. Foot-patrol officers ranked "helping the public" as the second most important part of their job; by contrast, motor patrol officers ranked it fifth. The data suggest that the positive benefits of foot patrol on attitudes are a two-way street.

New Questions, New Approaches

The Kansas City and Newark patrol experiments were major watersheds in thinking about the police. By questioning the traditional assumptions about patrol, the experiments encouraged creative new thinking. The finding that foot patrol reduced fear was encouraging. Also, as some observers pointed out, the experiments tested only the level of patrol and did not examine what patrol officers actually did while on duty. This new thinking led directly to the idea of community policing.[92]

For a discussion of community policing and other innovations, see Chapter 10.

Improving Traditional Patrol

In addition to community policing, many police departments have introduced innovations designed to improve the efficiency and effectiveness of traditional patrol. The most important innovations are discussed in this section.

Differential Response to Calls

Do the police really have to respond immediately to every call for service? As patrol officers have always known, many calls involve trivial matters. In addition to the proverbial "cat in a tree" call, most property crimes are cold crimes where the responding officer just takes a crime report. Given the huge volume of 911 calls and the burden they place on the police, is there a better way of providing service to the public?

Some police departments have responded to this issue by attempting to manage the calls-for-service workload more effectively. This approach rejects the traditional assumption that the police should respond as quickly as possible to every call.

Differential response involves classifying calls according to their seriousness. Calls receive (1) an immediate response by a sworn officer; (2) a delayed response by a sworn officer; or (3) no police response, with reports taken over the telephone, by mail, or by having the person come to a police station in person. Implementing differential response requires written guidelines and careful training for communications center personnel.[93]

differential response

An evaluation of differential response experiments found it to be successful. In Greensboro, North Carolina, only about half (53.6 percent) of all calls received an immediate dispatch of a police officer; 19.5 percent received no dispatched officer at all (most were cold larcenies where a report was taken over the telephone); and another 26.9 percent received a delayed response. Both police officers and citizens were satisfied with differential response. Greensboro citizens expressed satisfaction with 90 percent of the alternative responses, except for walk-in reports. In the case of delayed police response, citizen satisfaction was directly related to "whether the caller was informed that a delay might occur." This finding confirmed earlier research suggesting that citizen expectations are not a fixed entity but are dependent on what the police tell people to expect.[94]

The evaluation also found that differential response improved the overall quality of the call-for-service system. The new procedures "(1) increased the amount of information obtained from callers; (2) provided callers with more accurate information on what to expect in terms of response to their calls; and (3) provided patrol officers with more detailed information on calls prior to arrival at the scene."[95]

Robert Worden's study of differential response in Lansing, Michigan, found that it was both efficient and equitable. Cold crimes and other low-priority calls received a delayed response, with a median response time of 16 minutes. More than 90 percent of the citizens were satisfied with this service. Other calls were handled by taking reports over the telephone (almost all were larceny and vandalism incidents). More than 90 percent of the citizens were satisfied with this service. Differential response was equitable in the sense that whites and racial and ethnic minorities were just as likely to be satisfied (although there was some variation in intensity: satisfied versus very satisfied).[96]

Telephone Reporting Units

Telephone reporting units (TRUs) handle calls by taking reports over the phone. Almost half of all reported crimes are larcenies and almost all of those are cold crimes in which the patrol officer would do nothing more than take a report. Many TRUs are staffed by officers on light duty due to injury. The TRUs handle anywhere from 10 to 20 percent of all calls on some shifts and up to 35 percent of all crime reports. One department found that TRUs took only half as long to take reports as patrol officers (16 versus 34 minutes).[97]

311 Nonemergency Numbers

Do patrol officers really need to respond to all the minor calls that come through the 911 system? When researchers first began studying routine patrol, one of the main things they noticed was how many calls involved minor incidents that did not require a sworn officer with arrest powers. They also noticed that these calls consumed much of a patrol officer's time. As a result, experts began thinking about ways to relieve the police of this burden. One recent solution is the development of 311 call systems for less serious situations.

The Baltimore Police Department pioneered an experimental 311 system in 1996. Only those calls that require the immediate presence of a police officer are routed to a 911 system dispatcher. Others are routed to the 311 system and either are referred to other agencies or receive a delayed police response. According to the city's 311 website, calls routed to the 311 system include calls about crimes not in

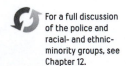

For a full discussion of the police and racial- and ethnic-minority groups, see Chapter 12.

progress, removing a dead animal, rodent problems, problems with traffic signs or signals, graffiti removal, sanitation problems, and other nonemergency situations.[98]

What happened as a result? Did the 311 system reduce the call workload for patrol officers as expected? Did officers have more time for serious crimes? The changes in call patterns in Baltimore were dramatic. The evidence indicates that most low-priority calls (priority categories 3, 4, and 5) shifted from 911 to 311. The number of 911 calls for the most serious situations (category 1) did increase, but the total number of 911-only calls fell by 35 percent (from 2 million to 1.3 million). An evaluation found that the overall impact of the 311 system was limited because the police department did not completely change its operations. It continued to dispatch officers to all calls, 311 and 911, thereby nullifying one of the most important goals of the 311 system: freeing officers from low-priority calls. Partly as a result, response times were not lowered. And for the same reason, officers did not experience an increase in uncommitted blocks of time.[99]

Non-English 911 Call Services

The face of America is changing. Immigration continues to bring to this country people from many different countries and cultures. A growing number of people in America do not speak English or have only weak command of English. This creates a major problem for the police, because they need to be able to receive and respond to calls from non-English speakers. Language barriers are one of the reasons Hispanic Americans are less likely to call the police for service. Police departments can subscribe to 24-hour interpreter services, which are offered for a fee by private companies. The largest company currently offers on-the-spot interpretation of 150 different languages. A patrol officer can call the toll-free number (the department pays an annual fee) and get an interpreter almost immediately.

Reverse 911

New communications and crime mapping technology has created reverse 911 systems. Instead of citizens calling the police, a reverse 911 system allows the police to call citizens. If a police department has important information about an event in a particular neighborhood, the system can identify telephone numbers in that area and call the residents. In Beech Grove, Indiana, for example, the system alerted businesses about a series of burglaries in their neighborhood. In another city, a missing child was located within 30 minutes by alerting people in the area. In 2013, reverse 911 was used by the Boston Police Department to notify residents to remain in their homes while they searched for the Boston marathon bombers. A reverse 911 system can be activated within five minutes following a reported incident and can flood the affected area with hundreds of calls an hour.[100]

Computers and Video Cameras in Patrol Cars

To enhance the efficiency of patrol operations, police departments have been placing computers in patrol cars. Field computers allow officers to both obtain information and file reports efficiently. By 2013, 90 percent of police agencies used computers in their patrol cars, up from 30 percent in 1990.[101] However, a study released in 2015 by Koper and colleagues showed that "mobile computing may have little if any direct, measurable impact on officers' ability to reduce crime in the field."[102]

Nonemergency Police Services (NEPS) in the Charlotte-Mecklenburg, North Carolina, Police Department

In partnership with 311, a citizen should call 311 in order to contact the Crime Reporting Unit (CRU). 311 personnel are trained to answer a wide variety of police-related questions, but will transfer the caller to the CRU if a police report is needed to be filed. 311 will also connect a caller with the CRU if they need to add something to a police report which has previously been filed.

Types of Non-Emergency Crime Reports

- ☐ Breaking and/or Entering of Storage/Utility Shed, or Detached Garage
- ☐ Breaking and/or Entering of Vehicle
- ☐ Communicating Threats
- ☐ Damage to Property
- ☐ Financial Identity Fraud
- ☐ Fraud
- ☐ Harassing Telephone Calls
- ☐ Indecent Exposure
- ☐ Larceny
- ☐ Simple Assault (Non-Domestic Violence Related)
- ☐ Supplements to Existing Police Reports
- ☐ Unauthorized Use of Motor Vehicle
- ☐ Worthless Check over $2000.00

Source: Reprinted by permission of the Charlotte-Mecklenburg Police Department website: www.charmeck.org/Departments/Police/Home.htm.

Police departments are also placing video cameras in patrol cars and on police officers, primarily as an accountability measure. In Arizona, sheriff's deputies working for the Maricopa County Sheriff's Office were required by a federal judge to wear body cameras as a consequence of a lawsuit over racial profiling. Video of controversial incidents document the behavior of both citizens and officers and can help to resolve controversies over, for example, whether an officer used excessive force. By 2013, LEMAS data indicated that about 68 percent of large local law enforcement agencies had video cameras in police cars and about 32 percent of local police agencies used body cameras.[103] These innovations are discussed in detail in Chapter 15.

Police Aides or Cadets

police aides

An alternative method of handling low-priority calls is to use nonsworn personnel, or **police aides.** Not all police tasks involve the need for a sworn police officer. The President's Crime Commission recommended the creation of a community service officer (CSO) to handle many of these routine assignments, thus freeing sworn officers for more critical tasks.[104] This approach is similar to the way other professions operate: delegating routine tasks to subprofessionals in training (for example, lawyers use law clerks, college professors use graduate assistants).

In an experiment in Worcester, Massachusetts, police service aides (PSAs) handled 24.7 percent of all calls and assisted in another 8.2 percent. These were nonemergency calls that did not require the presence of a sworn police officer. Citizens expressed satisfaction with the service they received from the PSAs and did not object to not having a sworn officer respond.[105] A Seattle CSO program was established in 1991; by 1993, it employed 17 CSOs supervised by a sworn sergeant and a sworn lieutenant. CSOs were specially trained in social services and worked primarily with street people. CSOs patrolled the downtown area on foot and referred homeless people to agencies providing shelter, food, clothing, and alcohol or drug abuse treatment.[106]

Police cadet programs are now common across the country. The Portland, Oregon, Police Cadet Program is typical of most programs. Cadets must be between the ages of 16 and 20, maintain a C average in high school with no failures, have no arrests or convictions, and be a U.S. citizen or have a valid immigration Green Card. Cadets participate in ride-alongs; assist sworn officers at crime scenes, traffic accidents, and traffic speed watches; and help with vacation house checks, parades, and other miscellaneous duties. Cadets do not have police powers, but they receive training on ethics, cultural awareness, defensive tactics, driving techniques, Oregon law, and other subjects.[107]

Directed Patrol and Hot Spots

Directed patrol gives patrol officers specific duties to perform during a specified time period while they are freed from normal 911 dispatches. Traditional patrol gives officers only a general mandate to patrol their beats and to respond to calls for service. A directed patrol program might, for example, involve instruction to look for specific persons or types of crimes, or to patrol certain areas intensively.[108]

directed patrol

Most police agencies today rely on directed patrol focused on hot spots, or those areas that receive a high volume of calls for service. An experiment in Minneapolis used a crackdown/back-off technique in which patrol officers would intensively patrol hot spots for short periods of time. The underlying assumption was that the impact of a short-term police presence would carry over because of residual deterrence.[109]

 For more discussion of hot-spots policing, see the case study in this chapter.

PERF surveyed 305 member agencies to better understand various strategies used in hot spots. They reported that no single method is used to define or identify a hot spot. Many police agencies use community input, administrative reports, and available agency data to identify a hot spot, which can be as small as a particular address or intersection or an area larger than a patrol beat. Although directed patrol was found to be one of the most common strategies used to respond to crime in hot spots, other strategies such as problem solving, targeting known offenders, and buy-and-bust stings were also found to be used frequently.[110]

Several randomized controlled trials have examined the impact of hot-spots policing on crime. A review of these studies reported that patrol directed toward hot spots has a modest but significant effect on reducing crime. The study emphasized that hot-spots policing strategies that incorporate problem-oriented policing reduce crime more than traditional directed patrol strategies.[111]

 We discuss the foundations and effectiveness of problem-oriented policing in Chapter 10.

Customer Feedback

A number of police agencies today are reaching out to the public to obtain feedback from those who have had contact with patrol officers. For example, the Seattle Police Department surveyed people who had called 911 to assess their satisfaction with the services they received. The customer feedback survey is a technique that many businesses (for example, automobile dealers, hospitals) use today to assess how they are doing and how they can improve their services.

A small number of studies have examined the effect of providing citizen feedback to officers. Most of these studies have shown this strategy to be ineffective at producing change. For example, the Lincoln, Nebraska, police department conducted surveys with those who had contact with their officers. Although some officers were randomly selected to receive the feedback, others were not provided the feedback until the end of the study period. The researchers found that the feedback did not have a significant impact on officer performance nor on their perceptions of the community they policed.[112] Another study, conducted in Schenectady and Syracuse, New York, collected feedback from citizens following their contact with the police and provided the information to police managers as part of monthly COMPSTAT meetings. Once again, no change in officer performance was detected in either city.[113]

Beyond Traditional Patrol

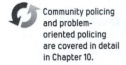

Community policing and problem-oriented policing are covered in detail in Chapter 10.

The most important innovations in policing look beyond traditional patrol. Advocates of community policing and problem-oriented policing argue that 911-driven policing is reactive and limited to isolated incidents. They argue that the police should be more proactive and, working closely with community residents, focus on underlying problems.

CASE STUDY

The Philadelphia Foot Patrol Experiment, by Jerry Ratcliffe et al.

Since the 1980s, it has long been the opinion of many police and criminology researchers that police foot patrols can improve community perception of the police and reduce fear of crime, but they don't prevent actual crime. Results from the Philadelphia Foot Patrol Experiment suggest that a more positive view of intelligence-led targeting of foot-patrol officers may be warranted.

On the invitation of the Philadelphia Police Department, police and academic researchers worked together to plan the Philadelphia Foot Patrol Experiment as a randomized controlled trial, using about 250 officers to patrol 60 violent crime locations during the summer of 2009.

Selecting Target Areas

During early 2009, violent crime reports were drawn from the incident database of the Philadelphia Police Department for 2006, 2007, and 2008. Violent crime here is defined as homicide, aggravated assault, and robberies not occurring indoors.

Incidents were weighted so crimes from 2008 counted 1.0, 2007 crimes counted 0.5, and 2006 crime events counted 0.25. In this way, more recent events had greater relevance in the creation of the target locations for 2009, but areas values could still retain a portion of the long-term hotspot component.

These weighted values were aggregated and summed to spatial units (called Thiessen polygons) centered on every street intersection in the city. This allowed the researchers to measure the city's crime centered on the nearest street corner to the crime incident. This resulted in a map of violent crime down to the nearest street corner. The top 5 percent of corners accounted in 2008 for 39 percent of robberies, 42 percent of aggravated assaults, and 33 percent of homicides.

Two PPD Regional Operations Commanders identified 129 potential foot beats, and from these 120 were selected for the experiment. Each area contained about 15 street intersections and 1.3 miles of roads. The foot beats were ranked by the weighted volume of violent crime and paired with a foot beat of similar crime rate. One from each pair was randomly selected to be a target beat, while the other became a control (or *comparison*) area.

What Did the Officers Do?

Officers generally patrolled in pairs with two pairs assigned to each foot patrol. They worked from Tuesday morning to Saturday night in two shifts (10 A.M. to 6 P.M., 6 P.M. to 2 A.M.). All patrol officers were provided with an initial criminal intelligence brief on their foot-patrol area by the criminal intelligence unit, as well as whatever information they gleaned from their initial orientation. Some officers engaged in considerable community-oriented work, speaking to community members and visiting child care centers and juvenile hangouts, while others were more crime oriented, stopping vehicles and conducting field interviews of pedestrians.

How Were the Results Analyzed?

We employed both an analysis of change scores and a linear regression model in which the crime value of the operational period serves as the dependent variable and the pre-operation crime level serves as a covariate. The linear regression model outcomes were examined in phases based on percentile levels of preintervention violence. To examine the issue of displacement, we also used Bowers and Johnson's weighted displacement quotient.

What Was the Result of the Experiment?

We found the violent crime hotspots had a reduction in violence of 85 offenses (with a net effect of 50 offenses once displacement is considered)—outperforming equivalent control areas by 22 percent; however, the benefits were only achieved in areas with a threshold level of pre-intervention violence. When that threshold was achieved (in our study an average of 5 violent crimes in the three months preintervention), target areas had significantly less violent crime during the operational period, even after accounting for natural regression to the mean. In summary, after twelve weeks and relative to the comparison areas:

- Violent crime in the target areas decreased 22 percent.
- Vehicle-related crime decreased 12 percent in the target areas.
- Drug-related incident detections increased 28 percent in the target areas.

- Pedestrian stops conducted by police increased 51 percent in the target areas.
- Vehicle stops and traffic enforcement increased 33 percent in the target areas.
- Arrests increased 13 percent in the target areas.

With the increased police activity, we estimate that in the target areas, one violent crime was reduced for every additional four arrests, 63 pedestrian stops and 25 traffic stops.

What About Displacement?

Studies show that sometimes crime is displaced to nearby areas, though more often it appears that nearby areas benefit from a diffusion of crime prevention. In Philadelphia, because some target areas were close to others, we combined some areas to examine the issue of displacement.

In the Philadelphia Foot Patrol Experiment, we did discover some modest displacement to surrounding streets, but that the displacement was less than the direct benefits achieved in the target areas. 85 crimes were prevented in the target area, offset by a 35 crime increase occurring in the displacement areas immediately surrounding target areas.

From this we can say that the overall reduction in violence indicates the foot patrols prevented 50 violent crimes during the summer.

What are the Key Points to Consider?

Target areas had 85 fewer violent incidents. Even with some displacement, the experiment was a success with a net reduction of 50 violent crimes over the summer of 2009.

Some displacement did occur, but the amount of crime displaced to areas around the foot beats was less than the total amount of violence prevented in the target areas.

The lack of a significant reduction in the less violent crime hotspots suggests that foot patrols are not a silver bullet to the problem of violence prevention. They may only be measurably effective in the highest crime areas. The relative lack of violent crime in other areas may warrant a more cost-effective approach to crime reduction, such as problem-oriented policing.

Pedestrian field interviews (where the public are stopped and often searched) increased by about 50 percent in the target areas, and vehicle stops and traffic enforcement increased by a third.

Source: Reprinted from Jerry Ratcliffe et al., *The Philadelphia Foot Patrol Experiment: Research in Brief* (Philadelphia: Temple University and the Philadelphia Police Department, February 2010), http://www.cla.temple.edu/cj/center-for-security-and-crime-science/the-philadelphia-foot-patrol-experiment/.

SUMMARY

Patrol is the backbone of policing. Despite many recent innovations in community policing, most police work involves patrol officers who patrol their assigned beats and respond to citizen calls for service. The patrol workload is dominated by calls for service and primarily involves noncriminal incidents. Thus, police work is best described as peacekeeping rather than crime fighting. The evidence suggests that increases in the level of patrol do not deter crime more effectively than lower levels of patrol. Innovations in patrol emphasize making more efficient use of patrol personnel and reducing the high volume of calls for service.

KEY TERMS

backbone of policing, 213
functions of patrol, 214
police–population ratio, 214
hot spot, 218
foot patrol, 219
officer-initiated activity, 220
watchman style, 221
legalistic style, 221

service style, 221
911 communications center, 223
communications center
   operators, 224
order maintenance calls, 228
service calls, 228
response time, 230
discovery time, 231

Kansas City Preventive Patrol
   Experiment, 234
residual deterrence, 236
Newark Foot Patrol
   Experiment, 236
differential response, 237
police aides, 240
directed patrol, 241

FOR DISCUSSION

1. The Philadelphia Foot Patrol Experiment represented a unique approach to crime prevention through patrol. Discuss how this approach is different from traditional patrol. What are the key elements of the experiment? What do foot patrol officers in this experiment do that is different from what basic patrol officers do? What is the relationship between the officers in this experiment and other patrol officers?

2. This experiment was a one-time special project. Discuss how this approach could be integrated into a police department on a permanent basis. What types of communities would it work best in, and in what communities might it not work as well? What problems would you anticipate? How could those problems be overcome through careful planning and administration?

3. You are the police chief in a department that is overwhelmed by 911 calls. Patrol officers have almost no time between calls and are frequently delayed in responding to calls. You have decided to adopt a 311 call system. What calls will be placed in the low-priority category? Which calls will receive top priority? How would you treat a "suspicious noise" call? What about a "noise next door" call?

INTERNET EXERCISE

What kinds of innovative patrol programs are currently operating around the country? Do a web search of police departments using www.officer.com as your starting point. Divide the class into teams and assign each team a different group of departments to research. For example, you might assign teams to different regions, or different size departments, or a range of departments of different sizes within particular regions.

Identify specific innovative patrol programs. Are there any programs listed on department websites? Describe the programs you find. Are they similar to programs described in this chapter? Or are they different in important ways? How are they different? Do the websites provide much detail about them? Are there any obvious patterns related to where these programs exist? Big departments versus small departments? One region of the country rather than others?

NOTES

1. James Q. Wilson, *Varieties of Police Behavior* (New York: Atheneum, 1973), 7; Michael Lipsky, *Street-Level Bureaucracy* (New York: Russell Sage, 1980).

2. National Advisory Commission on Criminal Justice Standards and Goals, *Police* (Washington, DC: U.S. Government Printing Office, 1973), 189; Wesley G. Skogan and Susan M. Hartnett, *Community Policing, Chicago Style* (New York: Oxford University Press, 1997), ch. 4.

3. T. A. Critchley, *A History of Police in England and Wales,* 2nd ed. (Montclair, NJ: Patterson Smith, 1972), 52.

4. O. W. Wilson and Roy C. McLaren, *Police Administration,* 4th ed. (New York: McGraw-Hill, 1977), 320.

5. U.S. Department of Justice, *The Police and Public Opinion* (Washington, DC: U.S. Government Printing Office, 1977), 39–40.

6. Albert Reiss, *The Police and the Public* (New Haven, CT: Yale University Press, 1971), 3.

7. Bureau of Justice Statistics, *Law Enforcement Management and Administrative Statistics, 1997* (Washington, DC: U.S. Department of Justice, 1999), table 8a.

8. Bureau of Justice Statistics, *Local Police Departments, 2013: Personnel, Policies, and Practices* (Washington, DC: U.S. Department of Justice, 2015).

9. Thomas B. Marvell and Carlisle E. Moody, "Specification Problems, Police Levels, and Crime Rates," *Criminology* 34 (November 1996): 609–646.

10. The original workload formula was developed by O. W. Wilson in 1941; see O. W. Wilson, *Distribution of Police Patrol Force* (Chicago: Public Administration Service, 1941). Excerpts are found in Wilson and McLaren, *Police Administration,* 633–55, appendix J.

11. Police Executive Research Forum, *Organizational Evaluation of the Omaha Police Division* (Washington, DC: Author, 1992).

12. Philadelphia Police Study Task Force, *Philadelphia and Its Police* (Philadelphia: The City, 1987), 49.

13. Police Executive Research Forum and the Police Foundation, *Survey of Police Operational and Administrative Practices–1981* (Washington, DC: PERF, 1981), 428–432.

14. James J. Fyfe, "Who Shoots? A Look at Officer Race and Police Shooting," *Journal of Police Science and Administration* 9 (December 1981): 373.

15. Bureau of Justice Statistics, *Household Poverty and Nonfatal Violent Victimization, 2008–2012* (Washington DC: U.S. Department of Justice, 2014).

16. Philadelphia Police Study Task Force, *Philadelphia and Its Police,* 48–49.

17. James L. O'Neill and Michael A. Cushing, *The Impact of Shift Work on Police Officers* (Washington, DC: Police Executive Research Forum, 1991).

18. Lawrence W. Sherman, James W. Shaw, and Dennis P. Rogan, *The Kansas City Gun Experiment* (Washington, DC: U.S. Department of Justice, 1995).

19. John Eck and Emily Eck, "Crime Place and Pollution," *Criminology and Public Policy* 11, no. 2 (2012): 281–316.

20. Anthony Braga, David Hureau, and Andrew Papachristos, "The Relevance of Micro Places in City Wide Robbery Trends," *Journal of Research in Crime and Delinquency* 48 (2011): 7–32; Anthony Braga, Andrew Papachristos, and David Hureau, "The Concentration and Stability of Gun Violence at Micro Places in Boston, 1980–2008," *Journal of Quantitative Criminology* 26 (2010): 33–53.

21. Lawrence W. Sherman, Patrick R. Gartin, and Michael E. Buerger, "Hot Spots of Predatory Crime: Routine Activities and the Criminology of Place," *Criminology* 27, no. 2 (1989): 27–55.

22. Bureau of Justice Statistics, *Law Enforcement Management and Administrative Statistics, 1997,* xv.

23. William A. Westley, *Violence and the Police* (Cambridge, MA: MIT Press, 1970), 35.

24. President's Commission on Law Enforcement and Administration of Justice, *Task Force Report: The Police* (Washington, DC: U.S. Government Printing Office, 1967), 54.

25. Bureau of Justice Statistics, *Local Police Departments, 1997* (Washington, DC: U.S. Government Printing Office, 2000).

26. Santa Barbara Police Department, "Tactical Patrol Force," available at www.sbpc.com.

27. "Officers Denounce Proposal for One-Person Patrol Cars," *New York Times,* February 16, 1996.

28. Bureau of Justice Statistics, *Law Enforcement Management and Administrative Statistics, 1997,* table 8a. Tom Jackman and Peter Hermann, "Police nationwide order officers to ride in pairs after Dallas police ambush." Washington Post. July 8, 2016. Found at https://www.washingtonpost.com/local/public-safety/dc-police-boost-patrols-after-snipers-in-dallas-kill-five-officers-wound-others/2016/07/08/9595063a-4508-11e6-88d0-6adee48be8bc_story.html

29. John E. Bodystun, Michael E. Sherry, and Nicholas Moelter, *Police Staffing in San Diego: One- or Two-Officer Units* (Washington, DC: The Police Foundation, 1977).

30. City of Buffalo, Press Release, July 17, 2003.

31. Philadelphia Police Task Force, *Philadelphia and Its Police,* 48.

32. Quoted in Jerome E. McElroy, Colleen A. Cosgrove, and Susan Sadd, *Community Policing: The CPOP in New York* (Newbury Park, CA: Sage, 1993), 133.

33. David H. Bayley and James Garofalo, "The Management of Violence by Police Patrol Officers," *Criminology* 27 (February 1989): 1–25.

34. Bureau of Justice Statistics, *Criminal Victimization in the United States, 1994* (Washington, DC: U.S. Government Printing Office, 1997), 100.

35. Wilson, *Varieties of Police Behavior.*

36. Christopher Commission, *Report of the Independent Commission on the Los Angeles Police Department* (Los Angeles: Author, 1991); Erwin Chermerinsky, *An Independent Analysis of the Los Angeles Police Department's Board of Inquiry Report on the Rampart Scandal* (Los Angeles: Police Protective League, 2000).

37. Bureau of Justice Statistics, *Performance Measures for the Criminal Justice System* (Washington, DC: U.S. Government Printing Office, 1993), 109–40, available at www.ncjrs.org, NCJ 193505.

38. McElroy, Cosgrove, and Sadd, *Community Policing,* 138.

39. Wilson and McLaren, *Police Administration,* 83.

40. Special Counsel to the Los Angeles Sheriff's Department, *9th Semiannual Report* (Los Angeles: Author, June 1998), 23.

41. Peter K. Manning, *Symbolic Communication: Signifying Calls and the Police Response* (Cambridge, MA: MIT Press, 1988), xiii.

42. Malcolm K. Sparrow, Mark H. Moore, and David M. Kennedy, *Beyond 911: A New Era for Policing* (New York: Basic Books, 1990).

43. Manning, *Symbolic Communication.*

44. George Antunes and Eric J. Scott, "Calling the Cops: Police Telephone Operators and Citizen Calls for Service," *Journal of Criminal Justice* 9, no. 2 (1981): 167.

45. "Licensing May Loom for 911 Dispatchers in Pa.," *Law Enforcement News* (May 15, 1995), 1.

46. Kent W. Colton, Margaret L. Brandeau, and James M. Tien, *A National Assessment of Police Command, Control, and Communications Systems* (Washington, DC: U.S. Government Printing Office, 1983); Bureau of Justice Statistics, *Local Police Departments, 2003* (Washington, DC: U.S. Government Printing Office, 2006), 11, available at www.ncjrs.org, NCJ 210118.

47. Tom McEwen, Deborah Spence, Russell Wolff, Julie Wartell, and Barbara Webster, *Call Management and Community Policing: A Guidebook for Law Enforcement* (Washington, DC: U.S. Department of Justice, 2003), 7.

48. Peter K. Manning, "Information Technologies and the Police," in Michael Tonry and Norval Morris, eds., *Modern Policing* (Chicago: University of Chicago Press, 1992), 349–398.

49. Manning, *Symbolic Communication,* 145.

50. Seattle Police Department, www.cityofseattle.net/police/.

51. Eric J. Scott, *Calls for Service: Citizen Demand and Initial Police Response* (Washington, DC: U.S. Government Printing Office, 1981).

52. Bayley and Garofalo, "The Management of Violence," 7.

53. James F. Gilsinan, "They Is Clowning Tough: 911 and the Social Construction of Reality," *Criminology* 27 (May 1989): 329–344.

54. Ibid.,

55. Manning, "Information Technologies and the Police," 371.

56. Sarah J. Tracy, "When Questioning Turns to Face Threat: An Interactional Sensitivity in 911 Call-Taking," *Western Journal of Communication* 66 (Spring 2002): 129–157.

57. Stephen D. Mastrofski, Roger B. Parks, Albert J. Reiss Jr., Robert E. Worden, Christina DeJong, Jeffrey B. Snipes, and William Terrill, *Systematic Observation of Public Police* (Washington, DC: U.S. Government Printing Office, 1998), 25.

58. Ibid.

59. Bureau of Justice Statistics, *Law Enforcement Management and Administrative Statistics, 1997,* table 9a.

60. McElroy, Cosgrove, and Sadd, *Community Policing: The CPOP in New York City,* 132–133.

61. Elaine Cumming, Ian Cumming, and Laura Edell, "Policeman as Philosopher, Guide, and Friend," *Social Problems* 12 (Winter 1965): 276–286.

62. Reiss, *The Police and the Public,* 73.

63. Arthur L. Stinchcombe, "Institutions of Privacy in the Determination of Police Administrative Practice," *American Journal of Sociology* 69 (September 1963): 150–160.

64. Reiss, *The Police and the Public,* 63.

65. Sherman, Gartin, and Buerger, "Hot Spots of Predatory Crime."

66. William Spelman and Dale K. Brown, *Calling the Police: Citizen Reporting of Serious Crime* (Washington, DC: U.S. Government Printing Office, 1984).

67. Kansas City Police Department, *Response Time Analysis: Executive Summary* (Washington, DC: U.S. Government Printing Office, 1978), 6; Gary W. Cordner, Jack R. Greene, and Tim S. Bynum, "The Sooner the Better: Some Effects of Police Response Time," in Richard R. Bennett, ed., *Police at Work* (Beverly Hills, CA: Sage, 1983), 145–164.

68. Cordner, Greene, and Bynum, "The Sooner the Better."

69. Spelman and Brown, *Calling the Police*, 74.

70. Frank F. Furstenburg Jr., and Charles F. Wellford, "Calling the Police: The Evaluation of Police Service," *Law and Society Review* 7 (Spring 1973): 393–406.

71. J. Thomas McEwen, Edward F. Connors III, and Marcia Cohen, *Evaluation of the Differential Police Response Field Test* (Washington, DC: U.S. Government Printing Office, 1986).

72. Wesley Skogan and Kathleen Frydl, eds., *Fairness and Effectiveness in Policing: The Evidence* (Washington, DC: National Academy of Sciences), 227.

73. Roger B. Parks, Stephen D. Mastrofski, Christina DeJong, and M. Kevin Gray, "How Officers Spend Their Time with the Community," *Justice Quarterly* 16, no. 3 (1999): 483–518.

74. Christine N. Famega, James Frank, and Lorraine Mazerolle, "Managing Police Patrol Time: The Role of Supervisor Directives," *Justice Quarterly* 22 (December 2005): 540–559.

75. Herman Goldstein, *The Drinking Drive in Madison: Project on the Development of a Problem-Oriented Approach to the Improvement of Policing,* vol. 2 (Madison: University of Wisconsin Law School, 1982), 67–68.

76. Jonathan Rubenstein, *City Police* (New York: Ballantine, 1974), 117–119.

77. National Institute of Justice, *Restrictive Policies for High-Speed Police Pursuits* (Washington, DC: U.S. Government Printing Office, 1989), 1.

78. Geoffrey P. Alpert and Roger D. Dunham, *Police Pursuit Driving: Controlling Responses to Emergency Situations* (New York: Greenwood Press, 1990), 37; L. Edward Wells and David N. Falcone, "Organizational Variables in Vehicle Pursuits by Police: The Impact of Policy on Practice," *Criminal Justice Policy Review* 6, no. 4 (1992): 317.

79. Wells and Falcone, "Organizational Variables in Vehicle Pursuits by Police," 324–325; Bureau of Justice Statistics, *Local Police Departments, 2000,* iv.

80. Alpert and Dunham, *Police Pursuit Driving,* 80.

81. Experiments regarding the effectiveness of patrol are reviewed in University of Maryland, *Preventing Crime: What Works, What Doesn't, What's Promising* (Washington, DC: U.S. Government Printing Office, 1997), ch. 8; see also John Eck and Edward Maguire, "Have Changes in Policing Reduced Violent Crime?" in A. Blumstein and J. Wallman, eds., *The Crime Drop in America* (New York: Cambridge University Press, 2000), ch. 7.

82. Discussed in James Q. Wilson, *Thinking about Crime* (New York: Basic Books, 1975), ch. 4.

83. George Kelling et al., *The Kansas City Preventive Patrol Experiment* (Washington, DC: The Police Foundation, 1974).

84. Lawrence W. Sherman and David Weisburd, "General Deterrent Effects of Police Patrol in Crime 'Hot Spots': A Randomized Controlled Trial," *Justice Quarterly* 12 (December 1995): 627–628.

85. Bureau of Justice Statistics, *Criminal Victimization in the United States, 1994,* 59.

86. Wesley G. Skogan and George E. Antunes, "Information, Apprehension, and Deterrence: Exploring the Limits of Police Productivity," *Journal of Criminal Justice* 7 (Fall 1979): 229.

87. Lawrence W. Sherman, "Police Crackdowns: Initial and Residual Deterrence," in Michael Tonry and Norval Morris, eds., *Crime and Justice: A Review of Research* (Chicago: University of Chicago, 1990), 1–48.

88. Richard C. Larson, "What Happened to Patrol Operations in Kansas City?" *Journal of Criminal Justice* 3, no. 4 (1975): 273.

89. Anthony M. Pate, "Experimenting with Foot Patrol: The Newark Experience," in Dennis P. Rosenbaum, ed., *Community Crime Prevention: Does It Work?* (Beverly Hills, CA: Sage, 1986), 155.

90. The Police Foundation, *The Newark Foot Patrol Experiment* (Washington, DC: The Police Foundation, 1981); Pate, "Experimenting with Foot Patrol."

91. The Police Foundation, *The Newark Foot Patrol Experiment,* 4–5.

92. James Q. Wilson and George L. Kelling, "Broken Windows: The Police and Neighborhood Safety," *Atlantic Monthly* 249 (March 1982): 29–38.

93. McEwen, Connors, and Cohen, *Evaluation of the Differential Police Response Field Test.*

94. Ibid., 102; Scott, *Calls for Service,* 97.

95. McEwen, Connors, and Cohen, *Evaluation of the Differential Police Response Field Test,* 8.

96. Robert E. Worden, "Toward Equity and Efficiency in Law Enforcement: Differential Police Response," *American Journal of Police* XII, no. 1 (1993): 1–32.

97. Margaret J. Levine and J. Thomas McEwen, *Patrol Deployment* (Washington, DC: U.S. Government Printing Office, 1985), 40–41.

98. U.S. Department of Justice, COPS Office, *311 for Non-Emergencies: Helping Communities One Call at a Time* (Washington, DC: U.S. Justice Department, August, 2003), 20.

99. Lorraine Mazerolle, Dennis Rogan, James Frank, Christine Famega, and John E. Eck, *Managing Calls to the Police with 911/311 Systems* (Washington, DC: Department of Justice, 2005), NCJ 206256.

100. Mike Johnson, "A New Twist on 911 Capability," *American City and County* 112 (December 1997): 10.

101. Bureau of Justice Statistics, *Local Police Departments, 2000,* iv; Bureau of Justice Statistics, *Local Police Departments, 2013*, 1.

102. Christopher S. Koper, Cynthia Lum, and Julie Hibdon, "The Uses and Impacts of Mobile Computing Technology in Hot Spots Policing," *Evaluation Review* 39, no. 6 (2015): 587–624.

103. Bureau of Justice Statistics, *Local Police Departments, 2013*, 1.

104. President's Commission on Law Enforcement and Administration of Justice, *The Challenge of Crime in a Free Society* (Washington, DC: U.S. U.S. Government Printing Office, 1967), 108–109.

105. James M. Tien and Richard C. Larson, "Police Service Aides: Paraprofessionals for Police," *Journal of Criminal Justice* 6 (Summer 1978): 117–131.

106. Martha R. Plotkin and Ortwin A. "Tony" Narr, *The Police Response to the Homeless: A Status Report* (Washington, DC: Police Executive Research Forum, 1993), 116–17, appendix C, 85–90.

107. Portland Police Bureau, www.portlandonline.com/police/.

108. Department of Justice, *Improving Patrol Productivity* (Washington, DC: U.S. Government Printing Office, 1977), ch. 4.

109. Lawrence W. Sherman and David Weisburd, "General Deterrent Effects of Police Patrol in Crime 'Hot Spots': A Randomized, Controlled Trial," *Justice Quarterly* 12 (December 1995): 625–648.

110. Christopher S. Koper, "Assessing the Practice of Hot Spots Policing: Survey Results from a National Convenience Sample of Local Police Agencies," *Journal of Contemporary Criminal Justice* (2014). doi:1043986214525079

111. Anthony A. Braga, Andrew V. Papachristos, and David M. Hureau, "The Effects of Hot Spots Policing on Crime: An Updated Systematic Review and Meta-Analysis," *Justice Quarterly* 31, no. 4 (2014): 633–663.

112. William Wells, Julie Horney, and Edward R. Maguire, "Patrol Officer Responses to Citizen Feedback: An Experimental Analysis," *Police Quarterly* 8, no. 2 (2005): 171–205.

113. Robert E. Worden and Sarah J. McLean, "Measuring, Managing, and Enhancing Procedural Justice in Policing: Promise and Pitfalls," prepared for delivery at the 2016 NACOLE Academic Symposium, April 22, 2016, John Jay College of Criminal Justice.

© McGraw-Hill Education/Christopher Kerrigan, photographer

C H A P T E R

8

Peacekeeping and Order Maintenance

CHAPTER OUTLINE

The Police Role

Calling the Police
Public Expectations
Police Response

Traffic Enforcement
Drunk-Driving Crackdowns

Policing Domestic Disputes
Defining Our Terms
The Prevalence of Domestic
Violence
Calling the Police

**Police Response to Domestic
Disturbances**
Factors Influencing the Arrest
Decision

A Revolution in Policy: Mandatory
Arrest
The Impact of Arrest on Domestic
Violence
Impact of Mandatory Arrest Laws
and Policies
Other Laws and Policies
The Future of Domestic Violence
Policy

Policing Prostitution
Policing the Homeless
Policing the Mentally Ill
Police Response to the Mentally Ill
Old Problems/New Programs
Policing People with HIV

Policing Juveniles
  Controversy over the Police Role
  Specialized Juvenile Units
  On-the-Street Encounters

The Issue of Race Discrimination
Crime Prevention Programs
CASE STUDY
Summary

Key Terms
For Discussion
Internet Exercises

Most police work involves peacekeeping and order maintenance, rather than crime fighting. People call the police for an infinite range of problems: arguments, fights, and domestic disputes; medical emergencies, including deaths, suicides, and injuries; assistance for dependent persons, including drunks, missing persons, and juvenile runaways; and public nuisances, including noise, trespassing, and suspicious persons. Exhibit 7–6 in the previous chapter (p. 225) provides Police Services Study (PSS) data on the frequency of these calls for service. Many order maintenance situations involve what are referred to as "special populations": the homeless, the mentally ill, and juveniles.[1] This chapter examines the peacekeeping and order maintenance activities of the police. It gives special attention to several specific situations that arise frequently and looks at the different police responses to them.

The Police Role

Order maintenance calls raise important questions about the police role. As we discussed in Chapter 1, some people view the police as crime fighters and think the noncrime calls are unimportant. Many police officers adopt this view and regard order maintenance calls as "garbage," "social work," or "bullshit."[2] This disparity between what the police actually do and what they value produces role conflict.

order maintenance

Some people, meanwhile, believe that noncrime calls are important, but primarily because they contribute to effective crime fighting. Stephen Mastrofski identifies four different ways that noncrime calls for service can help improve police effectiveness in dealing with crime: (1) The **crime prophylactic model** holds that police intervention can defuse potentially violent situations and prevent them from escalating into criminal violence; (2) the **police knowledge model** holds that noncrime calls give officers a broader exposure to the community with the result that they have more knowledge that will help them solve crimes; (3) the **social work model** holds that the latent coercive power of the police can help to steer potential lawbreakers into law-abiding behavior; and (4) the **community cooperation model** holds that effective responses to noncrime calls can help the police to establish greater credibility with the public.[3]

crime prophylactic model

police knowledge model

social work model

community cooperation model

All of these models, however, assume that crime fighting is the central part of the police role and that noncrime calls are subordinate to it. Most experts on policing today, however, argue that order maintenance is at least as important as crime fighting, if not more important.[4] It is a legitimate role for the police to resolve problems that people believe exist. An orderly and peaceful society is a better society. If the police did not respond to these problems, someone else would have to. Community policing, problem-oriented policing, and zero-tolerance policing are based on the idea that the police should focus on community problems, not all of which are crime related.[5]

 For a full discussion of community policing, problem-oriented policing, and zero-tolerance policing, see Chapter 10.

 For a full discussion of the role of policing order maintenance in crime control, see Chapter 9.

Calling the Police

Public Expectations

For a full discussion of the influence of communications technology, see Chapter 2.

In a classic analysis, Egon Bittner describes police work in terms of situations involving "something-that-ought-not-to-be-happening-and-about-which-someone-had-better-do-something-now!"[6] In short, a citizen believes there is a problem and wants something done about it. The modern police communications technology encouraged this expectation by creating the possibility that someone could respond to problems. The police encouraged people to call, and over time, people were socialized into the habit of "calling the cops."[7]

Citizens have different reasons for calling the police in noncrime situations. John C. Meyer identifies four specific expectations:[8]

1. *To maintain a social boundary:* People often want the police to remove someone they believe does not belong there. The victim of domestic violence, for example, may call the police to remove the assailant. Homeowners may want the police to disperse a group of teenagers from in front of their homes. In many of these situations, no actual crime has occurred: It is no crime to assemble peacefully on the street. In response, police officers often ask, encourage, or order people to leave. To a great extent, people comply with such requests even when they are not legally required to do so.
2. *To relieve unpleasant situations:* In many situations, someone calls the police because of noise, an argument, a family problem, or a dispute with neighbors. The role of the police is to restore order and keep the peace.
3. *Counterpunching:* In some disputes, someone calls the police about another person as a way of diverting attention from his or her own behavior. This is known as **counterpunching.**
4. *To obtain an emergency service:* People frequently call the police for emergency services: missing children, medical crises, suicide attempts, being locked out of their car or home, and so on.

counterpunching

Police Response

Police officers exercise great discretion in handling noncrime incidents. Typically, they handle situations informally and take no official action (for example, an arrest). Informal responses include a wide variety of verbal and nonverbal tactics. In their landmark study of New York City police officers, David Bayley and James Garofalo identified 20 different tactics that officers use in handling situations (see Exhibit 8–1).[9] The authors compared one group of experimental subject officers (ESOs) to a group of comparison subject officers (CSOs). The ESOs were nominated by other officers in the department to be especially skilled at handling conflict, and the CSOs were other officers who were randomly selected for the study.

Some officers are more active than others. Bayley and Garofalo found that the passive officers did nothing more than observe and take notes. The more active officers took control of the situation by asking questions, giving advice or information, or warning the persons involved. Some officers accepted the complainant's definition of the situation, whereas others rejected it.

EXHIBIT 8–1

Specific Actions Taken during Contact Stage by ESOs and CSOs—311 Nontraffic Encounters

Action*	ESOs		CSOs	
	Percentage	Number	Percentage	Number
Observed, stood by, took notes	4.4%	20	14.6%	26
Sought identity, relationships of parties	15.4	70	19.1	34
Questioned to elicit nature of problem	30.8	140	30.9	55
Asked citizens to "explain themselves"	16.0	73	7.3	13
Stated problem as police saw it	3.5	16	3.4	6
Verbally tried to defuse, "cool out" situation	11.0	50	4.5	8
Verbally restrained citizens (gave controlling orders)	5.9	27	2.8	5
Physically restrained citizens	2.2	10	0.6	1
Threatened physical force	1.1	5	2.2	4
Separated disputants in a nonphysical manner	2.9	13	4.5	8
Physically separated disputants	1.1	5	0.0	0
Requested dispersal of citizens	1.1	5	0.6	1
Ordered dispersal of citizens	0.7	3	2.8	5
Other	3.9	18	6.8	11
Total	100.0%	455	100.0%	177

*Up to five actions were coded for each officer.

Source: Specific Actions Taken During Contact Stage by ESOs and CSOs—311 Nontraffic Encounters. Copyright © American Society of Criminology.

Citizens generally comply with specific police requests. Mastrofski and colleagues found that citizens comply with police requests in 80 percent of all encounters. These incidents include requests to leave other people alone, to calm down and cease creating a disorder, to stop illegal behavior, and other miscellaneous requests. Compliance varies with the nature of the situation, the behavior of the officer, and the condition of the citizen. The more serious the situation, the less likely citizens are to comply. They are also less likely to comply with officers who approach the situation with a high degree of authoritativeness and/or who are disrespectful, and they are less likely to comply in situations occurring in private rather than in public places.[10]

Traffic Enforcement

Traffic enforcement activity is perhaps the most common type of order maintenance activity that the police carry out. Whereas citizen-initiated calls for service are heavily skewed toward a relatively small segment of any community, virtually all adult citizens drive cars, and minor violations of traffic laws are common. For example, about 10 percent (or 23.7 million people) of those ages 16 and older have a traffic-related contact with the police each year (see Exhibit 8–2). About half of these stops are for speeding.[11]

EXHIBIT 8–2

Number and Percentage of Drivers Stopped by Police, by Demographic Characteristics

Characteristic of Stopped Driver	Drivers Stopped by Police during Most Recent Contact	
	Number (in millions)	Percentage
Total	17.7	8.4%
Gender		
Male	10.3	9.9
Female	7.3	7.0
Ethnicity		
White	12.9	8.4
African American	1.8	8.8
Hispanic	2.0	9.1
Other	0.7	7.0
Two or more races	0.1	7.9
Age		
16–19	1.3	11.0
20–29	4.9	13.0
30–39	3.7	9.8
40–49	3.5	8.4
50–59	2.6	7.0
60 or older	1.7	4.1

Note: Detail may not add to total because of rounding.

Source: Christine Eith and Matthew R. Durose, *Contacts between Police & the Public, 2008* (Washington, DC: U.S. Government Printing Office, 2011).

Traffic stops are the source of low-level but significant friction between the police and the public. At the time of the stop, citizens resent being stopped, asked to produce identification, and ticketed. Because of the resentment by citizens at the time of the stop, police officers, in general, find traffic enforcement a distasteful task. However, research suggests that the public, after being stopped, understand why they are pulled over. About 85 percent of those stopped by the police believed that they were stopped for a legitimate reason—with whites and those stopped for speeding being the most likely to believe that they were stopped for a legitimate reason (see Exhibit 8–3).[12]

Traffic stops are also one of the most dangerous police tasks, in terms of officers killed or injured on duty, because some stops involve armed and dangerous criminals. Illya Lichtenburg and Alisa Smith reported that since 1988 about 13 percent of police deaths have occurred during routine traffic stops. During that same period, 9.4 percent of assaults on police were committed during traffic stops.[13]

The enforcement of traffic law violations varies widely from department to department. For example, police officers in Glendale, Arizona, write 50 percent more tickets than officers in Scottsdale, Arizona, even though both cities are approximately

EXHIBIT 8–3

Percentage of Stopped Drivers, by Ethnicity, Who Felt Police Stopped Them for a Legitimate Reason

Reason for Traffic Stop	Total	White	African American	Hispanic
All reasons	84.5%	86.3%	73.8%	82.5%
Speeding	90.0	91.8	78.7	88.7
Vehicle defect	82.6	86.8	60.7	84.3
Record check	89.1	91.6	83.5	82.4
Roadside check for drunk drivers	76.9	73.8	na	na
Seatbelt violation	84.7	84.7	86.6	79.0
Illegal turn or lane change	75.4	72.9	72.3	85.3
Stop sign/light violation	71.3	73.9	66.9	57.5

Note: na = not available.

Source: Christine Eith and Matthew R. Durose, *Contacts between Police & the Public, 2008* (Washington, DC: U.S. Government Printing Office, 2011).

the same size and are located in the same metropolitan area.[14] James Q. Wilson found similar variations in traffic law enforcement in his historic study of police organizations.[15]

Traffic enforcement policy is generally the result of formal or informal department policies. In some instances, community pressure dictates vigorous enforcement. In others, it is the decision of the top police administrator. Some departments have formal or informal quotas on traffic tickets for officers.[16] Police departments occasionally engage in highly publicized traffic enforcement crackdowns. There is mixed evidence about whether such efforts reduce traffic accidents or other crimes. For example, in Dayton, Ohio, the police department intensified enforcement in one high-traffic precinct over a six-month period. Officers were instructed to write many traffic tickets and to make frequent and highly visible traffic stops. This particular precinct and another precinct where no crackdown occurred were compared in terms of crime, arrests, and traffic accidents; the department found that the crackdown had no significant impact on any of these areas.[17]

There are three possible reasons the crackdown had no effect. First, it is possible that there is no relationship between enforcement effort and crime. That is to say, increased enforcement has no deterrent effect. Second, it is possible that the increased level of enforcement was too small to make any difference. (The same issue arose with respect to the Kansas City patrol experiment.) Third, it is possible that some effect occurred but that the methods used in the evaluation lacked sufficient statistical power to detect it.[18] Similar problems arise in other studies of police law enforcement programs.

For a full discussion on the Kansas City Preventive Patrol Experiment, see Chapter 7.

Drunk-Driving Crackdowns

In the 1980s, public concern led to a national crusade against drunk driving. Most states increased the penalties for drunk driving, federal regulations forced states to raise the legal drinking age to 21,[19] and local police departments intensified enforcement efforts.

Drunk-driving crackdowns included such tactics as random stops of drivers and road-blocks to stop all drivers. The goals were to apprehend actual drunk drivers and deter potential drunk drivers.

There is considerable debate over whether enforcement crackdowns reduce drunk driving. Evaluations of crackdowns in England and Scandinavia found short-term reductions in traffic fatalities followed by a return to previous levels.[20] Several factors appear to contribute to this phenomenon. The publicity surrounding a tough enforcement effort may cause changes in people's behavior. People drink less, or ask someone else to drive them home, or a friend stops them from driving. As the publicity surrounding the crackdown wears off, however, people return to their previous behavior patterns and drunk-driving fatalities increase.

The risk of arrest for drunk driving is extremely low. The probability of a police officer's spotting a drunk driver is limited by several factors. First, a very small percentage of all drivers are drunk: an estimated 5 percent of all drivers on an average evening, with a higher percentage on weekends. Second, relatively few police officers are on duty at any given moment relative to the number of cars on the road. Third, not all drivers who are drunk exhibit impaired driving.[21]

Each arrest, meanwhile, sharply reduces the probability of catching other drunk drivers. An arrest is an extremely time-consuming event, involving one or more officers for anywhere from one to four hours. For the duration, each officer is out of service, unable to make further arrests or to deter drunk driving through patrol. Finally, crackdowns are difficult to sustain. Police officers, like drinkers, slip back into their normal routines and reduce their level of arrest activity.

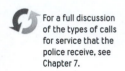 For a full discussion of the types of calls for service that the police receive, see Chapter 7.

The rate of alcohol-related traffic fatalities (based on the number of licensed vehicles and/or drivers) has declined steadily since the 1920s. Experts believe that several factors have contributed to this trend: safer cars, better roads and traffic safety measures, seat belts, air bags, and most recently the increase in the legal drinking age. The tough anti-drunk-driving enforcement programs have made, at best, some contribution to this trend, but they are only one part of a larger social control effort.[22]

Policing Domestic Disputes

Domestic disputes are an important order maintenance situation. Domestic incidents represented 4.5 percent of all calls in the PSS data.[23] Police response to domestic incidents has been a matter of great controversy since the 1980s. A revolution in public attitudes about domestic violence has led to new laws and policies, including increased criminal penalties, the development of intervention and treatment programs for batterers, and changes in police department policies.[24]

Defining Our Terms

domestic disturbance

There is much confusion about the police response to domestic incidents, in part because many people fail to distinguish between disputes and violent incidents. The police handle many situations that are labeled *disturbances*. These include bar fights, arguments between neighbors, and many other kinds of problems. A **domestic disturbance** is one involving two or more people engaged in an intimate relationship. This includes married or divorced couples, live-in lovers, or people who are on a first date. It includes problems between adults and their children or adults and their elderly parents. It also includes same-sex relationships. Only some of those—an estimated 33 percent—involve some form of *violence*.[25] The violence is usually an assault.

The Prevalence of Domestic Violence

The National Crime Victimization Survey (NCVS) estimated that, in 2013, 748,800 incidents of intimate partner violence occurred. An intimate partner was defined as a spouse, ex-spouse, boyfriend, or girlfriend.[26] Murray Straus and Richard Gelles, the two leading experts on the subject, have conducted a number of national surveys on domestic violence. They estimate that about 13 percent of all wives have experienced some form of **domestic violence,** and one-third of these have experienced severe violence.[27]

domestic violence

The Bureau of Justice Statistics reported that, in 2013, intimate partner violence represented 25 percent of all violent incidents against women. Researchers have reported that intimate partner violence has decreased substantially from 2004 to 2013. In particular, they have reported that intimate partner violence against women decreased by about 33 percent during this time period, with 1 million women being victimized in 2004, compared with about 748,000 in 2010. Violent victimization rates for women also declined during this period, falling from about 1.3 percent of women being the victim of a violent crime in 2004 to about 1.1 percent in 2013.[28]

Calling the Police

Many domestic violence victims do not call the police. NCVS data show that female victims of violence called the police only about 62 percent of the time.[29] The reporting of domestic violence varies by the status of the victim. Low-income people call the police most frequently. In a study of domestic violence in Omaha, Nebraska, 50 percent of the victims and 31 percent of the suspects were unemployed at the time of the police call. Only 7.4 percent of all calls to the police came from the western half of the city, which includes the middle- and upper-middle-class residential neighborhoods.[30] The NCVS found that nonwhite female victims are substantially more likely to call the police than are white female victims.[31]

Middle-class women are more likely to turn to private sources for help: a friend, a family member, a religious counselor, or a social worker. They are also more likely to be embarrassed about calling the police and worried about what neighbors or friends might think. Finally, the middle-income woman is more likely to be economically dependent on her spouse (especially if she is a housewife and he is the sole source of income). The low-income woman is more likely to have relatively more economic equality to her husband or male friend.[32]

There are several reasons victims of domestic violence do not call the police. According to NCVS data, most did not call the police because they regarded it as a private or trivial matter. About 4 percent did not call the police because they thought it was not important to the police, 3.4 percent did not call because they feared reprisal, and 2.9 percent did not call to protect the offender.[33]

Domestic violence is concentrated in certain families and nonexistent in most families. Consequently, repeat calls to the same address are a common occurrence. In the Omaha study, 65 percent of the suspects had previously been arrested for some

EXHIBIT 8-4

Factors Influencing Reporting Domestic Violence to the Police

Variable	Category	Incidents Reported	Incidents Not Reported
Most important reason for calling the police			
	It was a crime	30.2	—
	Protection from future attack	19.9	—
	To stop the incident	16.7	—
	Protection of others from future attack	5.4	—
	To punish the offender	3.5	—
	Duty to tell the police	2.6	—
	To catch the offender	2.1	—
	Other	19.6	
Most important reason for not calling the police			
	Private matter	—	22.8
	Trivial matter	—	18.1
	Not important to police	—	4.0
	Fear of reprisal	—	3.4
	Protecting the offender	—	2.9
	Other	—	48.8

Source: Richard Felson, Steven Messner, Anthony Hoskin, and Glenn Deane, "Reasons for Reporting and Not Reporting Domestic Violence to the Police," *Criminology* 40, no. 30 (2002): 617–647.

offense, 11 percent had been arrested for a past offense against the victim, and 3 percent had been arrested for an offense against the victim in the previous six months.[34] Gelles and Straus found the average female victim was battered three times a year.[35]

Police Response to Domestic Disturbances

Police officers exercise great discretion in handling domestic disturbances. The alternative responses include (1) arrest, (2) mediation, (3) separating the parties, (4) referral to a social service agency, or (5) no action at all. Arrest is not the most common response. As Mastrofski, Snipes, and Supina's study of police encounters (including all types of situations) found, rather than make an arrest, police officers often ask a person to cease illegal behavior.[36] Studies have found arrest rates ranging from a high of about 40 percent of all incidents to a low of about 12 percent. (Some studies, however, have not distinguished between violent incidents and disturbances, where no law has been broken and arrest is not an option.) A study of domestic violence in Kentucky found arrests in 41 percent of all violent incidents, but Donald Black's earlier study found arrests in only 25 percent of all violent felonies and 20 percent of all violent misdemeanors.[37]

Danger to Police in Domestic Disturbances

There is considerable controversy over the extent to which domestic disturbance calls pose a danger to police officers. Joel Garner and Elizabeth Clemmer's analysis of FBI data on officers killed or assaulted in the line of duty found that domestic disturbance calls ranked very low in terms of officers killed. Robbery and burglary were consistently the most dangerous kinds of incidents. There was mixed evidence with respect to assaults on officers. Some data indicate that domestic calls are the most dangerous situations, while others indicate that they rank third or lower.[a] Hirschel, Dean, and Lumb analyzed assault and injury rates relative to the frequency of calls for service for 10 categories of police activity. They found that "domestic disturbances ranked fourth in risk of officer assault and fifth in risk of officer injury."[b]

Domestic disturbances are often more frustrating than dangerous. The police are frequently able to resolve the immediate dispute, but they cannot do anything about the underlying cause—unemployment, alcohol or drug abuse, or psychological trouble. Black found that some officers deliberately drove slowly to a domestic disturbance, hoping the dispute would resolve itself before they arrived.[c]

Sources: [a]Joel Garner and Elizabeth Clemmer, *Danger to Police in Domestic Disturbances—A New Look* (Washington, DC: U.S. Government Printing Office, 1986); [b]J. David Hirschel, Charles Dean, and Richard Lumb, "The Relative Contribution of Domestic Violence to Assault and Injury of Police Officers" *Justice Quarterly* 11 (1994): 99–117; [c]Donald Black, "Dispute Settlement by the Police," in Donald Black, ed., *The Manners and Customs of the Police* (New York: Academic Press, 1980), 146.

Mediation includes a variety of kinds of verbal responses: talking sympathetically, talking in an unsympathetic or hostile manner, asking the complainant what she or he would like done, ordering the parties to be quiet, and threatening arrest. Officers often separate the parties to a dispute by asking one of them to leave the premises. If a person is the legal resident of the house or apartment, the police have no legal right to force him or her to leave. Again, to a great extent, people comply with police requests that they leave. In the Omaha domestic violence study, virtually all people left the premises when asked; moreover, couples remained apart an average of three days (70 hours), and 87 percent of the victims reported that the police intervention helped resolve the problem they were having.[38]

Police officers may also refer one or more of the parties to the dispute to social services: marriage counseling, alcohol or drug treatment, or legal aid (for those contemplating separation, divorce, and other legal matters). Although many departments provide officers with a list of social agencies, a police officer has no legal power to compel someone to seek professional help. One study found that officers chose this alternative in only 5 percent of all incidents.[39]

A police officer can also take no action whatsoever. One study examining the Boulder County Police Department reported that in about 20 percent of the cases, the police left the scene without taking any action.[40]

Factors Influencing the Arrest Decision

Historically, several factors have discouraged officers from making arrests in domestic violence situations. First, some officers regard domestic violence as a private matter—something to be dealt with by the family. Second, many officers have learned from experience that domestic violence arrests are often dismissed because the victim refuses to pursue the case. Third, victims of domestic violence often call the police for help but then ask them to do something other than make an arrest.[41] Fourth, an arrest is work. It requires the officer to perform many tasks (taking the suspect into custody, writing reports), some of which are potentially dangerous. An arrest also raises the visibility of the officer's work, bringing it to the attention of other officials who might find it improper. If an officer does not make an arrest, however, the situation remains hidden from others. As is true in other occupations, police officers often try to reduce their workload.[42] Fifth, police departments have traditionally not valued domestic violence arrests (which are regarded as order maintenance activities), placing a higher value on arrests for murder, rape, robbery, or narcotics.

A Revolution in Policy: Mandatory Arrest

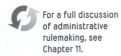

For a full discussion of administrative rulemaking, see Chapter 11.

A revolution in public attitudes toward domestic violence began in the 1970s. The women's movement identified spouse abuse as a major problem and demanded protection for victimized women. In two important lawsuits, women's groups in New York City and Oakland sued the local police departments, charging that they had denied women equal protection of the law by failing to arrest persons who had committed domestic assaults. The suits led to new department policies on police handling of domestic violence.[43] In *Bruno v. Codd* (1978), the New York City police agreed to adopt a written policy mandating arrest in cases of felonious assault (see Exhibit 8–5). The *Scott v. Hart* (1979) suit against the Oakland police resulted in a similar policy.[44]

Mandatory arrest policies represent one of the first attempts to control officer arrest discretion. The strategy of using written policies is called administrative rule-making, and it has also been used to control officer discretion in the use of deadly force, high-speed pursuits, and other areas of policing.[45]

The Impact of Arrest on Domestic Violence

Minneapolis Domestic Violence Experiment

Many people believe that arrest deters future domestic violence. The **Minneapolis Domestic Violence Experiment** (1981–1982) sought to determine the relative deterrent effect of arrest, mediation, and separation in misdemeanor domestic violence incidents. Cases were randomly assigned to one of the three treatments. Each officer carried a color-coded pad of report forms and handled each case according to the approach indicated by the top form. Investigators measured repeat violence over the next six months through follow-up interviews with victims and police department records of calls to the same address.[46]

The Minneapolis study found that arrest produced lower rates of repeat violence than separation or mediation. Rearrest occurred in 10 percent of the arrest cases, compared with 19 percent of the mediation incidents and 24 percent of the separation incidents. The experiment received considerable national attention and had a major impact on public policy. Between 1984 and 1986, the percentage of big-city police departments with "arrest preferred" policies increased from 10 to 46 percent.[47] Today, 99 percent of all municipal police departments have a written policy on domestic disputes (although not necessarily a mandatory arrest policy) and 46 percent have a special domestic violence unit.[48]

EXHIBIT 8–5

Summary of Results of Six Immediate Arrest Experiments, for Repeat Violence Against the Same Victim

	City					
Finding	Minneapolis	Omaha	Charlotte	Milwaukee	Colorado Springs	Miami
6-month deterrence, official measures	Yes	No	No	No	No	1 of 2
6-month deterrence, victim interviews	Yes	Border	No	No	Yes	Yes
6- to 12-month escalation, official measures	No	Yes	Yes	Yes	No	No
6- to 12-month escalation, victim interviews	*	No	No	No	No	No
30- to 60-day deterrence, official measures (any or same victim)	Yes	No	Border	Yes	No	1 of 2
30- to 60-day deterrence, victim interviews	Yes	Border	No	Yes	*	Yes
Escalation effect for unemployed	*	Yes	*	Yes	Yes	*
Deterrence for employed	*	Yes	*	Yes	Yes	*

*Key: relationship not reported.

Source: Lawrence W. Sherman with the assistance of Janell D. Schmidt and Dennis P. Rogan, *Policing Domestic Violence: Experiments and Dilemmas* (New York: Free Press, 1992), table 6.1, p. 129.

Critics have raised a number of serious questions about the Minneapolis experiment. Some police officers violated the integrity of the experiment by failing to handle the cases as directed, thereby undermining the random assignment of cases. A small percentage of the participating officers produced the majority of the arrests. They were also more likely to follow the rules of the experiment. When only their cases were examined, the deterrent effect disappeared.[49] There was also a great deal of attrition among the subjects. Only 62 percent of the victims (205 out of 330) could be located for an initial interview, and only 49 percent completed all 12 of the interviews.

Some critics argue that Lawrence W. Sherman, the director of the experiment, had "prematurely and unduly publicized" the results. It is unwise, they argue, to recommend major changes in public policy on the basis of only one study that had not yet been replicated.[50] The lack of replication is a general problem in police research. Many of the most important experiments, such as the Kansas City Preventive Patrol Experiment, have not been replicated at all. It is dangerous to base public policy on one or even a small number of experiments.[51]

 For more discussion of the Kansas City Preventive Patrol Experiment, see Chapter 7.

Replications of the Minneapolis experiment in other cities, in fact, failed to find a consistent deterrent effect of arrest. In Omaha, Charlotte, Colorado Springs, and Milwaukee, there was no deterrent effect found for arrest. Some of the findings of the Omaha, Milwaukee, and Colorado Springs experiments were particularly disturbing (see Exhibit 8–5). Arrest appeared to *escalate* violence among unemployed persons

SIDEBAR 8-2

Studying Your Local Police

Do the major law enforcement agencies in your area have written domestic violence policies? Obtain copies of those policies and compare them. Are they mandatory arrest or arrest pre-ferred policies? How much discretion do they leave to the officer? Do any of the agencies have special domestic violence units or programs? What do these programs involve?

compared with those who were employed. These data clearly indicate that arrest—at least from domestic violence—has different effects on different kinds of people.[52]

Impact of Mandatory Arrest Laws and Policies

Today, legislatures have taken three primary approaches with respect to incidents involving domestic violence: arrest is mandatory, arrest is preferred, and arrest is at the officer's discretion.[53] David Hirschel and colleagues reported that 22 states and the District of Columbia have statutes mandating arrest, 6 have statutes that state that the preferred response is arrest, and 11 states have statutes that grant the officers discretion in incidents involving domestic violence.[54]

The full impact of mandatory arrest laws and policies is still not known. First, some commentators have warned that mandatory arrest may discourage calls by per-sons who only want the police to calm the immediate situation. For example, early research by Margaret Martin reported that following the implementation of a manda-tory arrest statute in Connecticut, a dual arrest (meaning arresting both the offender and victim) was made in 33 percent of all police contacts for domestic violence. More recent research supported these findings.[55] Hirschel, in his national study of dual arrest, reported that although dual arrest was substantially less frequent than Martin suggested, statutes that mandate arrest result in an increased likelihood that the police arrest both individuals involved in the dispute.[56] Accordingly, mandatory arrest laws may have the unintended impact of deterring people from calling the po-lice for fear that they themselves may be arrested.[57] Second, mandatory arrest is likely to have a disproportionate impact on lower-class men, and poor African Amer-ican men in particular.[58] This is because these individuals often have no one to turn to for help other than the police. By contrast, the traditional no-arrest approach had a negative effect primarily on poor, African American women by denying them equal protection of the law.

Other Laws and Policies

In addition to mandatory arrest policies, many departments have added special train-ing for their officers in how to handle family violence situations. Surveys of victims, however, have failed to find greater satisfaction among those victims served by spe-cially trained officers than among those served by officers who have not received special training.[59]

At the same time, many states have revised their laws on domestic violence. For example, Iowa law directs the officer to identify and arrest the primary aggressor.

S I D E B A R   8 – 3

Domestic Violence by Police Officers

A 1996 federal law (known as the **Lautenberg Amendment***) prohibits anyone with a conviction for domestic violence from owning a firearm. The law has serious implications for both the police and the military because possession and possible use of a weapon is an essential part of the job. Police departments have been wrestling with how to respond to this law.*
The law presents several questions for consideration:

Lautenberg Amendment

1. Is the law good social policy? Is it appropriate to deny firearms to people with a record of domestic violence?

2. Is it fair, or even constitutional, for a law to be applied retroactively?

3. Should a person with any kind of criminal conviction be employed as a police officer?

At least eight states now require law enforcement agencies to develop written policies on the handling of domestic violence. Several other states expanded the arrest power, allowing the police to arrest in the case of misdemeanor assaults that did not occur in their presence.[60] Eighteen states mandate that police officers make an arrest for violation of a protection order. Traditionally, police did not have the power to arrest in these situations, with the result that many women's advocates regarded protection orders as worthless pieces of paper.[61]

The Future of Domestic Violence Policy

The future of police policy toward domestic disturbances and domestic violence is not clear. Mandatory arrest policies remain extremely popular, but the full impact of these policies is uncertain. In a comprehensive review of domestic violence policies, Jeffrey Fagan concludes that there is "weak or inconsistent evidence" on the deterrent effect of arrest, prosecution, protection orders, and batterer treatment.[62] Sherman, who directed the original Minneapolis experiment, no longer supports mandatory arrest in all situations.[63]

Policing Prostitution

Prostitution is a common problem in many communities across the country. It is estimated that there are about 250,000 full-time prostitutes in the nation who serve about 1.5 million customers a week.[64] One nationwide study found that about 14 percent of men have ever purchased sex from a prostitute and 1 percent had done so in the past year.[65] Gross revenue from prostitution is estimated at $7.2 billion to $9 billion a year in the United States.[66] Terance Miethe and Richard McCorkle note that there are five different types of prostitutes, including streetwalkers, bar girls, skeezers, brothel prostitutes, and call girls.

Streetwalkers, otherwise known as hustlers and hookers, work on the open streets. These prostitutes are the most visible to the public and police and are at the

streetwalkers

lower end of the social and economic scale of prostitution. Many streetwalkers are poor, minority women who have few other options for employment.[67]

bar girls

Bar girls, or b-girls, typically work out of bars or other entertainment establishments with the cooperation of management. Managers typically receive a percentage of the bar girls' revenue as a "referral" fee or sell bar girls overpriced drinks, which are paid for by the client. Bars near military bases have been a particularly popular location for bar girls to operate.[68]

skeezers

Skeezers are the newest type of prostitute, emerging in the 1980s with the introduction of crack cocaine. These prostitutes trade sex for crack cocaine and are almost always "crack addicts."[69] Research suggests that those who engage in sex for drugs are often the victims of major trauma and have serious mental health problems.[70]

brothel prostitutes

Brothel prostitutes typically work in large establishments owned by a single person or groups of individuals. Although legal brothels exist in only a few counties in Nevada, massage parlors and escort services have emerged as a new front for prostitutes. Many illegal brothels operate through a system of referrals and informal social networks.[71]

call girls

Call girls represent the upper end of the economic scale of prostitution. They cater to a more affluent customer and generally make their arrangements over the telephone. Because they are not on the street, their activities are not visible to either the public or the police. Prostitution of this sort may, however, come to the public's attention if the prostitutes are working out of a motel or apartment complex in a way that causes other people to notice, take offense, and complain.[72]

In most cities, police departments concentrate their enforcement efforts on streetwalkers—in part because streetwalkers are the most visible, but also because other types of prostitutes are more difficult to apprehend. However, in many cities, low-level streetwalking is also tolerated by the police. It is usually confined to certain parts of the central business district, where it is not seen by most of the public.

For instance, prostitution in Phoenix, Arizona, is restricted primarily to a two-mile strip of a major thoroughfare in the central part of the city. The police have reported that the area is fairly well organized in terms of the services offered by the prostitutes. One area of the strip consists of female prostitutes, a second area consists of male prostitutes, and a third area consists of transvestites. Historically, prostitution has been tolerated somewhat by the community as long as it is restricted to this area of the city and is not too obvious.

For the patrol officer, streetwalking is essentially an order maintenance problem similar to the policing of skid row. The primary police objectives are (1) to keep streetwalking confined to a limited area (containment) and (2) to prevent related disorders from breaking out (keep the peace).[73]

Prostitution is often accompanied by an ancillary crime: a more serious offense that results from prostitution. "Johns" may be robbed, or a prostitute may be assaulted by a pimp, manager, or customer. This problem has been magnified in the media as a consequence of the "Craigslist killer," who was suspected of killing at least one prostitute and harming several others. The case brought attention not only to the growing role of the Internet in prostitution but also to the risks that johns and prostitutes take when participating in such activity.

Arrests of prostitutes typically involve different motives. Conviction and punishment is not always the primary goal. Many arrests are designed to control streetwalking,

SIDEBAR 8-4

Sex Trafficking

Over the past several years there has been increased emphasis on responding to human sex trafficking. Under the Trafficking Victims Protection Act (TVPA), the U.S. Congress defined **sex trafficking** *as the recruitment, harboring, transportation, provision, or obtaining of a person for the purpose of a commercial sex act that is induced by force, fraud, or coercion, or when the person who is forced to perform the commercial sex act is under 18 years old. Little is known about the prevalence of the problem, however. One recent study of the largest police departments in the country reported that about 85 percent of large local police agencies report having a sex trafficking problem in their community. Sex trafficking victims were reported to be mostly females (90.9 percent), over 18 years old (65.8 percent), and from the United States (72.3 percent). About 70 percent of the large police agencies surveyed reported having a specialized unit or division responsible for addressing their community's sex trafficking problem. These units were often responsible for enforcing sex trafficking laws, linking victims to support services, and providing training and information to community groups.*

sex trafficking

1. Along with other students in your class conduct a web search to identify news stories about cases involving sex trafficking in a community selected by your instructor.

2. As a class, discuss whether the problem (as demonstrated through your review of sex trafficking cases appearing in the media) is serious, moderate, or minor.

3. Review news articles about the community's involvement in the prevention, intervention, and suppression of sex trafficking in the selected community.

4. As a class, discuss whether the community's response to the problem is consistent with the problem you identified through your review of sex trafficking cases appearing in the media.

---

either by confining it to a certain area or deterring it altogether. Convictions are usually for misdemeanors, with a sentence of, at most, several hundred dollars in fines and a few weeks or months in the county jail. The prostitutes themselves regard this as a routine business expense.[74]

Periodically, streetwalking increases to the point where it becomes more visible to the public. The resulting public outcry leads to a police crackdown: sweep arrests of all prostitutes. Like crackdowns related to other crimes, they have a short-term impact, after which things return to normal.

Policing prostitution is difficult for several reasons. Prostitution is a "victimless crime," with no complaining party.[75] This often means that the police must initiate investigations on their own. Wiretaps, informants, undercover work, and other covert investigative techniques raise a number of difficult legal and moral questions. Prostitution also involves behavior that many people regard as legitimate, or at least a private matter. The result is conflicting public attitudes about how vigorously the laws should be enforced. Another issue is that prostitution is often statutorily defined as a misdemeanor offense, which results in its often being a low priority for police officers. Policing prostitution is complicated further by the fact that enforcement is often selective, inconsistent, and arbitrary. Equal protection problems are raised by the traditional police practice of arresting only the prostitute (usually female) and ignoring the customer (usually male), even though both are guilty of violating the law against commercialized sex. Similarly, the informal practice of confining street-walking to a certain area of a city involves an illegal form of selective enforcement: enforcing the law in some areas but not others.[76]

Policing the Homeless

Homeless people represent another order maintenance problem for the police. The homeless problem increased significantly in the 1980s. There has been much contro-versy over the actual number of homeless people. The most recent figures from the U.S. Department of Housing and Urban Development estimate the total at about 564,708 people who are homeless.[77] The new homeless population includes more families than in the past, including more women and children. Some observers also believe there are more mentally ill persons among the homeless than in the past because of changes in mental health services.[78]

Skid row in Los Angeles in the 1990s included a designated "sleeping zone," an area of 50 square blocks where the homeless were allowed to sleep on the streets. A newspaper account found on one night a 69-year-old grandmother and a 32-year-old woman, pregnant with twins, struggling to get into their cardboard boxes for the night. An estimated 12,000 people lived in the neighborhood, most in single-room-occupancy hotels, although no one knows exactly how many homeless people sleep on the streets.[79]

The homeless problem creates a number of challenges for the police. Homeless people establish semipermanent camps in public parks, resist transport to homeless shelters, and sleep in bus stations and subways in some cities. Advocates for the homeless have filed lawsuits challenging both police actions and local ordinances designed to restrict the homeless. Some but not all of these suits have been success-ful.[80] The Police Executive Research Forum (PERF) surveyed police departments to determine how they were responding to the homeless problem. More than 70 percent of the departments located in large metropolitan areas reported that homeless people posed a major or moderate problem in the community.[81]

The current police response to the homeless problem, however, is little differ-ent than it was in the past. First, it is reactive, with the police responding to calls for service about a problem with a homeless person. This has led to a police strategy that places primary emphasis on addressing complainant concerns rather than proactively working on behalf of the homeless to prevent problems from occurring in the first place. Second, the current police strategy is based on the idea of containment. Police attempt to contain the homeless problem to one area of a community to minimize disorder and to keep the homeless out of public view.[82]

However, some police agencies have begun to use proactive strategies to ad-dress problems related to the homeless. For example, the Seattle Police Department uses community service officers (CSOs) to handle many of the homeless-related situations. A CSO street team refers homeless persons to shelters, alcohol and drug abuse treatment programs, and financial assistance services. During extremely cold weather, CSOs distribute clothes and sleeping bags that have been donated and patrol alleys looking for people who are in danger of death through exposure.[83]

Perhaps the most well-known, large-scale attempt at addressing homeless-related crime was conducted in Los Angeles. As mentioned earlier, the city of Los Angeles had a major problem associated with homelessness and related crime in the 1990s and early 2000s. Los Angeles's skid row was characterized as having not only the nation's largest concentration of homeless persons but also a large amount of serious crime such as robbery, gang violence, prostitution, open-air drug markets, and theft. In 2005, to respond to the problem, Chief William J. Bratton started a program called the Safe Cities Initiative (SCI). The SCI program was largely based on the zero-tolerance policing approach Bratton had implemented successfully in New York City. The SCI program started with the chief assigning 50 officers to the area. These officers were responsible for citing and fining those who were living in encampments. The goal was to reduce the high concentration of homeless persons in the area. Next, the police cracked down on public disorder in the area by citing and arresting individuals for public intoxication, prostitution, and drug use. Bratton believed that reducing disorder would eventually result in lower levels of crime. After a relatively short period of time, it was clear to the police that the program had its intended effect. A substantial number of the homeless persons soon left skid row, and their encampments were disbanded.[84] Richard Berk and John MacDonald further evaluated the SCI project by examining its impact on crime and disorder in the area over an eight-year period. In the end, the authors claimed that the program had a "meaningful but modest" impact on crime reduction. They also examined the surrounding neighborhoods to see whether crime simply moved to a nearby area and found that it had not.[85]

Although some people have promoted the program's success, others have suggested that it exemplifies a disturbing trend in policing. Michael White, in a response to Berk and MacDonald's work, noted that the zero-tolerance policing strategy taken on skid row by the Los Angeles Police Department (LAPD) represents a shift away from professional policing. He argues that good policing must go beyond mere crime fighting and embrace other responsibilities—including order maintenance and peacekeeping. He points out that policing has advanced substantially over the past two decades through the adoption of community policing and problem-oriented policing and that the LAPD could have employed strategies that might have had a more profound and long-term positive impact on the homeless and skid row. Instead, he argues, the LAPD employed a strategy associated with the criminalization of the homeless, rather than addressing the long-term systemic issues associated with homelessness and homeless-related crime.[86]

Policing the Mentally Ill

Mentally ill persons represent another important order maintenance problem for the police. The police usually become involved because someone defines the situation as a problem and no other solution is available. The exact frequency of mental illness incidents is difficult to determine precisely because of different definitions of mental illness. Most studies estimate that 7 to 10 percent of police contacts are with mentally ill persons.[87] Furthermore, those with mental illnesses are much more likely to be arrested than some other populations and are responsible for a large proportion of repeat calls for service.[88] In Massachusetts, for example, researchers found that 50 percent of

18- to 25-year-olds who had received services from the Massachusetts Department of Mental Health had been arrested in the 10 years following treatment.[89]

Police Response to the Mentally Ill

The police come into contact with the mentally ill in a number of ways. The most common way is in response to calls from family members (32 percent). Family members often try to handle problems by themselves, and when the situation becomes uncontrollable, they call the police. Businesspersons and landlords calling the police account for about one-third of cases involving police contact with mentally ill persons. Because mentally ill persons often live in and around the central business district, businesspersons often call the police to "shoo away" a mentally ill person who may be interfering with business.[90]

Mentally ill persons are also much more likely to be the victims of crime and, therefore, are more likely to come to the attention of the police. Linda Teplin and her colleagues reported that more than 25 percent of persons with severe mental illness were the victims of a crime in the past year. Even after controlling for demographic characteristics, those with serious mental illness were 11 times more likely to be the victim of a crime and 4 times more likely to be the victim of a serious violent crime, compared with the general population.[91]

However, more typically the police are called to the scene because a mentally ill person is seen as threatening. In one study, almost half of all incidents involving a mentally ill person involved the person having a weapon of some kind. Property damage also occurred in about 33 percent of police contacts with mentally ill persons.[92]

Because of the complexities of handling problems associated with mentally ill persons, a great amount of time is often required. Mark Pogrebin found that the average length of time for handling a mental health call was 74 minutes, which is significantly longer than for other order maintenance calls.[93]

Police officers exercise great discretion in handling the mentally ill. The basic options include (1) hospitalization, (2) arrest, and (3) informal disposition. One study found that 75 percent of contacts between the police and the mentally ill are handled through informal disposition. This typically involves the officer using informal tactics to calm a person down. Some observers have referred to this practice as **psychiatric first aid**.[94]

psychiatric first aid

When the situation cannot be handled informally, the officer may have to take a person with a mental illness to a hospital or jail. A number of factors are involved in deciding whether an individual should be hospitalized or arrested. These factors include the seriousness of the offense, officer training, alcohol or drug intoxication, and the offender's state of mind.[95] However, in communities with few mental health resources, police officers are sometimes inclined to arrest a mentally ill person for a misdemeanor. This practice is known as a **mercy booking.** In many jurisdictions, mental health care is more readily accessible in jails than in the community. In these communities, police officers make an arrest for a minor offense to ensure that a mentally ill person receives services to get the care that is needed.[96]

mercy booking

Depending on the circumstances and the community resources available, a mentally ill person might also be hospitalized by the police. One study reported that individuals who are hospitalized often exhibit suicidal behavior, have a history of

Characteristics of Patients Referred to a Psychiatric Emergency Service by Police

Characteristic	Percentage
Reason for referral	
Violence or threat toward officer	32%
Suicidal behavior	51
Violence in the emergency room	11
History of violence	49
Need for psychotropic medication in the emergency room	32
Need for restraint in the emergency room	8
Intoxicated	25
Suicidal in the emergency room	27
Other	17
Diagnosis	
Mood disorder	37
Psychosis	18
Substance use disorder	24
Axis IV pathology	
Mild	1
Moderate	66
Severe	33
Family history of mental illness	55

Source: Robert Redondo and Glenn Currier, "Characteristics of Patients Referred by Police to a Psychiatric Emergency Service," *Psychiatric Services* 54, no. 6 (2003): 804–806.

violence, are in need of psychotropic medication, have a mood disorder, or have a family history of mental illness.[97] (See Exhibit 8–6.)

Several institutional and legal factors have an impact on the police response. First, the law limits the ability of the police to commit someone to a mental health facility involuntarily. A person can be committed only if he or she is a danger to self or to others. The paperwork required to meet this standard discourages officers from trying to commit people except in the most extreme cases.[98]

Second, mental health services are highly fragmented, consisting of a variety of hospitals, homeless shelters, and detoxification facilities. Most have their own admission criteria and refuse to accept people the police bring to them. In some instances, police officers go from one agency to another looking for one that will accept the mentally disordered person.

Old Problems/New Programs

Problems arising from overreliance on arrest and the prevalence of use of force in encounters with mentally ill persons led a number of police agencies to institute special policies, personnel, and procedures to improve the police response to mentally ill persons in crisis. The first generation of efforts, during the 1980s, focused largely on

POLICE *in* FOCUS | Akron Tailors Response to Safety Concerns and Repeat Calls for Law Enforcement and Mental Health Services

Overview

The Akron (Ohio) Crisis Intervention Team (CIT) was one of the first agencies to replicate the Memphis CIT Model. Although this community maintains fidelity to the model, they have made several adjustments to the core elements. For example, CIT officers in Akron have access to four emergency resources, rather than the single point of entry available in Memphis. This adaptation was made to ease the burden on any single mental health facility. Akron has also modified the CIT training to include a segment about being a CIT officer, including safety issues, duties, and officers' experiences.

Tailored Responses

Once CIT was implemented, Akron stakeholders determined the need for a supplemental program to address the needs of their "at-risk" population—those individuals who are repeat clients of both the criminal justice and mental health systems and who often fall through the systems' cracks. The "CIT Outreach Program" consists of a group of officers who team up with an outreach worker from Community Support Services (CSS). Officers in uniform ride together with a CSS worker in a marked cruiser to contact referrals and attempt to engage people in services. Akron reported that pairing a law enforcement officer with a

case worker to conduct followup can also facilitate information sharing, locating individuals, and increasing the safety of encounters.

Outreach teams can refer individuals to mental health and other services, such as elder care and drug addiction services. When the team encounters someone who does not qualify for an involuntary commitment order, they are often able to persuade the person to voluntarily go to CSS, where they are welcomed in the back door with dignity and discretion.

Unique Program Features

The CIT program coordinator in Akron maintains his patrol duties, which lends credibility to the program and assists in soliciting officer involvement. When the outreach team transports an individual in a marked cruiser, he or she rides without handcuffs in the back seat with the mental health case manager. The person may meet criteria for emergency mental health evaluation, but the officer allows the person to ride without handcuffs when the situation is under control. If the person is at risk of harming him- or herself or others, or attempts to leave, the police will then use handcuffs and transport as needed.

Source: Excerpt from Melissa Reuland, Laura Draper, and Blake Norton, *Improving Responses to People with Mental Illnesses: Tailoring Law Enforcement Initiatives to Individual Jurisdictions* (New York: Council of State Governments Justice Center, 2005).

officer training. Today, almost all police agencies provide their recruits with at least some training on mental health issues. However, the amount of time dedicated to these issues during academy training is limited—typically less than 6.5 hours—and most agencies provide less than one hour of post-academy in-service training per year on responding to mental health calls.[99]

The second generation of efforts, during the 1990s, aimed at improving the police response to problems involving the mentally ill by providing more specialized and focused responses. Today, about one-third of large police departments report that they have some type of specialized response for calls involving mentally ill persons. These specialized responses provide police officers with several options tailored to meet the needs of those with mental illnesses and link the mentally ill with community-based services.[100] Agencies that have a focused response to mentally ill persons typically employ one of the following three models:[101]

1. *Police-based specialized response:* This model involves sworn officers who have extensive training in responding to problems involving the mentally ill. These officers are responsible for responding to calls for service involving mentally ill persons and serve as a liaison to mental health agencies.
2. *Police-based specialized mental health response:* This model involves utilizing mental health professionals, not sworn officers, who are employed by the police department to respond to problems involving the mentally ill. The mental health professionals provide on-location and telephone advice to officers in the field.
3. *Mental-health-based specialized mental health response:* This model involves formal agreements and arrangements between police departments and community mental health organizations. The model is based on the use of mental health crisis teams (MCTs) that are dispatched by police officers to provide field-level services to those in need.

Policing People with HIV

In the 1980s, the human immunodeficiency virus (HIV) presented the police with a new set of problems. Because police officers often handle people with HIV, there is some risk of infection. Most of the risk involves police officers coming into contact with blood. Although HIV has been found in saliva or "spit," there is no known case in which an officer has contracted HIV from saliva. HIV cannot be transmitted through casual physical contact such as touching.[102]

The Centers for Disease Control and Prevention (CDC) estimates that about 1.2 million people in the United States are living with HIV.[103] No studies to date have systematically assessed the risk to police officers of being exposed to HIV, but research examining HIV among arrestees—a group of individuals with whom the police have frequent contact—shows that police officers' potential for exposure is higher than it is in many other occupations. This is largely a consequence of the shift in policy toward more aggressive enforcement involving substance abusers. In most cities across the country, about 60 to 70 percent of those who are arrested by the police are current drug users, many of whom are injection drug users, placing them at higher risk for HIV infection.[104]

Although the concern among police officers about contracting HIV is high, few if any officers have contracted the disease. A survey by the FBI reported that between 1981 and 1991, seven police officers contracted HIV from a work-related exposure. However, more recent research conducted by the CDC found that not a single officer in the United States has ever contracted HIV as a result of a work-related exposure.[105]

Jeanne Flavin points out that even though the risk of contracting HIV is low for police officers, it poses a unique threat. First, HIV is contracted through a small microbe rather than a readily observable threat, such as a person or situation. Second, if an officer is exposed to HIV, it takes three to six months to know whether or not the officer has contracted the virus. Third, unlike most threats that the police are exposed to, HIV is an incurable and deadly disease.[106]

As a consequence of the fear of contracting HIV, some officers have become reluctant to render medical assistance. In a study of one police department, 30 percent of officers stated that they avoid helping people because of their fear of contracting HIV.[107] In other studies, researchers have found that most police officers attempt to take precautions to minimize their chances of contracting the disease, such as wearing latex gloves when assisting someone who is bleeding. However, precautions are not always possible, and as a result, officers sometimes do not render assistance and instead wait for medical personnel to take care of any medical problems.[108]

The fear of contracting HIV has also led a number of police agencies to unofficially keep records of infected individuals. When the police agency receives a call for service, the dispatcher will notify the responding officer if the individual with whom the officer will be coming into contact is HIV positive. This practice is intended to protect officers from unknowingly placing themselves at risk. However, the collection of such information may lead to the violation of a person's right to privacy. Persons with HIV are often the subject of prejudice and discrimination. For example, in Kokomo, Indiana, a waiter lost his job as a consequence of a police officer's informing the restaurant's management that the waiter was HIV positive—information that the officer had obtained while working on the job. The waiter later sued the city of Kokomo and was awarded $60,000, and the police department was ordered to educate its officers on issues of confidentiality.[109]

A Justice Department report recommended that all law enforcement agencies provide HIV-related education and training for their officers and develop formal policies for the handling of HIV-positive individuals in routine encounters, arrest situations, and police lock-ups.[110] Approximately 86 percent of state police departments offer HIV training to recruits during basic training, and 78 percent offer it through in-service training.[111] Almost half of all agencies are required to offer such training to meet state legal requirements.

Policing Juveniles

Juveniles represent a special set of problems for the police. First, the police have a high level of contact with people under the age of 18. Young people are more likely than adults to be out on the street, where the police observe them. "Hanging out" on the corner or "cruising" in cars often produces citizen conflict over the proper use of public spaces.

Second, young people consistently express more negative attitudes toward the police than do older people. For example, one survey reported that 72 percent of people between the ages of 18 and 29 expressed favorable attitudes with respect to the fairness of the police, compared with 90 percent for people in the 40- to 49-year-old age group.[112]

Third, juveniles represent a significant aspect of the crime problem in the United States: 10.4 percent of all violent index crime arrests and 15 percent of all property crime arrests. Juveniles are involved in three crimes at a particularly high rate: 22.8 percent of all arson arrests, 18.8 percent of all disorderly conduct arrests, and 15 percent of all vandalism arrests.[113]

Controversy over the Police Role

Significant controversy exists over the proper police role in relation to juveniles. Some people favor a strict law enforcement role, emphasizing the arrest of offenders. Others prefer a crime prevention role, arguing that the police should emphasize helping young people who are at risk with advice, counseling, and alternatives to arrest.[114] However, because of increased public fear of crime and violent juvenile crime in particular, police departments have given greater emphasis to the law enforcement role in recent years. With the exception of programs such as G.R.E.A.T. (Gang Resistance Education and Training), traditional crime prevention programs have been deemphasized.

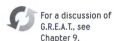

For a discussion of G.R.E.A.T., see Chapter 9.

Uncertain or conflicting department policies regarding juveniles often cause role conflict in police officers on the street. One report on police–juvenile operations pointed out that "crime prevention can be viewed as 'social work,' a role that police often see as taking time away from what they consider to be their primary role—the apprehension of criminals."[115]

Police response to juveniles is complicated by conflicting police responsibilities. The case of kids hanging out on the streets illustrates the problem. On the one hand, the police are expected to maintain order. To this end, a number of cities have passed curfews for juveniles and/or "gang loitering" ordinances. At the same time, however, the police have a responsibility to respect the rights of citizens. Young people have a First Amendment right to assemble in public.

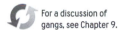

For a discussion of gangs, see Chapter 9.

Specialized Juvenile Units

Most police contacts with juveniles are divided between two units within the department: patrol and specialized juvenile units. Patrol officers have the most contact with juveniles as part of their normal patrol duty. They regularly see and have contact with groups of kids hanging out on the street corner, people they suspect to be gang members, and so on.

Most large police departments have special juvenile units. They are often referred to by such names as the juvenile division, the youth division, or the crime

---

SIDEBAR 8–5

Hot Spots of Juvenile Crime

In a first of its kind study, David Weisburd and his colleagues examined whether there were "hot spots" of juvenile crime in Seattle. The researchers mapped all of the incidents that were reported to the police in which a juvenile was involved. They found that juvenile crime was highly concentrated—with 50 percent of all juvenile crime occurring in fewer than 1 percent of street segments, and all juvenile crime occurring in less than 5 percent of street segments. They reported that these hot spots were characterized as areas frequented by youth such as schools and shops/malls, rather than private dwellings and bars, which are areas where adult criminality is more likely to take place. Weisburd et al. note that increasing the supervision and structure of juvenile activities in areas identified as hot spots might prevent delinquency and that place-based interventions led by place managers and the police are necessary to effectively respond to juvenile crime.

Source: David Weisburd, Elizabeth Groff, and Nancy Morris, "Hot Spots of Juvenile Crime: Findings from Seattle," *Juvenile Justice Bulletin* (Washington, DC: Office of Juvenile Justice and Delinquency Prevention, 2011).

prevention bureau. About 50 percent of all large local law enforcement agencies have a special juvenile unit. Many departments also have special child abuse and missing children units. The D.A.R.E. (Drug Abuse Resistance Education) program, through which police officers provide drug education in the schools, is popular. Currently, about 75 percent of school districts in the United States participate in the program.[116]

The responsibilities of traditional juvenile units typically include (1) investigating reports of juvenile crime, (2) arresting delinquents, (3) preparing cases for court, and (4) appearing in court. However, some juvenile units have other responsibilities as well. For example, the Minneapolis, Minnesota police department's juvenile division is responsible not only for investigating juvenile criminal behavior and the processing of cases but also provides short-term detention for arrested juveniles, ... maintains files on runaway and missing juveniles and juvenile criminal history records.[117]

Specialized juvenile units typically do not handle gang problems. Specialized gang units often deal with these problems.

On-the-Street Encounters

In their historic study examining police encounters with juveniles, Donald Black and Albert Reiss found that 72 percent of all encounters between police and juveniles were initiated by a telephone call. Officers appear to initiate contacts with juveniles at a slightly higher rate (28 percent of all contacts) than with adults.[118] This happens because young people are more likely than adults to be out on the street, and the police are more likely to regard juveniles as criminal suspects.

For a full discussion of the allocation and distribution of officers, see Chapter 7.

As is the case with all other police activities, officers exercise great discretion in dealing with juveniles on the street. The alternative police responses include the following:[119]

1. *Taking no official action:* This is the most common outcome. As is the case with domestic disputes and encounters with allegedly mentally disturbed people, the police dispose of situations informally, mainly just by talking with people. Talking may involve advising, warning, mediating disputes, or simply listening. In many instances, no arrest is made even though there are sufficient legal grounds to make an arrest.

2. *Taking a juvenile into custody but releasing him or her to a parent or guardian:* About 25 to 30 percent of all juveniles taken into custody are released in this fashion.[120]

3. *Taking the juvenile into custody and releasing him or her to another law enforcement or social service agency:* About 3 percent of all juveniles taken into custody are released in this fashion.[121]

4. *Arresting the juvenile and referring him or her to juvenile court:* About 71 percent of all juveniles taken into custody are referred to juvenile court. Some (about 7 percent of the total) are referred to criminal court for prosecution as adults.[122]

For a full discussion of police discretion, see Chapter 11.

Arrest discretion involving juveniles is influenced by the same situational factors that affect encounters with adults. These factors include the seriousness of the offense, the preference of the victim or complaining party, the relationship between complainant and suspect, and the demeanor of the suspect.[123]

The Issue of Race Discrimination

The police arrest proportionately far more African American juveniles than white. Several factors account for this disparity. First, police departments generally assign more patrol officers to minority neighborhoods than white neighborhoods and, consequently, observe minority youths more frequently.[124]

Second, minority youths are stopped and questioned at a higher rate than whites. Many racial profiling studies have found that minority youth are stopped and frisked, and their vehicles searched, at rates disproportionate to their presence in particular neighborhoods.[125]

Third, the racial disparity in arrests is associated with other factors that influence arrest decisions. Black and Reiss found that the higher arrest rate was explained in large part by greater African American involvement in serious crime. When seriousness of the suspected offense was controlled, blacks and whites were arrested at similar rates.[126] Lundman, meanwhile, found that black adults are more likely to ask the police to arrest the suspect than are white adults. Because most complainant–suspect situations are intraracial, black juveniles are arrested at a higher rate.[127]

Douglas Smith and colleagues, in a study of arrests involving persons of all ages, found that police are slightly more likely to make an arrest when the victim is white rather than African American. Other studies have also suggested that the police are more likely to arrest a juvenile when an adult is the complaining party.[128]

The demeanor of the suspect also influences police arrest decisions. In separate studies, Black and Reiss, as well as Werthman and Piliavin, found that African American juveniles expressed hostility toward the police more often than did whites and, as a consequence, were arrested at higher rates. Piliavin and Briar described the phenomenon as the "self-fulfilling consequences of the original set of police attitudes and behavior toward black youth." The police expect black juveniles to engage in more law breaking, stop and question them at a higher rate, and as a consequence create the perception of harassment and generate more hostile reactions.[129] David Klinger, however, has raised new questions about the role of demeanor in arrests, arguing that these earlier studies did not control for hostile behavior that occurred after the arrest and therefore could not have influenced the arrest itself.[130]

Crime Prevention Programs

Police crime prevention efforts have traditionally involved programs designed to steer juveniles away from criminal activity through education, counseling, or role modeling. The basic idea is for the police to present themselves as friends and helpers rather than as law enforcers.

Today, it is not uncommon for a police department to coordinate several youth-oriented programs as part of its prevention efforts. Examples include police athletic leagues, midnight basketball, wilderness clubs, and explorer and mentoring programs. Some current crime prevention programs are part of community policing. Under this model, police agencies work to build the capacity of neighborhoods to prevent crime. This is often accomplished by the police department coordinating community and social service organizations to focus on youth and neighborhoods that are at the highest risk for delinquency. In other words, the police department acts as a social service broker to ensure that those who need the most help have an opportunity to receive it.[131]

The most popular current crime prevention programs are D.A.R.E. and G.R.E.A.T., which attempt to prevent drug use, delinquency, and involvement in gangs and gang crime. These crime prevention strategies are covered in Chapter 9.

CASE STUDY

Responding to Chronically Inebriated Individuals in Seattle, Washington

Building on the research concerning alcoholism and homelessness, stakeholders in Seattle, Washington, developed a unique response that took aim at the enormous resource burdens chronically inebriated individuals were placing on the area. A group of 199 individuals who presented among the highest costs on the system were selected for no-cost housing in the Housing First residential facility. They were offered free meals and on-site health services, but there was no requirement for substance abuse treatment placed on them. Costs associated with these services averaged $1,220 per person per month. After one year, a program evaluation revealed that in the year preceding placement at Housing First, the program participants had incurred over $8 million in collective costs (jails, EMS, hospital, emergency department, detoxification, Medicare, and so forth). After one year in the program, participants' costs had dropped to $4 million. The average daily alcohol consumption among residents had dropped from 15.7 to 10.6 drinks per day. From these results, researchers concluded that stable housing, coupled with ready access to health services, while posing considerable up-front expense, could yield marked reduction in several related system costs (Levin, 2009). A subsequent study observed similar results: After one year in the Housing First residential program, average associated monthly costs per person dropped from $4,066 to $958. The total average monthly cost per person—after factoring in housing costs—was $2,449 (Larimer et al., 2009).

Source: Excerpt from Matthew Pate, *Chronic Public Inebriation*, Problem-Oriented Guide No. 68 (Washington, DC: Center for Problem-Oriented Policing, 2012), http://www.popcenter.org/problems/pdfs/chronic_public_inebriation.pdf.

SUMMARY

Order maintenance and peacekeeping is an important part of policing for the simple reason that most calls for service fall in this category. How the police respond to these calls raises the basic issues about the police role that we discussed in Chapter 1. How do we think about the police? What do we want them to do?

Traditionally, police officers regarded order maintenance calls as "garbage" and "social work," placing a higher value on crime fighting. Most experts today, however, argue that maintaining order and keeping the peace is a central aspect of policing.

Community policing, problem-oriented policing, and zero-tolerance policing place a high value on dealing with noncrime problems. Many order maintenance situations, moreover, involve special populations: the homeless, the mentally ill, and juveniles. If we think of the police in terms proposed by Herman Goldstein, as a general service agency providing a wide range of services to the public, it becomes important for police departments to develop special programs and procedures to improve the handling of these problem situations.[132]

KEY TERMS

order maintenance, 251
crime prophylactic model, 251
police knowledge model, 251
social work model, 251
community cooperation
    model, 251
counterpunching, 252

domestic disturbance, 256
domestic violence, 257
Minneapolis Domestic Violence
    Experiment, 260
Lautenberg Amendment, 263
streetwalkers, 263
bar girls, 264

skeezers, 264
brothel prostitutes, 264
call girls, 264
sex trafficking, 265
psychiatric first aid, 268
mercy booking, 268

FOR DISCUSSION

1. Describe four reasons the public calls the police in situations not involving a crime.
2. Explain how domestic violence policies evolved in local police departments across the United States.
3. Discuss the research findings on the impact of mandatory arrest for misdemeanor domestic violence.

4. Discuss the case study on responding to chronic inebriation in Seattle. As a class, discuss whether the program should be considered innovative, and the strengths and weaknesses of the approach.

INTERNET EXERCISES

Exercise 1 Visit the website www.lapdonline.org/detective_bureau/content_basic_view/1987 and check out the responsibilities of the Los Angeles Police Department's Vice Division. As a class, discuss the role of the police in responding to vice and how it might have changed over the past several decades.

Exercise 2 Visit http://ovc.ncjrs.gov/humantrafficking/publicawareness.html and watch Video 2 – "An Introduction to Sex Trafficking." Discuss the places where sex trafficking might be found in various communities and the complexities

related to the police identifying sex trafficking victims.

Exercise 3 Visit the website www.collegedrinkingprevention.gov to view the site College Drinking: Changing the Culture, created by the National Institute on Alcohol Abuse and Alcoholism (NIAAA). The site provides information on issues related to alcohol use among college students. Review the site and discuss as a class whether you believe such a website has an impact on college student alcohol use and other risky behavior such as drunk driving.

NOTES

1. Peter E. Finn and Monique Sullivan, *Police Response to Special Populations* (Washington, DC: U.S. Government Printing Office, 1988).
2. David Bayley, *Police for the Future* (New York: Oxford University Press, 1994).

3. Stephen Mastrofski, "The Police and Non-crime Services," in G. Whitaker and C. Phillips, eds., *Evaluating the Performance of Criminal Justice Agencies* (Beverly Hills, CA: Sage, 1983), 44–47.

4. Charles M. Katz, Vincent Webb, and David Schaefer, "An Assessment of the Impact of Quality of Life Policing on Crime and Disorder," *Justice Quarterly* 18, no. 4 (2001): 826–876.

5. Ibid.

6. Egon Bittner, "Florence Nightingale in Pursuit of Willie Sutton: A Theory of the Police," in Herbert Jacob, ed., *The Potential for Reform of Criminal Justice* (Beverly Hills, CA: Sage, 1974), 1–25.

7. Samuel Walker, *Popular Justice: A History of American Criminal Justice,* 2nd ed. (New York: Oxford University Press, 1998), 165–167.

8. John C. Meyer, "Patterns of Reporting Noncriminal Incidents to the Police," *Criminology* 12 (May 1974): 70–83.

9. David H. Bayley and James Garofalo, "The Management of Violence by Police Patrol Officers," *Criminology* 27 (February 1989): 1–25.

10. Stephen D. Mastrofski, Jeffrey B. Snipes, and Anne E. Supina, "Compliance on Demand: The Public's Response to Specific Requests," *Journal of Research in Crime and Delinquency* 33 (August 1996): 269–305; John McCluskey, Stephen Mastrofski, and Roger Parks, "To Acquiesce or Rebel: Predicting Citizen Compliance with Police Requests," *Police Quarterly* 2, no. 4 (1999): 389–416.

11. Christine Eith and Matthew R. Durose, *Contacts between Police & the Public, 2008* (Washington, DC: U.S. Government Printing Office, 2011).

12. Ibid.

13. Illya Lichtenberg and Alisa Smith, "How Dangerous Are Routine Police-Citizen Traffic Stops?" *Journal of Criminal Justice* 29 (2001): 419–428.

14. Arizona Criminal Justice Commission, *Crime and the Criminal Justice System in Arizona, The 2003 White Paper* (Phoenix: Arizona Criminal Justice Commission, 2003).

15. James Q. Wilson, *Varieties of Police Behavior* (New York: Atheneum, 1973), 95–99.

16. Ibid.

17. Alexander Weiss and Sally Freels, "The Effects of Aggressive Policing: The Dayton Traffic Enforcement Experiment," *American Journal of Police* XV, no. 3 (1996): 45–64.

18. Ibid.

19. James B. Jacobs, *Drunk Driving: An American Dilemma* (Chicago: University of Chicago Press, 1989); H. Laurence Ross, *Confronting Drunk Driving: Social Policy for Saving Lives* (New Haven, CT: Yale University Press, 1992).

20. Ross, *Confronting Drunk Driving.*

21. Ibid.; Jacobs, *Drunk Driving.*

22. Ibid.

23. Eric J. Scott, *Calls for Service: Citizen Demand and Initial Police Response* (Washington, DC: U.S. Government Printing Office, 1981); Craig D. Uchida, Laure Brooks, and Christopher S. Kopers, "Danger to Police during Domestic Encounters: Assaults on Baltimore County Police, 1984–1986," *Criminal Justice Policy Review* 2 (1987): 357–371.

24. Jeffrey Fagan, *The Criminalization of Domestic Violence: Promises and Limits* (Washington, DC: U.S. Government Printing Office, 1996); Lawrence W. Sherman, Janell Schmidt, and Dennis Rogan, *Policing Domestic Violence: Experiments and Dilemmas* (New York: Free Press, 1992).

25. Sherman, Schmidt, and Rogan, *Policing Domestic Violence.*

26. Jennifer Truman, *Criminal Victimization, 2010* (Washington, DC: U.S. Bureau of Justice Statistics, 2011).

27. Murray A. Straus and Richard J. Gelles, *Physical Violence in American Families: Risk Factors and Adaptation to Violence in 8,145 Families* (New Brunswick, NJ: Transaction, 1990).

28. Jennifer L. Truman and Lynn Langton, *Criminal Victimization, 2013* (Washington, DC: U.S. Bureau of Justice Statistics, 2014).

29. Shannan Catalano, *Intimate Partner Violence*, bjs.ojp.usdoj.gov/content/pub/pdf/ipvus.pdf.

30. Franklyn W. Dunford, David Huizinga, and Delbert S. Elliot, "The Role of Arrest in Domestic Assault: The Omaha Police Experiment," *Criminology* 28 (May 1990): 183–206. Some of these data appear in the unpublished technical report.

31. Catalano, *Intimate Partner Violence.*

32. Donald Black, "Dispute Settlement by the Police," in Donald Black, ed., *Manners and Customs of the Police* (New York: Academic Press, 1980), 125–126.

33. Richard Felson, Steven Messner, Anthony Hoskin, and Glenn Deane, "Reasons for Reporting and Not Reporting Domestic Violence to the Police," *Criminology* 40, no. 30 (2002): 617–647.

34. Dunford, Huizinga, and Elliot, "The Role of Arrest in Domestic Assault."

35. Richard J. Gelles and Murray A. Straus, *Intimate Violence: The Causes And Consequences of Abuse in the American Family* (New York: Simon & Schuster, 1988), 104.

36. Mastrofski, Snipes, and Supina, "Compliance on Demand."

37. Schulman, Mark A. A survey of spousal violence against women in Kentucky. US Department of Justice, Law Enforcement Assistance Administration, 1980.

38. Dunford, Huizinga, and Elliot, "The Role of Arrest in Domestic Assault."

39. Lynette Feder, "Police Handling of Domestic Violence Calls: An Overview and Further Investigation," *Women and Criminal Justice* 10, no. 2 (1999): 49–68.

40. Dana Jones and Joanne Belknap, "Police Responses to Battering in a Progressive Pro-Arrest Jurisdiction," *Justice Quarterly* 16, no. 2 (1999): 249–274.

41. Sherman, Schmidt, and Rogan, *Policing Domestic Violence.*

42. Albert Reiss, *The Police and the Public* (New Haven, CT: Yale University Press, 1971), 14.

43. Nancy Loving, *Responding to Spouse Abuse and Wife Beating: A Guide for Police* (Washington, DC: Police Executive Research Forum, 1980); Laurie Woods, "Litigation on Behalf of Battered Women," *Women's Rights Law Reporter* 5 (Fall 1978): 7–34.

44. Loving, *Responding to Spouse Abuse and Wife Beating.*

45. Samuel Walker, *Taming the System: The Control of Discretion in Criminal Justice, 1950–1990* (New York: Oxford University Press, 1993).

46. Lawrence W. Sherman and Richard A. Berk, "The Specific Deterrent Effect of Arrest for Domestic Assault," *American Sociological Review* 49, no. 2 (1984): 261–272; Sherman, Schmidt, and Rogan, *Policing Domestic Violence*, 91–96.

47. Sherman, Schmidt, and Rogan, *Policing Domestic Violence*, 110.

48. Bureau of Justice Statistics, *Law Enforcement Management and Administrative Statistics, 2000* (Washington, DC: U.S. Government Printing Office, 2004).

49. Patrick R. Gartin, "Examining Differential Officer Effects in the Minneapolis Domestic Violence Experiment," *American Journal of Police* 14, no. 3/4 (1995): 93–110.

50. Richard E. Lempert, "From the Editor," *Law and Society Review* 18, no. 4 (1984): 505–513; Lawrence W. Sherman and Ellen Cohn, "The Impact of Research on Legal Policy: The Minneapolis Domestic Violence Experiment," *Law and Society Review* 23, no. 1 (1989): 117–144; Richard Lempert, "Humility as a Virtue: On the Publicization of Policy-Relevant Research," *Law and Society Review* 23, no. 1 (1989): 145–161; Sherman, Schmidt, and Rogan, *Policing Domestic Violence,* 92–124.

51. University of Maryland, *Preventing Crime* (Washington, DC: U.S. Government Printing Office, 1997), ch. 8.

52. Sherman, Schmidt, and Rogan, *Policing Domestic Violence.*

53. David Hirschel, Eve Buzawa, April Pattavina, Don Faggiani, and Melissa Reuland, *Explaining the Prevalence, Context, and Consequences of Dual Arrest in Intimate Partner Cases* (Washington, DC: National Institute of Justice, 2007).

54. Ibid.

55. Margaret E. Martin, "Double Your Trouble: Dual Arrest in Family Violence," *Journal of Family Violence* 12, no. 2 (1997): 139–157.

56. Hirschel et al., *Explaining the Prevalence, Context, and Consequences of Dual Arrest.*

57. Martin, "Double Your Trouble."

58. Susan L. Miller, "Unintended Side Effects of Pro-Arrest Policies and Their Race and Class Implications for Battered Women: A Cautionary Note," *Criminal Justice Policy Review* 3, no. 3 (1989): 299–317.

59. National Institute of Justice, *Evaluation of Family Violence Training Programs* (Washington, DC: U.S. Government Printing Office, 1995).

60. Joan Zorza, "The Criminal Law of Misdemeanor Domestic Violence, 1970–1990," *Journal of Criminal Law and Criminology* 83 (1992): 240–279.

61. Barbara J. Hart, *State Codes on Domestic Violence* (Reno, NV: National Council of Juvenile and Family Court Judges, 1992); Eve Buzawa and Carl Buzawa, *Domestic Violence: The Criminal Justice Response* (Newbury Park, CA: Sage, 1990), 110–135.

62. Fagan, *The Criminalization of Domestic Violence,* 1.

63. Sherman, Schmidt, and Rogan, *Policing Domestic Violence,* 253.

64. Terance Miethe and Richard McCorkle, *Crime Profiles: The Anatomy of Dangerous Persons, Places, and Situations* (Los Angeles: Roxbury, 2001).

65. Martin A. Monto and Christine Milrod, "Ordinary or Peculiar Men? Comparing the Customers of Prostitutes with a Nationally Representative Sample of Men," *International Journal of Offender Therapy and Comparative Criminology* 58, no. 7 (2014): 802–820.

66. Miethe and McCorkle, *Crime Profiles.*

67. Ibid.

68. Ibid.

69. Ibid.

70. Ibid.

71. Mindy Fullilove, Anne Lown, and Robert Fullilove, "Crack Hos and Skeezers: Traumatic Experiences of Women Crack Users," *Journal of Sex Research* 29, no. 2 (1992): 275–287.

72. Miethe and McCorkle, *Crime Profiles,* 223–226.

73. Ibid.

74. Egon Bittner, "The Police on Skid Row: A Study of Peacekeeping," in Egon Bittner, ed., *Aspects of Police Work* (Boston: Northeastern University Press, 1990), 30–62.

75. Wayne R. LaFave, "Arrest to Control the Prostitute," in Wayne R. LaFave, ed., *Arrest* (Boston: Little, Brown, 1965), 450–464; Frederique Delacoste and Priscilla Alexander, *Sex Work* (San Francisco: Cleis Press, 1998); Michael Scott, *Street Prostitution* (Washington, DC: U.S. Government Printing Office, 2002).

76. LaFave, "Arrest to Control the Prostitute."

77. Meghan Henry, Azim Shivji, Tanya de Sousa, and Rebecca Cohen, *The 2015 Annual Homeless Assessment Report (AHAR) to Congress* (Washington, DC: U.S. Department of Housing and Urban Development, 2015).

78. Christopher Jencks, *The Homeless* (Cambridge, MA: Harvard University Press, 1994).

79. "Redevelopment Plans May Hem in Skid Row," *New York Times,* October 23, 1997, 1.

80. George L. Kelling and Catherine M. Coles, *Fixing Broken Windows* (New York: Free Press, 1996).

81. Colleen Cosgrove and Anne Grant, *National Survey of Municipal Police Departments on Urban Quality-of-Life Initiatives,* in Tara O'Connor Shelley and Anne C. Grant, eds., *Problem-Oriented Policing: Crime-Specific Problems, Critical Issues and Making POP Work* (Washington, DC: Police Executive Research Forum, 1998).

82. David Snow and Leon Anderson, *Down on Their Luck* (Berkeley: University of California Press, 1993).

83. Martha R. Plotkin and Ortwin A. Narr, *The Police Response to the Homeless: A Status Report* (Washington, DC: Police Executive Research Forum, 1993), appendix, C-85–C-116.

84. Richard Berk and John MacDonald, "Policing the Homeless: An Evaluation of Efforts to Reduce Homeless Related Crime," *Criminology & Public Policy* 9, no. 4 (2010): 813–840.

85. Ibid.

86. Michael White, "Jim Longstreet, Mike Marshall, and the Lost Art of Policing Skid Row," *Criminology & Public Policy* 9, no. 4 (2010): 883–896.

87. Judy Hails and Randy Borum, "Police Training and Specialized Approaches to Respond to People with Mental Illnesses," *Crime and Delinquency* 49, no. 1 (2003): 52–61.

88. Elizabeth Biebel and Gary Cordner, "Repeat Calls for People with Mental Illness: An Application of Hot Spot Analysis," *Police Forum* 13, no. 3 (July 2003): 1–3.

89. William Fisher, Kristen Roy-Bujnowski, Albert Grudzinskas, Jonathan Clayfield, Steven Banks, and Nancy Wolff, "Patterns and Prevalence of Arrest in a Statewide Cohort of Mental Health Care Consumers," *Psychiatric Services* 57, no. 11 (2006): 1623–1628.

90. Robert Panzarella and Justin Alicea, "Police Tactics in Incidents with Mentally Disturbed Persons," *Policing: International Journal of Police Strategies and Management* 20, no. 2 (1997): 339–356.

91. Linda Teplin, Gary McClelland, Karen Abram, and Dana Weiner, "Crime Victimization in Adults with Severe Mental Illness: Comparison with the National Crime Victimization Survey," *Archives of General Psychiatry* 62, no. 8 (2005): 911–921.

92. Robert Panzarella and Justin Alicea, "Police Tactics in Incidents with Mentally Disturbed Persons," *Policing: International Journal of Police Strategies and Management* 20, no. 2 (1997): 339–356.

93. Mark R. Pogrebin, "Police Responses for Mental Health Assistance," *Psychiatric Quarterly* 58, no. 1 (1986–87): 66–73.

94. Richard Lamb, Linda Weinberger, and Walter DeCuir, "The Police and Mental Health," *Psychiatric Services* 53, no. 10 (2002): 1266–1271.

95. Ibid.

96. Ibid.

97. Robert Redondo and Glenn Currier, "Characteristics of Patients Referred by Police to a Psychiatric Emergency Service," *Psychiatric Services* 54, no. 6 (2003): 804–806.

98. Lamb, Weinberger, and DeCuir, "The Police and Mental Health."

99. Judy Hails and Randy Borum, "Police Training and Specialized Approaches to Respond to People with Mental Illnesses," *Crime & Delinquency* 49 (2003): 52–61.

100. Melissa Reuland and Matt Schwarzfeld, *Improving Responses to People with Mental Illness* (New York: Council of State Governments Justice Center, 2008).

101. Ibid.

102. Minnesota Department of Health, *Facts of AIDS: A Law Enforcement Guide* (Minneapolis, MN: Department of Health, July 2003).

103. Centers for Disease Control and Prevention, *HIV in the United States: At a Glance*, http://www.cdc.gov/hiv/statistics/overview/ataglance.html

104. National Institute of Justice, *Annualized Site Reports, 2002* (Washington, DC: Author, 2003).

105. R. Alan Thompson and James Marquart, "Law Enforcement Responses to the HIV/AIDS Epidemic," *Policing: An International Journal of Police Strategies and Management* 21, no. 4 (1998): 648–665; Jeanne Flavin, "Police and HIV/AIDS: The Risk, the Reality, the Response," *American Journal of Criminal Justice* 23, no. 1 (1998): 33–58.

106. Flavin, "Police and HIV/AIDS."

107. C. Herlitz and B. Brorsson, "Facing AIDS: Reactions among Police Officers, Nurses and the General Public in Sweden," *Social Science Medicine* 30 (1990): 913–918.

108. Flavin, "Police and HIV/AIDS."

109. Ibid.

110. Theodore M. Hammett, "AIDS and the Law Enforcement Officer: Concerns and Policy Responses," *National Institute of Justice—Issues and Practices* (1987): 31.

111. Terry Edwards and Richard Tewksbury, "HIV/AIDS: State Police Training Practices and Personnel Policies," *American Journal of Police* 15, no. 1 (1996): 45–62.

112. W. S. Wilson Huang and Michael S. Vaughn, "Support and Confidence: Public Attitudes toward the Police," in Timothy J. Flanagan and Dennis R. Longmire, eds., *Americans View Crime and Justice: A National Public Opinion Survey* (Newbury Park, CA: Sage, 1996), 40.

113. Federal Bureau of Investigation, *2014 Crime in the United States*, table 36, https://www.fbi.gov/about-us/cjis/ucr/crime-in-the-u.s/2014/crime-in-the-u.s.-2014/tables/table-36.

114. National Institute for Juvenile Justice and Delinquency Prevention, *Police-Juvenile Operations: A Comparative Analysis of Standards and Practices,* vol. 2 (Washington, DC: U.S. Government Printing Office, n.d.), 3–10.

115. National Institute for Juvenile Justice, *Police-Juvenile Operations,* vol. 2, p. 3.

116. Drug Abuse Resistance Education (DARE) website at http://www.dare.org/about-d-a-r-e/.

117. See http://www.minneapolismn.gov/police/about/investigations/police_about_juvenile

118. Donald Black and Albert J. Reiss, "Police Control of Juveniles," *American Sociological Review* 35 (February 1970): 63–77.

119. Adapted from Office of Juvenile Justice and Delinquency Prevention, *Police-Juvenile Operations,* vol. 2, p. 57.

120. Office of Juvenile Justice and Delinquency Prevention, *Juvenile Offenders and Victims: A National Report* (Washington, DC: U.S. Government Printing Office, 1995).

121. Ibid.

122. Office of Juvenile Justice and Delinquency Prevention, *Juvenile Offenders and Victims: 2006 National Report* (Washington, DC: U.S. Government Printing Office, 2006).

123. Black and Reiss, "Police Control of Juveniles."

124. Samuel Walker, Cassia Spohn, and Miriam DeLone, *The Color of Justice,* 2nd ed. (Belmont, CA: Wadsworth, 2000), ch. 4.

125. J. McMahon, J. Garner, R. Davis, and A. Kraus, *How to Correctly Collect and Analyze Racial Profiling Data* (Washington, DC: U.S. Government Printing Office, 2002).

126. Black and Reiss, "Police Control of Juveniles."

127. Richard J. Lundman, "Police Control of Juveniles: A Replication," *Journal of Research in Crime and Delinquency* 15 (1978): 74–91.

128. Douglas A. Smith, Christy A. Visher, and Laura A. Davidson, "Equity and Discretionary Justice: The Influence of Race on Police Arrest Decisions," *Journal of Criminal Law and Criminology* 75 (Spring 1984): 234–249.

129. Carl Werthman and Irving Piliavin, "Gang Members and the Police," in David J. Bordua, ed., *The Police: Six Sociological Essays* (New York: Jorn Riley, 1968), 58–59.

130. David Klinger, "Demeanor or Crime? Why 'Hostile' Citizens Are More Likely to Be Arrested," *Criminology* 32 (1994): 475–493.

131. Gordon Bazemore and Scott Senjo, "Police Encounters with Juveniles Revisited," *Policing: An International Journal of Police Strategies and Management* 20, no. 1 (1997): 60–82.

132. Herman Goldstein, *Policing a Free Society* (Cambridge, MA: Ballinger, 1977).

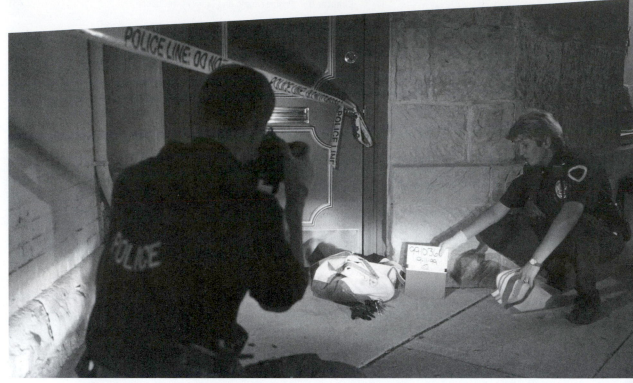

© Roylaty-Free/Corbis

CHAPTER

9

The Police and Crime

CHAPTER OUTLINE

The Police and Crime
    Crime Control Strategies
    Crime Control Assumptions
    Measuring Effectiveness
Preventing Crime
Apprehending Criminals
    Citizen Reporting of Crime
    Reporting and Unfounding Crimes
Criminal Investigation
    Myths about Detective Work
    The Organization of Detective Work
The Investigation Process
    The Preliminary Investigation
    Arrest Discretion

Follow-Up Investigations
The Reality of Detective Work
Case Screening
**Measuring the Effectiveness of
Criminal Investigation**
    The Clearance Rate
    Defining an Arrest
**Success and Failure in Solving
Crimes**
    Case Structural Factors
    Organizational Factors
    Environmental Factors
    Officer Productivity
    The Problem of Case
      Attrition

The Use of Eyewitness Identification, Criminalistics, and DNA in Investigations
Eyewitness Identification
Criminalistics
DNA
Improving Criminal Investigations
Special Investigative Techniques
Undercover Police Work
Informants
Policing Drugs
Drug Enforcement Strategies
Minorities and the War on Drugs
The Special Case of Marijuana
Demand Reduction: The D.A.R.E. Program

Policing Gangs and Gang-Related Crime
Gang Suppression
Gang Prevention: The G.R.E.A.T. Program
Policing Career Criminals
Policing Guns and Gun Crimes
Gun Suppression
Policing Hate Crime
The Scope and Nature of Hate Crime
The Police Response to Hate Crime

Policing and Terrorism
The Scope and Nature of Terrorism
Domestic Terrorism
Foreign Terrorism
Responding to Terrorism
CASE STUDY

Summary
Key Terms
For Discussion
Internet Exercises

C rime control is one of the major responsibilities of the police. This involves several specific activities in responding to criminal incidents, conducting criminal investigations, and arresting offenders. This chapter examines the crime control activities of the police. It describes what the police do and gives special attention to the popular myths that surround the subject of the police and crime.

The Police and Crime

People usually think about the subject of the police and crime in terms of patrol and arrests. The subject is actually far more complex, involving a number of different assumptions and strategies.

Crime Control Strategies

Lawrence W. Sherman provides the most systematic classification of the different crime control strategies used by the police or potentially available to them.[1] His classifications are discussed in the sections that follow.

Proactive versus Reactive

Some police anticrime strategies are **proactive,** in the sense that the police themselves initiate them. This reflects the police department's own sense of priorities. Most drug enforcement, for example, is proactive. Other strategies are **reactive,** in the sense that they occur in response to a citizen request for service. Citizen calls to report crimes involve a reactive police response.

proactive crime strategies

reactive crime strategies

General versus Specific

Some police activities are general in the sense that they are directed at the community at large and not at any particular crime. Routine preventive patrol is the most important general crime control strategy. Specific crime control activities, by contrast, are directed at particular crimes, places, offenders, or victims.

Particular Crimes. Routine patrol and the 911 system are general service activities that respond to any and all types of crimes. Other programs are directed at particular crimes. These include drunk-driving crackdowns, drug or gang crackdowns, or stakeouts designed to catch robbers.

Specific Places. Routine patrol serves the community at large with no particular geographic focus. Hot-spots programs, by contrast, are directed at specific places believed to be the centers of high levels of criminal activity.

Specific Offenders. Some anticrime activities are directed at particular offenders. The best examples are the repeat offender programs that target people suspected of currently committing high numbers of serious crimes.

Specific Victims. Some anticrime programs are directed at victims rather than offenders. The most important of these are the domestic violence programs and policies adopted by many police departments. Mandatory arrest policies, for example, are designed to protect victims of domestic assault from future violence.

Crime Control Assumptions
Police and Citizens

One of the basic issues with respect to the police and crime involves the underlying assumptions about the role of the police in relation to other social control mechanisms. Many people see the police, and the entire criminal justice system, as society's primary mechanism for controlling crime. As part of the professionalization movement, the police emphasized their crime-fighting role and staked out crime as their professional domain.[2] Many experts today believe that this definition of professionalism isolated the police and cut them off from the public. To correct this problem, advocates of community policing emphasize the development of close working relationships with neighborhood residents.[3] This approach is based on the assumption that citizens are coproducers of police services, including crime-fighting activities.[4]

Police and Other Social Institutions

A report on crime prevention programs by the University of Maryland places police activities in the context of other social institutions. The report argues that the traditional distinction between law enforcement and crime prevention is not valid. Law enforcement tactics such as arrest are designed to prevent crime, through either deterrence or incapacitation. Thus, it is appropriate to place all programs and institutions on a single crime prevention continuum.[5]

The report identifies seven institutions that play a role in preventing crime: communities, families, schools, labor markets, places (in the sense of specific locales), the police, and other criminal justice programs. This innovative approach makes two important points about crime prevention. First, it indicates that the police are only one of several institutions with some impact on crime and cannot be expected to bear the primary responsibility. Second, the report emphasizes the interdependence of the different institutions. Thus, effective school-based crime prevention programs depend on strong families, which in turn depend on healthy communities and good labor markets. Just as school programs are dependent on this larger social network, so is the effectiveness of police crime control programs.[6]

Measuring Effectiveness

Measuring the effectiveness of police crime control programs requires both meaningful definitions of what is to be measured as well as valid and reliable data on the expected outcomes. As is discussed later in this chapter, there are serious problems with the traditional measures of police effectiveness. Moreover, the move toward community policing and problem-oriented policing involves different assumptions about what the police do and, consequently, different measures of effectiveness.[7]

Preventing Crime

The primary crime prevention activity of the police is routine patrol. As explained in Chapter 7, the visible presence of police officers in the community is designed to deter individuals from committing a crime.

For a full discussion of the effectiveness of random preventive patrol, see Chapter 7.

Apart from officers who are responsible for random preventive patrol, many police agencies today have officers allocated toward crime prevention efforts—although their numbers are small. In the United States today, officers assigned to specialized crime prevention units account for only 3 percent of total officers.[8] Crime prevention officers are often responsible for meeting with citizens to explain how they can protect themselves from crime; working alongside neighborhood groups to establish and maintain neighborhood watch groups; and educating youth about drugs, crime, and gangs. These officers are typically housed in community relations units.

For a full discussion of community relations, see Chapter 12.

Police crime prevention strategies have undergone a revolution since the early 1980s. Instead of a peripheral activity, separated from the basic functions of patrol and criminal investigation, crime prevention is now seen as a central police activity.[9]

Crime prevention is a basic element of community policing and many problem-oriented policing programs.[10] The basic principle of community policing is that the police need to establish a better partnership with neighborhood residents. The underlying assumption is that citizens are coproducers of police services. This view of policing rejects the professional model of policing, which holds that the police and only the police have primary responsibility for crime control.[11]

For a full discussion of community policing and problem-oriented policing, see Chapter 10.

Community-based crime prevention programs include efforts to build neighborhood organizations, improve the physical appearance of the neighborhood, eradicate centers of drug activity, reduce truancy, and so on. In these programs, police officers act as planners, problem solvers, community organizers, and information exchange brokers. Their role is not to fight crime in the traditional manner (for example, with patrol and arrests) but to help citizens mobilize resources to prevent crime.[12]

Because community policing and problem-oriented policing crime prevention programs are so varied and are such an important part of contemporary policing, they are covered in detail in Chapter 10.

Apprehending Criminals

The second major crime-fighting responsibility of the police is to apprehend criminals once a crime has been committed. This process involves a complex set of social and organizational factors. The police must learn that a crime has been committed, officially record it as a crime, and then attempt to identify and arrest a suspect.

Citizen Reporting of Crime

Police learn about crimes through (1) citizen reports, (2) police officer on-view observations, and (3) police-initiated investigations. The first two are reactive responses; the third is a proactive response.

Most of the crimes that come to the attention of the police are the result of a citizen report. Reporting a crime is one of the most important discretionary decisions in the criminal process. In this sense, citizens are the real "gatekeepers" of the criminal justice system. Patrol officers rarely discover crimes in progress.

However, as seen in Exhibit 9–1, victims do not report most crimes to the police. According to the National Crime Victimization Survey (NCVS), only 46 percent of victims of violent crimes and 37 percent of victims of property crimes report the crime to the police.[13] The nonreporting of crime has important implications for the police, because they cannot be held responsible for solving crimes they do not know about.

The reporting of crime varies according to the type of crime and situational factors related to individual crimes. Generally, citizens are more likely to report

---

EXHIBIT 9–1

Reporting of Crime to the Police

	Percentage Reported to Police
Violent crime	**46.0%**
Rape/sexual assault	33.6
Robbery	60.9
Aggravated assault	58.4
Simple assault	40.0
Property crime	**37.0**
Burglary	60.0
Motor vehicle theft	83.3
Theft	29.0

Source: Bureau of Justice Statistics, *Criminal Victimization, 2014* (Washington, DC: U.S. Government Printing Office, 2015).

SIDEBAR 9-1

What If All Crimes Were Reported

What would happen if victims reported all crimes to the police? Would more arrests and fewer crimes result? Probably not. First, the police workload would increase enormously. There would be many more calls for service and about 200 percent more reported crimes. Patrol officers and detectives would be swamped. Second, most of these additional crimes would be the less serious crimes. The NCVS data indicate that victims report the more serious crimes at a relatively high rate. Third, there is no reason to assume that there would be that many more arrests. As we will see later (pp. 295–296), the police are able to solve crimes when there is a good lead at the outset. There is no reason to assume that they would solve many of the additional burglaries and larcenies where there are no good leads.

In short, are we better off because citizens use their discretion not to report most crimes?

serious crimes than minor crimes, violent crimes rather than property crimes, crimes where there is personal injury rather than those without injury, crimes involving a high dollar loss more than those with little loss, and so on. African Americans and those with lower incomes are more likely to report a crime than are whites and those with higher incomes. Women report property crimes less often than males do but are more likely to report a violent crime to the police. Except for teenagers, who report crime at a significantly lower rate, age does not influence the reporting of crime.[14]

As seen in Exhibit 9–2, victims often do not report crimes because they do not think the crime is that important or because they do not think anything can be done about it. Victims also regard certain crimes as private or personal matters or believe that they should be reported to other officials. Perception of the offender also affects the decision not to report a crime. According to the NCVS, about 8 percent of those not reporting a victimization indicated that they thought the offender or others would retaliate if they reported the crime to the police, and 5 percent did not report the crime because they did not want the offender to get into trouble.[15]

EXHIBIT 9-2

Reasons Violence Was Not Reported to the Police

Reason for Not Reporting	Percentage
Private or personal matter	18%
Reported to another official	16
Not important enough to report	18
Police would not or could not do anything	16
Fear of reprisal	8
Did not want to get the offender in trouble	5
Other reason	19

Source: Bureau of Justice Statistics, *National Crime Victimization Survey, 2006–2010* (Washington, DC: U.S. Government Printing Office, 2012).

Reporting and Unfounding Crimes

After a citizen reports a crime, the police must make an official record of it in order to enter it in the Uniform Crime Reporting (UCR) system. Police officers often do not complete a crime report, however. This is called **unfounding a crime.** Donald Black found that police completed official crime reports for 64 percent of all crimes in which no suspect was present, even though the complainant alleged a crime had occurred.[16]

There is no penalty—in the law, in FBI regulations, or in police department policy—for a police officer not completing a crime report. This is an area of unregulated police discretion.

A police officer's decision to complete a crime report is affected by the same factors that influence arrest decisions. Black found that the police were more likely to record serious crimes, crimes in which the complainant clearly expressed a preference for a crime report, crimes committed by strangers, and crimes in which the complainant was deferential to the officer.[17]

There are several reasons a police officer might unfound a crime. First, citizens do not always understand the criminal law and may believe that something is a crime when in fact it is not. For example, in Chicago, 58 percent of all calls to the police were defined as a crime by the citizen, but only 17 percent of all calls to the police were recorded as crime-related by the police.[18]

Second, there may be insufficient evidence to convince the officer that a crime was committed. For instance, a citizen may report an attempted break-in, but the officer finds no physical evidence to support this allegation. The resident may have heard a storm door banging in the wind. These examples represent the proper exercise of discretion.

Third, officers may abuse their discretion in unfounding crimes. A police officer may unfound a report of assault, for example, because of bias against the victim. Police officers may not make an arrest in a suspected assault incident when they perceive nonconforming behavior on the part of the victim: drinking or using drugs, being in the "wrong place," or being involved in questionable activity.

On a number of occasions, police departments have been caught systematically unfounding crimes to lower their crime rates. Most recently, police agencies in Atlanta, Baltimore, New Orleans, New York City, and Philadelphia have been identified as fudging crime reports in an effort to demonstrate that they have been successful in fighting crime.[19]

John Eterno and colleagues examined this issue further by surveying 1,770 retired New York City police officers about their knowledge of the manipulation of New York City Police Department (NYPD) crime report data. They reported that the manipulation of crime data in the NYPD has been fairly common since 1980 and became even more common after 2001. About 55 percent of those who retired between 2002 and 2012 self-reported that they had personal knowledge of manipulation "to make crime numbers look better." The authors found that increased manipulation was largely a consequence of the NYPD's implementation of COMPSTAT (see Chapter 4), which increased pressure on officers to show declines in crime, even if it meant "gaming numbers" by downgrading index crimes to less serious offenses.[20]

Crime reports can also be altered later. A crime can be either unfounded completely or changed to a lesser criminal offense. Thus, a rape can be changed to

POLICE *in* FOCUS | NYPD Manipulation of Crime Statistics

The NYPD recently confirmed what many had suspected. They were manipulating crime statistics in an effort to keep crime statistics low. It was learned that commanders were quietly informing sergeants, and sergeants were quietly informing officers, to keep the crime statistics down. Officers used various strategies. Sometimes they simply downgraded a felony to a misdemeanor, other times they diplomatically convinced victims not to file a complaint, but on some occasions they simply did not assign a case number to an event. State assemblypersons were hearing complaints that crime victims would check on the progress of their case and learn that the event or incident was never officially recorded. Other critics have also pointed out that the NYPD has created policies to purposefully keep crime statistics down. They cite a 2009 policy that required robbery victims to go to the station house to report a crime. Although administrators argued that the policy would help investigators get the information more quickly than if it were routed through a patrol officer, critics argued that it meant fewer crimes were reported to the police because victims had to wait for hours to file a police report at the station.

Although a number of outside critics raised these concerns, it was not until September 2009, when Officer Adrian Schoolcraft of the 81st Precinct in Brooklyn reported these problems to Internal Affairs, that broader attention was placed on the issue and the police department conducted an internal investigation. Shortly after Officer Schoolcraft made his complaint, and presented audiotapes as evidence, he was allegedly harassed at work by fellow officers. In addition, he alleges that senior officers picked him up at his apartment, placed him in handcuffs, and took him to the psychiatric ward of a local hospital where he was detained for six days for being an "emotionally disturbed person." Schoolcraft maintains that the police department took these actions in an effort to silence him.

Source: Al Baker and Joseph Goldstein, "Police Tactic: Keeping Crime Reports off the Books," *New York Times*, December 30, 2011, www.nytimes.com/2011/12/31/nyregion/nypd-leaves-offenses-unrecorded-to-keep-crime-rates-down.html?pagewanted=all; Chris Francescani, "NYPD Report Confirms Manipulation of Crime Stats," *Chicago Tribune*, March 9, 2012, www.chicagotribune.com/sns-rt-crime-newyorkstatistics-correctedl2e8e941f-20120309,0,7269806.story.

an assault or a robbery to a larceny or an assault. If the change is based on new information about the crime, it is legitimate. If it is done simply to lower the crime rate, however, it is illegitimate. Recording a crime in a lower category can alter the public's perception of community safety. The news media and the public tend to focus their attention on a few "high-fear" crimes: murder, robbery, rape, and burglary. Recording a robbery as a larceny makes the community appear safer than it really is.

Criminal Investigation

Once a crime has come to the attention of the police, it has been officially recorded, and no suspect has been immediately arrested, the criminal investigation process begins.

Myths about Detective Work

Criminal investigation, or detective work, is surrounded by myths. Movies and television police shows usually portray detective work as exciting and dangerous. Individual detectives are presented as heroic characters, possessing either great personal courage or extraordinary skill. The media often foster the idea that a good detective "can solve any crime," if he or she is only given the freedom and enough time to do it.[21]

There is no empirical basis for any of these myths. Moreover, they have several harmful effects on the public and the police. First, they create unreasonable public expectations about the ability of the police to control crime. This results in public dissatisfaction when the police fail to solve a crime. Second, the glamorous image of detective work leads many officers to regard it as *real* police work and to devalue routine patrol work.[22] Some detectives, in fact, imitate the behavior they see in the movies. Herman Goldstein observes that "many of the techniques employed by detectives today are more heavily influenced by a desire to imitate stereotypes than by a rational plan for solving crimes."[23]

The Organization of Detective Work

Criminal investigation is typically located in a separate unit of the department (except in small departments). Nationally, only about 15 percent of all sworn officers are assigned to detective units.[24] Large departments have specialized units devoted to particular types of crime (for example, homicide, property crimes). Medium-sized departments usually have a separate but unspecialized unit in which detectives handle all types of crime. Very small departments often have no specialized detective unit.

Assignment as a detective is generally considered a high-status assignment by most police officers. In most departments, it is a discretionary assignment—and one of the greatest rewards that a police chief has to hand out. In 40 percent of departments, it is a separate rank, with higher pay than patrol officers, and must be obtained through a competitive process.[25]

Detective work appeals to officers for several reasons. It offers greater opportunity to control one's work and to exercise initiative. Patrol work, by contrast, is largely reactive, in response to citizen calls. (Community policing, meanwhile, is designed to give patrol officers more responsibility for initiating activity.) Detectives have considerable discretion over which cases to work on, how much time to spend on each case, and how to investigate the case. Working in civilian clothes enhances the sense of individuality and frees detectives from citizens' stereotyped reactions based on the uniform.

Criminal investigation also offers a clearly defined measure of success: arrest of the suspect. The quality of work can be measured in terms of the number of arrests, the importance of a particular arrest (for example, an arrest related to a highly publicized crime), and the percentage of arrests resulting in conviction.[26] Patrol work, by contrast, involves mainly order maintenance and peacekeeping activities, for which there have never been any real performance measures.[27]

Not all detective assignments are the same, however. William B. Sanders points out that "the status of an individual detective is linked to the kinds of crimes he investigates."[28] Homicide traditionally occupies the highest status, followed by robbery and sexual assault. Investigating the more serious crimes carries greater moral significance because of the harm involved. Homicide units also have the smallest workloads and the highest clearance rates. Property crime units (burglary and larceny), by contrast, rank lowest in terms of moral significance and also have the highest workloads and the lowest clearance rates.

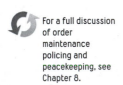

For a full discussion of order maintenance policing and peacekeeping, see Chapter 8.

Vice units such as narcotics and prostitution are a special case. Because they involve victimless crimes, they require proactive police work, asking officers to exercise initiative. Undercover work also requires special skill, involves the greatest dangers, and poses the greatest moral hazards. Traditionally, the worst police corruption has been found in vice units.[29] For these reasons, some police officers do not seek assignment in vice units (discussed later in this chapter).[30]

For a full discussion
of police corruption,
see Chapter 13.

The Investigation Process

The process of investigating a crime consists of two basic stages: the preliminary investigation and the follow-up investigation.

The Preliminary Investigation

The **preliminary investigation** consists of five basic steps: (1) identifying and arresting any suspects, (2) providing aid to any victims in need of medical attention, (3) securing the crime scene to prevent loss of evidence, (4) collecting all relevant physical evidence, and (5) preparing a preliminary report.[31]

preliminary investigation

In practice, patrol officers rather than detectives make about 80 percent of all arrests.[32] The explanation for this is simple. Most arrests occur because a suspect is on the scene or immediately identifiable and nearby. For those crimes where the suspect is not immediately arrested and there is no good information about him or her, arrests are relatively rare. Patrol officers, in short, handle the easy arrests, whereas detectives are assigned those that are inherently difficult to solve.

Arrest Discretion

Police officers exercise great discretion in making arrests. Black found that officers make arrests in only about half of the situations where there is sufficient legal basis for an arrest.[33] In a number of situations, officers simply ask the person to stop the illegal behavior. For example, in Indianapolis, Indiana, and St. Petersburg, Florida, 80 percent of the citizens were compliant with the officer's request.[34]

The decision to arrest is influenced by a number of situational factors. Generally, the probability of arrest rises when the evidence is relatively strong, the crime is more serious in nature, the victim requests an arrest, the victim and suspect are strangers rather than acquaintances, and the suspect is hostile or disrespectful toward the officer.[35]

A recent meta-analysis of the effect of suspect race on officers' arrest decisions showed that race also plays an important role in the decision to arrest. Tammy Rinehart-Kochel and her colleagues analyzed 40 research reports that examined this issue. They reported that "the chances of a minority suspect being arrested were found to be 30 percent greater than a white suspect."[36] These findings might partially explain why about half of all African Americans males are arrested by age 23.[37]

Arrest discretion
with respect to
domestic violence
situations and
juveniles is
discussed in more
detail in Chapter 8.

Follow-Up Investigations

A case is assigned to the detective bureau for follow-up investigation after an arrest has been made or if there has been no arrest. A Police Executive Research Forum

(PERF) study divided follow-up investigations into three categories of activities: routine, secondary, and tertiary activities.[38]

Routine activities include interviewing victims and checking the crime scene. These steps are taken in about 90 percent of all burglaries and robberies. Secondary activities include canvassing for witnesses, interviewing other people, interviewing witnesses, discussing the case with supervisors, and collecting physical evidence. Tertiary activities include discussing the case with patrol officers, interviewing suspects, discussing the case with other detectives, checking department records, checking the National Crime Information Center (NCIC) computer files, checking other records, interviewing informants, and conducting stakeouts.

The Reality of Detective Work

Contrary to popular belief, detective work is neither glamorous nor exciting. The RAND Corporation conducted the first detailed evaluation of detective units in the early 1970s, surveying 153 police departments by mail and interviewing officials in 29 departments. The study found detective work to be superficial, routine, and nonproductive. Many crimes receive only "superficial" attention, and some are not investigated at all. For example, detectives worked only 30 percent of all residential burglaries and 18 percent of all larcenies. Moreover, most investigative work involves "reviewing reports, documenting files, and attempting to locate and interview victims."[39] Most cases receive one day or less of investigative work, and most of that work involves paperwork: transferring information from one set of reports to another.

A PERF study of burglary and robbery investigations, meanwhile, found that about 25 percent of all burglary cases receive slightly less than two hours of investigative work, and only 11.9 percent are investigated for three days or more (at an average of about one hour per day). Only 24.8 percent of the robberies, meanwhile, are investigated for two days or more.[40] Harold Pepinsky argues that "most detectives spend the bulk of their time at their desks, going through papers and using the telephone."[41]

Case Screening

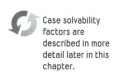

Case solvability factors are described in more detail later in this chapter.

In practice, detectives routinely screen cases, deciding how much effort to put into different cases. Screening decisions are based primarily on the seriousness of the crime and the existence of evidence that is likely to lead to an arrest. Some police agencies have adopted formal screening procedures based on "case solvability factors." These factors have in the past been shown to be highly related to the probability that a crime will be solved. Research has shown that, when taken together, case solvability factors can accurately predict 67 to 93 percent of investigative outcomes. These procedures are most often used by burglary, robbery, and auto theft detectives.[42]

nominal caseload

workable caseload

actual caseload

The PERF study found that a detective's caseload consists of three components. The **nominal caseload** includes all cases assigned to that officer. The **workable caseload** includes those cases "that have sufficient leads and therefore are worth attempting to solve." Finally, the **actual caseload** includes those cases "actually worked by detectives."[43]

Measuring the Effectiveness of Criminal Investigation

The Clearance Rate

The traditional measure of success in criminal investigation is the **clearance rate.**[44] The FBI defines a crime as cleared when the police have "identified the offender, have sufficient evidence to charge him, and actually take him into custody, or in exceptional instances, when some element beyond police control precludes taking the offender into custody."[45]

clearance rate

Nationally, only about 20 percent of index crimes are cleared. Exhibit 9–3 indicates national clearance rates for the eight UCR index crimes.

The clearance rate is not a reliable performance measure for several reasons.[46] First, it is based on reported crimes, and because only about 39 percent of all crimes are reported, the *true* clearance rate is much lower than the *official* rate. Only 60 percent of all burglaries are reported; therefore, the police clear only about 8 percent of all burglaries, rather than 14 percent.

Second, despite the UCR guidelines, police departments do not use the same criteria for clearing crimes. The PERF study, for example, found that, in one city, only 58 percent of the burglary cases recorded as cleared were actually cleared by an arrest.[47]

Third, the data can be manipulated to produce an artificially higher official clearance rate.[48] If officials unfound a large number of crimes, for example, this will lower the denominator and produce a higher percentage of crimes cleared. Alternatively, officials can attribute additional crimes to a suspect in custody and record them as cleared. This also raises the official clearance rate. In some instances, attributing additional crimes to a suspect is legitimate. There may be some evidence that the suspect did commit these other crimes, but not enough to present to the prosecutor. In this situation, there is no reason to look for another suspect. Last, police can manipulate the official clearance rate by the misuse of exceptional clearance. In other words, detectives may clear crimes even though there is no evidence to connect them with any suspect. For example, the Maricopa County Sheriff's Office was found to be clearing cases without even investigating them. One report indicated that 75 to 82 percent of solved crimes between 2006 and 2008 were cleared by exception.[49]

EXHIBIT 9–3

Crimes Cleared by Arrest or Exceptional Means, 2014

Murder and nonnegligent manslaughter	64.5%
Forcible rape	38.5
Robbery	29.6
Aggravated assault	56.3
Burglary	13.6
Larceny-theft	23.0
Motor vehicle theft	12.8

Source: Federal Bureau of Investigation, *Crime in the United States, 2014* (Washington, DC: U.S. Government Printing Office, 2015).

Cleared by Exception

The Uniform Crime Report Handbook *states the following policy for clearing a crime by exception: "If agencies can answer all of the following questions in the affirmative, they can clear the offense exceptionally for the purpose of reporting to UCR.*

1. Has the investigation definitely established the identity of the offender?
2. Is there enough information to support an arrest, charge, and turning over to the court for prosecution?
3. Is the exact location of the offender known so that the subject could be taken into custody now?
4. Is there some reason outside law enforcement control that precludes arresting, charging, and prosecuting the offender?"

However, while the FBI's guidelines are mandated, police departments vary substantially in their interpretation of the guidelines, and an agency's interpretation of policy can greatly influence their clearance rate. The following example shows five agencies that are all located in the Phoenix metropolitan area. It shows that the Phoenix Police Department rarely clears its crimes through exception (0.08 percent), followed by the Mesa Police Department (6 percent), the Glendale Police Department (11 percent), the Scottsdale Police Department (24 percent), and the Maricopa County Sheriff's Department (89 percent). Because clearance rates are sometimes used as a means of evaluating the effectiveness of an agency's ability to investigate and solve crime, some agencies interpret UCR policy more "liberally" than others as a means of inflating their clearance rates.

Cases Cleared by Exception by Agency in the Phoenix Metropolitan Area, 2008

Cases Cleared	Number of by Exception	Percentage Cleared
Phoenix Police Department	29,043	0.08%
Mesa Police Department	4,938	6.0
Glendale Police Department	8,933	11.0
Scottsdale Police Department	6,687	24.0
Maricopa County Sheriff's Office	7,265	89.0

Source: Joe Dana, "Many MCSO Cases Solved without Arrests," 12 News, January 19, 2010, www.azcentral.com/12news/news/articles/2010/01/15/20100115mcsocases01152010-CR.html.

Clearance rate data, along with the entire UCR system, are not audited by outsiders. A Police Foundation study, for example, found wide variation in the quality of arrest data,[50] and there is good reason to assume that similar variations exist with respect to official clearance rate data.

Defining an Arrest

Official data on arrests are also extremely problematic. The event referred to as an arrest has four different dimensions: legal, behavioral, subjective, and official.[51]

legally arrested

An individual is **legally arrested** or in custody when deprived of his or her liberty by legal authority. A police officer must have the intent to arrest, must communicate that intent to the person, and must take the person into custody.[52] Many people are detained on the street and then released. Others are taken to the police station and later released. During the time they were in the custody of the police and not free to leave, they were legally under arrest.[53]

Someone is **behaviorally arrested** when a police officer performs any of a number of actions: a stop (in which the officer tells the individual not to leave), a verbal statement that the person is "under arrest," or physically restraining a person.

behaviorally arrested

Someone is **subjectively arrested** whenever the person believes he or she is not free to go. A police officer may regard an encounter as only a stop, but the individual may believe he or she is under arrest.

subjectively arrested

An individual is **officially arrested** only when the police make an official arrest report of it. Practices on maintaining arrest records vary greatly from department to department, however, and may even vary within individual departments. Departments do not make arrest reports at the same stage in the process as detaining and taking someone into custody. A Police Foundation study found that only 16 percent of police departments always record an arrest whenever any restraint has been imposed on the suspect; only 11 percent always record an arrest whenever a suspect is brought to the station house. All departments make a record whenever the suspect is booked.[54]

officially arrested

The result is that in many departments, a lot of people are legally arrested (in custody on the street or at the station house) but no official record is made of these arrests. The lack of standard procedures makes it difficult if not impossible to use arrest data to compare departments. A police department that records all arrests at an early stage, for example, will appear to be working harder and engaging in more aggressive crime-fighting than one that records arrests only at the booking stage. In fact, the two departments might be taking people into custody at exactly the same rate. The official data are not a reliable indicator of their real levels of activity.

Success and Failure in Solving Crimes

The police solve only 20 percent of all index crimes each year. As Exhibit 9–3 indicates, they are far more successful in solving some crimes than others. Researchers have focused on three **case solvability factors** to examine their influence on investigative effectiveness: case structural factors, organizational factors, and environmental factors.

case solvability factors

Case Structural Factors

Case structural factors are related to the crime that was committed and that the police are investigating. For example, the presence or absence of a good lead is a structural factor, in the sense that it is related to the nature of the crime and independent of police effort. Research has repeatedly shown that the single most important factor in solving a crime is whether the police immediately obtain the name or description of a suspect. For instance, the data in Exhibit 9–4 represent a sample of 1,905 crimes investigated by the Los Angeles Police Department. The department cleared 86 percent of the 349 crimes in which a suspect was named, but only 12 percent of those in which a suspect was not named.[55]

Albert Reiss and David Bordua argue that most cleared crimes "solve themselves in the sense that the violator is 'known' to the complainant or to the police at

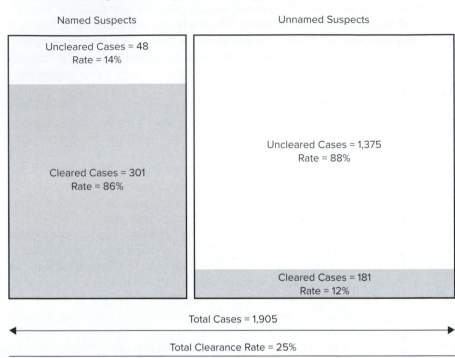

EXHIBIT 9–4

Crimes Cleared by the Los Angeles Police Department

Named Suspects

Unnamed Suspects

Uncleared Cases = 48
Rate = 14%

Cleared Cases = 301
Rate = 86%

Uncleared Cases = 1,375
Rate = 88%

Cleared Cases = 181
Rate = 12%

Total Cases = 1,905

Total Clearance Rate = 25%

the time the crime initially comes to the attention of the police."[56] Clearance rates are highest for violent crime because they involve direct contact between offender and victim. Few property crimes involve the same kind of direct contact and, consequently, have low clearance rates. Robbery is a violent crime but is usually committed by a stranger, resulting in low rates of identification and low clearance rates.

Detective screening of cases (described earlier) is based primarily on whether or not there is a good lead at the outset. Sanders found that "robberies, rapes, and assaults were typified as having leads, since the victim serves as a witness."[57] Burglaries and thefts, by contrast, were routinely considered not to have leads.

Organizational Factors

The impact of organizational factors on the success and failure in solving crimes has also been examined closely. Many of these studies have found that changes in police effort—more detectives, more or different levels of training, different management practices—have little effect on clearance rates. The RAND study of criminal investigation concluded that clearance rates are not higher when there are more detectives, when they put more effort into cases, or when they receive more training.[58] Even though detectives complain about being overworked, and do in fact have very heavy caseloads, the lack of resources is not the primary factor that keeps clearance rates low.

However, subsequent research by John Eck, and also Steven Brandl and James Frank, reached less pessimistic conclusions than the RAND study. These investigators argue that investigative effort does make a difference. Their analyses involve a "triage" model that categorizes cases according to the strength of the evidence: weak, moderate, or strong. Brandl and Frank found that the probability of arrest in moderate-evidence burglary and robbery cases increased as a result of more investigative effort.[59]

Environmental Factors

Environmental factors, though rarely discussed, have a significant impact on clearance rates—even though the police have no control over them. Environmental factors are characteristics of the community in which the police work. These might include the size of the community, the types of crimes committed in the community, the community's economic structure, and the characteristics of the community's residents. Gary Cordner examined the influence of organizational and environmental factors on clearance rates. He concluded that "environment-level variables have more influence than organization-level variables on police agency investigative effectiveness."[60]

Cordner points out that community size is perhaps the most important environmental factor. Small communities have many advantages when it comes to solving crimes. In small communities, residents are more likely to observe and recognize suspicious behavior and to recognize suspects than are residents in large cities. Likewise, officers in small communities are more likely to be knowledgeable about crime patterns and are more familiar with those who are more likely to be involved in criminal activity.

A study conducted by the Phoenix Police Department exemplifies the influence of community environment on case solvability. Since 2000, the police department's homicide clearance rate had been hovering between 30 and 50 percent, compared with 60 percent for similar-sized cities. Police officials found that the city's poor clearance rate was largely attributable to homicides involving Hispanic residents. Hispanics accounted for 61 percent of homicides, of which only 21 percent were solved. Police officials believed that their inability to solve these crimes was a result of the lack of community cohesion in the Hispanic community and problems surrounding the immigration of Mexicans into Arizona.[61]

Officer Productivity

There are significant differences in the productivity of detectives, as measured by the number of arrests. Some detectives make far more arrests than others. Productivity depends on a number of factors. Detectives assigned to high-solvability crimes such as robbery will have more chances to make arrests than those assigned to low-solvability crimes such as burglary. Nonetheless, it is also clear that, given the same assignment, some officers work harder and make more arrests than others. Lucius Riccio and John Heaphy found that the number of arrests for index crimes ranges from a low of 2.18 to a high of 12.06 per officer.[62]

More important than the total number of arrests is the *quality* of arrests—that is, whether the arrests lead to prosecution and conviction for a felony. For example, the Institute of Law and Society found that in one department 15 percent of the officers made more than half of the arrests that resulted in a conviction.[63]

The Problem of Case Attrition

Only about half of all felony arrests result in conviction of the suspect.[64] These data raise serious questions about whether the attrition is the result of poor police work or some other factor. In California, it was determined that 11 percent of persons arrested were released by the police, 15 percent of those arrested were declined for prosecution by prosecutors, and 18 percent of the cases resulted in dismissal or acquittal.[65] The total attrition rate was 44 percent. (And this analysis did not take into account persons who were legally arrested by the police but for whom no arrest report was made.) Joan Petersilia and colleagues attempted to identify those aspects of police work that were associated with high case attrition rates. They found that department practices explained little of the variation among the 25 departments studied. These practices included a case-screening process, a modus operandi (MO) file, a known offender file, a special victim/witness program, and other elements. Departments that used arrest statistics as a performance measure had lower clearance rates than departments that did not. The report did find that attrition rates were somewhat lower in cities that spent more money per arrest, a figure that seemed to indicate a connection between clearance rates and the availability of greater resources.[66]

An INSLAW study found that detectives expressed little interest in the performance measures associated with low attrition rates. None of the detectives interviewed knew what percentage of their cases were rejected by prosecutors. No supervisor reported evaluating detectives on the basis of the percentage of cases that resulted in convictions. None of the detectives expressed interest in feedback from prosecutors about the quality of their work.[67]

The Use of Eyewitness Identification, Criminalistics, and DNA in Investigations

Eyewitness Identification

Although victim and witness identification of suspects is extremely important in solving crimes, eyewitness identifications are also problematic. The victim is often traumatized by the crime, frequently has only an incomplete description of the suspect, may exaggerate certain features (such as height or weight), or may resort to stereotyping in the sense of being unable to distinguish the individual features of a member of a certain racial or ethnic group. Psychologist Elizabeth Loftus, the leading expert on the subject, warns that despite the importance of eyewitness identifications, they are "not always reliable," due to all the problems associated with human perception and memory.[68] It is unclear how often eyewitnesses are wrong, but one study indicated that of 230 people who have been exonerated through DNA testing procedures, more than 75 percent involved cases of mistaken identification.[69]

A report from the National Research Council made several recommendations to law enforcement agencies to address the problem: (1) train police on factors that impact eyewitness testimony, (2) video record processes associated with eyewitness identification, (3) use standardized witness instructions, (4) use double-blind line-up and photo array procedures, and (5) document how confident the eyewitness is in his or her identification.[70]

Criminalistics

Technical specialists from the crime lab may be used in some investigations. Large departments maintain their own criminalistics specialists, whereas the smaller departments use the services of either a neighboring large department or a state police agency. Virtually all police departments, including the smallest, have technical services available to them through cooperative arrangements with other agencies.[71]

Despite the great publicity they receive, fingerprints are rarely an important factor in solving crimes. A major part of the problem is that it is difficult to obtain useful prints. For example, New York City police are able to obtain a usable print in only 10 percent of all burglaries. Even when prints were obtained, only 3 percent led to an arrest. This meant that of the 126,028 burglaries occurring in New York City (in the year of the study), only 300 resulted in an arrest as a result of using fingerprints.[72]

DNA

Since the late 1980s, scientists have been able to use forensic DNA to accurately identify those from whom the DNA was obtained. DNA exists in all cellular material— such as blood, skin, bone, semen, saliva, and perspiration. Officers can collect DNA from many items, such as napkins, clothing, glasses, and many objects that humans come into contact with. The FBI notes that it only takes a few cells from a person to recover DNA.[73]

SIDEBAR 9-3

Live Scan and Arrestee DNA in North Carolina

In preparation for arrestee DNA collection, the North Carolina State Crime Lab and the Department of Justice Information Technologies Division worked with local law enforcement to install modifications to existing Live Scan terminals in each of the state's 100 counties. The new machines facilitate the screening and collection of arrestee DNA through the following process:

1. When an individual is arrested, the arresting officer brings him or her to a booking station and uses the Live Scan terminal to select charge information from a pick list of options.

2. If the machine indicates that the charge qualifies for DNA collection, the officer completes additional fields and submits the arrestee's fingerprints to the state repository to see if a DNA profile is already on file.

3. Following identity verification and confirmation that a DNA profile is not already in the system, collecting officers print a DNA collection card and mail the sample to the State Crime Lab.

4. Upon receipt, the laboratory checks three bar codes associated with the collection card, the collection kit, and the mailing pouch before processing. It will also verify that the correct offense was recorded. The laboratory rejects samples that were incorrectly obtained and sends them back to the collecting agency for destruction.

Source: Excerpt from Julie E. Samuels, Elizabeth H. Davies, and Dwight B. Pope, "Collecting DNA at Arrest: Policies, Practices, and Implications" (Washington, DC: Urban Institute, 2013). Unpublished research report submitted to the U.S. Department of Justice.

forensic index

convicted offender index

All DNA data obtained from local, state, and federal law enforcement officers is forwarded to the FBI. To manage all the data, the FBI created a National DNA Indexing System (NDIS). The system was designed to store two types of data. The first is **forensic index** data, which contains DNA profiles from genetic evidence gathered from crime scenes. The second type of data stored by the NDIS system is **convicted offender index** data. Convicted offender index data contain genetic information on offenders who have been required to provide blood samples for genetic typing. All states today collect DNA data from offenders convicted of particular crimes. Some states, such as Louisiana, allow the police to take DNA from any arrestee.[74] As part of this program, scientists working for the FBI store genetic profiles in a computer database. Forensic laboratories exchange these data electronically so that if a match results, the FBI can notify the agency investigating the crime. The process typically takes only three to seven days.[75]

Although the use of DNA evidence has garnered a great deal of attention in the media, the extent of influence that it has had on police investigations is still unclear. One study in New York City reported that DNA was rarely used in homicide investigations and that, when it was used, it did not increase the probability of the case being solved. The authors reported that, during the study period, DNA was collected, analyzed, and available for use in only 6.7 percent of the cases, and detectives used the evidence only as a "tool of last resort."[76] Another study, however, reported that DNA was helpful in clearing burglary cases. Specifically, the researchers worked with five police departments across the county and asked them to collect biological samples from a randomly selected number of burglary cases. The authors reported that when DNA evidence was used in addition to traditional investigative techniques, cases were twice as likely to result in an arrest of a suspect.[77]

Improving Criminal Investigations

Today, the most dramatic proposals for improving criminal investigations have been related to community policing. Although community policing is discussed at greater length in Chapter 10, here we present the three major changes in investigations that have been inspired by community policing to improve the effectiveness of detectives.[78]

First, the movement toward community policing has resulted in structural changes involving investigative units. Whereas criminal investigators in the past were typically assigned to "headquarters," many of today's investigators have been moved out of the office and into the field by being assigned to a particular geographic area such as a beat or precinct. This change is an effort by departments to increase communication and cooperation between investigators and patrol officers and the public. It is believed that assigning investigators to a particular area will result in the investigators becoming more knowledgeable about crime patterns and developing stronger relationships with the residents and officers who live and work in the area to which the investigator is assigned.

For example, in Albuquerque, New Mexico, the police department abolished all specialized investigative units such as homicide, robbery, and burglary units and created general investigative units within each command area. Detectives were then responsible for investigating all crimes within the command area to which they were assigned, rather than being responsible for investigating only one type of crime. This, the chief argued, would lead to greater cooperation between the patrol officers and the detectives and would result in commanders being geographically accountable for all crime in their command areas.[79]

Second, many departments have made procedural changes consistent with community policing in an effort to be more successful in their criminal investigations. In particular, many agencies are adopting procedures and practices that permit greater intergovernmental cooperation. In the past, most agencies, and their investigators, rarely permitted "outsiders" to assist them in investigating and developing responses to crimes. However, as community policing began to permeate police investigations, police organizations and investigators began to appreciate the assistance of other criminal justice organizations and community service organizations in developing broader responses to crime. Today, for example, it is not uncommon to have homicide review teams that comprise local, state, and federal officials from a variety of agencies, who review homicide files to develop more effective strategies to investigate and respond to homicides.

Third, some of the most innovative departments are making functional changes to the role and responsibility of the investigator. For example, the Spokane County Sheriff's Office has given primary responsibility for problem solving to detectives. The administration believed that detectives had the most flexibility in their schedules and had the most complete and readily available information on crimes in the department. Other agencies, such as the Mesa, Arizona, police department, are requiring investigators (who have large amounts of information readily available at their fingertips because of their role in neighborhood investigations) to attend community meetings to educate residents about crimes and how to prevent them.

Special Investigative Techniques

Undercover Police Work

Undercover police work presents a number of special problems for the police.[80] First, it involves deliberate deception by the officer: lying about who he or she is. The danger is that officers become socialized into the habit of lying and may be tempted to lie in other contexts as well, such as when testifying under oath.

Second, an officer working undercover associates with criminals and attempts to become their friend. This socialization can erode the values and standards of policing. Ties to peer officers and family are weakened. Some officers have "gone native," embraced the criminal subculture, and become criminals themselves.

Third, undercover officers are often subject to less direct supervision than other officers. This is particularly true of deep undercover operations in which the officer must spend weeks or months attempting to penetrate a criminal enterprise. The Knapp Commission found that detectives in the New York City Special Investigative Unit, for example, did not see their supervisors for weeks, and this contributed to the corruption.[81]

Traditionally, police departments have had few if any meaningful controls over undercover work. Officers learned how to work undercover through informal training by veteran officers.[82]

To prevent possible abuses, police departments have instituted formal controls over undercover work. The Commission on Accreditation requires law enforcement agencies to have "written procedures for conducting vice, drug, and organized crime surveillance, undercover, decoy, and raid operations." These procedures should cover such activities as "supplying officers with false identities, disguises, and necessary credentials," "designating a single person as supervisor and coordinator," and "providing close supervision."[83]

Informants

Informants are an important source of information about criminal activity. They are especially useful in victimless crimes and other covert criminal activity. Informants have special knowledge because they are often criminals themselves or are associated with criminals. Developing a group of informants is part of the art of police work. Jonathan Rubinstein observes that "vice information is a commodity, and the patrolman learns that he must buy it on a restricted market."[84]

J. Mitchell Miller examined how individuals became informants by interviewing 84 former informants in several southern states. He found that there were four types of informants: the hammered informant, the mercenary informant, the vengeful informant, and the police buff. **Hammered informants** were those individuals who agreed to be an informant because of the stress associated with their arrest. Many informants were drug users, or low- to mid-level drug dealers, and they were willing to become informants to avoid arrest or other formal sanction. **Mercenary informants** were motivated by money. They provided the police with information whenever they had information to sell. Miller noted that these informants were potentially the most problematic because there was a greater chance for these individuals to falsify evidence so that they could be paid. **Vengeful informants** served as a source of information to exact revenge on someone on whom they wanted to inflict harm. These included individuals who they believed cheated them out of money and former lovers who felt jilted. **Police buffs** were the fourth type of informant. These individuals were supportive of the police and provided them with information often on a one-time basis because of their access to a particular type of information. They rarely served as informants on a continuing basis.[85]

The use of informants, however, creates a number of potential problems. First, the police are involved in an exchange relationship with someone who is usually a known criminal offender. The police must give something in order to obtain the information they want. The most valuable commodity is a promise of leniency: an agreement either not to arrest or to recommend leniency to the prosecutor or judge. With respect to not arresting an offender, there are serious moral questions about the police knowingly overlooking criminal activity. Critics argue that the relationship compromises the integrity of the police and sets the stage for corruption. New York City police officers in the 1970s provided their informants with drugs, thereby turning the officers into drug dealers.[86] The information provided by informants may be questionable. Informants may invent information simply to please their handlers or provide information only against their enemies. Jerome Skolnick found that, in "Westville," narcotics detectives allowed their informants to steal, while burglary detectives allowed their informants to engage in drug dealing.[87] The practice remains

hammered informants

mercenary informants

vengeful informants

police buffs

just as rampant today. The FBI reported that it gave its informants permission to commit a crime 5,658 times in 2011.[88] The danger, as Gary Marx points out, is that the informer begins "to control the sworn agent rather than the reverse."[89]

To control the potential problems involved in the use of informants, the Commission on Accreditation for Law Enforcement Agencies (CALEA) accreditation standards require that police departments maintain a set of "policies and procedures" covering the master file of informants, the "security of the informant file," "criteria for paying informants," and other "precautions to be taken with informants."[90] A joint Bureau of Justice Assistance–PERF report recommended that "all understandings with a criminal informant should be put in the form of a written agreement."[91]

Policing Drugs

By the end of the 1980s, drugs represented the most serious problem facing the police, the criminal justice system, and American society as a whole. An epidemic of crack cocaine usage led to unstable drug markets in many large urban cities across the United States. The competition for control of drug markets produced a dramatic increase in homicides. Although the subculture of crack use had declined by the early to mid-1990s, and along with it general levels of violence, the nation still expends a substantial amount of resources toward combating the drug problem.[92] According to a White House report, the United States spends about $14.6 billion on domestic enforcement, interdiction, and international drug control efforts; $9.6 billion on drug treatment; and $1.3 billion on drug prevention.[93]

Drug Enforcement Strategies

Local police employ two basic strategies to combat illegal drug trafficking and use. The traditional **supply reduction strategy** includes four different tactics. The first is the simple buy-and-bust strategy: Undercover officers purchase drugs and then arrest the dealers. A second and related strategy is to attempt to disrupt the drug syndicate by "trading up": arresting low-level dealers and offering them leniency in return for information about higher-level dealers.[94] A third strategy involves penetrating the drug syndicate through long-term undercover work. The fourth is the drug crackdown, an intensive enforcement effort concentrated in a specific area over a limited period of time.[95]

supply reduction strategy

The **demand reduction strategy** involves attempting to reduce the demand for drugs on the part of potential users. This strategy includes drug education programs such as D.A.R.E. (described later in this chapter).

demand reduction strategy

The traditional supply reduction strategies have never proved to be effective. Illegal drug use continues to remain at high levels, and drug trafficking is open and rampant in the poorest neighborhoods. Several reasons explain this failure.

First, there is no persuasive evidence that the threat of arrest, per se, deters drug use or sale (or deters any other form of criminal activity, for that matter). Second, through what is known as the "replacement effect," new drug dealers quickly replace those who are arrested. Particularly in poor neighborhoods where legitimate career opportunities are limited, the incapacitation of dealers does not affect the

Drug Use Among Arrestees

Data collected as part of the Arizona Arrestee Information Network (AARIN) shows that police officers have regular contact with the drug-using population. Analysis of urine specimens taken from a random sample of recently booked male arrestees in Maricopa County, Arizona, found that 41.9 percent tested positive for marijuana, 14 percent for cocaine, 21.7 percent for methamphetamines, and 7.8 percent for opiates.

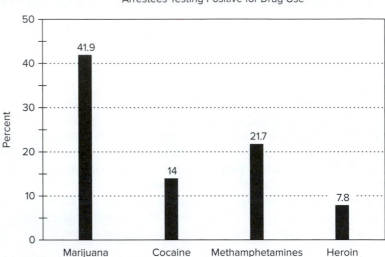

Arrestees Testing Positive for Drug Use

Source: Michael White, *AARIN Annual Adult Report* (Phoenix: Arizona State University, April 2012).

demand for new dealers. Third, the strategy of arresting low-level dealers and trading up to get key individuals in drug trafficking organizations has never proved to be effective in disrupting these organizations.[96]

An important question is, "Why do the police continue to engage in these activities despite their apparent ineffectiveness?" Peter Manning argues that drug arrests are made for their "dramaturgical effect": They generate publicity and create the appearance of doing something about the drug problem.[97] As John Crank and Robert Langworthy argue, police organizations exist in a larger social and political environment and need to create at least the impression that they are handling the problems that are within their professional domains.[98]

Minorities and the War on Drugs

A significant disparity exists in the arrest of racial and ethnic minorities for drug offenses. The National Household Survey has found that African Americans are only somewhat more likely than whites to be using illegal drugs in any given month (10.5 versus 9.5 percent, respectively).[99] Yet African Americans are arrested for drug offenses two and a half times more often than whites. Roughly 855 per 100,000 African

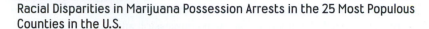

EXHIBIT 9–5

Racial Disparities in Marijuana Possession Arrests in the 25 Most Populous Counties in the U.S.

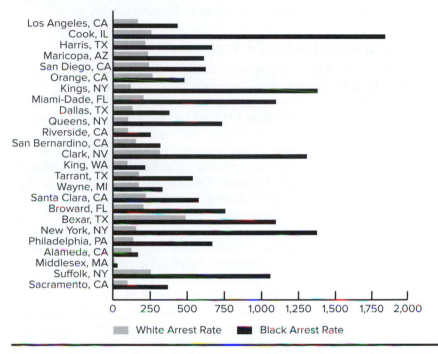

Source: Dylan Matthews June 4, 2013, The black/white marijuana arrest gap, in nine charts, Washington Post, Acess at https://www.washingtonpost.com/news/wonk/wp/2013/06/04/the-blackwhite-marijuana-arrest-gap-in-nine-charts/n on July 15, 2016.

Americans are arrested for a drug offense, compared to 328 per 100,000 whites.[100] As seen in Exhibit 9–5, disparities in arrests for drug offenses appear to be more pronounced in some communities than in others.

Many critics argue that the racial disparity in drug arrests is the result of department policies that deliberately target minority neighborhoods. As Thomas Castellano and Craig Uchida point out, "Drug arrests are largely police-initiated (proactive) rather than citizen-initiated (reactive)." As a result, "local drug arrest rates and patterns are largely dependent upon the arrest policies and enforcement priorities in police departments."[101] That is to say, it is not the result of discriminatory decisions by individual officers on the street, but of policy decisions made by commanders.

The Special Case of Marijuana

The landscape for drug enforcement has changed substantially over the past several years. Marijuana has been legalized for medical use in about half of all states and for recreational use in four states. The impact of the medicalization and legalization of marijuana on the police is still relatively unknown. One issue that has come to the forefront is that marijuana is being grown and sold in states where it has been legalized and is being trafficked to states where marijuana remains illegal. For example, following the medicalization of marijuana in Colorado, rates of arrests for possession and sale of marijuana increased significantly in bordering counties in Nebraska.[102] Therefore, although the legalization of marijuana might reduce the level of law enforcement resources needed to address marijuana possession and sale in some states, it might increase the level of resources needed to do the same in other states.

Demand Reduction: The D.A.R.E. Program

D.A.R.E.

Perhaps the most popular demand reduction strategy is the drug education program known as **D.A.R.E.** (Drug Abuse Resistance Education). D.A.R.E. originated with the Los Angeles Police Department in cooperation with the Los Angeles public schools in 1983. The program consists of 17 hour-long classroom sessions conducted by a sworn police officer. The program provides information about illegal drugs and their consequences as well as training in social skills to help resist illegal drug use.[103]

The D.A.R.E. program is extremely popular. According to D.A.R.E. officials, the program is operating in about 75 percent of the nation's school districts and has been adopted in 44 foreign countries.[104] Several factors explain the program's popularity. First, it addresses parent concerns about juvenile drug abuse. Second, there is a widespread belief that education is an effective approach. Third, both police and public school officials want to appear to be doing something about the drug problem.

Most evaluations of D.A.R.E. have not found any significant reduction in actual drug use as a result of the program. Critics of these evaluations have claimed, however, that most of them have been limited to one-year follow-up periods.[105] Two major studies examined the long-term impact of the D.A.R.E. program. One study examined the effects of the D.A.R.E. program 6 years after it had been administered, and the other, 10 years after it was administered. Both studies randomly assigned students to either a group that received the D.A.R.E. program or a group that did not receive the program. Both studies also measured the effects of D.A.R.E. on students' attitudes, beliefs, social skills, and drug use behaviors. The program had no measurable impact on those who participated in the program, compared with those who did not.[106]

Policing Gangs and Gang-Related Crime

In 1982, Walter Miller reported that only 27 percent of cities with populations of 100,000 or more had a gang problem, noting that the gang problem was largely isolated in America's largest cities.[107] Today, however, the street gang can be found in every state and in almost every major city throughout the United States. The National Youth Gang Survey, a survey of police departments across the country, reported that youth gangs are active in about 85 percent of large cities. Additionally, the survey reported that 30,700 gangs and 850,000 gang members are active in the United States.[108]

As a result, public officials and researchers have claimed that the increase in gangs is responsible for much of the rise in youth violence and drug use among youth. These claims have been substantiated in that studies of official records have consistently found that gang members are disproportionately involved in criminal activity. For example, in Mesa, Arizona, the police department discovered that when comparing the arrest records of documented gang members with a similar group of nondocumented delinquent youth, gang members were about twice as likely to have ever been arrested for a violent, weapon, drug, or status offense such as truancy or alcohol possession. Additionally, gang members were arrested for these offenses about four times as often as nondocumented delinquent youth.[109]

Local police rely primarily on two strategies to combat gang problems. One strategy is suppression; the other relies on prevention.

Gang Suppression

The growth of gangs since the early 1990s has been accompanied by the development and growth of specialized law enforcement responses to gangs. Traditionally, the police response to gangs and gang-related problems was to assign responsibility for gang control to existing units, such as patrol, juvenile bureaus, community relations, investigations, and crime prevention.[110] However, in the 1980s many police departments established specialized units for gang control, including what is commonly referred to as the police gang unit. A police gang unit is a secondary or tertiary functional division within a police organization. It has at least one sworn officer whose sole function is to engage in gang control efforts.[111] Therefore, by their very nature, police gang units are specialized; have their own unique administrative policies and procedures, which are often distinct from the rest of the department; and have a front line of experts who are uniquely trained and dedicated to perform specific and focused duties.

The Bureau of Justice Assistance reported that special gang units existed in about one-third of all large local law enforcement agencies with 100 or more sworn officers. Most of these gang units had been established since 2004. About 33 percent of the gang units reported that they spent most of their time collecting, maintaining, and disseminating intelligence; another 32 percent said that they spent most of their time on investigations; and 13 percent said that they spent most of their time on suppression. Only 4 percent said that they focused primarily on prevention. The remaining gang units (25 percent) indicated that they supported other units on gang-related matters.[112]

Although specialized police gang units represent a relatively new feature in American policing, they are part of an overall trend among many police departments to create specialized units to address unique law enforcement problems such as repeat offenders, domestic violence, and hate crimes. Such units are created to focus departmental resources, energy, and skill on the reduction of gangs and gang-related activity. Additionally, such an approach is intended to be a symbolic act, signifying to the community, gang members, and police officers that the police department is taking the gang problem seriously.[113]

Not only do gang units symbolize the commitment the police have toward eradicating the gang problem, but they are also symbolic of a moral crusade in which the police are battling against gangs. This is often conveyed to the public through the unit's or task force's name. For example, a task force located in Arizona uses the name Gang and Immigration Intelligence Team Enforcement Mission (GIITEM), and the Los Angeles Sheriff's Department uses GET (Gang Enforcement Team). Such names express a Hollywood-like image that the police are at war with gangs and that the gang problem can be solved as long as we intensify our efforts against them.

One of the few studies to examine the effectiveness of police gang units was conducted by Malcolm Klein and his colleagues in Los Angeles. The authors compared gang-designated homicide cases to non-gang-designated homicide cases in both the Los Angeles Police Department and the Los Angeles Sheriff's Department. The authors reported that gang-designated cases were significantly more likely to have a greater number of (1) pages of investigation, (2) interviews conducted, (3) witness addresses, and (4) suspects charged than non-gang-designated cases. Klein and his colleagues also reported that in both departments, homicide cases that were investigated by the special gang unit were significantly more likely to be cleared, compared with those that were not investigated by the special gang unit. As a result, it appears, at least initially, that gang units may contribute special knowledge that aids in the investigation of gang crimes.[114]

Gang Prevention: The G.R.E.A.T. Program

G.R.E.A.T.

The most popular police-led gang prevention program is called the Gang Resistance Education and Training (G.R.E.A.T.) program. The Phoenix Police Department established the program in 1991, modeling it after the D.A.R.E. program. **G.R.E.A.T.** is a nine-week class, led by a uniformed police officer, offered once a week to middle school students. The program introduces students to conflict resolution skills, cultural sensitivity, and the problems that are associated with gangs and gang-related behavior. Today, G.R.E.A.T. operates in all 50 states and several foreign countries.[115]

As of yet there have been few evaluations of the G.R.E.A.T. program. One of the most thorough studies used a multisite longitudinal design to evaluate the effectiveness of the gang prevention program. The researchers used a randomized controlled trial involving about 4,000 students from 31 schools in 7 cities (half were randomly selected to receive the G.R.E.A.T. program and the other half did not receive the program). Both groups were surveyed six times over five years. Over the study period, students who participated in the G.R.E.A.T. program were less likely to join a gang compared with those who had not been exposed to the program. Furthermore, the researchers reported that the program resulted in more positive attitudes about the police. The program, however, had no impact on delinquent activity.[116]

Policing Career Criminals

In the 1980s, several police departments experimented with programs to target career criminals, defined as people believed to be currently committing a high rate of offenses. This idea was based on the Wolfgang birth cohort study, which estimated that a small number of people (6 percent of any group of young men) commit an extremely high percentage of all serious crime.[117] Arresting, convicting, and imprisoning these career criminals, it was argued, would yield tremendous payoff in terms of crime reduction.[118]

Repeat offender programs consist of three different types: (1) targeting suspected high-rate offenders for surveillance and arrest, (2) special warrant service for suspected high-rate offenders who have outstanding warrants or are wanted for probation or parole violations, and (3) case-enhancement programs to provide prosecutors with full information about the criminal histories of high-rate offenders.[119]

The Repeat Offender Program (ROP) in Washington, D.C., involved a team of 88 officers (later reduced to 60) assigned to locate and arrest persons believed to be committing five or more index crimes per week. The suspects were selected on the basis of information provided by other police department units. Suspects remained on the list for 72 hours. Officers in the ROP team sought to locate the suspects through information in existing criminal records, supplemented by information available from the Department of Motor Vehicles, the phone company, and other sources. Many of the targeted individuals were already being sought on outstanding arrest warrants.[120]

An evaluation of ROP by the Police Foundation compared 212 suspects assigned to the ROP unit with a group of 212 similar suspects. The arrest activity of ROP unit officers was also compared with the activity of a control group of officers. The evaluation found that ROP "increased the likelihood of arrest of targeted repeat offenders." Half of the suspects in the experimental group (106 out of 212) were arrested by ROP officers (another 17 were arrested by other officers), compared with only 4 percent (8 out of 212) in the control group.

Other data, however, raised some questions about the efficiency of the program. ROP officers made fewer arrests than comparison officers (although most of the additional arrests by the comparison officers were for nonserious crimes). The ROP program cost $60,000 in direct expenses and took officers away from other police responsibilities, raising serious questions about the cost-effectiveness of the program.[121]

Policing Guns and Gun Crimes

Firearms, particularly handguns, are a serious problem in the United States. It is estimated that there are approximately 300 million guns in the United States, with about half of them owned for the purpose of self-defense.[122] However, data from the NCVS found that for every gun used in self-defense, six are used to commit a crime.[123] Steven Messner and Richard Rosenfeld note that the United States stands above all other industrialized nations with regard to the number of guns used in crime and the rates at which those crimes occur.[124] However, gun crime is down. The NCVS indicates that gun crime decreased by 69 percent between 1993 and 2011 (the latest years for which data were made available). Still, about 70 percent of homicides, 26 percent of robberies, and 31 percent of aggravated assaults were committed with a gun. Victims of gun-related homicide are more likely to be black, male, and 18- to 24-years-old (see Exhibit 9–6).

Gun Suppression

Police agencies have experimented with a number of strategies to reduce gun crime, such as gun buy-back programs and vigorous enforcement of gun-related laws, but these strategies have typically met with failure.[125] Today, some of the most innovative strategies to address gun violence have focused on directed patrol and the formation of interagency task forces.

The **Kansas City Gun Experiment** is perhaps the best-known directed patrol effort aimed at reducing gun violence. The experiment represented a combination of

Kansas City Gun Experiment

EXHIBIT 9–6

Firearm Homicides per 1,000 Persons Age 12 or Older by Ethnicity, Gender, and Age

Characteristic	Rate
Ethnicity	
White	1.9
Black	14.6
American Indian	2.7
Asian	1.0
Hispanic	3.8
Gender	
Male	6.2
Female	1.1
Age	
11 or younger	0.3
12 to 17	2.8
18 to 24	10.7
24 to 34	8.1
35 to 49	3.6
50 or older	1.4

Source: Bureau of Justice Statistics, "Firearm Violence, 1993–2011," *National Crime Victimization Survey, 2013* (Washington, DC: Author, 2014).

both problem-oriented policing, by focusing on a particular problem, and directed patrol, by concentrating on particular areas of high criminal activity.[126]

The experiment targeted a high-crime precinct of Kansas City where the murder rate in 1991 was 177 per 100,000, compared with a national rate of about 10 per 100,000. For a period of 29 weeks in 1992 and 1993, an extra pair of two-officer patrol cars patrolled the area for six hours at night between 7 P.M. and 1 A.M. The officers were directed to stop vehicles with people they believed to be carrying illegal handguns. The officers were directed to make only legally justified stops (for example, for traffic law violations) and then make legally justified searches for weapons (for example, search incident to an arrest). The underlying assumption was that this program would reduce crime both by removing guns from the streets and by sending a deterrent message about aggressive enforcement in the area.

During the course of the experiment, the special unit officers seized 29 guns, and another 47 guns were seized in the target beat by other officers. Gun crimes fell by 49 percent in the target beat, compared with a 4 percent increase in a control beat. Changes in gun crimes in other beats across the city were mixed. There was no evidence of either displacement of gun crimes or the diffusion of benefits. The experiment suggested the potential positive effect of hot-spots-oriented anticrime programs. A replication of the gun experiment in Indianapolis found similar results.[127]

Another example of an innovative gun violence reduction project is Project Safe Neighborhood (PSN). The program was established by President George W. Bush in 2001 to encourage criminal justice agencies to work together to reduce

---

SIDEBAR 9–5

Gun Buy-Back Programs

One popular approach to addressing gun crime is gun buy-back programs. These programs advocate individuals and families turning in their guns to the police, or another organization, with no questions asked. Individuals are not asked their names, nor is any other identifying information collected. In return, the individual who turns in the gun is typically offered an incentive such as cash or a gift card to a local store. The belief is that by reducing the supply of guns, gun crime will decrease. Through meta-analyses, Matthew Makarios and Travis Pratt examined 16 studies that evaluated the impact of gun buy-back programs. They reported that the programs had no impact on gun crime.

Source: Matthew D. Makarios and Travis C. Pratt, "The Effectiveness of Policies and Programs That Attempt to Reduce Firearm Violence: A Meta-Analysis," *Crime & Delinquency* 58 (2012): 222–244.

---

gun violence. The goals of this program are (1) to increase the capacity of PSN task forces to design data-driven strategies that produce measurable decreases in firearm-related violent crime and (2) to improve the long-term ability of federal, state, and local partners (including police agencies) to work together to understand, prosecute, and prevent firearm-related violent crime within their jurisdictions. More than 90 local projects based on the PSN model were funded by the Bush administration.[128]

Policing Hate Crime

Hate crimes, or bias-motivated crimes, represent a relatively new problem for the police. This is because hate crimes are not separate and distinct crimes, per se, but are offenses that are motivated by the offender's bias. The Hate Crimes Statistics Act of 1990 defined a hate crime as "a criminal offense against a person or property motivated in whole or in part by the offender's bias against a race, religion, disability, ethnic/national origin, or sexual orientation."[129] Because motivation is subjective, it is often difficult for police officers to determine if an offense was motivated by bias.

hate crimes

The Scope and Nature of Hate Crime

According to the NCVS, from 2007 through 2011, victims experienced an average of 259,700 bias crimes. As seen in Exhibit 9–7, most of these crimes were motivated by racial (54 percent) or ethnic (30 percent) bias, religion (21 percent), and sexual orientation bias (18 percent). (Percentages do not sum to 100 percent because individuals can report more than one type of bias motivating their victimization.) Only about 24 percent of victims reported the crime to the police, and victims reported a variety of reasons for not doing so. The most common reasons given by victims were that the police could not or would not help (24 percent), or they handled the victimization in another way, such as by reporting it to a school official or by handling it privately (23 percent). Others stated that they did not report it to the police because they felt that it was not important enough (18 percent).[130]

EXHIBIT 9–7

Victims' Accounts of Suspected Hate Crime Motivation, 2007–2011

Race	54%
Association	31
Ethnicity	30
Religion	21
Sexual orientation	18
Perceived characteristics	13
Disability	14

Note: Details do not add up to 100 percent because victims can report more than one type of motivation for the hate crime.

Source: Nathan Sandholz, Lynn Langton, and Michael Planty, *Hate Crime Victimization, 2003–2011* (Washington, DC: U.S. Bureau of Justice Statistics, 2013), table 2.

The FBI notes that hate crimes have five characteristics: (1) Hate crimes involve a higher level of assaults against persons than crimes generally; (2) hate crimes are generally more violent—about two-thirds of bias crime incidents are crimes against persons and the remaining one-third are crimes against property; (3) attacks are often preceded by a series of confrontations and incidents that escalate in severity; (4) hate crimes are more likely than other criminal activity to be committed by groups of perpetrators; and (5) most crimes against persons are committed by someone the victim knows, whereas hate crimes are more likely to be committed by strangers.

The Police Response to Hate Crime

In response to rising concern about bias crimes, a number of police departments have created specialized bias crime units. These units, like gang units, are intended to focus departmental resources and energy in an effort to increase the department's effectiveness in combating hate crimes and to signify to the community that the police department is taking hate crimes seriously. Susan Martin argues that there are three other reasons for singling out hate crimes for special attention.

> *First, because these offenses are based on who the victims are, they tend to cause victims greater difficulty in coming to terms with their victimization. Second, hate crimes appear to have particularly deleterious effects on communities, raising levels of mistrust, fear, and intergroup tensions. Third, because many of these crimes are not very serious in terms of penal law, they would otherwise receive very little or no police attention.[131]*

A number of alternative organizational structures have been established by police departments to combat hate crimes. For example, the New York City Bias Incident Investigation Unit (BIIU) is a centralized unit with a number of bureaucratic features. Officers who encounter what they believe to be a bias crime are required to notify their supervisors, who are in turn required to notify their commander. The commander then performs a preliminary investigation, and if the offense is verified, the Operations Unit is notified, which in turn notifies the Bias Crime Unit.[132]

Conversely, the Baltimore County Police Department uses a decentralized strategy. The department did not establish a specialized bias crime unit, but rather delegates patrol officers, as part of their community policing duties, to address such problems. If the precinct commander believes that an incident requires additional attention, the commander may request assistance from the Investigations, Community Relations, or Intelligence divisions.[133]

External evaluations have been conducted in both departments to determine the effectiveness of their strategies. In New York City, it was found that investigators in the special bias crime unit investigated more allegations of bias crimes and cleared more bias crimes than investigators assigned to a comparable group of nonbias crimes. Additionally, the victims of bias crimes expressed higher rates of satisfaction with the police response than did victims in the comparison group. The higher clearance rate was particularly surprising, because bias crimes are usually committed by strangers, whereas nonbias crimes are often committed by someone the victim knows. The fact that the investigators were able to clear offenses with less evidence suggests that the intensive investigative efforts by the special unit resulted in the higher clearance rate.[134]

Similarly, in Baltimore, verified bias crimes received more extensive and intensive investigation and were more likely to be cleared, compared with similar nonbias crimes. The researchers found that the administration had communicated to patrol officers that bias crimes were to be taken seriously and that the patrol officers took the problem seriously.[135]

Policing and Terrorism

The Scope and Nature of Terrorism

Terrorism is defined by the FBI as "the unlawful use of force or violence against persons or property to intimidate or coerce a government, the civilian population, or any segment thereof in furtherance of political or social objectives."[136]

Contrary to popular opinion, the number of terrorist attacks in the United States has declined significantly and most (80 percent) do not result in someone being harmed. From 1970 through 2013, there had been more than 2,600 terrorist attacks, with about half of these taking place in the 1970s alone. From 1991 through 2000, the United States experienced, on average, about 41 terrorist attacks a year, compared to about 16 a year between 2002 and 2010. Since 1970, there have been about 3,500 fatalities from terrorism, with about 85 percent of these fatalities occurring on September 11, 2001.[137] When discussing terrorism, it is helpful to differentiate between two types of terrorism: domestic and foreign.

terrorism

Domestic Terrorism

Domestic terrorism is planned and carried out by Americans on American soil. This is by far the most common type of terrorism. It accounts for more than 80 percent of terrorist incidents.[138] The National Consortium for the Study of Terrorism and Responses to Terrorism (START) at the University of Maryland has constructed a Global Terrorism Database, which tracks terrorist attacks around the world. They reported that, since 2000, about half of all terrorist incidents in the United States have been traced back to the Earth Liberation Front (ELF) and the Animal Liberation Front

domestic terrorism

(ALF).[139] ELF opposes forest destruction, new development, sport-utility vehicles, and globalization in general.[140] For instance, ELF was associated with the destruction of three luxury homes valued at $7 million near Seattle, Washington.[141] ALF, by contrast, aims to save animals, disrupt animal abuse, and expose companies that abuse animals.[142] According to the Global Terrorism Database, ALF was involved in only 1 of the 38 terrorist incidents that occurred in the United States in 2015,[143] which suggests that its involvement in domestic terrorism might be declining. According to the database, the most lethal attack since 9/11 was committed by Syed Rizwan Farook and Tashfeen Malik, who killed 14 and injured 17 at a holiday party on December 2, 2015.

Foreign Terrorism

foreign terrorism

Foreign terrorism involves terrorist activities coordinated and perpetrated by foreign persons or countries against the United States. These terrorist attacks take place both within and outside the borders of the United States. The worst foreign terrorist attack in United States history took place on September 11, 2001, involving four separate but coordinated aircraft hijackings by al-Qaeda operatives. Almost 3,000 persons were killed—many of whom were firefighters and police officers.

The consequences of the September 11 attacks were not limited to the victims and their families. Citizens across the country were substantially affected. A RAND survey showed that after the attack, 11 percent of adult Americans had trouble sleeping, 14 percent had difficulty concentrating, and 30 percent felt very upset when something reminded them of what happened. Additionally, 47 percent of children in the country were worried about their own and their family's safety.[144]

This attack was not the first or last involving foreign terrorists in general or Islamic terrorists in particular. For example, prior to 9/11, Ramzi Ahmed and Eyad Mahmoud Ismail Najim bombed the World Trade Center in 1993, and embassies in Kenya and Tanzania were bombed in 1998.[145] Post 9/11, Umar Farouk Abdulmutallab, on December 25, 2009, attempted to blow up a Northwest Airlines flight containing 253 passengers on their way from Amsterdam to Detroit. Also, on September 11, 2012, U.S. government facilities in Benghazi, Libya, were attacked, which resulted in the deaths of Ambassador Christopher Stevens and Sean Smith. It is suspected that al-Qaeda in the Lands of the Islamic Maghreb (AQLIM) was responsible for the attack.[146]

Responding to Terrorism

For a full discussion of the Department of Homeland Security, see Chapter 3.

In response to the terrorist attacks on 9/11, President Bush created the Department of Homeland Security, which is responsible for coordinating 22 previously separate agencies for the purpose of protecting the United States against terrorist attacks. As part of its mission, the Department of Homeland Security is also responsible for facilitating the President's plan to strengthen homeland security.

First, President Bush's plan provided $3.5 billion to first responders, such as police, firefighters, and medical personnel, to pay for training, equipment, and local antiterrorism planning. Second, about $11 billion was allocated to enhanced border security. Particular emphasis was placed on increasing the number of U.S. Coast Guard and Customs Service personnel and creating an enhanced entry–exit visa database and tracking system. Third, $6 billion was dedicated to defending the country against bioterrorism. In particular, the monies were used to boost research on new vaccines and medicines and to develop diagnostic tests to detect bioterrorist attacks. Last, $700 million was used to improve the federal government's capacity to gather and share intelligence with other federal agencies, as well as with state and city governments.[147]

The FBI also made a number of changes to respond to terrorism in the wake of 9/11. Most significant, it created an Intelligence Branch, which is focused on increasing the FBI's intelligence and analysis capacity related to terrorism. The FBI increased the number of analysts focusing on international terrorism by 400 percent. The Intelligence Branch also hired "report officers," who are responsible for identifying key trends and distributing the intelligence to key personnel, and brought 25 Central Intelligence Agency (CIA) officers to the FBI offices to help facilitate the identification and dissemination of intelligence related to terrorism.[148]

Although there has been extensive discussion about the federal government's reorganization to prevent and respond to terrorism, little national attention has focused on the role of the local police in preventing and responding to terrorism.[149] This is somewhat surprising given that citizens are more likely to report suspected terrorist activities to their local police departments than to a federal law enforcement agency. One study conducted in the Phoenix metropolitan area reported that 95 percent of residents were likely to report suspected terrorist activity to local police officials, whereas only 61 percent stated that they would be likely to report suspected terrorist activity to a federal law enforcement agency.[150]

Many police departments have begun to work toward increasing their capacity to respond to terrorist incidents. For example, one nationwide survey of local agencies indicates that about 58 to 64 percent of local law enforcement agencies have created a plan to respond to a terrorist attack, 35 percent have purchased hazmat detection equipment, 34 percent have conducted risk assessments, 8 percent have employed intelligence analysts, and 6 percent have increased personnel to respond to terrorism.[151]

Politics and turf battles have been described as some of the biggest barriers to becoming more effective in the response to terrorism.[152] Problems related to turf battles have perhaps been most pronounced between local and federal agencies. Local police officials have been vocal about their belief that federal law enforcement agencies are unwilling to share critical information with them. Some local police departments have threatened to stop participating in the Department of Homeland Security's information-sharing programs unless they are given greater and more timely access to intelligence. Police chiefs from the largest cities in the nation say that they are treated like second-class citizens by the Department of Homeland Security, but at the same time are responsible for ensuring the safety of their residents and are expected to be the first to respond to security threats. Officials from the Department of Homeland Security agree that local agencies need access to high-level intelligence but fear that the intelligence will be misused or that it will be leaked to the public.[153]

In an attempt to address some of these issues, the NYPD developed what has become one of the most controversial responses by a local law enforcement agency to increase its capacity to prevent terrorism. Following the 9/11 terrorist attacks, then-commissioner Raymond Kelly hired one former CIA agent to provide him with advice on responding to terrorism, and worked to appoint an active CIA agent to serve as a liaison to the NYPD. This later resulted in the creation of NYPD's Demographics Unit—later known as a Zone Enforcement Unit, which was given responsibility for monitoring the Muslim community. Until much later, the unit and its activities were unknown to city council and other local and federal lawmakers. The unit, with the help of the CIA, relied on Middle Eastern NYPD police officers to covertly monitor, for example, Muslim-owned businesses, mosques, and Muslim student groups within universities. There is little evidence to suggest that the program has been effective, and has since been discontinued.[154] According to one commander of the unit, who testified in court in 2012, no leads or investigations have ever been generated through the surveillance program. Further, the FBI has noted that its officers were not permitted to review the unit's intelligence reports because it violated FBI policy, which prohibits the use of undercover officers to collect information on businesses and persons related to politics and religion when there is no cause.[155]

CASE STUDY

Untested Evidence in Law Enforcement Agencies

In 2009, the National Institute of Justice (NIJ) published the results of a nationwide survey of forensic evidence that had not been submitted by a police agency to the crime laboratory for analysis. More than 2,000 state and local law enforcement departments responded to the survey.

The findings revealed that, during 2002–2007, police had not submitted forensic evidence—including DNA, fingerprints, firearms and toolmarks—to a crime lab in:

- 18 percent of unsolved rapes.
- 14 percent of unsolved homicides.
- 23 percent of unsolved property crimes.

Although there are reasons police may not send forensic evidence to a lab—it may not be considered probative, the charges may have been dropped, or a guilty plea may already have been entered—the researchers at Research Triangle Institute, International, which conducted the survey, concluded that some police may not fully understand the value of evidence in developing new investigative leads.

Forty-four percent of the responding police departments said one of the reasons they did not send evidence to the lab was because a suspect had not been identified. Fifteen percent said they did not submit evidence because analysis had not been requested by a prosecutor. Three in 10 said they did not submit evidence because they were uncertain of its usefulness.

These are important findings because evidence can potentially identify a suspect in a so-called no suspect case. For example, DNA can identify a possible perpetrator through the Combined DNA Index System (CODIS), the national DNA database, and latent prints can identify a possible perpetrator through databases such as the national Integrated Automated Fingerprint Identification System (IAFIS).

The knowledge gap revealed in the NIJ survey—particularly among the nation's small departments (less than 25 officers)—could be due to a lack of training. Specialized training in these cases may have been beneficial and could have led to a different outcome. Also, 11 percent of the agencies that responded to the survey said that one reason they did not submit evidence was the lab's inability to produce timely results, and 6 percent said that the lab was not accepting new evidence because of a backlog.

When considering this knowledge gap, it is important to remember that CODIS did not become operational until the late 1990s and could still be considered relatively new. Whether some detectives do not forward evidence to the lab because they do not fully understand how a "no suspect" CODIS hit can aid their investigation—or because there are standing policies or other issues that prevent them from doing so—is an issue that merits further study.

Finally, it is important to understand what the NIJ survey did not determine. For example, the survey did not reveal how many of the cases not sent to a lab would actually have benefited from analysis. The survey also did not address the number of unsolved cases in which evidence had been analyzed in the past but now—with the benefit of larger offender databases and new forensic technologies—might be solved or yield investigative leads; for example, a latent print submitted to IAFIS several years ago with no successful match could yield a hit now.

Some of the police departments noted that their survey responses were based on estimates. Larger agencies (including large county and state agencies) reported difficulty in providing information about sexual assaults because these records are not maintained in a centralized system. Property crimes in larger agencies are typically investigated at the precinct level (where the case information would be maintained), and this may also be true for rape cases. Finally, it is important to note that the survey's findings are based on self-reported information; there was no independent verification of the data.

Despite these caveats, however, there is no doubt that the survey reveals problems with an ongoing lack of procedures and policies for collecting, processing, and storing forensic evidence, including cases of alleged sexual assault. Policies and practices for evidence retention vary widely from jurisdiction to jurisdiction, with one in five agencies saying that they were not sure whether they had such policies. Less than half of the police departments, for example, said they had a policy regarding the preservation of biological evidence in cases where the defendant was found guilty.

The researchers who performed the survey made a number of recommendations to address these issues, including:

- Training police on the benefits and use of forensic evidence, including protocols for sending cases to the lab for analysis.
- Creating (or improving) information management systems to track forensic evidence and enhance communication among the police, lab, and prosecutor's office. This could include connected evidence tracking systems, dedicated staff for case management, and regular team meetings for case review.
- Providing more storage capacity for analyzed and unanalyzed forensic evidence, and providing standardized evidence-retention policies.
- Providing more research to determine what proportion of the open cases could benefit from forensic testing and how such cases should be prioritized for testing.

Source: Excerpt from Nancy Ritter, "Untested Evidence in Law Enforcement Agencies," in *The Road Ahead: Unanalyzed Evidence in Sexual Assault Cases* (Washington, DC: National Institute of Justice, 2011), 3–4.

SUMMARY

Crime control is one of the major responsibilities of the police. Crime-related programs involve a number of different strategies and assumptions. There is mixed evidence about the effectiveness of these strategies in reducing crime, however. Patrol has only limited deterrent effect on crime. The police clear or solve only about 20 percent of all crimes that come to their attention. They are able to solve a high percentage of those crimes in which a suspect is immediately known. Many experts today argue that the most promising programs are crime prevention efforts embodied in community policing and problem-oriented policing programs.

KEY TERMS

proactive crime strategies, 283
reactive crime strategies, 283
unfounding a crime, 288
preliminary investigation, 291
nominal caseload, 292
workable caseload, 292
actual caseload, 292
clearance rate, 293
legally arrested, 294
behaviorally arrested, 295

subjectively arrested, 295
officially arrested, 295
case solvability factors, 295
forensic index, 300
convicted offender index, 300
hammered informants, 302
mercenary informants, 302
vengeful informants, 302
police buffs, 302
supply reduction strategy, 303

demand reduction strategy, 303
D.A.R.E., 306
G.R.E.A.T., 308
Kansas City Gun
   Experiment, 309
hate crimes, 311
terrorism, 313
domestic terrorism, 313
foreign terrorism, 314

FOR DISCUSSION

1. Get into groups and discuss what a hate crime is and whether you believe that police agencies should police "hate."

2. As discussed in the text, the police use two primary strategies to reduce drug use: supply reduction and demand reduction. As a class, discuss how recent legislation medicalizing and legalizing marijuana will impact these strategies.

3. As a class, discuss possible reasons that D.A.R.E. has continued to be used in classrooms across the country.

4. As a class, watch a television program or movie that focuses on an investigator or detective working in a local police department. Discuss the accuracy of the portrayal of the detective's work in light of what you have learned in class.

INTERNET EXERCISES

Exercise 1 Check out recent clearance rate data on the web. Check the most recent FBI UCR data. Have national clearance rates changed for any crimes? Check out the websites for some local police departments. Do they provide their clearance rates? If so, how do different departments compare with the national clearance rates for particular crimes?

Exercise 2 RAND Corporation has created a crime calculator. It allows the user to alter the number of police officers and examine how increases or reductions in personnel will impact crime and the costs associated with crime. Visit http://www.rand.org/jie/justice-policy/centers/quality-policing/cost-of-crime.html and input information for your community. Then make changes to the number of personnel in the agency to assess the potential impact on crime in your community.

Exercise 3 Visit the Global Terrorism Database (www.start.umd.edu/gtd) to examine current trends in terrorism around the globe.

NOTES

1. Lawrence W. Sherman, "Attacking Crime: Police and Crime Control," in Michael Tonry and Norval Morris, eds., *Modern Policing* (Chicago: University of Chicago Press, 1992), 159–230.
2. Jihong Zhoa, Ni He, and Nicholas Lovrich, "Community Policing: Did It Change the Basic Functions of Policing in the 1990s? A National Follow-Up Study," *Justice Quarterly* 20, no. 4 (2003): 697–794.
3. Vincent J. Webb and Charles M. Katz, "Citizen Ratings of the Importance of Community Policing," *Policing* 20, no. 1 (1997): 7–24.
4. Ibid.
5. Lawrence W. Sherman et al., *Preventing Crime* (Washington, DC: U.S. Government Printing Office, 1997).
6. Ibid.
7. Edward Maguire, "Measuring the Performance of Law Enforcement Agencies," CALEA Update Online, www.calea.org/newweb/newsletter/No83/measurement.htm.
8. David Bayley, *Police for the Future* (New York: Oxford University Press, 1994).
9. Ibid.
10. Jeffrey Roth, Jan Roehl, and Calvin Johnson, "Trends in the Adoption of Community Policing," in Wesley Skogan, ed., *Community Policing: Can It Work?* (Belmont, CA: Wadsworth, 2004).
11. Zhoa, He, and Lovrich, "Community Policing."
12. Wesley Skogan and Jeffrey Roth, "Introduction," in Wesley Skogan, ed., *Community Policing: Can It Work?* (Belmont, CA: Wadsworth, 2004), xvii–xxxiv.
13. Bureau of Justice Statistics, *Criminal Victimization, 2014* (Washington, DC: U.S. Government Printing Office, 2015).
14. Bureau of Justice Statistics, *Reporting Crime to the Police, 1992–2000* (Washington, DC: U.S. Government Printing Office, 2003).
15. Bureau of Justice Statistics, *National Criminal Victimization Survey, 2006–2010* (Washington, DC: U.S. Government Printing Office, 2012).
16. Donald Black, "Production of Crime Rates," in Donald Black, ed., *The Manners and Customs of the Police* (New York: Academic Press, 1980), 69.
17. Ibid.
18. Albert J. Reiss Jr., *The Police and the Public* (New Haven, CT: Yale University Press, 1974), 95.
19. Fred Grimm, "Cops' Number Game Not Unique," *Miami Herald,* March 9, 2004, 6b.
20. John A. Eterno, Arvind Verma, and Eli B. Silverman, "Police Manipulations of Crime Reporting: Insiders' Revelations," *Justice Quarterly* 33, no. 5 (2016): 811–835.
21. Herman Goldstein, *Policing a Free Society* (Cambridge, MA: Ballinger, 1977), 55–57. For example, see Carmine Motto and Dale June, *Undercover* (Boca Raton, FL: CRC Press, 2000), 1–2.
22. William A. Westley, *Violence and the Police* (Cambridge, MA: MIT Press, 1970), 36. For example, see Motto and June, *Undercover.*
23. Goldstein, *Policing a Free Society,* 55. For example, see Motto and June, *Undercover.*
24. Bayley, *Police for the Future.*
25. Mary Ann Wycoff and Colleen Cosgrove, *Investigations in the Community Policing Context: Final Report* (Washington, DC: Police Executive Research Forum, 2001).
26. William B. Sanders, *Detective Work: A Study of Criminal Investigations* (New York: Free Press, 1977), 39–47.
27. Geoffrey Alpert and Mark H. Moore, "Measuring Police Performance in the New Paradigm of Policing," in *Bureau of Justice Statistics, Performance Measures for the Criminal Justice System* (Washington, DC: U.S. Government Printing Office, 1993), 109–140.
28. Sanders, *Detective Work.*
29. Victor Kappeler, Richard Sluder, and Geoffrey Albert, *Forces of Deviance,* 2nd ed. (Prospect Heights, IL: Waveland Press, 1998); John Dombrink, "The Touchables: Vice and Police Corruption in the 1980s," in *Police Deviance,* 3rd ed. (Cincinnati: Anderson, 1994), 61–97.
30. David Giacapassi and Jerry Sparger, "Cognitive Dissonance in Vice Enforcement," *American Journal of Police* 10, no. 2 (1991): 39–51.

31. John E. Eck, *Solving Crimes: The Investigation of Burglary and Robbery* (Washington, DC: Police Executive Research Forum, 1983), 69–93.

32. Reiss, *The Police and the Public,* 104.

33. Donald Black, *Manners and Customs of the Police* (San Diego, CA: Academic Press, 1980).

34. John McCluskey, Stephen Mastrofski, and Rodger Parks, "To Acquiesce or Rebel: Predicting Citizen Compliance with Police Requests," *Police Quarterly* 2 (1999): 389–416.

35. Donald Black, "The Social Organization of Arrest," in W. Clinton Terry III, ed., *Policing Society* (New York: John Wiley, 1985), 290–309.

36. Tammy Rinehart-Kochel, David Wilson, and Stephen Mastrofski, "Effect of Suspect Race on Officers' Arrest Decisions," *Criminology* 49, no. 2 (2011): 473–512.

37. Robert Brame et al., "Demographic Patterns of Cumulative Arrest Prevalence by Ages 18 and 23," *Crime & Delinquency* 60, no. 3 (2014): 471–486.

38. Eck, *Solving Crimes,* 124–127.

39. Peter W. Greenwood et al., *The Criminal Investigation Process, vol. 1, Summary and Policy Implications* (Santa Monica, CA: Rand, 1975), 35.

40. Eck, *Solving Crimes*, 106–110.

41. Harold E. Pepinsky, "Police Decision Making," in Don Gottfredson, ed., *Decision Making in the Criminal Justice System* (Washington, DC: U.S. Government Printing Office, 1975), 27.

42. Wycoff and Cosgrove, *Investigations in the Community Policing Context.*

43. Eck, *Solving Crimes,* 250; Maguire, "Measuring the Performance of Law Enforcement Agencies."

44. Alpert and Moore, "Measuring Police Performance in the New Paradigm of Policing."

45. Federal Bureau of Investigation, *Crime in the United States, 1999* (Washington, DC: U.S. Government Printing Office, 2000).

46. Greenwood et al., *The Criminal Investigation Process,* 32.

47. Eck, *Solving Crimes,* 203.

48. Black, "The Production of Crime Rates"; Maguire, "Measuring the Performance of Law Enforcement Agencies."

49. Clint Bolick, *Justice Denied: The Improper Clearance of Unsolved Crimes by the Maricopa County Sheriff's Office* (Phoenix, AZ: Goldwater Institute, 2009).

50. Lawrence W. Sherman and Barry D. Glick, *The Quality of Police Arrest Statistics* (Washington, DC: The Police Foundation, 1984).

51. Edna Erez, "On the 'Dark Figure' of Arrest," *Journal of Police Science and Administration* 12 (December 1984): 431–440.

52. Steven H. Gifis, *Law Dictionary,* 2nd ed. (New York: Barron's, 1984), 28–29.

53. Floyd Feeney, *Arrests without Conviction* (Washington, DC: U.S. Government Printing Office, 1983).

54. Sherman and Glick, *The Quality of Police Arrest Statistics.*

55. President's Commission on Law Enforcement and Administration of Justice, *Task Force Report: The Police* (Washington, DC: U.S. Government Printing Office, 1967), 8.

56. Albert Reiss and David J. Bordua, "Environment and Organization: A Perspective on the Police," in D. J. Bordua, ed., *The Police: Six Sociological Essays* (New York: John Wiley, 1967), 43.

57. Sanders, *Detective Work,* 96.

58. Greenwood et al., *The Criminal Investigation Process.*

59. Steven G. Brandl and James Frank, "The Relationship between Evidence, Detective Effort, and the Disposition of Burglary and Robbery Investigations," *American Journal of Police* XIII, no. 3 (1994): 149–168.

60. Gary Cordner, "Police Agency Size and Investigative Effectiveness," *Journal of Criminal Justice* 17 (1989): 145–155.

61. Judi Villa and Ryan Konig, "Murders Go Unsolved as Smuggling Grows," *Arizona Republic*, November 9, 2003, 1.

62. Lucius J. Riccio and John F. Heaphy, "Apprehension Productivity of Police in Large U.S. Cities," *Journal of Criminal Justice* 5 (Winter 1977): 271–278.

63. Brian Forst et al., *Arrest Convictability as a Measure of Police Performance* (Washington, DC: U.S. Government Printing Office, 1982).

64. Bureau of Justice Statistics, *Felony Defendants in Large Urban Counties, 2000* (Washington, DC: U.S. Government Printing Office, 2003).

65. Joan Petersilia, *Racial Disparities in the Criminal Justice System* (Santa Monica, CA: Rand, 1983), 21.

66. Joan Petersilia, Allan Abrahamse, and James Q. Wilson, *Police Performance and Case Attrition* (Santa Monica, CA: Rand, 1987).

67. Brian Forst, Judith Lucianovic, and Sarah J. Cox, *What Happens after Arrest?* (Washington, DC: INSLAW, 1977).

68. Elizabeth Loftus, *Eyewitness Testimony* (Cambridge, MA: Harvard University Press, 1979), 7.

69. Gary Wells and Deah Quinlivan, "Suggestive Eyewitness Identification Procedures and the Supreme Court's Reliability Test in Light of Eyewitness Science: 30 Years Later," *Law and Human Behavior* 33 (2009): 1–24.

70. Committee on Scientific Approaches to Understanding and Maximizing the Validity and Reliability of Eyewitness Identification in Law Enforcement and the Courts et al., *Identifying the Culprit: Assessing Eyewitness Identification* (Washington, DC: National Academies Press, 2014), http://www.nap.edu/read/18891/chapter/1.

71. Elinor Ostrom et al., *Patterns of Metropolitan Policing* (Cambridge, MA: Ballinger, 1977), ch. 7.

72. *New York Times,* August 17, 1986.

73. John Smialek, Charlotte Word, and Arthur Westveer, "The Microscopic Slide: A Potential DNA Reservoir," *FBI Law Enforcement Bulletin* 69 (November 2000), 18–21.

74. Barry Fisher, *Techniques of Crime Scene Investigation* (Boca Raton, FL: CRC Press, 2004).

75. Smialek, Word, and Westveer, "The Microscopic Slide."

76. David Schroeder and Michael White, "Exploring the Use of DNA Evidence in Homicide Investigations: Implications for Detective Work and Case Clearance," *Police Quarterly* 12 (September 2009), 319–342.

77. Nancy Ritter, "DNA Solves Property Crimes," *National Institute of Justice Journal* 261 (October 2008).

78. Wycoff and Cosgrove, *Investigations in the Community Policing Context.*

79. Personal communication with Chief Galvin of the Albuquerque Police Department, 1999.

80. Gary T. Marx, *Undercover: Police Surveillance in America* (Berkeley: University of California Press, 1988).

81. Knapp Commission, *Report on Police Corruption* (New York: Braziller, 1973).

82. Marx, *Undercover,* 188–190.

83. Commission on Accreditation for Law Enforcement Agencies, *Standards for Law Enforcement Agencies,* 4th ed. (Fairfax, VA: CALEA, 1999), Standard 43.1.6.

84. Jonathan Rubenstein, *City Police* (New York: Ballantine, 1973), 381.

85. J. Mitchell Miller, "Becoming an Informant," *Justice Quarterly* 28, no. 2 (2011): 203–220.

86. Robert Daley, *Prince of the City* (Boston: Houghton Mifflin, 1978).

87. Jerome Skolnick, *Justice without Trial* (New York: Macmillan, 1994), 129.

88. Eric Velez-Villar, unclassified memo on the *Annual Otherwise Illegal Activity Report,* http://www.documentcloud.org/documents/742049-fbi-oia-report.html.

89. Marx, *Undercover.*

90. Commission on Law Enforcement Accreditation, *Standards for Law Enforcement Agencies,* 4th ed., Standard 42.2.9.

91. Bureau of Justice Assistance, *Informants and Undercover Investigations* (Washington, DC: U.S. Government Printing Office, 1990), 16.

92. Elliot Currie, *Reckoning: Drugs, the Cities, and the American Future* (New York: Hill and Wang, 1993); Bruce Johnson, Andrew Golub, and Eloise Dunlap, "The Rise and Decline of Hard Drugs, Drug Markets, and Violence in Inner-City New York," in Alfred Blumstein and Joel Wallman, eds., *The Crime Drop in America* (Cambridge, U.K.: Cambridge University Press, 2000).

93. National Drug Control Policy, *National Drug Control Strategy: FY 2015 Budget and Performance Summary* (Washington, DC: Executive Office of the President of the United States), https://www.whitehouse.gov/sites/default/files/ondcp/about-content/fy2015_summary.pdf.

94. Mark H. Moore, *Buy and Bust* (Lexington, MA: Lexington Books, 1977).

95. Lawrence W. Sherman, "Police Crackdowns: Initial and Residual Deterrence," in Michael Tonry and Norval Morris, eds., *Crime and Justice: A Review of Research* 12 (Chicago: University of Chicago Press, 1990), 1–48.

96. Currie, *Reckoning;* Arnold S. Trebach, *The Great Drug War* (New York: Macmillan, 1987).

97. Peter K. Manning, *The Narcs' Game* (Prospect Heights, IL: Waveland, 2004).

98. John Crank and Robert Langworthy, "An Institutional Perspective of Policy," *Journal of Criminal Law and Criminology* 83, no. 2 (1992), 338–363.

99. Center for Behavioral Health Statistics and Quality. (2014). *Behavioral Health Trends in the United States: Results from the 2013 National Survey on Drug Use and Health* (HHS Publication No. SMA 15-4927, NSDUH Series H-50), http://www.samhsa.gov/data/.

100. Federal Bureau of Investigation, *Crime in the United States, 2013* (Washington, DC: U.S. Government Printing Office, 2014).

101. Thomas C. Castellano and Craig G. Uchida, "Local Drug Enforcement, Prosecutors and Case Attrition: Theoretical Perspectives for the Drug War," *American Journal of Police* IX, no. 1 (1990): 147.

102. Jared M. Ellison and Ryan E. Spohn, "Borders Up in Smoke: Marijuana Enforcement in Nebraska after Colorado's Legalization of Medicinal Marijuana," *Criminal Justice Policy Review* (2015). doi:0887403415615649

103. U.S. Bureau of Justice Assistance, *An Introduction to DARE: Drug Abuse Resistance Education,* 2nd ed. (Washington, DC: U.S. Government Printing Office, 1991).

104. Retrieved from D.A.R.E. website at www.dare.com/home/about_dare.asp.

105. Susan T. Emmett et al., "How Effective Is Drug Abuse Resistance Education? A Meta-Analysis of Project DARE Outcome Evaluations," *American Journal of Public Health* 84 (September 1994): 1394–1401.

106. Dennis Rosenbaum and Gordon Hanson, "Assessing the Effects of School-Based Drug Education: A Six-Year Multi-Level Analysis of Project D.A.R.E," *Journal of Research in Crime and Delinquency* 35, no. 4 (1998): 381–412; Donald Lynam et al., "Project DARE: No Effects at 10-Year Follow-Up," *Journal of Consulting and Clinical Psychology* 67 (1999): 590–593.

107. Walter Miller, *Crime by Youth Gangs and Groups in the United States* (Washington, DC: U.S. Government Printing Office, 1982).

108. Arlen Egley, James Howell, and Meena Harris, *Highlights of the 2012 National Youth Gang Survey* (Washington, DC: Office of Juvenile Justice Delinquency Prevention, 2014).

109. Charles M. Katz, Vincent J. Webb, and David R. Schaefer, "The Validity of Police Gang Intelligence Lists: Examining the Differences in Delinquency between Documented Gang Members and Non-documented Delinquent Youth," *Police Quarterly* 3 (2000): 413–437.

110. C. Ronald Huff, *Gangs in America* (Newbury Park, CA: Sage, 1993); Jerome Needle and William Stapleton, *Police Handling of Youth Gangs, Reports of the National Juvenile Justice Assessment Centers* (Washington, DC: U.S. Government Printing Office, 1983).

111. Charles M. Katz, Edward Maguire, and Dennis Roncek, "The Creation of Specialized Police Gang Units: Testing Contingency, Social Threat, and Resource-Dependency Explanations," in *Policing:*

An International Journal of Police Strategies and Management 25, no. 3 (2002): 472–506.

112. Lynn Langton, *Gang Units in Large Local Law Enforcement Agencies, 2007* (Washington, DC: Office of Juvenile Justice and Delinquency Prevention, 2010).

113. Charles M. Katz, "The Establishment of a Police Gang Unit: An Examination of Organizational and Environmental Factors," *Criminology* 39, no. 1 (2001): 37–73.

114. Malcolm Klein, Margaret Gordon, and Cheryl Maxson, "The Impact of Police Investigations on Police Reported Rates of Gang and Nongang Homicides," *Criminology* 24 (1986): 489–511.

115. Finn-Aage Esbensen, *Preventing Adolescent Gang Involvement* (Washington, DC: Office of Juvenile Justice and Delinquency Prevention, 2000).

116. Finn-Aage Esbensen, Dana Peterson, Terrance J. Taylor, and D. Wayne Osgood, *Is G.R.E.A.T. Effective? Does the Program Prevent Gang Joining? Results from the National Evaluation of G.R.E.A.T.* (St. Louis: University of Missouri-St. Louis, 2012).

117. Marvin E. Wolfgang, Robert Figlio, and Thorsten Sellin, *Delinquency in a Birth Cohort* (Chicago: University of Chicago Press, 1972).

118. William Spelman, *Repeat Offender Programs for Law Enforcement* (Washington, DC: Police Executive Research Forum, 1990).

119. Ibid., 25–26.

120. Susan E. Martin and Lawrence W. Sherman, *Catching Career Criminals: The Washington DC Repeat Offender Project* (Washington, DC: The Police Foundation, 1986).

121. Ibid.

122. Drew DeSilver, "A Minority of Americans Own Guns, But Just How Many Is Unclear," Pew Research Center, June 4, 2013, http://www.pewresearch.org/fact-tank/2013/06/04/a-minority-of-americans-own-guns-but-just-how-many-is-unclear/; Pew Research Center, *Perspectives of Gun Owners, Non-Owners Why Own a Gun? Protection Is Now Top Reason* (Washington, DC: Author, 2013).

123. David Hemenway and Sara J. Solnick, "The Epidemiology of Self-Defense Gun Use: Evidence from the National Crime Victimization Surveys, 2007–2011," Preventive Medicine 79 (2015): 22–27.

124. Steven Messner and Richard Rosenfeld, *Crime and the American Dream* (Belmont, CA: Wadsworth, 1997).

125. Samuel Walker, *Sense and Nonsense about Crime and Drugs* (Belmont, CA: Wadsworth, 2000).

126. Lawrence W. Sherman, James W. Shaw, and Dennis P. Rogan, *The Kansas City Gun Experiment* (Washington, DC: U.S. Government Printing Office, 1995).

127. Edmund McGarrell, Steven Chermak, Alexander Weiss, and Jeremy Wilson, "Reducing Firearms Violence through Directed Police Patrol," *Criminology and Public Policy* 1, no. 1 (2001): 119–148.

128. U.S. Department of Justice, "Project Safe Neighborhoods," *USA Bulletin* 50, 1 (January 2002).

129. Lynn Langton and Michael Planty, *Hate Crime, 2003–2009* (Washington, DC: U.S. Bureau of Justice Statistics, 2011).

130. Bureau of Justice Statistics, "Firearm Violence, 1993–2011," in *National Crime Victimization Survey, 2013* (Washington, DC: Author, 2014).

131. Susan Martin, "Police and the Production of Hate Crimes: Continuity and Change in One Jurisdiction," *Police Quarterly* 2 (1999): 417–437.

132. James Garofalo and Susan Martin, *Bias-Motivated Crimes: Their Characteristics and the Law Enforcement Response* (Carbondale: Southern Illinois University, 1993).

133. Ibid.

134. Ibid.

135. Ibid.

136. Terrorist Research and Analytical Center, *Counter-Terrorism Section Intelligence Division, Terrorism in the United States 1982–1992* (Washington, DC: U.S. Department of Justice, Federal Bureau of Investigations, 1993).

137. Erin Miller, START, *Terrorist Attacks in the US between 1970 and 2013*, https://www.start.umd.edu/pubs/Overview%20of%20Terrorist%20Attacks%20in%20the%20US%201970-2013_1.pdf.

138. Christopher Hewitt, *Understanding Terrorism in America* (New York: Routledge, 2003). For more recent trends, see the Global Terrorism database at www.start.umd.edu/gtd/.

139. *Violent Extremism in the U.S.,* December 9, 2011, www.start.umd.edu/start/announcements/announcement.asp?id=277.

140. See ELF website at www.earthliberationfront.com/news/2004/011304r.shtml.

141. Miyoko Ohtake, "From Green to Black," *Newsweek,* March 6, 2008.

142. Found at www.start.umd.edu/start/data_collections/tops/terrorist_organization_profile.asp?id=14. http://www.animalliberationfront.com/ALFront/WhatisALF.htm

143. See START website at www.start.umd.edu/gtd/search/.

144. Mark A. Schuster et al., *After 9-11: Stress and Coping in America*. RAND Corporation, www.rand.org/publications/RB/RB4546/index.html.

145. Federal Bureau of Investigation, *Terrorism in the United States, 1999,* www.fbi.gov/publications/terror/terror99.pdf.

146. See START website at www.start.umd.edu/gtd/search/.

147. Found at www.dhs.gov/dhspublic/display?theme=12&content=19 on January 20, 2004.

148. Found at www.fbi.gov/terrorinfo/counterterrorism/analysis.htm on January 20, 2004.

149. Kadee L. Brisner and William R. King. "Organizational Permeability to Environmental Conditions Local Police Agency Assessments of Threats Posed by Disasters, Accidents, and Terrorism." *Police Quarterly* (2016): 1098611115626409.

150. Stephen Schnebly, Steve Ballance, and Charles Katz, *Data Sharing between the Police and the Public* (Phoenix: Arizona State University, 2006).

151. Cynthia Lum, Maria (Maki) Haberfeld, George Fachner, and Charles Lieberman, "Police Activities to Counter Terrorism: What We Know and What We Need to Know," in D. Weisburd et al., eds., *To Protect and to Serve: Policing in an Age of Terrorism* (New York: Springer, 2009), 101–141.

152. National Crime Prevention Council, *Building the Homeland Security Network: What Will It Take? The Wirthlin Report* (Washington, DC: National Crime Prevention Council, 2002).

153. Robert Block, "Big-City Police Chiefs Assail Homeland Security's Secrecy," *Wall Street Journal Online,* June 30, 2006, B1.

154. http://www.nytimes.com/2014/04/16/nyregion/police-unit-that-spied-on-muslims-is-disbanded.html?_r=0

155. Matt Apuzzo and Adam Goldman, "The NYPD Division of Un-American Activities," *New York Magazine*, August 25, 2013, http://nymag.com/news/features/nypd-demographics-unit-2013-9/; David Ariosto, "Surveillance Unit Produced No Terrorism Leads," CNN, August 22, 2012, http://www.cnn.com/2012/08/21/justice/new-york-nypd-surveillance-no-leads/.

© Peter Casolin/Alamy

Advances in Police Strategy

CHAPTER OUTLINE

Impetus for Change in Policing

The Roots of Community Policing: The Broken Windows Hypothesis

Types of Disorder

Characteristics of Community Policing

Community Partnerships

The Effectiveness of Community Partnerships

Organizational Change

Evidence of Organizational Change

Problem Solving

Pulling It All Together: Implementing Community Policing at the Departmental Level

Chicago Alternative Policing Strategy (CAPS) Program

Community Policing: Problems and Prospects

A Legitimate Police Role?

A Political Police?

Decentralization and Accountability

Impact on Poor and Minority Communities

Conflicting Community Interests

But Does Community Policing Work?

The Roots of Problem-Oriented Policing

The Problem-Solving Process

Scanning

Analysis

Response

Assessment

Effectiveness of Problem-Oriented Policing

Problem-Oriented Policing in Newport News

Problem-Oriented Policing in San Diego

The Boston Gun Project: Operation Cease Fire

The Future of Problem-Oriented Policing

Characteristics of Zero-Tolerance Policing

The Effectiveness of Zero-Tolerance Policing

Zero-Tolerance Policing in New York City

Operation Restoration

Potential Problems with Zero-Tolerance Policing

But Does Zero Tolerance Policing Work?

CASE STUDY

Summary

Key Terms

For Discussion

Internet Exercises

S ince the 1980s, community policing and its many variations have become the new orthodoxy of policing.[1] Community policing, its advocates argue, represents a new philosophy of policing aimed at increasing the quality of police efforts.[2] The philosophy was reenergized in 2015 with a series of recommendations made by the President's Task Force on 21st Century Policing. The task force recommended that local law enforcement agencies place greater emphasis on the core tenets of community policing. This chapter examines community policing, along with other advances in police strategy—problem-oriented policing and zero-tolerance policing—and discusses the assumptions, characteristics, and impacts of these strategies.

Impetus for Change in Policing

Community policing and problem-oriented policing originated in the late 1970s and early 1980s as a result of a series of crises in policing. First, the police–community relations problems of the 1960s had created a crisis of legitimacy. Local police departments were isolated and alienated from important segments of the community, particularly racial and ethnic minority populations.[3]

Second, recent research had undermined the assumptions of traditional police management and police reform. The Kansas City Preventive Patrol Experiment found that there were limits to the ability of traditional police patrol to deter crime. Studies of the criminal investigation process raised doubts about the ability of the police to significantly increase the number of arrests. Furthermore, research showed that faster response time does not usually increase the likelihood of arrests. In short, the traditional reforms of more police, more patrol, more detectives, and faster response time were seen as not likely to improve policing. At the same time, the traditional police goal of providing an immediate response to all citizen calls for service, regardless of the nature of the call, burdened the police with an enormous workload.

Third, experts recognized that the police role is extremely complex, involving many different tasks and responsibilities. It was discovered that only a small part of police work was related to criminal law enforcement and that most police work involved order maintenance and service activities. As a consequence, experts recognized that if the police were to become more effective, they were going to have to broaden their characterization of police work from one that focused exclusively on crime control to one that also focused on such issues as community quality of life, order maintenance, and fear of crime.

For a full discussion of the effectiveness of traditional police patrol, see Chapter 7.

For a full discussion of the effectiveness of criminal investigations, see Chapter 9.

For a full discussion of the police–community relations crisis of the 1960s, see Chapter 2.

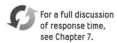

For a full discussion
of response time,
see Chapter 7.

For a full discussion
of the realities of
policing, see
Chapter 1.

Fourth, experts began to recognize the importance of citizens as coproducers of police services.[4] The police depend on citizens to report crime and to request help in dealing with disorder. The decision to arrest is influenced heavily by the expressed preference for arrest on the part of a citizen. Successful prosecution of offenders depends heavily on the cooperation of victims and witnesses. Even more important, informal social control at the neighborhood level was increasingly recognized as the key to limiting crime and disorder. In short, there was growing recognition that the police cannot control crime by themselves.

The Roots of Community Policing: The Broken Windows Hypothesis

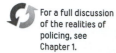

For a full discussion
of the type of work
performed by the
police, see Chapter 7.

broken windows

James Q. Wilson and George L. Kelling influenced the history of policing forever when they teamed together and wrote an essay entitled "Broken Windows" for *Atlantic Monthly* magazine. They argued that the police should focus their resources on disorder problems affecting the quality of neighborhood life.[5] In particular, they emphasized that the police should address those problems that create fear of crime and lead to neighborhood decay. The image of **broken windows** symbolizes the relationship among disorder, neighborhood decay, and crime. A broken window, Wilson and Kelling argue, is a sign that nobody cares about the appearance of the property. Left unrepaired, it encourages other neighborhood residents to neglect their property. This sets in motion a downward spiral of deterioration. Houses deteriorate, homeowners move out, residential buildings are converted to rental properties, houses are converted from single-family to multifamily dwellings, and some houses are abandoned. As the income level of the neighborhood declines, neighborhood stores close and property values decline. Gradually, crime in the neighborhood increases.[6] (See Exhibit 10–1.)

These initial signs of disorder include drunks hanging out on the street or groups of teenagers on street corners. Such events create fear for personal safety in the minds of law-abiding residents in the neighborhood. Out of fear, they stay at

EXHIBIT 10–1

Broken Windows Hypothesis

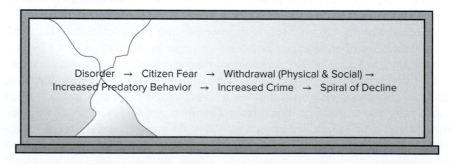

Disorder → Citizen Fear → Withdrawal (Physical & Social) → Increased Predatory Behavior → Increased Crime → Spiral of Decline

Source: George Kelling and William Bratton, "Declining Crime Rates: Insiders' Views of the New York City Story." Reprinted by special permission of Northwestern University School of Law, *The Journal of Criminal Law and Criminology*.

home and withdraw from active participation in the neighborhood. In extreme cases, they move out of the neighborhood altogether. The withdrawal of law-abiding citizens undermines the fabric of neighborhood life. The disorderly elements gain control of public areas, street corners, and parks; and the process of deterioration accelerates. The ultimate end of this process is serious predatory crime, such as burglary and robbery.

Wilson and Kelling maintain that traditional policing focuses on the end result of this process: serious crime. Yet the evidence indicates that the police officer's ability to fight crime is limited. They argue that the police should intervene at the beginning of the process of neighborhood deterioration—at the first signs of neglect and disorder.

Types of Disorder

Wilson and Kelling emphasize the importance of disorder rather than serious crime. Disorder is an extremely broad category. Skogan has distinguished between two major subcategories of disorder: social and physical. **Social disorder** includes such issues as public drinking, street corner gangs, street harassment, street-level drug sale and use, noisy neighbors, and commercial sex. **Physical disorder,** meanwhile, includes such problems as vandalism, dilapidation and abandonment of buildings, and rubbish.[7]

social disorder

physical disorder

Characteristics of Community Policing

Although about 88 percent of all local police departments today have instituted some form of **community policing**,[8] studies have illustrated that few in the law enforcement community understand the underlying concept. For example, one national survey of law enforcement agencies found that only about 50 percent of the police chiefs and sheriffs queried had a clear understanding of what community policing means.[9] Therefore, it should not be surprising that community policing has come to mean different things to different people. Popular strategies include instituting foot or bicycle patrols, establishing neighborhood police substations, identifying neighborhood problems, dealing with disorder, organizing community meetings, or conducting community surveys.[10] In fact, because the label of community policing has been attached to such a variety of activities and programs, some reformers express concern that community policing has come to mean anything that is new and innovative in American policing.[11]

community policing

Despite this confusion, there does appear to be a consensus about some of the basic elements of community policing, and how it differs from previous policing strategies. The most important difference is that community policing represents a *major change in the role of the police.* Whereas the police have traditionally defined their primary mission in terms of crime control, community policing seeks to broaden the police role to include dealing with such issues as fear of crime, order maintenance, conflict resolution, neighborhood decay, and social and physical disorder as basic functions of the police.

Stephen Mastrofski argues that this shift in primary mission of the police from serious crime to order maintenance is justified in two ways. First, reducing minor disorder may lead to a decrease in serious crime. The broken windows hypothesis, as

SIDEBAR 10-1

Broken Windows or Broken Theory?

Although there has been a great deal of discussion surrounding the broken windows hypothesis, little research has examined the relationship among disorder, fear, and serious crime. One of the few studies to examine this theory is Wesley Skogan's research that examined disorder and crime in 40 neighborhoods in six major cities. He found that perceptions of crime, fear of crime, and victimization are all related to physical and social disorder.[a]

However, Bernard Harcourt reexamined Skogan's data and concluded that his findings were driven largely by a few neighborhoods in which the relationship between disorder and crime was strong.[b] In particular, he found that if Skogan had excluded the neighborhoods of Newark, New Jersey, from his analyses, he would not have found a relationship between disorder and crime. Harcourt referred to this as the "Newark effect."

John Eck and Edward Maguire, addressing this debate, analyzed the data once again. They reported that had Skogan removed other neighborhoods from his analysis, outliers in which there was no relationship between disorder and crime, Skogan's finding of a relationship between disorder and crime would have been even stronger. They concluded that "Skogan's results are extremely sensitive to outliers and therefore do not provide a sound basis for policy."[c]

Robert Sampson and Stephen Raudenbush examined the issue further in Chicago and reported that disorder and crime are related to the same issue—social cohesion. Specifically, they found that when neighbors were less likely to intervene and help one another, both disorder and crime increased simultaneously.[d] Yily Xu and colleagues, by contrast, controlled for social cohesion in their study of the relationship between broken windows and crime in Colorado Springs, Colorado. The authors paid particular attention to the role of social cohesion and reported that physical and moral decay in a community both indirectly and directly resulted in crime.[e]

As a consequence, the proverbial jury is still out. There is no definitive evidence on whether disorder leads to crime or whether the connection between the two is spurious.

Source: [a]Wesley G. Skogan, *Disorder and Decline: Crime and the Spiral of Decay in American Neighborhoods* (New York: Free Press, 1990), 21–50; [b]Bernard Harcourt, "Reflecting on the Subject: A Critique of the Social Influence Conception of Deterrence, the Broken Windows Theory, and Order-Maintenance Policing New York Style," *Michigan Law Review* 97 (1998): 1–51; [c]John Eck and Edward Maguire, "Have Changes in Policing Reduced Violent Crime? An Assessment of the Evidence," in Alfred Blumstein and Joel Wallman, eds., *The Crime Drop in America* (Cambridge, UK: Cambridge University Press, 2000), 207–165; [d]Robert Sampson and Stephen Raudenbush, "Neighborhoods and Violent Crime: A Multi-Level Study of Collective Efficacy," *Science* 277 (1997): 918–925; [e]Yily Xu, Mora Fiedler, and Karl Flaming, "Discovering the Impact of Community Policing: The Broken Windows Thesis, Collective Efficacy, and Citizens' Judgment," *Journal of Research in Crime and Delinquency* 42 (2005): 147–186.

discussed earlier, asserts that an increase in community decay produces an increase in serious crime, and only by redirecting police services toward neighborhood deterioration and disorder can a community prevent crime. Second, he asserts that order maintenance is "justifiable in its own right in that it contributes to the establishment of a civil, livable environment in which citizens may, without fear, exercise their right to pursue their livelihood."[12]

In an ideal sense, then, community policing seeks to change the basic tenets most Americans, including the police, hold regarding police functions and priorities. Because the implementation of community policing involves a number of philosophical, organizational, strategic, and tactical changes,[13] it is helpful to focus on the three most commonly discussed targets of community policing reform: (1) community partnerships, (2) organizational change, and (3) problem solving.

Community Policing and Crime Reduction Recommendations Made by the President's Task Force on 21st Century Policing

4.1 Recommendation: Law enforcement agencies should develop and adopt policies and strategies that reinforce the importance of community engagement in managing public safety.

4.2 Recommendation: Community policing should be infused throughout the culture and organizational structure of law enforcement agencies.

4.3 Recommendation: Law enforcement agencies should engage in multidisciplinary, community team approaches for planning, implementing, and responding to crisis situations with complex causal factors.

4.4 Recommendation: Communities should support a culture and practice of policing that reflects the values of protection and promotion of the dignity of all, especially the most vulnerable.

4.5 Recommendation: Community policing emphasizes working with neighborhood residents to co-produce public safety. Law enforcement agencies should work with community residents to identify problems and collaborate on implementing solutions that produce meaningful results for the community.

4.6 Recommendation: Communities should adopt policies and programs that address the needs of children and youth most at risk for crime or violence and reduce aggressive law enforcement tactics that stigmatize youth and marginalize their participation in schools and communities.

4.7 Recommendation: Communities need to affirm and recognize the voices of youth in community decision making, facilitate youth-led research and problem solving, and develop and fund youth leadership training and life skills through positive youth/police collaboration and interactions.

Source: President's Task Force on 21st Century Policing, *Final Report of the President's Task Force on 21st Century Policing* (Washington, DC: Office of Community Oriented Policing Services, 2015), 41–50.

Community Partnerships

Community policing advocates assert that the most effective way of reducing community decay and disorder is through a collaborative relationship between the police and the community. This broadened view recognizes that cooperation between the police and the public will give police greater access to information provided by the community, which in turn will lead the police to be more responsive to the community's needs.[14] Accordingly, the community policing model stresses greater interaction between the police and the public, so that both entities act as **coproducers of crime control** and prevention.[15] Such a model, in an ideal sense, seeks to create a two-way working relationship between the community and the police, in which the police become more integrated into the local community and citizens assume an active role in crime control and prevention.[16]

coproducers of crime control

David Bayley, in his seminal book *The Police for the Future,* maintains that two elements are needed to successfully implement **community partnerships** between the police and the public: consultation and mobilization.

community partnerships

Consultation

Under community policing, agencies have sought to improve the quality of their crime control and prevention efforts by consulting with citizens in their community. This strategy is intended to help the community and police define and prioritize problems.

consultation

Consultation between the police and the public, usually done in the form of community meetings, serves four functions: (1) It provides a forum for citizens to express their problems and needs, (2) it allows the police to educate citizens about crime and disorder in their community, (3) it allows citizens to express complaints involving the police, and (4) it provides a forum for the police to inform the community about their successes and failures.[17] Most police agencies meet with community groups of one type or another (see Exhibit 10–2).[18]

For example, the Miami-Dade Police Department created the Marine Advisory Support Team (MAST) project as "an effort to facilitate community participation . . . and to bring together concerned parties to provide input and identify ways to improve service to the boating public and related interests." Representatives on the team included residents and businesses that lived and operated in and around Biscayne Bay as well as federal, state, and local law enforcement agencies that had jurisdiction over the bay. Once a month, MAST team members met to discuss crime and disorder. Aside from making agencies aware of problems, the meetings also led to the prioritization of community problems and to the sharing of resources to address the problems.[19] Many consultations between the police and public are not as formal, however. For instance, following the release of the President's Task Force on 21st Century Policing report, the Honolulu, Hawaii, police department instituted a "coffee with a cop" program in which the public has an opportunity to sit down and have coffee with the line-level officers who patrol their neighborhoods to discuss problems in the community and learn how the police department is responding to them.[20] Although ideally all four of the functions are fulfilled, research has found that partnerships between the police and the public vary in terms of the level of involvement of each partner and the expectations that each has of the other. In some agencies, community members are simply encouraged to act as the eyes and ears of the police. In other agencies, police officers speak at community meetings or work alongside citizen volunteers. In still

EXHIBIT 10–2

Percentage of Agencies with Partnerships with the Following Types of Groups

	Total	Municipal Police	Sheriff	State Law Enforcement
Advocacy groups	60%	64%	55%	33%
Business groups	59	67	45	36
Local public agencies	73	77	68	60
Neighborhood associations	74	81	66	29
Religious groups	49	54	44	16
Youth services organizations	59	66	51	27
Senior citizen groups	54	54	57	22

Source: Law Enforcement Management and Administrative Statistics, Bureau of Justice Statistics, 2007.

other agencies, formal relationships are established between the police and citizens in which the community works alongside the police to identify problems, develop possible solutions, and actively participate in responding to problems.[21]

Regardless, a distinctive characteristic of the police under community policing is that the police seek to reposition themselves so that they become an integral part of community life rather than remain distant and alienated from the community, as in years past. By embedding themselves within the community, "it is asserted that the police and public actually co-produce public safety."[22]

Mobilization

Because the police have recognized their own limitations in preventing crime and disorder, police agencies that have embraced community policing have mobilized the community for assistance. **Mobilization** comes in the form of such programs as Neighborhood Watch, Operation ID, and Crime Stoppers. These community organization strategies not only are a deterrent mechanism but also increase neighborhood cohesion and provide a forum for the police to inform the community of crime prevention techniques.[23] Bayley adds that although the majority of mobilization efforts have dealt with the general public, other municipal agencies can play a critical role in the prevention of crime: "Sanitation departments can haul away abandoned cars, parks and recreation agencies [can] open facilities at night or develop programs for young people, [and] fire and building inspectors [can] condemn abandoned buildings."[24]

mobilization

Accordingly, under community policing, the police expand the number of tools available to them, taking them beyond a reliance on arrest to solve problems. For example, they also use civil and administrative law to broaden their capacity to address quality-of-life concerns in neighborhoods. Many police agencies today work closely with zoning inspectors and other city officials to deal with problems related to local businesses that detract from a neighborhood's quality of life (for example, commercial sex shops, bars) as well as landlords and homeowners who fail to maintain their property in adequate condition.[25] In many communities today, it is not unusual for the police to partner with another agency within the city to address city code violations such as weeds, debris, inoperable vehicles, and graffiti to ensure the quality of life in neighborhoods.

For instance, in Portland, Oregon, the police department saw the number of drug houses increase from just a few to more than 200 in a single year. The police department did not have the time, or the resources, to address the problem using traditional methods such as undercover work. As an alternative strategy, they decided to mobilize landlords, the individuals who would be able to evict drug-dealing renters. In particular, the police department embarked on a program that educated and trained landlords about their rights and responsibilities. They taught landlords how to screen applicants, identify drug activity, evict tenants, and work with neighbors and the police. Over a two-year period more than 5,750 landlords, who oversaw 100,000 rental units, had received training.[26]

As such, community policing is largely focused on establishing and maintaining relationships between the police and the community—whether it be with citizens, community groups, or other public or private agencies—to address neighborhood crime and disorder problems. The police seek to broaden their role to one that is "seen as shifting from first government responder to social diagnostician and community mobilizer." Building linkages and relationships with others in the community allows the police to bring together a variety of services to address a specific issue or problem that may affect community safety.[27]

The Effectiveness of Community Partnerships

Foot Patrol

One of the most common ways police agencies have attempted to bring together the police and citizenry while attempting to reduce crime has been through the use of foot patrol. A number of evaluations that examined foot patrol in the 1980s reported that, although additional foot patrol did not reduce crime, it did increase feelings of safety. Moreover, citizens generalized these positive feelings to the police department—and not just to the foot patrol officers.[28] This finding has led some researchers to speculate that although the police might not be able to reduce crime, perhaps they can reduce fear of crime. And if people are less fearful, they might not withdraw from the communities, and the process of neighborhood deterioration might not begin.[29]

Other studies examining police efforts at increasing police–citizen interaction, however, have found that such strategies can be effective in reducing crime. For example, in Oakland and Birmingham, researchers found that both fear of crime and violent crime decreased substantially in beats where police officers made door-to-door contacts with residents.[30] In Houston, researchers examining community policing found that home visits by the police led to a decrease in violent crime and disorder in the city.[31] Most recently, in Philadelphia and Newark, researchers reported that violent crime was reduced in locations where foot patrol officers engaged in problem-oriented policing and in hot spots with high levels of violence where saturated foot patrol was implemented.[32]

Traditional random preventive foot patrol might not reduce crime (though it does offer other benefits such as reducing fear of crime), but strategies that increase police–citizen interaction and strategies in which foot patrol is problem focused (for example, problem-oriented policing or focusing on high-crime places) might be effective in reducing crime.

Neighborhood Watch

Neighborhood Watch programs are another popular community partnership strategy; however, they have repeatedly been found to have little impact on crime.[33] Research conducted in Britain, where some of the most comprehensive studies have taken place, has shown that "there is no strong evidence that Neighborhood Watch has prevented a single crime in Britain since its inception in the early 1980s."[34] These studies have found that Neighborhood Watch programs are typically more active, and have a closer working relationship with the police, in affluent suburban areas with little crime. Residents who live in areas with more crime, and who live in inner-city minority neighborhoods, have been less willing to participate in Neighborhood Watch programs or any other activities that involve partnership with the police.[35]

Policing Where "Community" Has Collapsed

One of the major questions surrounding community policing is whether it is a realistic strategy for the poorest and most crime-ravaged neighborhoods. Community organizing assumes that there is a viable community to help organize. The worst neighborhoods of many big cities—what some commentators call the "underclass"—are so devastated by unemployment, crime, and all the related social problems that no meaningful community remains. Most of the natural community leaders have left: those with stable employment, with families, and with a commitment to their neighborhood. In the absence of positive influences, gangs often become a focal point for young men's lives.

In their contribution to the *Perspectives on Policing* series, Hubert Williams and Patrick V. Murphy warned that "community-oriented approaches that are effective in most neighborhoods work less well, or not at all, in areas inhabited by low-income blacks and other minority groups."[36] Their point was confirmed by a University of Maryland report, *Preventing Crime,* in which Lawrence Sherman and his colleagues found that programs directed at families, schools, and communities tend to be most effective where they are needed least. They are least effective in the families, schools, and communities that need the most help. The Maryland report made a significant contribution to our understanding of crime prevention by emphasizing the interrelationship among families, schools, neighborhoods, and economic opportunities (what it called "labor markets").[37]

At the same time, communities in the traditional sense often do not exist in some newer and rapidly expanding cities. For instance, the Houston fear reduction experiment found that the city had an "almost nonexistent neighborhood life."[38]

It may be that community-organizing efforts help organize only the middle class. The fear reduction experiment in Houston and community-organizing programs in Minneapolis encountered the same phenomenon: They were more successful among middle-income people, homeowners, and whites than among the really poor, renters, and racial minorities.[39] Successful community organizing among white homeowners may be motivated by racism: their fear of blacks and Hispanics moving into the neighborhood. If this is the case, police-sponsored community-organizing activities may heighten racial conflict. A review of community-organizing efforts, in fact, reached the disturbing conclusion that the strongest community organizations it could identify "arose in response to impending or actual racial change." It would be tragic if community policing efforts assisted resistance to equal housing opportunity.[40]

Community partnership efforts in Chicago have challenged this often-cited criticism of community policing. Research conducted by Skogan and colleagues suggests that after four years of intensive efforts by the police to partner with the community, residents in crime-blighted areas in Chicago began to participate in neighborhood crime programs. They found that attendance at community meetings was highest among blacks who lived in high-crime areas and made less than $15,000 a year.[41]

Organizational Change

Community policing also calls for organizational change. Eck and Maguire argue that organizational change in agencies moving toward community policing is necessary for two reasons: "first, to stimulate and encourage officers to perform community policing functions; [and] second, to make the organization more flexible and amenable to developing community partnerships and creative problem solving strategies."[42] The authors maintain that agencies need to make changes in three organizational areas if they are to successfully implement community policing: (1) organizational structure, (2) organizational culture, and (3) management.

Organizational Structure

Police departments traditionally have been characterized by a highly centralized organizational design, whereas community policing organizations are decentralized. This means that they have fewer levels of management, have less specialization, and allow for more discretion on the part of the line officer.[43] A key assumption of community policing is that police agencies must remain flexible so that they can handle a variety of problems in different communities. To accomplish this, line officers are given a great deal of discretion in diagnosing local problems.[44]

The community policing organization is also characterized by consistently assigning officers to a particular neighborhood or geographic area. This strategy not only is intended to foster a sense of geographic responsibility but also is a means of holding officers accountable for what takes place in their beats. Community policing advocates also argue that this tactic "is necessary in order to take advantage of the particular knowledge that can come through greater police involvement in the community and feedback from it."[45]

Organizational Culture

Traditional police organizational culture stressed the importance of crime fighting. As a consequence, the transition to community policing has largely been a battle for the hearts and minds of police officers.[46] Many advocates of community policing articulate that with the implementation of community policing will come a "new breed" of police officers who will be much more knowledgeable about, and experienced in, problem solving and community interaction, and who will be much more productive and satisfied with their work.[47]

A number of police departments have attempted to change their agency's organizational culture by implementing organizational reforms such as using participative management styles that embrace police officer input in departmental decision making; providing formal training to officers on community partnerships, problem solving, and other community policing tactics; changing promotional standards so that officers who embrace community policing are advanced within the organization; and changing departmental evaluation standards so that evaluations reinforce the value of community policing activities.[48]

Management

The adoption of community policing also affects police management. In the past, police managers focused primarily on issues of control through discipline by emphasizing departmental rules and regulations.[49] In community policing, managers are expected to assist the neighborhood officer in developing community contacts, counsel the neighborhood officer on political issues, assist the neighborhood officer in acquiring resources, and facilitate training opportunities for the neighborhood officer. Therefore, community policing organizations are characterized by having more managers and fewer supervisors.[50]

For example, in St. Petersburg, Chief Goliath Davis made a number of management-oriented changes in an effort to enhance the department's community policing efforts. Prior to the changes, sergeants were responsible for supervising officers who were responding to calls for service, which coincidently conflicted with the sergeants' responsibility for supervising community policing officers. As such, the supervisors had little time to assist the officers with projects or to train new community policing officers. After a police and community retreat, Chief Davis made a number of organizational changes, including the addition of a shift community-police sergeant. This sergeant reported directly to the district major, instead of to the lieutenant and captain as regular patrol sergeants were required to do, and was solely responsible for managing community policing officers. This strategy, the chief argued, allowed the sergeants much more free time to work alongside officers and allowed them greater access to the resources required to address neighborhood crime and disorder.[51]

Evidence of Organizational Change

There has been little evidence suggesting that police organizations have changed their organizational structure as a consequence of implementing community policing. One study of police organizations found that police organizational structures had not changed significantly since 1987. In particular, the study found that police organizations were no more likely to have fewer rules or policies or fewer supervisory levels since the inception of community policing.[52]

Likewise, another national study suggested that the police have not changed their priorities to correspond with community policing principles. Jihong Zhao and colleagues examined the organizational priorities and core functions of more than 200 municipal police departments. They reported that "the core functional priorities of American policing largely remain closely modeled after the professional model; these priorities were not affected significantly by changes such as the addition of officers, the provision of funds for COP [community-orienting policing] training, or the adoption of COP programs."[53]

By contrast, altering the structure of the organization so that officers are permanently assigned to a beat has been found to have some beneficial effects. For example, permanent beat assignment in Chicago neighborhoods resulted in residents' reporting increased levels of police visibility, which was attributed to increased officer activity taking place as a consequence of the officers becoming more knowledgeable about the areas they were policing.[54] Similar findings were reported in Philadelphia, where police officers were permanently assigned to public housing areas. Officers who were permanently assigned to a public housing site were significantly more likely to initiate investigations, indicating an increased sense of officer ownership and responsibility, than officers who were not permanently assigned to a site.[55]

Research has shown that the occupational culture in many police agencies has changed significantly because of the implementation of community policing. Zhao and associates surveyed officers in one northwestern police department that was well known for practicing community policing. They found that the officers' occupational values changed significantly after the implementation of community policing. The researchers reported an increase in the values reflecting personal happiness, comfort, and security.[56] Other studies have similarly found that after community policing has been implemented in an agency, police officers' attitudes toward community policing gradually improve along with knowledge about community policing.[57]

Many police agencies have incorporated community-policing-related principles in their academy training curricula to help facilitate cultural change. Robin Haarr's research examining training in Arizona found that, although being given training in community policing principles has the desired effect, its impact dissipates quickly after the officer leaves the academy and is exposed to the work environment. The research also found that community policing principles were not reinforced during the recruits' field training experience.[58]

Generally, these findings suggest that training alone may not foster a police culture that is supportive of community policing, but they do suggest that police culture can change with the implementation of community policing, although the change will take a great deal of time.

Studies examining the changing role of management in community policing organizations have generally been positive. Mastrofski's examination of community policing in Indianapolis found that community policing may have changed the role of supervisors. Sergeants in Indianapolis were found to believe that performing supportive activities, such as helping officers work through problems in their neighborhoods, was much more important than performing constraining activities, such as enforcing departmental policies or monitoring officers.[59]

Problem Solving

problem solving

The last element of community policing is **problem solving.** Here, the police and the community engage in a cooperative effort to solve neighborhood problems. The defining feature of problem solving is that it requires the participants to identify the underlying causes of problems rather than simply respond to the problems themselves. Problem solving can be enacted in a number of ways: It can involve the police mobilizing and consulting with neighborhood residents, it can involve neighborhood residents (typically through neighborhood associations) identifying the root cause of a problem and mobilizing the police or another governmental service to address the problem, or it can be done by a neighborhood police officer who regularly confers with neighborhood residents as part of his or her regular duties. About one-third of local police agencies encourage officers to engage in problem-solving projects, and a slightly smaller proportion evaluate officers based on their involvement and success with problem solving (see Exhibit 10–3).[60]

Gary Cordner notes that problem solving, as performed in the course of community policing, is often confused with problem-oriented policing (discussed in the next section). Problem solving, he articulates, was adopted as part of community policing as a neighborhood-level strategy to address chronic problems. As such, he argues that problem-solving activities tend to be small in nature.[61] With this said,

---

EXHIBIT 10–3

Local Police Agency Involvement in Problem Solving

Actively encouraged patrol officers to engage in problem-solving projects	33%
Included problem-solving projects in criteria for evaluating patrol officers	30%

Source: Brian Reaves, *Local Police Departments, 2013: Personnel, Policies, and Practices* (Washington, DC: U.S. Bureau of Justice Statistics, 2015).

problem-oriented policing has become an important part of community policing in many police departments across the country. In practice, problem-oriented policing can be implemented alone or as part of community policing.

Because problem-solving and problem-oriented policing are often intertwined and examined together, we discuss their differences, characteristics, and impacts in greater detail in the next section.

Pulling It All Together: Implementing Community Policing at the Departmental Level

Although community policing has been said to be implemented in police agencies across the country, there has been little consensus about the extent to which community policing has been implemented on a departmentwide basis. Edward Maguire and Charles Katz, using data supplied by the Police Foundation, examined community policing in 1,600 police agencies. They found that agencies that claimed to have implemented community policing were more likely to embrace some elements of community policing than others. In particular, they found that police departments that had implemented community policing were more likely to perform patrol-level and organizational activities associated with community policing than they were to perform citizen and management activities associated with community policing. The authors conclude that "changes in the role of mid-management and citizens in community policing may be particularly difficult to implement because they require that police agencies make real and substantial changes in the way that they do business."[62]

Chicago Alternative Policing Strategy (CAPS) Program

The Chicago Alternative Policing Strategy (CAPS) program represents one of the most ambitious community policing efforts in the nation. With more than 12,000 sworn officers, the Chicago Police Department is the second largest in the country. For our purposes, it is also important for two additional reasons. First, CAPS is unique in that it began in 1993 and continues today. Second, and related, it remains one of the few long-term evaluations of community policing, which provides us with valuable insights into both the possibilities and the problems of implementing a new policing philosophy throughout a big-city department.[63]

The CAPS Plan

CAPS began with extensive planning, involving a number of experts from outside the police department. After much discussion and revision, CAPS was designed around six basic points:

1. *Involvement of the entire police department and the entire city:* Some community policing programs, by contrast, involve specialized units separate from the basic operations of the department and/or particular neighborhoods.
2. *Permanent beat assignments for officers:* To enhance officer knowledge of and involvement in neighborhood problems, officers would be given permanent beat assignments.

3. *A serious commitment to training:* If community policing truly represents a different philosophy, it is necessary to train officers regarding the new expectations about their job.
4. *Significant community involvement:* One of the basic principles of community policing is that it involves a high level of citizen input and partnership with the police.
5. *A close link between policing and the delivery of other city services:* CAPS was intended to address neighborhood problems by helping citizens mobilize other city agencies to improve the delivery of services.
6. *Emphasis on crime analysis:* A heavy emphasis was placed on geographic analysis of crime patterns, using sophisticated computer analysis, to identify problems.

CAPS leaders assumed at the outset that the program would take three to five years to implement. Although CAPS was implemented citywide, five districts were selected as prototype districts and were subjected to extensive evaluation. Each of these districts had a population of approximately 500,000 people—about the size of many big cities.

Obstacles to Change

Implementation of CAPS involved a number of major obstacles. The first was the problem of resources. Strong public opposition killed a proposed tax increase. Consultants, however, identified 1,600 officers in the department who could be reassigned to provide more efficient police services. Finally, the city obtained federal and state grants to hire more officers and support CAPS.

A second and related problem was strong public opposition to the planned closing of precinct station houses. Although designed as an efficiency measure, many residents felt that they were losing "their" police presence, and the proposal was killed.

A third and major problem involved getting the rank-and-file officers committed to CAPS. Unlike some other community policing programs, CAPS did not rely on volunteers. The police culture is highly resistant to change. Surveys of Chicago officers, however, found significant differences in attitudes within the rank and file. Generally, older officers, racial and ethnic minority officers, and female officers were more open to change than younger, white, and male officers. A majority of all officers were extremely pessimistic at the outset, believing that community policing would blur the lines of authority between police and citizens and put unreasonable demands on the police to solve all community problems.

The attitudes of the rank and file were related to another serious problem: supervision and performance evaluations. Because CAPS represented a new philosophy and a new role for the police, it required new forms of supervision and performance evaluation. Rank-and-file officers understandably asked what they were expected to do under CAPS and how they would be evaluated. This proved to be a major controversy and was never fully resolved.

Another major problem was the 911 system. The traditional approach to calls for service would pull officers away from problem-solving activities and dispatch officers outside their beats (thereby violating the beat integrity principle of the program). CAPS attempted to address this extremely difficult problem in several ways.

First, it capped the number of times officers could be dispatched out of their beats. Second, it created special rapid-response teams to handle critical incidents. Third, it attempted to limit the number of calls by developing new dispatching priorities.[64]

CAPS in Action

The heart of CAPS was citizen interaction with the police. This was attempted through a regular series of beat meetings, where citizens and beat officers would be able to discuss neighborhood problems and possible solutions.

As Wesley Skogan and Susan Hartnett point out, "Making beat meetings work was hard."[65] Officers thought meetings took time away from "real" police work. The typical meeting involved about 25 citizens and 5 officers, and took about an hour and a half. The agenda for each meeting was "just frank talk."[66] Attendance tended to be higher in African American neighborhoods, primarily because of concern about crime.

Exhibit 10–4 indicates the problems identified at beat meetings in five districts evaluated by Skogan and Hartnett. Drugs were clearly the problem of greatest concern.

EXHIBIT 10–4

Top Problems at Beat Meetings

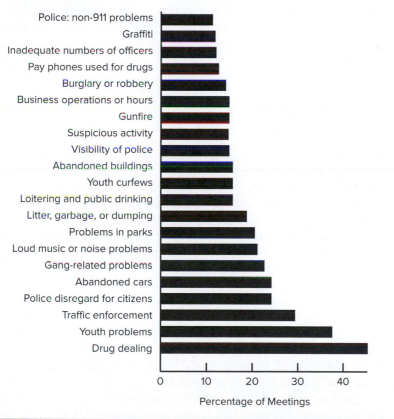

Source: Wesley G. Skogan and Susan M. Hartnett, *Community Policing: Chicago Style* (New York: Oxford University Press), 1997, figure 5–1.

Other crime-related issues were also mentioned frequently. Many of the problems fell into the disorder category: youth problems, loud music, and the like. Significantly, police disregard for citizens was the fourth most frequently mentioned problem, indicating that CAPS faced a significant problem in public distrust.

Observations of beat meetings found that the goal of police–citizen partnerships was not met. Police officers generally dominated meetings and controlled the agenda. The goals were met at a higher rate in some neighborhoods (Rogers Park) than in others (Morgan Park).

Getting other city agencies involved in problem solving was a major problem in Chicago. This has also been found to be a common problem in other cities that have attempted to implement community policing. An evaluation of community policing in eight cities, for example, had found that this effort failed in seven of them.[67] In Chicago, a special Mayor's Office of Inquiry and Information was responsible for seeing that other agencies cooperated with CAPS. The key instrument was a one-page service request form, which indicated a problem and the agency responsible for it. Specific requests involved replacement of missing street signs, closing or demolition of abandoned buildings, removal of graffiti, and towing of abandoned vehicles. These involved the physical decay category of disorder.

CAPS produced a number of different problem-solving activities. Under Operation Beat Feet, 60 residents in Rogers Park marched through part of the neighborhood at night in a form of "positive loitering" to deter potential criminals. Members of the Englewood community also conducted a march against drugs. Rogers Park residents initiated court action against the owner of a building that was the center of criminal activity. Morgan Park developed a Beatlink program that allowed business owners to contact patrol officers directly through beepers.

Evaluation of CAPS

A wide-ranging evaluation of CAPS found mixed results. Telephone surveys found a relatively high level of awareness of the program, but it also found that awareness did not increase as time went on. Citizens in most of the evaluation districts also reported seeing police officers more often than before. In most of the evaluation districts there was also an increase in the visibility of informal contacts between police and citizens. There were significant increases as well in public perceptions that the police were responding to their concerns and dealing with crime, along with reduced fear of crime. Especially important, more than 80 percent of the respondents indicated that police stopping too many people and being too tough was not a problem in their area. Consistent with previous surveys, African Americans (13 percent) were far more likely than whites (3 percent) to say that police use of excessive force was a problem.

In the end, CAPS met some but not all of its goals. Most important, officers did change the way they went about their jobs, spending more time on problem solving. There were significant perceived changes in the quality of life in the prototype districts: less crime, less fear, fewer gangs, and a greater sense of police responsiveness. It also led to the Chicago Police Department receiving consistent feedback from citizens through web-based community surveys for the purpose of enhancing discussions at police–community meetings. This innovation was credited with giving residents greater confidence to solve neighborhood problems and increased police officer satisfaction with their relationship to residents who attended their meetings.[68] The police department did not, however, succeed in fully implementing its crime-mapping program. There were also problems in achieving the desired level of citizen involvement.

The major achievement in Chicago is that some small but notable changes were accomplished in a citywide reorientation of policing. Most community policing projects in other cities have been small pilot projects, focusing on limited areas or problems, and usually involving volunteers. The CAPS experience suggested that a reorientation of a major police department was possible.

The program, however, has suffered some setbacks over the years. One major failure of CAPS was the inability to include some segments of the community. Latino renters, low-income households, and high school nongraduates in Chicago were the least aware of and least involved in CAPS. This is partially consistent with other community-oriented projects, which are generally more effective with whites and homeowners than racial and ethnic minorities and renters (see Exhibit 10–5). The other major problem was that CAPS resources were at least occasionally redirected to address special issues that arose in the city, and over time officers spent more time at headquarters than in the community. For example, in 2008, when the city was experiencing a spike in homicides, Mayor Richard Daley cut the department's CAPS

EXHIBIT 10–5

Personal Background and Awareness of CAPS

	1996	1998	2003
Number of cases	1,868	2,937	3,141
Percentage aware of CAPS	53%	79%	80%
Whites	52	78	81
Blacks	58	84	89
Latinos	51	73	70
Spanish speakers	47	65	56
English speakers	54	80	86
Age 18–29	46	76	69
Age 30–49	61	83	84
Age 50–64	53	80	86
Age 65+	46	65	77
Renters	50	75	74
Homeowners	58	83	85
Low income	48	69	68
Moderate income	59	84	86
Nongraduates	41	62	65
High school graduates	56	82	83
Females	50	76	80
Males	59	87	79

Note: All subgroup percentages are based on data weighted to standardize the racial composition of the samples across the years.

Source: Wesley Skogan, *Community Policing in Chicago, Year Ten: An Evaluation of Chicago's Alternative Policing Strategy* (Chicago: Illinois Criminal Justice Information Authority, 2004).

budget by 30 percent in an effort to put more officers on the streets. In 2013, Mayor Rahm Emanuel stated that the CAPS program was "bogged down by bureaucracy" and was suffering from decreased participation in beat meetings.[69]

In response, Emanuel slashed another $4.5 million from the city's budget for CAPS implementation and decentralized the program. Officers were moved from headquarters and placed in each of the city's 25 police districts. Commanders were made accountable for community policing and were assigned one CAPS sergeant, two CAPS officers, a community organizer, and a part-time youth service provider.[70]

Community Policing: Problems and Prospects

Although community policing is an important development, many unanswered questions about it remain.[71] Many advocates maintain that the era of community policing has already arrived.[72] Critics argue, however, that it is premature to claim that community policing either dominates contemporary policing or has proved to be a long-term success. A number of key questions about community policing need to be addressed.

A Legitimate Police Role?

One key issue in the community policing debate involves the question of the proper police role. Should police officers function as community organizers and work on housing problems and cleaning up vacant lots? Is this the proper role for a police officer with arrest power? Or should police officers spend their time and energy on serious crime?

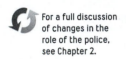

For a full discussion of changes in the role of the police, see Chapter 2.

There is no right or wrong answer to this question. It is a matter of policy choice. A community may define the police role in those terms, if it wishes to do so. Another community may prefer the more traditional police role. The fact that the police role has been defined one way for many years does not mean that it cannot be defined in a different way. Change is not impossible. As historians of the police point out, the crime-attack role that dominates today is not as traditional as many people think. In fact, it developed only over the past 50 years.

A Political Police?

Bayley warns that one aspect of changing the police role is the danger of involving the police in politics. One of the basic principles of Anglo-American law is the idea of clearly defined limits on all government power, and on the police in particular. Bayley refers to this as the "minimalist" tradition of policing.[73] These limits are embodied in the Bill of Rights. Community policing, however, expands the police role and erodes the traditional limits. Bayley refers to this as "maximalist" policing. Should police officers, for example, be going door to door, calling on law-abiding citizens when those people have not called the police? If the police organize community groups, there is the danger that they will turn into political advocacy groups that will lobby for candidates or issues that the police support.[74]

Furthermore, Bayley adds, the deeper the police delve into social structural issues to uncover the root causes of neighborhood problems, the greater the probability that they will place limitations on individual liberties. For example, after police officers in Portland, Oregon, researched the nature of increased citizen complaints about disorderly conduct around neighborhood mini-marts, they found that the sale of malt liquor and cheap wine was attracting gang members and transients. To remedy the problem, the officers asked the shop owners to voluntarily stop selling the malt liquor and cheap wine. However, the shop owners, who were all members of a single ethnic group, believed that the police had discriminatorily singled them out. The issue was eventually resolved, but the police officers learned that although encouraging social responsibility is part of their role within the community, it can have negative side effects.[75]

Decentralization and Accountability

One of the basic principles of community policing is decentralized decision making: giving rank-and-file officers more authority to decide what problems to work on and how to use their time. Decentralization, however, creates the problem of potential loss of control over police behavior, resulting in abuse of authority. As Herman Goldstein puts it, "How free should community officers be to select alternatives for solving problems?"[76]

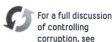

For a full discussion of controlling corruption, see Chapter 13.

Most of the gains in controlling police misconduct, including corruption and the use of force, have been achieved through centralized command and control. One major device has been administrative rulemaking: providing officers with written rules about what kinds of conduct are not permitted.

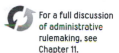

For a full discussion of administrative rulemaking, see Chapter 11.

An evaluation of the New York City Community Police Officer on Patrol (C-POP) program found that the traditional methods of supervising patrol officers were inappropriate for community policing. These methods are bureaucratic in nature, asking officers to account for the use of their time and their contacts with the public, and are designed primarily to control misbehavior. In New York City, there was special concern that giving officers too much leeway would lead to corruption—a recurring problem in the department. The C-POP program required sergeants to play more of a manager role than a strictly disciplinarian role. Sergeants had to assist officers in problem solving, represent the C-POP unit to the rest of the department (where there was some hostility), and represent it to the community.[77]

George Kelling and James Stewart warn of the dangers inherent in encouraging police officers to be responsive to community residents. A majority of the residents may demand things that are illegal or improper. Kelling and Stewart point out that "a neighborhood anti-crime group that consists exclusively of home owning whites in a racially mixed neighborhood" may only increase the level of racial conflict in the area.[78] Critics of community policing point to the "kick ass" policing style described in Wilson and Kelling's "Broken Windows." In that article, a Chicago police officer explains how the police remove gang members from a public housing project: "We kick ass." Wilson and Kelling note that this approach is not consistent "with any conception of due process and fair treatment."[79] The issue here is the tension between community demands for order and the requirements of due process and equal protection.

Chapter 13.

Impact on Poor and Minority Communities

Neil Websdale notes that community policing is particularly intrusive in the lives of poor, minority citizens. He explains that community policing increases surveillance in these communities through increased police presence mandates for those who live in public housing and through cracking down on minor "quality-of-life" infractions. He argues that the increased attention on poor minority communities, while welcome by some, results in increased arrests and subsequently the number of individuals incarcerated, leaving the community oftentimes with fewer men, who when released are even less likely to find jobs because of their criminal record.[80]

Conflicting Community Interests

Working with the community sounds wonderful in theory, but Michael Buerger's study of the Minneapolis RECAP program found that in some instances community interests conflicted with the objectives of an innovative police program. One program targeted shoplifting at convenience stores. It turned out, however, that corporate officials were more worried about potential lawsuits from customers than about shoplifting, which they tended to regard as a normal business expense. Some store owners, meanwhile, were afraid that a strong police presence would alienate and scare off their good customers. A proposal to exclude juveniles from stores after curfew conflicted with a larger corporate program to provide safe havens to children. The police also tried to discourage landlords from renting to suspected drug dealers. But many landlords preferred some drug dealers because they paid their rent on time, in cash, and generally tried to avoid attracting attention. In short, conflicting interests—especially financial interests—of some community residents can obstruct creative programs to solve community problems.[81]

But Does Community Policing Work?

The Office of Community Oriented Policing Services (COPS) commissioned a number of studies examining the effectiveness of community policing, the largest of which was conducted by Jihong Zhao and Quint Thurman. The researchers examined 6,100 cities over a six-year period to determine the impact of crime on community policing hiring initiatives (funded by the COPS Office). The authors concluded that the community policing strategy implemented under Bill Clinton's administration was extremely effective. They noted that "an increase in one dollar of innovative grant funding per resident has contributed to a decline of 12.26 violent crimes and 43.85 property crimes per 100,000 persons."[82]

Recently, however, Charlotte Gill and her colleagues conducted a meta-analysis of the 25 most methodologically sophisticated studies that examined the impact of community policing on crime, disorder, fear, legitimacy, and satisfaction with the police. They found that community policing resulted in significant improvements in the public's satisfaction with the police and reduced their concerns about disorder, but it had no significant impact on police legitimacy, crime, or fear of crime.[83]

The Roots of Problem-Oriented Policing

Herman Goldstein pioneered a new approach to the police role in 1979 with his concept of **problem-oriented policing.**[84] Goldstein had played a pivotal role in recognizing the complexity of the police role through his work with the American Bar Foundation Survey of Criminal Justice in the 1950s.[85] He then helped draft the American Bar Association (ABA) standards that emphasized the many different responsibilities of the police.[86] In his 1977 book, *Policing a Free Society,* Goldstein argues that we should think of the police as a government agency providing a wide range of miscellaneous services.[87]

problem-oriented policing

The central idea in Goldstein's initial article on problem-oriented policing was that the police had traditionally defined their role in terms of vague and general categories: crime, order maintenance, and service. In practice, however, each of these general categories includes many different kinds of problems. The category of crime, for example, includes murder, burglary, and drunk driving, each of which is a very different kind of social event. The category of disorder includes domestic disputes, mental health problems, public drunkenness, and many other problems. Goldstein argues that the police should take these categories and break them down into discrete problems and then develop specific responses to each one—in short, problem-oriented policing.[88]

Goldstein also points out that the traditional measures of police effectiveness are not useful. Not only are the data in the official Uniform Crime Reporting (UCR) system extremely problematic, but the UCR system collapses all crimes into one global category. A problem-oriented approach would require specific measures of effectiveness for specific problems.[89]

Along with a growing number of experts, Goldstein argues that the police are the prisoners of their communications system. The 911 system forces them into a reactive role: devoting most of their resources to responding to calls for service.[90] This reactive role means that the police think in terms of isolated incidents (calls). Goldstein argues that this prevents any serious planning with respect to underlying problems.

Exhibit 10–6 illustrates the differences between traditional, 911-driven, incident-based policing and problem-oriented policing. Under the traditional approach, each incident is handled as an isolated event. Police officers are concerned only with responding to each and every incident. Problem-oriented policing, by contrast, emphasizes the analysis of problems and developing appropriate solutions to respond to the problems. Such a model necessitates the decentralization of power within the police department so that line officers not only have the ability to identify problems but also are empowered to do something about them.[91]

Problem-oriented policing is often confused with community-oriented policing or is implemented as part of a department wide community policing strategy. However, as seen in Exhibit 10–10, on page 354, what differentiates problem-oriented policing from community policing is its emphasis on the end product of policing rather than the means by which policing is done.[92] Eck and Maguire note that "simply put, in community policing building a strong positive relationship between the public and the police is the goal. Addressing problems is secondary. Whereas in

Traditional versus Problem-Oriented Policing

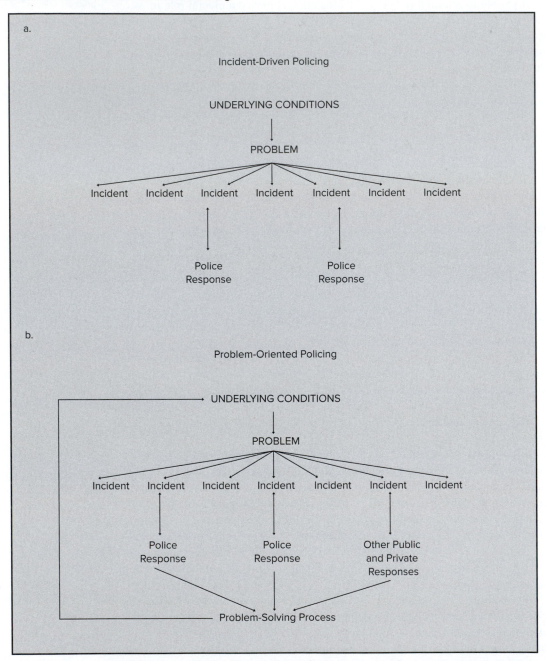

a.

Incident-Driven Policing

UNDERLYING CONDITIONS

PROBLEM

Incident   Incident   Incident   Incident   Incident   Incident   Incident

Police
Response

Police
Response

b.

Problem-Oriented Policing

UNDERLYING CONDITIONS

PROBLEM

Incident   Incident   Incident   Incident   Incident   Incident   Incident

Police
Response

Police
Response

Other Public
and Private
Responses

Problem-Solving Process

Source: John Eck and William Spelman, *Problem Solving: Problem-Oriented Policing in Newport News* (Washington, DC: PERF, 1987), Figure 1, p. 4.

problem-oriented policing the goal is to reduce problems of concern to the public. Close community partnerships are often important elements in addressing problems, but they are not the final objective."[93]

The Problem-Solving Process

John Eck and William Spelman point out that problem-oriented policing is typically implemented through a four-stage process known as **SARA:** (1) scanning, (2) analysis, (3) response, and (4) assessment (see Exhibit 10–7).

SARA

EXHIBIT 10–7

SARA Problem-Solving Model

Summary of Scanning Steps

Step 1

- Laundry list of potential problems.

Step 2

- Problems identified.

Step 3

- Problems prioritized.

Step 4

- State the specific problem.
- List examples of where the problem occurs.
- Which setting is causing the most difficulty?

Review and Preparation for Analysis

Hypothesis

- From what you already know, what do you think is causing the problem?
- General goal statement.
- How will data be gathered and reported?
- When will data collection begin?

Summary of Analysis Steps

Step 1

- What conditions or events precede the problem?
- What conditions or events accompany the problem?
- What are the problem's consequences?
- What harms result from the problem?

Step 2

- How often does the problem occur?
- How long has this been a problem?
- What is the duration of each occurrence of the problem?

Now that the data have been collected, should you continue with analysis or return to scanning and restate the problem?

Step 3

- Define a tentative goal.
- Identify resources that may be of assistance in solving the problem.
- What procedures, policies, or rules have been established to address the problem?

EXHIBIT 10–7	*(continued)*

Summary of Response Steps

Step 1

- Brainstorm possible interventions.

Step 2

- Consider feasibility and choose among alternatives.
- What needs to be done before the plan is implemented?
- Who will be responsible for preliminary actions?

Step 3

- Outline the plan and who might be responsible for each part.
- Will this plan accomplish all or part of the goal?
- State the specific goals this plan will accomplish.
- What are some ways data might be collected?

Step 4

- Realistically, what are the most likely problems with implementing the plan?
- What are some possible procedures to follow when the plan is not working or when it is not being implemented correctly?

Implement the Plan

Summary of Assessment Steps

Step 1

- Was the plan implemented?
- What was the goal as specified in the response?
- Was the goal attained?
- How do you know if the goal was attained?

Step 2

- What is likely to happen if the plan is removed?
- What is likely to happen if the plan remains in place?
- Identify new strategies to increase the effectiveness of the plan.
- How can the plan be monitored in the future?

Step 3

- Post-implementation planning
- Plan modification
- Follow-up assessment

Source: Police Executive Research Forum, *SARA Problem Solving Model,* www.policeforum.org/sara.html.

Scanning

scanning

The first stage of the SARA model is **scanning.** Scanning can be done in a number of ways. For example, over the course of their shift, the officers can look for and identify possible problems in their beat. Another strategy is for the officers to review calls for service and complaints to identify potential problems. Still another scanning strategy is to consult with residents who live or work in the officers' assigned area. However, the problems that are to be identified under the SARA model are not individual incidents with no association with one another, but rather problems that share some underlying cause.

Analysis

The second stage of the SARA model is **analysis.** This stage requires the police to collect information about the problem in an attempt to identify its scope, nature, and cause. This often leads to the police focusing on "three categories of problem characteristics: actors (victims, offenders, third parties), incidents (physical setting, social context, sequence of events), and past responses (by the community and its institutions)."[94]

analysis

Response

The third stage of the SARA model is **response.** The data collected during the analysis stage are used to develop a strategy to address the problem and implement a response. The response typically includes the use of alternative solutions that often incorporate the assistance of residents, other units within the police department, other government agencies, local businesses, private organizations, or any other person or group that might be able to help with the needed response. Problem-oriented policing emphasizes that the response should go beyond traditional crime control strategies and use strategies and tactics that will have an impact on the conditions that generate crime and disorder—rather than just treat the symptom itself (that is, crime and disorder). Such a strategy then attempts to give the police a greater number of tools to use.

response

Assessment

The last stage of the SARA model is **assessment.** The assessment involves an evaluation of the effectiveness of the response. It is intended to go beyond impressionistic or anecdotal evidence of success and incorporate rigorous feedback that allows the police to revise their response if it is not successful. The feedback also allows the police to reexamine whether or not they identified the problem correctly. Because the police use a wide variety of responses—as a consequence of the wide variety of problems they are required to address—no single type of assessment is possible. As such, the police are sometimes required to go beyond using existing data sources, such as calls for service, to measure, for example, changes in crime, and must collect and analyze nontraditional data, such as photographs, to measure, for example, changes in physical disorder.

assessment

Effectiveness of Problem-Oriented Policing

Evaluations of problem-oriented policing have generally been more positive than evaluations of community policing. This section reviews those projects that have used the strongest research designs or that have received a significant amount of national attention.

Problem-Oriented Policing in Newport News

The first significant problem-oriented policing experiment occurred in Newport News, Virginia. For several years, the police there had faced a high rate of burglaries in the New Briarfield apartment complex. Increased police presence in the area reduced reported burglaries by 60 percent, but when the officers were transferred to other areas, the burglary rate increased again. By 1984, the apartment complex was generating more calls for service than any other residential area in the city. At this point, the police department decided to abandon traditional methods and to experiment with problem-oriented policing.[95]

The project utilized the SARA model. The scanning phase began with an analysis of crime patterns in the area and an opinion survey of apartment residents. The survey helped reveal the extent to which the physical deterioration in the buildings contributed to burglaries. The police department task force assigned to New Briarfield responded with tactics that addressed the physical condition of the buildings. The police also organized a meeting of the various government agencies that had some responsibility for the housing project. Exhibit 10–8 lists the public agencies contacted. The purpose of the meeting was to develop a coordinated strategy to improve conditions in the complex. A police officer assigned to the project helped organize a tenants' group, which put pressure on city officials to make improvements in the apartments. Ultimately, however, a decision was made to demolish the apartments and relocate the residents.

Official statistics did indicate a drop in reported crime because of problem-oriented policing. More important, the activities of the officers represented a new role for the police in problem-oriented and community policing: conducting surveys of public opinion to identify neighborhood problems. By initiating the meetings

---

EXHIBIT 10–8

Public Agencies Contacted for Information on the New Briarfield Burglary Problem

Newport News City Agencies

Office of Business Licenses—business license records

Clerk of Courts—deed records

Department of Codes Compliance—building safety information

Fire Department—fire and arson data

Planning Department—land use and census data

Department of Public Works—street cleaning and sanitation information

Redevelopment and Housing Authority—data on housing subsidy programs

Tax Assessor's Office—property values and tax payments

State Agencies

Virginia Corporation Commission—corporate records

California Corporation Commission—corporate records

Federal Agencies

Federal Bureau of Investigation (local office)—fraud investigation issues

Internal Revenue Service—ownership patterns

Department of Housing and Urban Development (Washington, DC, central office)—housing standards and loan default data

Office of Management and Budget—multifamily housing problems and HUD assistance programs

---

Source: John E. Eck and William Spelman, *Problem-Solving: Problem-Oriented Policing in Newport News* (Washington, DC: Police Executive Research Forum, 1987), table 9, p. 70.

about the apartment complex, police officers were acting as community organizers or brokers of government services.

Problem-Oriented Policing in San Diego

The San Diego Police Department is widely recognized as a leader in problem-oriented policing throughout the world. The department has won national awards for problem-oriented policing projects, serves as the site for the annual international conference on problem-oriented policing, and is frequently used as a demonstration site for those wanting to learn how to engage in problem-oriented policing.

Cordner conducted one of the most thorough evaluations of the implementation of problem-oriented policing in San Diego by interviewing 320 officers throughout each of the agency's eight police districts and surveying about a quarter of the agency's patrol officers and their sergeants.[96]

He found that problem-oriented policing had had a major influence on the way policing was conducted in San Diego. For example, about 70 percent of officers indicated that they had used at least some principles of problem-oriented policing recently, and almost half stated that problem-oriented policing was a very important part of policing. Police officers also expressed that their supervisors were supportive and encouraged their problem-oriented policing efforts. Of particular interest was the finding that police officers in San Diego, while often relying on traditional policing strategies, frequently took advantage of a wide range of response options such as collaborating with other government agencies and working with the community to address a specific problem.

However, Cordner noted that most problem-oriented policing projects were not carried out in a "text book fashion." For example, most officers did not engage in sophisticated forms of scanning and analysis. Problems were mostly identified though personal observations and speaking with people. Few of the officers engaged in any form of crime analysis. Most of the officers focused on small-scale problems associated with drugs, transient/special populations, and public order. Less than 10 percent of officers worked on problems addressing crimes (other than drug-related problems).

Cordner's research in San Diego led him to conclude that, after almost two decades of implementing problem-oriented policing, officers had learned to implement the strategy but did not do so as formally or completely as that idealized by academics and policymakers.[97]

The Boston Gun Project: Operation Cease Fire

The Boston Gun Project was a problem-solving project that involved the Boston Police Department; the Bureau of Alcohol, Tobacco, and Firearms; federal and county prosecutors; county probation and patrol; City of Boston outreach workers; the Boston school police; and youth corrections. In the early 1990s, Boston was overwhelmed with an increase in youth homicides. Crime analysis revealed that there were, on average, 43 youth homicides per year in Boston between 1991 and 1995. After a thorough analysis facilitated by researchers at Harvard University, project participants found a strong illicit gun market providing firearms to youths. They also found that about 60 percent of the youths involved in the homicides were also associated with gangs that lived in three Boston neighborhoods.

The analyses led the project participants to believe that a successful response would have to include an attack on both the supply and demand for guns. A message was sent out to gang members that unless the shooting stopped, gang members would be closely scrutinized by law enforcement officials and there would be serious repercussions. "Gang members were told that drug markets would be shut down, warrants would be served, the street would swarm with law enforcement officials (including federal presence), bed checks would be performed on probationers, rooms would be searched by parole officers, unregistered cars would be taken away, and disorder offenses such as drinking in public would be pursued." In one case, a gang member who had been arrested on numerous other occasions for violent gang activity was found with a single bullet in his pocket. Because of his prior felony convictions, he was prosecuted as a career criminal and received 20 years in prison.[98]

The assessment found that the project had an impact on crime, fear of crime, and resident satisfaction with the police. Two years after the operation went into effect, youth gang homicides dropped by 70 percent. Fear of crime among residents who lived in the affected areas decreased by 21 percent, and the number of residents having faith in the police to prevent crime increased by about 33 percent.[99]

Based on the results of the Boston Gun Project, the federal government funded a large number of similar projects in communities across the country in an effort to respond to gun crime.[100] This specific approach to policing has come to be known as a **focused deterrence strategy,** or *pulling levers.* Although focused deterrence strategies were conceptualized within the framework of problem-oriented policing, it invokes principles that go well beyond the approach.[101] Heidi Bonner and colleagues explain that focused deterrence strategies rely on "enhancing the threat of criminal sanctions for the highest-risk offenders and deliberately communicating that threat in order to maximize its impact on offenders' behavior."[102] The strategy typically contains three elements. First, it focuses police attention on a small number of offenders in a small number of neighborhoods who are responsible for a disproportionate amount of crime. Second, the strategy calls for the police to establish a working group comprising other criminal justice agencies, as well as other key stakeholders, such as schools and the faith-based community, so that they can leverage a wide variety of sanctions. Third, the strategy employs the use of "call-ins" where the identified offenders are called into meetings with the police and others and they are put on notice that violence will not be tolerated. They are informed that if they are involved in violence they will be subject to the enhanced sanctions established by the working group. The strategy presupposes that these offenders will inform other offenders about their experience and how they too might be affected.[103]

focused deterrence strategy

The Future of Problem-Oriented Policing

By and large, criminologists and policymakers believe that the future of problem-oriented policing is bright. A number of fairly sophisticated tests of the strategy have found it to be effective. For example, Weisburd and his associates reviewed more than 5,500 evaluations of problem-oriented policing and identified those that used the most sophisticated research designs. They determined that the strategy, when implemented appropriately, results in a significant reduction in crime and disorder.

For instance, as one part of their analysis, they examined 45 studies that relied on a pretest/posttest research design. They found that, on average, the use of problem-oriented policing resulted in a 44 percent reduction in crime and disorder. The authors concluded that problem-oriented policing holds a substantial amount of promise and is a process that can be used effectively to address a wide number of problems.[104]

Characteristics of Zero-Tolerance Policing

Zero-tolerance policing, which is sometimes referred to as order maintenance policing or quality-of-life policing, is based on broken windows theory. It calls for the police to focus primarily on disorder, minor crime, and the appearance of crime.[105] It is characterized by interventions that aggressively enforce criminal and civil laws and that are conducted for the purpose of restoring order to communities. It is believed that through aggressive enforcement of laws aimed at combating disorder, residents will be more inclined to care for their communities, which will increase order, which in turn will lead to a reduction in the fear of crime and ultimately signal to potential criminals that law breaking will not be tolerated (see Exhibit 10–9).[106]

zero-tolerance policing

As shown in Exhibit 10–10, zero-tolerance policing differs from other policing strategies in a number of important ways. First, community policing and problem-oriented policing are based on the notion that the police should focus on crime prevention, whereas zero-tolerance policing focuses on a crime-attack model.[107] As such, Jack Green notes that "zero tolerance policing has its roots in the suppressive aspect of policing. In some respects it returns the police to a more traditional stance vis-à-vis law enforcement, a direction that is actively supported within many American police departments."[108]

Second, the strategy differentiates itself from community policing in that it is based on the presumption that the communities that need the police the most are also the least likely to have strong community social institutions. Therefore, although community policing is based on the idea that the community is a primary coproducer of crime control, zero-tolerance policing is based on the idea that the community may not be able to provide support for crime control strategies and that the police must take primary responsibility for crime control.[109]

EXHIBIT 10–9

The Social Influence of Zero-Tolerance Policing

Police Conduct→	Social Meaning→	Social Norm→	Impact on Community
Police remove visible signs of disorder	Community cares and criminals are no longer in control	Orderliness	Law-abiders feel safe and criminals stop committing crimes

Source: Dorothy Roberts, "Forward: Race, Vagueness, and the Social Meaning of Order-Maintenance Policing." Reprinted by special permission of Northwestern University School of Law, *The Journal of Criminal Law and Criminology.*

Comparisons of Social Interactions and Structural Components of Various Forms of Policing

Social Interaction or Structural Dimension	Traditional Policing	Community Policing	Problem-Oriented Policing	Zero-Tolerance Policing
Focus of policing	Law enforcement	Community building through crime prevention	Law, order, and fear problems	Order problems
Forms of intervention	Reactive, based on criminal law	Proactive, on criminal, civil, and administrative law	Mixed, on criminal, civil, and administrative law	Proactive, uses criminal, civil, and administrative law
Range of police activity	Narrow, crime focused	Broad, crime, order, fear, and quality-of-life focused	Narrow to broad, problem focused	Narrow, location and behavior focused
Level of discretion at line level	High and unaccountable	High and accountable to the community and local commanders	High and primarily accountable to the police administration	Low, but primarily accountable to the police administration
Focus of police culture	Inward, rejecting community	Outward, building partnerships	Mixed depending on problem, but analysis focused	Inward, focused on attacking the target problem
Locus of decision making	Police directed, minimizes the involvement of others	Community-police coproduction, joint responsibility and assessment	Varied, police identify problems but with community involvement/action	Police directed, some linkage to other agencies when necessary
Communication flow	Downward from police to community	Horizontal between police and community	Horizontal between police and community	Downward from police to community
Range of community involvement	Low and passive	High and active	Mixed, depending on problem set	Low and passive
Linkage with other agencies	Poor and intermittent	Participative and integrative in the overarching process	Participative and integrative depending on the problem set	Moderate and intermittent
Type of organization and command focus	Centralized command and control	Decentralized with community linkage	Decentralized with local command accountability to central administration	Centralized or decentralized but internal focus
Implications for organizational change/ development	Few, static organization fending off the environment	Many, dynamic organization focused on the environment and environmental interactions	Varied, focused on problem resolution but with import for organization intelligence and structure	Few, limited interventions focused on target problems, using many traditional methods
Measurement of success	Arrest and crime rates, particularly serious Part 1 crimes	Varied, crime, calls for service, fear reduction, use of public places, community linkages and contacts, safer neighborhoods	Varied, problems solved, minimized, displaced	Arrests, field stops, activity, location-specific reductions in targeted activity

Source: Jack R. Green, "Community Policing in America: Changing the Nature, Structure, and Function of the Police," in Julie Horney, ed., *Policies, Processes, and Decisions of the Criminal Justice System, Criminal Justice 2000,* vol. 3 (Washington, DC: Government Printing Office, 2000), p. 311.

Third, zero-tolerance policing differs from problem-oriented policing in that it does not attempt to carefully identify problems or thoroughly analyze the cause of problems.[110] Rather, zero-tolerance policing focuses on specific types of behavior. Minor crimes and disorder—such as urinating in public, fare-beating (not paying the fare on the subway by jumping the turnstiles), prostitution, loitering, aggressive pan-handling, graffiti, and "squeegeeing" (when boys and young men wash the windows of cars stopped at traffic lights and then demand payment)—are a major focus.[111]

Fourth, zero-tolerance policing is characterized by its focus on place-specific interventions. Prior studies examining hot spots have found that a small proportion of addresses account for a disproportionate amount of crime and disorder. Accordingly, a number of police departments across the country have begun to map crime, which allows them to direct zero-tolerance policing to hot spots.[112]

For a more thorough discussion of hot-spots policing, see Chapter 7.

Fifth, zero-tolerance policing differentiates itself from other police advances be-cause it culturally and organizationally represents a back-to-the-basics strategy. Its crime-fighting emphasis lends itself to a more militaristic organizational design that is both centralized and internally focused (information flowing from the administration to the line officer)—a mission and organizational structure that many police are more comfortable and familiar with. Additionally, unlike community policing and problem-oriented policing, because of the emphasis on proactive law enforcement, zero-tolerance policing does not require the police to make a fundamental change in police culture.[113]

The Effectiveness of Zero-Tolerance Policing

Although zero-tolerance policing has enjoyed much support among law enforcement officials, there has been little focus on its effectiveness. We now discuss police ef-forts in two cities in which zero-tolerance policing has been implemented and sub-jected to independent evaluation.

Zero-Tolerance Policing in New York City

Perhaps the best-known implementation of zero-tolerance policing has taken place in New York City. On the basis of the broken windows theory, Police Commissioner William Bratton and Mayor Rudolph Giuliani instituted a zero-tolerance policing strategy in 1993. Prior to this time, New York City was characterized by social dis-order (unlicensed peddlers, homelessness, street-level drug use), physical disorder (graffiti), and crime. There was an overall sense that the city was out of control.[114] Commissioner Bratton commented that, "I can recall coming in from the airport, fly-ing in to LaGuardia, and coming down that highway. It looked like something out of a futuristic movie in terms of graffiti on every highway wall, dirt on rubber tires that look like they have not been cleaned in years, burned out cars, litter everywhere."[115]

To address these problems, the New York City Police Department (NYPD) instituted a zero-tolerance strategy that focused enforcement efforts on order mainte-nance offenses such as aggressive panhandling, vandalism, public drunkenness, pub-lic urination, and prostitution.[116] The strategy was, once again, based on the notion that by focusing police resources on disorder and minor crime, the police department could restore order, which would eventually lead to a reduction in crime. An analysis of crime data suggests that the department's shift in philosophy had an immediate and significant impact on the behavior of the officers. The number of misdemeanor arrests in NYC, for example, jumped from 1993 through 1996, increasing from 133,446 to 205,277.[117]

Many observers credited the new policing strategy with the drop in serious crime in New York City in the mid- to late 1990s. Following the strategy's implementation in 1993, the overall crime rate dropped by 27 percent, homicides dropped by 40 percent, robbery dropped by 30 percent, and burglary dropped by 25 percent. These drops in crime were twice the national average, and they led a number of experts to conclude that zero-tolerance policing is more effective than other police strategies.[118]

A primary tactic used in NYC's zero-tolerance policing strategy was **stop and frisk, which is sometimes referred to as stop, question and frisk (SQF)**. SQF involved NYPD officers stopping a pedestrian for a minor infraction, questioning the individual, and then "frisking" for weapons.[119] Michael White and Henry Fradella explain that "[t]he combination of OMP [order maintenance policing] with 'gun oriented policing' was thought to act as a potential deterrent to gun related crimes because 'stopping people on minor infractions also made it riskier for criminals to carry guns in public'."[120] Between 2003 and 2011, the number of SQFs increased substantially, from about 160,000 to about 685,000.[121]

The policing tactic was hailed as a major crime control success. Crime in New York City declined substantially between 1990 and 2009. For example, homicides declined by 82 percent, rapes declined by 77 percent, and auto theft declined by 94 percent. Although crime did decline in other major cities across the United States, some academics noted that the decline was more pronounced in New York City, as shown in Exhibit 10–11.

However, much controversy remains over whether zero-tolerance policing and SQF deserve credit for this accomplishment. Although William Bratton, the police commissioner who instituted the policy, and criminologist George Kelling claim that zero-tolerance policing and its associated tactics were directly responsible,[122] others argue that the shift in strategy had little to no impact.

Richard Rosenfeld and his associates, for example, examined whether New York City's aggressive order maintenance policing strategy was associated with a reduction in homicides by comparing its homicide trend to 95 of the largest U.S. cities and controlling for factors known to be associated with violent crime. Their

stop, question, and frisk (SQF)

 For a more thorough discussion of SQF, see Chapter 12.

EXHIBIT 10–11

Crime Patterns in Six Cities, 1990–2009

	Homicide	Rape	Robbery	Assault	Burglary	Auto Theft	Larceny
New York	−82%	−77%	−84%	−67%	−86%	−94%	−63%
Los Angeles	−71	−59	−69	−78	−68	−68	−58
Houston	−64	−56	−37	−20	−51	−74	−30
San Diego	−75	−39	−63	−57	−66	−67	−56
San Jose	−36	−49	−19	−46	−47	−66	−54
Boston	−68	−54	−65	−52	−73	−89	−52

Source: Michael White and Henry Fradella, *Stop and Frisk* (New York: New York University Press, 2016), 88.

analysis indicated that New York City's homicide trend did not vary significantly from the national average prior to the implementation of zero-tolerance policing, and its reduction in homicides after its implementation was not "atypical" of other large cities during that time.[123] Likewise, John MacDonald, Jeffery Fagan, and Amanda Geller examined the specific impact of SQF in New York City from 2004 through 2012 but controlled for the simultaneous concentration of police deployment (that is, hot-spots policing) that was also taking place. They concluded that "saturating high crime blocks with police helped reduce crime in New York City, . . . the bulk of the investigative [SQF] stops did not play an important role in the crime reductions."[124]

Operation Restoration

A systematic examination of the effects of zero-tolerance policing was also conducted in Chandler, Arizona.[125] In 1995, it became clear to the Chandler City Council that the innermost part of the city had experienced an increase in physical and social disorder. The area was characterized by homes with broken and missing windows, doors falling off hinges, and trash and debris cluttering properties. The area was also well known for having high crime rates, street-level drug dealing, and prostitution.

The city responded by moving the zoning enforcement responsibilities from the planning and development department to the police department. This unit became responsible for the reduction of physical disorder by enforcing city code violations. The police department also established a specialized unit to aggressively enforce order maintenance laws. The two units worked in tandem, focusing their resources on four zones that were each approximately one square mile in size. This project became known as Operation Restoration and was theoretically based on the broken windows hypothesis.

Findings from the study suggested that the project had a significant impact on public morals crimes (for example, prostitution), disorderly conduct, and physical disorder. Similar trends were also observed in the areas adjacent to the targeted area, suggesting that the project also had an impact on the surrounding area. These findings led the authors to conclude that cracking down on disorder and minor crime may not have a substantial impact on serious crime, but the benefits of such an approach may be limited to those problems that the project specifically focuses on—namely, physical and social disorder. It also led the researchers to question the theoretical foundations of zero-tolerance policing.

Potential Problems with Zero-Tolerance Policing

Although zero-tolerance policing and its associated tactics have become a popular policing strategy, a number of important questions remain. Critics have argued that there is no clear evidence that the strategy is effective in reducing crime, and others have questioned the negative impact that the strategy might have on communities.

Conflict between the Police and the Public

Zero-tolerance policing has been heavily criticized for encouraging officers to be overly aggressive. Some have gone as far as to refer to the policing strategy as "harassment policing."[126] For example, in one eight-block area of Brooklyn, the police stopped, questioned, and frisked 52,000 people over four years. There were only about 14,000 people living in the area, suggesting that the NYPD stopped each person in the area, on average, once a year. In one month, the police averaged more than 60 stops a day in the eight-block area.[127]

The issue was particularly pronounced among young people. Vera Institute surveyed about 500 residents ages 18–25 who lived in high-crime areas. They reported the following:

- 44 percent had been stopped 9 or more times by the police in their lifetime.
- 71 percent had been frisked at least once, and 64 percent said they had been searched.
- 46 percent said they had experienced physical force at the hands of police.
- About 25 percent said they were involved in a stop where the police officer displayed his or her weapon.
- 88 percent said that people in their neighborhood do not trust the police.
- About 40 percent said they would feel comfortable seeking help from the police if in trouble.
- About 25 percent said they would report someone who had committed a crime.[128]

Some observers believe that zero-tolerance policing tactics increase conflict between the police and the public, reduce support for the police, and result in few if any benefits.

Increase in Crime in the Long Run

Sherman points out that although zero-tolerance policing might have a short-term impact on the reduction of crime, it might also result in an increase in serious crime in the long term. He argues that an arrest record can have a significant impact on a person's immediate and future employment. Additionally, he points out that arrests for minor offenses can lead to further, more serious crime by making a person angrier and more defiant.[129]

Impact on Poor and Minority Communities

A number of critics point to the fact that zero-tolerance policing efforts are focused largely on the poor and minorities. In 2009, for example, 90 percent of those stopped by the NYPD were African American or Hispanic.[130] Harcourt explains that because zero-tolerance policing is focused on minor offenses such as loitering, panhandling, and public drinking, it will be directed primarily toward poorer communities, which, in turn, means minority communities. An examination of misdemeanor arrests shows that minorities are disproportionately arrested for misdemeanor offenses, compared to the percentage of minorities in the population. This trend is particularly strong for offenses, such as arrest for suspicion, that call for a great deal of discretion on the part of police officers. Accordingly, zero-tolerance policing may lead the police back down the path of losing legitimacy in the eyes of minorities and minorities again seeing the police as a punitive occupying force.[131]

Harcourt emphasizes that the ultra-poor, minorities, and other "cultural outsiders" may be the most affected. He states that "by handing over the informal power to define deviance to police officers and some community members, we may be enabling the repression of political, cultural, or sexual outsiders in a way that is antithetical to our conceptions of democratic theory or constitutional principles."[132]

An example of this can be found in Chandler, Arizona, where local businesses wanted day laborers—many of whom were illegal immigrants—removed from the streets for pandering because of their disruption of local business. In response, 30 Chandler police officers and six immigration officers performed a crackdown for five days on illegal immigrants. The response team searched houses, stopped drivers, detained pedestrians, and interrogated children on their way to school to inquire about citizenship. In all, 432 immigrants and two U.S. citizens were deported. After the roundup, the state's attorney general found several of the searches to have been conducted illegally, and a number of residents came forward and complained of being harassed and beaten by the police because of their nationality. Official arrest records detailed the extent of the discrimination. One immigration agent justifying an arrest in his report stated that he "immediately noticed a lack of personal hygiene displayed by the subject, and a strong odor common to illegal immigrants." The crackdown led to a $35 million lawsuit that was later settled out of court. (For a full discussion, see the section "Operation Restoration" earlier in this chapter.)[133]

A number of large communities—including New York City, Boston, Newark, Chicago, Philadelphia, and Miami—have begun to investigate and/or sue the police for engaging in discriminatory SQF practices. These investigations have revealed that SQF practices are pervasive and disproportionately impact those living in poor, minority communities. For example, in 2013, Newark police made 91 stops per 1,000 residents, a stop rate that was 11 times higher than the NYPD's. Although only 52 percent of the Newark population was black, 75 percent of those stopped were black. Similar patterns have been observed in Chicago and Philadelphia.[134]

In New York City, the federal court ruled in *Floyd v. the City of New York* (2013) that NYPD's SQF tactics were unconstitutional. The court, as a consequence, appointed a monitor to ensure that policies, training, supervision, and discipline changed to be in compliance with court orders; required that the communities most affected by SQF be involved in reform efforts; and required a pilot test of body-worn cameras. Although matters are still being finalized in the courts through appeals, the use of SQF has declined dramatically. In 2014, the NYPD recorded fewer than 46,000 stops, compared to about 200,000 in 2013.[135]

But Does Zero-Tolerance Policing Work?

Several studies have examined the effectiveness of zero-tolerance policing. Anthony Braga and others conducted a meta-analysis of the evaluation results to understand the impact of this form of policing on violence, property crime, drug crime, and disorder offenses. They reported that zero-tolerance policing does not have a significant impact on reducing crime. Their findings in the context of other research studies suggest that focusing on misdemeanor offenses and disorder alone may have no impact on crime but may result in reduced legitimacy and increased conflict between the police and those living in poor, minority communities.[136]

CASE STUDY

Using Social Media as a Virtual Form of Neighborhood Watch in Sacramento, California

The Sacramento Police Department (SPD) recently implemented Nextdoor, a social network application that brings together neighbors and provides the police with a platform to communicate with residents within geographically defined neighborhoods. Nextdoor, the police say, brings together neighbors to form a virtual neighborhood watch, where neighbors can collaborate to identify and respond to problems, and it allows the police to target communication to specific neighborhoods. Although in some law enforcement agencies, social media applications are managed centrally through their public information offices, Nextdoor allows neighbors and police officers to communicate directly with one another. In Sacramento, more than 22,000 neighbors and 80 police officers participate in the program. Every 30 days, the police department makes about 4,000 posts and has about 10,000 responses from the community. The SPD states that they have had more than 14,000 interactions with the community that would not have occurred if not for Nextdoor. The SPD emphasized the cost-effectiveness of the program. Nextdoor is free to access and use, and it required only about 100 hours of work from a few officers to plan, implement, and train fellow officers and the public. The SPD notes that Nextdoor has resulted in the number of neighborhood watch groups growing from 183 to 338, and is partially responsible for the city's 15 percent decline in crime. Learn more about Nextdoor and its implications for community policing in your neighborhood at https://nextdoor.com.

Source: Alliance for Innovation Case Study Application by the City of Sacramento, California, *Rebuilding and Reconnecting: Making the Transition to Geographic Policing and Expanding Community Engagement through the Use of Social Media and Virtual Neighborhood Watch,* Case Study for 2015 Transforming Local Government Conference, tlgconference.org/modules/showdocument.aspx?documentid=494.

SUMMARY

For many police officials, community policing, problem-oriented policing, and zero-tolerance policing are simply buzzwords that mask traditional policing, or policing that many police officers believe they have been practicing for decades.[137] Nonetheless, the ideas of community policing, problem-oriented policing, and zero-tolerance policing have inspired remarkable advances in American policing. Bayley concludes that the last decade of the twentieth century may have been the most creative period in policing since the modern police officer was put onto the streets of London in 1829.[138]

As a final note, Goldstein and Skolnick and Bayley all point out that we should not be too quick to argue that the advances involved in these strategies have not proved to be effective. Neither have most of the activities labeled "traditional" policing. As we have already learned, patrol (Chapter 7), criminal investigation (Chapter 9), and other activities are rarely subjected to rigorous evaluations, and even fewer evaluations have proved them to be effective.[139]

KEY TERMS

broken windows, 326	consultation, 330	analysis, 349
social disorder, 327	mobilization, 331	response, 349
physical disorder, 327	problem solving, 336	assessment, 349
community policing, 327	problem-oriented policing, 345	focused deterrence strategy, 352
coproducers of crime control, 329	SARA, 347	zero-tolerance policing, 353
community partnerships, 329	scanning, 348	stop, question, and frisk, 356

FOR DISCUSSION

Are the law enforcement agencies in your community doing community policing, problem-oriented policing, or zero-tolerance policing? Discuss the activities of your local agency:

1. What label is used to describe the program?
2. What is the content of the program (community meetings, intensive drug enforcement, coordinated activities with non-criminal-justice programs)?
3. Is the program department wide or operated by a special unit?
4. Has it been evaluated, and if so, what were the results of that evaluation?
5. If your agency is not engaged in community policing, problem-oriented policing, or zero-tolerance policing, find out why.

INTERNET EXERCISES

Exercise 1 Visit the Center for Problem-Oriented Policing website at http://www.popcenter.org/learning/goldstein_interview/, and watch one of the eight interviews between Herman Goldstein and Samuel Walker to learn more about the origins of problem-oriented policing.

Exercise 2 Visit http://cops.usdoj.gov/html/dispatch/index.asp and click on the most recent version of the Office of Community Oriented Policing's online magazine *Community Policing*

Dispatch to find out about community policing projects that have been recognized as important. Pick one project and discuss how it makes an important contribution to policing today.

Exercise 3 Many police agencies describe their community policing, problem-oriented policing, and zero-tolerance policing programs on the web. Check out the website for several departments in your region of the country. What can you learn? Do they describe their programs in detail that is useful to you?

NOTES

1. John Eck and Dennis Rosenbaum, "The New Police Order: Effectiveness, Equity, and Efficiency in Community Policing," in Dennis Rosenbaum, ed., *The Challenge of Community Policing: Testing the Promises* (Thousand Oaks, CA: Sage, 1994).
2. Jack R. Greene and Stephen D. Mastrofski, *Community Policing: Rhetoric or Reality* (New York: Praeger, 1988).
3. George L. Kelling and Mark H. Moore, "The Evolving Strategy of Policing," *Perspectives on Policing,* no. 4 (Washington, DC: U.S. Government Printing Office, 1988), 8; John P. Crank, "Watchman and Community: Myth and Institutionalization in Policing," *Law and Society Review* 28, no. 2 (1994): 325–351.

4. Wesley G. Skogan and George E. Antunes, "Information, Apprehension, and Deterrence: Exploring the Limits of Police Productivity," *Journal of Criminal Justice* 7 (Fall 1979): 232; James Frank, Steven G. Brandl, Robert E. Worden, and Timothy S. Bynum, "Citizen Involvement in the Coproduction of Police Outputs," *Journal of Crime and Justice* XIX, no. 2 (1996): 1–30.

5. James Q. Wilson and George L. Kelling, "Broken Windows: The Police and Neighborhood Safety," *Atlantic Monthly* 249 (March 1982): 29–38.

6. Wesley G. Skogan, *Disorder and Decline: Crime and the Spiral of Decay in American Neighborhoods* (New York: Free Press, 1990), 21–50.

7. Ibid.

8. Brian Reaves, *Local Police Departments, 2013: Personnel, Policies, and Practices* (Washington, DC: U.S. Bureau of Justice Statistics, 2015).

9. Mary Ann Wycoff, *Community Policing Strategies* (Washington, DC: National Institute of Justice, 1995).

10. Dennis Rosenbaum, ed., *The Challenge of Community Policing: Testing the Promises* (Thousand Oaks, CA: Sage, 1994).

11. David Bayley, *Policing in America: Assessment and Prospects* (Washington, DC: Police Foundation, 1998); Jerome Skolnick and David Bayley, "Theme and Variation in Community Policing," in Michael Tonry and Norval Morris, eds., *Crime and Justice: A Review of the Research* (Chicago: University of Chicago Press, 1988).

12. Stephen Mastrofski, "Community Policing as Reform: A Cautionary Tale," in Stephen Mastrofski and Jack Greene, eds., *Community Policing: Rhetoric or Reality* (New York: Praeger, 1988); the preceding section was taken from Edward Maguire and Charles Katz, "The Validity and Reliability of Police Agencies' Community Policing Claims," presented on November 22, 1997, at the annual meeting of the American Society of Criminology in San Diego, California.

13. Gary Cordner, "Community Policing: Elements and Effects," in Roger Dunham and Geoffrey Alpert, eds., *Critical Issues in Policing* (Prospect Heights, IL: Waveland, 1997).

14. Community Policing Consortium, *Understanding Community Policing: A Framework for Action* (Washington, DC: U.S. Bureau of Justice Assistance, 1994).

15. Jerome Skolnick and David Bayley, *The New Blue Line: Police Innovation in Six American Cities* (New York: Free Press, 1986).

16. The preceding paragraph was taken from Maguire and Katz, "The Validity and Reliability of Police Agencies' Community Policing Claims."

17. David Bayley, *Police for the Future* (New York: Oxford Press, 1994).

18. *Law Enforcement Management and Administrative Statistics, 2007.* Author analysis. Data available at http://bjs.ojp.usdoj.gov/index.cfm?ty5dcdetail &iid5248.

19. Daniel W. Flynn, *Defining the "Community" in Community Policing* (Washington, DC: Police Executive Research Forum, 1998).

20. COPS Office, 2016. President's Task Force on 21st Century Policing: One-Year Progress Report, Washington, DC: Office of Community Oriented Policing Services.

21. Community Policing Consortium, *Understanding Community Policing: A Framework for Action.*

22. Jack Green, "Community Policing in America: Changing the Nature, Structure, and Function of the Police," in Julie Horney, ed., *Policies, Processes, and Decisions of the Criminal Justice System* (Washington, DC: National Institute of Justice, 2000).

23. David Carter, "Community Alliance," in Larry Hoover, ed., *Police Management: Issues and Perspectives* (Washington, DC: Police Executive Research Forum, 1992).

24. David Bayley, *Police for the Future;* the preceding paragraph was taken from Maguire and Katz, "The Validity and Reliability of Police Agencies' Community Policing Claims."

25. Green, "Community Policing in America: Changing the Nature, Structure, and Function of the Police."

26. E. J. Williams, "Enforcing Social Responsibility and the Expanding Domain of the Police: Notes from the Portland Experience," *Crime & Delinquency* 42, no. 2 (1996): 309–323.

27. Green, "Community Policing in America," 314.

28. The Police Foundation, *The Newark Foot Patrol Experiment* (Washington, DC: The Police Foundation, 1981).

29. James Q. Wilson and George L. Kelling, "Making Neighborhoods Safe," *Atlantic Monthly* 263 (1989): 46–53.

30. Craig Uchida, Brian Forst, and Sampson Annon, *Modern Policing and the Control of Illegal Drugs: Testing New Strategies in Two American Cities, Final Report* (Washington, DC: The Police Foundation, 1992).

31. Wesley Skogan, "The Impact of Community Policing on Neighborhood Residents: A Cross-Site Analysis," in Dennis Rosenbaum, ed., *The Challenge of Community Policing* (Thousand Oaks, CA: Sage, 1994), 167–181.

32. Jerry Ratcliff, Travis Taniguishi, Elizabeth Groff, and Jennifer Wood, "The Philadelphia Foot Patrol Experiment," *Criminology* 49, no. 3 (2011): 795–831.

33. David Kessler and Sheila Duncan, "The Impact of Community Policing in Four Houston Neighborhoods," *Evaluation Review* 20 (1996): 627–669.

34. Trevor Bennett, "Community Policing on the Ground: Developments in Britain," in Dennis Rosenbaum, ed., *The Challenge of Community Policing* (Thousand Oaks, CA: Sage, 1994), 240.

35. Ibid.

36. Hubert Williams and Patrick V. Murphy, "The Evolving Strategy of Police: A Minority View," *Perspectives on Policing* no. 13 (1990): 12.

37. University of Maryland, *Preventing Crime: What Works, What Doesn't, What's Promising—A Report to the Attorney General of the United States* (Washington, DC: U.S. Department of Justice, Office of Justice Programs, 1997), 8–1 to 8–58.

38. Skogan, *Disorder and Decline*, 95.

39. Ibid., 148.

40. Wesley G. Skogan, "Fear of Crime and Neighborhood Change," in Albert Reiss and Michael Tonry, eds., *Communities and Crime* (Chicago: University of Chicago Press, 1986), 222.

41. Wesley Skogan, Susan Hartnett, Jill DuBois, Jennifer Comey, Karla Twedt-Ball, and Erik Gudell, *Public Involvement: Community Policing in Chicago* (Washington, DC: National Institute of Justice, 2000).

42. John Eck and Edward Maguire, "Have Changes in Policing Reduced Violent Crime? An Assessment of the Evidence," in Alfred Blumstein and Joel Wallman, eds., *The Crime Drop in America* (Cambridge, UK: Cambridge University Press, 2000), 207–265.

43. Green, "Community Policing in America."

44. Jerome Skolnick and David Bayley, *Community Policing: Issues and Practices around the World* (Washington, DC: National Institute of Justice, 1988); Bayley, *Police for the Future*.

45. Skolnick and Bayley, *Community Policing* (Washington, DC: National Institute of Justice, 1988), 14.

46. Arthur Lurigio and Wesley Skogan, "Winning the Hearts and Minds of Police Officers," in Ronald Glensor, Mark Correia, and Kenneth Peak, eds., *Policing Communities* (Los Angeles: Roxbury Publishing, 2000).

47. Ibid.

48. Deb Weisel and John Eck, "Toward a Practical Approach to Organizational Change," in Ronald Glensor, Mark Correia, and Kenneth Peak, eds., *Policing Communities* (Los Angeles: Roxbury Publishing, 2000).

49. Stephen Mastrofski, Roger Parks, and Robert Worden, *Community Policing in Action: Lessons from an Observational Study* (Washington, DC: National Institute of Justice, 1998).

50. R. Trojanowicz and B. Bucqueroux, *Toward Development of Meaningful and Effective Performance Evaluations* (East Lansing, MI: National Center for Community Policing, 1992); Bayley, *Police for the Future.*

51. Dennis J. Stevens, *Case Studies in Community Policing* (Upper Saddle River, NJ: Prentice Hall, 2000–2001).

52. Edward Maguire, "Structural Change in Large Municipal Police Organizations during the Community Policing Era," *Justice Quarterly* 14, no. 3 (1997): 547–576.

53. Jihong Zhao, Nicholas Lovrich, and Hank Robinson, "Community Policing: Is It Changing the Basic Functions of Policing?" *Journal of Criminal Justice* 29 (2001): 373–400.

54. Wesley G. Skogan and Susan M. Hartnett, *Community Policing, Chicago Style* (New York: Oxford University Press, 1997).

55. Robert Kane, "Permanent Beat Assignment in Association with Community Policing: Assessing the Impact on Police Officers' Field Activity," *Justice Quarterly* 17, no. 2 (2000): 259–280.

56. Jihong Zhao, Ni He, and Nicholas Lovrich, "Value Change among Police Officers at a Time of Organizational Reform: A Follow-Up Study Using Rokeach Values," *Policing: An International Journal of Police Strategies and Management* 22, no. 2 (1999), 152–170.

57. Dennis Rosenbaum, Sandy Yeh, and Deanna Wilkinson, "Impact of Community Policing on Police Personnel: A Quasi-Experimental Test," *Crime and Delinquency* 40, no. 3 (1994): 331–353.

58. Robin Haarr, "The Impact of Community Policing Training and Program Implementation on Police Personnel: A Final Report," presented to the National Institute of Justice, 2000.

59. Mastrofski, Parks, and Worden, *Community Policing in Action.*

60. Bureau of Justice Statistics, *Law Enforcement Management and Administrative Statistics, 2000* (Washington, DC: U.S. Government Printing Office, 2004).

61. Gary Cordner, "Problem-Oriented Policing vs. Zero Tolerance," in Tara O'Connor Shelly and Anne Grant, eds., *Problem Oriented Policing* (Washington, DC: Police Executive Research Forum, 1998).

62. Edward Maguire and Charles Katz, "Community Policing Loose Coupling and Sensemaking in American Police Agencies," *Justice Quarterly* 19, no. 3, 501–534.

63. Skogan and Hartnett, *Community Policing: Chicago Style.*

64. Ibid., 67–68.

65. Ibid., 113.

66. Ibid., 114.

67. Susan Sadd and Randolph Grinc, "Innovative Neighborhood Policing: An Evaluation of Community Policing Programs in Eight Cities," in Dennis P. Rosenbaum, ed., *The Challenge of Community Policing: Testing the Promises* (Thousand Oaks, CA: Sage, 1994), 27–52.

68. Lisa M. Graziano, Dennis P. Rosenbaum, and Amie M. Schuck, "Building Group Capacity for Problem Solving and Police–Community Partnerships through Survey Feedback and Training: A Randomized Control Trial within Chicago's Community Policing Program," *Journal of Experimental Criminology* 10, no. 1 (2014): 79–103.

69. Lolly Bowean, "Chicago Police Look to Revamp CAPS," *Chicago Tribune*, February 25, 2013.

70. Ted Cox, "Chicago Police Department Shifts Community Policing Program to Districts," DNAinfo Chicago, January 8, 2013, www.dnainfo.com/chicago.

71. David Bayley, "Community Policing: A Report from the Devil's Advocate," in Jack R. Greene and Stephen D. Mastrofski, eds., *Community Policing: Rhetoric or Reality* (New York: Praeger, 1988), 225–237.

72. George L. Kelling and Mark H. Moore, "The Evolving Strategy of Policing," *Perspective on Policing,* no. 4 (Washington, DC: U.S. Government Printing Office, 1988).

73. Bayley, *Police for the Future*, 126–128.

74. Bayley, "Community Policing: A Report from the Devil's Advocate."

75. Williams, "Enforcing Social Responsibility and the Expanding Domain of the Police."

76. Herman Goldstein, "Toward Community-Oriented Policing," *Crime and Delinquency* 33 (January 1987): 12.

77. Jerome McElroy, Colleen Cosgrove, and Susan Sadd, *Community Policing: The CPOP in New York* (Newbury Park, CA: Sage, 1993).

78. George L. Kelling and James K. Stewart, "Neighborhoods and Police: The Maintenance of Civil Authority," *Perspectives on Policing* 10 (1989): 4.

79. Wilson and Kelling, "Broken Windows."

80. Neil Websdale, *Policing the Poor* (Boston: Northeastern University, 2001).

81. Michael E. Buerger, "The Problems of Problem-Solving: Resistance, Interdependencies, and Conflicting Interests," *American Journal of Police* XIII, no. 3 (1994), 1–36.

82. Jihong "Solomon" Zhao and Quint Thurman, *A National Evaluation of the Effects of COPS Grants on Crime from 1994 to 1999* (Omaha: University of Nebraska at Omaha, December 2001), 2.

83. Charlotte Gill, David Weisburd, Cody W. Telep, Zoe Vitter, and Trevor Bennett, "Community-Oriented Policing to Reduce Crime, Disorder, and Fear and Increase Satisfaction and Legitimacy among Citizens: A Systematic Review," *Journal of Experimental Criminology* 10, no. 4 (2014): 399–428.

84. Herman Goldstein, "Improving Policing: A Problem-Oriented Approach," *Crime and Delinquency* 25 (1979): 236–258; Herman Goldstein, *Problem-Oriented Policing* (New York: McGraw-Hill, 1990).

85. Samuel Walker, "Origins of the Contemporary Criminal Justice Paradigm: The American Bar Foundation Survey, 1953–1969," *Justice Quarterly* 9 (March 1992): 47–76.

86. American Bar Association, *Standards Relating to the Urban Police Function,* 2nd ed. (Boston: Little, Brown, 1980), Standard 1–2.2.

87. Herman Goldstein, *Policing a Free Society* (Cambridge, MA: Ballinger, 1977).

88. Goldstein, "Improving Policing."

89. See the discussion in Geoffrey Alpert and Mark H. Moore, "Measuring Police Performance in the New Paradigm of Policing," in Department of Justice, *Performance Measures for the Criminal Justice System* (Washington, DC: U.S. Government Printing Office, 1993), 109–140.

90. Malcolm K. Sparrow, Mark H. Moore, and David M. Kennedy, *Beyond 911* (New York: Basic Books, 1990).

91. Green, "Community Policing in America."

92. John Eck and William Spelman, "Who Ya Gonna Call: The Police as Problem Busters," *Crime and Delinquency* 33 (1987): 31–52.

93. Eck and Maguire, "Have Changes in Policing Reduced Violent Crime?, 47–48.

94. John Eck and William Spelman, *Problem Solving: Problem-Oriented Policing in Newport News* (Washington, DC: Police Executive Research Forum, 1987), 47.

95. Ibid.

96. Gary Cordner and Elizabeth Perkins Biebel, "Problem-Oriented Policing in Practice," *Criminology and Public Policy* 4, no. 2 (2005), 155–180.

97. Ibid.

98. David Kennedy, *Juvenile Gun Violence and Gun Markets in Boston* (Washington, DC: National Institute of Justice, 1997).

99. *Operation Cease Fire* (Boston: Boston Police Department, 1998).

100. Ibid.

101. Edward Maguire, personal communication March 23, 2012.

102. Heidi S. Bonner, Robert E. Worden, and Sarah J. McLean, *Focused Deterrence Initiatives: A Synopsis* (Albany, NY: Finn Institute, 2008).

103. Edmund McGarrell, Steven Chermak, Jeremy Wilson, and Nicholas Corsaro, "Reducing Homicide through a Lever Pulling Strategy," *Justice Quarterly* 23, no. 2 (2006): 214–231.

104. David Weisburd, Cody Telep, Joshua Hinkle, and John Eck, "Is Problem-Oriented Policing Effective in Reducing Crime and Disorder?" *Criminology and Public Policy* 9, no. 1 (2010): 139–172.

105. Cordner, "Problem-Oriented Policing vs. Zero Tolerance."

106. Dorothy Roberts, "Forward: Race, Vagueness, and the Social Meaning of Order-Maintenance Policing," *Journal of Criminal Law & Criminology* 89, no. 3 (1992): 811.

107. Green, "Community Policing in America."

108. Ibid., 318.

109. Ibid.

110. Cordner, "Problem-Oriented Policing vs. Zero Tolerance."

111. George Kelling and Catherine Coles, *Fixing Broken Windows* (New York: Free Press, 1996).

112. Green, "Community Policing in America."

113. Ibid.

114. William Bratton, "Remark: New Strategies for Combating Crime in New York City," *Fordham Urban Journal* 23 (1996): 781–785.

115. Ibid.

116. Dan Kahn, "Social Influence, Social Meaning, and Deterrence," *Virginia Law Review* 83, (1997): 349–395.

117. Bernard Harcourt, "Reflecting on the Subject: A Critique of the Social Influence Conception of Deterrence, the Broken Windows Theory, and Order Maintenance Policing New York Style," *Michigan Law Review* 97 (1998): 291–389.

118. Kahn, "Social Influence, Social Meaning, and Deterrence."

119. Michael White and Henry Fradella, *Stop and Frisk* (New York: New York University Press, 2016).

120. Ibid.

121. Weston Morrow, *Examining the Potential for Racial/Ethnic Disparities in Use of Force During NYPD Stop and Frisk Activities* (PhD dissertation, Arizona State University, 2015).

122. William Bratton, *Turnaround: How America's Top Cop Reversed the Crime Epidemic* (New York: Random House, 1998).

123. Richard Rosenfeld, Robert Fornango, and Eric Baumer, "Did Cease Fire, COMPSTAT, and EXILE Reduce Homicide," *Criminology and Public Policy* 4, no. 3 (2005): 414–477.

124. John MacDonald, Jeffrey Fagan, and Amanda Geller, "The Effects of Local Police Surges on Crime and Arrests in New York City," PLoS ONE 11, no. 6 (2016): e0157223. doi:10.1371/journal.pone.0157223

125. Charles M. Katz, Vincent J. Webb, and David R. Schaefer, "An Assessment of the Impact of Quality-of-Life Policing on Crime and Disorder," *Justice Quarterly* 18, 4 (2001): 825–876.

126. Robert Panzarella, "Bratton Reinvents 'Harassment Model' of Policing," *Law Enforcement News* (June 15–30, 1998): 13–15.

127. Ray Rivera et al., "A Few Blocks, 4 Years, 52,000 Police Stops," *New York Times*, July 12, 2010, A1.

128. Jennifer Fratello, Andrés F. Rengifo, and Jennifer Trone, *Coming of Age with Stop and Frisk: Experiences, Self-Perceptions, and Public Safety Implications* (New York: Vera Institute of Justice, 2013).

129. Lawrence Sherman, "Policing for Crime Prevention," *Preventing Crime: What Works, What Doesn't, What's Promising—A Report to the Attorney General of the United States*, 8–1 to 8–58.

130. Al Baker, "City Minorities More Likely to be Frisked," *New York Times*, May 13, 2010, A1.
131. Green, "Community Policing in America"
132. Harcourt, "Reflecting on the Subject," 48.
133. Christian Parenti, *Lockdown America: Police and Prisons in the Age of Crisis* (New York: Verso, 2000).
134. White and Fradella, *Stop and Frisk*.
135. Ibid.
136. Anthony A. Braga, Brandon C. Welsh, and Cory Schnell, "Can Policing Disorder Reduce Crime? A Systematic Review and Meta-Analysis," *Journal of Research in Crime and Delinquency* 52, no. 4 (2015): 567–588.
137. Ronald D. Hunter and Thomas Barker, "BS and Buzzwords: The New Police Operational Style," *American Journal of Police* 12, no. 3 (1993), 157–168.
138. Bayley, *Police for the Future*, 101.
139. Goldstein, "Toward Community-Oriented Policing," 27; Skolnick and Bayley, *The New Blue Line*.

© Hill Street Studios/Getty Images

PART IV

Issues in Policing

CHAPTER **11** Police Discretion

CHAPTER **12** Legitimacy and Police-Community Relations

CHAPTER **13** Police Corruption

CHAPTER **14** Accountability of the Police

© Hill Street Studios/Getty Images

Police Discretion

CHAPTER OUTLINE

Discretion in Police Work
A Definition of Discretion
New Perspectives on Police Discretion
    A Short History of the Study of
      Police Discretion
    A Richer Understanding of Police-
      Citizen Encounters
    Potential Abuse of Discretion
    Positive Uses of Discretion
Decision Points and Decision Makers
    Patrol Officers' Decisions
    Detectives' Decisions
    Police Managers' Decisions
Underlying Sources of Police
Discretion
    The Nature of the Criminal Law
    Conflicting Public Expectations
    Social and Medical Issues

    The Work Environment of Policing
    Limited Police Resources
Factors Limiting Patrol Officer
Discretion
    Legal Factors
    Administrative Factors
    Organizational Culture Factors
Factors Influencing Discretionary
Arrest Decisions
    Situational Factors
    Organizational Factors
    Social and Political Factors
The Control of Discretion
    The Need for Control
    Abolish Discretion?
    Enhancing Professional Judgment
    Informal Bureaucratic Controls

Administrative Rulemaking: Controls through Written Policies
Examples of Administrative Rulemaking
Principles of Administrative Rulemaking
Contributions of Written Rules
The Impact of Administrative Rulemaking

Ensuring Compliance with Rules
Codifying Rules: The Standard Operating Procedure Manual
Systematic Rulemaking
Citizen Oversight and Policymaking
The Limits of Administrative Rulemaking

CASE STUDY

Summary
Key Terms
For Discussion
Internet Exercises

P olice officers routinely exercise discretion while doing their jobs. They make important decisions that affect citizens' lives and liberty: whether or not to stop a car, whether or not to make an arrest, and so on. This chapter examines the phenomenon of police discretion. It covers the underlying reasons for discretion, how discretion is used, the problems that result from its misuse, and different strategies for controlling it.

Discretion in Police Work

A police officer patrolling a city park sees three young men hanging out together. He investigates and finds they are drinking beer in public in violation of a local ordinance. At least one and possibly two of them may be underage. The officer confiscates the beer, pours it out, and tells them to get out of the park. He could have issued citations but exercised his discretion not to do so.

This incident is typical of police discretion. Officers routinely decide not to arrest people who are obviously breaking the law. Other examples of discretion include the following:

- **Domestic dispute arrests.** Donald Black found that police arrested only 58 percent of people suspected of committing felonious assault in domestic violence situations.[1] That is, 42 percent of people suspected of committing a felonious domestic violence assault were allowed to go free, and left in a position to immediately assault the victim again.

- **Mental health commitments.** Linda Teplin reported that only 11.8 percent of persons judged mentally disordered were referred to a medical facility.[2] Police regularly deal with people having a mental health crisis. Only a few are arrested; many incidents are minor and officers resolve the situation by simply restoring order.

- **Traffic enforcement.** Traffic stops are the most common form of contact between the police and the public. In 2011, almost half (42 percent) of all contacts with the police involved a traffic stop. In 2011, police officers used their discretion to issue 4.8 percent of all white drivers a ticket, compared with 7 percent of African American and 6.2 percent of Hispanic drivers.[3]

For a full discussion
of policing domestic
disputes, see
Chapter 8.

- **Deadly force.** In 2015, 40 percent of people shot and killed by the police who were unarmed were African American, a clear racial disparity based on population data. What this means is that a large number of whites in roughly similar situations, who were also unarmed, were not shot. The decision to use deadly force is the ultimate life-and-death discretionary decision made by police officers.[4]

A Definition of Discretion

discretion

In his pioneering work on the subject, law professor Kenneth C. Davis defined **discretion** as (1) an official action (2) by a criminal justice official (3) based on that individual's judgment about the best course of action.[5] Discretion operates in the gap between what the law states and an official taking no action at all.

Discretion pervades the entire criminal justice system. Wayne LaFave argues that "it is helpful to look at the total criminal justice system as a series of interrelated discretionary choices."[6] Police officers decide to arrest or not arrest. An arrest is dismissed at the police station because the sergeant thinks there is insufficient evidence. A judge sets a very high bail of $100,000 that the defendant cannot raise. Another judge excludes evidence because of an unconstitutional search and seizure. One judge sentences someone convicted of assault to probation and another person to prison for essentially the same crime. The parole board decides to release one inmate on parole, but not another inmate with roughly the same criminal history. Finally, a judge sentences some people convicted of first-degree murder to the death penalty while sentencing others convicted of the same offense to life imprisonment.

New Perspectives on Police Discretion

A Short History of the Study of Police Discretion

Our understanding of police discretion has gone through several periods, ranging from complete denial to today's sophisticated efforts by officers on how to better use their discretion through detailed policies and training over those policies. The four different eras of our understanding of police discretion are as follows:

era of denial

1. *The era of denial:* Prior to the mid-1960s, there was virtually no recognition that police officers routinely exercise discretion.[7] During the **era of denial,** police officials regularly denied that officers did not enforce all the laws. In some states, in fact, failing to enforce the law was a crime. Police leaders refused to acknowledge the fact that officers exercised discretion because they did not want to have to explain to the public what they were doing and why.
2. *The "discovery" of discretion era:* The research project that "discovered" discretion involved the field observational studies of policing by the American Bar Foundation in the mid-1950s.[8] The 1967 President's Crime Commission was the first authoritative body to argue that police departments should adopt policies to control such important decisions as the use of deadly force.[9] The first person to fully address the issue of discretion was Kenneth C. Davis in his 1975 book, *Police Discretion.*[10]

3. *The controlling discretion era:* The open recognition of police discretion, the recommendation of the President's Crime Commission, and the work of Kenneth C. Davis and Herman Goldstein led to the first efforts by police departments to control discretion.[11] The strategy for control involved what is known in the law as administrative rulemaking. In brief, administrative rulemaking involves police departments developing their own rules on how officers should handle such incidents as the use of deadly force, high-speed pursuits, responding to persons experiencing mental health crises, and many more. Administrative rulemaking is today a basic part of police management. Much of this chapter is devoted to how it operates in practice.[12]

4. *The era of training for the exercise of discretion:* One of the most important recent developments in police training (which we discussed in Chapter 5) is a new emphasis on preparing officers to understand and utilize the broad range of options available to best handle difficult situations.[13] Underlying this new development is the goal of reducing officer use of force, including by de-escalating potentially violent situations. Additionally, there is increased recognition that many incidents often change significantly as they unfold, sometimes in a matter of minutes. The best thinking in police training today, as explained in Chapter 5, seeks to teach officers how to assess and continually reassess an incident, choose the right course of action (that is, use their discretion), and change that course of action when appropriate.

For a detailed discussion of innovations in police training related to the exercise of discretion, see Chapter 5.

A Richer Understanding of Police–Citizen Encounters

Another important development related to police discretion is the growth of a richer understanding of the complexity of police–citizen encounters. To an unfortunate degree, public thinking about police shootings, for example, has been shaped by the idea of a "split-second decision." This idea assumes that a person with a weapon appears suddenly, and the officer has no choice but to use deadly force. Traditional research on discretion, meanwhile, has generally used dichotomous variables: shoot/no shoot, arrest/no arrest, physical force/no force, and so on. In reality, however, most incidents, as we have already suggested, are scenarios that unfold over time, and often change in important ways.

Jennifer Schulenberg's research is particularly valuable in reconceptualizing the exercise of discretion. Conceptualizing a police–citizen encounter in terms of an arrest/no arrest dichotomy does not adequately capture all that happens in the incident. Her study takes into account other aspects of the encounter: first, "conversational directives" and officer requests for information; and second, police assistance to someone at the scene of the incident.[14] In a particular incident, an officer has to choose between these different responses. And within each response, there are choices to be made about what kind of information to ask for, what kind of assistance to render, and so on.

The new thinking about police training, as we learned in Chapter 5, is the need to train officers to continually assess and reassess the incident and to consider a different course of action.[15] If a situation suddenly becomes more dangerous and poses

Police Discretion in an Unfolding Disturbance Call

Stage 1: Officer dispatched to 911 call about a "disturbance."

　　Officer response: How should the officer prepare himself or herself for the call?

Stage 2: Officer arrives on scene and discovers that there is a mentally ill person acting out.

　　Officer response: What actions should the officer take? Call for backup? Handle the situation alone?

Stage 3: The mentally ill person says he will kill the officer.

　　Officer response: Should the officer change his or her plan of action? If so, in what way? Draw his or her weapon? Call for backup (if not done already)? Attempt verbal de-escalation?

Stage 4: The mentally ill person picks up a baseball bat.

　　Officer response: What should the officer do? Order the person to drop the bat? Threaten to shoot him? Attempt verbal de-escalation?

Stage 5: The mentally ill person says, "Go ahead and shoot me. I want to die."

　　Officer response: What should the officer do now? Shoot him? Try more verbal de-escalation?

Stage 6: The mentally ill person throws the bat away. (It is now at a safe distance from him.)

　　Officer response: What should the officer do now? Order him to lie on the ground? Threaten arrest?

Stage 7: The mentally ill person falls to the ground, crying.

　　Officer response: Now what should the officer do?

Final stage: What should the officer do to bring the incident to an end?

---

a threat to someone, including the officer, the use of force becomes the better choice. But if a situation suddenly becomes less dangerous—say, for example, the mentally ill person becomes less angry and belligerent—de-escalation becomes the better choice. The training director from the Los Angeles Police Department explained that, in the past, they "told recruits to sit down, shut up, and listen for six months." Today, they want "to create officers who are self-motivated, interdependent, community-motivated critical thinkers and problem-solvers."[16]

Potential Abuse of Discretion

Discretion can be misused in several different ways:

- **Discrimination.** The misuse of discretion can involve discrimination against racial or ethnic minorities. The New York City Police Department's aggressive stop and frisk program was declared unconstitutional, in part, because of discrimination against African Americans and Hispanics in violation of the Fourteenth Amendment.[17] Racial profiling in traffic stops has also been a major controversy.[18]

- **Denial of due process.** Deliberately harassing suspected drug dealers, prostitutes, and pimps to chase them out of the neighborhood rather than arresting them is an abuse of discretion.[19]

- **Systematic under-enforcement of the law.** Systematic under-enforcement of the law—for example, tolerating after-hours clubs in a certain neighborhood—can damage the quality of life in that area. Historically, the police tolerated gambling, prostitution, and after-hours clubs in poor and racial minority neighborhoods.[20] In his classic study of American race relations in the 1940s, Gunnar Myrdal found that, in the South, where segregation prevailed, the police did not make arrests for crimes committed by whites against African Americans and often did not arrest African Americans for crimes against other African Americans.[21]

- **Poor personnel management.** Effective supervision requires clear performance standards. Officers need to be provided clear guidelines regarding how they are to handle different situations. If there are no guidelines and discretion is completely unregulated, it is impossible to fairly evaluate the officers' performance. A sergeant may give one officer a high performance evaluation and another officer a poor one, but without any evidence of how well the two officers comply with department policies.[22]

- **Inconsistent policy.** If officers on the street make decisions inconsistent with department policy, the policy will not be carried out in a consistent and fair manner. A 2015 report on the Philadelphia Police Department training program found inconsistent policies and training on use of force. Different parts of the department's policies contradicted each other.[23]

 For a full discussion of racial and ethnic discrimination arising from the misuse of discretion, see Chapter 12.

Positive Uses of Discretion

A patrol officer is dispatched to an attempted burglary call at 1 A.M. The residents were sleeping and heard the sound of a break-in. The officer investigates but finds no evidence of an attempted break-in (for example, no marks on any door or window). He tells the residents that it must have been some noise, does not complete a crime report, and leaves. The officer has used his or her discretion to "unfound" a crime because of a lack of evidence. This is an example of a **positive use of discretion.**

positive use of discretion

In fact, unfounding crimes is very common.[24] In the preceding example, it represents a good choice. But it can be abused. If officers regularly unfound domestic assaults, it has several bad results: It keeps the official crime rate artificially low, leads to an understatement of the prevalence of domestic violence in the community, and leaves many victims vulnerable to be assaulted again by the same person.

Discretion can be used in proper ways, to promote effective and efficient police work. Examples include the following:

- **The use of good judgment.** In one of the earlier examples we have cited, the police officer exercised his or her professional judgment in determining that no crime had been committed and that there should be no crime report. In this case, there was no objective evidence of a crime and therefore no basis for a crime report. Recent changes in training in the Los Angeles Police Department involve an emphasis on training officers to continually assess and reassess difficult incidents to adjust their actions as the situation changes and use their judgment about the most reasonable response.[25]

- **Efficient use of scarce police resources.** The police cannot possibly enforce all of the criminal laws. They do not have enough officers to arrest everyone who violates the law, and the courts could not handle all of the cases.[26] By using good judgment to concentrate on the more serious crimes (for example, robberies) and disregard less serious ones (for example, kids drinking in the park), the police can make more efficient use of their time. Kenneth C. Davis comments in this regard that "[t]he common sense of the officers very often prevails over the legislative excesses in criminal legislation."[27]

- **Individualized justice.** The proper use of discretion can allow officers to individualize justice and choose the best course of action for particular events. A juvenile may have in fact violated the law, but in the case of a relatively minor offense, an arrest might not be the best response for that individual. The President's Task Force on 21st Century Policing, for example, recommended that police departments "consider adopting preferences for seeking 'least harm' resolutions, such as diversion programs or warnings and citations in lieu of arrest for minor infractions" (Action Item 4.1.1).[28]

- **Sound public policy.** The proper use of discretion can allow police departments to make sound judgments about public policy, in the sense of what is best for the whole community, or what is the best solution for the underlying problem. Many homeless people, for example, do things that could justify an arrest (for example, camping out in public parks, where they might technically be obstructing the sidewalk). Arresting them, however, might not be the best way to treat homelessness. Similarly, as we just pointed out, the President's Task Force recommended utilizing nonarrest alternatives for juveniles who have committed minor infractions.

For a discussion of innovations in police training designed to improve the judgment of police officers in police–citizen encounters, see Chapter 5.

Another example involves marijuana policy. Public attitudes are changing about whether marijuana possession for recreational purposes should be a crime, and several states have decriminalized mere possession for that purpose. Additionally, a 2013 ACLU report on marijuana arrests found that African American males are 3.7 times more likely than whites to be arrested for marijuana possession.[29] For these reasons, some experts argue that, even without a change in the law, it would be a sound public policy for the police to simply deemphasize arrests for marijuana possession.

Decision Points and Decision Makers

Police discretion is not limited to patrol officers, and not only to the decision to arrest or not arrest. Officers at different ranks make discretionary decisions covering a wide range of actions. The following sections list some of the major discretionary decisions made by officers in different assignments.[30]

Patrol Officers' Decisions

Discretionary decisions by patrol officers related to *law enforcement* situations include the following:

- To patrol an area more intensively than normal.
- To conduct a high-speed pursuit.
- To stop, question, and frisk a suspect.
- To make an arrest.
- To use physical or deadly force.

Decisions by patrol officers in *order maintenance* situations include the following:

- To mediate a domestic dispute rather than make an arrest.
- To suggest or even tell one of the people in a disorder situation to leave the premises.
- To refer a person to a social service agency (for example, alcohol abuse treatment).
- To commit a mentally disturbed person to a mental health facility.

Detectives' Decisions

Decisions by detectives related to *criminal investigations* include the following:

- To stop investigating a crime because of a lack of good leads.
- To seek a warrant for a search.
- To conduct a stakeout.
- To question or not question a potential suspect.

Police Managers' Decisions

Police managers, including chiefs and other high-ranking department officials, make discretionary decisions about *law enforcement policy* and priorities. These include the following:

- To adopt community policing or problem-oriented policing.
- To give high priority to traffic law violations.
- To ignore minor drug offenses such as possession of small amounts of marijuana.
- To crack down on prostitution.
- To give social gambling low priority.

Underlying Sources of Police Discretion

Discretion is the result of several sources related to the nature of policing itself.

The Nature of the Criminal Law

It is often said that if all the laws in this country were fully enforced, we would all be in jail or prison. There is a lot of truth to this statement. The **broad scope of the criminal law** in the United States creates significant problems for the police, which they deal with through the exercise of their discretion.

broad scope of the criminal law

Consider the following example. Two officers are dispatched to a bar on the basis of a reported disorder. They arrive and calm things down. It is clear that hostile words were exchanged between two people. One of them probably said something about "getting" the other guy. Did these words constitute a threat of assault? The guy who made the remark had a pool cue in his hand and may have moved it in a threatening manner. Did this constitute threat with a dangerous weapon? The responding officers have to decide whether to make any arrests.

POLICE in FOCUS

Avoiding Crime-Fighting Strategies That Harm Communities

It is now recognized that police departments have adopted some aggressive crime-fighting strategies that harm police–community relations. These include aggressive stop and frisk programs; intensive patrol of high-crime neighborhoods, where the police presence begins to appear to be like a military occupation; and zero-tolerance policing, in which police officers focus on minor offenses such as loitering or urinating in public.

Choosing such programs are an example of discretionary decisions by police managers. The question is whether the cost in terms of police–community relations—in particular, in trust and confidence in the police—outweighs whatever gains there might be in terms of crime control.

In 1968, after four years of riots all across the country, the Kerner Commission concluded that aggressive anti-crime programs damage community relations. Forty-seven years later, the President's Task Force on 21st Century Policing drew the same conclusion. It recommended that "[l]aw enforcement agencies should consider the potential damage to public trust when implementing crime fighting strategies" (Recommendation 1.6). The report noted that "numerous witnesses" had told the task force about the damage done by aggressive anti-crime policies in the public hearings it held around the country.

Source: National Advisory Commission Civil Disorders, *Report* (New York: Bantam Books, 1968), 304; President's Task Force Report on 21st Century Policing, *Final Report* (Washington, DC: U.S. Department of Justice, 2015), 16.

The nature of the criminal law demands that officers exercise discretion. The law defines particular crimes—assault, for example—but officers on the street have to determine whether the facts of a particular case fit the definition. Offenses such as disorderly conduct or public nuisance are particularly vague, opening the door for the greatest exercise and possible abuse of discretion. Many observers of the American legal system express concern about the "overreach" or "over-breadth" of the criminal law, the fact that it covers so many behaviors that the police could not possibly fully enforce.[31]

Conflicting Public Expectations

One of the main reasons the criminal law in the United States covers so many different kinds of behavior is that the American people have conflicting public expectations about what behavior should be illegal. The most obvious conflicts occur between people or business interests that want to keep streets and neighborhoods free of crime and disorder. This often results in pressure on the police to try to keep "undesirable-looking" people out of those areas through frequent stops and frisks, arrests for obstructing a public walkway, or simply telling people to move on. If someone is clearly breaking the law, by obstructing a sidewalk or urinating in public, an arrest is justified. But if the person is simply poor and unemployed, and looks shabby, there is no legal justification for an arrest. Being poor is a condition, not an act. There is a long history in the United States of cities and states enacting vagrancy laws to keep poor and/or unemployed people out of areas where other people do not want them.[32]

The law criminalizes a lot of activity that many people also regard as acceptable recreation: gambling, drinking, and certain forms of private sexual behavior, for instance. In recent decades, the law has changed significantly on some of these issues. Legal gambling in the form of poker and blackjack used to be available only in Las Vegas, where the state had legalized it long ago. Gambling on horse racing was limited to a few states. Today, gambling casinos exist all across the country. Illegal gambling on sports remains a huge enterprise nationwide, but how many police departments or state law enforcement agencies devote any effort to enforcing the law on this activity? The Supreme Court declared sodomy laws, which criminalized sex between two people of the same sex, to be unconstitutional. A number of states have legalized the medical use of marijuana, and by 2016 four states and the District of Columbia had legalized the recreational use of that drug.[33] In short, public opinion about different kinds of behavior continues to change, and the courts have also decriminalized certain behaviors.

Officers are often caught between these conflicting expectations and use their discretion about the best course of action. As we noted in Chapter 6, pp. 196–198, these pressures are often a source of job stress.[34]

Social and Medical Issues

The criminal law is widely used to deal with social and medical issues such as home-lessness, chronic alcohol abuse, or mental health problems.[35] The problem of people with mental health problems has gotten significantly worse in recent years, because of serious problems with the mental health systems across the country. A study of police discretion in the handling of mentally ill people in Canada found that the lack of community mental health services, particularly after normal business hours, put serious limits on the options available to officers there.[36] One senior commander in the Portland, Oregon, police department told Justice Department investigators in 2012 that, during his career, police encounters with mentally ill people had increased from "a couple of times a month to a couple of times a day."[37] Police officers on the street have to use their discretion about whether to arrest a mentally disturbed person, refer him or her to a social service program, or simply restore order to the situation and leave.

The Work Environment of Policing

The 911 communications center receives a call about a disturbance in an apartment, and two patrol officers are dispatched to the scene. They arrive to find clear evidence of a physical assault: The woman is bruised, and the man may also have been hit. The department has a mandatory arrest policy directing officers to make an arrest where there is evidence of a felonious assault. It is about 20 minutes until shift change, the officers are tired from a busy night of 911 calls, and so they just give the two people a verbal warning and leave. In effect, the officers have undermined the department's mandatory arrest policy. Decisions, in short, are often made on the basis of the immediate circumstances of the job on at a given moment.

For a discussion of the organizational work environment of policing, see Chapter 6.

This example illustrates one of the special features of police work: The lowest-ranking employees—patrol officers—exercise the greatest amount of discretion. James Q. Wilson comments that, in policing, "discretion increases as one moves down the organizational hierarchy."[38] For this reason, patrol officers have been

street-level bureaucrats   described as **street-level bureaucrats.** They make the decisions that produce actual police policy that people receive.[39]

In most organizations, the crucial decisions are made at the top of the organization. In wartime, generals decide when and where to attack. Foot solders carry out their orders; it is not their job to think about what to do. Policing is very different. Although the criminal law and police department policies state what is supposed to be done, it is the officer on the street who makes the decision about what will actually happen. The case of a minor in possession of alcohol is a great example. The law and police policy say that is illegal behavior and that the juvenile should be arrested. But the officer, for a variety of reasons, may decide not to arrest. In effect, the officer decides what "the law" really is. Later in this chapter, we discuss the various reasons that can affect an officer's decision in this kind of situation.

Through their discretion to arrest or not arrest, police officers are the *gatekeepers* of the entire criminal justice system. They determine the system's workload. If they do not arrest, there is no case for the rest of the system to handle. Police discretion, in short, determines *actual* public policy, which is not the same what the law says or a department's *official* policy. If police officers systematically do not make arrests for possession of small amounts of marijuana, for example, they effectively decriminalize that offense.

Jerome Skolnick observed years ago that "police work constitutes the most secluded part of an already secluded system of criminal justice and therefore offers the greatest opportunity for arbitrary behavior."[40] Three aspects of the work environment contribute to the exercise of discretion. Patrol officers work alone or in pairs. The Project on Policing Neighborhoods observed patrol work in two cities and found that in half of all encounters with citizens only one officer was present.[41] In many critical incidents, there is no direct supervision by a sergeant (often the sergeant arrives after the important decisions are made). Many police–citizen encounters occur in private places (domestic disturbance calls are the best example), with no other observers present—observers who might be able to testify about the officer's behavior.[42]

low-visibility work   For all these reasons, policing has been described as **low-visibility work.**[43]

Hidden from public view, police officers have tremendous opportunity to choose whatever course of action they prefer, and this work environment creates the opportunity for using and potentially abusing discretion.

Limited Police Resources

It is Saturday night, and the 911 communications center is flooded with calls for service. Patrol officers are running from one call to another, and for about two hours there are always several calls waiting for dispatch. On one call, the patrol officer could make an arrest for disorderly conduct in a parking lot outside of a bar. But there are other calls waiting, some of which involve more serious incidents, so the officer gives the person a stern warning and moves on to another call.

There are only so many officers on duty at any one time, and they have only so much time during a regular shift. In addition, they are often short handed because of sick leave or vacations by other members of their unit. Calls continue to come into the 911 system. Patrol officers cannot possibly handle every situation that comes up, and they have to exercise their discretion about how to use their time.[44] Adding to the problem is the simple fact that an arrest is a time-consuming event. Arresting, transporting, and booking a suspect may take one to three hours. Some arrests, moreover, may involve more than one officer.[45]

Finally, the economic recession that began in 2008, and continues to affect many city budgets, has aggravated the problem of short-handed police departments. Many have not been able to hire enough officers to completely replace those who have retired, resigned, or been fired. A 2013 Police Executive Research Forum report on the economic crisis reported that many police chiefs said that coping with the economic crisis had become "the dominant part of their job in recent years."[46]

Factors Limiting Patrol Officer Discretion

Police officers may work alone most of the time, and spend most of their time free of any direct supervision by their sergeants, but they are not completely free to do just anything they want. A patrol officer's discretion is limited and controlled by a number of different factors.[47]

Legal Factors

The law imposes significant constraints on police officer actions.

The Criminal Law

The criminal law specifies the behaviors that are criminal. A police officer cannot arrest a person for no reason. Admittedly, however, offenses such as disturbing the peace and public nuisance are so vague that officers can abuse them.

The Law of Criminal Procedure

The law of criminal procedure limits police discretion with requirements for searches and seizure and interrogations. The U.S. Supreme Court and state courts have fleshed out these statutes, most famously in such decisions as *Mapp v. Ohio* on searches and *Miranda v. Arizona* on interrogations. In pretrial hearings and at trial, defense attorneys challenge officer conduct under these decisions, and the prosecution runs the risk of having evidence or confessions excluded, and thereby losing the case.

Officers can covertly work around the law. They can, for example, conduct a search that is unconstitutional under the Fourth Amendment if it were scrutinized carefully. But they do so knowing that it's wrong, and that if they go too far and do this too many times, they might get caught. Much depends on the quality of supervision in the department and whether their immediate supervisors allow them to do things that are wrong. In the end, though, the law does set important limits on officer behavior.

Administrative Factors

Department Policy

Department policies provide the basic guidance to officers on what they may and may not do. The process of controlling discretion through written policies is known as administrative rulemaking. Policies cover the use of deadly force, physical force, handling of people who are have a mental health crisis, and many other situations.

 For a discussion of the impact of department policies on the police officer exercise of discretion, see Chapter 14.

Supervision

The enforcement of department policies is the responsibility of supervisors. For a patrol officer, that means a sergeant who signs off on all arrests, approves use-of-force reports, and has the authority to write up an officer for violating a department policy. Street sergeants have different styles of work; some are strict "rule-enforcers," while others act more as "friends" of the officers under their command and often try to shield them from discipline.[48] The quality of supervision depends heavily on the *span of control,* the number of officers under one supervisor's command. A span of control of eight to one is the generally recommended ratio. If a street supervisor has responsibility for more than eight patrol officers, the quality of supervision begins to erode.

Organizational Culture Factors

Police Officer Subculture

In Chapter 6, we discussed the police officer subculture. It has a powerful informal impact on officer conduct, including the exercise of discretion. If officers know that other officers will not report any misconduct to supervisors, their misconduct will continue. The 2016 report of the mayor's task force on the Chicago Police Department, for example, found that the "code of silence" among officers was a major barrier to accountability.[49]

Factors Influencing Discretionary Arrest Decisions

The exercise of discretion in arrest situations is influenced by a number of factors.

Situational Factors

situational factors

Police discretion is influenced by the circumstances of each situation. Studies of the decision to arrest, for example, have found that it is affected by several **situational factors.**

Seriousness of the Crime

The more serious the crime, the more likely the officer is to make an arrest. Black found that officers made arrests in 58 percent of suspected felonies but in only 44 percent of suspected misdemeanors. He concluded that "the probability of arrest is higher in legally serious crime situations than those of a relatively minor nature."[50] Seriousness of the situation also affects the handling of mental illness incidents. The more serious the disorder, or the more likely it is to offend other people, the higher the probability of arrest or commitment to a medical facility.[51]

The seriousness of an offense is a legal factor, and consequently is a legitimate factor for an officer to take into account in exercising his or her discretion. Not arresting a minor for possession of alcohol is a reasonable exercise of discretion, but not arresting someone for a felonious assault in a domestic violence situation is not a reasonable choice.

Strength of the Evidence

The police are more likely to arrest in situations where the evidence of the crime is strong. In crimes against persons, and in many property crimes, the primary evidence is the testimony of a victim or witness. When that kind of evidence or testimony does not exist, arrest is much less likely.[52]

The strength of the evidence is a major factor in whether or not a suspect will be convicted if arrested. Therefore, it is a reasonable exercise of discretion for an officer not to make an arrest where the evidence is weak.

Preference of the Victim

Two officers respond to a domestic disturbance call. There is some evidence that the man hit the woman. One of the officers asks the woman, "Do you want us to take him in?" She says "no." The other officer asks, "Are you sure? We can, you know." She says "no" again. The officers warn the man and leave.

The **preference of the victim** is likely to have a significant impact on whether a suspect would be convicted if arrested. If the victim refuses to cooperate with the prosecutor, the case will almost certainly be dismissed. Therefore, it is a reasonable exercise of discretion to not make an arrest if the victim clearly indicates that he or she does not want an arrest.

A number of studies have found that an arrest is more likely when the victim or complaining party asks for an arrest. Conversely, police are unlikely to arrest when the victim clearly indicates that he or she does not want an arrest. Black found that "arrest practices sharply reflect the preferences of citizen complainants."[53]

preference of the victim

Relationship between Victim and Suspect

Arrests are more likely when the victim and offender are strangers and are less likely when the two parties are married. In the past, police officers regarded domestic violence incidents as private matters and did not arrest abusive husbands.[54] Recent mandatory arrest policies are designed to ensure arrest in all felonious assault cases, regardless of the relationship of the two parties.

The relationship of the victim and the suspect is an extra-legal factor, and therefore should not be a factor in an officer's decision about whether to arrest. For the police to systematically not arrest husbands in domestic violence incidents is a form of sex discrimination and a denial of equal protection of the law.

Demeanor of the Suspect

Black and others found that the **demeanor of the suspect** is an important factor in arrest decisions: "The probability of arrest and officer use of force increases when a suspect is disrespectful toward the police."[55]

demeanor of the suspect

The demeanor of the suspect—rudeness or verbal disrespect of the officer—is an extra-legal factor and therefore is not a reasonable factor for an officer to take into account in an arrest decision. If the suspect assaults or threatens the officer, of course, that constitutes a separate offense and is a reasonable basis for deciding to arrest.

The demeanor of the suspect is a complex phenomenon, however. Klinger argues that in many situations the disrespect occurred *after* the arrest and, therefore, was a consequence and not a cause of the arrest.[56] At the same time, citizen hostility or disrespect can be triggered by the officer's demeanor or action. In an important breakthrough, Roger Dunham and Geoffrey Alpert studied the sequence of events in a set of police–citizen interactions. They found that the demeanor of both officers and citizens changed as the encounter developed. In about one-quarter of the encounters,

> ### S I D E B A R   11–2
>
> ## Discussion: Legal and Extralegal Factors in Officer Discretion
>
> *The situational factors affecting police discretion fall into two categories: legal and extralegal. Legal factors are those related to the legality of the conduct involved, such as the seriousness of the crime and the strength of the evidence. Extralegal factors are those that have nothing to do with legality of the conduct involved, such as the relationship of the offender and the victim.*
>
> - Most experts argue that legal factors are appropriate for an officer to take into consideration. Do you agree?
> - Is it appropriate for an officer to take into consideration the seriousness of the crime when deciding whether or not to make an arrest? Explain why. If you think it is not appropriate, explain why not.
> - Is it appropriate for an officer to take into consideration the strength of the evidence when deciding whether to make an arrest? Explain why. If you think it is not appropriate, explain why not.

the officer's demeanor changed. In half of those cases, the officer's demeanor changed for the better (that is, became more respectful), and in the other half, it changed for the worse (that is, became less respectful). Meanwhile, in slightly more than half of all encounters (52 percent), the citizen's demeanor improved, while in the other 48 percent it got worse.[57] The significant insight in Dunham and Alpert's study is that police–citizen encounters are *fluid,* with attitudes and behavior on both sides often changing. It misrepresents reality to record incidents at a single moment in time.

Officers have the capacity to shape how a particular incident unfolds. The new emphasis in police training, as we discussed in Chapter 5, is on officer decision-making as incidents unfold. There is particular emphasis on de-escalation to avoid uses of force. Through the use of body language, questions, attempts to change the subject, and other strategies, an officer can turn an encounter away from conflict and into a peaceful resolution. Choosing de-escalation is an important discretionary decision.[58]

Most police–citizen interactions are routine and uneventful, with neither side exhibiting disrespect to the other or using force. Stephen Mastrofski and colleagues investigated the extent to which citizens comply with requests from police officers by observing 346 interactions in which officers asked or told a citizen (or citizens) to do something: (1) leave another person or persons alone, (2) calm down or cease being disorderly, or (3) cease illegal behavior. Citizens complied with officer requests in 78 percent of the observed cases. Failure to comply increased the chances of arrest. In 28 percent of the failure-to-comply cases, the officer made an arrest.[59]

Characteristics of the Victim

Some decisions are based on characteristics of the victim, reflecting a moral judgment about the victim by the police officer. Gary LaFree found substantial evidence that police officers discounted the allegations of rape victims whose lifestyle was nonconformist, as indicated for example by their clothing or grooming.[60] This involved women who did not fit traditional middle-class standards of women's behavior. Christy Visher found that women who conform to traditional gender role stereotypes are likely to be treated more leniently than men who are suspected of the same offense. Women who violate gender role expectations, however, do not receive preferential treatment.[61]

The characteristics of the crime victim are extra-legal factors and therefore are not a legitimate basis for an officer deciding whether or not to arrest. Arresting people because of their race or ethnicity, of course, is a blatant form of discrimination, as is arresting or not arresting someone because of his or her gender.

Race, Ethnicity, and Gender of the Citizen

There is also evidence that arrest decisions are based on race. A review of 40 research reports determined that non-white suspects are significantly more likely to be arrested, compared to white suspects, even when taking into consideration the relevant situational factors. Likewise, the ethnicity of the victim has been found to be related to arrest.[62] For example, Douglas Smith and colleagues found that police officers were more responsive to white victims who complained about black suspects, particularly in property crimes.[63]

The "driving while black" controversy suggests that in some traffic enforcement situations, decisions to stop drivers are heavily influenced by race and ethnicity. In Maryland and New Jersey, data from surveys of traffic enforcement patterns indicate that state troopers were stopping a disproportionate number of African American drivers on interstate highways.[64] The New York City Police Department's controversial stop and frisk program was found to be unconstitutional in 2013 because it targeted African American and Hispanic people.[65]

Characteristics of the Neighborhood

The immediate work environment also influences police discretion. James F. Fyfe found that officers working in high-crime neighborhoods fired their weapons more than twice as often as officers working in low-crime areas.[66] Higher-crime areas have more incidents (especially robberies) in which an officer is likely to confront an armed criminal and use deadly force in response. Smith and colleagues, meanwhile, found that police officers were more likely to make arrests in low-income neighborhoods than in higher-income areas, with the result that poor whites and poor blacks were more likely to be arrested than people in higher-income areas.[67] Arrests for vagrancy are rare on skid row but more common when a homeless person wanders into the central business district.[68]

David Klinger's seminal work on negotiating order in patrol work provides a neighborhood-level theory of the police response to crime. He maintains that the police response to crime is contingent on neighborhood levels of crime. Contrary to Smith and colleagues' findings, Klinger argues that as neighborhood levels of crime increase, officer workload also increases, resulting in patrol officers having less time to respond to less serious neighborhood problems. Patrol officers in turn become more cynical about the quality of life in the neighborhood and are less likely to believe that victims are worthy of their attention. As a consequence, officers working in high-crime neighborhoods are less likely to enforce the law. Klinger's theory suggests that officer discretion in enforcing the law is heavily influenced by the neighborhood in which they work.[69]

Characteristics of the Individual Officer

Many people believe that different kinds of officers will act differently on the street—meaning that they will exercise their discretion in a different manner. As we discussed in Chapter 6, studies of police behavior have not found any significant differences in the performance of white, African American or Hispanic officers, or in the performance of male and female officers.

For a discussion of the influence of different supervisors' styles of work, see Chapter 6.

Officers also have different styles of work. In his observational research on Los Angeles police officers, criminologist Steve Herbert found that they had labels to describe their fellow officers. "Hard chargers" were active, often aggressive officers who would volunteer to handle potentially dangerous situations, and enjoyed the excitement of high-speed pursuits. Some others, meanwhile, were labeled "station queens" because they were seen as avoiding danger.[70]

Summary

In the end, what we know about police officer discretion is that it is extremely complex and influenced by a number of different factors at the situational level. At the same time, however, as the preceding discussion indicates, there are clear patterns in how different factors influence discretion. This does not mean, for example, that police officers always make arrests in the more serious crime situations, but it does mean that they generally do so. In short, police exercise of discretion has a certain degree of predictability.

Organizational Factors

Official Department Policy

For a more detailed discussion of the impact of written department policies on police discretion, see "The Control of Discretion" section later in this chapter, as well as Chapter 14.

Official department policies have a powerful influence over police discretion. Fyfe found that a restrictive "defense of life" shooting policy adopted by the New York City Police Department in 1972 reduced firearms discharges 30 percent over the next three and a half years.[71] Shootings of unarmed fleeing felons in Memphis in the 1970s disappeared following the adoption of a similarly restrictive shooting policy.[72] Restrictive policies on high-speed pursuits reduce the number of pursuits. Alpert found that pursuits in the Miami-Dade Police Department declined 82 percent after the introduction of a restrictive policy. In Omaha, meanwhile, pursuits increased 600 percent after a permissive policy was reintroduced.[73]

Informal Organizational Culture

informal organizational culture

Police departments also have their own **informal organizational culture** that influences officer discretion. In his classic study *Varieties of Police Behavior,* Wilson identifies three different organizational styles of policing: watchman, legalistic, and service.[74] Historically, the Los Angeles Police Department had a reputation for a legalistic style that involved aggressive crime-fighting tactics (for example, high rates of field interrogations and arrests). Chicago and some other departments had a watchman style that put much less emphasis on arrest activity.[75]

The organizational culture of a police department is not necessarily established by written policy. It is more the impact of values and traditions that are communicated informally among officers. In a comparison of six police departments, the

Project on Policing Neighborhoods found that the percentage of officer-initiated contacts with citizens ranged from a low of about 20 percent in some departments to a high of 50 percent in others. These different patterns of work activity obviously reflect different informal norms about patrol activity in the six departments.[76]

Police departments often send conflicting messages to their officers. In a study of the handling of people with mental health problems, Schulenberg found that the agencies, on the one hand, wanted informal, non-arrest resolution of incidents. Arrests take time and involve paperwork. This is especially a problem when there are many 911 calls. On the other hand, however, for the "monthlies"—the record of police activity, supervisors wanted arrests and citations.[77] These conflicting pressures put considerable stress on police officers.

Social and Political Factors

Local Political Culture

In almost every state, there are small towns where, according to local folklore, you want to be sure to drive right at the speed limit. These towns have reputations for making a lot of arrests for speeding.

Police officer discretion is also influenced by the **local political culture.** One community might place a high priority on, for example, traffic enforcement, with the result that the police department engages in aggressive enforcement.[78] Another community might place a very high priority on order maintenance, with the result that the police aggressively enforce laws on disturbing the peace, loitering, and so on. Local political culture influences police departments informally (for example, through communication from elected officials or other community leaders) and not necessarily through written policy.[79]

local political culture

The most notorious recent case of local political culture influencing the police involves Ferguson, Missouri. A Justice Department investigation found—what local residents long knew—that the city was using the police department to generate revenue to support city government through traffic tickets, fines for other arrests, and other court fees. The investigation found emails from city officials to the police chief warning of a possible budget crisis and the need to increase revenue-generating police activity. The result of this pressure was a pattern of often-unjustified arrests of African American residents and a resulting hostility to the police.[80] Similarly, many people believe that other small towns in America maintain police "speed traps" solely for the purpose of generating revenue to support their city government.[81]

The Control of Discretion

The Need for Control

Virtually all experts agree on the need to control police discretion in order to prevent abuse of police authority. Earlier, we discussed the problems that can result from the misuse of discretion. Both Davis and Goldstein argue that the first step toward controlling police discretion is admitting that it exists, that it can create problems, and that control is necessary.[82] During the era of denial, the police denied that they exercise discretion, claiming, instead, that they fully enforce all laws.

myth of full enforcement

The so-called **myth of full enforcement** and denial of discretion existed for several reasons.[83] First, the police wanted to maintain a public image of authority. They believed that admitting that they sometimes do not enforce the law would undermine their authority in encounters with citizens. It would give suspects a basis for challenging an arrest, with comments like "Why me?" and "You don't arrest everyone."

Second, if the police admitted that they do not arrest everyone, it would raise serious questions about equal protection of the law. Equal protection is a major legal issue, particularly with respect to stops and frisks, traffic stops, and arrests. The issue of striking a balance between the hypothetical extremes of full enforcement and arresting no one is resolved today through *guided discretion,* in which formal police department policies outline the factors that officers should take into account when making a discretionary decision. When deciding whether to pursue a fleeing vehicle, for example, an officer should take into account the seriousness of the suspected offense and road conditions that are dangerous and might result in an accident that endangers members of the public.

Third, to admit that the police exercise discretion in enforcing certain laws would raise questions about all police policies and how departments determine what their enforcement policies are. Traditionally, police leaders clung to the myth of full enforcement so they would not have to answer questions about these issues. Only in recent years have police departments opted for openness and transparency and begun placing their policy manuals on their websites.

Fourth, most states have laws requiring the police to enforce all laws fully. Some states have criminal penalties for police and other officials who do not enforce the law. For this reason, some legal scholars in the past questioned whether police discretion is legal.[84] That position is not taken seriously today, however.

Finally, denying that discretion exists allows supervisors to avoid closely reviewing officer behavior and developing performance expectations. Commanders can justify this neglect on the grounds that they trust the professional judgment of officers on the street.[85]

Davis, Goldstein, and other experts argue that the myth of full enforcement creates a number of serious problems. Most important, it represents a denial of the basic reality of police work. As mentioned earlier, it creates potential due process and equal protection problems, increases the likelihood of police–community relations problems, makes it difficult to manage personnel effectively, and makes meaningful planning impossible.[86]

Abolish Discretion?

In one of the first studies of police discretion, Joseph Goldstein (not to be confused with Herman Goldstein) concluded that it was illegal and should be abolished.[87] He and others have argued that the police do not have the legal authority to nullify the criminal law by not arresting a criminal offender. Virtually all experts today reject the idea of abolishing discretion. They argue that discretion is both inevitable and, as was pointed out earlier in this chapter, can often be used for positive purposes.

The debate over abolishing police discretion parallels similar debates over how to control discretion in other parts of the criminal justice system: plea bargaining, sentencing, parole release, and so forth. In those other areas, there is now a general consensus that attempting to **abolish discretion** is both unwise in principle and impossible in practice. The consensus is that the best response is to regulate and control discretion through written rules. Sentencing guidelines that leave judges some room for discretion are a good example of this approach.[88]

abolish discretion

Enhancing Professional Judgment

When you go to a doctor because of some symptoms that worry you, the doctor asks a series of questions and decides what tests to give you. He or she decides in some cases that there is nothing really wrong with you; in other cases the doctor refers you to a specialist for further tests; and in many cases, the doctor diagnoses what is medically wrong and prescribes a medication. The doctor does not follow any rigid set of rules or consult a policy manual in making these decisions but relies on a combination of experience and professional judgment.

Enhancing the professional judgment of police officers is one method of controlling discretion. This represents the professional model employed in medicine, law, and education. In these occupations, practitioners are granted broad discretion to make judgments about how to handle specific incidents. Control is exercised through the process of screening, training, and socializing members of the profession. Admission standards to medical schools, for example, are very high; medical school training is long and rigorous; and the training process serves to socialize prospective doctors into the culture of the profession. Once a doctor is licensed, he or she is expected to make professional judgments without direct supervision.[89]

 For a discussion of improved training to enhance the professional judgment of police officers, see Chapter 5.

Many police experts, however, argue that the traditional professional model does not apply to policing. First, recruitment standards are low, compared with law and medicine. Preservice training is very short (six months even in the best departments), compared with these other professions (three years for law school). Second, the peer culture of policing has often tolerated and even covered up improper behavior.[90] Third, policing has been described as a craft rather than a profession. That is to say, it involves a set of skills that are learned through practice. There is no body of specialized professional knowledge equivalent to the body of knowledge that the tax lawyer or the heart specialist possesses. Police officers are generalists rather than specialists. For all these reasons, James Q. Wilson argues that "the police are not in any of these senses professionals."[91] Consequently, the traditional professional model of controlling discretion is not applicable to policing.

The recent innovations in police training, as we discussed in Chapter 5, put greater emphasis on officers using their judgment to assess and reassess incidents as they unfold, and to be ready to alter their tactics as the situation changes.[92] Training officers to understand that they have the capacity to make tactical decisions that can prevent having to use force in many situations is a way of enhancing their professional judgment.

Informal Bureaucratic Controls

To a certain extent, police discretion is controlled by the bureaucratic setting of the criminal justice system. An arrest, for example, raises the "visibility" of a police officer's behavior. The arrest is reviewed by a supervisor, a prosecutor, a defense attorney, and one or more judges. A competent defense attorney will challenge improper or illegal behavior and may succeed in persuading the judge to dismiss the case. In short, a police officer is not totally free to act out his or her prejudices. Albert Reiss, for example, found that about 75 percent of the officers in his field study made verbal expressions of racial prejudice in the presence of the observers. Yet the data on arrests did not indicate any direct pattern of race discrimination.[93] Evidently, they knew they could not consistently act on the basis of their prejudices, although it does happen in many instances in policing. In short, police officer attitudes do not automatically translate into behavior. Bureaucratic procedures, involving routine review by other persons, constrain officers' behavior.

Administrative Rulemaking: Controls through Written Policies

administrative rulemaking

The method of controlling discretion that has evolved is through the use of written policies that guide the police officer's exercise of discretion. This approach is called **administrative rulemaking.** It is currently the dominant approach in police management, and the police department policy and procedure manual (different names are used in some departments) is today a basic tool of modern police management. On many issues, such as use of deadly force and domestic violence, state laws reinforce police department policies. For the most part, however, department policies have the advantage of being able to be more detailed than state laws and also being much easier to revise.

Administrative rulemaking seeks to guide the exercise of police discretion through written departmental policies. These policies typically specify (1) what an officer *must* do in certain situations, (2) what he or she *may not do* in those situations, and (3) what factors an officer should take into consideration in deciding on a course of action. Virtually all experts on policing endorse this approach. The Commission on Accreditation for Law Enforcement Agencies (CALEA) accreditation *Standards for Law Enforcement Agencies* require that "a written directive governs procedures for assuring compliance with all applicable constitutional requirements."[94] The American Bar Association standards for police include a similar recommendation (see Exhibit 11–1).[95]

Examples of Administrative Rulemaking

- **Deadly force.** The defense-of-life standard for the use of deadly force clearly spells out when deadly force may be used (threat to the life of the officer or another person) and when it may not be used (an unarmed fleeing felon).[96]

EXHIBIT 11–1

American Bar Association Standard 1–4.3 Administrative Rule Making

Police discretion can best be structured and controlled through the process of administrative rule making by police agencies. Police administrators should, therefore, give the highest priority to the formulation of administrative rules governing the exercise of discretion, particularly in the areas of selective enforcement, investigative techniques, and enforcement methods.

Source: Excerpt from American Bar Association, *Standards on Urban Police Function*, http://www.americanbar.org/publications/criminal_justice_section_archive/crimjust_standards_urbanpolice.html.

Many department policies also include specific prohibitions on the use of warning shots, shots to wound, or shots at moving vehicles. (See Exhibit 11–2.)

- **Domestic violence.** Mandatory arrest policies on domestic violence instruct police officers that they must make an arrest when a felonious assault has occurred. Many experts argue that a mandatory arrest policy is too rigid and does not allow officers to take into account relevant facts in particular domestic violence incidents. A more widely used alternative involves *arrest-preferred policies,* which state that arrest is the expected action in the case of felonious assault but allow the officers a range of discretion in misdemeanor assaults depending on various circumstances.[97]

- **High-speed pursuits.** Department policies on high-speed pursuits instruct officers to consider the seriousness of the suspected offense, road conditions, the presence of pedestrians, and other potential risks before initiating a pursuit. In the case of many suspected lesser offenses, the risks involved in a high-speed pursuit do not justify the risks of a pursuit, particularly if some dangerous conditions such as rain or snow exist.[98]

EXHIBIT 11–2

Use of Deadly Force Policy, Minneapolis, Minnesota Police Department, 2016

5-305 AUTHORIZED USE OF DEADLY FORCE (08/17/07)

Minn. Stat. §609.066 sub. 2—"The use of deadly force by a peace officer in the line of duty is justified only when necessary:

- To protect the peace officer or another from apparent death or great bodily harm;
- To effect the arrest or capture, or prevent the escape, of a person whom the peace officer knows or has reasonable grounds to believe has committed or attempted to commit a felony involving the use or threatened use of deadly force, or;
- To effect the arrest or capture, or prevent the escape, of a person who the officer knows or has reasonable grounds to believe has committed or attempted to commit a felony if the officer reasonably believes that the person will cause death or great bodily harm if the person's apprehension is delayed."

In addition to Minn. Stat. §609.066, MPD policies shall utilize the United States Supreme Court decision in Tennessee vs Garner as a guideline for the use of deadly force.

The Tennessee vs Garner case references that:

"Apprehension by the use of deadly force is a seizure subject to the Fourth Amendment's reasonableness requirement."

"The use of deadly force to prevent the escape of all felony suspects, whatever the circumstances, is constitutionally unreasonable."

Sworn MPD employees shall recognize that:

- For the safety of the public, warning shots shall not be fired.
- The use of a firearm, vehicle, less-lethal or non-lethal weapon, or other improvised weapon may constitute the use of deadly force.
- This policy does not prevent a sworn employee from drawing a firearm, or being prepared to use a firearm in threatening situations.

Source: Excerpt from Minneapolis Police Department, *Policy and Procedure Manual, Section 5-300 Use of Force,* http://www.ci.minneapolis.mn.us/police/policy/mpdpolicy_5-300_5-300.

- **Respectful language.** To curb offensive and disrespectful language by police officers, particularly racial, ethnic or gender slurs, the President's Task Force on 21st Century Policing recommended that law enforcement agencies should "adopt policies directing officers to speak to individuals with respect."[99]

Principles of Administrative Rulemaking

Kenneth C. Davis, a leading authority on administrative law, describes the principles of administrative rulemaking in terms of a strategy to fill the gap between law and practice.[100] Laws are written in very broad language. The criminal law, for example, describes categories of criminal behavior in general terms ("threat to do serious bodily harm"). In practice, someone has to use his or her discretion to apply these general definitions to a specific situation. Administrative rulemaking fills in the gap between what the law states and the choices an officer could make by providing additional detail on how to handle specific situations. The specific objectives of administrative rulemaking, according to Davis, are **confining discretion,** structuring discretion, and checking discretion:[101]

confining discretion

- **Confining discretion.** Rules confine discretion by "fixing the boundaries." The defense-of-life standard on the use of deadly force, for example, fixes the boundaries by clearly indicating situations where an officer may not shoot: for example, fleeing felons, at moving vehicles, and as warning shots. A typical mandatory arrest policy on domestic violence fixes the boundaries by instructing officers that an arrest is required if there is a felonious assault.
- **Structuring discretion.** Discretion is structured when there is a rational system for guiding police officers' exercise of discretion. As Davis puts it, a structured policy says to the officer: "Within the area in which you have discretionary power, let your discretion by guided by these goals and principles."[102] With respect to high-speed police pursuits, for example, policies typically prohibit pursuits in residential neighborhoods and school zones. The goal underlying this policy is to protect the lives of neighborhood residents and school children and their parents. The principle is that their lives are more important than the arrest of a fleeing criminal suspect.
- **Checking discretion.** Discretion is checked when decisions are reviewed by another person. The use of deadly force is checked by the requirement that officers fill out reports after each firearms discharge and by having those reports automatically reviewed by supervisors.[103] This process puts officers on notice that their decisions will be examined by other people, including the chief of police. A police department use of force review board, which reviews patterns of force incidents for the purpose of identifying needed changes in policy or training, serves as an additional check on discretion.

Contributions of Written Rules

A patrol officer sees a car he believes is stolen and starts to make a traffic stop by turning on his flashing lights. Suddenly, the suspect car accelerates in an obvious attempt to flee. The officer has to make a quick decision: pursue or not pursue? He knows the roads are wet and dangerously slick and sees that the fleeing vehicle is headed for a residential area or school zone where there are high risks to people and children. The officer knows that the department's high-speed pursuit policy advises against pursuits when road conditions and traffic levels might pose a danger to innocent bystanders, and decides not to pursue. Instead, he or she calls in the identity of the fleeing vehicle to the 911 dispatcher.

Written rules offer obvious advantages. They provide direction for officers on how to handle critical incidents. In a Justice Department report, *"Broken Windows" and Police Discretion,* George L. Kelling argues that, for the police to effectively address quality-of-life issues in neighborhoods, officers need clear guidance in the form of rules that tell them both what they should do and what they should not do.[104] Should they strictly enforce the minor-in-possession-of-alcohol offense in all instances, for example? Is the offense really that serious? Is it that important, given all the other more serious offenses facing the police?

Written policies promote consistent performance throughout the department. This helps ensure equal protection of the law, which in turn promotes better police–community relations by reducing or, it is hoped, eliminating many potential lawsuits against police departments.

Written policies also provide the basis for effective supervision. They provide officers with clear guidance on how to respond to certain situations, and when they fail to follow policy, supervisors have a clear and rational basis for disciplinary action.[105] In this regard, clear policies protect officers against unfair evaluations by supervisors. In the face of what seems like an unfair evaluation, an officer can point out that he or she acted consistent with department policy.

Additionally, officers are more likely to respect and comply with rules that are clear and are enforced consistently. The President's Task Force on 21st Century Policing recommended that officers be involved in the development of department policies because that gives them a sense of ownership of those policies (see Exhibit 11–3).[106] Herman Goldstein further argues that police officers are more likely to comply with policies that are developed internally by the department than with rules imposed on them by outsiders.[107] For this reason, the President's Task Force on 21st Century Policing strongly recommended that police departments apply procedural justice to their internal management.[108]

Having rules and making them public, moreover, eliminates the secrecy surrounding police activities and officer discretion. It informs the public about what official policy is and creates the opportunity for public debate over what policy would be best for the community. Both Kenneth C. Davis and Herman Goldstein argue that a system of open rulemaking would create an atmosphere of openness that would have a positive effect on police–community relations.[109] The President's Task Force made a similar recommendation for the same reason.[110]

Finally, in an important 2016 report on use of force, the Police Executive Research Forum argued that police departments policies are embraced by courts in decisions on policing and as a result become established legal standards, relevant to other cases in other jurisdictions. The report cited a Virginia case in which the U.S. Court of Appeals for the Fourth Circuit ruled that an officer had used excessive force in the use of an electronic control weapon, and based its decision in part on a model policy developed by PERF and the COPS Office of the Justice Department.[111]

EXHIBIT 11–3

The President's Task Force on 21st Century Policing on Police Department Policies and Policy Manuals

The President's Task Force in 2015 made three recommendations related to police department policies and their policy manuals:

1. Action Item 1.3.1 recommends that "law enforcement agencies should make all department policies available for public review . . . ."
2. Action Item 1.4.1 recommends that in order to "achieve internal legitimacy, law enforcement agencies should involve employees in the process of developing policies and procedures."
3. Action Item 1.5.1 recommends that "law enforcement agencies should involve the community in the process of developing and evaluating policies and procedures."

Source: President's Task Force on 21st Century Policing, *Final Report* (Washington, DC: Department of Justice, 2015), http://www.cops.usdoj.gov/pdf/taskforce/taskforce_finalreport.pdf.

The basic argument in favor of administrative rulemaking is that it is more effective than other means. Abolishing discretion is not realistic. Allowing unlimited discretion is unacceptable because it opens the door to potential abuse, for example, in the form of inappropriate use of force or discrimination.

The Impact of Administrative Rulemaking

There is persuasive evidence that administrative rulemaking has produced some significant improvements in policing. After a comprehensive review of police research, the National Academy of Sciences concluded that "clear administrative guidelines regarding the use of force, coupled with consistently imposed sanctions for misconduct, reduces the incidence of excessive force."[112] For example, Fyfe found that a restrictive policy on deadly force adopted by the New York City Police Department in 1972 reduced the weekly average number of firearms discharges by about one-third (29.1 percent).[113] Alpert's study of high-speed pursuit policies found that when restrictive policies were adopted, there was a reduction in the number of pursuits, accidents, and injuries to both officers and citizens.[114] In the Los Angeles Sheriff's Department, the number of citizens bitten by canine unit dogs declined by 90 percent after the department put in place new controls over how the dogs could be deployed.[115]

In their 2016 book on stop and frisk, the first thorough study of the subject, Michael D. White and Henry F. Fradella concluded that "previous efforts at discretion control [discussed above] offer important lessons for stop and frisk."[116] That is the administrative rulemaking principles of clear written polices, a mandatory officer reporting requirement, and an automatic review of officer reports can effectively control officer conduct and greatly reduce illegal stop and frisk practices.

For a discussion of the impact of written rules on police use of deadly force, see Chapter 14.

Ensuring Compliance with Rules

Rules designed to control discretion are effective only if officers comply with them fully. The basic strategy for ensuring compliance is to require officers to file a written report after each incident, and to have each report automatically reviewed by

---

SIDEBAR 11-3

Case Study: Impact of a More Restrictive Policy on Use of Electroconductive Weapons

An evaluation of the impact of a new and more restrictive policy on the use of electroconductive (ECW) weapons (popularly known by their trademarked name TASER), in the Dallas, Texas, police department found that it significantly reduced the use of the weapon. Dallas at the time of the study was a city with a population of 1.2 million people and a police force of about 3,500 sworn officers.

The original policy, implemented in 2005, stated that officers could deploy an ECW in cases of defensive resistance, *which covered any kind of physical noncompliance against a police officer. It would cover, for example, a person going limp or falling into a fetal position. After about one year, the department revised the policy to permit deployment of an ECW only in the case of* active aggression. *This is a far more restrictive policy that, for example, would not permit ECW deployment against someone in a fetal position. (A more commonly used term is* aggressive resistance *to an officer.)*

The evaluation examined 399 ECW deployments: 292 under the original policy and 107 under the new policy. Deployments of ECW climbed steadily in the first five months of the original policy and then fell sharply in the remaining three months. With only some month-to-month fluctuation, ECW deployment remained significantly under the new policy. The authors of the evaluation concluded that the findings "suggest that officers will follow policy directives intended to guide" ECW deployment.

Source: Stephen A. Bishopp, David A. Klinger, and Robert G. Morris, "An Examination of the Effect of a Policy Change on Police Use of TASERs," *Criminal Justice Policy Review* 26, no. 7 (2015): 727–746.

---

supervisors. The CALEA accreditation standards, for example, require a police officer to file a written report whenever he or she "discharges a firearm," causes "injury or death of another person," uses "lethal or less-than-lethal weapons," or "applies physical force as defined by the agency."[117]

Compliance with use-of-force policies is a major problem in American policing. Justice Department investigations of police departments with significant problems related to excessive force have found that in "troubled" departments, officers sometimes do not file reports, and when they do they often omit important details (for example, reporting they used a lower level of force than they actually used), or falsify aspects of the incident (for example, claiming that the person was more resistant than was actually the case), and the sergeants simply approve officer reports without critically examining them. The Justice Department's investigation of the Cleveland police department, for example, found that supervisors' review of force reports often "appear to be designed from the outset to justify the officers' actions."[118]

To ensure compliance with policies, Justice Department consent decrees require sergeants to critically review officer use-of-force reports; to demand more detail where reports lack detail; and when a report remains unsatisfactory, to report the officer for violating department policy. The Justice Department report on the Newark, New Jersey, police department, for example, found that officer force reports were often "insufficient to permit meaningful review," in particular, failing "to describe the actions that prompted the use of force."[119] Ensuring that sergeants do their duty in this regard, however, is yet another problem. The solution is to have

compliance with use-of-force rules

command officers (lieutenants and captains, for example) closely supervise sergeants under their command. In the end, the department as a whole has to have a commitment to accountability, and this requires both a strong commitment and effective leadership from the chief of police.

An important factor influencing compliance with department policies is the nature of the event. Firearms discharges are, by definition, high-visibility events: They occur in public areas and are accompanied by a loud noise and the presence of at least one citizen, along with other potential witnesses. There is also the evidence from the officer's weapon, and from the body of the person who was shot (for example, whether he was shot in the chest or in the back). High-speed pursuits also are public events, occurring in the streets where many people can observe them. Events of this sort provide a powerful incentive for officers to complete reports as required and to provide accurate detail. In these cases, too many factors could provide evidence that contradicts an officer's report.

Domestic violence incidents, however, are very low-visibility events. They typically occur in private homes, usually with no witnesses other than the immediate parties. Thus, it is easier for the officer to ignore both the policy and the reporting requirement.[120] Stops and frisks on the street are also often low-visibility events. Although they occur in public, in many instances there are no witnesses to the stop. The same is true for many arrests and searches incident to arrests.

Codifying Rules: The Standard Operating Procedure Manual

standard operation procedure manual

Written rules and policies are collected and codified in a department's **standard operating procedure manual** (SOP manual; also known as the policy manual, or policy and procedure manual). The SOP manual is the central tool of modern police management. The typical SOP manual in a big-city department is several hundred pages long.

Many police departments now place their SOP manuals on their websites. The Seattle, Minneapolis, San Francisco, and Washington, D.C., police departments offer four examples. (See Sidebar 11–4.) The President's Task Force on 21st Century Policing Action Item 14.1 recommended that departments make their policy manuals publicly available as a way of building community trust and confidence in the police.[121]

SIDEBAR 11–4

SOPs on the Web

An increasing number of police departments place their policy and procedure manuals on the web. They include the following:

- Seattle Police Department: http://www.seattle.gov/police-manual
- Minneapolis Police Department: http://www.ci.minneapolis.mn.us/police/policy/index.htm
- San Francisco Police Department: http://sanfranciscopolice.org/sf-police-general-orders
- Washington, DC, Metropolitan Police Department: http://mpdc.dc.gov/page/written-directives-standard-operating-procedures

---

Placing SOP manuals on websites has several positive effects. First, it is a step in the direction of greater openness and transparency. It allows citizens to know what their department's policies are. This increases public understanding and trust, which promotes better police–community relations. Second, it promotes reform. Citizens and local professional groups can compare their department's policy on a particular subject. They might find that the policy—use of Tasers, for example—is not consistent with most other departments and should be changed.

SOP manuals have certain limits. First, they have traditionally overemphasized relatively trivial issues (such as proper uniforms) and ignored critical issues in the use of law enforcement power (such as the use of informants or the use of choke holds). In recent years, although departments have adopted written policies on deadly force and pursuits, other important issues remain uncovered by a policy. Many departments still do not have policies on the use of informants or on arrest discretion in situations other than domestic violence.

A second problem is the erratic "crisis management" process by which manuals develop. New policies are typically adopted in response to an immediate crisis: a lawsuit or a community protest. Peter Manning quotes a British police sergeant as saying that his department's procedures manual represented "140 years of screw-ups. Every time something goes wrong, they make a rule about it."[122] The result of crisis management is that SOP manuals are generally unsystematic. Some areas of police discretion are covered, but many are not. Manuals are often not revised for many years, and, as a result, important subjects are not reviewed or updated.

One consequence of the crisis management approach to the growth of SOP manuals is that new policies are often not consistent with existing policies that cover the same topic. The Inspector General for the New York City Police Department in 2015, for example, found that the department's policies did not provide a consistent definition of "force," making it extremely difficult for officers to provide consistent use of force reports.[123] To correct for this problems, departments need to regularly review their SOP manuals to look for possible inconsistencies.

Systematic Rulemaking

Leading experts on police discretion have urged the police to engage in systematic rulemaking. Davis and Goldstein argue that a systematic approach allows the police to anticipate problems before they become crises and represents a professional approach to planning. Despite these recommendations, police departments have not engaged in systematic planning. Davis pointed out in his classic book in the 1970s that the "research and planning" units in many police departments are usually occupied with trivial matters.[124]

Walker and Archbold argue that **systematic rulemaking** should involve proactively developing written policies for every "critical incident" in police work.[125] A critical incident is any police activity that implicates the life, liberty, or health and safety of people. In the past, too much policy making has been reactive, a response to a controversial incident which exposed the limits of a department's existing policy or the lack of a policy altogether.

Several attempts have been made to encourage systematic rulemaking. The CALEA accreditation *Standards for Law Enforcement Agencies* require accredited

systematic rulemaking

departments to have a system of written directives governing police policy.[126] In 1987, the International Association of Chiefs of Police (IACP) established the National Law Enforcement Policy Center, which began publishing model policies on specific discretionary decision points.[127] The Police Executive Research Forum also develops model policies on various aspects of police work. Finally, a number of citizen review agencies engage in policy review, recommending new policies in areas that have generated citizen complaints.[128]

Wayne Schmidt proposes that to make administrative rulemaking systematic, each state should create an administrative council on law enforcement. This agency would have the authority to develop policies for all local police departments in the state.[129] Walker recommended that states enact laws requiring police departments to develop rules on a specific set of critical decision points.[130] To a certain extent, this approach already exists for some decisions. Police use of deadly force, for example, is covered by state statute. The 1985 Supreme Court decision in *Tennessee v. Garner* ruled as unconstitutional state laws embodying the "fleeing felon" standard. Police department deadly force policies adopted in the wake of Garner, however, have added many more details on when officers can and cannot shoot. Some states have enacted laws governing police pursuits. Walker's proposal would require the police to adopt rules on a broader range of police decision points.

Citizen Oversight and Policymaking

Some citizen oversight agencies also contribute to rulemaking through a process known as *policy review*. Police auditors (also known as inspectors general) have the authority to review any and every aspect of the operations in the agency under their jurisdiction. When they identify problems, they have the authority to make recommendations in a public report.[131]

For a detailed discussion of citizen oversight of the police, see Chapter 14.

The Inspector General for the New York City Police Department, for example, issues regular reports in important issues, including use of force policies and the use of choke holds by officers.[132] The Special Counsel to the Los Angeles Sheriff's Department, for example, in 2003 found a serious problem with foot pursuits by officers. There was no formal policy in the department governing foot pursuits. Additionally, the report found that they were very dangerous events, resulting in unnecessary uses of force against the suspect, injuries and sometime deaths to officers, and dangers to community residents. The Special Counsel recommended a policy, which the department adopted.[133] Finally, White and Fradella argue that citizen oversight agencies based on the auditor model can "periodically investigate" police department practices to ensure that stops and frisks are being conducted in a legal manner.[134]

The Limits of Administrative Rulemaking

Administrative rulemaking also has some important limitations. First, it is impossible to write a rule that covers every possible situation. Life is complex, and police officers routinely encounter very complex, challenging and possibly dangerous situations. And as we have mentioned several times already, police-citizen encounters often change as they unfold. No policy manual could possibly cover all the possible situations. In the end, police officers have to use their *discretion* about what course of action is best. A good policy can, however, confine discretion by establishing the outer limits of what is permissible and defining factors that an officer should take into account before acting.

Second, formal rules may encourage evasion or lying. The exclusionary rule, for example, may encourage officers to lie about how they obtain evidence. With respect to narcotics, observers cited the "dropsy" phenomenon: Officers lied, claiming that the suspect dropped the narcotics on the ground (thus making the seizure legal).[135] Fyfe found that in New York City the number of reported "accidental" firearms discharges increased after the restrictive shooting policy was implemented, suggesting that officers were using this category to cover improper shootings. But accidents as a percentage of all shootings increased only from 3 to 9 percent of all discharges, suggesting that if this did represent an attempt to evade policy, it was still rather limited.[136]

Finally, elaborate rules may only create a negative atmosphere in the department where officers believe that the rules only exist to "get" them and, as a result, the officers do as little work as possible. As Kelling argues, in this kind of organizational environment officers are unlikely to engage in any creative, proactive police work.[137]

Police organizations have been characterized as punishment-centered bureaucracies, with many rules that tell officers what not to do and few rewards for positive police work. Part of the reason for this is that, historically, police managers have been concerned with control, in the sense of keeping officers from inappropriate behavior, with too little attention to guiding officers on the proper courses of action.

Walker replies to these criticisms by arguing that uncertainty is inherent in the nature of policing, that some rules are better than no rules at all, and that if officers evade rules, the task is to ensure greater compliance and not to throw out the rules altogether.[138]

CASE STUDY

"Broken Windows" and Police Discretion

IV. Philosophy of Order Maintenance Practices

The New Haven Police Department will always use the least forceful means possible to achieve its purposes. While we will not hesitate to cite or arrest offenders, our approach, at all levels of organization, will be to attempt to get citizens to obey laws and ordinances as unintrusively as possible.

The first level of intervention, whether by managers, supervisors, or by police officers, will be to educate the public about civility, the consequences of incivility, and the laws that oblige citizens to behave in particular ways. This can be done in neighborhood meetings, in schools, or in interactions with citizens. Some citizens do not fully understand their obligations, and if those obligations—for example, regarding a noisy car or public drinking in parks—are patiently explained, they will adhere to the law.

The second level of intervention will be to remind citizens of their responsibilities if they are disorderly—that is, that they are breaking the law and subject to penalties if they persist. This too can be done in a variety of ways. It could be done by visiting a problem location and warning people that if their behavior continues they will be subject to penalties. Similarly, owners of locations that are chronic problems could be so warned by individual officers.

The final level of intervention will be law enforcement—the use of citation and arrest.

Having said that the least intrusive means of intervention will always be used should not be read to mean that in every incident police must start with education. Since police deal with incidents that have histories (for example, with problems), it may well be that in a particular incident the offenders might have a history of outrageous behavior that warrants forceful action at the outset of the encounter (for example, warning or citation).

Source: Excerpt from George Kelling, *"Broken Windows" and Police Discretion* (Washington, DC: U.S. Department of Justice, 1999), 50.

SUMMARY

Discretion is a pervasive part of policing. It is embedded in almost everything police officers on the street do, from routine patrol, to handling a disturbance call, to firing a weapon. Police chiefs also make important decisions, such as whether or not to adopt community policing. Officers routinely make critical decisions affecting the life and liberty of citizens. Uncontrolled discretion results in serious problems, including denial of due process and equal protection of the law.

Discretion can be controlled best through administrative rulemaking, a process that involves formal written department policies that cover critical issues such as the use of deadly force and the handling of domestic violence situations. Written policies do not completely eliminate discretion; they guide it by providing directions on what the officer should or should not do in certain situations. There is evidence that written policies have reduced the number of persons shot and killed by police.

KEY TERMS

discretion, 370
era of denial, 370
positive use of discretion, 373
broad scope of the criminal
    law, 375
street-level bureaucrats, 378
low-visibility work, 378

situational factors, 380
preference of the victim, 381
demeanor of the suspect, 381
informal organizational culture, 384
local political culture, 385
myth of full enforcement, 386
abolish discretion, 387

administrative rulemaking, 388
confining discretion, 390
compliance with use-of-force
    rules, 393
standard operating procedure
    manual, 394
systematic rulemaking, 395

FOR DISCUSSION

The New Haven Police Department policy calls for police officers to use a three-stage process in exercising discretion: (1) educate, (2) remind, and (3) enforce the law. As an in-class project, discuss experiences and perceptions regarding police discretion, following these steps:

1. As an in-class discussion, identify several different order maintenance situations where the police intervened (e.g., party with loud noise).
2. Survey the experiences of students in the class by having each student complete an anonymous report of (*a*) their experience with

one or more of these situations and (*b*) their experience/observation of the police response (e.g., warning, arrest, lecture).

3. With the instructor reading the anonymous reports, discuss the responses in class.

INTERNET EXERCISES

Exercise 1 Find three big-city police departments that have their SOP manuals on their web sites.

1. Compare their use of force policies. Are there significant differences among the three departments? Are some more detailed than others? Do any of them have a specific policy on de-escalation?
2. Compare their high-speed vehicle pursuit policies. Are some more restrictive than others? Do the policies permit or prohibit pursuits of people suspected of traffic violations (as opposed to violent or property crimes)?
3. Compare their domestic violence policies. Do any of them mandate arrest in certain situations? What kinds of situations? Do any of the departments not have a policy on arrests in domestic violence incidents?

Exercise 2 In response to allegations of racial profiling (an abuse of discretion), a number of law enforcement agencies have adopted new policies and procedures to control traffic enforcement activities by their officers.

What departments have taken these steps? Exactly what do these policies and procedures involve? Some policies involve only the collection of data on traffic stops. What other kinds of controls have been adopted?

Search the web for reports on racial profiling. Try key words "racial profiling" or "driving while black." Also, go to www.officer.com and look for some agency reports.

In class, discuss what policies and procedures you found. Do you think they will be effective in controlling discretion? Will data collection control discretion? That is, will officers avoid questionable actions if they know they have to report them? Or will data collection deter them from taking any kind of law enforcement action?

Exercise 3 One important area of police discretion involves the handling of domestic violence situations. A number of states have addressed this issue by enacting laws attempting to control police discretion. Some of these are "mandatory arrest" laws; some others are "arrest preferred" laws.

Research the law in your state. Is there a state statute related to domestic violence? Does it cover police discretion? Is it a mandatory arrest law? If not, how would you characterize it? Does the law provide guidelines for police officer handling of domestic violence? What do those guidelines say? In your opinion, do you think this law provides clear and effective guidance for police officers?

If your state does not have such a law, find one that does and study it with regard to the preceding questions.

State statutes can be found through some of the legal resource sites on the web. One starting point would be the Reference Desk site (www.refdesk.com). Another way to find states that have domestic violence laws would be to do a web search under the subject of domestic violence. See if any of those sites have reference material on state statutes.

NOTES

1. Donald Black, "The Social Organization of Arrest," in D. Black, *The Manners and Customs of the Police* (New York: Academic Press, 1980), 90.
2. Linda Teplin, *Keeping the Peace: Parameters of Police Discretion in Relation to the Mentally Disordered* (Washington, DC: Government Printing Office, 1986).
3. Bureau of Justice Statistics, *Police Behavior During Traffic and Street Stops, 2011* (Washington, DC: U.S. Justice Department, 2013), Table 6.
4. Sandhya Somashekhar and Steven Rich, "Final Tally: Police Shot and Killed 986 People in 2015," *Washington Post* (January 6, 2016). https://www.washingtonpost.com/national/final-tally-police-shot-and-killed-984-people-in-2015/2016/01/05/3ec7a404-b3c5-11e5-a76a-0b5145e8679a_story.html
5. Kenneth Culp Davis, *Discretionary Justice: A Preliminary Inquiry* (Urbana: University of Illinois, 1971), 4.

6. Wayne R. LaFave, *Arrest* (Boston, Little, Brown, 1965), 9.

7. See the criticism of this attitude in Davis, *Police Discretion*, Ch. 3, "The Pervasive False Pretense of Full Enforcement, 52–78. Davis cites the Illinois full enforcement statute.

8. Samuel Walker, "Origins of the Contemporary Criminal Justice Paradigm: The American Bar Foundation Survey, 1953–1969," *Justice Quarterly* 9 (March 1002), 47–76.

9. President's Commission on Law Enforcement and the Administration of Justice, *The Challenge of Crime in a Free Society* (New York: Avon Books, 1968), 267.

10. Kenneth C. Davis, *Police Discretion* (St. Paul, MN: West, 1975).

11. President's Commission on Law Enforcement and Administration of Justice, *Task Force Report: The Police* (Washington, DC: Government Printing Office, 1967), 28–30 Davis, *Police Discretion*. Herman Goldstein, *Policing a Free Society* (Cambridge: Ballinger, 1977), 93-103.

12. Samuel Walker and Carol Archbold, *The New World of Police Accountability*, 2nd ed. (Thousand Oaks, CA: Sage, 2014).

13. Police Executive Research Forum, *Re-Engineering Training on Police Use of Force* (Washington, DC: PERF, 2015). http://www.policeforum.org/assets/reengineeringtraining1.pdf.

14. Jennifer L. Schulenberg, "Moving Beyond Arrest and Reconceptualizing Police Discretion: An Investigation into the Factors Affecting Conversation, Assistance, and Criminal Charges," *Police Quarterly* 20 No. 3, 2015), 244–271.

15. Police Executive Research Forum, *Re-Engineering Training on Police Use of Force*. http://www.policeforum.org/assets/reengineeringtraining1.pdf. Los Angeles Police Commission, Office of the Inspector General, *Ten Year Overview of Categorical Use of Force Investigations, Policy, and Training* (Los Angeles: Office of the Inspector General, March 10, 2016). http://media.wix.com/ugd/b2dd23_3139a5342cc34ce2860af75368 87f149.pdf.

16. Police Executive Research Forum, *Re-Engineering Training of Police Use of Force*, 59.

17. *Floyd et al., v. City of New York* (2013).

18. American Civil Liberties Union, *Driving While Black: Racial Profiling on Our Nation's Highways* (New York: ACLU, 1999).

19. Davis, *Police Discretion*.

20. Samuel Walker, Cassia Spohn, and Miriam DeLone, *The Color of Justice*, 6th ed. (Belmont, CA: Cengage, 2018).

21. Gunnar Myrdal, *An American Dilemma: The Negro Problem and Modern Democracy* (New York: Harper and Row, 1942).

22. Frank J. Landy, *Performance Appraisal in Police Departments* (Washington, DC: The Police Foundation, 1977); Timothy N. Oettmeier and Mary Ann Wycoff, *Personnel Performance Evaluation in the Community Policing Context* (Washington, DC: PERF, 1997). http://www.policeforum.org/assets/docs/Free_Online_Documents/Community_Policing/personnel%20performance%20evaluations%20in%20the%20community%20policing%20context.pdf

23. George Fechner and Steven Carter, *An Assessment of Deadly Force in the Philadelphia Police Department* (Washington, DC: Department of Justice, 2015). http://media.philly.com/documents/COPS+Report.pdf.

24. Lawrence W. Sherman and Barry D. Glick, *The Quality of Police Arrest Statistics* (Washington, DC: The Police Foundation, 1984). http://pftest1.drupalgardens.com/sites/g/files/g798246/f/Sherman%20et%20al.%20(1984)%20-%20The%20Quality%20of%20Police%20Arrest%20Statistics.pdf.

25. Los Angeles Police Commission, Office of the Inspector General, *Ten Year Overview of Categorical Use of Force Investigations, Policy, and Training*.

26. Goldstein, *Policing a Free Society*, 9.

27. Davis, *Police Discretion*, 62–66.

28. President's Task Force on 21st Century Policing, *Final Report*, Action Item 4.1.1.

29. ACLU, *The War on Marijuana in Black and White*.

30. Herman Goldstein, *Policing a Free Society*, 94–101; Albert J. Reiss Jr., "Consequences of Compliance and Deterrence Models of Law Enforcement for the Exercise of Discretion," *Law and Contemporary Problems* 47 (Autumn 1984): 88–89.

31. One of the best criticisms of the overreach of the criminal law is Norval Morris and Gordon Hawkins, *The Honest Politicians Guide to Crime Control (*Chicago: University of Chicago Press, 1970).

32. Eric H. Monkkonen, *Walking to Work: Tramps in America, 1790-1935* (Lincoln: University of Nebraska Press, 1984).

33. State marijuana laws: http://www.governing.com/gov-data/state-marijuana-laws-map-medical-recreational.html.

34. LaFave, *Arrest*, 83–101.

35. Raymond T. Nimmer, *Two Million Unnecessary Arrests* (Chicago: American Bar Foundation, 1971).

36. Jennifer L. Schulenberg, "Police Decision-Making in the Grey Zone: The Dynamics of Police-Citizen Encounters with Mentally Ill Persons," *Criminal Justice and Behavior* 43 (April 2016), 473.

37. United States Department of Justice, Civil Rights Division, Letter to The Honorable Sam Adams, Mayor, City of Portland, *Investigation of the Portland Police Bureau* (September 12, 2012), 6–7. https://www.justice.gov/sites/default/files/crt/legacy/2012/09/17/ppb_findings_9-12-12.pdf.

38. James Q. Wilson, *Varieties of Police Behavior* (New York: Atheneum, 1973), 21.

39. Michael Lipsky, *Street-Level Bureaucracy: Dilemmas of the Individual in Public Services* (New York: Russell Sage, 1968); Janet Coble Vinzant and Lane Crothers, *Street-Level Leadership: Discretion and Legitimacy in Front-Line Public Service* (Washington, DC: Georgetown University Press, 1998).

40. Jerome Skolnick, *Justice without Trial*, 3rd ed. (New York: Macmillan, 1994), 13.

41. Albert Reiss, *The Police and the Public* (New Haven, CT: Yale University Press, 1971); Stephen D. Mastrofski, Roger B. Parks, Albert J. Reiss Jr., Robert E. Worden, Christina DeJong, Jeffrey B. Snipes, and William Terrill, *Systematic Observation of Public Police: Applying Field Research Methods to Policy Issues* (Washington, DC: Department of Justice, 1998), 25.

42. Herman Goldstein, "Administrative Problems in Controlling the Exercise of Police Authority," *Journal of Criminal Law, Criminology, and Police Science* 58, no. 2 (1967): 165.

43. Joseph Goldstein, "Police Discretion Not to Invoke the Criminal Process: Low Visibility Decisions in the Administration of Justice," *Yale Law Journal* 69, no. 4 (1960): 543–88.

44. Herman Goldstein, *Policing a Free Society*, 9.

45. Davis, *Police Discretion*, 62–66.

46. Police Executive Research Forum, *Policing and the Economic Downturn: Striving for Efficiency is the New Normal* (Washington, DC: Police Executive Research Forum, 2013), 33. http://www.policeforum.org/assets/docs/Critical_Issues_Series/policing%20and%20the%20economic%20downturn%20-%20striving%20for%20

efficiency%20is%20the%20new%20normal%202013.pdf.

47. Steve Herbert, "Police Subculture Reconsidered," *Criminology* 36 no. 2 (1998): 343–68.

48. Robin S. Engel, How Police Supervisory Styles Influence Patrol Officer Behavior (Washington, DC: Department of Justice, 2003). https://www.ncjrs.gov/pdffiles1/nij/194078.pdf.

49. Chicago, *Police Accountability Task Force Report* (Chicago: Police Accountability Task Force, 2016). https://chicagopatf.org/.

50. Black, "The Social Organization of Arrest."

51. Teplin, *Keeping the Peace*.

52. Black, "The Social Organization of Arrest."

53. Ibid., 101.

54. Ibid., 104.

55. Ibid., 107–8; Albert Reiss, "Police Brutality—Answers to Key Questions," *Transaction* 5 (July–August 1968): 10–19.

56. David A. Klinger, "Demeanor or Crime? Why 'Hostile' Citizens Are More Likely to Be Arrested," *Criminology* 32, no. 3 (1994): 475–93.

57. Roger G. Dunham and Geoffrey P. Alpert, "Officer and Suspect Demeanor: A Qualitative Analysis of Change," *Police Quarterly* 12 (March 2009): 6–21.

58. Police Executive Research Forum, *An Integrated Approach to De-Escalation and Minimizing Use of Force* (Washington, DC: Police Executive Research Forum, 2012). http://www.policeforum.org/assets/docs/Critical_Issues_Series/an%20integrated%20approach%20to%20de-escalation%20and%20minimizing%20use%20of%20force%202012.pdf.

59. Stephen D. Mastrofski, Jeffrey B. Snipes, and Anne E. Supina, "Compliance on Demand: The Public's Response to Specific Police Requests," *Journal of Research in Crime and Delinquency* 33 (August 1996): 269–305.

60. Gary LaFree, *Rape and Criminal Justice* (Belmont, CA: Wadsworth, 1989), 76.

61. Christy A. Visher, "Gender, Police Arrest Decisions, and Notions of Chivalry," *Criminology* 21 (February 1983): 5–28.

62. Tammy Rinehart Kochel, David Wilson, and Stephen Mastrofski, "Effect of Suspect Race on Officers' Arrest Decisions," *Criminology* 49, no. 2 (2011): 473–512.

63. Douglas A. Smith, Christy A. Visher, and Laura A. Davidson, "Equity and Discretionary Justice: The Influence of Race on Police Arrest Decisions," *Journal of Criminal Law and Criminology* 75 (Spring 1984): 234–49.

64. American Civil Liberties Union, *Driving While Black* (New York: ACLU, 1999). https://www.aclu.org/report/driving-while-black-racial-profiling-our-nations-highways.

65. *Floyd, et al., v. City of New York* (2013). See the materials on the case on the Center for Constitutional Rights web site: www.ccrjustice.org.

66. James J. Fyfe, "Who Shoots? A Look at Officer Race and Police Shooting," *Journal of Police Science and Administration* 9 (December 1981): 367–82.

67. Smith, Visher, and Davidson, "Equity and Discretionary Justice."

68. Egon Bittner, "The Police on Skid Row: A Study in Peacekeeping," in Egon Bittner, *Aspects of Police Work* (Boston: Northeastern University Press, 1990), 30–62.

69. David A. Klinger, "Environment and Organization: Reviving a Perspective on the Police," *Annals of the American Academy* of *Political and Social Science* 593 (May 2004): 119–36; David Klinger, "Negotiating Order in Patrol Work," *Criminology* 35, no. 2 (1997): 277–306.

70. Herbert, "Police Subculture Reconsidered," 355–56.

71. James J. Fyfe, "Administrative Interventions on Police Shooting Discretion: An Empirical Examination," *Journal of Criminal Justice* 7 (Winter 1979): 309–23.

72. Jerry R. Sparger and David J. Giacopassi, "Memphis Revisited: A Reexamination of Police Shootings after the Garner Decision," *Justice Quarterly* 9 (June 1992): 211–25.

73. Geoffrey P. Alpert, *Police Pursuit: Policies and Training* (Washington, DC: Department of Justice, 1997).

74. Wilson, *Varieties of Police Behavior*.

75. Lou Cannon, *Official Negligence: How Rodney King and the Riots Changed Los Angeles and the LAPD* (New York: Times Books, 1997), Ch. 3.

76. Mastrofski et al., *Systematic Observation of Public Police*, 25.

77. Jennifer Schulenberg, "Police Decision-Making in the Grey Zone: The Dynamics of Police-Citizen Encounters with Mentally Ill Persons," *Criminal Justice and Behavior* 43 (April 2016), 473.

78. John A. Gardiner, *Traffic and the Police: Variations in Law-Enforcement Policy* (Cambridge, MA: Harvard University Press, 1969).

79. Wilson, *Varieties of Police Behavior*.

80. United States v. City of Ferguson, *Investigation of the Ferguson Police Department* (March 4, 2015).

https://www.justice.gov/sites/default/files/crt/legacy/2015/03/04/ferguson_findings_3-4-15.pdf

81. "7 Ways to Shut Down a Speed Trap," National Motorists Association Blog (October 30, 2007). https://www.motorists.org/blog/7-ways-to-shut-down-a-speed-trap/.

82. Davis, *Police Discretion*, 70–78; Goldstein, *Policing a Free Society*, 93–130.

83. Davis, *Police Discretion*, 52–78.

84. Ibid.; Ronald Allen, "The Police and Substantive Rulemaking: Reconciling Principle and Expediency," *University of Pennsylvania Law Review 125* (Spring 1976): 62–118.

85. H. Richard Uviller, "The Unworthy Victim: Police Discretion in the Credibility Call," *Law and Contemporary Problems* 47 (Autumn 1984): 28.

86. Davis, *Police Discretion*, 70–78; Joseph Goldstein, "Police Discretion Not to Invoke the Criminal Process," 146–47.

87. Joseph Goldstein, "Police Discretion Not to Invoke the Criminal Process."

88. Samuel Walker, *Taming the System: The Control of Discretion in Criminal Justice, 1950–1990* (New York: Oxford University Press, 1993).

89. Wilbert E. Moore, *The Professions: Roles and Rules* (New York: Russell Sage, 1970).

90. William A. Westley, *Violence and the Police: A Sociological Study of Law, Custom, and Morality* (Cambridge, MA: MIT Press, 1970).

91. Wilson, *Varieties of Police Behavior*, 20.

92. Los Angeles Police Commission, Office of the Inspector General, *Ten Year Overview of Categorical Use of Force Investigations, Policy, and Training.*

93. Reiss, *The Police and the Public*, 147.

94. Commission on Accreditation for Law Enforcement Agencies, *Standards for Law Enforcement Agencies*, 4th ed. (Fairfax, VA: CALEA, 1999), Standard 1.2.2.

95. American Bar Association, *Standards Relating to the Urban Police Function*, 2nd ed. (Boston: Little, Brown, 1980).

96. Fyfe, "Administrative Interventions on Police Shooting Discretion."

97. Lawrence W. Sherman, *Policing Domestic Violence* (New York: Free Press, 1992).

98. Geoffrey P. Alpert and Roger D. Dunham, *Police Pursuit Driving: Controlling Responses to Emergency Situations* (New York: Greenwood, 1990).

99. President's Task Force Report on 21st Century Policing, *Final Report*, Action Item 4.4.1, 45.

100. Davis, *Discretionary Justice*.
101. *Ibid.*
102. Davis, *Police Discretion*, 145.
103. Fyfe, "Administrative Interventions on Police Shooting Discretion."
104. George L. Kelling, *"Broken Windows" and Police Discretion* (Washington, DC: Department of Justice, 1999).
105. Walker, *Taming the System*.
106. President's Task Force on 21st Century Policing, *Final Report*.
107. Herman Goldstein, "Administrative Problems in Controlling the Exercise of Police Authority."
108. President's Task Force on 21st Century Policing, *Final Report*, Recommendation 1.4.
109. Davis, *Police Discretion*. Herman Goldstein, *Policing a Free Society*, 119–20.
110. President's Task Force on 21st. Century Policing, *Final Report*, Action Item 1.3.1.
111. Police Executive Research Forum, *Guiding Principles on Use of Force* (Washington, DC: Police Executive Research Forum, 2016, 18.
112. Wesley G. Skogan and Kathleen Frydl, *Fairness and Effectiveness in Policing: The Evidence*, (Washington, DC: National Academies Press, 2004), 282.
113. Fyfe, "Administrative Interventions on Police Shooting Discretion."
114. Geoffrey P. Alpert, *Pursuit Policies and Training* (Washington, DC: Government Printing Office, 1997).
115. Merrick Bobb, *15th Semiannual Report* (Los Angeles: Police Assessment Resource Center, 2002), 99.
116. Michael D. White and Henry F. Fradella, *Stop and Frisk: The Use and Abuse of a Controversial Policing Tactic* (New York: New York University Press, 2016), 184.
117. CALEA, Standards for Law Enforcement Agencies, Standard 1.3.6.
118. United States v. Cleveland, Investigation of the Cleveland Division of Police (December 4, 2014), 5. https://www.justice.gov/sites/default/files/crt/legacy/2014/12/04/cleveland_findings_12-4-14.pdf.
119. United States Department of Justice, Civil Rights Division, *Investigation of the Newark Police Department* (July 22, 2014), 25. https://www.

justice.gov/sites/default/files/crt/legacy/2014/07/22/newark_findings_7-22-14.pdf
120. Walker, *Taming the System*.
121. President's Task Force on 21st Century Policing, *Final Report*, Action Item 1.4.1.
122. Peter K. Manning, *Police Work* (Cambridge, MA: MIT Press, 1977), 165.
123. Inspector General for the NYPD, *Police Use of Force in New York City: Findings and Recommendations on NYPD's Policies and Practices* (New York: Office of the Inspector General, 2015).
124. Davis, *Police Discretion*, 32–33.
125. Walker and Archbold, *The New World of Police Accountability*, 2nd ed., 65–103.
126. CALEA, *Standards for Law Enforcement Agencies*, Ch. 1.
127. IACP Model Policies: http://www.iacp.org/Model-Policies-Alphabetical-Order
128. PERF web site: http://www.policeforum.org/
129. Wayne Schmidt, "A Proposal for a Statewide Law Enforcement Administrative Law Council," *Journal of Police Science and Administration* 2, no. 2 (1974): 330–38.
130. Samuel Walker, "Controlling the Cops: A Legislative Approach to Police Rulemaking," *University of Detroit Law Review* 63 (Spring 1986): 361–91.
131. Samuel Walker, *Police Accountability: The Role of Citizen Oversight* (Belmont, CA: Wadsworth, 2001). See also Walker and Archbold, *The New World of Police Accountability*, 2nd ed., 65–103.
132. See the Inspector General's web site at http://www.1NYC.gov/site/oignypd/index.page.
133. Merrick Bobb, *16th Semiannual Report* (Los Angeles: Police Assessment Resource Center, 2003). www.parc.info.
134. White and Fradella, *Stop and Frisk*, 184.
135. Dallin H. Oaks, "Studying the Exclusionary Rule in Search and Seizure," *University of Chicago Law Review* 37 (1970): 665–757.
136. Fyfe, "Administrative Interventions on Police Shooting Discretion."
137. Kelling, *"Broken Windows" and Police Discretion*.
138. Walker, *Taming the System*.

© Brooks Kraft LLC/Sygma via Getty Images

12 Legitimacy and Police–Community Relations

CHAPTER OUTLINE

From Police–Community Relations to Legitimacy

The National Police Crisis, 2014–2016

Legitimacy and Procedural Justice

The Many Communities in Police–Community Relations

Understanding Race and Ethnicity

Official Data on Race and Ethnicity

The Major Racial and Ethnic Groups

Public Opinion about the Police

Factors That Affect Public Opinion about the Police

The Impact of Controversial Incidents

Additional Perspectives on the Police in American Society

The Police and American Society

The Police and Other Occupations

The American Police in International Perspective

Police Officer Perceptions of Citizens

Police–Citizen Interactions: Sources of Police–Community Relations Problems and Loss of Legitimacy

The Level of Neighborhood Police Protection

Delay in Responding to 911 Calls

Police Use of Deadly Force

Unconscious Bias and Police Use of Deadly Force

Use of Physical Force

Patterns in Officer Use of Force

Stops and Frisks

Arrests

Arrests and the War on Drugs

The Complex Interaction of
   Demeanor, Race, and Arrests

David Kennedy on the "Racial
   Divide"

Unconscious Bias, Stereotyping,
   and Arrests

Verbal Abuse and Racial and
   Ethnic Slurs

Traffic Enforcement and Racial
   Profiling

**Building Legitimacy and Improving
Police–Community Relations**

The Different Dimensions of Trust
   and Confidence in the Police

Engaging the Community

Perspective: The Failure of
   Police–Community Relations
   Units in the 1960s

Ending Police Misconduct

Engaging Immigrant Communities

Immigration and Cultural Barriers
   in Policing

Language Barriers in Policing

A Representative Police Force

Citizen Oversight of the Police

Assign Officers on the Basis of
   Race or Ethnicity?

Do Citizens Care about the
   Ethnicity of the Officer?

Special Training over Race and
   Ethnicity

Summary
Key Terms
For Discussion
Internet Exercises

A deep divide over trust in the police exists in American society. The police shoot-ing and brutality events of 2014 and 2016 created a national police crisis focused on the fatal shooting of African American men by the police. Tradition-ally, the racial issues surrounding policing were labeled the *police–community rela-tions problem.* This term originated with the racial disturbances of the 1960s (see Chapter 2). Today, police experts argue that although race relations are indeed a serious problem, the police have a much deeper problem of *legitimacy.* **Legitimacy** is defined as the belief that the police as a social institution are acting properly and effectively, and deserve public support. Police experts today argue that legitimacy can be built by procedural justice in routine police activities, in which police officers treat people with respect, explain the reason for the contact with an officer, and answer peoples' questions. Research indicates that when people are treated respectfully they are more like to accept the legitimacy of the person or the institution they are dealing with (and this applies not just to the police) and be more willing to cooperate and assist them. In policing, this means that people are more willing to report crimes and neighborhood problems, serve as witnesses in criminal cases, and participate in police-initiated community policing programs.

legitimacy

This chapter examines legitimacy and procedural justice, giving special atten-tion to its racial dimensions. It links the traditional police–community relations is-sues of police shootings, excessive force incidents, traffic stops, and other actions with the new emphasis on legitimacy and procedural justice.

From Police–Community Relations to Legitimacy

The National Police Crisis, 2014–2016

In Ferguson, Missouri, a suburb of St. Louis, a white police officer on August 9, 2014, shot and killed Michel Brown, an unarmed 18-year-old African American. Angry protests about the shooting began quickly. When Missouri authorities mobi-lized military equipment in response to the growing demonstrations, the protesters

police–community
relations

grew only angrier. Eventually, violence erupted, including property destruction and arson. Cable television news programs began carrying round-the-clock coverage of the crisis, and sympathy demonstrations occurred in other cities around the country.[1]

Soon it was clear there was a national crisis over **police–community relations.** The Ferguson events were compounded by news of the earlier July 2014 choking death of Eric Garner, an African American who was selling illegal cigarettes. New York City police officers sat on him and did not respond to his pleas, "I can't breathe!" Garner died of suffocation. A cell phone video recorded the incident, and it was broadcast over national television. Then, in early April 2015, a white police officer shot in the back and killed Walter Scott, a 50-year-old African American man who was moving away from the officer. That shooting was also recorded on a cell phone. A week later, on April 12, 2015, Freddie Gray, a 25-year-old African American, died in a Baltimore police van of neck injuries. Gray's death touched off protests and then arson and looting in Baltimore.

David Kennedy, one of the top experts on gun violence in America, argues that a deep "racial divide" exists between the police and the African American community, one that affects routine police-citizen encounters on the street.[2] (We discuss his argument on p. 428.) In their study of traffic stops in the Kansas City metropolitan area, meanwhile, Charles Epp and his colleagues found a similar "deep racial chasm" in peoples' experiences with traffic stops.[3]

The national police crisis, in short, is serious and as this chapter explains, touches on every aspect of policing, from decisions about crime fighting strategy to the conduct of officers in encounters with individuals on the street. As this chapter progresses, two important theme will emerge. First, in some cases the data does not seem to support the idea of a national police crisis. Policing is complex, however, and the discussion of that data in this chapter will put it in a broader context. Second, this chapter will explain how some police practices that negatively affect the African American community are not the result of bias on the part of individual officers. Instead, they are the result of institutionalized department policies, particularly crime fighting strategies, that result in systematic discriminatory practices.[4]

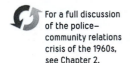

For a full discussion of the police–community relations crisis of the 1960s, see Chapter 2.

As the national police crisis grew, and the slogan "Black Lives Matter" became a rallying cry against police misconduct, President Barack Obama appointed the President's Task Force on 21st Century Policing to study the problem. It was the first presidential task force or commission devoted exclusively to the police in American history. The task force conducted public hearings across the country, and in the spring of 2015, issued a report with a sweeping set of recommendations for police reform, covering everything from police use of deadly force to police department hiring practices, and with a special emphasis on steps police departments should take to build public trust and confidence.[5] In Chapter 1, we discussed the main points of the task force report.[6]

Legitimacy and Procedural Justice

Experts in policing today now recognize that trust and confidence in the police is essential if the police are to do their jobs effectively. Public cooperation affects many basic police operations.[7] The police rely on the public to *report crimes* that occur. If a crime is not reported, the police cannot look for any suspects. They rely on people to *provide information* about particular crimes and neighborhood problems. The police need people, for example, to tell them about a drug house in the neighborhood. Both community policing and problem-oriented policing seek to build partnerships with neighborhood residents and groups to develop strategies to address crime and disorder. In particular, the police need people to *testify against criminals* in court. There is a major problem today with gang members intimidating potential witnesses from being witnesses against other gang members. The involvement of people in all of these activities is referred to as the "co-production" of police services.[8] The police cannot do it all themselves. They need neighborhood residents to participate actively in police-initiated programs to reduce crime and disorder.

Procedural justice is one of the keys to building legitimacy. Procedural justice focuses on how people are treated in, for example, employment settings or the activities of public agencies.[9] Specifically with respect to policing, procedural justice asks whether officers treat people equally, treat them with respect, explain the reason for the stop, and answer their questions. A growing body of research has found that people who are treated in a procedurally just manner are more likely to obey the law, cooperate with the police, have a more favorable opinion of the police department, and regard the police as legitimate. Additionally, people treated in a procedurally just manner are more likely to cooperate with both the police and community efforts to address crime and disorder.

Tom Tyler and Jeffrey Fagan surveyed 1,653 residents of New York City in 2002, and then 830 members of that cohort who could be located in 2004. Of the 830 in the second wave of interviews, 255 had at least one contact with the police since the first interview. This methodology, called a panel design, allowed in the second wave of interviews questions about respondents' experiences with the police since the initial interviews. The study was particularly timely, since New York City at that time was in the midst of a controversy over an aggressive stop and frisk program, which had generated protests and lawsuits, and which was eventually declared unconstitutional in 2013.[10]

The study found that "[r]espondents viewed the police as more legitimate if they [the police] made decisions fairly," and also "[i]f they treated people more justly." In the second wave of interviews, those respondents who had a "procedurally just" encounter with the police gave significantly higher ratings of police legitimacy than those who had no encounter since the first interview. Meanwhile, those who had an "unjust encounter" since the first interview "made significantly lower ratings of police legitimacy" than respondents who did not have an encounter since the first interview. In short, procedurally just policing matters in terms of whether people regard the police as legitimate.[11]

procedural justice

The Many Communities in Police–Community Relations

While the principal focus of the national police crisis is on the African American community, the social reality of America is that the police are responsible for many different communities, defined by social class, race and ethnicity, in some cases religion, and immigration status. The following section provides a quick overview of the different communities of color that exist in American society.

The experiences of different communities of color with the police are very different, and it is inappropriate to use blanket terms such as *minority groups* or *immigrants*. There is considerable evidence, for example, that African Americans and Hispanics have very different experiences with and different attitudes toward the police. Hispanics who are recent immigrants, moreover, have different experiences with the police than American-born Hispanics whose families have been here for several generations. Immigrants from Africa have very different experiences than African Americans. Native Americans, meanwhile, have a unique history in America. The term *minority groups* is inappropriate, for two reasons. First, it fails to distinguish between race and ethnicity, and assumes that all groups have roughly the same experience.[12] Second, in many cities and counties today, people of color are the majority population. Detroit is 83.4 percent African American, and Atlanta is 54 percent. El Paso is 80 percent Hispanic, and Miami is 69.4 percent. In the local context of these communities, who can be accurately described as the "majority" or the "minority"?

Understanding Race and Ethnicity

To intelligently discuss the issues related to the police and communities of color, it is important to get an accurate understanding of race and ethnicity.[13]

race

Race has traditionally been defined as referring to the major biological divisions of the people of the world. The traditional categories are Caucasian, Negroid, and Mongoloid. Anthropologists today, however, do not believe that these categories have any scientific validity. The surface differences that we observe, in skin color, hair texture, and body proportions, do not represent fundamental differences between people. Among African Americans, for example, there are people with the full range of skin tones, from light to very dark. People who are called "white," meanwhile, also come in a variety of skin tones. The American Anthropological Association's official 1998 statement declared that there is no scientific foundation for the traditional classification of human beings into distinct "races" that are identifiable by physical characteristics such as skin color, hair texture, and other features.[14]

ethnicity

Ethnicity refers to cultural differences, such as language, religion, family patterns, and food ways. Ethnicity is separate from race as a category. A person in the United States may be ethnically Hispanic, for example, but in terms of race can be either White, African American or Native American.[15] Among people of European background in the United States, all are considered white in terms of race, but they also come from a variety of nationalities, with separate traditions of language, religion, and so on.

Official Data on Race and Ethnicity

Official criminal justice data on race and ethnicity are important for understanding basic policy issues. It is important to know, for example, patterns of traffic stops by race and ethnicity, and the racial breakdown of people shot and killed by the police.

Criminal justice agencies use the U.S. Census categories of race and ethnicity.[16] The census, is a self-report system. Your race or ethnicity is whatever you tell the census it is. With regard to race, the official categories are White; Black or African American; American Indian and Alaska Native; Asian; and Pacific Islander. The U.S. Census now permits people of mixed racial background (for example, someone with a white father and an African American mother) to report themselves as mixed race. Ethnicity is a separate category in the census system. Thus, you report your race and then your ethnicity. Therefore, you can self-report as white/Hispanic, African American/non-Hispanic, or Native American/Hispanic, or whichever category is appropriate.

Official criminal justice data are problematic in a number of ways. Some agencies still use the "white/black" or "white/nonwhite" dichotomy. The FBI arrest data use "white/black," with the result that we do not know the arrest patterns for Hispanics.[17] Following the traditional but now discredited pattern, Hispanics are automatically classified as white by some agencies. An official, for example, may believe someone to be Hispanic and record it as such, without asking the person. The result is inconsistency and confusion. The report *Donde esta la justicia?* gives the hypothetical example of "Juanita," whose father is Puerto Rican and whose mother is African American. In Arizona, she would define her own race and ethnicity; in California, she would be classified as African American; and in Ohio, she would be listed as "biracial."[18]

The Major Racial and Ethnic Groups

In terms of the history of police–community relations, the most important racial group has been the African American community. Virtually every issue in policing involves controversies over race. This includes everything from employment practices to patterns of shootings. As was explained in Chapter 2, there have been several periods of mass urban violence. The 1968 Kerner Commission report found that many of the 1960s riots were provoked by an incident involving the police: the shooting of an African American by a police officer, or just a simple traffic stop. Complaints against the police included allegations of unjustified fatal shootings, use of excessive force, overly aggressive police tactics in stops and frisks, discrimination in traffic stops, and race discrimination in the recruiting and promoting of African Americans.[19] The national police crisis of 2014–2016 has primarily involved police fatal shootings of African Americans.

Recent immigration patterns have brought an increasing number of immigrants from Africa to the United States. Not only are African immigrants distinct from the African American community, they are divided by their country of origin, religion, and cultural practices.[20]

The Hispanic community has a very different history of relations with the police, compared with the African American community. It is diverse in terms of country of origin and immigration, with people from Mexico, Puerto Rico, and Central America and South America. Many are native-born Americans, while others are immigrants. In 2014, Hispanics represented 17 percent of the U.S. population. About two-thirds (64 percent) are of Mexican heritage, and one-third (35 percent) of all Hispanics are foreign born. Along with Asians, they are the fastest growing racial or ethnic group. It is estimated that between 10 and 15 percent of all Hispanics in the United States are undocumented immigrants (representing only half of the estimated

11 million undocumented immigrants in the United States in 2016). The number of undocumented Mexican immigrants began to decline in 2008, mainly because of the economic recession.[21] The issue of undocumented immigrants has in recent years become a major political issue. We discuss that issue, and the related issue of immigration enforcement, later in this chapter. Problems arise from prejudice on the part of non-Hispanics who stereotype all Hispanics as immigrants and/or undocumented immigrants.

Native Americans have a unique and complex relationship with American law enforcement. Native American tribes have the legal status of independent nations, with formal treaties with the U.S. government. (This is what exempts Native American reservations from state laws prohibiting gambling, for example.) Native American people live in both urban areas and on Native American reservations. A number of Native American tribes have their own tribal police forces.[22] A Justice Department report found that crime rates are much higher on reservations than in the general American population. Many tribal police departments are understaffed and lack sufficient equipment and resources to provide adequate police protection on reservations that encompass large geographic areas. In addition, there are often jurisdictional problems between tribal police and local police and sheriff's departments regarding the authority over offenses committed on reservations by Anglo Americans.[23] In urban areas, Native American people have many of the same problems with the police as do African Americans.

The Asian American community is also very diverse, including people whose national origin is Japan, China, Vietnam, Laos, Cambodia, and many other countries. In addition to having different national origins, Asian Americans speak different languages, practice different religions, and have different cultural traditions. And as a result, nationality groups are divided among long-standing American resident families and recent immigrants.

Arab Americans are also an extremely diverse group, with people of different national origins, religions, languages, and cultural traditions. Among the estimated 3.5 million Arab Americans in the United States, about a third (30 percent) trace their background to Lebanon, 12 percent to Egypt, and 9 percent to Syria. Most Arab Americans are native-born Americans, and more than 80 percent are American citizens. In terms of religion, many are Muslim, but others are Christian or members of other religious groups. The U.S. Census Bureau classifies Arab Americans as white or Caucasian. There is no definitive estimate of the Arab American population,

---

SIDEBAR 12-1

Not Just Race and Ethnicity: Gender and Sexual Preference

Police–community relations problems also exist with regard to other groups in society, particularly women, gay men, lesbians, and transgendered persons. With regard to women, there is a specific problem of some police officers targeting young women for traffic stops as a form of harassment. With regard to gay men, lesbians, and transgendered persons, the problem is one of disrespect and physical abuse.

Source: Amnesty International USA, *Stonewalled: Police Abuse and Misconduct Against Lesbian, Gay, and Transgendered People in the U.S.* (New York: Amnesty International USA, 2005).

however.[24] The major law enforcement problem related to the Arab American community is related to the war on terrorism and the terrorist attacks on September 11, 2001. Many Americans incorrectly assume that all Arabs are Muslims, and then unfairly stereotype all Muslims as terrorists. The result has been acts of discrimination against Arab Americans based on those two incorrect assumptions.

The incredible racial and ethnic diversity of the United States poses serious challenges in terms of languages, cultural practices, understanding of the American legal system, and attitudes about the police based on their native country experience.

Public Opinion about the Police

A good starting point for understanding police relations with the public is with public opinion about the police. What do people think about the police? How well do they rate their performance? As we will see, public opinion about the police is extremely complex and includes some contradictions that require explanation.

Surveys of **public attitudes toward the police** at both the national and local levels have been conducted since the 1960s. On the basic question of how people evaluate their local police, attitudes have been remarkably stable over that period.[25] Surveys consistently find that most Americans are satisfied with the police in their communities. In 2012, 84 percent of all Americans reported having confidence in the police (56 percent reported a "great deal" or "a lot"; 28 percent reported "some"). This represented 84 percent of white Americans, 76 percent of African Americans, and 85 percent of Hispanic Americans (see Exhibit 12–1).[26]

The fact that in 2012, 76 percent of African Americans expressed a positive attitude about the police appears to contradict the idea of a national police crisis. Part of the answer to this puzzle lies in the nature of the question in the survey. When people are asked a global question about how they rate the police, the responses have historically been quite positive. But when questions probe more deeply into specific issues such as perceptions of police use of force or whether respondents know someone who has had a bad experience with the police, the ratings by African Americans are much lower than it is for whites. (See our discussion of Sarah Stoutland's research on p. 437). A second consideration is that, as we will explain later in this chapter, police misconduct is concentrated among young African American men who live in high crime neighborhoods (or who travel into predominantly white neighborhoods). A public opinion survey that uses a nationally representative sample of the population does not capture the concentrated nature of police misconduct.

public attitudes toward police

Factors That Affect Public Opinion about the Police

Public attitudes about the police are influenced by a number of different factors. Here we take a closer look at the most important factors.

Race and Ethnicity

Race and ethnicity are the most important factors influencing attitudes toward the police. Survey since the 1960s have found a sharp difference between the attitudes of whites and African Americans. Exhibit 12–1 indicates that nearly twice as many African Americans as whites report "very little" confidence in the police.[27] The attitudes of

EXHIBIT 12–1

Reported Confidence in the Police, 2012

Demographic Characteristic	Great Deal/ Quite a Lot	Some	Very Little	None
Race				
White	57%	27%	14%	2%
Black	32	44	23	
Ethnicity				
Hispanic	57	28	13	x
Sex				
Male	59	24	14	2
Female	51	32	15	1
Age				
18–29 years	56	28	15	1
30–49	50	29	19	3
50–64	59	27	13	x
65 and older	61	28	10	x
Education				
College post-graduate	59	33	7	1
College graduate	63	28	8	1
Some college	50	28	20	2
High school graduate or less	55	27	16	2
Income				
$50,000–$74,000	58	30	10	1
$30,000–$49,999	55	27	17	x
Under $20,000	36	31	27	4

Source: Adapted from 2012 Gallup Poll. $N = 1,004$ adults, 18 years of age or older. Available in *Sourcebook of Criminal Justice Statistics* (Washington, DC: U.S. Bureau of Justice Statistics, 2012), table 2.12.

Hispanic Americans, meanwhile, are consistently less positive than whites but not as negative as African Americans.

The less positive attitudes of African Americans toward the police is easy to understand. Surveys of local communities have consistently found high levels of experiences with police misconduct among African Americans. In a survey of Cincinnati residents, 46.6 percent of African Americans indicated they had been personally "hassled" by the police, compared with only 9.6 percent of whites. *Hassled* was defined as being "stopped or watched closely by a police officer, even when you had done nothing wrong." Additionally, 66 percent of African Americans reported that someone they knew had been hassled, compared with only 12.5 percent of whites.[28] Among many African American families, there is much fear of the police. A number of news stories since 1997 have described how some African American and Hispanic parents made a special effort to teach their children to be very respectful of police officers, primarily because they were afraid their children might be arrested, beaten, or even shot if they displayed any disrespect to an officer.[29]

Social Class

Social class also has a major impact on attitudes toward the police. Exhibit 12–1 indicates that 27 percent of people with incomes below $20,000 have very little confidence in the police, compared with only 7 percent of people with incomes of $75,000 or greater. Ronald Weitzer interviewed 169 residents of Washington, D.C., representing three neighborhoods: one middle-class white, one middle-class African American, and one lower-income African American (there were not enough lower-income whites in the city for a fourth group). The residents of the lower-income African American neighborhood were seven times more likely than residents of the black middle-class neighborhood to believe that the police stop people on the street in their neighborhood without good reason and three times more likely than residents of the white middle-class neighborhood to believe this. Also, half (49 percent) of the residents of the lower-income African American neighborhood reported having seen the police use excessive force in their neighborhood, whereas none of the residents of the white middle-class neighborhood reported seeing excessive force incidents.[30] Along the same lines, Roger Dunham and Geoffrey Alpert found that attitudes about the police role in Miami vary according to social class as well as by race and ethnicity. Middle-class and lower-class African Americans do not share the same attitudes toward the police.[31]

Age

Age consistently ranks second to race and ethnicity as a factor in public attitudes toward the police. Exhibit 12–1 indicates that 16 percent of young people (between18 and 29 years old) and 22 percent of people between the ages of 30 and 49 had very little or no confidence in the police, compared with only 10 percent of people 65 years or older.

In a series of interviews with Chicago high school students by the Invisible Institute, one student argued, "They [the police] judge people by how old they are." "They think all teenagers are bad." Another charged that "they judge people by the way they look." A white female student added, "Just because you have a different color skin, or hair, or wear bizarre clothes doesn't mean you are a criminal."

The impact of age on attitudes toward the police is understandable. Young people spend more time out of the home than older and especially married people, and as a result have more contact with the police. Young men in high-crime neighborhoods are more likely to be stopped and questioned by the police than older people. Some of those contacts turn into conflict situations. Not only do people remember their own unpleasant encounters with the police, but they either see or hear of the unpleasant encounters their friends and acquaintances have experienced. As young people grow older, they generally marry and spend more time at home with their families and as a consequence are less likely to have contact with the police.

The combined impact of race, social class and age helps to explain the national police crisis. The result is a concentration of negative attitudes, based on bad experiences, in particular parts of American society.

Neighborhood Quality of Life

The quality of life in a neighborhood plays a major role in shaping attitudes toward the police. People who believe the police are effective in controlling crime in their neighborhood have greater confidence in the police. This is true for all racial and ethnic groups. The quality of neighborhood life is closely related to social class, as poor neighborhoods have higher levels of crime.[32]

Other Factors

A number of other factors also have some impact on attitudes toward the police. With respect to gender, there have generally been only slight differences in the attitudes of men and women toward the police. People who have been *victims of crime* consistently rate the police less favorably than do people who have not been victimized. They are angry about being victimized and direct that anger toward the police, the symbols of authority. *Level of education* has some impact on attitudes toward the police. People with only a high school education, or less, consistently rate the police less favorably than people with some college or more education. (Level of education, of course, is closely associated with social class.) In 2012, 18 percent of people with only a high school education or less had very little or no confidence in the police, compared with 8 percent of college graduates (See Exhibit 21–1).

Intercity Variations

When we look more closely at policing and public attitudes, we find that attitudes toward the police vary from city to city. A Bureau of Justice Statistics survey found that 93 percent of San Diego residents were satisfied with their police, compared with only 80 percent of Chicago residents and 78 percent of Washington, D.C., residents. Interestingly, the attitudes of whites and African Americans closely tracked each other from city to city. Both groups rated the San Diego police very high, and both rated the Chicago and Washington, D.C., police relatively low.[33]

The data suggest that the quality of policing varies from city to city, that people notice the quality, and that people of different races notice the difference. The data also suggest that police reform can have a positive impact on public attitudes. Hopefully, if a department implements procedural justice, people will notice the greater respect they receive from officers, and this will translate into more positive attitudes about the department.[34]

The Impact of Controversial Incidents

George Holliday never imagined that he would make the most famous videotape in the history of the police. On March 3, 1991, he stood on his apartment balcony and videotaped Los Angeles police officers repeatedly beating Rodney King. The tape was soon broadcast on television around the world, setting off a chain of dramatic events that included two criminal trials, a major riot (1992), and an independent investigation of the Los Angeles Police Department (LAPD). This one event had a significant impact on public attitudes about the police in Los Angeles, the United States, and the rest of the world.[35]

Stephen Tuch and Ronald Weitzer found that the Rodney King incident had a dramatic short-term effect on attitudes toward the LAPD. Prior to the incident, about 70 percent of whites consistently indicated they approved of the way the LAPD did its job. By May 1992, the figure had fallen to 40 percent. By 1993, however, responses of whites had returned to the 70 percent range. The percentage of African Americans approving of the LAPD fell even more dramatically (to only 14 percent in late March 1991), eventually returning to previous levels but at a slower rate than for whites.[36]

Additional Perspectives on the Police in American Society

The Police and American Society

Attitudes toward the police do not necessarily reflect personal experience with the police or the reputation of a particular department. In important respects attitudes about the police reflect attitudes toward American society, government, and race relations in general. People who express the greatest dissatisfaction with the police also have the most negative attitudes toward courts and judges, for example. They are more alienated from society and participate less in politics than people with more favorable attitudes toward the police.[37]

As many police experts have pointed out, the police play a symbolic role in American society as the agents of authority and the coercive power of the state. The badge, baton, and gun are the visible reminders of the police officer's power to use force, which Bittner argues is the defining aspect of the police role. Blumberg argues that the police are a "social lightning rod" for public attitudes about other social and political issues, while Niederhoffer calls the police officer a "Rorschach in uniform" —someone onto whom people project their fears and fantasies.[38] Thus, people who are the victims of discrimination, or who feel powerless or alienated from society, are likely to have more negative attitudes toward the police than people who feel powerful and integrated.

The Police and Other Occupations

If you do a web search for "lawyer jokes," you will quickly find many such jokes. Most of them characterize lawyers as unethical, amoral, and greedy. There are also a lot of jokes about police officers, particularly about them sitting in donut shops instead of patrolling the streets. Jokes about different occupations almost always reflect negative stereotypes that do not accurately represent the occupation in question or actual public attitudes.

Police officers regularly complain that they are always being criticized and do not get sufficient respect from the public. Public opinion surveys, however, indicate that the police rank very high compared with other institutions in American society. As Exhibit 12–2 indicates, the public has more confidence in the police than almost all other institutions, ranking behind only the military and small business. And as Exhibit 12–3 indicates, the police rank very high in terms of how the public perceives the honesty of different occupations.

EXHIBIT 12–2

Confidence in American Institutions, 2010

Institution	Percentage Expressing Confidence
The military	76%
Small business	66
The police	59
The church or organized religion	48
The medical system	40
The U.S. Supreme Court	36
The presidency	36
The public schools	34
The criminal justice system	27
Newspapers	25
Banks	23
Television news	22
Organized labor	20
Big business	19
Health maintenance organizations (HMOs)	19
Congress	11

Source: Lydia Sadd, "Congress Ranks Last in Confidence in Institutions," Gallup's 2010 Confidence in Institutions Poll, www.gallup.com/poll/141512/congress-ranks-last-confidence-institutions.aspx.

EXHIBIT 12–3

Ratings of Honesty and Ethical Standards of Occupations, 2010

Occupation	Percentage of Americans Rating It "Very High" or "High"
Nurses	81%
Grade school teachers	67
Medical doctors	66
Police	57
Clergy	53
Judges	47
Bankers	23
Lawyers	17
Car salespersons	7

Source: Jeffery Jones, Nurses Top Honesty and Ethics List for 11th Year, Gallup's annual Honesty and Ethics survey. Copyright © 2010 Gallup, Inc. All rights reserved. The content is used with permission; however, Gallup retains all rights of republication.

The American Police in International Perspective

American police also do very well compared with law enforcement agencies in other countries. A cross-national study conducted by Sanja Ivkovic found that American police enjoy one of the highest levels of public confidence in the world (see Exhibit 12–4).

EXHIBIT 12–4

Percent Expressing Confidence in Police, around the World

Finland	85%
Canada	84.1
Sweden	81.1
New Zealand	79.0
Netherlands	73.2
United States	71.2
Switzerland	68.6
Austria	67.8
France	66.5
Croatia	66.3
Italy	64.9
Spain	62.1
Belgium	51.0
Hungary	50.6
Yugoslavia	50.0
Romania	45.1
Ukraine	37.5
Russia	30.2
Slovakia	27.3
Lithuania	20.1

Source: Excerpts from Sanja Kutnjak Ivkovic, "A Comparative Study of Public Support for the Police," *International Criminal Justice Review* 18 (2008): 406–434.

Police Officer Perceptions of Citizens

It is important to also look at the other side of the police–public equation: the **attitudes of police officers** about the public. Police officers generally do not have an accurate perception of public attitudes toward them. In the 2014-2016 national police crisis, many police officers around the country were reportedly feeling under attack from the public. James Q. Wilson argues that police officers "probably exaggerate the extent of citizen hostility."[39] In his pioneering work on the police subculture, William A. Westley found that 73 percent of the officers thought that the public was "against the police, or hates the police." As we have seen, however, public opinion surveys do not support this view. Only a relatively small percentage of the American people say they have "very little" confidence in the police."[40] When a RAND survey of Cincinnati police officers asked officers if "citizens on the street act disrespectfully," half of the officers responded that half or more citizens were disrespectful. Yet, when asked if suspects forcibly resisted being arrested, only 7 percent said "usually." The police perception of public hostility is far greater than the actual experience of physical challenges to their authority.[41]

Several factors explain police officer misperception of public attitudes. Most important is the pattern of **selective contact** between police and the public. Officers do not have regular contact with a cross-section of the community. The 911 call system

attitudes of police officers

For a detailed discussion of the police subculture, see Chapter 6.

selective contact

brings them into contact with problem situations: a disorder incident, a residential burglary, a person having a mental health crisis, a robbery in progress, and so on. Few people are at their best in these situations. Even if the burglary victim is a law-abiding person who respects the police, he or she is likely to be very upset because of the burglary and may take out the frustration on the responding officer.

Police officers see humanity at its worst. They are the first responders who find the dead victim of a violent crime; the person suspected of several murders; the victim of severe child abuse; or the parents grieving over their son who was just shot and killed by a gang member. These situations would take a psychological toll on any person. Police officers get a steady diet of such situations, month by month and year by year. To maintain some degree of emotional stability, officers learn to become detached and not get emotionally involved in the tragedies they deal with. In a similar way, doctors in the hospital emergency room learn to keep a professional distance from the serious medical conditions they deal with. Unfortunately, for police officers, this "professional distance" can often be seen as cold indifference, and in that respect contribute to negative attitudes about the police. Additionally, the steady diet of human tragedy that officers encounter can give them a cynical view of humanity in general. They see that people can do terrible things, and they can easily begin to stereotype all people in that regard.[42]

For a discussion of routine police patrol work, see Chapter 7.

Low-income people, and people of color in particular, have a disproportionate level of contact with the police. Police departments deploy more patrol officers in their neighborhoods because of higher crime levels, and they are more likely than other Americans to call the police. This pattern of concentrated contact contributes to less favorable attitudes toward the police.[43]

selective perception and memory

Police officer attitudes are also shaped by **selective perception and memory,** particularly with respect to situations that involve conflict with people. In fact, only about 2 to 5 percent of all police contacts with citizens involve hostility or conflict. But, like most people, police officers are more likely to remember unpleasant events.[44] Donald Black found that young African American men were more likely than young white men to express hostility to the police. Consequently, officers tend to stereotype young African American males in terms of what Jerome Skolnick called the "symbolic assailant" and a potential source of conflict.[45]

Police–Citizen Interactions: Sources of Police–Community Relations Problems and Loss of Legitimacy

How do we explain the apparent contradiction between the generally favorable ratings given to the police and the long history of police–community relations problems, along with the President's Task Force conclusion that there is a crisis of confidence and trust in the police?

We can answer these questions by examining specific aspects of policing. As we have already discussed, single-question public opinion surveys do not adequately address the complexity of the police role in society, the many tasks they perform, and the different actions they take. In the sections that follow, we examine the different aspects that create tensions between the police and different groups, and between the police and communities of color in particular.[46]

The Level of Neighborhood Police Protection

A recurring allegation by leaders in many African American communities is that the police fail to provide adequate police protection. Yet, police departments routinely assign more patrol to high-crime neighborhoods, which includes poor African American areas. Do the police provide too much or too little protection? Most Americans, when asked what they would like from the police, say they want more police protection. Stoutland's research (see p. 437) explored the question of whether people believe the police share their concerns about the neighborhood as one of four dimensions of trust in the police.[47] Weitzer and Tuch found that whites, African Americans, and Hispanics all express strong support for more police patrol and surveillance of high-crime areas.[48]

Historically, African Americans were the victims of underenforcement of the law. Gunnar Myrdal's classic study of race relations in America found that during the period of institutionalized segregation in the South, the police disregarded many crimes in the African American community. The result was **four systems of justice,** depending on the racial components of the offender–victim relationship: (1) Crimes by whites against whites were handled as "normal" crimes; (2) crimes by whites against African Americans were rarely prosecuted, if at all; (3) crimes by African Americans against whites received the harshest response; and (4) crimes by African Americans against African Americans were often ignored.[49] In the 1960s, the President's Crime Commission and the Kerner Commission both reported that in major cities outside the South, African American community leaders alleged that the police did not provide adequate police protection, including being late in responding to calls for service.[50]

four systems of justice

Failure to enforce the law in minority neighborhoods has often involved crimes of vice. Historically, gambling, after-hours drinking, prostitution, and drugs were allowed to exist in low-income and racial-minority neighborhoods. Tolerating vice crimes harms low-income and racial-minority communities in several ways. First, it breeds disrespect for the law and the police, partly because of the corruption that usually accompanies it. The Knapp Commission investigation of police corruption in New York City found that the monthly vice payoffs to police in the predominantly African American areas of Harlem averaged $1,500 (or $7,255 in 2016 dollars), compared with $300 ($1,451 in 2016) in predominantly white downtown precincts.[51]

Second, underenforcement of the law exposes law-abiding citizens in communities of color to prostitution, drug dealing, and related crimes such as shootings and robberies. These crimes expose individuals and their families to personal risk, lower the quality of life in the neighborhood, and increase the risk that juveniles will engage in crime themselves.[52]

The question of whether the police under-police or over-police neighborhoods illuminates an important contradiction in policing. In practice, the policing of a neighborhood can *simultaneously* involve underenforcement and overenforcement. On the same shift, patrol officers can both stop many young men on the street and deliberately respond slowly to a 911 call. On one block, the officers responding to a violent domestic assault choose not to arrest the assailant, even though the victim is bleeding and there is obvious cause for a felony arrest. One block over, however, two police officers stop, question, and frisk three young African American men on the street, even though the officers do not have any reasonable suspicion that the men are committing or are about to commit a crime. To repeat a point we made earlier, policing is complex; contradictory things can happen in the same neighborhood within hours or even minutes of each other.

Delay in Responding to 911 Calls

Several studies of police work found that patrol officers often deliberately delayed responding to calls for service, especially in the case of family disturbances.[53] In an early study, Frank Furstenburg and Charles Wellford's interviews with citizens in Baltimore who had called the police found that African American citizens perceived greater delays than whites. A higher percentage of whites reported the police responding in less than five minutes, while nearly twice as many blacks as whites reported that the police took more than 15 minutes to respond. A more recent study of a high-crime, predominantly African American neighborhood in St. Louis found that "most complaints about policing centered around poor police response." This included delayed response time and complete failure to respond to a 911 call.[54, 55]

In short, there is some truth to the allegation of inadequate police protection (underenforcement) in low-income and neighborhoods of color. In the next section, we will see how, at the same time, certain police practices also support the allegation of unfair treatment of young males in the same neighborhoods (overenforcement).

Police Use of Deadly Force

The fatal shooting of Michael Brown in Ferguson, Missouri, in August 2014 touched off angry protests that eventually led to property destruction and arson.[56] The release of the police video in Chicago, in November 2015, showing a police officer fatally shooting Laquan McDonald in the back touched off massive protests and calls for the resignation of the mayor.[57] Historically, the fatal shooting of African American men by the police has been the most explosive issue in police–community relations. Exhibit 12–5 summarizes shootings by Chicago police officers between 2008 and 2015.

EXHIBIT 12–5

Shootings by Chicago Police (person hit or killed), by Race and Ethnicity, 2008–2015

	Number and Percentage Shot	Proportion of City Population
African American	299 (74%)	32.9%
Hispanic	55 (14)	28.9
White	33 (8)	31.7
Total	387	

Note: --- (data not provided).

Source: Police Accountability Task Force, *Recommendations for Reform: Restoring Trust between the Chicago Police and the Communities They Serve* (Chicago: Author, April 2016), 7, https://chicagopatf.org/wp-content/uploads/2016/04/PATF_Final_Report_4_13_16-1.pdf.

In 2014, people were shocked to discover that the United States did not have complete and reliable data on the number of persons shot and killed by the police every year. The Ferguson shooting prompted a team of reporters from the *Washington Post* to look deeply into the issue and begin compiling as complete a list as possible for 2015. They discovered that the police shot and killed twice as many people (986 in 2015) as the FBI's data had been indicating in recent years (it reported 444 in 2014, the most recent figures available). The official FBI data involve a voluntary system, in which police departments are not required to report shooting data. The lack of a complete data on police shootings suggests an indifference to the issue. The *Washington Post* data, moreover, indicated that African Americans were three times more likely to be shot by the police than whites. Further, they represented 40 percent of all the people who were unarmed but shot and killed.[58]

The pattern of racial disparities in police shootings has existed for decades, although there have been some significant changes over time. As result of better policies to control officer use of deadly force, the ratio of African Americans to whites shot and killed by the police had declined from 6 to 1, or even 8 to 1 in the late 1960s and early 1970s, compared to the recent estimate of 3 to 1. In short, no matter how bad the situation appears today, it was even worse in past.[59]

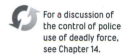

For a discussion of the control of police use of deadly force, see Chapter 14.

The long-term reduction in the number of police shootings since the mid-1970s is the result of two major factors. The first was the more restrictive use-of-deadly-force policy adopted by the New York City Police Department (NYPD) in 1972. The policy replaced the **fleeing-felon rule,** which allowed police officers to shoot and killed a fleeing unarmed burglary suspect, with the restrictive *defense-of-life* policy, which allows officers to use deadly force only where there is an imminent threat of death or serious bodily injury to the officer or some other person. James J. Fyfe evaluated the new NYPD policy and found the annual average number of shots fired declined by 30 percent. The greatest reduction occurred in fleeing-felon situations.[60] Other departments around the country soon began adopting the defense-of-life rule. We examine the 1972 NYPD policy and other controls over police use of deadly force in more detail in Chapter 14.

fleeing-felon rule

The second major factor affecting police use of deadly force was the 1985 Supreme Court ruling in *Tennessee v. Garner*. Edward Garner was a slightly built (weighing 110 pounds) 15-year-old unarmed African American who was shot and killed by two Memphis, Tennessee, police officers while fleeing a suspected burglary. He had in his possession a stolen purse containing $10. A lawsuit brought by his family resulted in the landmark Supreme Court case that bears his name. The Court ruled that the fleeing-felon rule, under which the Memphis officers acted, was unconstitutional. The decision accelerated the trend toward adoption of the defense-of-life standard, which greatly restricts the use of deadly force by police officers.[61]

In addition to the perceived injustice of many police shootings, particularly when the person was unarmed, community members have also been critical of the lack of information available about shooting incidents and the lack of independent investigations of such incidents. As a result, the President's Task Force in 2015 recommended that "[w]hen serious incidents occur, including those involving alleged police misconduct, agencies should communicate with citizens and the media swiftly, openly, and neutrally, respecting areas where the law requires confidentiality" (Action Item 1.3.2). The lack of information about excessive force or shooting incidents allows rumors and misinformation to spread, aggravating already-tense community relations. Additionally, the task force recommended mandatory "external and independent criminal investigations in cases of police use of force resulting in death, officer-involved shootings resulting in injury or death, or in-custody deaths" (Action Item 2.2.2). Many people do not trust police departments to investigate themselves, particularly in shooting cases, and investigations by independent external agencies will serve to build trust and confidence.[62]

Unconscious Bias and Police Use of Deadly Force

unconscious stereotypes and bias

There is growing recognition of the role of **unconscious stereotypes and bias** regarding race and ethnicity in police use of deadly force. Many Americans hold stereotypes about race and ethnicity, and police officers are no exception. Stereotypical biases are often so deeply rooted that people are not conscious of them.

In policing, the most important stereotype is the association of African American men with "dangerousness." Acting on that belief, officers are more likely to stop and frisk young African American men in the belief that they are gang members or active criminals who are carrying weapons. Another common stereotype is the association of Hispanics with immigration, with Hispanic individuals being treated as immigrants even though they are natural-born Americans. Men, meanwhile, are also stereotyped as being potentially more dangerous than women. Lorie Fridell, director of the Fair and Impartial Policing Project, explained how many police recruits underestimate the dangerousness of women and, for example, in training situations do not search for a gun that might be tucked in a woman's back "because they stereotype women as not being a threat."[63]

Research using computer simulations of encounters between police officers and suspects of different races or ethnicities has found that the decision to use deadly force is affected by racial or ethnic stereotypes. One study involved three different groups of participants in a videogame simulation of scenarios of armed and unarmed white and African American men. The groups included Denver police officers, community residents, and a second group of police officers who were attending a training seminar. Participants were presented with 25 images each of an armed white, unarmed white, armed African American, and unarmed African American. The unarmed people held objects that were not weapons, such as wallets or cell phones. Participants were instructed to shoot as quickly as possible anyone who appeared to be an "imminent threat," and to push the "don't-shoot" button as quickly as possible for those who did not pose an imminent threat.[64]

The study found "robust racial bias" in the speed with which both the officers and the non-officers fired their simulated weapons. In terms of accurately assessing imminent threats, the citizen participants were less accurate than the police officers, meaning they were more likely to see an imminent threat from the African American images where one did not exist. In a replication study, participants were forced to make their decisions more quickly, and as a result the error rate increased significantly. Other studies have confirmed the role of racial stereotypes in the decision to use deadly force.

The Fair and Impartial Policing Project conducts training on unconscious bias for rank-and-file officers and supervisors as a means of reducing unconscious bias in policing.[65]

POLICE in FOCUS | Does Skin Tone Matter?

Does a person's skin tone matter in policing? Are African Americans or Hispanics who are very dark skinned more likely to be stopped, arrested, or even shot than people who are light skinned?

In a pioneering study, Karletta M. White investigated the impact of skin tone on being stopped by the police. The most recent survey in the National Longitudinal Study of Adolescent Health (generally referred to as ADD Health) involved in-home surveys, in which investigators recorded the respondents' skin tone on a five-point scale (black, dark brown, medium brown, light brown, white). Respondents reported their own race and identity, and also their experience in being stopped by the police.

White found that "skin tone is related to the likelihood of being stopped or arrested by the police" for African Americans. In particular, "the odds of being stopped or arrested increase significantly" the darker the person's skin. The findings with regard to Hispanics, however, were ambiguous, because of the small number of dark-skinned Hispanics. More research on the issue of skin tone is needed. If skin tone affects police decisions to stop people, does it also have an effect on police shootings or use of physical force?

Source: Karletta M. White, "The Salience of Skin Tone: Effects on the Exercise of Police Enforcement Authority," *Ethnic and Racial Studies* 38, no. 6 (2015): 993–1010.

Use of Physical Force

Allegations of excessive force by police (often referred to as "police brutality") is the second most serious source of police–community relations tensions. The issue of excessive physical force is particularly complex. Police officers are authorized by department policies to use force in certain situations: to protect themselves, to effect an arrest, to overcome resistance, and to bring a dangerous situation under control. The relevant question is, "When is the use of force excessive?"[66] The Commission on Accreditation for Law Enforcement Agencies (CALEA) accreditation standards state that officers "will use only the force necessary to accomplish lawful objectives." Excessive force is any level of force more than is necessary to fulfill a lawful objective.[67] A police officer is not justified in using physical force in response to mere disrespect, for example.

Measuring police use of force is difficult, First, force incidents are relatively infrequent. Studies involving direct observation of police generally estimate that officers use force in about 1 to 2 percent of all encounters with people. It is further estimated that about two-thirds of all uses of force are justified, and about one-third are unjustified or excessive.[68] The 2011 Police-Public Contact Survey found that police officers used force in 1.5 percent of all encounters with citizens, and threatened to use force in another 3.4 percent of encounters.[69]

Many people believe the 1 to 2 percent estimate of police use of force is far too low. The estimate, however, acquires a different meaning when measured in terms of all police–citizen encounters in a particular city. Consider the case of Omaha, Nebraska, with a population of about 400,000 people and a police force of 850 sworn officers. The department responded to 223,000 emergency (911) calls plus 37,638 officer-initiated traffic stops in 2014, for a total of about 260,000 police–citizen contacts. If we assume that force is used in 1.5 percent of all encounters, then force was used an estimated 3,900 times that year (remember, this is an *estimate* and not an actual count). One-third of that figure yields an estimate of 1,287 excessive force incidents, or 3.5 excessive force incidents each and every day.[70] (As an exercise, you can analyze the data for your own city.)

Moreover, as Albert Reiss points out, use-of-force incidents accumulate over time with the result that "a sizeable minority of citizens experience police misconduct at one time or another."[71] And because most force incidents involve young, low-income men, with a disproportionate representation of racial and ethnic minorities, this group of people will have a strong perception of police harassment.

Patterns in Officer Use of Force

Police use of force is not a random event. Studies have consistently found general patterns in the use of force. Certain situational factors explain when police officers are more likely to use force. Officers are more likely to use force against criminal suspects (about 4 to 6 percent of all encounters with suspects), male suspects, African American males, and citizens who were drunk and/or antagonistic to the police. Physical resistance or disrespect to a police officer significantly increases the likelihood of use of force.[72] The discussion on p. 441 lists six steps that police departments can take to reduce the use of force by officers, including de-escalation.

force factor

Geoffrey Alpert developed the **force factor** framework, which examines police officer behavior in relation to the citizen's actions. If an officer uses force when there is no resistance or threat on the part of the citizen, then the force is considered excessive. In one police department, Alpert found that officers used more force than was indicated by citizen behavior in 19 percent of all cases, and less force than was indicated in 32 percent of all cases.[73]

A Police Foundation national survey of police officers yielded a different perspective on officer use of force. Many officers concede that other officers use excessive force. The survey found that 21.7 percent of all officers agree that officers in their own departments sometimes, often, or always use more force than is necessary to make an arrest. The survey found a significant gap in the perceptions of white and African American officers. More than half of the African American officers (57.1 percent) agreed that officers are more likely to use physical force against African Americans and other minorities than against whites in similar situations. Only 5.1 percent of the white officers agreed with that statement. African American officers also agreed more than white officers (54.4 percent versus 8.8 percent) that the police are more likely to use force against poor people than middle-class citizens.[74]

Critics of the police assume that excessive force incidents primarily involve white officer interactions with people of color. Reiss, however, found that white and African American officers were about equally likely to use force and were most likely to use force against members of their own race.[75] Citizen complaint data from San Jose and New York City, meanwhile, indicate that white, African American, and Hispanic officers receive citizen complaints at rates equal to their presence on the police force.[76] In short, the use of force is primarily a function of the police role and situational factors rather than the race or ethnicity of officers.

As we learned in Chapter 5, there is today a special emphasis on police departments developing policies and training on de-escalation, so that officers can use verbal and nonverbal techniques to prevent encounters with citizens that have the potential for escalating into conflict from ending with that result. Police experts argue that de-escalation can avoid violence, injury to both parties, lawsuits against the department, and damage to community relations.[77]

Stops and Frisks

Stopping and questioning people on the street, and frisking some of them, is a traditional police practice. The police believe that stops will both successfully identify criminal suspects and send a deterrent message to other potential offenders. But do the police have a right to stop and question someone?[78]

The Supreme Court ruled in *Terry v. Ohio* that a "stop" (which is not an arrest) is constitutional if the officer has *reasonable suspicion* that a person is committing or about the commit a crime. The officer, however, must have some specific reason for the suspicion. The Court also ruled that an officer may "frisk" (which is less intrusive than a search) a stopped person through a pat-down in order to determine if the person has a weapon. The purpose of a frisk is limited to ensuring officer safety and not to search for evidence of contraband.[79]

For more than a decade, New York City was embroiled in a major controversy over the NYPD's aggressive **stop and frisk** program. Despite community protests that it targeted African Americans and Hispanics, the number of stops increased from 97,296 in 2002 to 685,724 in 2011. Over half of those stopped (55.7 percent) were frisked. Young African American and Hispanic males between the ages of 14 and 24 accounted for 41.6 percent of all stops in 2011, even though they represented only 4.7 percent of the city's population. The frisks were extremely unproductive. Only 1.9 percent of all frisks resulted in the finding of a weapon.[80]

stop and frisk

In 2013, a U.S. District Court ruled the NYPD practices to be an unconstitutional violation of the Fourteenth Amendment guarantee of equal protection of the law, and also the Fourth Amendment protection against unreasonable searches and seizures. The court ordered the NYPD to revise its stop and frisk policy, including developing an improved stop and frisk report form, and also to improve its training of officers on the law of stops and frisks. In short, the court-ordered reforms followed the policy approach discussed in this chapter with regard to deadly force, excessive force, and traffic stops.[81]

A pattern of stops without legal justification not only is illegal but also can have a devastating effect on attitudes toward the police and the perceived legitimacy of the police. In a study of street stops by police in New York City (in the midst of the stop and frisk controversy), Tom Tyler and colleagues argue that for young people in particular, stops by the police are "teachable moments" that have a significant impact on their attitudes toward the police and the larger society. The police are "the primary face of the state" and, for many young people, the first real contact with authority they experience as they are growing up. The study involved 1,261 young men between the ages of 18 and 26 from different neighborhoods in the city. The respondents represented a racially and ethnically balanced sample, but interestingly 82.9 percent reported having been stopped by the police at some point in their lives, and 43.5 percent had been stopped in the past year (either on the street or in a car). These data provide a revealing glimpse into the intensity of the NYPD stop and frisk program. The number of times individuals had been stopped by the police did not have a significant impact on attitudes toward police legitimacy, but the "intrusiveness" of stops had a very significant effect, with *intrusiveness* defined in terms of officer use of force or threatened use of force, or humiliating or disrespectful treatment. The perceived legitimacy of the respondents' experience affected three self-reported law-related behaviors: criminal behavior, cooperating with the police, and cooperating with the legal system. In the end, the authors conclude that "legitimacy matters."[82]

In terms of ensuring that stop and frisk practices are constitutional, White and Fradella argue that "previous efforts of discretion control," for example with respect to police use of deadly force, "officer important lessons" for effectively controlling officer conduct. Additionally, they argue that the police auditor model of citizen oversight (see our discussion on p. 444) can help to ensure that a department's stop and frisk practices continue to comply with the law.[83]

The NYPD's aggressive stop and frisk program was a classic example of the kind of heavy-handed crime-fighting policy that the Kerner Commission in 1968 argued damaged relations with the community, and which the President's Task Force also criticized for the same reason in 2015.[84] The impact of the program represents a form of *institutionalized discrimination* because it arises from an organization's policy and not from acts of individual officer discrimination (see the discussion on p. 433).

Arrests

African Americans are arrested more often than whites relative to their proportions in the population. In 2014, African Americans represented 12 percent of the population but 56 percent of all arrests for robbery, 30 percent of all arrests for burglary, and 13 percent of arrests for drunk driving. The data clearly indicate considerable variation in the racial distribution of arrests by different types of crime (African Americans are more often arrested for robbery, while drunk driving arrests overwhelmingly involve whites. And as we discuss shortly, arrests for drug offenses represent a particularly contentious issue.) Arrest is an extremely common experience for young African American men in the inner city. The Sentencing Project estimated in 2016 that African American men who were born in 2001 have a 1 in 3 chance of imprisonment, compared with 1 in 17 for white men.[85] One of the major collateral consequences of arrest, moreover, is that it tends to increase racially disparate decisions in later stages of the criminal justice system (bail, sentencing, etc.), increasing the overall racial disparities in the criminal justice system.[86]

Observational studies of police arrest practices have found a complex pattern of factors that influence officers in making arrests. The most important situational factors include the seriousness of the offense, the strength of the evidence, whether or not the victim wants an arrest, the relationship of the victim to the offender (with a higher probability of arrest if they are strangers), and the demeanor of the suspect. Race or ethnicity have not been identified as the direct *cause* of arrests. This important matter is extremely complex, however, as race or ethnicity is closely interrelated with some other factors. Overall, the research indicates that race is a factor in arrests.

Tammy Rinehart Kochel and colleagues undertook a systematic review of all available studies of police arrests and found that "race matters." Even after controlling for other variables, they found "a clear pattern of evidence" that "minorities and Blacks have higher odds of arrest" than whites. On average, the probability of arrest for an African American was 30 percent higher than for a white person.[87]

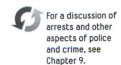

For a discussion of arrests and other aspects of police and crime, see Chapter 9.

The role of race and ethnicity becomes clearer when we look more closely at particular aspects of arrests, especially the war on drugs and the influence of a suspect's demeanor in influencing a police officer's decision.

Arrests and the War on Drugs

The greatest racial disparities in arrest involve drug offenses. In 2014, African Americans accounted for 30 percent of all drug-related arrests. The 2014 Monitoring the Future survey of drug use, however, found that among high school seniors, self-reported marijuana use was nearly identical for whites (35.1 percent), African Americans (35.9 percent), and Hispanics (37.1 percent).[88] The data on patterns of drug usage suggest that the police target African Americans for drug enforcement. The war on drugs has directly contributed to the enormous U.S. prison population, which Michelle Alexander has labeled "mass incarceration."[89]

One aspect of the **war on drugs** that has gotten steadily worse in recent years involves arrests for marijuana possession. A 2013 American Civil Liberties Union report found that nationwide between 2001 and 2010, there were over 8 million marijuana arrests, accounting for half of all drug arrests, and that the number had been steadily increasing every year. African Americans were 3.73 times more likely than whites to be arrested for marijuana possession.[90] The enormous disparity in arrests for marijuana possession is not consistent with patterns of marijuana usage reported by the Monitoring the Future survey.[91]

war on drugs

The Complex Interaction of Demeanor, Race, and Arrests

Studies have consistently found that the **demeanor of the suspect** has an important effect on officers' decisions to arrest. (See Sidebar 12–3.) The subject of demeanor, however, is extremely complex.

demeanor of the suspect

In a pioneering study, Donald Black found that African Americans were more likely to be antagonistic to the police than whites, and more likely to be arrested for that reason.[92] However, in many instances the hostile demeanor of the suspect is provoked by the police officer. Bayley and also Mastrofski and Parks argue that police officers approach encounters with citizens with a "script" representing their preliminary perception of the situation. Thus, an officer may begin with an expectation of conflict and, through verbal or nonverbal ways, communicate a hostile attitude toward the person, which in turn provokes a hostile response. That hostility then provokes an arrest. Additionally, as we discuss shortly, there has been a pattern of disrespectful and offensive language used by police officers, including racial and ethnic slurs. Offensive language of this sort can easily provoke a response that the officer can use to justify an arrest.[93]

Christy Lopez, meanwhile, argues that many arrests for disorderly conduct or resisting arrest in fact involved the officer improperly responding to perceived disrespect

S I D E B A R   1 2 – 2

The Complex Dimensions of Police–Citizen Demeanor

The patterns of demeanor of citizens and police officers are extremely complex. Dunham and Alpert point out that almost all studies measure the subjects' behavior at one point. Common sense, however, tells us that our behavior often changes in response to someone else's conduct. Dunham and Alpert confirmed this in a study of police–citizen interactions in Savannah, Georgia, where they observed the sequence of events in encounters.

The demeanor of citizens and police officers changed in about one-fourth of all encounters. With both citizens and officers, their demeanor improved (i.e., became more civil) in half the cases and changed for the worse (i.e., became less civil) in the other half. Most important, both citizen and officer demeanor changed in reaction to the demeanor or behavior of the other person.

Dunham and Alpert argue that the last point has enormous implications for police training. Officers need to be trained on how their conduct affects citizens, and taught techniques for de-escalating potential confrontations and gaining cooperation. (One such technique is known as "verbal judo.") This would probably reduce the number of use-of-force incidents and citizen complaints. As discussed in Chapter 5, one of the most important recent developments in police training involves tactical decision-making, which involves training officers to constantly reassess a situation and adjust their response as the situation changes. If a suspect becomes less threatening, for example, officers choose de-escalation and avoid the use of force.

Source: Roger G. Dunham and Geoffrey P. Alpert, "Officer and Suspect Demeanor: A Qualitative Analysis of Change," *Police Quarterly* 12 (March 2009): 6–21. Police Executive Research Forum, Re-Engineering Training on Police Use of Force (Washington, DC: Police Executive Research Forum, 2015).

by the person involved. Disrespect, in terms of a facial expression or not answering a question, is not a crime. These kinds of arrests have been labeled "contempt of cop." The officer makes the arrest to punish the person for not showing what he or she feels is the proper respect.[94]

David Kennedy on the "Racial Divide"

racial divide

David Kennedy, one of the leading experts on gun violence reduction, developed the argument about scripts in a provocative argument on what he sees as a deep "**racial divide**" in policing African American neighborhoods. He argues that both sides in police–citizen encounters have inherited narratives about the other side and that there is no real dialogue between the two. The police narrative is that in high-crime neighborhoods, no one cares, that the "moral backbone" of these communities collapses, that no one tells criminals to stop, and that there is no "community" left to partner with. As a result, many officers approach an encounter with negative attitudes about the people in the encounter. The community narrative is that there is a conspiracy to destroy African American communities, that the police are a part of it, and that the government introduced the drug "crack" as part of this conspiracy. In addition, there is a community memory of recent or even long-past incidents of police shootings or use of excessive force.[95]

The result of these two narratives is that in an encounter on the street, both the young African American man and the police officer bring deeply embedded suspicions, and are very likely to either communicate those attitudes to the other person and/or interpret that person's words or looks as hostile. In many such situations, the encounter quickly escalates to overt conflict and an arrest. Kennedy argues that both of these narratives contain exaggerations and falsehoods and that it is necessary to get past them if we are to develop effective solutions to the problems of drugs and gun violence in high-crime, African American neighborhoods. Ideally, training officers in procedural justice, and having officers treat people on the street with greater respect, can break the cycle of mutual distrust and build more positive police-community relations.

Unconscious Bias, Stereotyping, and Arrests

As we discussed earlier on the subject of deadly force, unconscious bias is a general problem in America, and it affects the police as it does people in other occupations. In policing, unconscious stereotypes about criminal behavior and/or dangerousness can lead to unjustified arrests. An African American resident of Washington, D.C., for example, explained how he and his friends perceive police practices: "If they [the police] stop a white guy at three in the morning, they'll figure he was working late and he's on his way home to see his wife. [They] stop a black person at three in the morning and figure he was up to no good, always assuming the worst when it's some-one of color." The perception of harassment by the police is very strong, especially with regard to police-initiated stops on the street. These actions are referred to as *pedestrian stops* or *field interrogations*. Stops are sometimes accompanied by searches.

Jerome Skolnick pointed out many years ago that police officers are trained to be suspicious and, from experience, develop a visual "shorthand" for suspects, based on visual cues. Inevitably, this involves a certain amount of **stereotyping,** by gender, age, and race. Skolnick concludes that "a disposition to stereotype is an integral part of the policeman's world."[96] Training over unconscious bias can hopefully help officers to recognize unconscious biases they may have and as a result reduce actions improperly based on racial stereotypes.[97]

stereotyping

SIDEBAR 12–3

Abuse of Sexual Minorities

Surveys of gay and lesbian people have found a pattern of police abuse directed toward them. Reports of police abuse range from a high of 30 percent of respondents to a low of 8 percent. In addition to abuse, gay and lesbian people also experience ordinary disrespect from some police officers. Where it occurs, mistreatment of gay and lesbian people reflects, in part, prejudice against people who do not have conventional lifestyles. Abuse also reflects a sense that, in many instances, gay and lesbian people are vulnerable and powerless because filing a complaint or a suit would identify them as gay or lesbian. Some police departments have responded to this problem in several different ways. Some departments actively recruit gay and lesbian officers. Some have established active outreach or liaison programs with the gay and lesbian community. Many departments incorporate material on equal treatment of gay and lesbian people in their regular human relations training.

Source: Amnesty International USA, *Stonewalled: Police Abuse and Misconduct Against Lesbian, Gay, and Transgendered People in the United States* (New York: Author, 2005).

Verbal Abuse and Racial and Ethnic Slurs

Insulting, abusive, and offensive language, especially racial and ethnic slurs, have a long and tragic history in American policing. In 1967, a half century ago, the President's Crime Commission found that "verbal discourtesy" by officers occurred in 15 percent of all police–citizen encounters.[98] This estimate would make it far more prevalent than uses of force. More recently, in 2016, a San Francisco police officer resigned when it was revealed that he had been sending racist and homophobic text messages to other officers in the department. It was the second offensive text message scandal in the department in two years.[99] Offensive language by police officers involves not just race and ethnicity, but also gender, sexual preference, social class, and lifestyle.

verbal abuse

As Samuel Walker testified before the President's Task Force on 21st Century Policing, **verbal abuse** causes several harms. First, it inflicts psychological injury to the person it is directed toward. It communicates the message that the person is not a full member of society, entitled to basic respect from government officials. Second, when verbal disrespect is repeated over time to African Americans or Hispanics, it creates a pervasive distrust of the police in their communities. Third, offensive language in some encounters provokes a hostile response toward the officer, which then leads to an escalation into a violent encounter and officer use of force. Fourth, if offensive language by officers goes unpunished by the department it undermines standards of professionalism in the department. Officers learn by experience that they will not be disciplined for such conduct.[100]

Most police departments have long had formal policies prohibiting offensive language. The Minneapolis police department's Code of Conduct, for example, directs officers to "Be courteous, respectful, police and professional."[101] These policies, however, are often not enforced. For this reason, the President's Task Force in 2015 recommended that "[b]ecause offensive or harsh language can escalate a minor situation, law enforcement agencies should underscore the importance of language used and adopt policies directing officers to speak to individuals with respect" (Action Item 4.4.1).[102] Enforcing such policies is difficult, however. When someone files a citizen complaint about rude or insulting language, there is often no independent witness to the event, making it virtually impossible to sustain the complaint. Training over procedural justice, with its emphasis on treating people with respect, can directly address officer use of offensive language.

Traffic Enforcement and Racial Profiling

racial profiling

Around 1999–2000, a series of incidents involving traffic stops made the issue of **racial profiling** a national controversy. The allegation was that the police systematically stopped African American drivers solely on the basis of their race, and not because of any traffic violation or suspected criminal activity. The practice was given the label "driving while black."[103] The controversy exposed the fact that little was known about police traffic enforcement activities. The only major study of the subject was a book, *Traffic and the Police,* published in 1969.[104] As a result of the controversy, the Bureau of Justice Statistics began a series of national surveys of traffic enforcement known as the Police-Public Contact Survey, which has greatly enriched our knowledge about police traffic enforcement patterns. One major finding was that

EXHIBIT 12–6

Traffic Stop Outcomes, by Race and Ethnicity, 2011

Race/Ethnicity of Driver	Action Taken by Officer (percentage of all drivers of each race/ethnicity)		
	Ticketed	Warned	Searched
White	4.8%	3.6%	2.3%
African American	7.0	3.5	6.3
Hispanic	6.2	2.8	6.6

Source: Bureau of Justice Statistics, *Police Behavior During Traffic and Street Stops, 2011* (Washington, DC: U.S. Department of Justice, 2013), tables 5, 7.

the traffic stop is the most common form of public contact with the police, accounting for about half of all contacts.

The Police-Public Contact Survey has consistently found patterns of racial and ethnic disparities related to stops, searches, and tickets or arrests. The 2011 survey, for example, found that 15 percent of Native American drivers reported being stopped by the police, compared with 12.8 percent of African American, 10.4 percent of Hispanic, 9.8 percent of white, and 9.4 percent of Asian American drivers. (The survey, which is conducted in cooperation with the U.S. Census Bureau, uses a self-report system.) In 2011 there were also disparities among drivers who were ticketed: 8 percent of African American, 6.2 percent of Hispanic, and 4.8 percent of white drivers. The greatest disparities involved searches by the police: 6.6 percent of Hispanic drivers and 6.3 percent of African American drivers were searched, compared with only 2.3 percent of white drivers.[105]

Not all traffic stops are the same, however, particularly with respect to their impact on the people stopped. In a study of traffic stops in the Kansas City, Missouri, metropolitan area, using both qualitative and quantitative methods, Charles Epp and colleagues found "a deep racial chasm" based on the pattern of different kinds of stops.[106]

There are two basic kinds of stops. First, there are traffic safety stops, which are mainly for speeding, suspected drunk driving, or other traffic code violations. Then there are **investigatory stops,** where the purpose is to investigate the driver (and/or passengers) for possible criminal law violations, such as possession of a weapon or drugs, or an outstanding warrant. Most traffic safety stops are nondiscretionary: For example, the car is dangerously speeding or weaving, and the officer really has no choice about stopping the vehicle. Investigatory stops, by contrast, are made at the discretion of the officer. Frequently, officers use a pretext for the stop, such as a minor violation: a burned-out tail light, failure to signal for a lane change, or something similar.

investigatory stops

Epp and his colleagues argue that investigatory stops are at the heart of the racial profiling controversy, because African Americans are subject to far more investigatory stops than whites. In their study, they found that 40 percent of African Americans under the age of 25 were likely to be stopped in any year, compared with only 13 percent of whites. In fact, African American women were more likely to be stopped than white men (about 17 percent versus 13 percent). Investigatory stops are far more intrusive and personally offensive than traffic safety stops. According to Epp and his colleagues, they are "deeply resented" by African Americans. In such stops, the officer is looking for something incriminating about *you*, as opposed to being concerned about your driving. With traffic safety stops, most drivers, regardless of race, know they were speeding or that they had been drinking. The stop, in short, is not about you; it's about your driving. An investigatory stop, on the other hand, is about *you*, and a suspicion of criminal activity. And because it is about you, according to Epp and his colleagues, such stops are regarded as "deeply unfair."[107] The intrusive and offensive nature of investigatory stops, the authors argue, significantly undermines trust in the police. The effect is both personal (being singled out as a suspicious person) and cumulative. As many members of the African American community share their stories about traffic stops with other members of their community, it erodes trust in the police even among people who have themselves not been stopped. Epp and his colleagues found that 37 percent of the African Americans they surveyed had heard a story of police disrespect, compared with only 15 percent of whites. The overall experience for African Americans, they found, is one of "ongoing, pervasive surveillance," an outcome that directly undermines the legitimacy of the police. [108]

Investigatory traffic stops are generally not the product of bias on the part of individual officers. Too often it is an *institutionalized departmental practice*: part of a broader strategy to use traffic stops as a crime-fighting strategy. In short, it is not a matter of bad people making bad decisions; it is a matter of an organizational policy choice made for what is believed to be a good reason: fighting crime. This was just one of the reasons the President's Task force recommended that "[l]aw enforcement agencies should consider the potential damage to public trust when implementing crime fighting strategies" (Recommendation 1.5). The damage done to police–community relations may far outweigh the potential advantages of a particular strategy for fighting crime.

The book by Epp and his colleagues, *Pulled Over,* further argues that the police practice of investigatory traffic stops has an impact that goes far beyond the police and the criminal justice system. Investigatory stops "convey powerful messages about citizenship and equality." The message is that you are not a full member of our society. The sense of constant surveillance and being the object of suspicion has a profound alienating impact.

Discrimination versus Disparity

discrimination versus disparities

Virtually every study of traffic stops data has found evidence of racial or ethnic *disparities* in stops and searches. The racial profiling controversy presents difficult issues related to determining whether or not a pattern of racial discrimination, as opposed to statistical disparities, exists. See the "Police in Focus" for a discussion of **discrimination versus disparities.**

Interpreting Traffic Stop Data

Virtually every study of traffic stops has found a pattern of racial or ethnic *disparities* in traffic stops. Disparities in stops, searches, uses of force, and arrests are consistent

POLICE in FOCUS | Discrimination versus Disparities

Traffic stop data raise the important issue of discrimination versus disparities. Discrimination is defined as differential *treatment* based on some *extralegal* category such as race, ethnicity, or gender. If an employer refuses to hire members of a certain ethnic group, for example, that represents discrimination. Disparity, by contrast, refers to *different outcomes* that are not necessarily caused by differential treatment. Most college students, for example, are between the age of 18 and their early 20s. This is not the result of discrimination, but because of the normal life course: Younger people have not completed high school, and middle-aged people have either finished college or do not plan to attend.

Disparities in traffic stops do not necessarily involve discrimination. A number of different factors could explain why one group is stopped more often than other groups, including differences in driving behavior, or motor vehicle law violations such as expired license plates or a broken headlight. To prove in a lawsuit that a racial disparity involves discrimination, the plaintiffs need to provide evidence that persuades the court that the disparity cannot be explained by legitimate factors. The best recent example was the successful suit against the NYPD's stop and frisk program, in which plaintiffs presented evidence by expert witnesses that the disparate percentage of stops against African Americans and Hispanics was overwhelming, that in many of the stops the police officers lacked reasonable suspicion for a legal stop, and that the disparity could not be explained by the crime rates in local neighborhoods.

There are different forms and degrees of discrimination. The figure represents the discrimination–disparity continuum developed by Samuel Walker, Cassia Spohn, and Miriam DeLone.

Discrimination–Disparity Continuum

Systematic Discrimination	Institutionalized Discrimination	Contextual Discrimination	Individual Acts of Discrimination	Pure Justice

Definitions

Systematic discrimination—Discrimination at all stages of the criminal justice system, at all times, and in all places.

Institutionalized discrimination—Racial and ethnic disparities in outcomes that are the result of the application of racially neutral factors such as prior criminal record, employment status, demeanor, etc.

Contextual discrimination—Discrimination found in particular contexts or circumstances (e.g., certain regions, particular crimes, special victim—offender relationships).

Individual acts of discrimination—Discrimination that results from the acts of particular individuals but is not characteristic of entire agencies or the criminal justice system as a whole.

Pure justice—No racial or ethnic discrimination at all.

Source: Samuel Walker, Cassia Spohn, and Miriam DeLone, *The Color of Justice; Race, Ethnicity and Crime in America*, 6th ed. (Belmont, CA: Cengage, 2018).

in the Police-Public Contact Surveys. The question is, what standard or benchmark should be used to determine if a disparity involves discrimination.[109]

Local studies have generally used the racial composition of the residential population of the area as the **benchmark** to determine whether there are more stops of a particular group than the population would warrant (Exhibit 12–7). Population data, however, do not indicate who is *actually driving* on the roads or which drivers are

benchmark

EXHIBIT 12-7

Alternative Benchmarks for Studying Traffic Stop Data

1. **Resident population data.** Convenient, but does not measure the driving population or driving behavior.
2. **Direct observation.** Expensive, but provides good evidence on the driving population and driving behavior.
3. **Internal benchmarking.** Relatively convenient, and provides valuable comparisons of peer officer behavior.
4. **Nonfault traffic accident data.** Convenient and a useful proxy measure of driving population by demographic characteristics.

Source: Adapted from Lorie A. Fridell, *By the Numbers: A Guide for Analyzing Race Data from Vehicle Stops* (Washington, DC: Police Executive Research Forum, 2004).

violating a traffic law. African Americans may be driving more or violating traffic laws at a higher or lower rate than white drivers. In fact, whites report driving drunk at a significantly higher rate than African Americans, according to the Monitoring the Future survey. Young African Americans, meanwhile, are less likely than whites to own cars.[110]

An alternative benchmark involves *"nonfault" traffic accident data.* Drivers who are involved in a traffic accident, but are not themselves at fault, represent a random selection of all drivers. (Drivers who are at fault are not a representative sample of all drivers, for obvious reasons.) Nonfault traffic accident data have the advantage of being readily available and inexpensive to analyze.

The best benchmark data come from systematic *direct observation* of particular roadways (see Exhibit 12–7). Trained observers observe the racial breakdown of all drivers and the racial breakdown of those drivers who are speeding. This technique provides a valid and reliable estimate of who is actually at risk for a traffic stop on that particular roadway. Unfortunately, such observation is extremely expensive to conduct and requires careful training and supervision of observers.

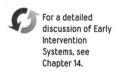 For a detailed discussion of Early Intervention Systems, see Chapter 14.

Another alternative benchmark focusing on police officers is called *internal benchmarking.* This approach compares traffic stops of officers working in the same precinct or area. It can identify any officer or officers who stop significantly more African American or Hispanic drivers than their peers. The data do not prove discriminatory behavior, but they raise questions about an officer's performance that become the basis for administrative review of the officer's performance. Because it involves a comparison of officers within the same department, internal benchmarking is not useful if all officers are engaging in racial profiling. Internal benchmarking can be accomplished through an Early Intervention System (EIS), a computerized database on officer performance, which many departments have adopted (see Chapter 14).[111]

The Different Contexts of Racial Profiling

Racial profiling can occur in one of three different contexts. The first, which we have already discussed, involves department policy. The war on drugs is one example. Drug enforcement activities often target African Americans or Hispanics because officers believe these groups are likely to be engaged in drug trafficking.[112] An aggressive anti-crime strategy that emphasizes traffic stops can also lead to strong racial disparities.

As we have already discussed, Epp and his colleagues concluded that investigatory stops, which African Americans regarded as particularly intrusive and offensive, were the product of department crime-fighting strategies.

A second context involves police stopping citizens who appear to be *out of place*. This might include, for example, an African American who is in a predominantly white neighborhood or a white person in a predominantly African American neighborhood. In their study of traffic stops in a white suburban community that bordered on a predominantly African American city, Albert Meehan and Michael Ponder found that *place* makes a difference. African American drivers were somewhat more likely to be stopped than whites, were more than twice as likely to be the subject of a query, and were more likely to be stopped and queried in predominantly white neighborhoods. Significantly, white drivers were queried at the same rate regardless of the location. This study supports the argument that the police are more likely to stop drivers who in their judgment are "out of place."[113]

Police Justifications for Racial and Ethnic Disparities in Traffic Enforcement

Police and some social scientists offer explanations for racial and ethnic disparities in traffic stops. The major argument is that African Americans and Hispanics are more likely to be engaged in criminal activity, and drug trafficking, in particular. The conservative writer Heather MacDonald makes this point in arguing that racial profiling is a "myth".[114] The FBI data on arrests do indicate different levels of involvement according to the type of crime. But the matter is more complex than those data suggest.

Critics argue that using arrest data involves circular reasoning: Racial and ethnic minorities are stopped and arrested more often than whites, producing higher arrest rates that, in turn, justify higher rates of stops and arrests. The National Survey on Drug Use and Health consistently finds that reported use of illegal drugs is only slightly higher among African Americans than among whites, whereas use among Hispanics is lower than among either of the other groups.[115] Observational studies of traffic patterns on both Maryland and New Jersey interstate highways, meanwhile, found that white and African American drivers were equally likely to be speeding and that there was no justification for stopping African American drivers at a higher rate.

The San Jose Police Department, in a report on its traffic stop patterns, explained the racial and ethnic disparities on the grounds that Hispanic and African American neighborhoods are assigned higher levels of patrol because they have higher crime rates and calls for service than other neighborhoods. Consequently, the report argues, residents of those neighborhoods are more exposed to observation by police officers and therefore more likely to be stopped than drivers in areas with lower levels of police presence.[116] The mere presence of a larger number of police officers, however, does not explain the traffic enforcement priorities of those officers. The question is not how many police officers there are in a particular neighborhood; the relevant question is what they do in terms of law enforcement.

Racial profiling remains a controversy in America. To end profiling and the appearance of profiling, the President's Task Force recommended that "[l]aw enforcement agencies should adopt and enforce policies prohibiting profiling and discrimination based on race, ethnicity, national origin, religion, age, gender, gender identity/expression, sexual orientation, immigration status, disability, housing status, occupation, or language fluency" (Recommendation 2.13).[117] The policy discussed in the next section is a valuable guide for the police on when race and ethnicity can and cannot be used in law enforcement actions.

The Legitimate Use of Race and Ethnicity in Police Work

Race and ethnicity can legitimately be used in police work, but only under limited circumstances. The Police Executive Research Forum (PERF) in 2001 issued a report, *Racially Biased Policing: A Principled Response,* with a model policy on when race or ethnicity can and cannot be used.

First, a police officer cannot stop or arrest a person *solely* on the basis of race or ethnicity. An officer cannot make a traffic stop just because the driver is African American. Such a stop would clearly violate the Fourteenth Amendment guarantee of equal protection of the law.

Second, the police cannot use race or ethnicity when it is one element in a *general profile* of criminal suspects. That is, the police cannot use a general profile that, for example, directs officers to look for African American males, or young Hispanic males who are wearing baggy jeans.

Third, the police may use race or ethnicity when it is *one element in the description of a specific criminal suspect,* and where that information is based on *credible information* from a *reliable source.* In the case of a convenience store robbery, for example, the police can rely on information from the victim that describes the suspect as a young, stocky male, with a beard, wearing a blue baseball cap, and who is African American (or white, or Hispanic).

In short, race and ethnicity can be used in law enforcement, but only when subject to strict controls that limit it to situations where there is individualized suspicion about a suspect. The NYPD's aggressive stop and frisk program, which was declared unconstitutional in 2013, is an example of a program that had no strict controls over the use of race and ethnicity.[118]

Building Legitimacy and Improving Police–Community Relations

As we discussed at the beginning of this chapter, what used to be called the police–community relations problem is now understood as a much deeper issue of legitimacy. The specific issues that were of concern regarding police–community relations remain important issues today: unjustified shootings, use of excessive force, and others. The next section links those long-standing concerns with the new perspectives of legitimacy and procedural justice.

The Different Dimensions of Trust and Confidence in the Police

We have covered a number of specific police–citizen interactions in which illegal or inappropriate police actions undermine trust and confidence in the police. There are several different **dimensions of trust and confidence** in the police, however, and they are shaped by a number of other considerations. Surveys that frame the issue in a single question (for example, "How much confidence do you have?") fail to capture all the different dimensions.

dimensions of trust and confidence

SIDEBAR 12–4

Stoutland's Dimensions of Trust

Trust dimension 1: *Priorities.* Do people feel that the police share their concerns about the neighborhood? Stoutland's focus groups found that many residents feel they do not, and believe the police concentrate too narrowly on short-term crime reduction rather than broader quality-of-life issues.

Trust dimension 2: *Competence.* Do people feel the police have the knowledge and skills to achieve their objectives? Most of the focus group participants who had noticed increased police crime-fighting efforts felt it had reduced drug-related crime.

Trust dimension 3: *Dependability.* Do people feel the police can be counted on to fulfill their promises? With respect to drug-related crime, most focus group participants believe the police can be depended on to follow through on their promise to reduce crime.

Trust dimension 4: *Respect.* Do people feel that the police treat them respectfully? Lack of respect from the police was one of the strongest themes to emerge from the focus groups. Many participants expressed anger at the way they felt the police treat them. In addition to rudeness, some participants felt the police fail to respond when called about an incident in the neighborhood. Finally, many participants felt that the police violated their rights, and in particular harassed young people.

Source: Sara E. Stoutland, "The Multiple Dimensions of Trust in Resident/Police Relations in Boston," *Journal of Research in Crime and Delinquency* 38 (August 2001): 226–256.

Stoutland probed deeper into public attitudes about the police in a series of focus groups and individual interviews with young people, parents, and professional youth workers in four high-crime neighborhoods in Boston. The interviews identified four separate dimensions of trust in the police. (See Sidebar 12–4.) The questions include the following: (1) Do the police "share our priorities or motives," and specifically do they share residents' concerns about crime in the neighborhood? (2) "Are the police competent," meaning do they have the "knowledge and skills" to accomplish their tasks? (3) "Are they dependable in fulfilling their responsibilities?"—including do they have the resources needed to do their job well? and (4) "Are they respectful?"—including being "courteous and fair in their interactions" with people?[119]

Overall, and particularly important, the interviews found that people were able to distinguish between the different aspects of police work and officer conduct. Many respondents believed that the police were too focused on crime reduction and gave insufficient attention to broader quality-of-life issues. A number of participants wanted the police create "sustainable security," which would involve developing more and more effective resources related to mental health, education, and service programs for young people. Many respondents believed that the police were competent with respect to short-term crime reduction, and that recent efforts (which involved the highly publicized Boston Gun Project)[120] had reduced gun violence in their neighborhoods.

In terms of respectful treatment, however, respondents had strong negative opinions. Many mentioned specific instances when they were treated with disrespect. One mother, for example, said that officers at the local police station made fun of her for bringing a complaint about a relatively minor issue. Others complained about the police failing to respond when they reported an incident. Several said the police did not respond to a gunfight until 20 minutes after they reported it. Stories of police harassment by participants were "rampant" in the interviews. Several referred to the police department as "the biggest gang in the city." One person recalled being stopped for just standing outside smoking a cigarette, questioned, and then thrown to the ground. At the same time, however, some participants mentioned specific officers who had been "consistently respectful."

Particularly interesting, Stoutland observed, many people understood that the police needed to be tough in fighting crime in a high-crime neighborhood—for example, needing to conduct street stops, but resented the disrespect shown to people who were not criminals, and in particular people who sought their assistance. In short, people support tough but respectful police crime-fighting.

Wesley Skogan's study of people who had been stopped by the police showed that attitudes toward the police were much more favorable among people who felt that officers treated them fairly and if the officers explained the situation to them, were polite, and paid attention to what they said. African Americans and Spanish-speaking Latinos, however, were far less likely to say that the police explained the reason they had been stopped. Less than half of the African Americans and Latinos thought the police were polite, and both groups were more likely to say the police treated them unfairly. Nonetheless, Skogan's study found that, in general, people notice how they are treated by police officers and it makes a difference in how they view the police.[121]

Engaging the Community

Engaging the community involves taking a number of steps in which members of the community are active participants in the process of policing and feel that they are an accepted part of that process. The President's Task Force on 21st Century Policing made a number of recommendations on how departments can engage the community.[122]

The principles of procedural justice emphasize the importance of *giving people a voice* in the decisions that affect them. This includes the employees of a major corporation and the person who is stopped for an alleged traffic violation. To this end, the President's Task Force recommended that "[l]aw enforcement agencies should schedule regular forums and meetings where all community members can interact with police and help influence programs and policy" (Action Item 4.5.1). Such events give people an opportunity to ask questions about police operations and express their grievances. Too often, unfortunately, such public meetings are only occasional events, usually occurring in the wake of a crisis (typically a shooting or beating incident). After the crisis has passed, no more meetings are held. Public meetings should occur regularly, crisis or no crisis, and be held in different parts of the community. The Chicago community policing program (known as CAPS), for example, held regular "beat meetings" in neighborhoods.[123]

The President's Task Force also recommended that members of the public be informed about official department policies and also about police activities. To accomplish this, the task force recommended that "law enforcement agencies should make all department policies available for public review and regularly post on the department's website information about stops, summonses, arrests, reported crime, and other law enforcement data aggregated by demographics" (Action Item 1.3.1). The traditional secrecy of American police departments, and their unwillingness to share information and explain what they are doing, has long been a source of distrust among segments of the community.

Not only should departments make their official policies available to the public, but the task force recommended that law enforcement agencies "should involve the community in the process of developing and evaluating policies and procedures" (Action Item 1.5.1). Involving the public builds trust, confidence, and legitimacy. People are far more likely to have confidence in a policy—for example, on the handling of domestic violence incidents—if they have had an opportunity to participate in the development of that policy. Public participation, moreover, allows for contributions from people with expertise or experience on the subject. In the case of domestic violence, that would include academic experts on the subject, staff members at local domestic violence social service agencies, and people who have been the victims of domestic violence themselves.

As discussed several times in this chapter, certain crime-fighting strategies do considerable harm to community relations and, as a consequence, undermine the legitimacy of the local law enforcement agency. The Kerner Commission pointed this out in 1968, and the President's Task Force made the same point 47 years later in 2015. To address this problem, the President's Task Force recommended that "[l]aw enforcement agencies should collaborate with community members to develop policies and strategies in communities and neighborhoods disproportionately affected by crime for deploying resources that aim to reduce crime by improving relationships, greater community engagement, and cooperation" (Recommendation 2.1). The perspective of the communities affected by a certain policy—stops and frisks, for example, or an intensive anti–drunk driving campaign—can serve to modify a proposed or existing policy and mitigate some of the harm. The fact that community residents can participate in the policymaking process helps to build trust and confidence in whatever policy eventually results.

Finally, police departments must talk candidly about their past mistakes. The President's Task Force specifically recommended that "[l]aw enforcement agencies should acknowledge the role of policing in past and present injustice and discrimination and how it is a hurdle to the promotion of community trust" (Recommendation 1.2). The report of the Chicago police accountability task force appointed following the release of the video showing the killing of Laquan McDonald (described earlier in this chapter) candidly discussed the racism in the Chicago Police Department. In its 2016 report, the task force stated bluntly, "Racism and maltreatment at the hands of the police have been consistent complaints from communities of color for decades." The report then went on to make a sweeping set of reforms to end this long pattern and to create a police department committed to treating all people equally.[124]

Perspective: The Failure of Police–Community Relations Units in the 1960s

The President's Task Force recommendations regarding **engaging the community** should be understood in the context of the failures of the police–community relations programs that appeared in the 1960s in response to the urban riots of the period.

Many big-city police departments created special **police–community relations (PCR) units,** which operated programs designed to improve relations with

engaging the community

police–community relations (PCR) units

For a detailed discussion of the police–community relations crisis of the 1960s, see Chapter 2.

ride-along programs

communities of color. PCR unit officers spent most of their time speaking in schools and to community groups. The problem with PCR units is that they were separate from basic police operations of patrol, traffic, and criminal investigation, and had no impact on the police actions (shootings, uses of force) that were the primary source of community tensions with the police. Most PCR units had disappeared by the early 1970s.[125]

Departments also created (and many still maintain) **ride-along programs,** which allow citizens to ride in a patrol car for a few hours and observe police work first-hand. The weakness of ride-along programs, then and now, is that they attract people who already have a positive attitude about the police, rather than people who have criticisms. Also, like PCR units, ride-alongs have no impact on police operations that are the source of tensions with the community.[126]

Some large metropolitan police departments also created neighborhood storefront offices, staffed by PCR unit officers, in an effort to provide a more convenient access for community residents. Police headquarters buildings are often forbidding places for many citizens and can be difficult to reach. Neighborhood offices, however, proved to be expensive to operate, and like the other PCR programs did not address the police actions that create police-community tensions.[127]

Finally, many police chiefs created advisory committees, composed of selected community leaders, to provide advice on police issues. In practice, however, the members of such committees were selected by the chief and had no real credibility with many community residents. Members also had no special expertise on policing and consequently were not able to understand the details of policing or make constructive recommendations. The President's Crime Commission concluded that existing advisory commissions were ineffective.[128]

In the end, special PCR programs were judged not to be effective. The President's Crime Commission found that African American community leaders regarded them as "public relations puff" and a "deliberate con game." A Justice Department report found them "marginal to the operations of the police department," with little or no relationship to patrol or criminal investigation activities.[129] As the next section explains, the basic failure of all the PCR programs of the 1960s was that they did not directly address the police practices on the street—shootings, use of force, and other abuses—that were the main sources of police–community tensions.

Ending Police Misconduct

The most significant barriers to trust and confidence in the police is police officer misconduct. We have devoted much of this chapter to discussions of unjustified police shootings, the use of excessive force, discriminatory arrests, and unconstitutional stops and frisks, and intrusive traffic stops. We have discussed several important research studies that have shown that people notice how they are treated by police officers, and that rudeness, failure to treat people with respect, and a sense of unfairness causes people to have low confidence and trust in the police. Along with engaging communities, as we just discussed, the first steps in building legitimacy include ending unacceptable police practices.

We have also discussed some of the reforms that can reduce unacceptable police actions. For instance,

- Adopting the defense-of-life policy on the use of deadly force
- Discontinuing aggressive crime-fighting strategies that harm communities
- Adopting the PERF model policy on the proper use of race and ethnicity
- Ending offensive language by officers directed toward citizens.
- Including procedural justice in police training and ensuring that officers practice it on the street.
- Adopting a policy of de-escalation for police-citizen encounters, including it in training, and ensuring that officers use it in encounters with citizens.

We discuss these and more policies and practices in Chapter 14, on police accountability. The main point is that improper and unacceptable police actions do not need to continue. There are different ways to effectively address and correct bad policing.

Engaging Immigrant Communities

Immigration trends are changing the face of the United States. The percentage of the population that is foreign born increased from 6.2 percent in 1980 to 13.1 percent in 2013. An estimated 12 million undocumented immigrants are currently living in the United States. Contrary to widespread belief, only about half of the undocumented came from Mexico, with other countries accounting for the other half.[130]

The increase in immigration has created new challenges for American policing. First, immigration law enforcement is the responsibility of the federal government. State and local law enforcement officers have no authority to enforce immigration laws, except where a local agency has a formal agreement to do so under the Immigration and Customs Enforcement (ICE) 287(g) program. The **287(g) agreements** permit local police to enforce immigration law after they have received required training from ICE personnel. By mid-2016, 32 law enforcement agencies in 16 states had signed a 287(g) agreement with ICE.[131] State and local law enforcement agencies can arrest an undocumented immigrant for a conventional criminal law violation: murder, burglary, drunk driving, and so on. A 2008 survey of local law enforcement executives found most were not prepared to address the issue of undocumented immigrants. Less than half had a policy regarding policing immigrants, and only 45 percent of departments offered training on the issue.[132]

Many local police departments do not want to become involved in the **enforcement of federal immigration laws.** More than 70 percent of the local law enforcement executives in 2008 believed that immigration enforcement is the responsibility of the federal government. In fact, many of the largest cities (New York, Los Angeles, San Francisco, Washington, D.C., Chicago, Baltimore, Boston, Detroit, Minneapolis, St. Louis, Newark, Philadelphia, Austin, and Seattle) have passed ordinances and/or resolutions limiting their local police agency's ability to enforce immigration laws. Likewise, four states (Alaska, Montana, New Mexico, and Oregon) have passed legislation that bans the use of local resources for immigration enforcement.

Local police officials and political leaders worry that involving local police departments in identifying and deporting undocumented immigrants would alienate them from local immigrant communities with whom they are trying to develop positive

287(g) agreements

enforcement of federal immigration laws

relations. They emphasized that illegal immigrants are often the most vulnerable to victimization because they are often afraid to tell the police about the crime for fear of deportation.[133] The Major Cities Chiefs Association, which represents chiefs from 57 large urban police departments, warned that local enforcement of immigration laws would undermine trust and cooperation.[134]

Immigration and Cultural Barriers in Policing

cultural competence

An important aspect of conflict between the police and some racial and ethnic groups is a lack of **cultural competence** on the part of police officers. Cultural competence is defined as the ability to understand and respond appropriately to differences in the languages, traditions, lifestyles, and patterns of communication of different racial or ethnic groups. This is a special problem in communities that have recently experienced significant immigration of people from Latin America, Asia, or Africa. The city of Minneapolis, for example, has over 20,000 immigrants from Somalia. The Minneapolis police need to be able to communicate with and understand the cultural traditions of Somali people.

The report *Donde esta la justicia?* points out the negative impact of one difference in styles of communication: "Avoiding direct eye contact is considered respectful in many Latin nations," but in the United States doing so can be perceived as "a sign of disrespect or deceptiveness" by criminal justice officials. The report cited the case of a judge who interpreted the downcast eyes of a Latino juvenile as an admission of guilt and, consequently, gave him a long sentence.[135]

How different immigrant groups relate to the police and to crime problems depends in part on how well they are assimilated into the local political power structure. A survey of six racial and ethnic groups in New York City found significant differences in how they respond to an incident of family violence, for example. Among Dominicans and Colombians, about 80 percent said they would be "very likely" to report it to the police. Only 66 percent of African Americans and 65 percent of Asian Indians said they would report it. There were similar differences in the likelihood of reporting a break-in or a drug sale. The key factor in explaining these differences was the degree to which a group had a sense of community empowerment. Members of groups were more likely to report a crime if they believed their racial or ethnic community "was likely to work together to solve local problems" and also if they believed their community had political power. Feelings of powerlessness reduced the likelihood of reporting crimes. In short, racial and ethnic groups have very different experiences in this country, and these differences explain how they relate to the police.[136]

Language Barriers in Policing

A police officer in a midwestern city, assigned to patrol the part of town that is the center of the growing Hispanic community, explained, "The way I figure, we're here to provide a service and if you can't provide a service to a certain group of people, then you're not doing your job." The officer was referring specifically to being able to communicate with community residents who do not speak English.[137]

Police work involves communication between people. As we learned in Chapter 5, many police departments put special emphasis on communication skills in their new officer recruitment efforts. In the case of people who do not speak English, or do not speak it well, **language barriers** create potentially serious obstructions to the delivery of high-quality police services. Barriers are likely to arise when the citizen speaks a language other than English that the responding officer does not speak. If the officer is bilingual—for example, able to speak both English and Spanish—these barriers can be overcome.[138]

Language skills make a big difference in how people relate to the police. Skogan conducted the first survey of English-speaking and non-English-speaking Hispanics and found significant differences in relations with the police. Hispanics who did not speak English were much less likely to report crimes or to report a neighborhood problem to the police. As a result, many offenders remain unpunished and many victims are vulnerable to repeat victimization.

A study of potential Spanish-language barriers in one midwestern city found some minor problems and delays but no serious problems because of language. Potential language barriers represented only 15 percent of all police–citizen contacts in the precinct that is the center of that city's Hispanic community. Delays occurred in 87 percent of those contacts, and frustration on the part of either the citizen or the officer occurred in 73 percent. Some conflict occurred in 27 percent of the calls because of language barriers, but none of those situations involved serious conflict (for example, use of force by either party). Generally, officers who lacked a command of Spanish "muddled through" their interactions with Spanish-speaking citizens. They either utilized "street Spanish" (a few basic phrases they had learned on the job), used command Spanish (which they had learned through formal training), or found a bystander who could translate.[139]

Police departments are responding to the changing demographics of their communities in different ways. One of the most important responses is to ensure that officers can communicate with people who do not speak English. Some police departments, for example, offer incentive pay to bilingual officers. The National Crime Prevention Council, meanwhile, urges police departments to hire officers from recently arrived immigrant groups who can serve as liaisons between the police and newly arrived ethnic communities. Some departments offer training in street Spanish to equip their officers with the basic words and phrases necessary for police work. As mentioned in Chapter 7, departments have the option of subscribing to 911 interpreter services to handle calls from people who speak different languages. Citizen oversight agencies publish informational material and complaint forms in various languages for people who want to file a complaint against a police officer. The Seattle Office of Professional Accountability publishes brochures in nine languages other than English, including Spanish, Korean, and Arabic, on how to file a complaint against a police officer.[140]

To ensure the ability of the police to serve all members of the community, including people who do not speak English, or have only a limited command of English, the President's Task Force recommended that "[l]aw enforcement agencies should ensure reasonable and equitable language access for all persons who have encounters with police or who enter the criminal justice system" (Action Item 1.9.2).

A Representative Police Force

Employment discrimination by police departments on the basis of race, ethnicity, and gender has been a long-standing problem in policing. We discussed the recruitment of

African Americans, Hispanics, and women in detail in Chapter 5, and the performance of the three groups in Chapter 6.

For a detailed discussion of diversity and affirmative action, see Chapter 5.

The President's Task Force recognized the importance of developing a police force that represents the community, and consequently recommended that "[l]aw enforcement agencies should strive to create a workforce that contains a broad range of diversity including race, gender, language, life experience, and cultural background to improve understanding and effectiveness in dealing with all communities" (Recommendation 1.8). The CALEA accreditation standards, meanwhile, recommend that each law enforcement agency have "minority group and female employees in the sworn law enforcement ranks in approximate proportion to the makeup of the available work force in the agency's law enforcement service community."[141]

Citizen Oversight of the Police

An African American resident of Milwaukee told the U.S. Civil Rights Commission that "people who have police complaints are literally afraid to go down to the fire and police commission and fill out these complaints." A 1978 U.S. Civil Rights Commission report on Memphis found that "the single most aggravating factor is the failure of the existing internal and external mechanisms which purportedly exist to prevent and combat" police misconduct.[142]

Traditionally, and still today in most police departments, citizen complaints are investigated by the internal affairs unit (sometimes called the professional standards unit). There has been a long history of allegations that internal affairs investigators do not investigate complaints thoroughly or fairly. In response, civil right groups have demanded independent citizen oversight of the police. Since the 1970s, there has been a dramatic growth in citizen oversight agencies. There are now over 100 police or sheriff's departments that have some form of citizen oversight. The principle of citizen oversight is that people are more likely to have trust and confidence in the police if their complaints are investigated by an agency independent of the police department.[143]

Two basic forms of citizen oversight exist. One is the civilian review board, which investigates individual citizen complaints and makes a recommendation to the chief on whether the complaint should be sustained or not sustained. Civilian review boards exist in New York City, San Francisco, and many other cities. The other form of citizen oversight in the police auditor or inspector general model. In this approach, an independent agency has the authority to examine any issue within the police department where there may be a problem, and to issue public reports with recommendations for improvement. Auditors/inspectors general do not investigate individual citizen complaints; their function is to address problems with police department policies and practices.

The President's Task Force recommended that "[s]ome form of civilian oversight of law enforcement is important in order to strengthen trust with the community. Every community should define the appropriate form and structure of civilian oversight to meet the needs of that community" (Recommendation 2.8). We discuss the different forms of citizen oversight in detail in Chapter 14, on police accountability.

Assign Officers on the Basis of Race or Ethnicity?

Some people believe that it would help improve police–community relations if African American officers were assigned to the African American community and if Hispanic officers were assigned to the Hispanic community. This idea rests on the assumption that officers who police members of their own racial or ethnic group will relate better to community people and also better understand community problems.

This idea runs into a number of legal and sociological problems. Making police officer assignments on the basis of race would be illegal under the 1964 Civil Rights Act. It would also "ghettoize" both African American and Hispanic officers, confining them to a limited range of assignments and denying them the broader range of assignments that are important in gaining promotion. Sociologically, urban communities are always in constant flux in terms of their racial composition. Some previously all-white communities have become predominantly African American or Hispanic. Through "gentrification," some neighborhoods change from being poor and African American to upper middle-class and white. Because of this constant change, there are no fixed boundaries between what are called "the black community" and "the white community."[144]

Finally, this idea is extremely unpopular with American citizens. In their national survey of public attitudes, Weitzer and Tuch found that more than 90 percent of whites, African Americans, and Hispanics reject the idea. Surveys in Washington, D.C., and New York City, in fact, found that most people prefer mixed-race patrol teams. Moreover, they have very clear ideas about the value of such teams. First, mixed-race teams of officers are likely to educate each other about differences in race, ethnicity, culture, and communities. Second, mixed-race teams are more likely to result in equal treatment of citizens. Third, mixed-race teams have an important symbolic value regarding equality and integration.[145]

Do Citizens Care about the Ethnicity of the Officer?

Do people who have contact with the police care about the race or ethnicity of the officer or officers who respond? Weitzer interviewed 169 residents of three neighborhoods in Washington, D.C.: one middle-class African American, one middle-class white, and one lower-income African American (there were not enough low-income whites in the city to allow for surveying of that category). Two-thirds of the middle-class residents, white and African American, reported that they could see no difference between white and African American officers. Residents in the lower-income African American neighborhood were more likely to see differences, but their perceptions were mixed. Some saw white officers being more courteous and African American officers being less courteous than their counterparts. Only 13 percent of the residents of the lower-income African American neighborhood expressed a preference for having mostly African American officers in their neighborhood. Generally, the overwhelming number of respondents in all neighborhoods either expressed a preference for racially mixed teams of officers or said that the race of officers doesn't matter.[146]

Special Training over Race and Ethnicity

Police training programs, as we learned in Chapter 5, have improved dramatically over the past 30 years. Not only has the average length of preservice training more than doubled, but most police academies have either added or greatly expanded their coverage of race relations and human relations.[147]

race relations training

No research, however, has established a direct connection between police academy **race relations training** programs and better police performance. A number of experts question the value of classroom-only training on race and ethnicity. A review of cultural diversity training programs for police found that the content of these programs had not changed much since the 1960s, that they tended to perpetuate negative stereotypes of racial minorities, and that they focused on individual officers and ignored problems related to the organization as a whole.[148] Geoffrey Alpert and colleagues, meanwhile, argue that "mere classroom training" on issues of race relations "is insufficient." They stress the importance of on-the-street police behavior and recommend that both new recruits and veteran officers "experiment with methods of communicating with members of racial and cultural groups other than their own."[149]

The most relevant training programs involve training over specific department policies designed to curb bias in policing. The PERF model policy on the use of race and ethnicity, for example, provides specific guidance on when officers may and may not use peoples' race or ethnicity in basic police operations, such as street stops, traffic stops, and arrests. Training on unconscious bias helps officers to recognize unconscious racial or ethnic stereotypes they might hold, and also to make a conscious effort not to act on them. As we learned in Chapter 5, police training needs to be scenario based, or reality based, and not lecture based. Finally, as already mentioned, the President's Task Force recommended that "[l]aw enforcement agencies should engage community members in the training process" (Recommendation 5.2).

SUMMARY

Public trust and confidence in the police is a serious issue in American policing. The police cannot function effectively in addressing crime and disorder without the active cooperation of ordinary citizens. Although the problem of legitimacy affects all Americans, there are special problems related to police relations with the African American community, which has a long and tragic history. There is evidence of racial discrimination in police shootings, the use of force, traffic stops, and other areas of police activity. The recent focus on procedural justice has provided a pathway toward correcting many of these problems. Research has indicated that trust and confidence in the police is higher when officers treat people with respect, explain what they are doing, and answer people's questions. Finally, the President's Task Force on 21st Century Policing has offered a broad array of recommendations on how police departments can improve their operations, reduce officer misconduct, and build trust and confidence in the police among the people they serve.

KEY TERMS

legitimacy, 405
police–community relations, 406
procedural justice, 407
race, 408
ethnicity, 408
public attitudes toward police, 411

attitudes of police officers, 417
selective contact, 417
selective perception and memory, 418
four systems of justice, 419
fleeing-felon rule, 421

unconscious stereotypes and bias, 422
force factor, 424
stop and frisk, 425
war on drugs, 427
demeanor of the suspect, 427
racial divide, 428

stereotyping, 429
verbal abuse, 430
racial profiling, 430
investigatory stops, 431
discrimination vs. disparities, 432
benchmark, 433

dimensions of trust and
    confidence, 436
engaging the community, 439
police–community relations
    (PCR) units, 439
ride-along programs, 440

287(g) agreements, 441
enforcement of federal
    immigration laws, 441
cultural competence, 442
language barriers, 443
race relations training, 446

FOR DISCUSSION

1. Discuss whether you think racial profiling takes place in your community, and how it has possibly impacted the relationship between the police and the community.
2. As a class, discuss the issues associated with assigning officers on the basis of race or ethnicity.
3. Divide the class into several groups. Each group should discuss what steps, if any, they would take to address racial profiling in their agency if they were a chief of police.

INTERNET EXERCISES

Exercise 1 Pick four police departments, based on a rational selection process (four different geographic regions, four different sizes, four departments in one state, etc.). Visit their websites. Search their sites to determine the following: (1) Do they have a special PCR program or unit? (2) If not, do they have a community policing or problem-solving program that addresses the old PCR problems? (3) Do they have any special programs regarding new immigrants to the community? (4) Do they have any special reports or information regarding efforts to build trust and legitimacy?

Compare the information you are able to find. How would you rank these departments? Do some appear to be doing a better job than others? Does one department stand out compared with the others?

Report your findings in class. How many departments report having any program? What do those programs consist of (e.g., citizen attitude surveys, ride-along programs, citizen police academies)?

Exercise 2 Visit www.nij.gov/multimedia/presenter/presenter-tyler/ and watch a presentation on "Legitimacy and Community Cooperation with Law Enforcement" by Tom Tyler. As a class, discuss how the interactions between the police and public affect police legitimacy.

NOTES

1. U.S. Department of Justice, Civil Rights Division, *Investigation of the Ferguson Police Department* (2015), https://www.justice.gov/sites/default/files/opa/press-releases/attachments/2015/03/04/ferguson_police_department_report.pdf.
2. David M. Kennedy, *Don't Shoot: One Man, A Street Fellowship, and the End of Violence in Inner-City America* (New York: Bloomsbury, 2011), "Across the Racial Divide," 124–155.
3. Charles R. Epp, Steven Maynard-Moody, and Donald Haider-Markel, *Pulled Over: How Police Stops Define Race and Citizenship* (Chicago: University of Chicago Press, 2014).
4. Samuel Walker, Cassia Spohn and Miriam De Lone, *The Color of Justice: Race, Ethnicity, and Crime in America*, 6th ed. (Belmont: Cengage, 2018).
5. President's Task Force Report on 21st Century Policing, *Final Report* (Washington, DC:

Department of Justice, 2015), http://www.cops. usdoj.gov/pdf/taskforce/taskforce_finalreport.pdf.

6. For this emphasis, see earlier editions of this book, *The Police in America*, editions 1 through 7.

7. See the discussion in Tom R. Tyler and Jeffrey Fagan, "Legitimacy and Cooperation: Why Do People Help the Police Fight Crime in the Communities?" *Ohio State Journal of Criminal Law* 6 (2008): 231–275.

8. President's Task Force on 21st Century Policing, *Final Report,* Recommendation 4.5.

9. Tom Tyler, *Why People Obey the Law* (New Haven, CT: Yale University Press, 1990).

10. Tyler and Fagan, "Legitimacy and Cooperation."

11. See the research and discussion in Tammy Rinehart Kochel, "Can Police Legitimacy Promote Collective Efficacy," *Justice Quarterly* 29 (June 2012): 384–419.

12. Discussed in Walker, Spohn, and DeLone, *The Color of Justice,* 6th ed. .

13. Ibid.

14. American Anthropological Association, *Statement on Race*, May 17, 1998, available on the organization's website at www.aaanet.org.

15. Definitions of race and ethnicity are discussed in Walker, Spohn, and DeLone, *The Color of Justice*, 6th ed., 6–12.

16. Office of Management and Budget, *Standards for the Classification of Federal Data on Race and Ethnicity* (August 28, 1995), https://www. whitehouse.gov/omb/fedreg_race-ethnicity.

17. See Federal Bureau of Investigation, *Crime in the United States, 2014*, https://www.fbi.gov/about-us/ cjis/ucr/crime-in-the-u.s/2014/crime-in-the-u.s.-2014.

18. Francisco A. Villarruel and Nancy E. Walker, *Donde esta la justicia?* (Washington, DC: Building Blocks for Youth, 2002), 46, http://cclp.org/ documents/BBY/Donde.pdf.

19. National Advisory Commission on Civil Disorders, *Report* (New York: Bantam Books, 1968).

20. Monica Anderson, *A Rising Share of the U.S. Black Population is Foreign Born* (Washington, DC: Pew Research Center, 2015).

21. Jens Manuel Krogstad and Jeffrey S. Passel*, 5 Facts About Illegal Immigration in the U.S.* (Washington, DC: Pew Research Center, 2015), http://www.pewresearch.org/fact-tank/2015/11/19/5-facts-about-illegal-immigration-in-the-u-s/.

22. Executive Committee for Indian Country Law Enforcement Improvements, *Final Report to the Attorney General and the Secretary of the Interior* (Washington, DC: Author, October 1997); Eileen Luna, "The Growth and Development of Tribal Police," *Journal of Contemporary Criminal Justice* 14 (February 1998): 75–86.

23. Marianne O. Nielsen and Robert A. Silverman, eds., *Native Americans, Crime, and Justice* (Boulder, CO: Westview, 1996).

24. Information is available on the website of the Arab American Institute, at www.aaiusa.org.

25. Steven A. Tuch and Ronald Weitzer, "Racial Differences in Attitudes toward the Police," *Public Opinion Quarterly* 61 (1997): 642–663.

26. Ronald Weitzer and Steven A. Tuch, *Race and Policing in America: Conflict and Reform* (New York: Cambridge University Press, 2006), 41.

27. Mark Hugo Lopez and Gretchen Livingston, *Hispanics and the Criminal Justice System: Low Confidence, High Exposure* (Los Angeles: Pew Hispanic Center, 2009); President's Commission on Law Enforcement and Administration of Justice, *The Challenge of Crime in a Free Society* (New York: Avon Books, 1968), 256.

28. Sandra Lee Browning, Francis T. Cullen, Liqun Cao, Renee Kopache, and Thomas J. Stevenson, "Race and Getting Hassled by the Police: A Research Note*," Police Studies* 17, no. 1 (1994): 1–11.

29 . "From Some Parents, Warnings about Police," *New York Times,* October 23, 1997, A18.

30. Ronald Weitzer, "Citizens' Perceptions of Police Misconduct: Race and Neighborhood Context," *Justice Quarterly* 16 (December 1999): 1101–1128.

31. Roger G. Dunham and Geoffrey P. Alpert, "Neighborhood Differences in Attitudes toward Policing: Evidence for a Mixed-Strategy Model of Policing in a Multi-Ethnic Setting," *Journal of Criminal Law and Criminology* 79, no. 2 (1988): 504–523.

32. Weitzer and Tuch, *Race and Policing in Americ,* 45.

33. Bureau of Justice Statistics, *Criminal Victimization and Perceptions of Community Safety in 12 Cities* (Washington, DC: U.S. Government Printing Office, 1998), http://www.bjs.gov/content/pub/pdf/ cvpcs98.pdf.

34. The idea that procedural justice by police officers will result in improved public attitudes about the police is the central argument in President's Task Force on 21st Century Policing, *Final Report.*

35. The events of March 3, 1991, are described in detail in Jerome H. Skolnick and James J. Fyfe, *Above the Law* (New York: Free Press, 1993), 1–3.

36. Tuch and Weitzer, "Racial Differences in Attitudes toward the Police," 647–649.

37. Stan L. Albrecht and Miles Green, "Attitudes toward the Police and the Larger Attitude Complex," *Criminology* 15 (May 1977): 67–86.

38. Egon Bittner, "The Functions of the Police in Urban Society," in Egon Bittner, *Aspects of Police Work* (Boston: Northeastern University Press, 1990), 89–232; Abraham Blumberg, *Criminal Justice*, 2nd ed. (New York: New Viewpoints, 1979), 58; Arthur Niederhoffer, *Behind the Shield: The Police in Urban Society* (Garden City, NY: Anchor Books, 1967), p. 1.

39. James Q. Wilson, *Varieties of Police Behavior* (New York: Atheneum, 1973), 28.

40. William A. Westley, *Violence and the Police* (Cambridge, MA: MIT Press, 1970), 93.

41. Greg Ridgeway et al., *Police-Community Relations in Cincinnati: Year Two Evaluation Report* (Santa Monica: RAND Corporation, 2006), 72.

42. Lawrence W. Sherman, Patrick R. Gartin, and Michael E. Buerger, "Hot Spots of Predatory Crime: Routine Activities and the Criminology of Place," *Criminology* 27, no. 1 (1989): 27–55.

43. Albert Reiss, *The Police and the Public* (New Haven, CT: Yale University Press, 1971).

44. Robert E. Worden, "The 'Causes' of Police Brutality: Theory and Evidence," in W. A. Geller and H. Toch, eds., *And Justice for All* (Washington, DC: Police Executive Research Forum, 1995), 44; John A. Groeger, *Memory and Remembering: Everyday Memory in Context* (New York: Addison Wesley, 1997), 189–196.

45. Donald Black, "The Social Organization of Arrest," in Donald Black, *The Manners and Customs of the Police* (New York: Academic Press, 1980), 85–108; Kennedy, *Don't Shoot.*; David Kennedy, "Drugs, Race and Common Ground: Reflections on the High Point Intervention," *NIJ Journal* 262 (March 2009): 12–17.

46. U.S. Department of Justice, Civil Rights Division, *Re: Albuquerque Police Department* (April 10, 2014), https://www.justice.gov/sites/default/files/crt/legacy/2014/04/10/apd_findings_4-10-14.pdf.

47. Sara E. Stoutland, "The Multiple Dimensions of Trust in Resident/Police Relations in Boston,"

48. Weitzer and Tuch, *Race and Policing in America,* 150–152.

49. Gunnar Myrdal, *An American Dilemma: The Negro Problem and Modern Democracy* (New York: Harper and Brothers, 1944); Samuel Walker, "'A Strange Atmosphere of Consistent Illegality': Myrdal on 'The Police and Other Public Contacts,'" in O. Clayton, ed., *An American Dilemma Revisited* (New York: Russell Sage, 1996), 226–246; Guy B. Johnson, "The Negro and Crime," *Annals of the American Academy of Political and Social Science* 217 (September 1941): 93–104.

50. National Advisory Commission on Civil Disorders, *Report*, 307–309.

51. The Knapp Commission, *Report on Police Corruption* (New York: Braziller, 1973), 75.

52. National Advisory Commission on Civil Disorders, *Report*, 307–308.

53. Black, *The Manners and Customs of the Police*, 117; Richard J. Lundman, "Domestic Police-Citizen Encounters," *Journal of Police Science and Administration* 2 (March 1974): 25.

54. Frank Furstenburg and Charles Wellford, "Calling the Police: The Evaluation of Police Service," *Law and Society Review* 7 (Spring 1973): 402; Carolyn M. Ward, "Policing in the Hyde Park Neighborhood, St. Louis: Racial Bias, Political Pressure, and Community Policing," *Crime, Law, and Social Change,* 26, no. 2 (1996): 169.

55. Stoutland, "The Multiple Dimensions of Trust in Resident/Police Relations in Boston."

56. U.S. Department of Justice, Civil Rights Division, *Investigation of the Ferguson Police Department* (2015).

57. Police Accountability Task Force, *Recommendations for Reform: Restoring Trust between the Chicago Police and the Communities They Serve* (Chicago: Author, April 2016), https://chicagopatf.org/.

58. "Final Tally: Police Shot and Killed 986 People in 2015," *Washington Post,* January 6, 2015, https://www.washingtonpost.com/national/final-tally-police-shot-and-killed-984-people-in-2015/2016/01/05/3ec7a404-b3c5-11e5-a76a-0b5145e8679a_story.html; Federal Bureau of Investigation, *Crime in the United States, 2014, Expanded Homicide Data*, table 14, https://www.

Journal of Research in Crime and Delinquency 38 (August 2001), 226–256.

fbi.gov/about-us/cjis/ucr/crime-in-the-u.s/2014/crime-in-the-u.s.-2014/tables/expanded-homicide-data/expanded_homicide_data_table_14_justifiable_homicide_by_weapon_law_enforcement_2010–2014.xls.

59. James J. Fyfe, "Blind Justice: Police Shootings in Memphis," *Journal of Criminal Law and Criminology* 73, no. 2 (1982): 707–722.

60. William A. Geller and Michael S. Scott, *Deadly Force: What We Know* (Washington, DC: Police Executive Research Forum, 1992); James J. Fyfe, "Administrative Interventions on Police Shooting Discretion: An Empirical Assessment," *Journal of Criminal Justice* 7 (Winter 1979): 309–323.

61. *Tennessee v. Garner*, 471 U.S. 1 (1985).

62. President's Task Force on 21st Century Policing, *Final Report*.

63. Lorie Fridell, quoted in Police Executive Research Forum, *Re-Engineering Training on Police Use of Force* (Washington, DC: Author, 2015), 37–38, http://www.policeforum.org/assets/reengineeringtraining1.pdf.

64. Joshua Correll, Bernadette Park, Charles M. Judd, Bernd Wittenbrink, Melody S. Sadler, and Tracie Keesee, "Across the Thin Blue Line: Police Officers and Racial Bias in the Decision to Shoot," *Journal of Personality and Social Psychology* 92, no. 6 (2007): 1006–1023. The article and other publications on unconscious bias are available on the Fair and Impartial Policing Project website at http://www.fairimpartialpolicing.com/.

65. Fair and Impartial Policing Project website at http://www.fairimpartialpolicing.com/.

66. See the findings and discussion in Geoffrey P. Alpert and Roger G. Dunham, *Understanding Police Use of Force: Officers, Suspects, and Reciprocity* (New York: Cambridge University Press, 2004).

67. Commission on Accreditation for Law Enforcement Agencies, *Standards for Law Enforcement Agencies*, 4th ed. (Fairfax, VA: Author, 1999), Standard 1.3.1, http://www.calea.org/.

68. Kenneth Adams, "Measuring the Prevalence of Police Abuse of Force," in W. A. Geller and H. Toch, eds., *And Justice for All* (Washington, DC: Police Executive Research Forum, 1995), 61–97; Reiss, *The Police and the Public*, 142.

69. Bureau of Justice Statistics, *Police Behavior During Traffic and Street Stops, 2011* (Washington, DC: U.S. Department of Justice,

2013), table 9, http://www.bjs.gov/content/pub/pdf/pbtss11.pdf.

70. Omaha Police Department, *Annual Report 2014*, http://opd.ci.omaha.ne.us/images/Annual_Reports/2014AnnualReportFinal.pdf.

71. Reiss, *The Police and the Public*, 151.

72. Worden, "The 'Causes' of Police Brutality: Theory and Evidence on Police Use of Force," 52.

73. Geoffrey P. Alpert, "The Force Factor: Measuring and Assessing Police use of Force and Suspect Resistance," in Bureau of Justice Statistics, *Use of Force by Police: Overview of National and Local Data* (Washington, DC: U.S. Government Printing Office, 1999), 45–60, https://www.ncjrs.gov/pdffiles1/nij/176330-1.pdf.

74. David Weisburd and Rosann Greenspan, *Police Attitudes Toward Abuse of Authority: Findings from a National Study* (Washington, DC: The Police Foundation, 2000), http://www.policefoundation.org/wp-content/uploads/2015/06/Weisburd-et-al.-2001-The-Abuse-of-Police-Authority.pdf.

75. Albert Reiss, "Police Brutality—Answers to Key Questions," *Transaction* 5 (July–August 1968): 10–19.

76. San Jose Independent Police Auditor, *Annual Report 2006* (San Jose, CA: City of San Jose, 2007), 51; New York Civilian Complaint Review Board, *Status Report, January–December 2007* (New York: CCRB, 2008), table 11.

77. Police Executive Research Forum, *Re-Engineering Training on Police Use of Force* (Washington, DC: Author, 2015), http://www.policeforum.org/assets/reengineeringtraining1.pdf.

78. The best discussion of the stop and frisk controversy is Michael D. White and Henry F. Fradella, *Stop and Frisk: The Use and Abuse of a Controversial Policing Tactic* (New York: New York University Press. 2016).

79. *Terry v. Ohio* 392 U.S. 1 (1968).

80. New York Civil Liberties Union, *Stop and Frisk 2011. NYCLU Briefing* (New York: Author, 2012), www.nyclu.org. Additional details about the case are available at www.ccrjustice.org. Information on the NYPD stop and frisk controversy is available at the Center for Constitutional Rights website at www.ccrjustice.org.

81. *Floyd, et al., v. City of New York*, (2013). For materials related to the case, see www.ccrjustice.org.

82. Tom R. Tyler, Jeffrey Fagan, and Amanda Geller, "Street Stops and Police Legitimacy: Teachable Moments in Young Men's Legal Socialization,"

Journal of Empirical Legal Studies 11 (December 2014), 751–785.

83. Whte and Fradella, *Stop and Frisk*, 184.

84. National Advisory Commission on Civil Disorders, *Report*; President's Task Force Report on 21st Century Policing, *Final Report*.

85. Nazgol Ghandnoosh, *Black Lives Matter: Eliminating Racial Inequity in the Criminal Justice System* (Washington, DC: The Sentencing Project, 2015), http://www.sentencingproject.org/publications/black-lives-matter-eliminating-racial-inequity-in-the-criminal-justice-system/. See also the earlier estimate in Robert Tillman, "The Size of the 'Criminal Population,' The Prevalence and Incidence of Adult Arrest," *Criminology* 25 (August 1987): 561–579.

86. Kimberly Kempf Leonard, "Minority Youths and Juvenile Justice: Disproportionate Minority Contact After Nearly 20 Years of Reform Efforts," *Youth Violence and Juvenile Justice* 5 (January 2007): 80.

87. Tammy Rinehart Kochel, David B. Wilson, and Stephen D. Mastrofski, "Effects of Suspect Race on Officers' Arrest Decisions," *Criminology* 49, no. 2 (2011): 473–511.

88. Federal Bureau of Investigation, *Crime in the United States, 2014,* "Arrests," table 43; Richard A. Micch, Lloyd D. Johnston, Patrick O'Malley, Jerald Bachman, and John E. Schulenberg, *National Survey Results on Drug Use 1975–2014*, vol. 1 (Ann Arbor: Monitoring the Future, 2014), table 4‑6, http://www.monitoringthefuture.org/pubs/monographs/mtf-vol1_2014.pdf.

89. Michelle Alexander, *The New Jim Crow: Mass Incarceration in the Age of Colorblindness* (New York: Free Press, 2010).

90. American Civil Liberties Union, *The War on Marijuana in Black and White* (New York: Author, 2013), https://www.aclu.org/report/war-marijuana-black-and-white.

91. Miech et al., *National Survey Results on Drug Use 1975–2014,* vol. 1, table 4–6.

92. Black, "The Social Organization of Arrest"; David A. Klinger, "Demeanor or Crime? Why 'Hostile' Citizens Are More Likely to Be Arrested," *Criminology* 32, no. 3 (1994): 475–493.

93. Samuel Walker, Testimony, President's Task Force on 21st Century Policing, *Final Report*.

94. Christy Lopez, *Disorderly (Mis)Conduct: The Problem with 'Contempt of Cop' Arrests* (Washington, DC: American Constitution Society,

2010), https://www.acslaw.org/sites/default/files/Lopez_Contempt_of_Cop.pdf.

95. Kennedy, *Don't Shoot.*; David Kennedy, "Drugs, Race and Common Ground: Reflections on the High Point Intervention," *NIJ Journal* 262 (March 2009): 12–17.

96. Jerome Skolnick, *The Police and the Urban Ghetto* (Chicago: American Bar Foundation, 1968).

97. Quoted in Weitzer, "Racialized Policing," 137.

98. Cited in National Advisory Commission on Civil Disorders, *Report*, 302–303.

99. "New Racist Texting Scandal at SFPD Points to Problems All Over," *San Francisco Chronicle,* April 27, 2016, http://www.sfchronicle.com/opinion/editorials/article/New-racist-texting-scandal-at-SFPD-points-to-7379813.php.

100. Samuel Walker, Testimony, President's Task Force on 21st Century Policing, *Final Report,* Action Item 4.4.1.

101. Minneapolis Police Department, Policy and Procedure Manual, Section 5-104.01, "Professional Policing."

102. Walker, Testimony, President's Task Force on 21st Century Policing.

103. ACLU, *Driving While Black: Racial Profiling on our Nation's Highways* (New York: Author, 1999), https://www.aclu.org/report/driving-while-black-racial-profiling-our-nations-highways; David Harris, *Profiles in Injustice: Why Racial Profiling Cannot Work* (New York: The New Press, 2002).

104. John A. Gardiner, *Traffic and the Police: Variations in Law-Enforcement Policy* (Cambridge: Harvard University Press, 1969).

105. Bureau of Justice Studies, *Police Behavior During Traffic and Street Stops*, 2011.

106. Epp, Maynard-Moody, and Hader-Markel, *Pulled Over.*

107. Ibid.

108. Epp et al., *Pulled Over.*

109. Lorie Fridell, *By the Numbers: A Guide for Analyzing Race Data from Vehicle Stops* (Washington, DC: Police Executive Research Forum, 2004), http://www.justice.utah.gov/Documents/Research/Race/PERF%20by%20the%20Numbers.pdf.

110. L. D. Johnston, J. G. Bachman, and P. M. O'Malley, *Monitoring the Future: Questionnaire Responses from the Nation's High School Seniors, 2009* (Ann Arbor, MI: Institute for Social Research, 2009), question C27, 26.

111. Samuel Walker, *Early Intervention Systems for Law Enforcement Agencies: A Planning and Management Guide* (Washington, DC: Department of Justice, 2003), http://www.cops.usdoj.gov/html/cd_rom/inaction1/pubs/EarlyInterventionSystemsLawEnforcement.pdf.

112. ACLU, *Driving While Black*; Harris, *Profiles in Injustice*.

113. Albert J. Meehan and Michael C. Ponder, "Race and Place: The Ecology of Racial Profiling African American Motorists," *Justice Quarterly* 19 (September 2002), 399–430.

114. Heather MacDonald, *Are Cops Racist?* (Chicago: Ivan Dee, 2003).

115. National Survey of Household Drug Use.

116. San Jose Police Department, *Vehicle Stop Demographic Study: First Report* (San Jose: Author, 1999).

117. Police Executive Research Forum, *Racially Biased Policing: A Principled Response* (Washington, DC: Author, 2001), ch. 4, http://www.policeforum.org/assets/docs/Free_Online_Documents/Racially-Biased_Policing/racially%20biased%20policing%20-%20a%20principled%20response%202001.pdf.

118. *Floyd v. City of New York* (2013).

119. Stoutland, "The Multiple Dimensions of Trust in Resident/Police Relations in Boston."

120. National Institute of Justice, *Reducing Gun Violence: The Boston Gun Project's Operation Ceasefire* (Washington, DC: Department of Justice, 2001), https://www.ncjrs.gov/pdffiles1/nij/188741.pdf.

121. Wesley G. Skogan, "Citizen Satisfaction with Police Encounters," *Police Quarterly* 8 (September 2005), 298–321.

122. President's Task Force on 21st Century Policing, *Final Report*.

123. Wesley G. Skogan and Susan M. Hartnett, *Community Policing, Chicago Style* (New York: Oxford University Press, 1997).

124. Police Accountability Task Force, *Recommendations for Reform*.

125. Fred A. Klyman and Joanna Kruckenberg, "A National Survey of Police–Community Relations Units," *Journal of Police Science and Administration* 7 (March 1979): 74; Charles E. Reasons and Bernard A. Wirth, "Police–Community Relations Units: A National Survey," *Journal of Social Issues* 31 (Winter 1975): 27–34.

126. Reasons and Wirth, "Police Community Relations Units."

127. Ibid.

128. President's Commission on Law Enforcement and Administration of Justice, *Task Force Report: The Police*.

129. U.S. Department of Justice, *Improving Police/Community Relations* (Washington, DC: U.S. Government Printing Office, 1973), 3–4.

130. Pew Research Center, *U.S. Foreign-Born Population Trends* (Washington, DC: Pew Research Center, 2015), http://www.pewhispanic.org/2015/09/28/chapter-5-u-s-foreign-born-population-trends/.

131. U.S. Immigration and Customs Enforcement, *Fact Sheet: Delegation of Immigration Authority Section 287 (g) Immigration and Nationality Act* (n.d.), https://www.ice.gov/factsheets/287g.

132. Scott Decker, Paul Lewis, Doris Provine, and Monica Varsanyi, *Immigration and Local Policing* (Washington, DC: The Police Foundation, 2015), http://www.policefoundation.org/wp-content/uploads/2015/06/Appendix-G_0.pdf.

133. Jessica Saunders, Nelson Lim, and Don Prosnitz, *Enforcing Immigration Law at the State and Local Levels* (Santa Monica, CA: RAND Corporation, 2010).

134. Judy Keen, "Big Cities Reluctant to Target Illegals," *USA Today*, usatoday.com

135. Villarruel and Walker, *Donde esta la justicia?*, 46, http://cclp.org/documents/BBY/Donde.pdf.

136. Robert C. Davis and Nicole J. Henderson, "Willingness to Report Crimes: The Role of Ethnic Group Membership and Community Efficacy," *Crime and Delinquency* 49 (October 2003): 564–580.

137. Leigh Herbst and Samuel Walker, "Language Barriers in the Delivery of Police Services," *Journal of Criminal Justice* 29, no. 4 (2001): 329–340.

138. Robert C. Davis and Edna Erez, *Immigrant Populations as Victims: Toward a Multicultural Criminal Justice System* (Washington, DC: U.S. Department of Justice, 1998), http://www.ncdsv.org/images/NIJ_ImmigrantPopulationsAsVictimsTowardAmulticulturalCJsystem_5-1998.pdf.

139. Herbst and Walker, "Language Barriers in the Delivery of Police Services."

140. Seattle Police Department, Office of Professional Accountability, http://www.seattle.gov/opa.

141. Commission on Accreditation for Law Enforcement Agencies, *Standards for Law Enforcement Agencies*, Standard 31.2.1, www.calea.org.

142. U.S. Civil Rights Commission, *Police Protection of the African American Community in Milwaukee* (Washington, DC: U.S. Government Printing Office, 1994), 45; U.S. Civil Rights Commission, Tennessee Advisory Committee, *Civic Crisis–Civic Challenge: Police Community Relations in Memphis* (Washington, DC: U.S. Government Printing Office, 1978), 1, 88.

143. Samuel Walker, *Police Accountability: The Role of Citizen Oversight* (Belmont: Wadsworth, 2001).

144. Reiss, *The Police and the Public*,

145. Weitzer and Tuch, *Race and Policing in America*, 112–116.

146. Ronald Weitzer, "White, Black, or Blue Cops? Race and Citizen Assessment of Police Officers," *Journal of Criminal Justice* 28 (2000): 313–324.

147. Thomas M. Frost and Magnus E. Sherry, *San Diego Community Profile: Final Report* (Washington, DC: The Police Foundation, 1975).

148. Jerome L. Blakemore, David Barlow, and Deborah L. Padgett, "From the Classroom to the Community: Introducing Process in Police Diversity Training," *Police Studies* XVIII, no. 1 (1995): 71–83.

149. Geoffrey P. Alpert, William C. Smith, and Daniel Watters, "Implications of the Rodney King Beating," *Criminal Law Bulletin* 28 (September–October 1992): 477.

© David McNew/Getty Images

C H A P T E R

13 Police Corruption

CHAPTER OUTLINE

A Definition of Police Corruption

The Costs of Police Corruption

Types of Corruption

Gratuities

Bribes

Theft and Burglary

Sexual Misconduct

Internal Corruption

Corruption and Brutality

Levels of Corruption

Pervasiveness of Corruption within a Police Organization

Theories of Police Corruption

Individual Officer Explanations

Social Structural Explanations

Neighborhood Explanations

The Nature of Police Work

The Police Organization

The Police Subculture

Becoming Corrupt

The Moral Careers of Individual Officers

Corrupting Organizations

Controlling Corruption

Internal Corruption Control Strategies

The Attitude of the Chief

Rules and Regulations

Managing Anticorruption Investigations

Investigative Tactics

Cracking the "Blue Curtain"

Proactive Integrity Tests
Effective Supervision
Rewarding the Good Officers
Personnel Recruitment
Field Training
**External Corruption Control
Approaches**
Special Investigations
Criminal Prosecution

Mobilizing Public Opinion
Altering the External Environment
The Limits of Anticorruption Efforts
CASE STUDY
Summary
Key Terms
For Discussion
Internet Exercises

" **F**or as long as there have been police," Lawrence Sherman observes, "there has been police corruption."[1] Corruption is one of the oldest and most persistent problems in American policing. Historians have found evidence of bribery in the earliest years of colonial America. Although a number of police departments have successfully reduced corruption in recent years, it persists as a major problem in some departments today. In the 1990s, for example, the Mollen Commission found serious corruption in the New York City Police Department (NYPD). Officers were found on the payroll of drug dealers, earning up to $4,000 a week.[2] In the early 2000s, an investigation into the Los Angeles Police Department (LAPD) found serious corruption in the organization. Officers in the Rampart Division of the LAPD were found to be involved in the theft of drugs, bank robbery, false imprisonment, planting evidence, and the beating of arrestees.[3] Similarly, in 2014, an investigation into the Philadelphia Police Department found serious corruption among six narcotics officers. The officers were found to be extorting cash and drugs from drug dealers through beatings, kidnappings, and threats, and through arrests in which they would jail drug dealers for a short period of time so that they could burglarize their homes.[4]

This chapter examines the nature of police corruption, the factors that cause it, and strategies for controlling it.

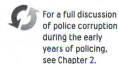

For a full discussion of police corruption during the early years of policing, see Chapter 2.

A Definition of Police Corruption

Herman Goldstein defines **police corruption** as "acts involving the misuse of authority by a police officer in a manner designed to produce personal gain for himself or for others."[5] The two key elements are (1) misuse of authority and (2) personal gain.

Corruption is only one form of misconduct or deviant behavior by police officers. Thomas Barker and David Carter's typology of police deviance distinguishes between occupational deviance and abuse of authority. **Occupational deviance** includes criminal and noncriminal behavior "committed during the course of normal work activities or committed under the guise of the police officer's authority." This includes improper behavior that is not illegal, such as sleeping on the job. **Abuse of authority** includes an action by a police officer "that tends to injure, insult, trespass upon human dignity . . . and/or violate an inherent legal right" of a citizen.[6] An illegal arrest or use of excessive force is wrong but does not involve any personal gain. Some illegal activity by a police officer, meanwhile, is not occupational deviance. A

police corruption

occupational deviance

abuse of authority

E X H I B I T   13–1

Rules and Regulations, Phoenix Police Department
Operations Order 3.13
Acceptance of Gifts or Rewards

(1) Employees will not solicit or accept, either directly or indirectly, rewards or gratuities for performance of duties or in exchange for police services and will not use their position to seek favors of any kind, for example:

- The acceptance of free or discounted meals from any commercial establishment other than those offered to the general public
- The acceptance of free or discounted rent other than those offered to the general public
- Solicitation of off-duty work from victims, suspects, witnesses, or businesses

(2) Employees will not engage in any business transaction with a person in police custody.

(3) Employees will not engage in bribery or extortion.

Source: Phoenix Police Department, "Operations Orders", Operations Order 3.13, page 2. [Revised 06/14]

criminal assault on a friend or family member by an off-duty police officer is a private act. Finally, some actions are unwise but not necessarily illegal. Some police departments, for example, do not allow their officers to receive free meals at restaurants. Taking a free meal is a violation of department policy but not a crime. Exhibit 13–1 represents an excerpt from the personnel standards of the Phoenix Police Department, indicating behavior that is prohibited.

The Costs of Police Corruption

Corruption imposes high costs on the police, the criminal justice system, and society. First, a corrupt act by a police officer is a criminal act. Criminal activity by a police officer undermines the basic integrity of law enforcement.

Second, corruption usually protects other criminal activity. Historically, corruption protected gambling syndicates, which were the major source of income for organized crime. More recently, corruption has often been related to drug trafficking. A Government Accounting Office report revealed that about half of all police officers convicted as a consequence of FBI-led corruption cases were convicted for drug-related offenses.[7]

Third, police corruption undermines the effectiveness of the criminal justice system. The New York City Commission to Combat Police Corruption argues that "The honesty and integrity of police officers is . . . critical to the workings of the criminal justice system."[8] Officers routinely testify in court, and if they have a reputation for dishonesty, their credibility in criminal cases is damaged. In 2010, for example, about 200 criminal cases were dropped or convictions were vacated because of revelations that police officers in Camden, New Jersey, were among other things framing individuals by planting drugs on them and lying on police reports.[9]

Fourth, corruption undermines the professionalism of a police department. Effective discipline becomes impossible if supervisors are corrupt and threatened with exposure by officers under their command. Corruption encourages police lying, as officers protect one another. Lying to protect oneself or other officers can then spread to other areas of policing, such as covering up excessive use of force.[10]

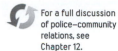

For a full discussion of police–community relations, see Chapter 12.

Fifth, as former *New York Times* reporter David Burnham argues, corruption is "a secret tax totaling millions of dollars a year" on individual citizens of New York City.[11] In some instances, it is a direct tax, as when corrupt police extract bribes from businesses.

Sixth, corruption undermines public confidence in the police. The belief that a department is corrupt undermines respect for officers and public support for the department as a whole. This has a special impact on police–community relations. Illegal vice activities have generally been relegated to low-income and racial-minority neighborhoods. Ronald Weitzer and Steven Tuch, in their national study of citizen perceptions of police misconduct, found that minorities were significantly more likely than whites to believe that it is very common or fairly common for police officers in their city's police department to engage in corruption (see Exhibit 13–2).[12]

For a full discussion of the perceived honesty of the police, see Chapter 12.

The Mollen Commission's report on police corruption in New York City addressed this issue only indirectly. It noted that the worst examples of corruption and brutality existed "particularly in crime-ridden, drug-infested precincts, often with large minority populations."[13] It did not, however, specifically discuss the point that the officers in these areas probably felt free to engage in rampant corruption and brutality because they perceived the residents to be politically powerless.

On the positive side, public opinion polls consistently indicate that the police rank relatively high compared with other occupations in terms of perceived honesty and integrity. In a 2015 Gallup poll, for example, the police ranked fifth out of 21 occupations, just ahead of clergy and much higher than congresspersons, bankers, and business executives.[14]

The percentage of white Americans rating the honesty and ethical standards of the police as "high" or "very high" rose between the 1977 and 2001, but then began to decline somewhat through 2015. Most years, the ratings by nonwhites are lower than those of whites.[15]

EXHIBIT 13–2

How Common Do You Think Corruption (Such as Taking Bribes, Involvement in Drug Trade) Is in Your City's Police Department?

	Whites	Blacks	Hispanics
Very common	6%	22%	9%
Fairly common	11	26	20
Not very common	50	41	47
Not at all common	33	11	24
Number of respondents	613	555	592

Source: Ronald Weitzer and Steven Tuch, *Rethinking Minority Attitudes toward the Police: Final Technical Report* (Washington, DC: National Institute of Justice, June 26, 2004).

Types of Corruption

Corruption takes many different forms. Some forms are far more serious than others. For some activities, such as receiving free meals, there is debate over whether the activity should be defined as corruption. Different corrupt acts have different causes and call for different control strategies.[16]

Gratuities

gratuities

The most common form of police corruption involves **gratuities:** free meals, free dry cleaning, or discounts on other purchases. Some departments prohibit gratuities, whereas others do not. One survey found that only half of all police departments had written policies mentioning free meals—and not all of those policies clearly prohibited the practice.[17]

Gratuities involve mixed motives on the part of businesspeople. In some cases, they represent a sincere effort to thank police officers for doing a dangerous job to protect the community. In other cases, they reflect self-interest: the belief that the presence of police cars near their stores will deter robbers and burglars or the expectation that the police will return the favor by providing extra patrol coverage in the area. For example, one survey conducted in Reno, Nevada, found that about 33 percent of those who offer police officers free gifts such as coffee and meals explicitly stated that they expected special favors in return.[18]

People who believe that the police should never be allowed to receive gratuities argue that they open the door to more serious forms of corruption.[19] Gratuities encourage officers to believe they are entitled to special privileges and may lead them to demand such privileges. The Knapp Commission, which investigated New York City corruption in the early 1970s, made a distinction between **grass eaters** (who passively accept what is offered to them) and **meat eaters** (who aggressively demand favors).[20]

grass eaters
meat eaters

A survey of North Carolina residents found very mixed opinions about police accepting gratuities. Only 36 percent believed it was inappropriate for a police officer to accept an occasional free coffee, nonalcoholic drink, or discounted meal when on duty. At the same time, however, only 23 percent thought accepting a meal when off duty was appropriate.[21]

Bribes

bribes

Accepting **bribes** not to enforce the law is a far more serious form of corruption. Some bribes are isolated acts, such as when an officer takes money not to write a traffic ticket. Other bribes are more systematic, particularly regular payoffs to protect a drug operation. Historically, the most serious police corruption has involved regular payoffs to protect an ongoing illegal activity—prostitution, after-hours drinking, or narcotics. In New York City, regular payoffs were referred to as "the pad." New York City police officers "on the pad" were found to receive up to $850 a month to protect a single dealer.[22] More recently, nine police officers in Georgia were convicted of accepting cash payments for protecting drug deals.[23]

Corrupt officers can also be bribed to sell information about criminal investigations, either before or after arrests are made. A tip about an investigation may help

POLICE *in* FOCUS | At What Price a "Freebie"? The Real Cost of Police Corruption

Jim Ruiz, a retired police sergeant from New Orleans turned professor, recounts his experiences with receiving gratuities as a police officer in a candid and well-framed analysis of the ethical issue. He points out that most academic discussions of police accepting gratuities focus on single events of free coffee, sodas, or a free or discounted meal and do not frame their analysis as a percentage of an officer's income or the cumulative amount they receive from gratuities each year. Ruiz's experiences and observations led him to a conservative estimate that police officers receive approximately $8,713 a year in gratuities and that if these "gifts" were taxed, the sum would be significantly higher. He points out that policymakers and academics should not overlook the substantial amount of gratuities that police officers cumulatively receive over a year and that gratuities comprise a substantial proportion of an officer's compensation (up to 30 to 40 percent of an officer's income).

As a class, discuss whether you believe that a police department should have a policy on gratuities and what that policy should be. If departmental policies are believed to be needed to control the practice, discuss which strategies could be used to address the issue.

"Conservative List" and Cost of Common Gratuities

Gratuities	Annual Cost
Coffee/soda	$494.00
Doughnuts	444.60
Lunch	1,482.00
Cigarettes	2,002.00
Alcohol	2,496.00
Laundry	962.50
Movie theater	832.00
Total annual gratuities	$8,713.10

Source: Jim Ruiz and Christine Bono, "At What Price a 'Freebie'? The Real Cost of Police Gratuities," *Criminal Justice Ethics* 23, no. 1 (2004): 44–54.

drug dealers avoid arrest. Robert Daley reported in 1978 that New York City detectives regularly sold information to defense attorneys about pending cases. Officers took money in exchange for altering their testimony, "forgetting" important points on the witness stand, destroying evidence, or revealing important points about the prosecution's case.[24] A person engaged in a civil lawsuit against someone else may bribe a police officer for damaging information about that person contained in police files. In the past, before bail reform, police officers frequently took kickbacks for referring arrested persons to certain bail bondsmen or defense attorneys.

Some bribes protect illegal activities, whereas others support legitimate businesses. David Burnham found that New York City building contractors regularly paid the police $50 a week to avoid being ticketed for such violations as double-parking or blocking streets and sidewalks.[25] In 2016 the FBI alleged that several officers assigned to the licensing division of the NYPD expedited gun license applications for cash and gifts.[26]

It is important to point out that although bribery is still a problem in many police agencies across the country, police officers in the United States ask for bribes far less often than police officers in many other countries do. The most comprehensive study to date surveyed citizens around the globe on whether they had been asked to pay a bribe to a police officer. The United States ranked 17th out of 41 counties—ranking just below many of the developed countries, but above undeveloped and third-world countries (see Exhibit 13–3).[27]

EXHIBIT 13–3

International Survey on Bribe Payments

Nation	Percentage of Respondents Asked to Pay a Police Officer Last Year	Nation	Percentage of Respondents Asked to Pay a Police Officer Last Year
England and Wales	0.00%	Poland	2.36%
France	0.00	Chechnya	2.38
Netherlands	0.00	Belarus	2.61
Scotland	0.00	Costa Rica	2.63
Sweden	0.00	Ukraine	3.30
Switzerland	0.00	South Africa	3.50
Canada	0.16	Paraguay	3.92
Slovenia	0.28	India	4.26
Botswana	0.63	Lithuania	4.37
Macedonia	0.72	Slovak Rep.	4.61
Austria	0.75	Kyrgyz Rep.	5.23
Mongolia	0.77	Croatia	6.84
Malta	0.93	Yugoslavia	7.09
Albania	1.13	Brazil	8.90
Hungary	1.35	Georgia	9.18
Estonia	1.46	Russia	9.90
United States	1.50	Bolivia	11.34
Philippines	1.56	Bulgaria	13.54
Romania	1.63	Indonesia	17.64
Latvia	1.73	Argentina	20.92
Zimbabwe	2.20		
		Average	4.59

Source: From "To Serve and Collect: Measuring Police Corruption," Sanja Kutnjak Ivkovic in *Journal of Criminal Law and Criminology* 93. Copyright © 2003. Reprinted by special permission of Northwestern University School of Law, *The Journal of Criminal Law and Criminology.*

Theft and Burglary

Theft or burglary by officers on duty is a particularly serious form of corruption. One example involves officers taking money from people arrested for drunkenness. The victim often has a hard time remembering how much money he or she actually had, much less convincing anyone that the officer stole any money. Another example involves officers who steal property, money, or drugs from the police department's property room. In the 1990s, 40 police officers in New Orleans were arrested for bank robbery, auto theft, and other illegal acts. An additional 200 officers were later reprimanded, fired, or retired as a consequence of criminal activity.[28]

Narcotics arrests offer special temptations for theft. Officers making a drug raid usually find large amounts of both money and drugs. For example, the "River Cops" case in Miami, Florida, revealed that a large number of police officers were involved in the stealing and selling of cocaine. Upon further scrutiny of police activities, 19 officers were arrested, convicted, and sentenced to prison, and 70 officers were fired.[29]

Similarly, the Mollen Commission found that corrupt officers in New York City stole drugs, money, and guns from drug dealers. One officer took $32,000 in money and goods in one theft. In some instances, officers arranged for phony 911 calls that allowed them to enter business premises and steal goods.[30]

Sexual Misconduct

Sexual misconduct by the police is perhaps the least discussed but one of the most common forms of misconduct. One study examining media reports indicated that about 13 percent of misconduct reports involved sexual misconduct.[31] The International Association of Chiefs of Police (IACP) defines sexual misconduct as "any behavior by an officer that takes advantage of the officer's position in law enforcement to misuse authority and power (including force) in order to commit a sexual act, initiate sexual contact with another person, or respond to a perceived sexually motivated cue (for a subtle suggestion to an overt action) from another person."[32]

sexual misconduct

According to the IACP there are the following forms of police sexual misconduct:

1. Sexual contact, including rape and sexual assault.
2. Sexual shakedowns, such as when the officer receives sexual favors in exchange for not arresting the individual.
3. Gratuitous physical contact, including inappropriate frisks.
4. Officer- or citizen-initiated sexual contact or behavior while on duty, even among consenting individuals.
5. Sexual harassment of colleagues.
6. Unnecessary contacts, such as calling a witness or victim of a crime for sexually motivated reasons.
7. Voyeuristic actions, including looking through windows for sexually motivated reasons.[33]

Several reports have provided insight into sexual misconduct by the police, suggesting that it might be more common than once believed. *The Associated Press* examined law enforcement licensing records from 41 states and reported that from 2009 through 2014 about 1,000 officers lost their law enforcement licenses because of sexual misconduct or a sex offense.[34] Philip Stinson and his colleagues looked further at the issue using the Google News search engine. They found reports of 548 police sex-related crimes during their three-year study period. In about 73 percent of the cases, officers were arrested for victimizing a juvenile. Although these findings might be biased because they are only representative of cases identified through the media, which are more likely to reflect serious cases of misconduct, they suggest that much more research is needed to understand the problem.[35] Over the past few years, the Cato Institute's National Police Misconduct Reporting Project has tracked police misconduct throughout the United States. In its 2010 report, the Cato Institute identified 4,861 cases of police misconduct involving 6,613 officers and 6,826 victims. As seen in Exhibit 13–4, the report identified sexual misconduct as the second most common form of misconduct. The report estimated that about $346,512,800 was spent on misconduct-related civil judgements and settlements.[36]

EXHIBIT 13–4

Misconduct by Type

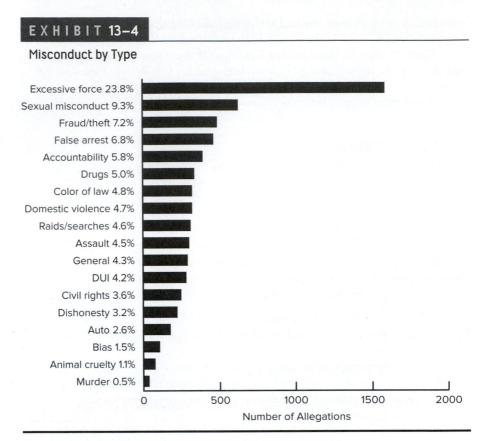

Excessive force 23.8%	
Sexual misconduct 9.3%	
Fraud/theft 7.2%	
False arrest 6.8%	
Accountability 5.8%	
Drugs 5.0%	
Color of law 4.8%	
Domestic violence 4.7%	
Raids/searches 4.6%	
Assault 4.5%	
General 4.3%	
DUI 4.2%	
Civil rights 3.6%	
Dishonesty 3.2%	
Auto 2.6%	
Bias 1.5%	
Animal cruelty 1.1%	
Murder 0.5%	

Number of Allegations (0, 500, 1000, 1500, 2000)

Source: Adapted from *Cato Institute's National Police Misconduct Reporting Project,* 2010.

There are four primary explanations for police sexual misconduct. The first is lack of training and written policies. Police chiefs report that their officers receive little formal training or guidance on sexual misconduct; as a consequence, police officers have little understanding of police sexual misconduct and the consequences they might face if they are caught engaging in such behavior. The second is that many of the victims of police sexual misconduct do not make a complaint to the police department. This is because victims often fear retaliation for making a complaint or fear that their complaint will not be treated seriously by the police department. Third, police work provides officers with numerous opportunities to engage in sexual misconduct. The combination of an unsupervised work environment and the authority officers possess over certain people in certain situations provides for ample opportunities for sexual misconduct. Also, some people (sometimes called "cop groupies") are attracted to police officers, which provides for frequent temptation in the field. Last, police culture provides protection to police officers who engage in sexual misconduct because fellow officers often keep quiet about such behavior.[37]

The Cost of Police Misconduct in the 10 Largest Local Police Departments, 2010–2014

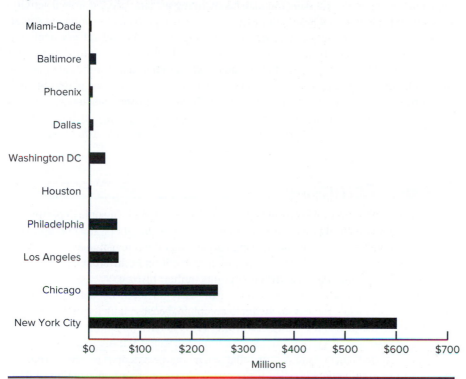

Source: Zusha Elinson and Dan Frosch, "Cost of Police-Misconduct Cases Soars in Big U.S. Cities," *Wall Street Journal,* July 15, 2015, http://www.wsj.com/articles/cost-of-police-misconduct-cases-soars-in-big-u-s-cities-1437013834.

Internal Corruption

In very corrupt departments, promotions or favored assignments must be purchased with bribes. During the nineteenth century, payment for promotion was so systematic in the New York City police department that there was a printed schedule of the "price list" for each rank.[38] The Knapp Commission found a "widespread" pattern of police officers bribing other officers "to gain favorable assignments." It was rumored that a bribe of between $500 and $2,000 could gain assignment as a detective.[39]

Corruption and Brutality

The Mollen Commission argues that a new form of corruption emerged in the 1980s and 1990s, characterized by a convergence of corruption and brutality. Officers brutally beat drug dealers, stole their drugs and money, and then sold the drugs to other dealers or other officers. Not all corruption involved brutality, and not all brutality in the department was associated with corruption. Nonetheless, the two were closely related. Particularly disturbing was the extent to which officers testified that brutality was their "rite of initiation" into other forms of misconduct: "Once the line was crossed without consequences, it was easier to abuse their authority in other ways, including corruption."[40]

The most notorious case to date may involve officers from the LAPD's Rampart Division, in which officers were found to be engaging in "hard core" criminal activity. Officers in the Rampart CRASH unit, which was considered an elite antigang squad, were found to be actively attacking known gang members and falsely accusing individuals of crimes that they did not commit. Investigation into the scandal disclosed that officers routinely choked and punched individuals for the sole purpose of intimidating them. In one case, officers used a suspect as a "human battering ram" and thrust his face continuously into a wall. In several other instances, officers planted drugs on suspects to make arrests. Corrupt sergeants in the division promoted these activities by giving out awards for misdeeds. One officer was given an award for shooting an unarmed innocent person.[41]

Levels of Corruption

The level of corruption varies from department to department. In some departments, corrupt acts involve only an occasional deviant officer. In others, the corruption is systemic through the department. Sherman argues that the relevant question is, Why are there different kinds and amounts of police corruption in different communities, and in the same communities at different points in their history?[42]

Measuring the level of corruption is extremely difficult. By definition, it is a covert crime. Typically there is no victim to complain, because both the officer and the person paying the officer are guilty of a crime. Surveys have found that only 5 percent of those approached by a police officer for a bribe report the activity to the police.[43]

As a consequence, there is little reliable data on the extent of police corruption. Most of the available data consist of the revelations of corruption scandals and reports of investigations that usually follow major scandals. A few researchers, however, have attempted to survey the public and police officials to examine this issue, but most of these studies have not been systematic and typically ask questions about perceptions of corruption rather than participation in it.[44]

The seminal piece of research on the topic was conducted by Robert Kane and Mike White in their analysis of the life and career histories of all officers who were involuntarily separated from the NYPD from 1975 through 1996. They found that few officers were found to have been involved in corruption or other forms of police misconduct. The data indicated that 1,543 officers (out of about 78,000 who were employed over the period) had engaged in career-ending misconduct, which represented about 2 percent of all officers employed over the period.[45]

As seen in Exhibit 13–5, the 1,543 officers generated 2,465 charges. The majority of offenses against officers were administrative in nature, followed by drug offenses (e.g., sale, possession), profit-motivated crime, off-duty crimes against persons, obstruction of justice, off-duty public order crimes, on-duty abuse (i.e., excessive force), and conduct on probation. Accordingly, the authors found that few of the officers were disciplined for activities associated with corruption.

Kane and White also examined risk and protective factors associated with career-ending police misconduct in the NYPD. They concluded that those officers

EXHIBIT 13–5

Charge Specifications against NYPD Officers, 1975–1996

Charge Specifications	Percent (Number)
Administrative/failure to perform	30.1% (742)
Drugs	19.0 (468)
Profit-motivated crimes	15.7 (387)
Off-duty crimes against persons	11.6 (286)
Obstruction of justice	10.8 (266)
Off-duty public order crimes	5.8 (144)
On-duty abuses	4.8 (119)
Conduct on probation	2.2 (53)
Total	100.0 (2,465)

who were black, had a criminal history, and had documented problems in prior jobs were the most likely to be separated from the police department for serious misconduct. Conversely, those who had an associate's or baccalaureate degree and those who performed well in the academy were significantly less likely to engage in career-ending misconduct.

Pervasiveness of Corruption within a Police Organization

Sherman identified different levels of corruption, using a three-part typology based on "the pervasiveness of corruption, its organization, and the sources of bribes."[46]

Type I: Rotten Apples and Rotten Pockets

The least serious form of corruption exists when it involves only a few police officers acting on their own. The **rotten apple** theory describes a situation in which only a few officers are independently engaged in corrupt acts. A **rotten pocket** exists when several corrupt officers cooperate with one another. An example of a rotten pocket is a group of narcotics officers stealing money or drugs during a narcotics raid. The Mollen Commission found corruption centered in crews. In the Thirtieth Precinct of the NYPD, for example, groups of three to five officers worked semi-independently, protecting and assisting each other.[47]

rotten apple
rotten pocket

Type II: Pervasive Unorganized Corruption

Corruption reaches a higher degree of intensity when it has "a majority of personnel who are corrupt, but who have little relationship to each other."[48] In **pervasive unorganized corruption,** many officers may be taking bribes for not issuing traffic tickets, for example, but the officers are not actively cooperating with one another.

pervasive unorganized corruption

Type III: Pervasive Organized Corruption

The most serious form of corruption exists at an organized level that penetrates the higher levels of the department. An example of this **pervasive organized corruption** is a systematic payoff to protect illegal activities, with the payoff

pervasive organized corruption

shared among all members of a unit and their supervisors. In his study of one West Coast city, William Chambliss describes how one restaurant owner had to pay $200 a month to the beat officers (the sum was divided equally among them) and $250 a month to the higher-ranking officers (also divided among several officers). Failure to pay meant that the owner faced frequent citations for building code violations.[49] The Knapp Commission found that in New York City, a newly assigned plainclothes detective was not entitled to a share of the payoffs for about two months until he was checked out for reliability. The earnings lost by this delay were made up in the form of two months' "severance pay" when the officer left the division.[50]

Theories of Police Corruption

Theories of police corruption fall into six different categories, depending on whether they focus on the individual officer, the social structure, the neighborhood, the nature of police work, the police organization, or the police subculture.

Individual Officer Explanations

The most popular explanation of police corruption is the so-called rotten apple theory. It is appealing because it emphasizes the moral failings of one or more individuals, provides convenient scapegoats, and avoids dealing with more difficult issues. It also points in the direction of a simple remedy.

Police officials prefer the rotten apple theory because it allows them to blame a few individuals without having to investigate larger problems in the department. The department can appear to solve the problem by firing the guilty officers. The rotten apple theory also appeals to private citizens, because they can understand personal guilt more easily than complex legal or organizational issues. Further, the theory allows citizens to avoid considering the extent to which police corruption may be rooted in their own preferences for illegal activity.

Most experts, however, believe that the rotten apple theory fails to adequately explain most police corruption. It does not account for the long history of corruption or its pervasiveness in certain departments. How could so many "bad" people be concentrated in one organization? Nor does it explain why some honest people become corrupt. Studies of police recruitment indicate that most people attracted to policing are not morally inferior; they are rather average people, attracted to policing for the same reasons that people choose other careers.[51] Finally, the rotten apple theory does not explain why some police departments have long histories of corruption while others are relatively free of corruption. The Knapp Commission concluded that "the rotten-apple doctrine has in many ways been a basic obstacle to meaningful reform."[52]

Social Structural Explanations

Most experts explain police corruption in terms of the American social structure. In their view, closely related aspects of the criminal law, cultural conflict, and politics encourage and sustain corruption.[53]

The Criminal Law

The criminal law is a major cause of much police corruption. State and federal laws prohibit or seek to regulate many activities that people regard as legitimate recreation or matters of private choice. These include gambling, alcohol and drug consumption, and various sexual practices. The basic problem is a conflict of cultures and lifestyles. Some people believe these activities are immoral and harmful, while others believe they are acceptable and not harmful to others.[54]

Prohibition in the 1920s is an excellent example of the extent to which an industry will arise to provide products or services that have been outlawed. The providers of illegal goods and services have a self-interest in maintaining their enterprise. The profits from these nontaxed enterprises provide sufficient revenue to corrupt the administration of justice—to bribe police, prosecutors, and judges as needed. Police corruption, then, is a routine business expense—an "insurance policy" designed to guarantee continuation of the enterprise. Eric Schlosser reported that organized crime and illicit activities were a major part of the American economy. Roughly 4.6 percent of America's gross domestic product (GDP), or about $650 billion, was related to the nation's "shadow economy."[55] The greatest proportion of the revenue is believed to be generated through drug trafficking and sales. Drug sales alone are believed to total about $60 billion a year.[56]

Criminal syndicates have sufficient financial resources to support candidates for political office who, in turn, may use their power to influence the administration of justice, including, for example, blocking the investigation of certain criminal activities. In 1935, V. O. Key noted a change in the nature of police corruption as the delivery of vice services became more centralized and criminal syndicates took on the characteristics of legitimate big business enterprises.[57]

The law also includes many regulatory ordinances that contribute to police corruption. Laws prohibiting double-parking, for example, are designed to facilitate the smooth flow of traffic, but some business owners are afraid that tough enforcement will deny them some customers. Particularly in cities with congested central business districts, there have been payoffs to the police to ignore certain traffic law violations.

The example of regulatory ordinances illustrates an important distinction between different types of corruption. Some forms of corruption involve the use of deviant means to further deviant goals. An example is bribery to protect illegal drug sales. Other forms of corruption involve deviant means to achieve legitimate goals. An example is a bribe to sustain a profitable business.

Chambliss emphasizes the intimate connection between the law, the political structure, the police, and criminal activity. "Organized crime," he argues, "becomes not something that exists outside law and government but is instead a creation of them." Chambliss adds that "the people who run the organizations which supply the vices in American cities are members of the business, political, and law enforcement communities—not simply members of a criminal society."[58]

Cultural Conflict

The criminal law is a reflection of the cultural diversity of American society. Different groups have used the law to prohibit behavior that offends their values. Other groups, however, regard the same behavior as legitimate. McMullen argues that conflict over the goals of the legal system is a basic precondition for corruption: "A high level of corruption is the result of a wide divergence among the attitudes, aims, and methods of the government of a country and those of the society in which they operate."[59]

Local Political Culture

The level of corruption in a police department is heavily influenced by the local political culture. Sherman argues that there will be less corruption in "communities with a more public-regarding ethos." Some communities develop traditions of efficient and honest public service, whereas others develop self-serving, or "private-regarding," traditions that encourage corruption.[60] Police corruption persists in New York City and New Orleans because corruption pervades other parts of government. But police corruption has been largely eliminated in cities such as Charlotte, North Carolina, and Portland, Oregon, where the local political culture emphasizes good government.

Although an important factor, the concept of political culture has not been clearly defined or investigated. It is not clear why some cities and counties have a different political culture or exactly how it affects law enforcement.

Neighborhood Explanations

Just as some individuals are responsible for corruption, and some organizations foster corruption, Robert Kane argues that some neighborhoods influence the deviant patterns of police officers assigned to an area. He points out that since the 1930s, researchers have known that crime and delinquency are strongly related to neighborhoods that are characterized by social disorganization (i.e., neighborhoods with high levels of poverty, high population turnover, high racial diversity, and low levels of informal social control). Kane maintains that because police officers work in socially disorganized neighborhoods where they are subject to many of the same neighborhood problems that lead to increases in crime among residents, such factors might also explain police misconduct.

To examine this issue, he collected data on the number of police officers terminated and dismissed by the NYPD between 1975 and 1996. He then linked this information to where the officers were assigned at the time of the incident(s) that led to their separation and whether the officer was dismissed because of police misconduct or corruption. Kane found that corruption was significantly more likely to take place in neighborhoods where there was a great amount of population turnover, poverty, and unemployment; and where there was a high proportion of foreign-born residents and persons who had low levels of education.[61]

The Nature of Police Work

Thomas Barker argues that the "occupational setting" of police work "provides the police officer with more than ample opportunity for a wide range of deviant activities."[62] Three aspects of police work contribute to police corruption. First, police work exposes officers to many opportunities to be corrupt. The police enforce the law, and inevitably, some people seek to avoid arrest by offering a bribe. Thus, officers face constant temptations from people seeking to corrupt them. Organized crime syndicates, in particular, have enormous financial resources at their disposal. This helps to explain why corruption has generally been worst among vice and narcotics officers. Second, policing is **low-visibility work**.[63] Officers generally work alone or in pairs, with no direct supervision. The risk of being caught is often very low. Detectives work with even less direct supervision than patrol officers. Thus, they face the greatest temptations and have the lowest risk of being caught.

low-visibility work

Third, the impact of police work on officer attitudes also contributes indirectly to corruption. Herman Goldstein argues that "the average officer—especially in large cities—sees the worst side of humanity. He is exposed to a steady diet of wrongdoing. He becomes intimately familiar with the ways people prey on one another." As a result, officers easily develop a cynical attitude toward people. Constant exposure to wrongdoing can lead to the belief that "everyone does it."[64]

The Police Organization

Some departments have more corruption than others, while others have succeeded in reducing it. The most important organizational variable is leadership: the quality of management and supervision. Corruption flourishes in departments that tolerate it. Assuming that temptations or "invitations" to corruption are prevalent in all communities, individual officers are more likely to succumb if they believe they won't be caught or, if they are caught, the punishment will not be severe.

Carl Klockars and colleagues examined the impact of organizational culture on corruption in 30 police departments across the country. They found that officers, regardless of the police organization that they worked for, ranked the seriousness of various types of corruption similarly. However, they found that officers in departments that scored high on organizational integrity were more likely to expect to be severely disciplined if caught committing a corrupt act than officers in departments that scored low on organizational integrity. They also found that officers in departments that scored high on organizational integrity were more likely to believe that officers should be severely disciplined for engaging in corrupt acts.[65] Such findings suggest that although police officers view the seriousness of various forms of corruption similarly, officers in organizations that do not tolerate corruption may be less tempted to engage in corruption.

Robin Haarr emphasizes the importance of organizational commitment and its relationship with police deviance. In her examination of patrol officers in one midwestern police department, she found that officers with a low level of organizational commitment were more likely to engage in work avoidance and police misconduct such as sex with prostitutes and unnecessary use of force. By contrast, officers with a high level of organizational commitment were more likely to engage in deviance *for* the organization, such as falsifying arrest reports and lying in court to increase work productivity.[66]

The Police Subculture

The occupational subculture of policing is a major factor both in creating police corruption, by initiating officers into corrupt activities, and in sustaining it, by covering up corrupt activities by other officers.

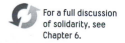

For a full discussion of solidarity, see Chapter 6.

In his classic study of the police subculture, William Westley reported in 1970 that officers were willing to lie to cover up an illegal act by another officer.[67] More recent studies suggest that little has changed since that time. In a survey of 925 officers from 121 police departments, David Weisburd and colleagues reported that 52.4 percent of officers thought that it is not unusual for a police officer to turn a blind eye to improper conduct by other officers, and only 39 percent of officers agreed that police officers would report serious criminal violations involving abuse of authority by fellow officers.[68]

This is in large part a consequence of peer pressure, which is particularly strong among police officers. The police subculture puts a high value on loyalty and group solidarity. Officers defend one another in the face of criticism because they expect their colleagues to come to their aid as well. This kind of group solidarity, however, tends to foster lying and cover-ups.[69] Officers who are not loyal to other officers are often ostracized in the police department. One national survey of police officers reported that 67 percent of police officers believed that an officer who reports another officer's misconduct is likely to be given the cold shoulder by his or her fellow officers.

Becoming Corrupt

The Moral Careers of Individual Officers

With few exceptions, police officers are honest at the outset of their careers. (The exceptions are those individuals who have prior histories of criminal activity and who are not rejected during recruitment.) The Mollen Commission found that "most corrupt officers start off as honest and idealistic." In fact, "some of the most notoriously corrupt cops in the [New York City] Department were ideal recruits on paper."[70] Officers who do become corrupt typically go through a process involving a series of stages that move from lesser to greater tolerance of and/or involvement in corrupt activities. Sherman describes this process as the **"moral career" of a police officer.**[71]

The moral career of a corrupt officer begins with relatively minor gratuities. The officer begins to regard free meals as a normal part of the job. Peer pressure is extremely important in this first stage. The new officer is introduced to corrupt acts by veteran officers. Sherman writes that the "moral experience about accepting these perks usually occurs in the recruit's first days on duty, and the peer pressure to accept them is great."[72] The Mollen Commission found that in New York the unpunished use of excessive force initiated many officers into patterns of misconduct, including corruption.[73]

At the same time, the officer is under pressure from citizens offering bribes. There are many stories of free meals being forced on police officers even though they are willing to pay.

The second and third stages of becoming corrupt, according to Sherman, involve regulatory offenses. An officer accepts a free drink from a bar owner and allows the bar to remain open after the legal closing hour, or the officer takes a bribe from a driver who has exceeded the speed limit. Peer pressure is important if the officer knows that other officers routinely do the same thing. At this point, the individual officer is still passively accepting such offers.

At some point, the officer becoming corrupt changes from one who only passively accepts gratuities (the "grass eater") into one who aggressively solicits bribes (the "meat eater").[74] Corrupt acts begin to involve more serious violations of the law, become more systematic, and involve larger amounts of money; the officer begins to initiate corrupt acts. The fourth, fifth, and sixth stages in Sherman's hypothetical model involve regular payoffs for the protection of such activities as prostitution and narcotics trafficking. Sherman points out that "accepting narcotics graft . . . is the most difficult moral experience of all." Officers must adjust their self-image to accept the fact that they are actively assisting the sale and distribution of what they know to be an illegal and destructive drug. At this point, the moral career of the officer is complete. The officer has reached the final point of not just accepting but actively furthering illegal and harmful activities.

Corrupting Organizations

Entire organizations become corrupt as they move through similar stages from less serious to more serious corruption. The "moral career" of a department can be viewed as moving through the various stages identified by Sherman. Initially, corruption involves isolated individuals or a few isolated groups. When virtually all officers are engaged in corrupt acts, the second and third stages have been reached. The final stages involve "pervasive organized corruption," in which virtually all officers are engaged in systematic arrangements with criminal elements. A police department becomes progressively corrupt because the department's leadership does not actively combat corruption.

Controlling Corruption

Controlling police corruption is extremely difficult. The history of the police indicates that many apparently successful reform efforts have been only temporary. Herman Goldstein observes that "the history of reform provides many illustrations of elaborate attempts to eliminate dishonesty followed by rapid reversion to prior practices."[75] In New York City, for example, there were corruption scandals followed by special investigations every 20 years from the 1890s to the 1990s. Each investigation made recommendations for reform, and yet corruption continued to flourish.

At the same time, however, there are examples of police departments that have successfully reduced or eliminated corruption: Los Angeles and Oakland in the 1950s. Sherman calls the reform of the Oakland police department during the same period "one of the most lasting of any American police agency."[76]

The control of corruption involves two different tasks. The first is to prevent it from occurring in the first place. The second is to reduce and eliminate it once it exists. There are two basic approaches to the control of corruption. One involves *internal* approaches, including activities undertaken by a police department itself. The other involves *external* approaches, including agencies outside of the department.

Internal Corruption Control Strategies

There are several components of an effective internal corruption control program.

The Attitude of the Chief

Experts agree that successful control of corruption begins with the attitude of the chief administrator. The head of the department must make it clear that corruption will not be tolerated. The Mollen Commission argued that "commitment to integrity cannot be just an abstract value. It must be reflected not only in the words, but in the deeds, of the Police Commissioner, the Department's top commanders, and the field supervisors who shape the attitudes of the rank and file."[77] The known examples of successful corruption control all involved strong action by chiefs: William Parker in Los Angeles, Wyman Vernon in Oakland, Clarence Kelley in Kansas City, and Patrick V. Murphy in New York City.

For a full discussion of administrative rulemaking, see Chapter 11.

A police chief faces certain risks in taking a strong public stand against corruption. Open discussion of the subject is an admission of existing or possible wrongdoing. The Mollen Commission found that anticorruption mechanisms in New York City failed in part because department officials did not want any bad publicity. As a result, allegations of corruption were not investigated.[78]

Rules and Regulations

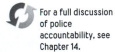

For a full discussion of police accountability, see Chapter 14.

The second step in a corruption control process involves clearly defining what actions will not be tolerated. One way to draw the line clearly is to develop written policies that specify forbidden acts. The use of written policies, or what is known as administrative rulemaking, is also used to control police discretion and to achieve police accountability. Carter and Barker argue that administrative rules on corruption serve six basic purposes. They "(1) inform officers of expected standards of behavior; (2) inform the community about those standards; (3) establish the basis for consistency in police operations; (4) provide grounds for discipline and counseling of errant officers; (5) provide standards for officer supervision; and (6) give direction for officer training."[79]

There is much disagreement over where to draw the line on some issues.[80] Not all law enforcement officials believe that it is necessary or possible to prohibit free meals or other discounts, for example. A Police Foundation survey of Oregon state police officers found that 62 percent did not think it was proper for officers to accept discounts even if they were offered to other customers, while 20 percent thought it was acceptable.[81]

Other leaders, however, argue that the line must be drawn prohibiting all gratuities. Patrick V. Murphy told his officers, "Except for your paycheck there is no such thing as a clean buck."[82] William Parker in Los Angeles and O. W. Wilson in Chicago believed that even a free cup of coffee compromised the integrity of the police. The argument against all gratuities is premised on the belief that this one small step creates a climate in which successively larger steps become possible. Other experts, however, argue that anticorruption efforts should focus on serious acts of corruption.

Managing Anticorruption Investigations

The effective control of corruption requires meaningful investigation of suspected corruption by the department itself. Typically, this is the responsibility of the internal affairs unit (IAU) or office of professional standards. (See Exhibit 13–6.)

A successful anticorruption effort requires several elements. As already noted, it first needs the strong backing of the chief executive. The IACP recommends that the unit commander "should report directly to or have regular access to the chief,"

E X H I B I T   13–6

Internal Affairs Unit, St. Petersburg Police Department

VI.   Internal Affairs Division

   A.   Purpose of the Internal Affairs Division

      1.   To conduct thorough investigations and make fair and impartial evaluations of allegations made against employees, upon receipt of an allegation or complaint of misconduct against the Department or its employees, or as may be directed by the Chief of Police.

      2.   To make random inspections to ensure proper conduct and integrity in the following areas:

         a.   Audit and destruction of controlled substances seized by the Department

         b.   Use of cellular phones

         c.   Bail bond procedures

         d.   Wrecker service

         e.   Random substance testing

   B.   Organization and Staffing

      1.   The Internal Affairs Division shall report directly to the Chief of Police. The Division will be staffed by such personnel as directed by the Chief and assigned to such duty hours as directed by the Division Commander.

      2.   The Commander of the Internal Affairs Division shall advise the Chief of Police of the receipt of each Formal Complaint or potential formal complaint, as necessary. In no case shall this exceed seven (7) calendar days from the time the information was received.

Source: St. Petersburg Police Department Internal Affairs Report, 2005.

because the chief is ultimately responsible for discipline.[83] The Mollen Commission, however, found that in New York City, command officers sent clear messages to corruption investigators that they should not aggressively pursue reports of corruption. The most notorious officer in that scandal, Michael Dowd, was in fact arrested on drug charges by suburban Suffolk County police—not by New York City police.[84]

Second, an IAU needs a sufficient number of personnel to handle the investigative workload. Patrick V. Murphy increased the size of the Internal Affairs Division in the NYPD, bringing the ratio of investigators to officers from 1 to 533 line officers, to 1 to 64. Sherman found investigator-to-officer ratios of 1 to 110 and 1 to 216 in two other departments he studied.[85] Murphy also decentralized anticorruption by creating a network of field internal affairs units (FIAUs). Twenty years later, however, the Mollen Commission found that the Internal Affairs Division investigated few corruption allegations, while most cases were delegated to the FIAUs, which were then too overloaded to conduct effective investigations.[86] The problem was not necessarily the structure of the anticorruption effort but the lack of administrative commitment to make it work effectively.

There is disagreement over whether anticorruption efforts should be centralized or decentralized within the department. Most police departments have centralized the management of investigations, with the commander of the IAU reporting directly to the chief. However, some agencies, such as New York City, take a different approach by decentralizing their anticorruption efforts.[87]

Staffing IAUs is a problem in many departments. Police officers generally do not like IAUs, regarding them as "snitches," and do not want the assignment themselves. Interviews with current and former internal affairs officers in one southwestern metropolitan area found many examples of the stigma attached to internal affairs assignments. One officer was told by a friend, "You're crazy, what the hell do you want to work there for?" Another was told, "I thought you were better than that."[88]

From the perspective of many officers, internal affairs violates the norms of group solidarity. Also, many officers regard internal affairs investigations as more intrusive than criminal investigations. Under the ***Garrity* ruling,** an officer can be disciplined and even dismissed for refusing to answer questions by internal affairs (although anything the officer discloses cannot then be used against him or her in a criminal prosecution). Finally, many officers believe that internal affairs is biased and out to "get" certain officers.[89]

In some departments, because of union contracts, the chief has no choice over who is assigned to the IAU. Common sense suggests that someone who does not want the assignment, or who may have a problematic performance record, is not likely to be an aggressive anticorruption investigator. In other departments, the chief has full control over assignment to the IAU, and it is a preferred assignment that is considered a key to promotion.

Garrity ruling

Investigative Tactics

The major obstacle facing anticorruption investigations is the same one that all detectives face: obtaining credible evidence. Corruption is often a victimless crime with no complaining party. Investigators usually have to initiate investigations on their own. In corrupt departments, the major problem has always been the "blue curtain," the refusal of officers to testify against corrupt officers. Even honest officers are reluctant to inform on their colleagues.

Successful investigations have often relied on a few corrupt officers who decided to cooperate with investigators. In the New York City scandal of the 1970s, for example, Robert Leuci provided the most important evidence for investigators. The officer did so, however, only at a tremendous personal cost: ostracism within the department and even potential threats against his life. Similarly, in the Los Angeles Rampart scandal, it was not until after officer Rafael Perez was arrested for auto theft, forgery, and the sale of cocaine—and was offered a reduced prison sentence—that he provided departmental investigators with information that broke open the case.[90]

Cracking the "Blue Curtain"

The so-called **blue curtain of silence**—the refusal of officers to testify against other officers—is one of the major factors protecting police corruption. In Los Angeles and New York City, new initiatives have been developed to catch and punish officers who give false testimony. In the late 1990s in Los Angeles, the inspector general for the Police Commission launched a new effort to identify officers who give "false and misleading testimony" in investigations.[91] The Commission to Combat Police Corruption, established in the wake of the Mollen Commission investigation, reviewed the police department's handling of perjury cases and concluded that "the penalties imposed for lying are insufficient." It recommended that officers be automatically terminated for lying unless there were special circumstances.[92]

Some police agencies have found that such policies actually serve to reinforce the code of silence. For example, in Los Angeles, the Rampart Independent Review Panel reported that there are a variety of reasons that officers do not immediately come forward to report an incident, including friendship, loyalty, and fear of retaliation. However, the panel found that officers often reconsider their decision, especially if they witness repeated misconduct by the same officer. It argued that policies that punish officers for failing to report misconduct immediately discourage officers from reporting misconduct later, and further serve to reinforce the need for secrecy.[93]

Proactive Integrity Tests

The use of integrity tests is another strategy used by police departments to identify corrupt officers. This strategy, while used infrequently, involves targeting officers who are under suspicion, called *directed integrity tests,* or the random selection of officers, called *randomized integrity tests,* and attempting to stimulate officers into engaging in corruption. For example, an officer might be called to the scene of a proposed burglary. As part of the integrity test, no one would be at the supposed crime scene and there might be jewelry or cash left in the open. Because of the burglary, the officer might steal the jewelry or cash and attempt to "blame" the theft on the supposed offender.

For example, New York City used this strategy in the wake of both the Knapp Commission in the 1970s and the Mollen Commission in the 1990s. In the 1970s, they found that between 12 and 34 percent of the officers tested failed the integrity

blue curtain of silence

test, depending on the district. In 1995 and 1996, about 2,500 police officers were tested, of whom fewer than 1 percent failed the test. The police department believed that this was evidence of their success in combating corruption.[94]

Similarly, in response to a series of corruption scandals, the New Orleans Police Department created a Public Integrity Division in the mid-1990s. The division began conducting integrity tests of police officers to identify corruption. Official reports from the last year integrity tests were performed showed that all 48 of the officers tested passed.[95] Today few agencies use directed integrity tests.

Effective Supervision

Standards of integrity also require effective supervision of routine officer behavior. Herman Goldstein comments that "corruption thrives best in poorly run organizations where lines of authority are vague and supervision is minimal."[96] If officers learn from experience that their day-to-day behavior is not being monitored, or that they are not being disciplined for minor neglect of duty, they will conclude that corrupt acts will not be discovered. Historically, departments with reputations for pervasive corruption have also had reputations for general inefficiency. In 2015, a systematic review of misconduct within the San Diego Police Department by the Department of Justice found that budget cuts resulted in a reduced number of first-line supervisors who were also not well trained for their positions and due to department regulations were often unable to access the department's early warning system.[97]

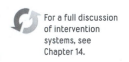

For a full discussion of intervention systems, see Chapter 14.

Officers themselves argue that good first-line supervision is perhaps the best way to control police deviance. For example, in one national survey, "almost 90 percent of officers believed that good first-line supervisors are effective in preventing police officers from abusing their authority." In focus group sessions, supervisors agreed, articulating that supervisors, through good role modeling and mentoring, can prevent police deviance.[98]

As a means of enhancing supervision, the IACP and the Justice Department's police integrity conference both recommend early warning systems to identify officers with chronic problems. Early warning systems are designed not just to punish officers but also to "address, and hopefully resolve, problems early in their development."[99]

Rewarding the Good Officers

Experts on police corruption argue that corruption flourishes because police departments fail to reward the honest officers. As Herman Goldstein points out: "Many competent officers have found that to have reported corruption even once had the effect of permanently impairing their careers."[100] The Mollen Commission argued that "reforms must focus on making honest officers feel responsible for keeping their fellow officers honest, and ridding themselves of corrupt ones." Unfortunately, it found that honest officers "were often discouraged from doing so." Officers were told not to report corruption, and when they did report corrupt officers, the information was ignored.[101]

Personnel Recruitment

Effective screening of recruits is an important element in controlling corruption. Unfortunately, however, it is not always possible to spot potentially corrupt officers

The Five Most Corrupt U.S. Police Officers in U.S. History

5. Louis Eppolito and Stephen Caracappa

Louis Eppolito and Stephen Caracappa worked for the NYPD but in reality, they worked for the mafia. Caracappa was a member of the Organized Crime Homicide Unit investigating the very people he was working for. The two former partners were taking orders for the Lucchese crime family and served as hitmen as well as moles in the NYPD. In 2006, Eppolito and Caracappa were convicted of racketeering, obstruction of justice, extortion, and eight counts of murder and conspiracy.

4. Joseph Miedzianowski

Joseph Miedzianowski was a Chicago police officer labeled as the most corrupt cop. Miedzianowski served as both police officer and drug kingpin, using his knowledge of the streets and gangs to shake down drug dealers. For most of his 22-year career, Miedzianowski would run the Chicago Gangs Unit, while running his own drug gang at the same time. Miedzianowski would be convicted of 10 counts, including drug conspiracy and racketeering, in 2001.

3. David Mack and Rafael Perez

David Mack and Rafael Perez worked together for the LAPD Rampart division, but they also worked for Death Row Records and were members of the Bloods gang. Mack would receive the LAPD Medal of Honor for killing a drug dealer who allegedly pulled a gun on him. But he would also later be convicted of robbing a bank and be implicated in the murder of rapper Notorious BIG. Perez shot and framed an unarmed gang member during his tenure and stole eight pounds of cocaine from an LAPD evidence locker.

2. Jon Burge

Jon Burge is a former Chicago Police Department detective who oversaw the torture of hundreds of black men, resulting in false confessions between 1972 and 1991. Burge would burn suspects with radiators and cigarettes and electrocute their testicles. Although Burge was protected by the statute of limitations for his crimes, he was convicted for lying about the torture in January 2012.

1. Robert Gisevius, Kenneth Bowen, and Anthony Villavaso

Robert Gisevius, Kenneth Bowen, and Anthony Villavaso were members of the New Orleans Police Department during Hurricane Katrina. They were charged with first-degree murder for killing 17-year-old James Brissette, who was innocent and unarmed, during Hurricane Katrina on the Danzinger bridge. Brisette was simply looking for shelter in the hurricane and cops pounced on him. Bowen, Gisevius, Villavaso, and another officer, Robert Faulcon, were found guilty of falsifying reports and false prosecution in the conspiracy to cover-up the shooting.

Source: Excerpt from "The Top 5 Most Corrupt U.S. Police Officers of All-Time," http://newstalkcleveland.com/discussion-2/were/the-top-5-most-corrupt-u-s-police-officers-of-all-time/.

at this stage. The Mollen Commission found that some of the most corrupt officers were ideal recruits in terms of their backgrounds.[102]

The police departments in Miami, Washington, D.C., and Los Angeles have had major corruption scandals as a result of hiring officers with crime and drug-related histories. The problem, however, was that these departments were under political pressure to hire more officers and did not conduct the normal background checks.[103] For example, officers involved in the Rampart scandal in Los Angeles were found to have criminal records, financial problems, histories of violent behavior, and drug problems. Upon further investigation, the department found that these officers were all hired in the late 1980s and early 1990s, a time when the department compromised its hiring protocol in an effort to quickly fill empty positions within the police department.[104]

Today, among all large local law enforcement agencies, 98 percent report using criminal record checks, 97 percent report using background investigations, and 78 percent report using credit history checks as a screening method for selecting new officers.[105] Background investigations of job applicants are regarded as an essential part of an effective anticorruption effort. Experience indicates that persons with prior arrest records (even without convictions) and particularly people with prior involvement with drugs are extremely high risk in terms of becoming corrupt if employed as police officers.

There is considerable disagreement among police departments over whether applicants should be automatically eliminated on the basis of any prior criminal activity and/or drug involvement. Virtually all agencies refuse to hire anyone with a felony conviction. With respect to drugs, the IACP argues that the ideal standard should be "no prior drug abuse of any kind."[106] However, given the extent of drug usage in contemporary society, maintaining an absolute standard would screen out a large percentage of applicants. Generally, most departments are willing to hire individuals with some prior drug history, making distinctions between experimentation, use, and abuse. Most departments are willing to accept individuals with some minor usage or experimentation but not recent and/or heavy use.

Many departments have initiated drug-testing programs to identify both applicants and currently employed officers who are involved with drugs. One survey of police agencies found that 89 percent of all departments gave drug-screening tests to applicants.[107] Another study reported that of those departments that had some kind of drug-testing program, several tested officers currently in or seeking transfer to "sensitive" assignments (internal affairs, vice, or narcotics units). Officers found to be using drugs were not necessarily dismissed automatically. Many departments indicated that they preferred offering counseling to the officers.[108]

Field Training

Field training is also believed to have a substantial effect on the trainee's future involvement in police misconduct. Field training officers (FTOs) are responsible for the trainees' initial exposure to work place norms, attitudes, values, and behaviors. The trainees' expression of these attitudes and behaviors are reinforced through formal and informal rewards and punishments and can have a lasting impact on the trainees' career. A recent study of FTOs impact on trainee future misconduct in the

Dallas Police Department suggested that about 25 percent of the variation in post-supervision misconduct could be attributed to FTOs.[109] These findings suggest that FTOs play a vital role in preventing future police misconduct.

External Corruption Control Approaches

Once corruption exists in a department, it is extremely difficult to eliminate. Often, the internal mechanisms of control have broken down or, in the case of pervasive corruption, are inadequate to the task. In those situations, external corruption control strategies may be necessary.

Special Investigations

Because of the difficulties in investigating corruption, special investigation commissions have sometimes been used. The Knapp Commission investigated the New York City police in the early 1970s, and the Mollen Commission conducted another investigation in the 1990s. Similarly, the Christopher Commission in the 1990s investigated allegations of police abuse in Los Angeles. In 2016, the Chicago Police Accountability Task Force investigated the Chicago Police Department on matters related to brutality, racism, and misconduct.

In New Orleans, in an effort to fight corruption and misconduct, there have been at least two external corruption control approaches that involve special investigations. In the first, two FBI agents were assigned to work full time in the New Orleans Police Department in 2011. The agents worked with the Public Integrity Bureau to investigate allegations of corruption and to assist with the in-service training of local police officers.[110] The second involved the city's inviting the Department of Justice's Civil Rights Division to conduct an independent investigation into patterns and practices of unconstitutional conduct.[111]

Special commissions have the advantage of being independent of the police department. However, commissioners may lack intimate knowledge of the inner, day-to-day workings of the department. Also, external investigations arouse the hostility of the rank and file, aggravating the existing tendency of the police to close ranks and refuse to cooperate.

Criminal Prosecution

Because police corruption involves violations of the criminal law, prosecution under state law is one potential remedy. Criminal offenses include specific corruption-related offenses, theft, possession and sale of narcotics, and perjury.

Although no nationwide data are available on the number of state prosecutions of police officers for corruption, an analysis of officers arrested, convicted, and imprisoned can shed some light on the criminal justice system's ability to convict and punish corrupt officers. Sanja Ivkovich's historical analysis of the effectiveness of this strategy suggests that few officers are seriously punished for engaging in corruption. For example, over the course of the Knapp Commission, 137 cases involving corruption were forwarded to the prosecutor's office, in which two-thirds of defendants were convicted or pled guilty. About 61 percent of those convicted were released or given a suspended sentence, and only five officers were sentenced to prison for one year or longer.[112]

Another remedy is to prosecute cases of local police corruption using federal laws. Federal prosecutors have fewer ties to local criminal justice officials, allowing them to be more independent in their investigations. One of the most extensive studies to examine the prosecution of corruption cases was conducted by Kathryn Malee and John Gardiner. These researchers compiled data from all corruption cases prosecuted in Chicago and Cook County between 1970 and 1987. During this 16-year period, there were 114 cases involving corruption. Malee and Gardiner reported that federal prosecutors were 10 times more likely to prosecute the case than were county prosecutors.[113]

Criminal prosecution of alleged corruption is, in many respects, easier than prosecution of excessive force complaints. It is usually easier to prove, for example, that an officer received a bribe—and had criminal intent to receive it—than that an officer had criminal intent in beating someone. Nonetheless, there are reasons to question the effectiveness of criminal prosecution, by itself, as a long-term remedy for police corruption. In almost all of the investigations of corruption in the NYPD, officers have been prosecuted and convicted. And yet, corruption persists. The lesson appears to be that criminal prosecution can remove individual officers but cannot eliminate the factors that cause corruption.

SIDEBAR 13–4

DOJ Inquiries Focus on Corruption, Misconduct

When the Department of Justice investigates a police agency, generally the allegations involve public corruption or misconduct. Here are examples of the types of cases the Department of Justice has brought against law enforcement agencies in the past few years.

Cleveland Division of Police

In March 2013, following a series of highly publicized use-of-force incidents that suggested critical flaws exist in use-of-force policies, procedures, and practices within the Cleveland Division of Police (CDP), in Cleveland, Ohio, we opened an investigation pursuant to the Violent Crime Control and Law Enforcement Act of 1994 that focused on CDP's use of force, including deadly force. The investigation, which concluded in December 2014, revealed that CDP engages in a pattern or practice of using excessive force in violation of the Fourth Amendment of the United States Constitution. We also determined that structural deficiencies and practices, including insufficient accountability, inadequate training and equipment, ineffective policies, and inadequate engagement with the community, contribute to CDP's use of excessive force. As an initial step to address these findings, the Justice Department and the City of Cleveland signed a statement of principles that commits both parties to work together to develop a court enforceable consent decree, overseen by a monitor, that requires certain reforms.

Ferguson Police Department

In September 2014, the Department of Justice opened an investigation of the Ferguson Police Department (FPD) pursuant to the Violent Crime Control and Law Enforcement Act of 1994, the Omnibus Crime Control and Safe Streets Act of 1968, and Title VI of the Civil Rights Act of 1964. The investigation focused on allegations that Ferguson law enforcement engaged in a pattern or practice of violations of the Constitution and federal statutory law. On March 4, 2015, DOJ announced the results of the investigation, finding that FPD's police and municipal court practices systematically violate the First, Fourth and Fourteenth Amendments. DOJ determined that FPD's approach to law enforcement is unduly focused on revenue generation and that its practices both reflect and exacerbate existing race bias. As a result, Ferguson's law enforcement practices discriminate against African Americans and decrease trust between the Ferguson community and law enforcement, hampering FPD's ability to ensure public safety.

Maricopa County Sheriff's Office

In March 2009, we opened an investigation of the Maricopa County Sheriff's Office (MCSO) pursuant to Section 14141 of the Violent Crime Control and Law Enforcement Act of 1994 and Title VI of the Civil Rights Act of 1964 (Title VI). MCSO refused to cooperate with our investigation, and we filed suit under Title VI to obtain the information we needed, which MCSO agreed to provide in June 2011, settling this suit. After completing our investigation, on December 15, 2011, we announced our findings. We found that MCSO engaged in a pattern of misconduct that violated the Constitution and federal law. Specifically, we found that MCSO engaged in a policy of stopping, detaining, and investigating persons of Hispanic ancestry based on their race, in traffic and during worksite raids; failed to provide language access assistance to Hispanic jail inmates with Limited English Proficiency (LEP); and unlawfully retaliated against individuals who complained about or criticized MCSO's practices.

We attempted to work with MCSO to reach an agreement to remedy the unlawful conduct we found, but we could not resolve our claims without litigation. We filed suit against Sheriff Arpaio and Maricopa County on the above grounds in May 2012. The Court granted summary judgment in our favor on the discriminatory policing claim in June 2015. We reached a partial settlement with Sheriff Arpaio and Maricopa County in July 2015, resolving the remaining claims concerning conduct in worksite raids, retaliation, and language access requirements for Hispanic LEP inmates in MCSO jails.

In May 2013, in a parallel law suit, Melendres v. Arpaio, the federal district court of Arizona found that MCSO had engaged in unlawful discrimination against Hispanic persons in its traffic enforcement operations. In October 2013, the court issued an injunction, ordering MCSO to undergo reforms to prevent further discriminatory law enforcement practices, and appointed an independent monitor to oversee implementation of the injunction. In August 2015, we requested, and were granted intervention in Melendres, to join the case as a Plaintiff-Intervenor. We are now working with Plaintiffs and the independent monitor to ensure that MCSO meaningfully implements the court-ordered reforms required by the injunctive order.

New Orleans Police Department

On May 15, 2010, we opened an investigation of the New Orleans Police Department (NOPD) pursuant to the Violent Crime Control and Law Enforcement Act of 1994, the Omnibus Crime Control and Safe Streets Act of 1968, and Title VI of the Civil Rights Act of 1964. Following a comprehensive investigation, on March 17, 2011, we announced our findings. We found that the NOPD has engaged in patterns of misconduct that violate the Constitution and federal law, including a pattern or practice of excessive force, and of illegal stops, searches, and arrests. We found also a pattern or practice of gender discrimination in the Department's under-enforcement and under-investigation of violence against women. We further found strong indications of discriminatory policing based on racial, ethnic, and LGBT bias, as well as a failure to provide critical police services to language minority communities. On July 24, 2012, we reached a settlement resolving our investigation and asked the Court to make our settlement an order enforceable by the Court. The documents here provide more information about the investigation, the Justice Department's findings, settlement, and next steps.

Source: Excerpts from U.S. Department of Justice, *Special Litigation Section Case Summaries,* https://www.justice.gov/crt/special-litigation-section-case-summaries#mcso-summ.

Mobilizing Public Opinion

Many experts argue that police corruption flourishes in certain departments because of a local political culture that tolerates it. Controlling corruption, therefore, requires mobilizing public opinion. The media play a major role in shaping public opinion about corruption. The media often expose the existence of corruption and set in motion the reform process. *New York Times* reporter David Burnham, for example, was instrumental in exposing corruption in the NYPD in the 1970s. His front-page article on corruption on April 25, 1970, led to the Knapp Commission investigation.[114]

It is worth noting that the *Times* took up the issue only after both the mayor and high-ranking officials in the police department had refused to follow up on the allegations brought to them by officers Frank Serpico and David Durk.

More recently, Gina Barton of the *Journal Sentinel* in Milwaukee reported that 93 police officers, or about 5 percent of the Milwaukee Police Department, were disciplined for acts that violated the law. She reported that many of the officers who were involved in misconduct such as sexual assault, domestic violence, driving while intoxicated, and shoplifting were never prosecuted or disciplined. She shed light on the issue by requesting the records of all 93 officers, which took two years and a fee of $7,500, and created an interactive website where residents could view those officers who were involved in misconduct and the outcome of departmental sanctions and criminal prosecutions. The website can be viewed at http://archive.jsonline.com/watchdog/131991558.html. The story and website illustrate how new technologies can play a powerful role in mobilizing public opinion on police misconduct.[115]

Relying on the media has certain limitations, however. Media-generated scandals tend to be short lived. Both the media and the public have very short attention spans, and they quickly turn to other crises. The media also tend to cover the most dramatic aspects of a scandal, usually focusing on individuals who become scapegoats. The underlying causes of corruption are complex and do not offer a dramatic newsworthy event. Finally, scandals tend to produce dramatic responses, such as the removal or transfer of certain officers, which does not necessarily address the underlying problem. Departments often reassign personnel in response to a scandal. Allan Kornblum found that mass transfers in New York City affected honest officers as well as corrupt ones and failed to address the underlying causes of corruption.[116]

Altering the External Environment

Sherman argues that police departments are not completely at the mercy of the external political environment. He cites Oakland in the 1950s, where a reform-minded police chief influenced that environment by threatening to arrest politicians who were involved in gambling and other illegal activities. The threat helped to reduce corruption both in the police department and in the city as a whole. The result was a new political environment that was less supportive of corruption.[117]

The Limits of Anticorruption Efforts

Frank Anechiarico and James B. Jacobs argue that anticorruption efforts not only have been ineffective but also have made government itself ineffective. In their view, rules and regulations designed to prevent corruption limit the capacity of government agencies to be creative and flexible in carrying out their basic missions.[118]

The Anechiarico-Jacobs argument is a provocative one. As they point out, corruption has persisted in the NYPD despite special investigations every 20 years since the 1890s. Nonetheless, their argument suffers from two flaws. Most important, it is almost entirely specific to New York. Other cities do not have the same level of corruption as New York, and police departments in other cities have successfully reduced corruption.[119]

CASE STUDY

Hurricane Katrina and the New Orleans Police Department

On August 29, 2005, New Orleans experienced substantial destruction in the wake of Hurricane Katrina, which resulted in the breach of a levy and subsequent massive flooding throughout 80 percent of the city. While a mandatory evacuation resulted in most residents leaving the city, between 50,000 and 100,000 residents were left behind to largely fend for themselves. Massive numbers of police officers were needed for humanitarian and rescue efforts and to combat lawlessness in the streets following the hurricane. However, NOPD executives quickly realized that they did not have the number of officers available for service that they had anticipated. Initially, it was unclear whether missing officers were attending to family problems, were simply unable to report for duty due to being stranded, or were absent without leave.

Following the initiation of rescue efforts, Chief Compass estimated that 500 officers, or 36 percent of the department, had deserted. News reports also began to show videos of police officers looting department stores for nonessential items, such as electronics and jewelry. The latest police department statistics show that problems associated with desertion were not as problematic as initially believed. However, they do suggest that police misconduct immediately following Hurricane Katrina will have a devastating impact on the New Orleans police department for some time to come. In the end,

- 66 officers were fired for desertion.
- 11 officers were fired for neglecting their duties.
- 41 officers resigned because of police misconduct.
- An undisclosed number were suspended without pay for police misconduct.

Altogether, it is estimated that NOPD lost about 7 percent of its officers after investigations of police misconduct were completed.

Sources: Kevin Johnson, "Katrina Made Police Choose between Duty and Loved Ones," *USA Today*, February 21, 2006, www.usatoday.com/educate/college/firstyear/articles/20060226.htm; Willoughby Anderson, "This Isn't Representative of Our Department," unpublished manuscript.

SUMMARY

Police corruption remains one of the most serious problems in policing. Not only does it have a long history, but the current drug problem threatens to make it even worse. Controlling corruption is

extremely difficult. Corruption is not simply the result of a few bad apples but is deeply rooted in the nature of American society and the criminal law, and is influenced by such factors as the neighborhood where the police officer works and the unit to which he or she is assigned. Despite these problems, there are some hopeful signs. A few departments have succeeded in reducing or eliminating corruption through effective control techniques.

KEY TERMS

police corruption, 455
occupational deviance, 455
abuse of authority, 455
gratuities, 458
grass eaters, 458
meat eaters, 458
bribes, 458

sexual misconduct, 461
rotten apple, 465
rotten pocket, 465
pervasive unorganized
     corruption, 465
pervasive organized
     corruption, 465

low-visibility work, 469
"moral career" of a police
     officer, 471
Garrity ruling, 474
blue curtain of silence, 475

FOR DISCUSSION

1. What are the costs of corruption?
2. What are the five types of corruption? Give an example of each.
3. What are grass eaters and meat eaters? Which type of officer causes the greatest amount of harm to a community?

4. Explain the three levels of corruption, and give an example of each.
5. Identify the six different theories of police corruption. Explain which theory you believe best explains why police corruption occurs.

INTERNET EXERCISES

Exercise 1 Visit the website www.policeabuse.com. Select one of the many complaints registered on the website by the public about a police officer working for a police agency and attempt to assess the quality of the complaint. What did the complainant focus on? What did the complainant not address that should have been addressed. As a class, discuss the strengths and weaknesses of the complaint.

Exercise 2 Do some research on corruption in your local police department by visiting the city newspaper's website. How often has there been a corruption scandal? Have there been any patterns

(e.g., involvement in drugs, prostitution, gambling)? How has the department typically handled the problems? Has the department typically blamed the problems on a few "bad apples," or has it tried to address the root causes of the problems?

Exercise 3 Visit the Chicago Police Accountability Task Force website at https://chicagopatf.org and see its report on police misconduct. As a class, discuss what the agency does well with regard to addressing misconduct and what it needs to do better.

NOTES

1. Lawrence W. Sherman, ed., *Police Corruption: A Sociological Perspective* (Garden City, NY: Anchor Books, 1974), 1.
2. Mollen Commission to Investigate Allegations of Police Corruption, *Commission Report* (New York: Author, 1994).

3. Bernard Parks, *Rampart Area Corruption Incident: Public Report* (Los Angeles: Los Angeles Police Department, 2000).
4. Maryclaire Dale, "6 Philly Narcotics Cops Charged in Corruption Case," https://www.policeone.com/

officer-misconduct-internal-affairs/articles/7418612-6-Philly-narcotics-cops-charged-in-corruption-case/.

5. Herman Goldstein, *Police Corruption: A Perspective on Its Nature and Control* (Washington, DC: The Police Foundation, 1975), 3.

6. Thomas Barker and David L. Carter, "A Typology of Police Deviance," in T. Barker and D. L. Carter, eds., *Police Deviance,* 2nd ed. (Cincinnati, OH: Anderson, 1991), 3–12.

7. Government Accounting Office, *Report to the Honorable Charles B. Rangel, House of Representatives, Law Enforcement: Information on Drug-Related Police Corruption* (Washington, DC: U.S. Government Printing Office, 1998), 35.

8. New York City Commission to Combat Police Corruption, *The New York City Police Department's Disciplinary System* (New York: The Commission, 1996), 10.

9. "185 Camden Cases Tossed, 'Corrupt' Police Work Blamed," *New York Post,* April 3, 2010, http://nypost.com/2010/04/03/185-camden-cases-tossed-corrupt-police-work-blamed/.

10. William A. Westley, *Violence and the Police* (Cambridge, MA: MIT Press, 1970), 109–152.

11. David Burnham, "How Police Corruption Is Built into the System—And a Few Ideas for What to Do about It," in Lawrence W. Sherman, ed., *Police Corruption: A Sociological Perspective* (Garden City, NY: Anchor Books, 1974), 305.

12. Ronald Weitzer and Steven Tuch, *Rethinking Minority Attitudes toward the Police: Final Technical Report* (Washington, DC: National Institute of Justice, June 26, 2004).

13. Mollen Commission, *Commission Report,* 45.

14. The Gallup Organization, "Honesty/Ethics in Professions," Gallup Poll, December 2–6, 2015, http://www.gallup.com/poll/1654/honesty-ethics-professions.aspx?version=print.

15. The Gallup Organization, "Americans' Faith in Honesty, Ethics of Police Rebounds," Gallup Poll, December 21, 2105, http://www.gallup.com/poll/187874/americans-faith-honesty-ethics-police-rebounds.aspx.

16. Goldstein, *Police Corruption,* 16–22.

17. Tom Barker and Robert O. Wells, "Police Administrators' Attitudes toward the Definition and Control of Police Deviance," *Law Enforcement Bulletin,* March 1982, 11.

18. Robert Sigler and Timothy Dees, "Public Perception of Petty Corruption in Law Enforcement," *Journal of Police Science and Administration* 14 (1988): 18.

19. Richard Kania, "Should We Tell the Police to Say 'Yes' to Gratuities?" *Criminal Justice Ethics* 7, no. 2 (1982): 37–49.

20. Knapp Commission, *Report on Police Corruption* (New York: George Braziller, 1973), 4.

21. Mark Jones, "Police Gratuities and Public Opinion," *Police Forum,* October 1997, 6–11.

22. Victor Kappeler, Richard Sluder, and Geoffrey Alpert, *Forces of Deviance: Understanding the Dark Side of Policing* (Prospect Heights, IL: Waveland, 1994).

23. Federal Bureau of Investigation, "Nine Law Enforcement Officers Sentenced for Protecting Drug Dealers," August 6, 2014, https://www.fbi.gov/atlanta/press-releases/2014/nine-law-enforcement-officers-sentenced-for-protecting-drug-dealers.

24. Robert Daley, *Prince of the City* (Boston: Houghton Mifflin, 1978).

25. Burnham, "How Police Corruption Is Built into the System—And a Few Ideas for What to Do about It," 305.

26. Lia Eustachewich, Larry Celona, and Bruce Golding, "Orthodox Jewish Leader Alelgedly Bragged about NYPD Bribes for Pistol Permits," *New York Post,* April 18, 2016, http://nypost.com/2016/04/18/shomrim-leader-busted-amid-nypd-corruption-probe/.

27. Sanja Kutnjak Ivkovich, "To Serve and Collect: Measuring Police Corruption," *Journal of Criminal Law and Criminology* 93 (2003): 593–649.

28. Kappeler, Sluder, and Alpert, *Forces of Deviance: Understanding the Dark Side of Policing.*

29. Ibid.

30. Mollen Commission, *Commission Report,* 22–31.

31. *NPMSRP 2009 Semi-Annual Police Misconduct Statistics Report,* http://www.ucimc.org/content/national-police-misconduct-statistics-released.

32. International Association of Chiefs of Police, *Addressing Sexual Offenses and Misconduct by Law Enforcement* (Alexandria, VA: Author, 2011).

33. Ibid.

34. Matt Sedensky and Nomaan Merchant, "AP: Hundreds of Officers Lose Licenses Over Sex Misconduct," Associated Press, November 1, 2015, http://bigstory.ap.org/article/fd1d4d05e561462a85abe50e7eaed4ec/ap-hundreds-officers-lose-licenses-over-sex-misconduct.

35. Philip Matthew Stinson, John Liederbach, Steven L. Brewer, and Brooke E. Mathna, "Police Sexual Misconduct: A National Scale Study of Arrested

Officers," *Criminal Justice Policy Review* 26, no. 7 (2015): 665–690.

36. Cato Institute, *The Cato Institute's National Police Misconduct Reporting Project, 2010 Annual Report,*" http://www.policemisconduct.net/statistics/2010-annual-report/#Summary.

37. Timothy Maher, "Police Chiefs' Views on Police Sexual Misconduct," *Police Practice and Research* 9, no. 3 (2008): 239–250.

38. Jay Stuart Berman, *Police Administration and Progressive Reform: Theodore Roosevelt as Police Commissioner of New York* (New York: Greenwood Press, 1987).

39. Knapp Commission, *Report on Police Corruption,* 3, 167–168.

40. Mollen Commission, *Commission Report,* 47.

41. "Testimony: Alleged Corrupt LAPD Cops Gave Each Other Awards," CNN.com, February 10, 2000, www.cnn.com/2000/us/02/10/lapd.scandal/; "Outside Probe of LAPD Corruption Scandal Demanded," CNN.com, February 16, 2000, www.cnn.com/2000/us/02/16/lapd.scandal/.

42. Sherman, ed., *Police Corruption,* 3.

43. Ivkovich, "To Serve and Collect."

44. See the attempt to resolve this problem in Lawrence W. Sherman, *Scandal and Reform: Controlling Police Corruption* (Berkeley: University of California Press, 1978).

45. Robert J. Kane and Mike White, "Bad Cops: A Study of Career-Ending Misconduct Among New York City Police Officers." *Criminology & Public Policy* 8, no 4 (2009): 737–768.

46. Sherman, ed., *Police Corruption,* 7.

47. Mollen Commission, *Commission Report,* 17.

48. Sherman, ed., *Police Corruption,* 9.

49. William Chambliss, "The Police and Organized Vice in a Western City," in Lawrence W. Sherman, ed., *Police Corruption: A Sociological Perspective* (Garden City, NY: Anchor Books, 1974), 153–170.

50. Knapp Commission, *Report on Police Corruption,* 74.

51. David H. Bayley and Harold Mendelsohn, *Minorities and the Police* (New York: Free Press, 1969), 1–33.

52. Knapp Commission, *Report on Police Corruption,* 7.

53. Goldstein, *Police Corruption,* 32–38.

54. Robert F. Meier and Gilbert Geis, *Victimless Crime?* (Los Angeles: Roxbury, 1997).

55. Eric Schlosser, *Reefer Madness* (New York: Houghton Mifflin Company, 2003).

56. Commission on Behavioral and Social Sciences and Education, National Research Council, Committee on Law and Justice, *Transnational Organized Crime: Summary of a Workshop* (Washington, DC: National Academies Press, 1999).

57. V. O. Key, "Police Graft," *American Journal of Sociology* 40 (March 1935): 624–636.

58. Chambliss, "The Police and Organized Vice," 154.

59. M. McMullen, "A Theory of Corruption," *Sociological Review* 9 (June 1961): 184–185.

60. Sherman, ed., *Police Corruption,* 16–17.

61. Robert Kane, "The Social Ecology of Police Misconduct," *Criminology* 40, no. 4 (2002): 867–896.

62. Thomas Barker, "Peer Group Support for Police Occupational Deviance," *Criminology* 15 (November 1977): 353–366.

63. Joseph Goldstein, "Police Discretion Not to Invoke the Criminal Process: Low-Visibility Decisions in the Administration of Justice," *Yale Law Journal* 69, no. 4 (1960): 543–588.

64. Goldstein, *Police Corruption,* 25.

65. Carl Klockars, Sanja Ivkovich, William Harver, and Maria Haberfeld, *The Measurement of Police Integrity* (Washington, DC: National Institute of Justice, 2000).

66. Robin Haarr, "They're Making a Bad Name for the Department: Exploring the Link between Organizational Commitment and Police Occupational Deviance in a Police Patrol Bureau," *Policing: An International Journal of Police Strategy and Management* 20, no. 4 (1997): 786–817.

67. Westley, *Violence and the Police.*

68. David Weisburd and Rosann Greenspan, *Police Attitudes toward Abuse of Authority: Findings from a National Study* (Washington, DC: National Institute of Justice, 2000).

69. Westley, *Violence and the Police.*

70. Mollen Commission, *Commission Report,* 5, 20.

71. Lawrence W. Sherman, "Becoming Bent: Moral Careers of Corrupt Policemen," in Lawrence W. Sherman, ed., *Police Corruption: A Sociological Perspective* (Garden City, NY: Anchor Books, 1974), 191–208.

72. Ibid., 199.

73. Mollen Commission, *Commission Report,* 47.

74. Knapp Commission, *Report on Police Corruption,* 4.

75. Goldstein, *Police Corruption,* 37.

76. Sherman, *Scandal and Reform: Controlling Police Corruption,* xxxiv.

77. Mollen Commission, *Commission Report,* 112.

78. Ibid., 70–109.

79. David L. Carter and Thomas Barker, "Administrative Guidance and Control of Police Officer Behavior: Policies, Procedures, and Rules," in T. Barker and D. L. Carter, eds., *Police Deviance,* 2nd ed. (Cincinnati, OH: Anderson, 1991), 22–23.

80. Kania, "Should We Tell the Police to Say 'Yes' to Gratuities?"

81. Karen Amendola, *Assessing Law Enforcement Ethics: A Summary Report Based on the Study Conducted with the Oregon Department of State Police* (Washington, DC: The Police Foundation, 1996), 12.

82. Goldstein, *Police Corruption,* 29.

83. International Association of Chiefs of Police, *Building Integrity and Reducing Drug Corruption in Police Departments* (Washington, DC: Office of Justice Programs, U.S. Department of Justice, September 1989), 68.

84. Mollen Commission, *Commission Report.*

85. Sherman, ed., *Police Corruption,* 10.

86. Mollen Commission, *Commission Report,* 85–90.

87. Sherman, ed., *Police Corruption,* 8.

88. Aogán Mulcahy, "'Headhunter' or 'Real Cop': Identity in the World of Internal Affairs Officers," *Journal of Contemporary Ethnography* 24 (April 1995): 99–130.

89. Ibid.; *Garrity v. New Jersey,* 385 U.S. 493 (1967).

90. Parks, *Rampart Area Corruption Incident.*

91. Inspector General, *First Annual Report* (Los Angeles: Los Angeles Police Commission, 1997).

92. New York Commission to Combat Police Corruption, *The New York City Police Department's Disciplinary System: How the Department Disciplines Members Who Make False Statements* (August 1998), 32, 39.

93. Richard Drooyan, *Report of the Rampart Independent Review Panel* (Los Angeles: November 16, 2000).

94. Ivkovich, "To Serve and Collect," 593–649.

95. New Orleans Police Department, *2003 Annual Report* (New Orleans: City of New Orleans, 2004).

96. Goldstein, *Police Corruption,* 42.

97. Police Executive Research Forum, *Critical Response Technical Assessment Review: Police Accountability—Findings and National Implications of an Assessment of the San Diego Police Department* (Washington, DC: Office of Community Oriented Policing Services, 2015).

98. Weisburd and Greenspan, *Police Attitudes toward Abuse of Authority: Findings from a National Study,* 6.

99. Department of Justice, *Police Integrity* (Washington, DC: U.S. Government Printing Office, 1997).

100. Goldstein, *Police Corruption,* 50–51.

101. Mollen Commission, *Commission Report,* 5.

102. Ibid., 20.

103. "D.C. Police Force Still Paying for Two-Year Hiring Spree," *Washington Post,* August 28, 1994, p. 1; Parks, *Rampart Area Corruption Incident.*

104. Parks, *Rampart Area Corruption Incident.*

105. Bureau of Justice Statistics, *Law Enforcement Management and Administrative Statistics, 2000* (Washington, DC: Bureau of Justice Statistics, 2004).

106. International Association of Chiefs of Police, *Building Integrity and Reducing Drug Corruption in Police Departments,* 26.

107. Bureau of Justice Statistics, *Law Enforcement Management and Administrative Statistics, 2000.*

108. J. Thomas McEwen, Barbara Manili, and Edward Connors, *Employee Drug-Testing Policies in Police Departments* (Washington, DC: U.S. Government Printing Office, 1986).

109. Ryan M. Getty, John L. Worrall, and Robert G. Morris, "How Far from the Tree Does the Apple Fall? Field Training Officers, Their Trainees, and Allegations of Misconduct," *Crime & Delinquency* 62, no. 6 (2016): 821–839.

110. Brendan McCarthy, "FBI to Assign Two Agents to Work in New Orleans Police Department's Internal Affairs Unit," *The Times-Picayune,* September 12, 2011, www.nola.com/crime/index.ssf/2011/09/fbi_two_assign_two_agents_to_w.html.

111. Department of Justice, *Investigation of the New Orleans Police Department* (Washington, DC: Author, 2011).

112. Ivkovich, "To Serve and Collect," 593–649.

113. Kathryn Malee and John Gardiner, "Measurement Issues in the Study of Official Corruption: A Chicago Example," *Corruption and Reform* 2 (1987): 267–278.

114. David Burnham, *The Role of the Media in Controlling Corruption* (New York: John Jay College, 1977).

115. Gina Barton, "At Least 93 Milwaukee Police Officers Have Been Disciplined for Violating Law," *Journal Sentinel,* October 23, 2011, www.jsonline.com/watchdog/watchdogreports/at-least-93-milwaukee-police-officers-have-been-disciplined-for-violating-law-132268408.html.

116. Allan Kornblum, *The Moral Hazards* (Lexington, MA: D. C. Heath, 1976), 58–59.

117. Sherman, ed., *Scandal and Reform,* 140–145.

118. Frank Anechiarico and James B. Jacobs, *The Pursuit of Absolute Integrity* (Chicago: University of Chicago Press, 1996).

119. Comments, Samuel Walker, "Author Meets Critics," American Society of Criminology, Annual Meeting, 1997.

© Steve Hix/Somos Images/Fuse/Getty Images

14 Accountability of the Police

CHAPTER OUTLINE

What Do We Mean by Police Accountability?

The Dilemmas of Policing in a Democracy

A Historical Perspective on Accountability

Accountability for *What* the Police Do

The Traditional Approach to Measuring Police Effectiveness

Alternative Measures and Their Limitations

COMPSTAT: A Neighborhood-Focused Approach

Accountability for *How* the Police Do Their Job

Internal Mechanisms of Accountability

Routine Supervision of Patrol Officers

Coaching, Mentoring, Leading, and Helping

Organizational Culture and Accountability

Command-Level Review of Force Incidents: The Emerging Standard

Corrective Action: Informal and Formal

Performance Evaluations

Internal Affairs/Professional Standards Units

The Discipline Process

Appropriate Levels of Discipline

Openness and Transparency for
  Disciplinary Actions

Standards for Investigating
  Citizen Complaints

Using Discipline Records in
  Personnel Decisions

The "Code of Silence"

Early Intervention Systems

Officers with Performance
  Problems

The Nature and Purpose of an EIS

Performance Indicators and
  Thresholds

Interventions for Officers

The Multiple Goals of an EIS

The Effectiveness of an EIS

Risk Management and Police Legal
  Advisors

**Accreditation for Law
  Enforcement Agencies**

The Nature of Accreditation

Pros and Cons of Accreditation

**External Mechanisms of
  Accountability**

Guiding the Police through the
  Political Process

The Courts and the Police

Federal "Pattern or Practice" Suits

The Collaborative Reform Team
  Approach: An Alternative to
  Litigation

Injunctions to Stop Patterns of
  Police Misconduct

Criminal Prosecution of Police
  Officers

Citizen Oversight of the Police

Blue-Ribbon Commissions

The Digital Revolution and Police
  Accountability

The News Media as a Police
  Accountability Mechanism

Public Interest Groups and
  Accountability

**Accountability and Crime Control:
  A Trade-Off?**

**Conclusion: A Mixed Approach to
  Police Accountability**

CASE STUDY

Summary

Key Terms

Internet Exercises

On July 17, 2014, New York City police officers arrested Eric Garner, who was selling illegal (untaxed) single cigarettes on Long Island. A confrontation ensued, and the lead officer placed Garner in a chokehold and took him to the ground while four other officers helped to restrain him. Garner began to cry repeatedly, "I can't breathe!" The officers did not respond and get off him, and he soon died. A bystander captured the horrifying incident on a cell phone video, which was broadcast on television around the country.

Garner's death and the fatal shooting of Michael Brown by a police officer in Ferguson, Missouri, three weeks later sparked a national police crisis. Many people protested in the streets, and others asked questions: How could such things happen? Are the police completely out of control? Are they not accountable for their actions?

This chapter seeks to provide answers to those questions. The chapter addresses other important questions, as well: What do we mean by police accountability? What mechanisms do we have for holding officers accountable for their actions? The courts? Internal affairs units? Citizen oversight? Do they work? Are they effective in holding police officers accountable to the law, to police department policies, and to standards of decency and justice? By the end of the chapter, you will have a broad overview of the mixed approach to police accountability that exists in the United States.

What Do We Mean by Police Accountability?

Accountability means having to answer for your conduct: explaining what you did, and answering questions about your conduct if there appears to be a problem. Accountability applies to both law enforcement agencies and individual officers. Accountability is a

accountability

489

fundamental aspect of a democratic society. The police and other government agencies answer to the public. Elected officials such as mayors, governors, and presidents of the United States answer directly to the voters. In turn, they are responsible for holding law enforcement agencies under their jurisdiction accountable for their performance.

two dimensions

What are the police accountable for? There are **two dimensions** to this question. The National Academy of Sciences argues that the police in America have a dual mandate: effectiveness and fairness.[1] They are expected to control crime and disorder effectively *and* be professional, fair, and lawful. In other words, the police should be held accountable for *what* they do and *how* they do it. Community policing and problem-oriented policing are strategies for improving police response to crime and disorder. At the same time, individual police officers are accountable for how they do their jobs. In these two areas of accountability, there has been tremendous change and innovation in recent years. This chapter examines the most important innovations.

For further discussion of community policing, see Chapter 10.

The Dilemmas of Policing in a Democracy

The principle of accountability distinguishes democratic from totalitarian societies. In totalitarian regimes, the police do not have to answer to either the public or the law. They are, literally, "lawless." When communism collapsed in the Soviet Union in late 1991, and the country began the transition to democracy, criminologist Louise Shelley commented that "for the first time in seventy years . . . the regular police (*militsiia*) were expected to abide by the rule of law."[2]

Policing in a democracy is not easy, however. The public often demands that the police do things that are not lawful: stopping and questioning people who they think are "suspicious" looking; arresting or using other tactics to keep unemployed or homeless people out of commercial areas. As Jerome Skolnick argued in his classic work *Justice Without Trial,* the demand for effective crime control often conflicts with the requirements of the law.[3] "Suspicious looking," for instance, is usually a code word for people of a different race or ethnicity. Being unemployed or homeless, meanwhile, is a condition, and not a crime that would justify arrest. If police officers beat confessions out of people (as they did back in the 1930s, according to the famous Wickersham Commission report), they might solve more crimes, but it would involve buying effectiveness at the price of legality and respect for human decency.[4]

A Historical Perspective on Accountability

In the Los Angeles Police Department (LAPD), before the mid-1960s, there was "an automatic inquiry whenever an officer damaged a department motor vehicle," but not until 1965 year was there a similar investigation when an officer "inflicted a wound on a person."[5] Meaningful accountability is a relatively recent development in American policing. Throughout most of their history, as we learned in Chapter 2, the police were not accountable at all. Police departments were corrupt and inefficient, and individual officers evaded duty and assaulted citizens without fear of being disciplined. Elected officials used the police for graft, protection of illegal enterprises, and getting jobs for their friends. They took almost no interest in controlling officer misconduct.

Procedures for holding officers accountable began to develop slowly in the late 1950s. The Supreme Court issued a series of decisions imposing constitutional standards on routine police work, particularly searches and interrogations. In the 1970s, police departments began to develop written rules on deadly force, pursuits, and other actions to control police officer behavior. Serious rethinking about what the police do and how they can more effectively address crime and disorder began in the 1980s, with the emergence of community policing and problem-oriented policing. The leaders of these movements argued that the police needed to focus on neighborhood-level problems, develop strategies for addressing specific problems or community concerns, and also develop working partnerships with individuals and groups in those neighborhoods. In the 1990s, systems such as COMPSTAT and early interventions systems emerged to review both crime control effectiveness and individual officer conduct.[6] Yet, as the events of 2014–2016 made clear, much more needs to be done.

Accountability for *What* the Police Do

The Traditional Approach to Measuring Police Effectiveness

The central problem regarding police accountability is that policing is a human service. Police officers deal with people in an unbelievable range of situations: as victims of crime, as parties to a domestic dispute, as mentally ill people, and as criminal offenders. Measuring the effectiveness of both a department as a whole and individual officers in those incidents is a major challenge.

The police role involves law enforcement, order maintenance, and service. Traditionally, however, police performance was measured almost entirely in terms of the crime rate, ignoring the order maintenance and service roles of the police. Other crime-related measures included the clearance rate and 911 call response times.[7]

As discussed in Chapter 9, the **crime rate** is not a valid or reliable measure of police performance. The official FBI Uniform Crime Reporting (UCR) crime rate is limited to eight index crimes, with no data on white-collar crime, organized crime, and drug offenses. Also, the UCR program records only *reported* crime. As we have learned from the National Crime Victimization Survey (NCVS), two-thirds of all crimes are not reported to the police: In 2014, only 44.6 percent of all assaults were reported, and only 29 percent of thefts were reported.[8] The first important point is that the police cannot be held responsible for solving crimes they do not know about. A second important point is that even among crimes that are reported to the police, police officers routinely *unfound* them, meaning they do not complete an official crime report of the incident. As a result, the incident does not become part of the official crime rate. Additionally, some crime reports are lost, changed because of new information, or deliberately changed as way to keep the official crime rate low. Throughout police history there have been scandals in which the police were caught deliberately manipulating crime data. In Milwaukee, for example, an investigation by the *Milwaukee Journal-Sentinel* in 2012 found that the police department had downgraded the seriousness of "hundreds" of assault cases, which had the effect of lowering the city's violent crime rate.[9] Because police departments vary considerably in terms of the quality of their crime records systems, the UCR data are not a reliable performance measure for comparing different departments. Finally, the UCR data are not independently audited to ensure professional record keeping.

crime rate

For a discussion of official police data on crime, see Chapter 9.

Official arrest data, which are used to compute the clearance rate, are also not reliable. Lawrence Sherman and Barry Glick found great variation among police departments in how they record arrests. Some complete an official arrest report only when a suspect is booked, whereas others make a report whenever a suspect is detained and questioned. For these reasons, arrest data and the resulting clearance rates are not reliable for comparing different departments.[10]

The clearance rate is the percentage of reported crimes solved or cleared by the police, and it is also not a reliable performance measure. The denominator, the official number of robberies, for example, is not reliable. Officers responding to many robberies may have recorded them as assaults. (This is often legitimate, because a robbery includes the "lesser included offense" of an assault. In other words, in the act of committing a robbery, the offender also commits an assault.) And the number of arrests can be easily manipulated, for example, by attributing several other unsolved crimes to a person who has just been arrested.

Most important, however, the crime rate and clearance rate do not measure the order maintenance and service-related activities of the police, which represent 70 to 80 percent of all police work. There are no data, for example, on police handling of disorder situations, such as domestic violence incidents or situations involving a mentally ill person. Some police departments may do a much better job of handling such situations, but there are no performance data that would measure that.

Alternative Measures and Their Limitations

The community policing movement and problem-oriented policing, because they focus on the full range of neighborhood problems (for example, nuisances that create fear, signs of disorder and neighborhood decay), created a need for police performance measures other than the official UCR crime rate. Several alternative measures of the quality of police services have been considered, but all have serious limitations.

Citizen Complaints

Citizen complaints are a possible measure of department performance, on the assumption that a high rate of citizen complaints for one police department compared with other departments indicates a high rate of police misconduct. There are a number of problems with official citizen complaint data, however. First, only a small percentage of people who have an unpleasant experience with the police ever file an official complaint. Most people think it is not worth the effort and/or do not think anything will be done with their complaint. The official complaint rate (number of complaints per 100 officers, or per 1,000 local residents) can mean one of two completely different things. A high complaint rate might mean that there is a lot of officer misconduct. But it could also mean that people generally have a lot of confidence in the complaint system and that it is worthwhile filing a complaint. Similarly, a low complaint rate could mean that there is little officer misconduct, or that people have almost no confidence in the complaint system.[11]

Civil Litigation and Damage Awards

In 2012, New York City paid out $64 million in lawsuits involving the police department. The amount had been rising steadily over five years, and totaled $264.4 million from 2008 to 2012.[12] Cities across the country are paying out vast sums of money every year because of suits against their police departments (see the section "Civil Suits against the Police").

Civil litigation and damage awards to plaintiffs are also a problematic measure of police performance. The fact that one city pays out millions of dollars for police misconduct does not necessarily mean it is that much worse than other cities that pay less. In some cities, the city legal department has a policy of settling many cases without going to trial. They simply want to avoid the time, trouble, and uncertainty of contested trials. This policy, however, has the effect of encouraging lawyers to bring more cases. Some cities, by contrast, have a policy of not settling and instead force the plaintiffs' lawyers to go to trial. This policy discourages lawyers from bringing cases.

The dollar volume of payouts is also problematic as a measure of police performance, since there is always a time lag between the misconduct incident and the settlement or trial verdict. In serious misconduct cases the lag can involve several years. The result is that the total payouts for 2015 do not measure the quality of policing in that year. A large payout of $5 million in 2015 may involve a type of misconduct (for example, misuse of an electroconductive weapon) that has since been corrected by a new policy limiting the behavior that led to the payout.[13]

Surveys of Public Opinion

Regular surveys of public opinion have some potential for measuring community perceptions of how a police department is doing. It is possible to survey contacts with the police and how people feel they were treated. Surveys can also specify the variations by neighborhood, race, ethnicity, and income. Regular surveys over time can also track any important changes in public attitudes. Unfortunately, public opinion surveys are expensive, and few police departments are prepared to divert funds from more basic police services.

The city auditor in Portland, Oregon, annually surveys the community about conditions in the city and about city services. In 2015, for example, it found that the percentage of people rating the police "very good or good" rose from 59 percent in 2011 to 63 percent in 2015. Ratings of the fire department in the same period were stable, while the ratings of street maintenance fell from 35 to 28 percent. In 2015, only 2 percent of all respondents said they felt unsafe walking alone in their neighborhood during the day, while 18 percent felt "unsafe or very unsafe" walking alone at night in their neighborhood. Only 38 percent of respondents felt the city was doing a "very good or good" job of "regulat[ing] conduct of Portland police officers."[14]

Another way for a police department to assess its performance and hold officers accountable is to survey those who involuntarily come into contact with the police. This can be done by interviewing recently booked arrestees and asking them their perceptions of their encounter with the police. In Los Angeles, as part of an evaluation of the federal consent decree, the research team interviewed 71 people within hours of their being detained by the police. Most had been detained at least three times in the past two years. Despite this high level of police contact, 39 respondents (55 percent) reported that the LAPD was doing an "excellent" or "good" job. Almost half, meanwhile, said that the LAPD had improved its professionalism and respect in the previous three years.[15]

COMPSTAT: A Neighborhood-Focused Approach

Every other Thursday, about 30 officers with the Lowell, Massachusetts, police department, including the chief, top commanders, and some sergeants and patrol officers, meet in a conference room for the biweekly COMPSTAT meeting. The purpose of each meeting is to review neighborhood crime data from each of the department's three districts over the past three weeks. The review is designed to identify patterns in criminal activity and develop immediate and crime-specific responses.[16]

COMPSTAT is one of the most important innovations in police accountability. Developed by the New York City Police Department (NYPD) in the 1990s, it has been adopted by many departments across the country. COMPSTAT involves the timely collection of data on crime and calls for service, with regular command staff meetings to analyze the data and discuss focused responses to the most serious problems or to new problems. Precinct or area commanders can be held directly accountable for what they are doing about conditions in the areas for which they are responsible. The focused responses might involve one of the recent innovations in policing, such as hot-spots policing or focused deterrence.

For a detailed discussion of COMPSTAT, see Chapter 4.

COMPSTAT can serve as an accountability measure in several ways. First, it provides *timely data* on crime and disorder at the neighborhood level. In many programs the crime data are available within 24 hours. Second, with its specific *geographic focus,* COMPSTAT can assess how the police are doing in different areas. Third, and particularly important, COMPSTAT focuses on *internal accountability,* by holding precinct commanders responsible for crime problems in their areas. In the history of American policing, COMPSTAT is the first systematic effort to hold precinct commanders accountable for conditions in the areas under their command. Finally, it also emphasizes innovative *problem solving,* with precinct commanders expected to develop timely and relevant responses to crime problems.

Accountability for *How* the Police Do Their Job

The other important area of accountability involves *how* the police do their job. This refers specifically to the conduct of police officers in their contacts with people. Do they use excessive force on a regular basis? If an officer does, is he or she investigated thoroughly and fairly by the department? If the excessive force allegation is sustained, is the officer appropriately disciplined? Does a department have in place a procedure for systematically reviewing certain actions, such as street stops, traffic stops, uses of force, and high-speed vehicle pursuits? Does the department have a process for identifying the "lessons learned" from questionable use-of-force incidents, for example, and then providing feedback for possible revisions of department policy, training, or supervision? The Las Vegas Metropolitan Police Department, following a Justice Department review, strengthened its use-of-force review board to include a process of identifying problems that arose in particular force incidents (poor officer tactics, or training failures, for example) and then providing feedback to the relevant police commanders for corrective action.[17]

Internal Mechanisms of Accountability

Primary responsibility for holding police officers accountable for their actions lies with the police department itself. Herman Goldstein argues that "the nature of the police function is such that primary dependence for the control of police conduct must continue to be placed upon internal systems of control."[18] These systems include routine supervision, officers' reports on critical incidents, periodic performance evaluations, and investigation of alleged misconduct by the internal affairs (IA) or professional standards unit.

As Sidebar 14–1 outlines, a comprehensive system of internal accountability consists of many steps, beginning with officers and their sergeants on the street and rising up through higher levels of command in a police department. The **PTSR framework** refers to *policy, training, supervision,* and *review.* The key point is that all four components are necessary for a comprehensive accountability process. If one is inadequate, it undermines the effect of the others. A department, for example, can have an excellent use-of-force policy, and do a first-rate job of training its officers, but if on-the-street supervision is inadequate, the value of that policy and training is lost.

PTSR framework

Routine Supervision of Patrol Officers

A newspaper report described the midnight shift in the Suffolk County, New York, police department as the "lost battalion." It found that officers "can go for hours without speaking to a supervisor, or weeks without having contact with their precinct's top managers."[19] The department was failing to provide routine supervision—

SIDEBAR 14–1

The PTSR Framework: A Comprehensive Model of Internal Police Accountability

Policy
   The department has a state-of-the-art policy on use of deadly force, use of physical force, de-escalation, the handling of domestic violence incidents, etc.
Training
   The department's training unit trains officers on the precise meaning of each policy, using the best new training methods (role playing, computer simulations, as few lectures as possible; see Chapter 5).
Supervision
   Sergeants closely supervise officers under their command, holding them strictly accountable for compliance with department policies and training. (See the discussion of the elements of close supervision in Sidebar 14–2.)
Review
   The department has a process for reviewing patterns in past critical incidents (uses of deadly force, high-speed vehicle pursuits, etc.) for the purpose of identifying problems that need to be corrected through changes to the department's policy, better training, or improved supervision.

Source: Samuel Walker and Carol Archbold, *The New World of Police Accountability*, 2nd ed. (Thousand Oaks: Sage, 2014), 16–20.

S I D E B A R 14–2

The Elements of Close and Effective Supervision

1. A state-of-the-art policy on force (or other police action)

2. A requirement that officers complete a written use-of-force report before the end of the shift

3. A requirement that officers who use force answer questions from supervisors about the use of force

4. A requirement that sergeants critically review officer use-of-force reports, and ask for more detail or for clarifications when needed

5. A requirement that sergeants collect any evidence, search for witnesses, question witnesses, and question witness officers at the scene of the incident

6. A requirement that sergeants complete a use-of-force report before the end of the shift, and report any excessive use of force if justified by the evidence

7. A force investigation team (FIT) to provide experienced investigators for each serious use of force incident

8. A use-of-force review board (UFRB) to look for patterns of problems that need to be corrected

9. Officer use-of-force reports entered into department's early intervention system (EIS)

the kind recommended in police management textbooks since the 1940s—to officers working between midnight and 8 A.M. The report was prompted by a series of allegations that male officers in the department had stopped, harassed, and even abused young, single, female drivers.

routine supervision

Routine supervision of officers on the street is the cornerstone of a system of accountability in a law enforcement agency. A Police Foundation survey of police officers found that almost 90 percent agree that "good first-line supervisors can help prevent police officers from abusing their authority."[20]

The Span of Control

In the mid-1990s, the Los Angeles County Sheriff's Department experienced a number of officer-involved shooting incidents by officers assigned to the Century Station. An investigation by Special Counsel Merrick Bobb—the police auditor for the department—found that the source of the problem was not a few "bad apples" but bad management practices. Most serious, Bobb found that at times each sergeant was supervising 20 to 25 officers, a ratio that far exceeded the department's own standard of 8 to 1.[21]

span of control

The ratio of sergeants to officers is referred to as the **span of control.** The theory of span of control assumes that any supervisor can effectively supervise only a limited number of people.[22] In policing, the recommended span of control is between 8 and 10 patrol officers for each sergeant. When the recommended span of control is exceeded, supervision may deteriorate, and as a result the quality of officer performance will deteriorate and improper actions will occur. Maintaining the proper span of control is difficult in police departments, however, because of promotions, transfers or budget issues. Following a series of sexual abuse incidents involving officers, a 2015 investigation found that the San Diego Police Department experienced serious accountability problems because of budget cuts that caused a high use of interim sergeants who had not been officially promoted and, therefore, had not received formal training for supervisors.[23]

How Sergeants Supervise

Darrel Stephens, former chief of the Charlotte-Mecklenburg Police Department, points out that sergeants are largely responsible for setting departmental expectations and "translating the department's mission, vision, values, policies, rules and regulations into operational practice." They are the ones who have the most contact with patrol officers and the public, and determine what is acceptable performance and what is not.[24]

Supervision by sergeants involves a number of different activities. First, they are expected to *monitor* officers under their command on a regular basis, either through face-to-face meetings or over the police radio. Second, in the case of potentially serious incidents, they are expected to *appear at the scene,* provide advice if needed, and if necessary take command of the situation. Third, they *review officers' reports,* including arrest and use-of-force reports. (All part of a department's efforts to control officer use of force.) Fourth, sergeants are expected to *advise, counsel, and mentor* officers under their command whenever their performance is less than satisfactory and to instruct them on proper procedure. Fifth, if a sergeant becomes aware that an officer has violated a department policy or committed some act of misconduct, he or she is expected to *file a report with the internal affairs unit* or the office of professional standards, which would then investigate the allegation. Sixth, sergeants prepare the regular performance evaluations of officers under their command.[25]

Robin Engel analyzed the work styles of supervisors and found four different approaches to supervision and discipline. *Supportive supervisors* define their role in terms of protecting officers under their command "from criticism and discipline" by upper management. *Traditional supervisors,* on the other hand, "expect aggressive enforcement" and "are more likely to punish patrol officers" than are other categories of supervisors. **Innovative supervisors** "generally encourage their officers to embrace new philosophies and methods of policing." Finally, *active supervisors* lead by example and are "heavily involved in the field alongside subordinates while controlling patrol officers' behavior."[26] The style of supervision can make a difference in the overall quality of a police department. If most sergeants use the supportive style, misconduct will often not be punished, and the public will suffer as a result. A large number of innovative supervisors, by contrast, will mean that the department is more likely to successfully implement important new developments such as de-escalation and procedural justice.

innovative supervisors

When Supervision Fails

Sergeants often develop close personal ties with the officers under their command. This can affect their ability to supervise properly. They may become unwilling to criticize those officers and exercise the proper level of control and discipline. These relationships represent an important part of the police subculture. Personal relationships involve not just sergeants, but extend to higher ranking command officers. In a

 For a discussion of the police subculture, see Chapter 6.

review of the Los Angeles Sheriff's Department early intervention system (discussed later in this chapter), Special Counsel Merrick Bobb found that captains were frequently strong advocates for officers under their command, arguing that they should not be placed on performance review in which their performance would be monitored to correct performance problems.[27]

The quality of policing suffers when sergeants fail to provide close and effective supervision of officers under their command. The Department of Justice (DOJ) investigation of the Cleveland, Ohio, police department in 2014 provided a revealing picture of a pattern of sergeants failing to perform their basic job duties. The DOJ report found, for example, that "[u]ntil recently, when a use of force incident occurred, each officer at the scene was not required to write a report documenting the incident." In addition, sergeants typically "conduct[ed] insufficient reviews of officers' use of less lethal force." In particular, they made "little effort to determine the level of force that was used and whether it was justified." Even worse, sergeants in some cases sought "to justify a use of force that, on its face, was unreasonable." The DOJ investigators "almost never found" cases where sergeants reported that the force used was unreasonable.[28]

Coaching, Mentoring, Leading, and Helping

The role of supervisors in holding officers accountable includes more than imposing formal discipline. The section on "Expectations for Supervisory Personnel" in the *Standard Operating Procedure Manual* of the Madison, Wisconsin, police department, for example, explains that supervisors are expected to "[e]ngage in activity to coach, consult, and guide personnel" in the department. This includes "providing advice and interpreting [department] procedures." Additionally, they are expected to "[d]iscover existing weaknesses within [their] area of responsibility and address inadequacies to see that corrective action is taken."[29]

employee assistance program

Supervising officers also involves helping them when they have problems. Most city or county governments maintain **employee assistance programs** (EAPs), which provide counseling services for officers experiencing serious stress, family problems, substance abuse, depression, or thoughts of suicide. An active sergeant who is closely monitoring his or her officers should be able to spot significant personal problems, initiate a discussion with an officer, and if necessary recommend contacting the EAP office. Participation in an EAP is confidential, and no record is placed in an officer's discipline file. An active sergeant, who is in close touch with his or her officers will recognize the signs of extreme stress and take steps to get help for any officer who might be suicidal.[30]

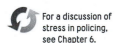 For a discussion of stress in policing, see Chapter 6.

Organizational Culture and Accountability

The LAPD in 2000 delivered a devastating criticism of its own personnel evaluation system: "Our personnel evaluations have little or no credibility at any level in the organization." This criticism was delivered by the LAPD's internal Board of Inquiry report on the highly publicized Rampart scandal. The report's chapter on the department's integrity systems, meanwhile, identified more than 30 policies and procedures designed to ensure integrity and accountability. Yet it concluded that all these systems had not prevented the Rampart scandal from occurring. In short, what the official policies stated on paper were not translated into actual practice.[31]

The findings of the Board of Inquiry report raised a general problem with personnel evaluations and other internal accountability mechanisms. There is an important distinction between meaningful accountability, where actions have consequences, and superficial accountability, where an organization has elaborate policies and forms but does not use them in any meaningful way.

Whether or not meaningful discipline occurs depends on the **organizational culture** of a police department. The Chemerinsky report on the LAPD's Board of Inquiry report argued that "every police department has a culture—the unwritten rules, mores, customs, codes, values, and outlooks—that creates the policing environment and style." The culture of the LAPD, it concluded, involves the enforcement of "voluminous rules and regulations, some of them very petty." While petty rules are enforced, serious misconduct is covered up. First, the "code of silence" results in officers being reluctant to report misconduct by other officers (discussed later in this chapter). Second, when they do report misconduct, officers are not only *not* rewarded for doing so but often are punished by the department.[32] In fact, in 2000, 90 current and former LAPD officers filed suit against the department for having been demoted or otherwise punished for reporting misconduct by other officers.

organizational culture

Command-Level Review of Force Incidents: The Emerging Standard

Ensuring that sergeants critically review officer use-of-force reports is the cornerstone of a police department's commitment to accountability. It does not stop there, however. The culture of a department with respect to accountability, particularly with regard to use of force, depends on additional reviews at higher levels. The emerging standard of accountability requires **command-level reviews** that take three different forms: force investigation teams, use-of-force review boards, and early intervention systems.

command-level review

A force investigation team (FIT) is a specialized unit that responds immediately to all serious uses of force. This includes shootings, serious physical force incidents, and other incidents as determined by the department. Traditionally, force incidents have been investigated by the immediate supervisor on the scene. A FIT, however, involves investigators who have the "appropriate expertise, independence, and investigative skills" for handling such cases. FIT investigators are also more independent than an immediate supervisor, who is likely to have developed close personal ties to the involved officer. The first task of a FIT is to roll out immediately to the scene of an incident. All officers at the scene should be separated, to ensure that they do not attempt to create a false scenario that would justify whatever force was used, to secure all evidence, and to locate any witnesses to the incident. If the incident involved possible criminal conduct by an officer, the local prosecutor is to be immediately notified. Finally, the FIT will complete a preliminary report of the incident.[33]

A **use-of-force review board** (UFRB) conducts a higher level review of force incidents than the FIT. As an indication of its importance, it is often chaired by a deputy chief. The UFRB reviews each FIT report with several purposes in mind. First, it determines whether the use of force violated department policy, and if so it refers

use-of-force review board

the case to internal affairs for disciplinary action. Second, and particularly important, it reviews the incident to determine (in the words of the New Orleans consent decree) "whether the incident raises policy, training, equipment, or tactical concerns."[34] If it does, the UFRB refers the issue to the appropriate unit in the department. As we learned in Chapter 5, the new thinking about controlling police use of force includes a focus on officer tactical decisions that can either make use of force more likely or alternatively lead to a resolution of the incident where force is not necessary. If the UFRB identifies an issue with the tactics used by the officer in a particular case, it can refer the matter to the training unit with a recommendation for greater emphasis on the tactical choices available to officers. Alternatively, the UFRB review might find that the department's policy on, for example, the handling of mentally ill people, is not clear on a certain point. In that case, it would refer the issue to the chief of police with a recommendation that the policy be reexamined and possibly revised.

As we learned in Chapter 5, one of the most important developments in police training involves preparing officers to assess the situation in a difficult encounter and to consider alternatives that might avoid the need to use force. Reviewing past incidents is a valuable way to understand what choices were made and what alternatives might have been better choices.[35] The process of reviewing past use-of-force incidents and using the lessons learned to make improvements in policy, training, and supervision represents what William A. Geller called police departments becoming "learning organizations."[36]

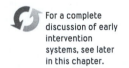 For a complete discussion of early intervention systems, see later in this chapter.

The third command-level review of force incidents involves an early intervention system, which is an administrative tool for identifying officers with repeated performance problems and referring them for corrective action.

Corrective Action: Informal and Formal

One important task for supervisors is to take corrective action to improve the performance of officers under their command. Some of these actions can be *informal.* After a police–citizen encounter, for example, a sergeant might talk to an officer, pointing out that he or she was rude to a citizen or that the officer created a potential danger for herself by the way she placed herself at the scene. A sergeant might notice that another officer appears to have a lot of things on his mind or be in a hostile mood. Like employees in other occupations, police officers are often affected by family problems. The sergeant in this case might just talk with the officer about the situation or suggest referral to a counselling program.[37]

A number of departments have *formal* programs for improving officer performance. A sergeant might refer an officer for retraining on traffic stop or use-of-force tactics, for example. The Los Angeles Sheriff's Department has a formal peer officer support program. This consists of officers who have received 40 hours of training and are available to talk with other officers on a strictly confidential basis. As mentioned earlier, most departments also participate in formal EAPs, where an officer can receive professional counseling related to depression, family problems, or substance abuse.[38]

Performance Evaluations

performance evaluations

Writing regular **performance evaluations** of officers under their command is an important task for sergeants. Annual (or more frequent) evaluations by an immediate supervisor are designed to provide feedback to employees by identifying areas of outstanding, acceptable, or inadequate performance. Identifying areas of inadequate performance is intended to provide feedback to the officer so that he or she has an opportunity to improve. Performance evaluations are also used when officers apply for promotion.

As discussed in Chapter 6, standard performance evaluations in police departments have a number of serious problems. A Police Executive Research Forum (PERF) report found that "most performance evaluations currently used by police do not reflect the work officers do."[39]

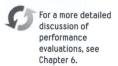

For a more detailed discussion of performance evaluations, see Chapter 6.

Internal Affairs/Professional Standards Units

The **internal affairs** or professional standards unit is responsible for investigating alleged officer misconduct by police officers. Investigations are either *reactive,* in response to a citizen complaint or official report, or *proactive,* when the department has some evidence of possible misconduct by an officer. The report on *Standards and Guidelines for Internal Affairs* argues that "Internal Affairs is not an isolated agency function. It is integral to a more complex interrelationship among entities within the agency." In short, internal affairs does not merely deal with discipline but has an important impact on operations in the entire organization.[40]

internal affairs

Internal affairs officers occupy a difficult position within police departments. Because they investigate other officers, they face hostility from the rank and file. Officers assigned to IAUs are often regarded as "snitches" for the chief. A study of IAUs in a metropolitan area in the Southwest quoted an internal affairs lieutenant as saying, "They are a bunch of headhunters, and they're headhunters for the police chief." Many officers do not want to serve in internal affairs because they may have to investigate friends. One officer who requested the assignment said of his friends, "[they] thought I was nuts."[41]

The effectiveness of IAUs depends on several factors. Most important are the attitude and the actions of the chief. Virtually all experts on policing agree that the chief must communicate to officers that misconduct will not be tolerated and then follow up with appropriate discipline against officers who are in fact found guilty.[42]

IAUs also need sufficient resources. They need to have enough investigators, given the size of the department, to handle their assigned tasks effectively. Following the Rampart scandal in Los Angeles, a report found the LAPD's Internal Affairs Group "underfunded and understaffed."[43] Following the famous corruption scandal in New York City in the 1970s (often referred to as the Serpico scandal), the new police commissioner Patrick V. Murphy increased the ratio of internal affairs investigators to officers from 1:533 to 1:64.[44]

If adequate staffing is not maintained, however, police abuses can easily worsen. In New York City, the anticorruption reforms instituted by Commissioner Murphy in the early 1970s were allowed to erode, with the result that in the mid-1980s another major corruption scandal erupted in the department.[45] Between 2009 and 2012, the San Diego Police Department, which long had a good national reputation for its commitment to community policing and other issues, was struck by a series of scandals involving sexual abuse by its officers. One officer was convicted and sentenced to prison for sexual assault of women while on the job. A review of the department concluded that one of the contributing factors had been a reduction in the number of officers assigned to internal affairs, with the result that the department was less able to investigate suspected officer misconduct.[46]

Selecting officers for internal affairs presents some difficult issues. Many officers do not want that assignment because of the stigma associated with investigating fellow officers. The NYPD began "drafting" officers for a two-year assignment to internal affairs, even if they did not want the assignment. An assessment of the experiment raised the question of having internal affairs "staffed largely by people who do not want to be there." Would that result in poor performance? The assessment found some morale problems (related to issues such as the loss of overtime opportunities) but no serious performance problems.[47] Another issue involves allowing officers to serve for long periods of time in internal affairs. On the one hand, they gain valuable experience in the difficult task of investigating fellow officers. On the other hand, however, they may eventually become too comfortable in the assignment and begin to give officers the benefit of the doubt in too many cases.

Training for internal affairs investigators is important. Many departments provide no special training related to investigating citizen complaints or corruption allegations. A PERF evaluation of a midwestern police department in 1992 found that "no formal training is provided [for new internal affairs investigators;] all training is on the job."[48] Most internal affairs officers had prior experience in criminal investigation; however, investigating fellow officers is very different from investigating criminals. A report by Jayson Wechter, a staff member with the San Francisco Office of Citizen Complaints, argues that investigating citizen complaints is especially difficult. "Allegations of police misconduct are emotionally charged," he argues, and "[c]omplainants may feel deeply violated and expect the complaint investigator to provide them with justice." Internal affairs officers are faced with conflicting demands: to be fair to the complainant while also being loyal to the department. All organizations have a tendency to be self-protective in the face of outside criticisms. Investigators are naturally inclined to believe the officer rather than the citizen.[49]

The Discipline Process

Police Discipline: A Case for Change, by Darrel W. Stephens, the respected former chief of the Charlotte-Mecklenburg Police Department, is one of the most thoughtful discussions of the long-standing problems with police disciplinary procedures and the direction change should take. The first issue is the need for effective supervision on the street, discussed earlier. One major problem is that the focus of police disciplinary systems "is predominantly punishment, not behavior change."[50] An officer who receives a suspension of one or two days for excessive force returns to the job resentful over the discipline having learned nothing about the proper use of force, which would prevent use of excessive force in the future. The use of early intervention systems (described later in this chapter) addresses that problem by identifying officers with patterns of problematic behavior and then, in a nondisciplinary fashion, providing retraining designed to improve officers' performance.

Disciplinary procedures often take too long to complete and, as Stephens points out, often do not appear to be fair in the eyes of the officer.[51] The San Jose Independent Police Auditor, for example, found that in 2014 the department closed 26 percent of all complaints *after* the 300-day deadline required by state law. In 2015, the speed of investigations improved, and only 15 percent were beyond the 300-day deadline.[52] There is an old saying that "justice delayed is justice denied," and it applies to police discipline. When an investigation takes many months to complete, the complainant experiences delayed justice, while the officer is left with uncertainty about his or her fate. The problem of perceived unfairness of a disciplinary action can be addressed if the department adopts procedural justice in its internal procedures, as recommended by the President's Task Force on 21st Century Policing.[53] Procedural justice in this context involves the command officer explaining to the officer what he or she did, what was wrong about the conduct, which department policy it violated, and the general expectations of the department in terms of performance.

Appropriate Levels of Discipline

Disciplinary actions against officers is a subject surrounded by mystery. Police departments do not release information on what discipline, if any, an officer received for a controversial excessive force case. As discussed in Chapter 12, the belief among members of the community that officers who have committed misconduct are given a "slap on the wrist" or not disciplined at all is a major source of police–community relations problems. We do not know what the "going rate" is for officer misconduct. We do not know what discipline officers generally receive for an incident involving use of offensive language or for use of force (for example, slamming someone up against a car). As a result, we do not know whether some departments are genuinely tough on excessive force while others are weak. By comparison, sentences in criminal courts are public information, and researchers are able to determine which courts are tough on gun crimes or drunk driving, and which ones are not.[54]

Fair and consistent discipline requires that the level of discipline imposed be appropriate for the proven misconduct and that the same level of discipline be applied in all roughly similar cases. A 2003 report by the Philadelphia Integrity and Accountability Office found that almost half of the officers who were found guilty by the Internal Affairs Bureau between 2000 and 2003 were "never formally disciplined."[55] The Office of Independent Review in the Los Angeles Sheriff's Department found that in about half of all minor discipline cases, the officer never undertook the required action (for example, attending substance abuse counseling or an anger management class).[56] A 2000 report to the Los Angeles Police Commission found a lack of guidelines for the Internal Affairs Group; as a result, disciplinary actions were arbitrary and inconsistent. Favoritism for certain officers and inconsistent discipline create serious morale problems among rank-and-file officers.[57]

A number of departments have had problems with respect to patterns of discriminatory disciplinary actions against African American, Hispanic, or female officers, or against officers who have criticized the department. To address the problem of unfair and inconsistent discipline, some departments have adopted a **discipline matrix,** to structure disciplinary actions. In essence, a discipline matrix is similar to the sentencing guidelines used in the courts. One axis of the matrix specifies the seriousness of the officer's current offense (for example, verbal abuse, use of excessive force with no injury, use of excessive force with injury). The other axis specifies the officer's discipline history (for example, reprimands, one-day suspension, five-day

discipline matrix

suspension). A matrix typically allows for some discretion by specifying a minimum or maximum penalty (as do most sentencing guidelines). The settlement of a suit against the Oakland, California, police department required the department to develop a matrix. A discipline matrix, Stephens explains, not only lets "employees know in advance" what discipline to expect" but also it "will help make the sanctions applied both fair and consistent."[58] Stephens believes that officers prefer a disciplinary matrix because they provide them with a clearer understanding of departmental sanctions. He also notes that a matrix saves officers time and the department time and money because once an officer has been found to have committed an act of misconduct, the discipline outcome is clear and nonnegotiable.[59]

Openness and Transparency for Disciplinary Actions

In almost all police departments, disciplinary actions are not public records. Disclosure of the discipline an officer receives for a particular incident is not considered a public record, and disclosure is barred by police union contract in many departments. This is generally not true of terminations, which are public events where an announcement is made to the news media. In the case of a controversial excessive force case, however, the public never learns whether the officer was disciplined, and if so whether the action taken was a suspension, a reprimand, or something else.

The secrecy surrounding police discipline is the source of much public mistrust of the police, as it feeds community suspicion that the police never disciplines its officers. Steven Zansberg and Pamela Campos argue that there is a "compelling public interest" in the public release of at least some police internal affairs files. Officers have a right to privacy, they concede, and there is much information in the investigative files on cases that should not be released. But, they argue, public disclosure should include "the results of the investigation, such as documents reflecting whether charges were sustained and whether any discipline was imposed."[60]

Standards for Investigating Citizen Complaints

The principles of fairness, thoroughness, and respect for due process impose significant demands on citizen complaint investigators. In the interests of fairness, for example, they must treat the complainant and the officer equally. In particular, they may not give an automatic preference to the views of the officer. Thoroughness requires that they seek out all possible evidence. Fairness also means that they cannot discount the testimony of the complainant because of the way he or she dresses or is groomed, and of course there can be no bias on the basis of race, ethnicity, gender, sexual preference, or social class. Investigators should actively canvass the scene of the incident and the immediate neighborhood for possible witnesses. The resolution of the complaint investigation must be clearly related to the facts of the case.

The state of New Jersey has a unique law under which the state attorney general is empowered to develop standards for the citizen complaint procedures of local police departments. The 2000 Internal Affairs Policy and Procedures (IAPP) law requires that each department accept complaints "from any person, including anonymous sources"; that internal affairs should travel to the complainant's home or other

location for the interview if the complainant is unable to travel; among other requirements.[61] A 2009 investigation by the American Civil Liberties Union of New Jersey,
however, found that police departments were routinely violating the attorney general's guidelines. More than 60 percent of all departments, for example, required
citizens to file complaints in person, in violation of the guidelines.[62]

Using Discipline Records in Personnel Decisions

The 1991 **Christopher Commission** report on the LAPD found that the department
did not use officer discipline records in promotion or reassignment decisions. As a
result, officers with reprimands or suspensions were often being promoted.[63] The
failure of police departments to take disciplinary records into account when making
promotion decisions or assignments to important specialty units is a serious problem.

    In response to this problem, the consent decree with the City of Oakland required
the department to take into account "Prior Disciplinary History as an Aggravating
Factor" in discipline cases. Specifically, it directed that "[f]actors which may be
considered in the weighing process include, but are not limited to: . . . [t]he nature and
seriousness of any prior violation; . . . [t]he number of prior violations; . . . [t]he length
of time between prior violations and the current case;" and other disciplinary matters.[64]

Christopher Commission

The "Code of Silence"

The city of Chicago was in turmoil in late 2015 following the release of a police
video showing an officer shooting Laquan McDonald in the back more than a year
earlier. Chicago mayor Rahm Emanuel made the startling statement in December
2015 that "[t]he short answer is, yes," there is a **code of silence** in the Chicago
Police Department. This was the first time any mayor or high-ranking police official
had admitted there was a pattern of secrecy and lying about police misconduct.[65] The
Invisible Institute, an activist organization in Chicago addressing police misconduct,
followed up with a four-part series of articles on the code of silence in the Chicago
police department detailing how the code of silence served not only to protect a corrupt
officer engaged in narcotics trafficking but also to protect retaliation against whistle-
blower officers who had broken the code in an effort to expose the corruption.[66]

code of silence

    The code of silence (also known as the "blue curtain") is defined as the unwill-
ingness of police officers to report misconduct by other officers. In some cases, they
simply say nothing. But in other cases, they deliberately lie in their official reports or
on the stand in a trial. Lying under oath, of course, is perjury, a criminal offense.
Police experts have long claimed that the code of silence is one of the greatest barriers to police accountability. In an officer-involved shooting or excessive force incident, the crucial evidence about what happened is the testimony of witness officers.

    The code of silence is a major part of the organizational culture of policing.
William Westley identified the code of silence in his pioneering study of the police
subculture.[67] The Christopher Commission found that the code of silence was a major factor in protecting abuse of force by Los Angeles police officers.[68] A national
survey of police officers by the Police Foundation in the 1990s found that slightly
more than half (52.4 percent) agreed that "it is not unusual for a police officer to turn
a blind eye to improper police conduct by other officers."[69]

A corrupt New York City police officer explained the code of silence in blunt terms. Asked by the Mollen Commission investigating corruption in the early 1990s if he was ever afraid that one of his fellow officers might turn him in, he answered, "Never." "Why not?" commission investigators asked. "Because it was the Blue Wall of Silence. Cops don't tell on cops." Anyone who might report his corrupt activities would "be labeled as a rat."[70]

Officers lying in court to protect either themselves or other officers is believed to be so common that a term exists to describe it: "testilying."[71] In surveys where their anonymity is assured, officers freely admit to the existence of the code of silence. The National Institute of Ethics surveyed 3,714 police officers and police academy recruits from 42 different states about the code of silence between 1999 and 2000. The survey confirmed the widespread existence of the code: 79 percent of the recruits said that the code of silence exists throughout the country; 52 percent said that the code of silence does not bother them; and 46 percent said they would not report another officer who had sex while on duty. Asked what they thought would happen to them if they reported misconduct by a fellow officer, veteran officers responded that they would be "ostracized" (177 out of 1,157 officers); the officer would be fired (88 officers); "I would be fired" (73 officers), and "I would be blackballed" (59 officers).[72]

There have been few efforts to break the code of silence and to punish officers for giving false testimony in investigations of officer misconduct.[73] The San Diego Police Department has a formal policy requiring officers to report misconduct by other officers. Policy 9.33 states that "[i]f any member [of the department] has credible knowledge of another member's misconduct," the officer shall first attempt to stop it and then "report the misconduct to a supervisor as soon as possible."[74] Other departments have similar policies, but there is no evidence that those departments have in fact broken the traditional code of silence.

Early Intervention Systems

Officers with Performance Problems

In its investigation of the LAPD, following the highly publicized 1991 beating of Rodney King, the Christopher Commission identified 44 "problem" officers. They averaged 7.6 complaints for excessive force or improper tactics in the period studied, compared with only 0.6 for all other officers.[75]

Media stories about other departments reported a similar pattern of a few officers with much higher rates of uses of force or citizen complaints. In Kansas City, 2 percent of the officers were responsible for 50 percent of all citizen complaints. Two officers in the Boston Police Department accumulated 24 citizen complaints each between 1981 and 1990. For one officer, three of the complaints were sustained, but for the other officer none of the 24 complaints was sustained. Overall, 11 percent of the Boston officers received 62 percent of all complaints.[76]

For decades, according to Samuel Walker, it was a "dirty little secret" in policing that a small number of officers had repeated performance problems. As Herman Goldstein observed as far back as 1977, "Such officers are well-known to their supervisors, to the top administrators, to their peers, and to the residents of the areas in which they work." Officers in the department, including higher level command officers, knew about this, but until the 1990s nothing was ever done about it.[77] That changed in the 1990s, with the emergence of **early intervention systems** (EIS) as a major police accountability tool, with the capacity to identify the "problem" officers.

early intervention systems

The Nature and Purpose of EIS

An EIS is a computerized database of officer performance on a number of indicators. Analysis of the data can identify those officers with high rates of uses of force, citizen complaints, or other behaviors. Officers identified by the system are selected for non-disciplinary intervention by the department, which may consist of counseling by their immediate supervisor, special retraining to address the causes of their performance problem, or referral to professional counseling for such issues as substance abuse, family problems, or other matters affecting their performance.[78]

An EIS is not part of the disciplinary system. An officer cannot be disciplined because he or she was identified by the EIS (but can be disciplined by internal affairs for one of the incidents contained in the EIS database), and participation in the EIS is not entered into an officer's disciplinary record. An EIS is also not a predictive tool. That is, it is not designed to predict the performance of officers. The purpose of an EIS is to examine past performance and then to help officers improve their performance by identifying performance problems early (hence, it is an *early* intervention). Police commanders explain the purpose of an EIS in terms of "saving officers' careers."

EISs are included in the mandated reforms of all of the consent decrees and settlements arising from Justice Department investigations of law enforcement agencies with a "pattern or practice" of abuse of citizens (described later in this chapter). In the New Jersey State Police, for example, the court-ordered EIS is known as the Management Awareness and Personnel Performance System (MAPPS); in the Cincinnati Police Department, it is called the Risk Management System.[79]

Performance Indicators and Thresholds

The number of performance indicators in an EIS varies. Some systems are large, with 15 or more indicators, whereas others are small, with only 5 indicators. The 2015 consent decree between the Justice Department and the Cleveland, Ohio, police department, mandated an Officer Intervention Program with 16 performance indicators (see Exhibit 14–1).

Performance data in an EIS can be revealing about officers' performance, and often the underlying circumstances of their personal lives that are affecting their performance. Excessive use of sick leave can often be a sign that an officer is having a drinking problem and using sick leave to deal with hangovers. Resisting arrest charges filed by an officer, especially when there is no other arrest charge generally suggests that an officer is using the resisting arrest charge to cover his or her own use of force. And, after all, if there is no other arrest charge, what could the person have been "resisting"?

An EIS with a large number of indicators can provide a more complete picture of an officer and his or her performance. Merrick Bobb, one of the leading experts on police accountability, argues that "the longer profiles are a gold mine of information about when and how deputies got in trouble during their careers."[80] But large systems

---

EXHIBIT 14–1

Performance Indicators in the Cleveland, Ohio, Police Department (CDP) EIS

a. all uses of force
b. all ECW [electroconductive weapon] applications and accidental discharges involving a subject
c. all injuries and deaths to persons in custody
d. all critical firearm discharges
e. incidents involving the reportable pointing of a firearm at a person
f. the number of OC [pepper] spray applications
g. canine bites
h. vehicle pursuits and traffic collisions involving CDP equipment
i. civilian complaints, whether filed with CDP, OPS, or the Mayor's office
j. judicial proceedings where an officer is the subject of a protective or restraining order, other than a temporary restraining order dealing solely with financial matters. Officers will be required to report to their supervisors if they become the subject of a protective or restraining order, other than a temporary restraining order dealing solely with financial matters
k. failures to record incidents with CDP's body worn cameras that are required to be recorded under CDP's body worn camera policy
l. instances in which CDP is informed that a court has made a negative credibility determination regarding a CDP officer, or that a motion was granted on the grounds of a constitutional violation by a CDP officer
m. all disciplinary action taken against officers
n. all documented non-disciplinary corrective action required of officers
o. sick leave usage, especially in concert with regular days off and holidays; and
p. all criminal proceedings initiated against an officer, and all civil lawsuits served upon the City and/or its officers or agents, resulting from the actions of CDP officers.

Source: United States v. City of Cleveland, Consent Decree (2015), Para. 328, p. 76, https://www.justice.gov/sites/default/files/crt/legacy/2015/05/27/cleveland_agreement_5-26-15.pdf.

---

are more difficult to manage in terms of entering timely and accurate data. Smaller systems are easier to manage but do not capture as broad a picture of the officer.

Rank-and-file officers often object to the inclusion in an EIS database of unsustained citizen complaints and uses of force that were not found to be justified. They argue that in both cases the officer was not found to have done anything wrong. EIS experts and command-level officers reply that the point of an EIS is to look for *patterns* of officer behavior that may indicate deeper problems. Police commanders argue that a pattern of unsustained citizen complaints that is significantly higher than for other officers, even though none of the complaints was sustained, is an indicator of performance problems that need to be addressed. The fact that an officer uses force, justified or not, significantly more often than other officers is a warning of performance problems that might result in a serious incident in the future.

When all the performance data are analyzed, officers whose conduct exceeds certain thresholds are identified as possibly in need of intervention. The thresholds used by the Los Angeles Sheriff's Department involved 6 or more complaints in the last three years, 6 or more serious uses of force in the last three years, 10 or more less serious uses of force in the last three years, and 2 or more shootings in the last three years.[81]

SIDEBAR 14-3

The Components of an Early Intervention System

Identification
Performance indicators
Analysis of data
Identification of officers with performance problems
Selection
Assessment of identified officers
Selection of officers for intervention
Intervention
Effort to improve officer performance
Supervisor's counseling
Special training
Referral to professional counseling
Follow-Up
Monitor officer's performance, postintervention

Source: Samuel Walker, *Early Intervention Systems for Law Enforcement Agencies: A Planning and Management Guide* (Washington, DC: U.S. Department of Justice, 2003).

There is no consensus of opinion or national standard for the right number of performance indicators, what those indicators should be, or the best thresholds. A rigid formula (e.g., x number of complaints in y months), however, does not take into account different assignments and work environments. An officer assigned to a high-crime neighborhood is likely to use force more often than an officer working a low-crime area, because of the more frequent arrests. As a result, many departments use a peer-group comparison formula, according to which officers are compared to other officers working the same or similar assignment.[82]

Most departments use a two-stage process for identifying and selecting officers for intervention (see Sidebar 14–3). The EIS performance data *identify* officers who might need intervention. In the Los Angeles Sheriff's Department, a committee of command officers reviews these officers and selects some for intervention, called **performance review.** The committee reviews all the available evidence and *selects* some for intervention. There are often legitimate reasons why, for example, an officer had a high number of uses of force (a high level of gang activity and resulting arrests in his or her precinct). Only some officers are finally referred for intervention.[83] In the Los Angeles Sheriff's Department between 1996 and 2002, for example, the EIS identified 1,213 officers for possible intervention, but only 235 (or 19 percent) were selected to be placed on performance review.[84]

performance review

Interventions for Officers

Interventions take many forms, including counseling by the officer's immediate supervisor. Typically, the supervisor discusses the performance problems identified by the EIS and offers advice on how to handle certain situations in a more professional manner and in compliance with department policy. In such instances, the sergeant is playing the coaching role discussed earlier. The intervention might involve retraining on a particular police tactic, as indicated by the EIS data. An officer, for example, might have received many complaints for rudeness in handling traffic stops. The beauty of an EIS is that it can often pinpoint the exact nature of an officer's performance problems. Many officer performance problems are the result of personal issues, such as family problems, alcohol abuse, or financial pressures. The intervention in these cases would involve referral either to the city or country EAP or to professional counseling in the appropriate area.

The existence of an EIS can encourage supervisors to speak to an officer even before he or she has been flagged by the EIS. A PERF report on intervention strategies found some departments in which sergeants said they were able to spot behavior changes in officers that suggested personal problems, such as a normally outgoing officer becoming very quiet and withdrawn, an officer whose joking with fellow officers becomes hostile, or an officer whose paperwork becomes sloppy. The sergeants made an effort to talk with officers informally, often referring them to peer officers who had experienced similar problems for help, or recommending professional counseling.[85]

The Multiple Goals of an EIS

An EIS has several goals, related to different target audiences:

- **Individual officers.** An EIS is designed primarily to improve the performance of officers whose performance indicates they are having problems dealing effectively with citizens.

- **Supervisors.** An EIS can also address problems with supervisors, for example, by identifying sergeants who have a high number of officers under their command who are identified by the EIS data. Merrick Bobb explains that an EIS can "look at the acts of commission and omission by management that allowed the behavior [of rank-and-file officers] to occur in the first place."[86]

- **The department.** An EIS has the capacity to improve a department as a whole by documenting trends in use of force or citizen complaints. It can document that officers from a certain recruit class are more prone to be identified by the system, suggesting either recruitment or training problems specific to that recruit class. The MAPPS system in the New Jersey State Police, according to a monitors' report, "moved beyond [a] narrow focus in its use of MAPPS to focus on systemic organizational issues and to craft solutions to those issues before they negatively impact the organization in any significant way." The New Jersey State Police had moved beyond what was required by the consent decree to engage in proactive problem-solving regarding traffic stops and other issues. For example, it was developing a database on officer off-duty misconduct.[87]

- **Openness and Police–community relations.** An EIS can help improve police–community relations. The department can release aggregate numbers of officers selected for intervention (without officer names because of privacy considerations) and the types of interventions provided as a way of demonstrating to the public that it is monitoring officer conduct and taking appropriate corrective action when needed.

The Effectiveness of an EIS

An officer in a large police department in the southeastern United States was involved in a high number of use-of-force incidents. After she was identified by the department's EIS, the performance review found that she had a special fear of being struck in the face and scarred. Because she was not asserting control of conflict encounters, she was frequently attacked and had to use her baton to gain control. The EIS intervention involved special training in defensive tactics that allowed her to assert control while feeling protected. As a result, her performance improved significantly.[88]

The case described here provides anecdotal evidence about the success of an early intervention system. Other more systematic research also indicates that EISs are successful in reducing officer use of force and citizen complaints. A National Institute of Justice evaluation of three EISs found that they were effective in identifying officers with performance problems and in correcting their performance. In Minneapolis the average number of citizen complaints against officers who were subject to intervention dropped by 67 percent after one year. In the Miami-Dade Police Department, only 4 percent of the officers selected for intervention had no use-of-force reports before intervention, whereas 50 percent had no reports following intervention.[89]

A survey of police managers with EIS experience found positive assessments of their systems. The managers overwhelmingly reported that their EISs improved management and supervision: 65 percent reported a positive effect; 21 percent reported a "mixed" effect; and most important, only 2 percent said that it had a negative effect on management and supervision (12 percent had no opinion). Only 6 percent of managers observed that their EISs had a negative impact on officer morale. Sergeants commented that they had been able to evaluate the strengths and weaknesses of their squads even before meeting with them. Command officers stated that they were now able to intervene with help before misconduct occurred that required discipline.[90]

Managers also reported that their EISs helped to improve supervision. One manager pointed out that the system identifies officers with performance problems and thereby focuses supervisors' efforts to improve the quality of policing.

EISs are far from perfect. In fact, their power and complexity create many problems. A police department with an EIS has to have good records systems on all of the performance indicators. The data have to be accurate and entered into the EIS in a timely fashion. The computer provides data outputs but cannot make judgments about which officers need intervention. And the computer cannot deliver the counseling or retraining needed to improve an officer's performance. Top management in the department has to keep a continuously vigilant eye on the EIS to make sure that all the components work properly and effectively. Many police departments, in fact, have had serious problems in getting and keeping their systems fully up to speed. Investigations in 2015 alone found that the EISs in San Diego and Chicago were not working well.[91]

Risk Management and Police Legal Advisors

Risk management is a process used widely in private industry and in health care agencies to reduce the cost associated with lawsuits against the organization. The basic principle of risk management is that the organization collects systematic data on litigation costs, analyzes the causes of the lawsuits, and takes steps to reduce or eliminate the causes. If a police department is often sued for property damage when

risk management

officers break down doors while serving warrants, for instance, the department can provide officers with training on this issue and/or develop written policies to reduce property damage.

Carol Archbold outlines the five basic components of a risk management program:

1. Identifying risks (for example, high-speed pursuits), the frequency of their occurrence, and the resulting severity of the losses
2. Exploring methods to manage and control the exposure to each of the risks
3. Choosing an appropriate and effective response to manage and control each risk
4. Implementing the response
5. Evaluating the effectiveness of the chosen response[92]

The most aggressive risk management program involved the work of the (now-disbanded) Special Counsel to the Los Angeles Sheriff's Department. Special Counsel Merrick Bobb regularly reported data on the number of suits filed against the department and the annual litigation costs. To help reduce litigation costs, Bobb and his staff investigated and made recommendations for reform in a wide range of issues that result in misconduct and lawsuits, including use of deadly force, use of physical force, foot pursuits, deployment of the canine unit, and many others.[93]

police legal advisor

A related approach to accountability is the **police legal advisor,** a lawyer or team of lawyers employed by the police department itself. The purpose of a police legal advisor is preventive: to review police policies and activities to prevent actions that might violate the law, harm citizens, or produce a lawsuit. The Charlotte-Mecklenburg, North Carolina, police department's Office of the Police Attorney, which reports directly to the chief of police, in 2016 had a staff of five attorneys and two legal assistants. In the past, it published a regular *Police Law Bulletin,* which summarized recent court decisions affecting the police, along with other relevant legal information.[94]

Risk management has not been adopted widely in American law enforcement. Archbold's survey of police legal advisors and risk management units found that none of the 354 law enforcement agencies examined had a risk manager or risk management unit internal to the department. In those departments where there was a risk management unit, it was located in some other office of local government. Few of those departments with a risk management program or a police legal advisor, moreover, collected and published data on the impact of their efforts on litigation costs.[95]

Accreditation for Law Enforcement Agencies

The Nature of Accreditation

accreditation

Accreditation is a process of professional self-regulation, and it is used in virtually all professions: law, medicine, education, and others. An accreditation process for law enforcement was created in 1979. A coalition of the leading professional associations created the Commission on Accreditation for Law Enforcement Agencies (CALEA). The group originally included representatives from the International Association of Chiefs of Police, the National Sheriffs' Association, the National Organization of

Black Law Enforcement Executives, and PERF. CALEA published its first set of standards for law enforcement agencies in 1983 and accredited the first police departments in 1984. By 2009, more than 750 agencies had been accredited.[96]

CALEA establishes minimum standards for all law enforcement agencies. Some standards are mandatory; others are recommended but optional. Some standards are mandatory for large agencies, but not for small ones. The most recent edition of the standards includes more than 445 specific standards. Accredited departments are required, for example, to have a written policy on the use of force and the use of deadly force, a system of written directives for all rules and regulations, an affirmative action plan, a system for handling citizen complaints, and so on.[97]

Pros and Cons of Accreditation

Advocates of accreditation argue that it is an essential aspect of any occupation that aspires to professional status. Self-governance is preferable to regulation and control by external groups, they argue, because members of the profession know the field best.[98] The CALEA website (www.calea.org) has a page titled "Accreditation Works!" It includes statements by police chiefs on how accreditation has benefited their departments. Some examples include the following:[99]

- **Reduced insurance costs.** The chief of the Kingsport, Tennessee, police department (99 sworn officers) reported that accreditation resulted in a $100 per officer reduction in annual insurance costs, for a savings of about $10,000 per year.
- **Improved use-of-force reporting.** The Concord, California, police department reported that the accreditation process pointed out that the department was not following its own policy in reviewing officer use-of-force reports. Accreditation corrected this problem.

Accreditation also has serious limits, however. First, it is a voluntary process. Police departments suffer no penalty for not being accredited. In education, lack of accreditation means that students' credits or degrees may not be accepted by other institutions and that the institution may not be eligible for federal education funds. Second, some critics argue that accreditation process sets only minimum standards but do not define the optimum standards of excellence. That is, they define the "floor" but not the "ceiling." Most of the CALEA standards, for example, require that a department have a written policy on a particular issue. But with the exception of the use of force and a few others, the CALEA standards fail to specify what that policy should be. Third, a number of law enforcement officials believe that the accreditation process is too expensive and time consuming.

External Mechanisms of Accountability

Guiding the Police through the Political Process

In the **American political system,** primary responsibility for the control of law enforcement agencies lies with local city, county and state governments. Elected mayors and city council members control municipal police departments. Mayors choose police chiefs,

American political system

while city councils have a major voice in police departments through the budget. Sheriffs are directly elected by the people, while elected county boards control sheriff's departments' budgets. In the end, these elected officials are the principal ways we hold our law enforcement agencies accountable. Samuel Walker argues that the American police are not "out of control," as many critics of the police charge. Police departments are under the direct control of local officials. The central problem, however, is not "a lack of democratic control, but from a rather well-functioning process of democratic governance in the pursuit of the wrong values": crime control at any cost rather than respectful and constitutional policing; racial superiority rather than equal protection.[100]

As Walker argues, democratic self-government has not always led to professional, respectful, and constitutional policing. As we learned in Chapter 2, American police departments in the nineteenth century were completely corrupt, inefficient, and brutal. The local elected officials wanted it that way: They saw the police department primarily as a source of patronage jobs and payoffs for not enforcing the law. The most blatant example of political control of the police for unjust ends involved the racially segregated states of the Southeast, where enforcing the racial caste system was the principal function of the police.[101]

A century of police reform since the early twentieth century has brought many significant improvements in policing, but it also has left many problems uncorrected. The civil rights movement in the 1960s exposed discriminatory practices in every aspect of policing, from recruitment to the use of excessive force.[102] And in recent years, Justice Department investigations of police misconduct in Ferguson, Missouri, Baltimore, Maryland, and other cities have exposed serious deficiencies in local police departments.

The formal structure of governance for a police or sheriff's department is only the beginning. Elected officials have to make a commitment to high standards of professionalism for their law enforcement agencies and hire competent and committed chief executives.

Although elected officials are the primary means by which law enforcement agencies are held accountable in the American system of constitutional democracy, additional forms of external accountability exist. They include the courts, citizen oversight agencies, the news media, and public interest groups.

The Courts and the Police

The Supreme Court and the Police

In one of the most famous cases ever decided by the U.S. Supreme Court, Cleveland police officers barged into Dolree Mapp's house on May 23, 1957, waving what they said was a search warrant. They had previously been to the house looking for a suspect they thought was hiding there. When they could not find the suspect, they arrested Mapp for possession of obscene literature, which she had in the house. Mapp was convicted, but she appealed and eventually took her case to the Supreme Court. No copy of the alleged search warrant was ever found, either in police files or in any court, and there was strong suspicion that the police did not actually have a warrant. The U.S. Supreme Court overturned Mapp's conviction.[103]

Mapp v. Ohio

The ***Mapp v. Ohio*** (1961) decision is still one of the most controversial in the history of the Supreme Court. The Court ruled that the evidence against Mapp had been obtained illegally, violating her Fourth Amendment right to protection against "unreasonable searches and seizures." The Court imposed the **exclusionary rule,** which holds that "all evidence obtained by searches and seizures in violation of the Constitution is, by that same authority, inadmissible in a state court." The Court had previously applied the exclusionary rule to federal criminal proceedings in 1914 (*Weeks v. United States*). *Mapp* applied the exclusionary rule to state and local police through the Fourteenth Amendment, which holds that no state may deprive one of its citizens' due process of law. Thus, the Court set national standards for all police agencies and assumed the role of policing local police.[104]

exclusionary rule

The judicial branch of government is an important but indirect part of the process of governing the police. Courts at all levels of government play some role in holding the police accountable. At bail settings, preliminary hearings, and trials, local court judges rule on many issues in a way that serve as a check on the police, consistent with the constitutional principle of checks and balances.[105]

The Impact of Supreme Court Decisions

What impact do Supreme Court decisions have on the police? Has the *Mapp* decision eliminated illegal searches? Has **Miranda v. Arizona** ended coercive interrogations and ensured that criminal suspects have an attorney before police questioning becomes accusatory? Or, are the critics of the Supreme Court right that these decisions have made it difficult for the police to fight crime? These questions are part of a 50-year debate over the role of the Supreme Court and the police that continues today.[106]

Miranda v. Arizona

Law professor Paul Cassell was almost single-handedly responsible for bringing a case before the Supreme Court in 2000, asking it to overturn the original *Miranda* decision. Cassell's research estimated that *Miranda* had resulted in serious costs to society's ability to fight crime. Cassell did not succeed, however. In *U.S. v. Dickerson* (2000), the Supreme Court rejected his argument and reaffirmed the *Miranda* warning in a seven-to-two decision. Cassell's efforts were part of a long debate over the impact of the Supreme Court on the police. In this instance, his own evidence did not support his conclusion. He estimated that *Miranda* results in a net loss of convictions in only 3.8 percent of all criminal cases. Many observers did not find this to be a significant impact. And, in fact, 84 percent of the suspects in his study voluntarily waived their *Miranda* rights and confessed.[107]

Richard Leo observed interrogations in one West Coast police department (and observed videotapes of interrogations in others) and found that 78 percent of the suspects waived their *Miranda* rights and talked to the police. He also found, however, that in 30 percent of the cases, the police lied to the suspect by falsely claiming they had a confession from a partner or had some other incriminating evidence. In short, the police found ways to evade the specific intent of *Miranda* through a variety of devices. And they also have found ways to evade the requirements of other Supreme Court decisions such as the exclusionary rule. In short, Supreme Court decisions are not self-enforcing, and they require voluntary cooperation on the part of police officers. (See Sidebar 14–4.)

Despite criticisms of *Mapp v. Ohio*, studies have found that the exclusionary rule does not limit the crime-fighting capacity of the police. The rule is largely confined to drug and weapons cases that raise issues of how the police obtained the evidence. Reviewing criminal cases in Boston, Sheldon Krantz found that "very few

The Long-Term Impact of Supreme Court Decisions: Leo's Argument

Based on his observational studies of the impact of Miranda on interrogations, Richard Leo argues that the decision has had four "profound" long-term effects.

First, "Miranda has had a civilizing influence on police behavior inside the interrogation room." The decision has helped to eliminate the brutal tactics—documented in the 1931 report Lawlessness in Law Enforcement—that the police used to get confessions.

Second, Leo argues, Miranda has helped to change and transform the culture of policing, defining a moral and legal standard that is always in the mind of officers when conducting interrogations.

Third, Miranda and other Supreme Court decisions have heightened public awareness of constitutional rights. Citizens' knowledge of their rights, meanwhile, serves as a check on police behavior, because they feel empowered to challenge unjust officer behavior.

Fourth, Miranda has stimulated the police to develop more sophisticated interrogation techniques. In some respects, this has been a good development, because the police have abandoned coercive or brutal techniques. But at the same time, as Leo's research makes clear, some of the new techniques involve subtle tricks that undermine the spirit and intent of Miranda.

Source: Richard A. Leo and George C. Thomas III, *The Miranda Debate: Law, Justice, and Policing* (Boston: Northeastern University Press, 1998), 217–219.

motions to suppress evidence are raised, and very few of these are granted." Motions to suppress evidence were raised in only 48 of 512 district court cases (or 9.4 percent), and only 10 of those 48 motions were granted. Thus, the defendant was successful in only 20.8 percent of the motions and 1.9 percent of all cases. A General Accounting Office (GAO) study found that defense attorneys filed motions to suppress evidence in only 11 percent of 2,804 cases. Less than 20 percent of those motions were successful, producing an overall success rate of 2.2 percent.[108]

Supporters of the Supreme Court decisions on the police argue that they had three positive effects. First, the Court defined basic principles of due process. Second, decisions such as *Mapp* and *Miranda* created penalties for police misconduct (excluding the evidence or the confession). This served as a basic mechanism of accountability. Third, the decisions stimulated police reform, including improvements in recruitment, training, and supervision.[109]

Myron Orfield's interviews with Chicago narcotics officers found several positive effects of the exclusionary rule. The *Mapp* decision led to better training of officers, including closer supervision of warrants by prosecutors. Detectives were also more likely to use warrants than to conduct impulsive warrantless searches. Many officers indicated that the exclusionary rule was a good thing that helped to maintain high standards of professionalism.[110]

The Supreme Court decisions also increased public awareness about the details of police procedures. This knowledge, and the resulting citizen demands for their rights, constrains the police, preventing many abuses. Increased awareness of individual rights also raises public expectations about police performance and generates pressure for continued police reform.

There are also significant limitations on the Supreme Court as a mechanism of police accountability. First, the Court cannot supervise day-to-day police operations and ensure that officers are complying with its decisions.[111] Second, most police work does not involve an arrest and, therefore, never comes before a court. An individual has a remedy only if he or she is arrested and convicted. Third, the police may or may not be informed about current court decisions. Stephen Wasby found that small-town police in Massachusetts and Illinois did not receive information of Court decisions in a systematic fashion in the 1970s.[112] Fourth, some critics argue that Court-imposed rules only encourage evasion or lying by police officers. Finally, the exercise of rights may become an empty formality, with little real meaning. Both Cassell and Leo, for example, found that most suspects waive their right to silence and agree to be interrogated by the police.

Civil Suits against the Police

Between 2004 and 2014, the City of Chicago paid out about $662 million **damage awards** for police misconduct, an average of about $60 million a year. One case involved a $10.25 million award to a man who spent 26 years in prison after torture by Chicago police officers who coerced him to confess. The City of Baltimore paid out $12 million in damage awards between 2010 and mid-2015. New York City paid $6 million to the family of Eric Garner, whose death was discussed at the beginning of this chapter.[113]

damage awards

Across the country, cities and counties continue to pay out huge settlements in police abuse cases. Yet, there is no revolt among local tax payers. Police departments take no steps to end the officer conduct that lead to these settlements. Mayors and city council members do not demand the necessary police reforms.

Many civil rights activists and lawyers believe that civil suits against police departments for abusive actions will bring about police reform. Their assumption has been that driving up the financial cost of police misconduct will force cities and counties to reform their departments, by improving policies and supervision, so that abuse and the resulting lawsuits and damage awards will decline. The evidence of the continued suits and payouts suggests that the assumption is flawed. The key to the problem is that local governments are irresponsible, particularly with respect to the police, and do not act in a rational and fiscally responsible way. The reality is that, for the most part, one agency of local government commits the abuse, a second agency defends the city in court, and a third agency writes the check to the plaintiffs. There is no feedback, no process of learning from mistakes and taking the appropriate corrective action. Edward Littlejohn's study of police misconduct litigation in Detroit through the 1970s found that suits produced few reforms.[114]

It is also true that, apart from the highly publicized and expensive cases, people who sue the police rarely win, and if they do they do not win much. Lawsuits are expensive and time consuming. If the harm done is only minor, it is difficult to even get a lawyer to take the case. A report on civil litigation on police misconduct found that even among those cases where the plaintiff won, the average award was only 10 percent of the initial claim. The median award, in fact, was only $8,000.[115]

A more positive view of the impact of litigation emerges when we look at the issue from a broader long-term perspective. Charles Epp takes a broad national and long-term perspective in *Making Rights Real*. He argues that since the 1960s litigation against police misconduct has had a profound effect on police accountability. Law enforcement officials and experts began to develop internal accountability procedures in the late 1960s (all of which are discussed in this chapter). Civil rights lawyers, meanwhile, addressed police problems through litigation seeking systemic police reform (for example, in the form of constitutional standards for searches, interrogations, and use of deadly force). Epp argues that the litigators succeeded in "legalizing" the field of accountability, that is, establishing legal standards for a wide range of police activities. (Supreme Court decisions on police practices have the same effect.) As a result, the ever-present threat of litigation has become a driving force behind many police-initiated reforms. In this respect, suits against the police became a dominant force in the development of most of the accountability measures discussed in this chapter.[116]

Law professor Joanna Schwartz identifies another benefit of litigation, arguing that civil suits against police department generate a "vast amount of information" about policing and officer misconduct. Yet, only a "small but growing" number of departments make an effort to use that information "to identify personnel and policy problems."[117] Using litigation information on a systematic basis has the potential to be an extremely valuable accountability mechanism.

The rising cost of civil suits over officer misconduct has prompted some cities and counties to take proactive steps to reduce misconduct. In Los Angeles, following the Rodney King incident, the Los Angeles County Board of Supervisors created the Kolts Commission to study the Los Angeles Sheriff's Department to determine if it had serious problems related to use of force or other issues. The commission found not only a high dollar volume of civil suit payouts but also a small group of deputies with performance records of high rates of misconduct. As a result, the County Board created the Special Counsel to the Los Angeles Sheriff's Department in 1993 as a permanent citizen oversight body to regularly audit the Sheriff's Department. The Los Angeles Sheriff's Department, meanwhile, created an early intervention system to address the issue of officers with performance problems. The result was improvements in several areas of the department. Particularly important, the docket of excessive force lawsuits fell from an average of 300 in fiscal years 1992–1993 and 1993–1994 to about 63 between 2002 and 2004.[118]

Federal "Pattern or Practice" Suits

consent decree

A 1997 **consent decree** against the Pittsburgh Police Department ordered sweeping changes in its management and accountability procedures. The decree ordered the department to develop a data system on all officer uses of force (something it did not have), to create an early intervention system, and to require officers to record the race and ethnicity of all persons they stopped for questioning, including pedestrians and motor vehicle drivers.[119]

The Pittsburgh consent decree was the first of about 30 settlements resulting from lawsuits brought by the Civil Rights Division of the U.S. Department of Justice. The 1994 Violent Crime Control Act authorized the Justice Department to bring

pattern or practice of abuse

civil suits against law enforcement agencies where there is a "**pattern or practice of abuse**" of citizens' rights (see Exhibit 14–2). In addition to Pittsburgh, the Justice Department sued the New Jersey State Police, the LAPD, the Cincinnati, Ferguson, Missouri, and Cleveland police department, among others.[120]

Pattern or practice investigations are settled through a consent decree, a memorandum of agreement (MOA), or an investigative findings letter. A consent decree or a

---

EXHIBIT 14–2

Section 14141, 1994 Violent Crime Control Act

It shall be unlawful for any governmental authority, or any agent thereof, or any person acting on behalf of a governmental authority, to engage in a pattern or practice of conduct by law enforcement officers or by officials or employees of any governmental agency with responsibility for the administration of juvenile justice or the incarceration of juveniles that deprives persons of rights, privileges, or immunities secured or protected by the Constitution or laws of the United States.

MOA involves mandatory reforms related to accountability and is supervised by a federal judge. The judge appoints a monitor to oversee the implementation of the court-ordered reforms. (Investigative findings letters, by contrast, identify problems and recommend certain reforms, but they are not enforced by a court.) The Justice Department defines a "pattern or practice" of police misconduct as more than "sporadic bad incidents or the actions of the occasional bad officer" and requires "information indicating a pattern of misconduct or systemic practices underlying the misconduct."[121]

In addition to federal pattern or practice suits, other cases have been brought by state attorneys general and private plaintiffs. The attorney general of California brought a civil suit against the Riverside, California, police department because of a series of excessive-force incidents. The suit resulted in a consent decree similar to those in the cases brought by the Justice Department.[122] In Oakland, California, a private lawsuit involving abuses by a secret gang of officers in the department (the "Riders") resulted in a settlement that was essentially identical to the federal consent decrees.[123]

Pattern or Practice Case Reforms

The settlements in the Justice Department "pattern or practice" cases embody a common set of reforms, which include the following:

- **Use-of-force policy, reporting, documentation, and review.** Settlements have ordered police departments to develop a state-of-the-art policy on officer use of force; to require officers to complete use-of-force incident reports immediately after each incident; to require sergeants to critically review officer reports; and to require the department to systematically review use-of-force incidents.

- **Early intervention system.** Settlements have required police departments to create an EIS, which can monitor officer performance, identify officers with performance problems, and provide interventions to correct those performance problems.

- **Improved citizen complaint procedures.** Settlements have required police departments to revise their procedures for receiving and investigating citizen complaints, to make them more open and accessible to potential complainants.

- **Officer training.** Consent decrees generally require improvements in training to cover new use-of-force policies and other departmental changes.

The more recent federal consent decrees have added provisions for a formal community voice in the implementation of the required reforms. In Seattle, for example, the Community Police Commission had a direct role in the development of the new use-of-force policy for the Seattle Police Department and the inclusion of a de-escalation component in that policy. Adding a community voice to the reform process, it is believed, gives the consent decree and its reforms greater credibility and legitimacy among community members. Additionally, recent federal consent decrees have given police union representatives a role in the reform process, as members of the Community Police Commission in Seattle and in Cleveland, Ohio.[124]

The settlement of the federal investigation of the Cincinnati Police Department was unique because it paralleled a separate settlement of several private race discrimination suits against the police department. The Justice Department settlement ordered accountability-related reforms similar to those in other cities. The settlement of the private lawsuits, labeled the Collaborative Agreement, ordered the police department to adopt problem-oriented policing and to work closely with community groups in developing new strategies for addressing crime and disorder. The Cincinnati Collaborative Agreement is the only settlement that has ordered a department to change its policing strategy.[125]

The Cincinnati Collaborative Agreement has proven to be extremely influential, as the Justice Department began including a similar model of community involvement in its settlements in Seattle, Cleveland, and other cities. The federal judge in the New York City stop and frisk case, meanwhile, also ordered a collaborative process for developing the new stop and frisk policies, training, and supervision for the NYPD.[126]

The Role of Court-Appointed Monitors

independent monitor

Consent decree and MOA settlements include the appointment by the court of an **independent monitor.** Monitors have several functions. The most important are to oversee implementation of the court-ordered reforms and to report on progress to the judge. Monitors also assist police department in implementing the reforms, serving as a resource in providing model use-of-force policies or training programs, for example. Monitors also prod departments that are not making progress. The monitor in Washington, D.C., for example, reported in June 2002 that "[d]espite substantial efforts in the past several months to compensate for an extraordinarily slow start, [the department] has failed to accomplish virtually all of the milestones identified in the MOA within the time periods specified."[127] The monitor's prodding played a major role in prodding the department to make a greater effort, and by 2008 it had made substantial progress in implementing the required reforms.

The Impact of Consent Decrees

Do consent decrees and MOAs achieve their intended results? Are the court-ordered reforms actually implemented, and are departments more accountable as a result? In each case, the federal judge lifts the consent decree only when the monitor reports that the police department has substantially complied with all the required reforms. The monitor in the New Jersey State Police case, for example, concluded in December 2007 that the "New Jersey State Police appear to have reached a watershed moment during the last two reporting periods. Ample evidence exists to suggest that the agency has become self-monitoring and self-correcting to a degree not often observed in American law enforcement.[128] Similarly, the monitor in Cincinnati in August 2008 found that the "City of Cincinnati is now in a very different situation than it was in 2002. In the five years of the MOA and the six years of the [Collaborative Agreement], the City made significant changes in the way it polices Cincinnati. The CPD has improved its training, its policies and procedures, its investigations of uses of force and citizen complaints, its risk management and its accountability."[129] Monitors' reports, however, do not address the question of whether the reforms in the department in question will endure or simply fade away if the department returns to its previous unprofessional ways.

The most thorough evaluation to date is the 2009 Harvard University evaluation of the LAPD under a consent decree. The evaluation concluded that Los Angeles police officers were working harder and smarter. "We found the LAPD much changed from eight years ago," it reported. Public satisfaction had risen, with 83 percent of the public saying the department is now "doing a good or excellent job." Particularly important, "the frequency of the use of serious force has fallen each year since 2004." Although some officers feel that the requirements of the consent decree inhibit their law enforcement activity, "there is no objective sign of so-called 'de-policing'" (the idea that officers reduce their enforcement activities out of fear of being disciplined). In fact, since the consent decree took effect, the number of both pedestrian stops and motor vehicle stops since 2002 had doubled, but particularly important, a greater percentage of stops resulted in arrest. This suggests that the stops were "good stops," based on legitimate legal reasons and not illegitimate stops based on race or ethnicity.[130]

In short, these evaluations indicate court-ordered reform, supported by an independent monitor, can bring about significant change in a large, previously troubled police department. Samuel Walker and Morgan Macdonald argue that federal intervention is an effective and necessary response to "troubled" police departments that, before Justice Department intervention, had seemed to be incapable of reforming themselves.[131]

Further evidence about the positive impact of federal pattern or practice cases comes from police chiefs and command officers who have been through the experience. As commissioner of the Washington, D.C., police department, Charles Ramsey had actually invited the Justice Department to investigate. He argued that "the end result was very positive. Shootings dropped 80 percent and ... remained low." Also, "it gave us credibility with the public." An LAPD commander said that although the consent decree eventually cost $15 million, "the money was well spent in terms of preventing future litigation and gaining credibility with the community."[132]

Nonetheless, controversy over the impact of federal pattern or practice investigations continues. Some critics argue that the court-ordered reforms are too expensive for local governments.[133] The issue of the "cost" for court-ordered reforms is complex. As noted earlier, many police departments have been paying out huge damage awards related to police misconduct. Reducing those costs is a net savings that offsets the cost of the reforms. Additionally, police misconduct imposes huge human and social costs in terms of people who are shot and killed or physically abused by the police. These costs are borne by the individuals involved, their families, and the communities in which they live. The broader cost to community relations cannot be measured by standard accounting methods. Others worry about the danger that the reforms will not endure over the long haul and that departments will revert to their old ways. There remains, however, the question of whether court-ordered reforms will endure and a consent decree is ended.[134]

The Collaborative Reform Team Approach: An Alternative to Litigation

The Office of Community Oriented Policing Services (popularly known as the COPS Office) in the U.S. Justice Department developed three new technical assistance programs as alternatives to seeking police reform through litigation. The Collaborative Reform, Critical Response, and Research and Best Practices programs are voluntary and initiated when a police department requests assistance. By mid-2016, the Collaborative Reform program was involved with 12 police departments, including Milwaukee and San Francisco. The Critical Response program, meanwhile, was involved with 11 departments, including San Diego, Minneapolis, and Tampa.[135]

collaborative reform

      Collaborative reform is a comprehensive "long-term, holistic strategy" that seeks to "improve trust between police agencies and the communities they serve" through "organizational transformation." With its emphasis on organizational change, collaborative reform resembles the Civil Rights Division's "pattern or practice" litigation approach, except that it is voluntary.

      In 2012, the Collaborative Reform program completed an investigation of officer-involved shootings in the Las Vegas Metropolitan Police Department, conducted by an independent consulting group, CNA. The department requested assistance in response to public controversy over a series of fatal shootings by department officers, a series of critical articles in a local newspaper, and the possibility of a community request for a Justice Department civil rights investigation. The investigation found significant deficiencies in the use-of-force policy, training, and investigation of shooting incidents, and made a set of recommendations for reform in each area. With respect to the investigation of shooting incidents, for example, the report recommended the department restore the previously abolished specialized Force Investigation Team to ensure "accurate, thorough, and fair investigations" of officer-involved shootings. With respect to training, the investigation found that the department did not require training on de-escalation, and recommended that it make de-escalation training an annual requirement.[136] The investigation found that tactical errors by officers often contributed in some way to the ultimate use of deadly force. They included many radio communications problems, such as miscommunications with the dispatcher and failure to use the radio to update officers en route to the scene, officers getting too close to a potentially dangerous person and officers failing to slow down the unfolding events and gain time to make better tactical decisions.[137] The findings were consistent with the recommendations of the 2015 PERF report *Re-Engineering Training on Police Use of Force,* discussed in Chapter 5.[138]

      Some civil rights activists oppose the Collaborative Reform and Critical Incident programs because, unlike consent decrees, they lack a court-enforced reform element. The Justice Department's Special Litigation Section, which conducts the pattern or practice investigations, however, is a very small unit, and does not have the staff needed to investigate every police department where abuses exist. Additionally, the fact that a number of abuse cases exist in a given police department does not necessarily mean that a pattern or practice of violations of civil rights exists, one that is sufficient to support a consent decree.

Injunctions to Stop Patterns of Police Misconduct

In response to police practices that systematically violate citizen rights, some civil rights groups have sought court injunctions against the police department ordering an end to alleged practices. If, for example, police officers are systematically stopping, questioning, and frisking all African American males in a community—without regard for individualized suspicion—members of that group can seek an injunction ordering the practice stopped. Injunctions, however, have not been an effective remedy for police misconduct. In *Rizzo v. Goode* (1976), the U.S. Supreme Court held that the plaintiffs had failed to prove that the police chief and other city officials were directly responsible for the alleged police misconduct, and had not proved that the plaintiffs themselves were likely to be the targets of this misconduct in the future.[139] In short, injunctions have never been an effective tool for police accountability.

Criminal Prosecution of Police Officers

In the 2014 Ferguson, Missouri, controversy over the fatal shooting of Michael Brown, the refusal of the local grand jury to indict the officer who shot him provoked further public outrage and protests. In fact, criminal prosecutions of police officers are extremely rare. Between 2005 and 2014, an average of only five officers were charged with murder or manslaughter, and only one in five were convicted. The number of indictments rose to 12 in the first 10 months of 2015, largely because of the intense public interest in police shootings since the Ferguson events.[140]

Successful **criminal prosecution** of a police officer is extremely difficult. First, local prosecutors routinely work closely with the police and are reluctant to bring criminal charges against them. The Criminal Division of the U.S. Justice Department is extremely small and has responsibility for many other types of criminal activity.[141] Second, in the case of allegations of police use of excessive force, it is often difficult to prove that the officer had *criminal intent*. A police officer can always claim that his or her actions were a legitimate exercise of police powers under the circumstances (for example, that the person was violently resisting). The successful 1993 conviction on federal charges of three Los Angeles police officers involved in the Rodney King beating was a relatively rare exception (and it followed their acquittal on state criminal charges the year before). Convictions are much easier to obtain in corruption cases, where there is less ambiguity about the facts than there is in use-of-force cases. Third, convictions are difficult to obtain because, as a Vera Institute report concluded, juries are often sympathetic to police officers and "suspicious of victims" of police abuse.[142]

Criminal prosecution by itself appears to have limited deterrent effect in departments where other effective controls do not exist. A number of New York City police officers were prosecuted and convicted in the scandals of the 1970s and 1980s, yet the Mollen Commission found serious criminal law violations in the 1990s.[143] Evidently, the officers were not deterred by the prosecutions and convictions in the previous years.

criminal prosecution

Citizen Oversight of the Police

Since the 1960s, civil rights groups have demanded citizen oversight of police departments. They argue that police departments do not investigate citizen complaints thoroughly or fairly, and as a result police misconduct goes unpunished. As an alternative, civil rights groups have demanded the creation of **citizen oversight** (also called external review or civilian review) of the police. Citizen oversight is defined as a process by which people who are not sworn officers are involved in some way in the review of citizen complaints against police officers or police department policies and practices. Citizen oversight rests on the assumption that, because of the police subculture, police officers cannot objectively investigate complaints against fellow officers. Citizen oversight has grown tremendously since the early 1980s. In almost all big cities, there is now some form of oversight agency.[144] Additionally, there is a national professional association of citizen oversight staff and board members, the National Association for Civilian Oversight of Law Enforcement (NACOLE).[145]

Historically, police departments were hostile to people seeking to file a complaint against an officer. The Kerner Commission, appointed to study the riots of the 1960s, found many instances of complainants being turned away for trying to file a complaint. The police regarded complaints as threats to their authority.[146] Today, there is a new paradigm for citizen complaints. First, a complaint represents a citizen exercising his or her First Amendment right to petition government. A fair and thorough review should then determine whether the complaint is justified. Second, police officials now recognize that citizen complaints are a valuable source of management information about the quality of policing. Even when complaints are not sustained, they are an indicator of possible performance problems for certain officers or with regard to certain situations (for example, the handling of homeless people). For this reason, all complaints need to be accepted, investigated, and then reviewed. Complaints are a standard performance indicator in early intervention systems.[147]

There are now two models of citizen oversight of the police: civilian review boards and police auditors/inspectors general, with different missions based on different models of police reform (see Exhibit 14–3).[148]

EXHIBIT 14–3

Two Models of Citizen Oversight

	Civilian Review Boards	Police Auditors/ Inspectors General
Primary activity	Review citizen complaints	Investigate department policies and practices
Output	Findings on merits of complaints	Reports on problems in the department, with recommendations for improvement
Goals	Thorough and fair investigations of complaint; recommendations for discipline, where appropriate	Improve the organizations

Civilian Review Boards

A **civilian review board** is a local agency independent of the police or sheriff's depart-   civilian review board
ment, with the responsibility of reviewing citizen complaints against the police. After
its review, the agency makes a recommendation to the chief about the disposition of the
complaint: sustained, unsustained, unfounded, or exonerated. The recommendations
are not binding, however.

There are many varieties of civilian review boards. The San Francisco Office
of Citizen Complaints, the New York Civilian Complaint Review Board (CCRB),
and the Washington, D.C., Office of Police Complaints have original jurisdiction
over citizen complaints, meaning that they conduct the investigation of all complaints. Other review boards review the internal affairs complaint investigation file.
They have the authority to agree or disagree with the internal affairs investigation.
Some have the authority to send a case file back to internal affairs if it finds that the
investigation was inadequate.[149]

Civilian review boards have a mixed record. Overall, they sustain only about
10 percent of all the complaints they review. In 2014, the New York City CCRB
substantiated ("sustained") only 3.9 percent of all force allegations, which was actually twice the 2013 figure of 1.8 percent.[150] The San Francisco Office of Citizen
Complaints, meanwhile, sustained 8.2 percent of all complaints in 2014.[151] Most
review boards have limited investigatory power. Most do not have subpoena power
and cannot compel the testimony of the police officer against whom the complaint
was made or any witness officers. Most review boards also do not have the staff resources that would allow them to investigate and develop additional information
about complaints.

Police Auditors or Inspectors General

The second form of citizen oversight is the **police auditor or inspector general.**   police auditor or
These agencies do not investigate individual citizen complaints. Instead, their role   inspector general
is to audit, investigate, or monitor the policies and practices of the police department.
This includes the complaint process; policies on use of force and other police actions; and procedures related to traffic stops, foot pursuits, civil litigation against the
department, or any other aspect of the department. Auditor/inspector generals have
an unrestricted mandate in terms of what they choose to investigate. After examining
an issue, they issue public reports with recommendations. They do not have the
power to force their recommendations to be adopted, but their reports play an important role in transparency, providing detailed fact-based information about particular
police practices. The information is particularly valuable for the public, elected officials, and the news media. The process is sometimes referred to as **policy review.**   policy review
The San Jose Independent Police Auditor, for example, has made more than 100
policy recommendations since it was established in 1993. In their study of stops and
frisks by the police, White and Fradella argue that the police auditor model of citizen
oversight can, on an on-going basis, be an effective way of ensuring that a department's stop and frisk practices are consistent with the law and department policy.[152]

New York City created an inspector general in 2013, and it soon issued a series
of reports on lawsuits against the police department, the NYPD's use-of-force policies, and body-worn cameras. The report on lawsuits, for instance, found that in the

previous decade lawsuits had cost the city over $202 million and recommended that the police department, the city Comptroller's Office and the Law Department could do a much better job of collecting and analyzing litigation data and identifying ways to improve the quality of policing.[153]

Goals and Objectives of Oversight Agencies

Civilian review boards and police auditors/inspector generals have different goals and objectives. Review boards focus on individual complaints for the purpose of determining whether or not the police officer is guilty of abusing the citizen and/or violating department rules. The basic goal is to ensure justice in individual cases. An underlying assumption is that independent review of citizen complaints will result in more discipline of officers, and more discipline in turn will deter future misconduct more effectively than the traditional internal affairs investigation of complaints. Police auditors, by contrast, focus on the organization, with the goal of bringing about organizational change. (In this respect, police auditors have the same goal as Justice Department pattern or practice investigations.) The long-term goal is to effect change that will prevent future misconduct.[154]

community outreach   **Community outreach** is one activity through which review boards and police auditors seek to increase public understanding. Outreach activities can include neighborhood meetings, public forums on particular issues or controversies, publishing brochures explaining police operations and the complaint process, and publishing reports on issues of concern to the public. The Office of Police Complaints in Washington, DC, for example, has regularly investigated and made recommendations on a wide range of police issues.[155]

Citizen Oversight: Pro and Con

Police critics of citizen oversight argue that (1) it intrudes on the professional independence of the police, (2) people who are not police officers are not qualified to review police operations, (3) it is expensive and unnecessarily duplicates the work of internal affairs, and (4) internal affairs units sustain more complaints against police officers.[156] Advocates of citizen review, by contrast, argue that it serves to open up police departments, ending their historic isolation from the public. They cite evidence that the number of citizen complaints is higher in cities with some form of external review, suggesting that it enhances public confidence in the complaint process.[157]

There have been few evaluations of citizen review procedures. Part of the difficulty is that citizen complaint review agencies have multiple goals: providing a more satisfactory complaint review process for both complainants and officers; conducting thorough and fair complaints investigations; sustaining more complaints than police internal affairs units; helping to discipline more officers than in the past; deterring future officer misconduct; improving public attitudes about the police. Police auditors/inspectors general are more easily evaluated: identifying recommendations made for departmental policy change; assessing the adoption of recommendations; evaluating the impact of the policy changes on the quality of policing.[158]

In short, some forms of citizen review appear to be relatively more effective than others. Effectiveness depends on several factors, including the agency's definition of its role, its resources, the quality of its staff, and the degree of political support it receives from the community.

Blue-Ribbon Commissions

In April 2016, the Chicago Police Accountability Task Force issued a blistering report on problems in the Chicago Police Department. In blunt terms, it cited a long history of race discrimination by police officers, particularly with regard to fatal shootings of citizens. It also found that the existing police accountability mechanisms did not function effectively, including both the internal police department systems and the external Independent Police Review Authority. The report concluded with a broad set of recommendations for reform.[159]

The 2016 Chicago Police Accountability Task Force and the 2015 President's Task Force on 21st Century Policing are the latest in a long line of "blue-ribbon" commissions that have investigated the police in America.[160] **Blue-ribbon commissions** are special one-time groups that investigate a problem and issue a report with recommendations for change. There have been both national and local commissions on the police. National commissions bring together the leading experts in the field and define minimum standards for the police that can then be used to seek improvements in local departments.

blue-ribbon commissions

Earlier blue-ribbon commissions have included the 1931 Wickersham Commission, which issued a powerful exposé of the "third degree," defined as "the inflicting of pain, physical or mental, to extract confessions or statements" from suspected criminals.[161] The President's Crime Commission (1965–1967) sponsored important research on the police, particularly the work of Albert J. Reiss and Donald Black, referred to many times in this book.[162] The 1968 Kerner Commission investigated the causes of the 1960s riots. The 1991 Christopher Commission examined the problems in the LAPD following the beating of Rodney King earlier that year.

The great weakness of blue-ribbon commissions, however, is that they are temporary agencies that disband after issuing their final reports. As a result, they have no enforcement powers to implement their recommendations, and no ability to do follow-up and monitor whether their recommendations are implemented. The President's Task Force on 21st Century Policing has attempted to overcome this problem by issuing a separate implementation guide.[163] Samuel Walker argues that this limitation has been overcome by the new institution of the police auditor or inspector general, described earlier in this chapter.[164]

The Digital Revolution and Police Accountability

Someone with a cell phone camera just happened to be watching on April 4, 2015, when a North Charleston, South Carolina, police officer shot and killed 50-year-old Walter Scott as he was running away. Scott was unarmed, and there was no threat of any kind to the officer. The cell phone video was broadcast across the country, adding fuel to the national fire over police shootings that had begun in August 2014 in Ferguson, Missouri. It was one of several incidents of police shootings or excessive force to be recorded in the tumultuous period that began with Ferguson.

The **digital revolution in communications** is revolutionizing police accountability. Cell phone cameras are everywhere and can quickly and inexpensively record

digital revolution in communications

police officers at work. As in the North Charleston case, people can see firsthand incidents of police misconduct. The revolution began on March 3, 1991, when George Holliday recorded the beating of Rodney King by Los Angeles police officers on a videotape.[165] Many people in America once believed that completely unjustified police shootings simply did not occur. Now they can see such things on the evening news. We don't yet know the full impact of the digital revolution, but it will certainly be profound.

Cell phone cameras are only one part of the revolution. Possibly even more profound in terms of impact are police-worn body cameras, which are rapidly being adopted by police departments, and which record police encounters of all varieties in terms of seriousness. They will provide the best record of police encounters we will ever have. Even so, the resulting recordings are not a perfect record of what happens. Some things can happen—possibly important things—before the office turns on the camera. And the camera does not record things that are outside the view of its lens. Nonetheless, the recordings are far more complete and objective than the later testimony of either the officer or the person.

At this point in time we do not know exactly what the impact of body cameras and other new technologies will be. Nor do we know what new technologies might develop in the near future. The only thing we can be certain of is that whatever develops will almost certainly have an impact on police accountability.

The News Media as a Police Accountability Mechanism

The fatal shooting of Michael Brown in Ferguson, Missouri, touched off a national controversy over police shootings. As reporters dug into the subject, it was revealed that there was no reliable count of the number of people shot and killed by the police each year. A team of reporters from the *Washington Post* began a systematic count of all shootings in 2015, using every possible source (official reports, local news media accounts, social media, and the like). Their story, "Final Tally," in January 2016 reported that the police had shot and killed 986 people in 2015. The shocking part of the story was that this figure was about twice what the FBI had been reporting every year (444 in 2014, for example).[166]

The *Post* story of police shootings is the most recent example of how the news media function as a form of police accountability: investigating, assembling facts, and reporting a story that has a significant impact on public knowledge about policing. There have been many similar examples in the past. *New York Times* reporter David Burnham in a front-page story of April 25, 1970, almost single-handedly exposed one of the biggest corruption scandals in the history of the NYPD. The scandal is often referred by the name "Serpico," after NYPD officer Frank Serpico, who testified against corrupt officers. Following Burnham's revelations, the mayor of New York appointed the Knapp Commission to investigate corruption in the NYPD. A number of officers were convicted of corrupt acts, and the mayor brought in Patrick V. Murphy as police commissioner to clean up the department.[167]

In Chicago, activist journalists and lawyers with the Invisible Institute created the Citizens Police Data Project, and after many years of effort, succeeded in late 2015 in obtaining the release of 56,000 misconduct complaint records involving more than 8.500 Chicago police officers. In October 2016, public records requests by Chicago's two major daily newspapers succeeded in obtaining the release of 125,180 complaint records reaching back to 1967. Both sets of documents provided an unprecedented view of alleged officer misconduct and how the Chicago police department responded to citizen complaints.[168]

The news media play an important role in police accountability.[169] On a day-to-day basis, the media report on what the police are doing, including everything from human interest stories in which an officer saves a child's life to officer misconduct in a major excessive-force incident. Media accounts inform the public and elected officials and, it is hoped, help them to make intelligent political choices related to policing.

At the same time, the news media often contribute to police problems. First, they tend to emphasize sensational stories, especially violent crimes, and do not provide balanced coverage of routine police activities which are mainly not dramatic. As a result, the media present a distorted picture of police work by focusing primarily on crime-fighting. The media tend to emphasize the negative aspects of policing. They will give considerable coverage to a questionable shooting by a police officer, for example, but not cover the fact that there are long periods with no shootings. One of the unwritten rules of the news media is that good news is not news.

Public Interest Groups and Accountability

The Center for Constitutional Rights sued the NYPD over its aggressive stop and frisk program, charging that it violated both the Fourth Amendment protection against unreasonable searches and seizures and the Fourteenth Amendment guarantee of equal protection of the law. The case lasted for more than 10 years, and in 2013, a federal District Court agreed, ordering the NYPD to reform its policies, training, and supervision.[170]

The New York stop and frisk case is only one example of the role that **public interest groups** have played in police accountability. Historically, civil rights and civil liberties groups at both the national and local levels have challenged abusive and unconstitutional police practices. In 1999, the American Civil Liberties Union (ACLU) issued the report *Driving While Black,* which was the first national report on racial profiling in traffic enforcement.[171] Forty-five years earlier, the ACLU of Ohio filed an amicus brief in the *Mapp v. Ohio* case, which influenced the Supreme Court in its landmark decision on the exclusionary rule.[172]

public interest groups

The ACLU is a private, nonprofit public interest organization. Private groups play an important role in police accountability. For the most part, they have been involved in attacking police misconduct. The National Association for the Advancement of Colored People (NAACP) has a long record of fighting police use of excessive force against African Americans.[173] The ACLU was responsible for some of the most important Supreme Court cases involving the police. ACLU briefs were the basis for the Court's decisions in the landmark *Mapp* and *Miranda* cases, for example. The ACLU has been the leading advocate of citizen review of the police in New York City, Los Angeles, and many other cities. At the same time, the ACLU has defended the rights of police officers in cases involving, for example, grooming standards and department investigations of alleged police misconduct. The ACLU has published a handbook on *The Rights of Police Officers.*

Accountability and Crime Control: A Trade-Off?

Traditionally, many people have argued that a trade-off exists between accountability and effective crime control. In the 1960s, for example, critics of the police argued that the exclusionary rule (*Mapp. v. Ohio*), which excluded illegally obtained evidence of criminal cases, and the *Miranda* warning (*Miranda v. Arizona*), which guaranteed criminal suspects a right to remain silent, hindered police crime-fighting efforts.[174] In recent years, critics of consent decrees resulting from Justice Department civil rights investigations argue that the required strict policies on officer use of force and reporting requirements hinder the police.

accountability and crime control

The tension between **accountability and crime control** was best framed by Herbert Packer in his classic essay "Two Models of the Criminal Process." The crime control model envisions fewer formal restraints on criminal justice officials (and not just the police) for the purpose of effective crime control. The due process model envisions strict rules of procedures to govern criminal justice officials for the purpose of protecting the rights of citizens.

Increasing evidence, however, suggests that the accountability–crime control dichotomy is a false one. David Bayley argues forcefully that the alleged conflict between accountability (including formal due-process requirements) and crime control is a false dichotomy.[175] Several recent developments support the argument that strict accountability does not hinder effective crime control. These developments include the following:

- The Harvard University evaluation of the LAPD under a federal consent decree found that both officer uses of force and the crime rate decreased under the consent decree. In addition, police enforcement activities (traffic and street stops) increased during the period.[176]

- In New York City, the crime rate began to decrease before the police department sharply increased the number of stops and frisks, and crime remained low after it backed off and drastically reduced the number of stops and frisks.[177]

- In Chicago, a new department policy on stops and searches resulted in a dramatic decline in stops and pat-downs (frisks), from 157,346 in early 2015 to 20,908 in an equivalent period in early 2016. Yet, this 87 percent decline in stops and pat-downs was accompanied by only a 6.9 percent reduction in the number of guns seized (from 1,413 to 1,316).[178] Chicago was experiencing a sharp increase in gun violence in early 2016, and some people blamed the restrictions on police stops and pat-downs. But in fact, the police were no less effective in seizing guns than they had been before the new policy went into effect.

The evidence strongly suggests that in Los Angeles, New York City, and Chicago, the police were "working smarter." They were complying with the law, court decisions, and department policies on respecting the rights of people, but with no adverse effect on their crime fighting activities. Samuel Walker argues that lawful and respectful policing positively contributes to more effective crime-fighting. If police officers are stopping people because of their race and/or without reasonable suspicion or probable cause, they are not only violating peoples' rights but also are wasting valuable police time with people who are not engaged in crime. When abusive tactics are stopped, police officers have more time available for carefully focused crime fighting activities that are more likely to be effective.[179]

Conclusion: A Mixed Approach to Police Accountability

There is no single best approach to police accountability. The situation in the United States today represents a **mixed approach to police accountability,** a blend of internal and external mechanisms (see Exhibit 14–4). In important respects, this reflects the concept of checks and balances, which is one of the fundamental principles of American democracy. Elected officials have significant control over police departments, but not total control. Police administrators have a great deal of autonomy, but not complete autonomy. The courts have some influence over policing, but only in limited areas. Citizens have some input, but not direct control over police operations. Viewed from a historical perspective, there has been a shift in the mix of internal and external forms of accountability. Direct political interference in policing declined as a result of the professionalization movement. Some other forms of external accountability—particularly the courts and citizen review—have grown in recent decades. At the same time, some forms of internal accountability have also grown, with the development of better mechanisms for the control of misconduct and the supervision of routine police work.

mixed approach to police accountability

EXHIBIT 14–4

A Mixed Approach to Police Accountability

Measures of Police Effectiveness
> The crime rate
> The clearance rate
> Regular surveys of public attitudes
> Systematic COMPSTAT data

Internal Mechanisms of Accountability
> Routine supervision of police officers
> Command-level review of force incidents
> Meaningful discipline of officers
> Early intervention systems
> Risk management and police legal advisors
> Accreditation of law enforcement agencies

External Mechanisms of Accountability
> Guiding the police through the political process
> Court decisions on police practices
> Civil suits against the police
> Federal "pattern or practice" suits
> The collaborative team approach
> Criminal prosecution of police officers
> Citizen oversight of the police
> Blue-ribbon commissions
> The digital revolution and police accountability
> The news media
> Public interest groups

CASE STUDY

Policing Los Angeles under a Consent Decree:
The Dynamics of Change at the LAPD: Executive Summary

The Los Angeles Police Department is today completing one of the most ambitious experiments in police reform ever attempted in an American city. After a decade of policing crises that began with the beating of Rodney King in 1991 and culminated in the Rampart police corruption scandal in 1999, the U.S. Department of Justice announced in May 2000 that it had accumulated enough evidence to sue the City of Los Angeles over a pattern-or-practice of police misconduct. Later that year, the city government entered a "consent decree" promising to adopt scores of reform measures under the supervision of the Federal Court.

The experiment in police reform in Los Angeles has two components: the consent decree produced by the Justice Department's intervention, and the leadership of Chief William Bratton, who since 2002 has focused the Department's attention simultaneously on reducing crime, improving morale, and complying fully with the consent decree. What has the experience in Los Angeles revealed about policing under a consent decree? Has the consent decree achieved its purpose? How is the Los Angeles Police Department controlling its use of force? What is the state of police-community relations? How rigorous is the governance and oversight of the LAPD? And how is the culture of the Department changing? Most importantly, as the LAPD has incorporated the policies and practices specified in the consent decree into its own operations and management, has the Department won the public's trust and confidence while reducing crime and bringing offenders to justice?

To answer those questions, we examined the LAPD using multiple research methods. We undertook hundreds of hours of participant observation from patrol to the command staff; we analyzed administrative data on crime, arrests, stops, civilian complaints, police personnel, and the use of force. We compiled surveys conducted over the last decade of police officers and residents of Los Angeles, and then conducted three surveys of our own, one of residents, another of LAPD officers, and a third of detainees recently arrested by the LAPD. Finally, we conducted a series of formal focus groups and structured interviews with police officers, public officials, and residents of Los Angeles. While some questions remain unanswered, this ranks among the most comprehensive assessments ever conducted of a police department outside of a time of crisis.

We found the LAPD much changed from eight years ago, and even more so in the last four or five years. Public satisfaction is up, with 83 percent of residents saying the LAPD is doing a good or excellent job; the frequency of the use of serious force has fallen each year since 2004. Despite the views of some officers that the consent decree inhibits them, there is no objective sign of so-called "de-policing" since 2002; indeed, we found that both the quantity and quality of enforcement activity have risen substantially over that period. The greater *quantity* is evident in the doubling of both pedestrian stops and motor vehicle stops since 2002, and in the rise in arrests over that same period. The greater *quality of stops* is evident in the higher proportion resulting in an arrest, and the *quality of arrests* is evident in the higher proportion in which the District Attorney files felony charges.

Our analysis confirmed what others have previously reported: that serious crime is down substantially in Los Angeles over this same period. Indeed, recorded crime is down in every police division in the city. A majority of Los Angeles residents no longer rate crime as a big problem, substantially down from only four years ago, and that is true among Black and Hispanic as well as White and Asian residents.

We asked residents specifically if they think the LAPD could police effectively while also respecting people's rights and policing within the law. More than twice as many residents see improvement than see deterioration, and the vast majority of each racial and ethnic group is hopeful that this kind of policing will soon be routine.

Both the management and the governance of the LAPD have also changed for the better under the decree. The officer tracking system known as TEAMS II is forcing supervisors to pay attention to officers who attract more civilian complaints or more frequently use force than their peers; and the management tool known as COMPSTAT has helped to transform the Department's captains into strategic commanders, accountable for reducing crime while maintaining integrity and building public trust in police, one of several initiatives that go well beyond what the consent decree requires. In terms of governance, the Police Commission and the Inspector General have, in particular, enhanced the scrutiny of the Department's use of force, and of its handling of civilian complaints.

We found persistent differences in the experience of policing among Hispanic residents of LA and more so for Black residents. More than two-thirds of Hispanic and Black residents think well of the job the LAPD is doing today, rating it as good or excellent; yet a substantial minority within each of these groups remains unsatisfied with the Department, and ten percent of Black residents report that almost none of the LAPD officers they encounter treat them and their friends and families with respect. We therefore found it encouraging that, when looking ahead to the next three years, Black residents of Los Angeles are among the most hopeful about the Department.

In sum, the evidence here shows that with both strong police leadership and strong police oversight, cities can enjoy both respectful and effective policing. The LAPD remains aggressive and is again proud, but community engagement and partnership is now part of the mainstream culture of the Department. The Department responds to crime and disorder with substantial force, but it is scrutinizing that force closely and it is accountable through many devices for its proper use. Will the management and oversight improvements persist if the consent decree ends? Better yet, will management and oversight become still stronger? While we cannot answer those questions in advance, the LAPD appears ready for that test.

Source: Christopher Stone, Todd Foglesong, and Christine M. Cole, "Executive Summary," *Policing Los Angeles Under a Consent Decree: The Dynamics of Change at the LAPD* (Cambridge, MA: Harvard Kennedy School, 2009), www.hks.harvard.edu/var/ezp_site/storage/fckeditor/file/pdfs/centers-programs/programs/criminal-justice/Harvard_LAPD_Report.pdf.

SUMMARY

Accountability of the police is a very complex subject. The two main issues involve accountability for police organizations and accountability for individual officers. There are no generally accepted accountability mechanisms that cover the many responsibilities of police organizations. The official crime rate has many flaws and covers only one small part of what the police do. There are many different mechanisms for holding individual police officers accountable. They are divided among internal and external mechanisms of accountability. Particularly important are the internal mechanisms that require officers to complete official reports on their actions, require their immediate supervisors to critically review those reports, and have

a process for command-level review of officer reports. Early intervention systems are also important. External accountability mechanisms include an effective citizen oversight agency, an aggressive and responsible local news media, and finally an active number of public interest groups with an interest in the police.

KEY TERMS

accountability, 489
two dimensions, 490
crime rate, 491
PTSR framework, 495
routine supervision, 496
span of control, 496
innovative supervisors, 497
employee assistance
    program, 498
organizational culture, 499
command-level review, 499
use-of-force review board, 499
performance evaluations, 500
internal affairs unit, 501
discipline matrix, 503
Christopher Commission, 505

code of silence, 505
early intervention systems, 507
performance review, 509
risk management, 511
police legal advisor, 512
accreditation, 512
American political system, 513
Mapp v. Ohio, 514
exclusionary rule, 515
Miranda v. Arizona, 515
damage awards, 517
consent decree, 518
pattern or practice of abuse, 518
independent monitor, 520
collaborative reform, 522
criminal prosecution, 523

citizen oversight, 524
civilian review board, 525
police auditor or inspector
    general, 525
policy review, 525
community outreach, 526
blue-ribbon commissions, 527
digital revolution in
    communications, 527
public interest groups, 529
accountability and crime
    control, 530
mixed approach to police
    accountability, 531

INTERNET EXERCISES

Exercise 1 About 30 law enforcement agencies have been sued for a "pattern or practice" of abusing the rights of citizens, and resolved the investigation with a consent decree, memorandum of agreement, or settlement agreement.

Examine the original Findings Letters for some of these departments. What picture of these departments emerges? How bad is police conduct, according to these investigations? Do you find the evidence persuasive to justify federal intervention and a set of court-ordered reforms? Examine, for example, the Findings Letters for the New Orleans Police Department (https://www.justice.gov/sites/default/files/crt/legacy/2011/03/17/nopd_report.pdf); for the Cleveland police department (https://www.justice.gov/sites/default/files/crt/legacy/2014/12/04/cleveland_findings_12-4-14.

pdf); and for the Ferguson, Missouri, police department (https://www.justice.gov/sites/default/files/crt/legacy/2015/03/04/ferguson_findings_3-4-15.pdf).

Exercise 2 The San Jose Independent Police Auditor (IPA) is an important citizen oversight agency. Find the IPA's website and review its annual reports from 1993 to the present. What has the San Jose IPA done over the years? What does it claim as its most important achievements? Do you believe these are valuable contributions to police accountability? Do you believe any of the activities of the IPA interfere with the management of the San Jose Police Department? If so, which activities? Discuss in class why you think these activities interfere with professional management.

NOTES

1. National Academy of Sciences, *Fairness and Effectiveness in Policing: The Evidence* (Washington, DC: National Academies Press, 2004).
2. Louise Shelley, "The Soviet Police and the Rule of Law," in David Weisburd and Craig Uchida, eds., *Police Innovation and Control of the Police* (New York: Springer-Verlag, 1993), 127.
3. Jerome H. Skolnick, *Justice Without Trial: Law Enforcement in Democratic Society*, 3rd ed. (New York, Macmillan, 1994).
4. National Commission on Law Observance and Enforcement, *Lawlessness in Law Enforcement* (1931, reprinted New York: Arno Press, 1969).
5. Paul Jacobs, *Prelude to Riot: A View of American from the Bottom* (New York: Vintage Books, 1968), 38.
6. Samuel Walker and Carol Archbold, *The New World of Police Accountability*, 2nd ed. (Thousand Oaks, CA: Sage, 2014); Samuel Walker, "Historical Roots of the Legal Control of Police Behavior," in David Weisburd and Craig Uchida, eds., *Police Innovation and Control of the Police* (New York: Springer-Verlag, 1993), 32–55.
7. Geoffrey P. Alpert and Mark H. Moore, "Measuring Police Performance in the New Paradigm of Policing," in Bureau of Justice Statistics, *Performance Measures for the Criminal Justice System* (Washington, DC: U.S. Government Printing Office, 1993), 109–42, http://www.bjs.gov/content/pub/pdf/pmcjs.pdf.
8. National Crime Victimization Survey, *Criminal Victimization, 2014* (Washington, DC: U.S. Department of Justice, 2015), table 6, http://www.bjs.gov/content/pub/pdf/cv14.pdf.
9. "Hundreds of Assault Cases Misreported by Milwaukee Police Department," *Milwaukee Journal-Sentinel,* May 22, 2012, http://www.jsonline.com/watchdog/watchdogreports/hundreds-of-assault-cases-misreported-by-milwaukee-police-department-v44ce4p-152862135.html.
10. Lawrence W. Sherman and Barry G. Glick, *The Quality of Police Arrest Statistics* (Washington, DC: The Police Foundation, 1984), http://pftest1.drupalgardens.com/sites/g/files/g798246/f/Sherman%20et%20al.%20(1984)%20-%20The%20Quality%20of%20Police%20Arrest%20Statistics.pdf.
11. Samuel Walker, *Police Accountability: The Role of Citizen Oversight* (Belmont: Wadsworth, 2001), 120–127.
12. City of New York, Office of the Comptroller, *Claims Report Fiscal 2012* (New York: Office of the Comptroller, 2013), http://comptroller.nyc.gov/reports/annual-claims-report/.
13. These issues are discussed in Walker and Archbold, *The New World of Police Accountability*, 45–48.
14. City Auditor, *2015 Community Survey* (Portland, OR: Office of the City Auditor, November 2015), https://www.portlandoregon.gov/auditservices/article/551383.
15. Christopher Stone, Todd Fogelsong, and Christine M. Cole, *Policing Los Angeles under a Consent Decree: The Dynamics of Change at the LAPD* (Cambridge, MA: Kennedy School, 2009), https://www.hks.harvard.edu/content/download/67474/1242706/version/1/file/Harvard_LAPD_Report.pdf.
16. James J. Willis, Stephen D. Mastrofski, and David Weisburd, "CompStat and Bureaucracy: A Case Study of Challenges and Opportunities for Change," *Justice Quarterly* 21 (September 2004): 463–496.
17. Collaborative Reform Process, *A Review of Officer-Involved Shootings in the Las Vegas Metropolitan Police Department* (Washington, DC: U.S. Department of Justice, 2012), 92–104, http://www.cops.usdoj.gov/pdf/e10129513-Collaborative-Reform-Process_FINAL.pdf.
18. Herman Goldstein, "Administrative Problems in Controlling the Exercise of Police Authority," *Journal of Criminal Law, Criminology, and Police Science* 58, no. 2 (1967): 171.
19. "The Lost Battalion," *Newsday*, February 2, 2001, 1.
20. David Weisburd and Rosann Greenspan, with Edwin E. Hamilton, Hubert Williams, and Kellie A. Bryant, *Police Attitudes Toward Abuse of Authority: Findings from a National Study* (Washington, DC: U.S. Department of Justice, 2000), 7, http://www.policefoundation.org/wp-content/uploads/2015/06/Weisburd-et-al.-2001-The-Abuse-of-Police-Authority.pdf.
21. Special Counsel Merrick Bobb, *9th Semiannual Report* (Los Angeles: Police Assessment Resource Center, 1998), 22–23, available at www.parc.info.
22. James J. Fyfe, Jack R. Greene, William F. Walsh, O. W. Wilson, and Roy Clinton McLaren, *Police Administration*, 5th ed. (New York: McGraw-Hill, 1997), 139.

23. Critical Response Technical Assessment Review, *Police Accountability—Findings and National Implications of the San Diego Police Department* (Washington, DC: U.S. Department of Justice, 2015), 61, https://www.sandiego.gov/sites/default/files/legacy/police/pdf/perfrpt.pdf.

24. Darrel W. Stephens, *Police Discipline: A Case for Change* (Washington DC: National Institute of Justice and the Harvard Kennedy School, 2011), https://www.ncjrs.gov/pdffiles1/nij/234052.pdf.

25. Adapted from *United States v. City of New Orleans, Consent Decree Regarding the New Orleans Police Department* (2013), Paragraph 306, https://www.justice.gov/sites/default/files/crt/legacy/2013/01/11/nopd_agreement_1-11-13.pdf; John Van Maanen, "The Boss: First-Line Supervision in an American Police Agency," in Maurice Punch, ed., *Control in the Police Organization* (Cambridge, MA: MIT Press, 1983), 275–317.

26. Robin Shepard Engel, *How Police Supervisory Styles Influence Patrol Officer Behavior* (Washington, DC: U.S. Department of Justice, 2003), https://www.ncjrs.gov/pdffiles1/nij/194078.pdf.

27. Special Counsel Merrick Bobb, *15th Semiannual Report* (Los Angeles: Police Assessment Resource Center, 2002), 53, http://static1.squarespace.com/static/5498b74ce4b01fe317ef2575/t/54fc7241e4b01792f1e96e86/1425830465117/15th+Semiannual+Report.pdf.

28. U.S. Department of Justice, Civil Rights Division *Investigation of the Cleveland Division of Police* (2014), 29, 31, https://www.justice.gov/sites/default/files/crt/legacy/2014/12/04/cleveland_findings_12-4-14.pdf.

29. Madison, Wisconsin, Police Department, "General Duties and Expectations of Employees, Expectations for Supervisory Personnel," *Standard Operating Procedure Manual*, http://www.cityofmadison.com/police/documents/sop/GenDutiesExp.pdf.

30. International Association Chiefs of Police, *Breaking the Silence on Law Enforcement Suicides* (Arlington, VA: IACP, 2014), http://www.theiacp.org/Portals/0/documents/pdfs/Suicide_Project/Officer_Suicide_Report.pdf.

31. Los Angeles Police Department, *Board of Inquiry into the Rampart Area Incident* (Los Angeles: LAPD, March 2000), Executive Summary, 7; Stone, Fogelsong, and Cole, *Policing Los Angeles under a Consent Decree.*

32. Erwin Chemerinsky, *An Independent Analysis of the Los Angeles Police Department's Board of Inquiry Report on the Rampart Scandal* (Los Angeles: Loyola, September 11, 2000), http://digitalcommons.lmu.edu/cgi/viewcontent.cgi?article=2262&context=llr.

33. *United States v. City of New Orleans*, Consent Decree (2013), Section K, Paragraphs 96–107.

34. Ibid.

35. Police Executive Research Forum, *Re-Engineering Training on Police Use of Force* (Washington, DC: Author, 2015), http://www.policeforum.org/assets/reengineeringtraining1.pdf.

36. William A. Geller, "Suppose We Were Really Serious about Police Departments Becoming 'Learning Organizations'," *National Institute of Justice Journal* (December 1997): 2–8, https://www.ncjrs.gov/pdffiles/jr000234.pdf.

37. Samuel Walker, Stacy Osnick Milligan, and Anna Berke, *Strategies for Intervening with Officers through Early Intervention Systems: A Guide for Front-Line Supervisors* (Washington, DC: Police Executive Research Forum, 2006), http://www.cops.usdoj.gov/pdf/publications/e01060004.pdf.

38. Ibid.

39. Timothy N. Oettmeier and Mary Ann Wycoff, *Personnel Performance Evaluations in the Community Policing Context* (Washington, DC: Police Executive Research Forum, 1997), 5, http://www.policeforum.org/assets/docs/Free_Online_Documents/Community_Policing/personnel%20performance%20evaluations%20in%20the%20community%20policing%20context.pdf.

40. Office of Community Oriented Policing, *Standards and Guidelines for Internal Affairs: Recommendations From a Community of Practice* (Washington, DC: Department of Justice, nd). https://static1.squarespace.com/static/5498b74ce4b01fe317ef2575/t/54affb83e4b066a5a28ad527/1420819331714/cops-p164-pub.pdf.

41. Aogan Mulcahy, "'Headhunter' or 'Real Cop'? Identity in the World of Internal Affairs Officers," *Journal of Contemporary Ethnography* 24 (April 1995): 106, 108.

42. Herman Goldstein, *Police Corruption* (Washington, DC: The Police Foundation, 1975), 40–41.

43. Los Angeles Police Commission, *Report of the Rampart Independent Review Panel* (Los Angeles: Author, 2001), 93–96, http://assets.lapdonline.org/assets/pdf/report_rampart_special_order_40.pdf.

44. Lawrence W. Sherman, *Controlling Police Corruption* (Washington, DC: U.S. Department of Justice, 1978), 10.

45. New York City, Commission to Investigate Allegations of Police Corruption and the Anti-Corruption Procedures of the Police Department [Mollen Commission], *Report* (New York: Author, 1994).

46. Critical Response Technical Assessment Review, *Police Accountability.*

47. New York City, Commission to Combat Police Corruption, *The New York City Police Department's Internal Affairs Bureau: A Survey of Former IAB Members* (March 2000), 3, http://www.nyc.gov/html/ccpc/assets/downloads/pdf/The-NYPDs-Internal-Affairs-Bureau-A-Survey-of-Former-IAB-Members-March-2000.pdf.

48. Police Executive Research Forum, *Organization Evaluation of the Omaha Police Division* (Washington DC: Author, 1992), 75.

49. Jayson Wechter, "Executive Summary," *Investigating Citizen Complaints Is Different: The Special Challenges of Investigating Citizen Complaints Against Police Officers* (Omaha: University of Nebraska at Omaha, 2004), http://samuelwalker.net/wp-content/uploads/2010/06/ICCID.pdf.

50. Stephens, *Police Discipline: A Case for Change,* 6.

51. Ibid., 7.

52. San Jose Independent Police Auditor, *2015 IPA Year End Report* (San Jose: Office of the Independent Police Auditor, 2016), 17, http://www.sanjoseca.gov/DocumentCenter/View/55841.

53. President's Task Force on 21st Century Policing, *Final Report* (Washington, DC: U.S. Department of Justice, 2015), http://www.cops.usdoj.gov/pdf/taskforce/taskforce_finalreport.pdf.

54. See, for example, Peter F. Nardulli, James Eisenstein, and Roy B. Flemming, *The Tenor of Justice: Criminal Courts and the Guilty Plea Process* (Urbana: University of Illinois Press, 1988).

55. Philadelphia Police Department, Integrity and Accountability Office, *Disciplinary System* (Philadelphia: Author, 2003).

56. Los Angeles Sheriff's Department, Office of Independent Review, *Second Annual Report* (Los Angeles: Author, 2003), 63.

57. Los Angeles Police Commission, *Report of the Rampart Independent Review Panel*, 97–99.

58. Stephens, *Police Discipline: A Case for Change*, 10.

59. Stephens, *Police Discipline: A Case for Change.*

60. Steven D. Zansberg and Pamela Campos, "Sunshine on the Thin Blue Line: Public Access to Police Internal Affairs Files," *Communications Lawyer* (Fall 2004): 34, http://heinonline.org/HOL/Page?handle=hein.journals/comlaw22&div=27&g_sent=1&collection=journals.

61. New Jersey Attorney General, *Internal Affairs Policy and Procedures* (Rev. November 2000), http://www.nj.gov/oag/dcj/agguide/internalaffairs2000v1_2.pdf.

62. ACLU of New Jersey, *The Crisis Continues Inside Police Internal Affairs* (Newark: Author, February 2103), https://www.aclu-nj.org/files/3413/6059/3876/ACLU_NJ_Internal_Affairs.pdf.

63. Christopher Commission, *Report of the Independent Commission on the Los Angeles Police Department,* 168–171.

64. *Allen v. City of Oakland*, Consent Decree (2003).

65. Chicago Police Accountability Task Force, *Recommendations for Reform: Restoring Trust between the Chicago Police and the Communities They Serve, Report* (Chicago: Author, 2016), 69, https://chicagopatf.org/wp-content/uploads/2016/04/PATF_Final_Report_4_13_16-1.pdf.

66. Jamie Kalven, "Code of Silence," (four parts) October 6, 2016. http://invisible.institute/codeofsilence.

67. William Westley, *Violence and the Police* (Cambridge, MA: MIT Press, 1970).

68. Christopher Commission, *Report of the Independent Commission on the Los Angeles Police Department*, 168–171.

69. David Weisburd et al., *The Abuse of Police Authority: A National Study of Police Officers' Attitudes* (Washington, DC: The Police Foundation, 2001), http://www.policefoundation.org/wp-content/uploads/2015/06/Weisburd-et-al.-2001-The-Abuse-of-Police-Authority.pdf.

70. Mollen Commission, *Report*, 53.

71. Christopher Slobogin, "Testilying: Police Perjury and What to Do About It," *University of Colorado Law Review* 67 (Fall 1996), http://www.constitution.org/lrev/slobogin_testilying.htm.

72. Neal Trautman, Director, National Institute of Ethics, *Police Code of Silence Facts Revealed*, International Association of Chiefs of Police, Annual Conference 2000, available at http://www.aele.org/loscode2000.html.

73. Public Advocate for the City of New York, *Disciplining Police: Solving the Problems of Police Misconduct* (New York: Author, 2000), 31–36.

74. Critical Response Technical Assessment Review, *Police Accountability*, 11.

75. Christopher Commission, *Report of the Independent Commission*, 38–48.

76. "Kansas City Police Go after Their 'Bad Boys'," *New York Times,* September 10, 1991; "Wave of Abuse Claims Laid to a Few Officers," *Boston Sunday Globe*, October 4, 1992, 1.

77. Walker and Archbold, *The New World of Police Accountability*, 137. One of the first discussions of the problem was in Herman Goldstein, *Policing a Free Society* (Cambridge, MA: Ballinger, 1977), 171–172; U.S. Commission on Civil Rights, *Who Is Guarding the Guardians? A Report on Police Practices* (Washington, DC: Author, 1981), finding 3.5, 81–86, https://babel.hathitrust.org/cgi/pt?id=uc 1.32106015219253;view=1up;seq=4.

78. Samuel Walker, *Early Intervention Systems for Law Enforcement Agencies: A Management and Planning Guide* (Washington, DC: U.S. Department of Justice, 2003), http://www.cops. usdoj.gov/html/cd_rom/inaction1/pubs/ EarlyInterventionSystemsLawEnforcement.pdf.

79. The Justice Department consent decrees and memoranda of agreement are available on the Special Litigation Section website at https://www.justice.gov/ crt/special-litigation-section-cases-and-matters0.

80. Special Counsel Merrick Bobb, *15th Semiannual Report*, 50.

81. Ibid., 41.

82. Walker, *Early Intervention Systems for Law Enforcement Agencies*, 30–33.

83. Special Counsel Merrick Bobb, *15th Semiannual Report*, 39–41.

84. Ibid., 39–40.

85. Walker, Milligan, and Berke, *Strategies for Intervening with Officers through Early Intervention Systems*.

86. Special Counsel Merrick Bobb, 15th *Semiannual Report*, 51–52.

87. New Jersey State Police, *Monitors' Seventeenth Report* (April 2009), vii, http://www.nj.gov/oag/ monitors-report-17.pdf.

88. Anecdote, field notes for Walker, *Early Intervention Systems for Law Enforcement Agencies: A Planning and Management Guide*.

89. Samuel Walker, Geoffrey P. Alpert, and Dennis J. Kenney, *Early Warning Systems: Responding to the Problem Police Officer* (Washington, DC: U.S. Department of Justice 2001), https://www.ncjrs. gov/pdffiles1/nij/188565.pdf.

90. Walker, *Early Intervention Systems for Law Enforcement Agencies*.

91. Critical Response Technical Assessment Review, *Police Accountability;* Chicago Police Accountability Task Force, *Recommendations for Reform.*

92. Walker and Archbold, *The New World of Police Accountability*, 211.

93. The reports of the Los Angeles Sheriff's Department Special Counsel are available at the Police Assessment Resource Center website at http://www.parc.info/resources/.

94. Charlotte-Mecklenburg Police Department, Police Attorney's Office, http://charmeck.org/city/ charlotte/CMPD/organization/PoliceChief/ PoliceAttorney/Pages/Home.aspx.

95. Carol A. Archbold, *Police Accountability, Risk Management, and Legal Advising* (New York: LFB Scholarly Publishing, 2004); Walker and Archbold, *The New World of Police Accountability*, ch. 7, 210–236.

96. Commission on the Accreditation of Law Enforcement Agencies website at www.calea.org.

97. Commission on Accreditation for Law Enforcement Agencies, *Standards for Law Enforcement*.

98. Jack Pearson, "National Accreditation: A Valuable Management Tool," in James J. Fyfe, ed., *Police Management Today* (Washington, DC: ICMA, 1985).

99. CALEA, "Accreditation Works!" http://www.calea. org/calea-update-magazine/accreditation-works/ case-studies.

100. Samuel Walker, "Governing the Police: Wrestling with the Problems of Democracy," *Chicago Law Forum* V. 2016: 615–660.

101. Samuel Walker, *A Critical History of Police Reform* (Lexington, MA: Lexington Books, 1977).

102. Samuel Walker, *Popular Justice: A History of American Criminal Justice*, 2nd ed. (New York: Oxford University Press, 1998).

103. *Mapp v. Ohio*, 367 U.S. 643 (1961); Carolyn Long, *Mapp v. Ohio: Guarding against Unreasonable Searches and Seizures* (Lawrence: University Press of Kansas, 2006).

104. Ibid.

105. Herman Goldstein, "Trial Judges and the Police," *Crime and Delinquency* 14 (January 1968): 14–25.

106. *Miranda v. Arizona*, 383 U.S. 436 (1966); Liva Baker*, Miranda: Crime, Law, and Politics* (New York: Atheneum, 1983); Richard A. Leo, *Police Interrogations and American Justice* (Cambridge, MA: Harvard University Press, 2008).

107. Paul G. Cassell and Bret S. Hayman, "Police Interrogation in the 1990s: An Empirical Study of the Effects of Miranda," *UCLA Law Review* 43 (February 1996): 860.

108. Sheldon Krantz et al., *Police Policymaking* (Lexington, MA: Lexington Books, 1979); Controller General of the United States, *Impact of the Exclusionary Rule on Federal Crime Prosecutions*, Report #GGD-79-45 (April 19, 1979), http://www.gao.gov/assets/130/126585.pdf.

109. Walker, "Historical Roots of Legal Control of Police Behavior."

110. Myron W. Orfield, Jr., "The Exclusionary Rule and Deterrence: An Empirical Study of Chicago Narcotics Officers," *University of Chicago Law Review* 54 (Summer 1987): 1016–1055.

111. Herman Goldstein, *Policing a Free Society*, ch. 7, "Controlling and Reviewing Police-Citizen Contacts," 157–186; Carl McGowan, "Rulemaking and the Police," *Michigan Law Review* 70 (March 1972): 659–694.

112. Stephen Wasby, *Small-Town Police and the Supreme Court* (Lexington, MA: Lexington Books, 1976).

113. "Chicago Police Misconduct Settlements Surge as the City Pays Out Millions in Taxpayer Dollars," *HuffPost Chicago* (March 14, 2013); "Baltimore Paid $4.4 Million for Claims against Police Officers in 2010," *Baltimore Sun*, July 25, 2015, http://www.baltimoresun.com/news/maryland/investigations/bs-md-sun-investigates-0726-lawsuits-20150725-story.html.

114. Edward J. Littlejohn, "Civil Liability and the Police Officer: The Need for New Deterrents to Police Misconduct," *University of Detroit Journal of Urban Law* 58 (1981): 365–431.

115. Charldean Newell, Janay Pollock, and Jerry Tweedy, "Financial Aspects of Police Liability," *ICMA Baseline Data Report* 24 (March–April 1992): 1–8.

116. Charles Epp, *Making Rights Real: Activists, Bureaucrats, and the Creation of the Legalistic State* (Chicago: University of Chicago Press, 2009).

117. Joanna C. Schwartz, "What Police Learn from Lawsuits," *Cardozo Law Review* 22, no. 3 (2010): 841–894.

118. Special Counsel James G. Kolts et al., *The Los Angeles County Sheriff's Department* (Los Angeles: Kolts Commission, 1992), 25–73, 157–167, http://www.clearinghouse.net/chDocs/public/PN-CA-0001-0023.pdf; Merrick J. Bobb, *1st Semiannual Report*.

119. *United States v. City of Pittsburgh* (W. D. Pa., 1997), https://www.justice.gov/crt/united-states-district-court-western-district-pennsylvania-united-states-america-plaintiff-v-0.

120. U.S. Department of Justice, Civil Rights Division, Special Litigation Section, https://www.justice.gov/crt/special-litigation-section.

121. Samuel Walker and Morgan Macdonald, "An Alternative Remedy for Police Misconduct: A Model State 'Pattern or Practice' Statute," *George Mason University Civil Rights Law Journal* 19, no. 3 (2009): 479–552.

122. *California v. City of Riverside* (2001), http://www.clearinghouse.net/chDocs/public/PN-CA-0014-0001.pdf.

123. *Allen v. City of Oakland* (2003).

124. Samuel Walker, "The Community Voice in Policing: Old Issues, New Evidence," *Criminal Justice Policy Review* 9 (August 2015): 1–16; *United States v. Cleveland, Consent Decree* (2015), 4–7.

125. *In re Cincinnati* (2002). https://www.cincinnati-oh.gov/police/linkservid/27A205F1-69E9-4446-BC18BD146CB73DF2/showMeta/0/.

126. *Floyd v. City of New York* (2013); Monitor's website, http://nypdmonitor.org/overview/.

127. Michael R. Bromwich, *Special Report of the Independent Monitor for the Metropolitan Police Department* (Washington, DC: Special Monitor, June 2002).

128. New Jersey State Police, "Executive Summary," *Sixteenth Monitors' Report* (August 2007), http://www.nj.gov/oag/monitors-report-16.pdf.

129. City of Cincinnati, *Independent Monitor's Final Report* (December 2008), 37.

130. Stone, Fogelsong, and Cole, *Policing Los Angeles under a Consent Decree*.

131. Walker and Macdonald, "An Alternative Remedy for Police Misconduct."

132. Police Executive Research Forum, *Civil Rights Investigations of Local Police: Lessons Learned* (Washington, DC: Author, 2013), 34, http://www.policeforum.org/assets/docs/Critical_Issues_Series/civil%20rights%20investigations%20of%20local%20police%20-%20lessons%20learned%202013.pdf.

133. See "Forced Reforms, Mixed Results," *Washington Post*, November 13, 2015, http://www.washingtonpost.com/sf/investigative/2015/11/13/

forced-reforms-mixed-results/; see also the reply, Samuel Walker, "When Policing Goes Wrong," *The Crime Report* (November 25, 2015), http://samuelwalker.net/wp-content/uploads/2015/12/WAPODOJstory.pdf.

134. Trent Ikerd and Samuel Walker, *Making Police Reforms Endure: The Keys for Success* (Washington, DC: U.S. Department of Justice, 2010), http://ric-zai-inc.com/Publications/cops-p176-pub.pdf; Samuel Walker, "Institutionalizing Police Accountability Reforms: The Problem of Making Police Reforms Endure," *St. Louis University Public Law Review*, XXXII, no. 1 (2012): 57–92.

135. U.S. Department of Justice, Office of Community Oriented Policing Services, Technical Assistance, http://www.cops.usdoj.gov/technicalassistance.

136. Collaborative Reform Process, *A Review of Officer-Involved Shootings in the Las Vegas Metropolitan Police Department* (Washington, DC: U.S. Department of Justice, 2012), 78, 94, http://www.cops.usdoj.gov/pdf/e10129513-Collaborative-Reform-Process_FINAL.pdf.

137. Ibid.

138. Police Executive Research Forum, *Re-Engineering Training on Police Use of Force.*

139. Monrad G. Paulson, "Securing Police Compliance with Constitutional Limitations," National Commission on the Causes and Prevention of Violence, *Law and Order Reconsidered* (New York: Bantam Books, 1970), 402–405; *Rizzo v. Goode*, 423 U.S. 362 (1976).

140. "Prosecution of U.S. Police for Killings Surges to Highest in Decade," *HuffPost Politics* (October 26, 2015), http://www.huffingtonpost.com/entry/prosecution-police-killings_us_562e26aee4b0ec0a3894eb23.

141. Vera Institute of Justice, *Prosecuting Police Misconduct* (New York: Author, 1998), http://www.vera.org/sites/default/files/resources/downloads/misconduct.pdf.

142. Ibid.

143. Mollen Commission, *Report.*

144. The history of citizen oversight is in Chapter 2 of Walker, *Police Accountability: The Role of Citizen Oversight.*

145. See NACOLE website at www.nacole.org.

146. National Advisory Commission on Civil Disorders [Kerner Commission], *Report* (New York: Bantam Books, 1968), 310–312.

147. Walker and Archbold, *The New World of Police Accountability*, 2nd ed., 105–107.

148. Joseph De Angelis, Richard Rosenthal and Brian Buchner, *Citizen Oversight of Law Enforcement: A Review of the Strengths and Weaknesses of Various Models* (Washington, DC: Department of Justice, 2016).

149. Walker, *Police Accountability: The Role of Citizen Oversight.*

150. New York City, Civilian Complaint Review Board, *2014 Annual Report*, xxii, http://www.nyc.gov/html/ccrb/downloads/pdf/2014-annual-report-rev2layout.pdf.

151. San Francisco, Office of Citizen Complaints, *2014 Annual Report*, 10, http://sfgov.org/occ/sites/sfgov.org.occ/files/OCC_2014.pdf.

152. Michael D. White and Hnery F. Fradella, *Stop and Frisk: The Use and Abuse of a Controversial Policing Tactic* (New York: New York University Press, 2016), p. 184.

153. New York City, Office of the Inspector General for the NYPD, *Using Data from Lawsuits and Legal Claims Involving NYPD to Improve Policing* (New York: Author, 2015), http://www1.nyc.gov/assets/oignypd/downloads/pdf/2015-04-20-litigation-data-report.pdf.

154. The goals of the different models are discussed in Walker, *Police Accountability.*

155. Washington, DC, Office of Police Complaints, "Policy Recommendations." http://policecomplaints.dc.gov/page/policy-recommendations.

156. Americans for Effective Law Enforcement, *Police Civilian Review Boards AELE Defense Manual, Brief 82-3* (San Francisco: Author, 1982).

157. The arguments on both sides are reviewed in Walker, *Police Accountability: The Role of Citizen Oversight*, 54–60.

158. These issues are discussed in Walker, *Police Accountability.*

159. Chicago Police Accountability Task Force, *Recommendations for Reform.*

160. Ibid.

161. National Commission on Law Observance and Enforcement, *The Third Degree* (1931; reprinted: New York: Arno Press, 1969), 153.

162. Samuel Walker, "Setting the Standards: The Efforts and Impacts of Blue-Ribbon Commissions on the Police," in W. A. Geller, ed., *Police Leadership in America: Crisis and Opportunity* (New York: Praeger, 1985), 354–370.

163. President's Task Force on 21st Century Policing, *Implementation Guide* (Washington, DC: U.S.

Department of Justice, 2015), http://www.cops.usdoj.gov/pdf/taskforce/Implementation_Guide.pdf.

164. Walker, *Police Accountability*; Walker and Archbold, *The New World of Police Accountability*, 2nd ed.

165. Lou Cannon, *Official Negligence: How Rodney King and the Riots Changed Los Angeles and the LAPD* (New York: Times Books, 1997).

166. "Final Tally," *Washington Post,* January 6, 2016, https://www.washingtonpost.com/national/final-tally-police-shot-and-killed-984-people-in-2015/2016/01/05/3ec7a404-b3c5-11e5-a76a-0b5145e8679a_story.html.

167. David Burnham, *The Role of the Media in Controlling Corruption* (New York: John Jay College, 1977).

168. Invisible Institute, Citizens Police Data Project. http://invisible.institute/police-data/. "Over 125K Complaints Against More Than 25K Chicago Cops," *Chicago Tribune*, October 14, 2016. http://www.chicagotribune.com/news/watchdog/.

169. See the contributions in "The Chief and the Media," in W. A. Geller, ed., *Police Leadership in America: Crisis and Opportunity* (New York: Praeger, 1985), 99–146.

170. *Floyd, et al., v. City of New York* (2013); information about the case is available at the Center for Constitutional Rights website at www.ccrjustice.org.

171. ACLU, *Driving While Black: Racial Profiling on Our Nation's Highways* (New York: Author, 1999), https://www.aclu.org/report/driving-while-black-racial-profiling-our-nations-highways.

172. Long, *Mapp v. Ohio*; on the history of the ACLU and police misconduct, see Samuel Walker, *In Defense of American Liberties: A History of the ACLU* (New York: Oxford University Press, 1990).

173. NAACP, *Beyond the Rodney King Story: An Investigation of Police Misconduct in Minority Communities* (Boston: Northeastern University Press, 1995).

174. Samuel Walker, *Popular Justice: A History of American Criminal Justice,* 2nd ed. (New York: Oxford University Press, 1998), 180–193.

175. David Bayley, "Law Enforcement and the Rule of Law: Is There a Tradeoff?" *Criminology and Public Policy* 2 (November 2002): 133–154.

176. Stone, Fogelsong, and Cole, *Policing Los Angeles under a Consent Decree.*

177. Information on the case is available on the website of the Center for Constitutional Rights at www.CCRJustice.org; New York Civil Liberties Union, *Stop and Frisk 2011: NYCLU Briefing* (New York: Author, 2012), http://www.nyclu.org/files/publications/NYCLU_2011_Stop-and-Frisk_Report.pdf; see also New York Civil Liberties Union, *NYC: Stop-and-Frisk Down, Safety Up* (New York: Author, 2015), http://www.nyclu.org/files/publications/stopfrisk_briefer_FINAL_20151210.pdf.

178. "Violence Surges in Chicago Even as Policing Debate Rages On," *New York Times*, March 28, 2016, http://www.nytimes.com/2016/03/29/us/violence-surges-in-chicago-even-as-policing-debate-rages-on.html?_r=0.

179. Samuel Walker, "The Consent Decree Does Not Hamper Crime Fighting," *East Bay Express*, September 26, 2012, http://samuelwalker.net/wp-content/uploads/2013/02/constitutionalpolicing.pdf.

© Colin Anderson/Getty Images

Challenges for a New Century

CHAPTER **15** The Future of Policing in America

PART V

© Colin Anderson/Getty Images

15 The Future of Policing in America

CHAPTER OUTLINE

Police Technology
  Major Technology Applications
  The Use of Technology in the Field
  The Future of Police Information
    Technology
  Technologically Advanced Weapons

Crime Analysis
  Types of Crime Analysis
  Crime Mapping

The Outlook for Police Employment
  Opportunities in Local, County, and
    State Law Enforcement

Local, County, and State Salaries
Opportunities in Federal Law
  Enforcement
Federal Salaries

The Future of Police Research
  Does Research Do Any Good?
  Politics and Research
  Police Practitioner—Researcher
    Relationships
  The Future of Federal Support for
    Research

Impact of the War on Terrorism
    Role Expansion
    Racial and Ethnic Profiling
    Personnel Challenges
    Role Change

CASE STUDY
Summary
Key Terms

For Discussion
Internet Exercises

Previous chapters have discussed various innovations and reforms that have taken place in many police agencies across the United States. In this chapter, we discuss what Edward Maguire and William King refer to as large-scale, macro-level trends. These are changes that have the potential to transform the landscape of policing in the future.[1] As you have probably discovered by now, there is a lot left to learn about policing today, and much more if we're to make predictions about its future. With this caveat, we discuss six areas of policing in which we believe current trends will have a profound and long-standing impact on police agencies in the future: (1) police technology, (2) crime analysis, (3) employment practices in law enforcement, (4) police research, and (5) the war on terrorism.

Police Technology

Perhaps one of the most influential changes taking place in policing today is related to information technology. Many police agencies use the Internet to convey information to the public, use cell phones to communicate with others while in the field, and use mobile computers to instantly retrieve information. However, it is clear that this is just the beginning and that advances in information technology will have a broad and powerful impact on policing in the future. According to Tom Steele, founder of the International Association of Chiefs of Police, Law Enforcement Information Managers Section,

> *We are just beginning to realize the significance of what is happening. There is not one—I repeat not one—area of the enforcement culture that will go untouched. The very essence of how we do business has been impacted through greater communications and information sharing. Over the next 15 to 20 years you will see the greatest redirection, reorganization, and modification of policing since Sir Robert Peel and the Metropolitan Police.[2]*

Major Technology Applications

Jim Chu, a police manager with the Vancouver, Canada, police department and a leading expert in police-related information technology, identifies four major applications that are of consequence to police agencies of the future: (1) database and information technology, (2) computer-aided dispatch, (3) records management systems, and (4) mobile computing.[3]

Database and Information Technology

In the past, police agencies relied on card file indexes, with cards containing basic information on suspects such as their name, date of birth, case number, and criminal history record. This system was particularly helpful to specialized units such as burglary, forgery, and sex crimes to assist them with identifying potential suspects in an area where a crime had occurred.

Some of the most progressive police departments today have either developed relational databases or are on their way to doing so. Computerized relational databases operate much like a card file index but are much more powerful. They allow the police to store and retrieve large amounts of information obtained from a variety of sources. For example, if a police officer is investigating a suspect in a crime, the officer can use a relational database to gather information from the department's criminal history records system, the gang unit's intelligence system, and the state's department of motor vehicles—all at one time.

Relational databases are useful not only for gathering and storing information on suspects and criminals but also for management purposes. They have the capacity to identify areas that need greater levels of police service and can provide trend information on criminal activity in specific neighborhoods. Relational databases can also be used to evaluate officers by tracking the number of arrests they make, the types of arrests they make, and the number of complaints against them.[4]

Computer-Aided Dispatch

computer-aided dispatch

Computer-aided dispatch (CAD) was first used in the 1970s as a method of more effectively and efficiently managing calls for service from the public. It was quickly realized that this system of service delivery had many advantages. First, it offered police departments a faster and more effective method of communicating with police officers in the field. Much like instant text messages, CAD systems allowed dispatchers to input relevant information into the system and send it instantaneously to officers' mobile computers. Unlike radio dispatch, the uniformity and clarity of the graphic display reduced officer confusion. Second, CAD systems enhance safety by monitoring officer status. If officers do not update their "field status" after they have responded to a call, the CAD system will automatically alert a dispatcher to contact someone to check on their safety. Third, CAD systems help dispatchers and officers prioritize calls for service. Various types of calls are precoded according to their seriousness and guide dispatchers and officers on appropriate action.

Records Management Systems

In the past, one of the most time-consuming activities engaged in by police agencies was the management of paperwork. In large police organizations, it was a hopeless effort that often resulted in frustration and loss of information. This was largely the consequence of complex processes in place for collecting, organizing, storing, and disseminating paper reports. All of the paper shuffling taking place in organizations led to too many opportunities for "lost paperwork" and resulted in administrators and officers rarely having all of the relevant information at their disposal.

records management systems

The advent of **records management systems** (RMSs) has solved many of the problems associated with the "paper tiger." Records management systems are used to input and organize information from different types of reports in one easy-to-access format. For example, officers who work in agencies that have adopted this technology often are not required to file written reports. Instead, all information is input into a mobile terminal and is transmitted to appropriate personnel. As such,

RMSs not only have reduced the amount of time that officers spend on paperwork but also have improved the accuracy of the information collected by the police. The computer programs in place in mobile terminals have quality-control features that prompt officers for certain types of information and ensure that the data entered are consistent and accurate.

RMS programs also allow for easy access to information. Some RMS programs allow numerous types of reports—such as crime reports, field interview contacts, traffic citations, booking reports, criminal history reports, and investigation reports—to be displayed at any time, on any computer terminal—permitting officers to access information faster and more easily.[5]

Mobile Computing

Before the early 1980s the only way for a supervisor or dispatcher to communicate with a police officer was through a call box or by mobile radio. It was even more difficult for a citizen to get a hold of a particular officer while he or she was in the field. Today, a number of methods are available for communicating with an officer (see Exhibit 15–1), each with its own strengths and weaknesses, and new methods are expected to be developed in the future.

 For a discussion of the impact of earlier technological innovations—the telephone, the two-way radio, and the police car—see Chapter 2.

Call boxes, first installed in 1877, were inefficient and ineffective compared with today's communication devices. Officers could access call boxes only at specific locations, and when they did have access to a call box, officers could obtain or convey only certain types of information—such as the location of a particular problem or the need for assistance. Mobile radios, which became popular in the 1930s, allowed officers to access communication at almost any geographic location and permitted communication among officers, supervisors, and dispatchers at almost any time. Cellular phones further enhanced the ability of officers to communicate with those outside of the police department who do not have access to a two-way radio. For example, officers responsible for particular areas or who work closely with businesses or neighborhood groups are now able to easily communicate with members of the community. Although the progression from the call box to the two-way radio and the cellular phone has substantially enhanced the capacity of police officials to communicate with each other and the community, the content of the information exchanged over these forms of media has changed only slightly. Typically, it is restricted to specific incidents or particular pieces of information.

EXHIBIT 15–1

Communication Devices

	Timely	Access to All Information
Call box	No	Not good
Mobile radio	Yes	Not good
Cellular phone	Yes	Not good
Mobile data terminal	Maybe	Better
Mobile workstation	Maybe	Very good

Source: Jim Chu, *Low Enforcement Information Technology* (New York: CRC Press, 2001). 148

Mobile computers and workstations have revolutionized the type and amount of information that patrol officers have at their disposal. In some of the most technologically advanced police departments, mobile computers and workstations are the primary mechanism that officers use to deposit and access information. For example, officers can input information that was formerly in written form directly into the computer. This not only eliminates all of the paper generated by reports but also makes the information available to all other police officials almost instantaneously. Mobile computing also permits anytime, anyplace access to the department's CAD and RMS, which can assist officers with stops and crime scene investigations. For example, if an officer pulls over a suspect for a traffic violation, he or she can instantly access the department's CAD and RMS by mobile computer and query information about the person who was pulled over. Officers, for example, can check the driver's criminal record, verify if the driver is the owner of the car, and determine if the person has any outstanding arrest warrants. Additionally, mobile computers facilitate investigations and information gathering by allowing officers to perform online text searches for needed information when they are in the field.[6]

The Use of Technology in the Field
COMPSTAT

For further discussion of COMPSTAT, see Chapter 4.

One of the most important innovations in police crime fighting is COMPSTAT. Using computerized data management, COMPSTAT provides timely data on crime and disorder by neighborhood. In most programs, police commanders meet weekly or monthly to analyze and discuss the data. At these meetings, precinct commanders are expected to have analyzed the data, identified problems, and already developed responses that will address new or changing patterns of crime and disorder in the areas under their command (for example, a series of residential burglaries on one block; a sharp increase in drug arrests in one area).[7]

Through COMPSTAT, computer technology offers the opportunity for greater police effectiveness than in the past. First, the data are current. Some programs provide data on a 24-hour basis. Second, computer technology facilitates analysis of trends and changes in crime and disorder. Third, the system facilitates crime mapping, allowing a focus on particular neighborhoods or even streets. Fourth, the system heightens the ability of the chief of police to hold precinct commanders accountable for crime and disorder in their areas.

Early Intervention Systems

For additional information on police accountability, see Chapter 14.

Early intervention systems (EISs) are an application of personnel records management for the purpose of increasing the accountability of police officers. An EIS is a computerized database with performance data on each officer. Systems vary, but most include data on officer use of force, citizen complaints, commendations, and officer involvement in civil suits against the department. Some EISs contain as many as 18 or 20 performance indicators.[8] The data permit commanders to analyze officer performance and to identify those officers who appear to have performance problems. The department can then refer these officers to some kind of intervention—

informal counseling, retraining, professional counseling—designed to correct their performance problems.[9]

License Plate Readers

Local police agencies across the country are beginning to use automated license plate readers, otherwise known as LPRs or tag readers. License plate readers are installed on police vehicles and fixed sites such as traffic intersections and highway entrances and exits. License plate readers became popular in the 1990s as a strategy used by the British military to deter Irish Republican Army attacks. The United States later adopted them to identify stolen cars and illegally parked cars.[10] For example, in Mesa, Arizona, LPRs are placed in patrol vehicles and on street corners to immediately alert patrol officers when a vehicle has been identified as stolen. Currently, there are five potential uses for license plate readers: (1) crime analysis, (2) alerts and hot lists, (3) tracking individuals, (4) identifying previously undetected crimes, and (5) revenue generation.

Some police departments may choose to use LPRs for tactical crime analysis (described later in this chapter). For example, an agency might have an LPR near a local bank that could help to identify vehicles that were in an area when a robbery occurred. Police agencies can also use LPRs to identify vehicles owned by persons of interest or those who pose a threat to law enforcement. These lists are referred to as "hot lists." Hot lists can be generated by a variety of sources including patrol officers, the National Insurance Crime Bureau, the Department of Homeland Security, the National Crime Information Center, and Amber Alerts. License plate readers notify police officers when a license plate on the hot list is observed so that the officer can take appropriate action. Additionally, LPRs are used to track individuals. Some jurisdictions may choose to track the movement of drug smugglers, gang members, fugitives, and those on parole or probation. The Department of Homeland Security might use the information to track the movement of those on terrorist watch lists, and local police departments could use LPRs to determine whether the license plates of registered sex offenders have entered a school or day care parking lot. License plate readers can also be used by the police to detect previously undetected crime. For instance, in many states a person's license can be suspended if the individual is found to be driving without insurance. However, this violation is rarely discovered by the police unless the person is pulled over for another reason. With the appropriate data-sharing agreements in place, LPRs have the potential to be used to detect those vehicles on the road that have not been insured and they could be used to identify vehicles associated with persons whose licenses have been suspended. Last, and related, some states revoke license plates and driver's licenses because drivers failed to pay a fine or owe taxes. LPRs could be used to bring those who owe the government money to the attention of the police.[11]

An emerging body of research has begun to examine the effectiveness of LPRs. One of the first studies examining LPR technology was conducted in Mesa, Arizona. The local police installed LPRs in four patrol vehicles. Each LPR was loaded twice a shift with information that would allow it to recognize a hot list of cars and license plates for the purpose of recovering stolen cars, arresting auto thieves, and reducing vehicle theft. The authors reported that the technology resulted in about eight times the number of plates being run through the information system when compared to those that were run using traditional techniques. This, in turn, resulted in (1) significantly more "hits" for vehicles involved in auto theft, (2) more hits for stolen license plates, (3) more arrests for auto theft, and (4) more recoveries of occupied stolen vehicles. The LPRs, however, were found not to have an impact on the level of auto theft in the community.[12]

Although police officials are excited about the prospects of LPR technology, some critics question their use. The American Civil Liberties Union (ACLU) recently released a study of almost 300 police agencies that showed that LPRs rarely alert officers to a wanted vehicle. As an example, in Maryland, for every 1 million license plates read, there are 2,000 alerts, of which "only 47 were potentially associated with more serious crimes—a stolen vehicle or license plate, a wanted person, a violent gang . . . ." As part of the report, the ACLU also raised serious questions about data retention and privacy. As part of LPR programs, law enforcement agencies collect and retain millions of records on the location of persons—through their license plates—and can later reanalyze the information to determine the exact location where the license plate was last observed or the area where the plate was most frequently observed.[13]

Some states, such as California and New Hampshire, are developing legislation that would limit the use of LPR technology, but there have been no legal precedents to address privacy rights issues raised by LPRs. Police advocacy groups claim that analogous cases have been seen before the courts in the past and suggest that LPRs do not violate constitutional privacy protections.[14]

Officer-Worn Body Cameras

Officer-worn body cameras record the events and interactions that take place between community members (for example, the public, suspects, and victims) and officers. A body-worn camera (BWC) can be worn in a multitude of places on the officer's body or head with the camera looking in the same direction as the officer. The video recordings can be used by the police to document statements, observations, behaviors, and other evidence and can simultaneously be used to prevent and deter unprofessional, illegal, and inappropriate behaviors by both the police and the public. Accordingly, this technology can be used to resolve disputes and build trust with the community by preserving a record of critical events.[15]

The police use BWC technology primarily for two purposes. First, it is used to increase police accountability. The technology has the potential to record misconduct, use of force, and other problem behavior or unprofessional conduct; conversely, it has the potential to be used by an officer to disprove an allegation of misbehavior and may defuse potentially violent interactions between the police and the community. Furthermore, the technology might deter officers from engaging in unprofessional conduct. As a consequence, some observers believe that the technology has the capacity to increase accountability among the public and the police; decrease citizen complaints; and result in increased perceptions of legitimacy, trust, and public satisfaction with the police. Another benefit of the technology is that it might reduce civil judgments against the police as a result of injuries or damage that might occur as a consequence of police misconduct or false claims about police misconduct.

Second, BWC technology has the potential to increase the effectiveness of the police response to crime. It is believed that recording officer-involved incidents will improve the level of recollection of the incidents when the officer is completing his or her field reports and later during court proceedings. The video can also be entered into evidence as further proof of the incident, which has the potential to lead to higher rates of arrest, charging, prosecution, and conviction.[16]

Several studies have examined the impact of BWCs. This body of literature has fairly consistently shown that BWCs are associated with a decline in officer use of force and complaints against the police. For example, in Rialto, California, BWCs were associated with an 89 percent decline in complaints, from 28 complaints 12 months prior to their implementation to 3 complaints after BWC were deployed. Similarly, use-of-force incidents decreased by 59 percent, from 61 incidents before BWCs to 25 after.[17] BWCs have also been helpful in prosecuting offenders. A study of the impact of BWC evidence on the case processing of domestic violence cases in Phoenix showed that those cases in which a BWC was present were more likely to result in an arrest, have charges filed, have cases furthered, result in a guilty plea, and result in a guilty verdict at trial.[18]

Body-worn cameras are not without their problems, however. They have been found to increase the amount of time officers spend on paperwork and are expensive to implement. For example in Wichita, Kansas, the city estimated that equipping its officers with BWCs would cost $927,200 in the first year, and that over 10 years, the program would cost over $6 million.[19]

Many more police agencies will be deploying BWCs soon. In 2015, President Barack Obama announced a $20 million Body-Worn Camera (BWC) Pilot Partnership Program initiative, which seeks to assist police agencies in purchasing and deploying BWCs in local law enforcement agencies across the nation.[20]

Social Media

Today, roughly 96 percent of law enforcement agencies use social media of some kind. The most frequent application of social media is through Facebook, Twitter, and YouTube. The police use social media for a variety purposes, including criminal investigations, providing emergency-related information, community outreach, crime prevention, recruitment, and background checks of job applicants.[21]

The Boston Police Department has frequently been cited as an exemplar in the use of social media, particularly following the 2013 Boston Marathon bombing. First, the police department used the agency's social media to immediately inform the public about the incident, and used it to provide near real-time information about news conferences, traffic conditions, and police operations. Second, the police department used social media to inform the public about inaccurate information and, in its place, to provide accurate and timely information. Third, they used social media to identify a primary suspect and asked for the public's assistance in identifying his location.[22]

There are several challenges to law enforcement's use of social media. One is that many agencies have a difficult time engaging the public through social media. One study of Facebook use among the 23 largest police agencies using social media showed that on average an agency has only about 2,600 followers, which represents a small proportion of residents in a jurisdiction.[23] Another is that it is difficult to control officers' use of their own social media sites, which can have an impact on an agency's interest and image. For example, defendants have used information (that is, thoughts and opinions) posted by police officers on their personal social media sites to discredit the officers involved in their arrest.[24]

Public Use of Technology and Accountability

The new technology is also widespread among the public and has emerged as a new form of police accountability. People have video cameras and cell phones with both audio and video capacity. The most famous use of the new technology was in the 1991 beating of Rodney King by Los Angeles police officers. The citizen videotape recording of the beating "went viral," in today's language, and aroused an enormous controversy. This incident was arguably the first time most people had viewed an incident of extreme police use of excessive force. Similar incidents—and public outcry—have occurred following the release of video showing excessive use of force resulting in the death of suspects in Chicago, New York City, and North Charleston, South Carolina. Technology, in this respect, has transformed controversies over police conduct. In the past, allegations of misconduct were often "swearing contests" between two sides, with no objective evidence to support either side. Visual or audio evidence has changed that. To be sure, video or audio recordings are not definitive, because they often do not capture the entire episode. They often do not record the initial part of the incident and or what happens outside the range of the camera or audio recorder. Nonetheless, technology has provided a new method for scrutinizing police conduct.

The Future of Police Information Technology

Since the terrorist attacks of September 11, 2001, increased priority has been placed on building the necessary infrastructure for law enforcement agencies to share information with one another. In most agencies today, the police have limited capacity to share information. One of the few exceptions is the National Crime Information Center, run by the FBI. The National Crime Information Center is a computerized database project that permits local agencies to report to the FBI a limited amount of information pertaining to criminal record history, fugitives, stolen property, and missing persons, and in turn provides the information to other agencies on demand.[25] The program, while valued by police, permits only a limited amount of information to be shared. As a consequence, a small number of police agencies across the country are beginning to develop technology that permits more detailed information to be shared.

One major innovation, which started as the Global Justice XML Data Model (GJXDM), and is today called the National Information Exchange Model (NIEM), allows criminal justice agencies to maintain their information in a standardized language, providing for increased opportunities for data sharing in a consistent format with partners across the criminal justice field. Unfortunately, information-sharing initiatives are generally complex, which greatly increases the risk of failure. One problem is that many police agencies do not have personnel with the required skills to facilitate data integration and information-sharing projects. This requires police agencies to hire outside consultants to develop and implement information-sharing capacities, expending a substantial amount of financial resources that the police do not often have. Another problem is that these projects require a great amount of trust and a willingness to share. Police agencies are highly fragmented organizations that often do not work well with one another and that are protective of information gathered by their people, on their "turf." Last, researchers from COPLINK, a fairly well-known company that specializes in information sharing (now owned by IBM), pointed out that agencies must see an immediate gain or benefit in order to be motivated to share information. Because information-sharing projects typically take years to plan and implement, there are almost no immediate rewards for police agencies.[26]

Although information sharing is difficult to implement, there is evidence regarding its benefits to the police. For example, Martin Zaworski examined the impact of the Automated Regional Justice Information System (ARJIS) on the performance of officers and investigators in the San Diego Sheriff's Department. The findings indicated that information-sharing technology in general increased effectiveness and job performance. More specifically, Zaworski reported that information-sharing technology increased arrest rates for patrol officers and improved case clearance rates for detectives. Additionally, the report indicated that officers were more satisfied with the data they had available to them to perform their job and believed that it enhanced officer safety due to increased officer knowledge in the field.[27]

Technologically Advanced Weapons

New technologically advanced forms of nonlethal weaponry are being developed to assist the police to subdue dangerous suspects. Perhaps the most well-known technological advancement in this area is the Thomas A. Swift Electric Rifle (TASER). A **Taser** is a battery-powered electromuscular device that fires two metal prongs, which are attached to a wire that delivers approximately 26 watts of electricity at more than 50,000 volts. The electricity causes substantial muscular pain and typically results in immobilization of the suspect. A short time after the electrical charges are stopped, there are reportedly few lasting effects other than irritation where the probes were located.[28] (*Note:* The word "Taser" is trademarked by TASER International.)

Taser

Today, approximately 12,000 police agencies have purchased Tasers or other similar products, and 260,000 have been issued to law enforcement officers.[29] The adoption of this technology is believed to help officers make arrests when the offender resists arrest and is thought to provide officers with an alternative to more lethal forms of force.[30]

The Phoenix Police Department has the largest number of Tasers. A departmental study of their use suggested that the implementation and use of Tasers successfully reduced injuries to suspects and officers. In one year, the Phoenix Police Department reported that among 475 incidents where a Taser could have been employed, it was used only 128 times. Only 9 percent of suspects Tasered were injured, compared to 33 percent of those who were not. Likewise, 2 percent of officers who used the Taser were injured, compared to 9 percent of officers who did not use the weapon.[31]

Several organizations, however, have condemned the use of Tasers. They argue that the weapon is more dangerous than the police admit or may be aware of. One report found that the weapon is 39 times more powerful than company official's claim, explaining that the Taser generated 704 watts of power compared to the 26 watts specified by the manufacturer. A 2015 report on the safety of Tasers indicated that in the United States about one person a week dies from a Taser-related incident.[32] Unfortunately, little independent research to date has examined the medical ramifications of Taser use. The independent research that has examined Taser use, however, has determined that only 0.3 percent of incidents involving Tasers result in moderate or serious injuries such as broken bones, loss of an eye, or serious head injury.[33]

Crime Analysis

Related to the shift in the use of technology is the employment of crime analysis by police departments. Crime analysis allows police agencies to make organizational and strategic decisions based on evidence rather than on guesswork. It allows agencies to make data-driven decisions with regard to the allocation of resources and predicting future criminal activity, and supports patrol officers and investigators in their technical decisions.

Timothy O'Shea and Keith Nicholls state that crime analysis consists of three functions:

1. To assess the nature, extent, and distribution of crime in order to efficiently and effectively allocate resources and deploy personnel.
2. To identify crime–suspect correlations to assist investigations.
3. To identify the conditions that facilitate crime and incivility so that policymakers may make informed decisions about prevention approaches.[34]

To accomplish these functions, crime analysts are responsible for a number of activities related to the collection, analysis, and dissemination of crime-related data. First, crime analysts are responsible for gathering, and sometimes entering, information that comes to the police. This information is typically collected through crime reports, calls for service, arrest reports, and field interview cards. Second, crime analysts are responsible for analyzing the data to determine patterns and trends in crime. This is often accomplished through the use of databases, complex statistical packages, and mapping software that require substantial training to use. Third, after a crime analyst has identified a pattern, the information is presented to the appropriate personnel, who use it to develop a response.[35]

Today, about 75 percent of police departments having more than 100 sworn officers have assigned at least one person to conduct crime analysis. These positions are usually staffed by a civilian because of the specialized training needed for the assignment and because civilians are less costly to employ when compared with sworn officers. About 72 percent of agencies that do have a crime analyst have placed them in a separate unit. This unit falls typically under an administrative division (44 percent) but may also fall under a detective division (27 percent) or patrol division (8 percent).[36]

Types of Crime Analysis

Deborah Osborne and Susan Wernicke describe three of the most common types of crime analysis used by police agencies, or potentially available to them: tactical, strategic, and administrative.[37]

Tactical Crime Analysis

tactical crime analysis
Tactical crime analysis typically involves the identification of specific crime problems in particular geographic areas. The goal of this type of analysis is to provide patrol officers and detectives with timely information that allows them to respond to crimes that are currently taking place. For example, a crime analyst might identify a

trend of auto burglaries, determining the typical location, time, and dates of the criminal activity. This information would provide patrol officers with information about where to direct their patrol activities and the time that this strategy might be most effective in capturing or deterring the offender(s).

Strategic Crime Analysis

Strategic crime analysis focuses on long-term crime trends. This information is used to develop strategic plans to address particular problems. Strategic crime analysis is different from tactical crime analysis in that the focus is on long-term planning and larger, more complex projects. A project conducted in Scottsdale, Arizona, provides an illustration. The Scottsdale Police Department Crime Analysis Unit discovered that over the course of years, open-garage-door burglaries were increasing. The crime analyst coordinated with patrol, community watch groups, and neighborhood associations to develop a strategic plan to prevent open-garage-door burglaries. The plan was implemented, and the strategy employed was repeated over the course of several years.

strategic crime analysis

Administrative Crime Analysis

Administrative crime analysis focuses on providing summary statistics and data to police managers. This information is often used by managers to better understand crime and disorder problems. For example, a chief of police might use the Uniform Crime Reporting data collected by the agency to compare the amount of crime in his or her community with that of similar jurisdictions. Similarly, district commanders might request daily crime reports to examine the amount and type of crime occurring in their districts so that they can stay better informed about crime in their areas of responsibility.

administrative crime analysis

Crime Mapping

Since the late 1980s police experts have come to recognize that some geographic areas have more crime than others. These areas have become known as hot spots. This has led some police departments' crime analysts to specialize in what has become known as **crime mapping.** Crime mapping permits analysts to identify spatial patterns and hot spots for different types of crimes. Today, about 13 percent of police departments engage in computerized crime mapping. About one-third of large police departments (with 100 or more sworn officers) currently use computer crime mapping, compared with 3 percent of smaller departments. One Arizona study found that even among those departments that use crime mapping, only half have crime analysts that are proficient in its use.[38] As such, the use of computerized crime mapping is still in its infancy and will take some time to be fully institutionalized within police agencies across the country.

 For additional discussion of hot spots, see Chapter 7.

crime mapping

Currently, the Department of Justice is allocating substantial resources to assist police agencies to adopt crime mapping.[39] This is because crime mapping allows the police to allocate resources in areas that have the most crime. In the past, this might have been done at the precinct and beat level by simply calculating the number of crimes that take place in each area. However, with crime maps the police are able to allocate resources to specific addresses, street corners, and blocks. Crime mapping can be used for a variety of other purposes as well. For example, it can be combined with other sources of data—such as census data, school boundary data, and property assessment data—to help the police understand the relationship among geographic

EXHIBIT 15–2

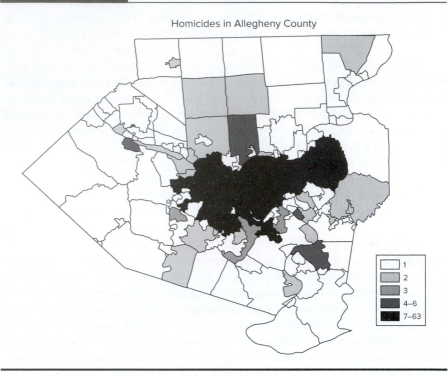

Homicides in Allegheny County

☐	1
▨	2
▨	3
▨	4–6
■	7–63

Source: Erin Dalton, "Violence in Pittsburgh: An Analysis," unpublished manuscript, 2005.

areas, crime, and community-level characteristics.[40] Some agencies also provide their officers with crime maps to keep them up-to-date on where crime is occurring in their patrol areas so that they can engage in proactive enforcement efforts when they are not responding to calls for service. Likewise, crime maps can be shared with the community to educate people about crime in their neighborhoods.[41]

Research funded by the National Institute of Justice reported that of agencies that use computerized crime mapping, 94 percent use it to inform officers and investigators of the location of crime, 56 percent use it to make resource allocation decisions, 49 percent use it to evaluate interventions, 47 percent use it to inform residents about crime activity and changes in their communities, and 44 percent use it to identify addresses where there are repeat calls for service.[42]

For an example of what crime mapping looks like, see Exhibit 15–2.

The Outlook for Police Employment

The employment outlook for those interested in a career in law enforcement appears bright. Greater concern about crime and delinquency, increasing threats to homeland security, and the need to replace police officers from the baby boom generation has resulted in an increasing demand for law enforcement officers that should last for years to come. For example, the Bureau of Labor Statistics reports that the demand for police officers is projected to increase 4 percent through 2024.[43]

Opportunities in Local, County, and State Law Enforcement

Most of the job opportunities available in law enforcement exist within city, county, and state agencies. However, jobs as a city police officer, county sheriff, or highway patrol officer are not the only available job options. A host of jobs are available that might be of greater interest to you or might provide you with an experience you might not have considered. These jobs can not only provide you with the experience and connections that can help you get the law enforcement career that you have always wanted, but they can also offer you a career for a lifetime.

Some of the most overlooked careers in policing are jobs held by civilians. Today, about one-third of all personnel employed by local, county, and state law enforcement agencies are civilians. Many police agencies hire civilians to enforce community physical disorder ordinances, facilitate community crime prevention, and collect evidence. Civilians are also used as crime analysts, strategic planners, and technicians of various kinds.

There are also a number of state agencies that grant individuals police powers to perform various regulatory functions. These jobs range from enforcing laws related to gambling, to inspecting factories for excess pollution, to regulating livestock and other farm animals. For example, an individual who is interested in policing but also has a strong interest in outdoor activities might consider working for a state agency that protects wildlife, such as the state department of agriculture, state department of parks and recreation, or the state department of fish and game. There is an agency to fit almost anyone's interest. For example, Exhibit 15–3 lists a variety of California state agencies that employ persons who possess police power.

EXHIBIT 15–3

California State Agencies That Possess Police Power

Department of Agriculture	Department of Employment	Department of Justice	Department of Fish and Game	California Horse Racing Board
Department of Alcoholic Beverage Control	Department of Finance	Department of Mental Hygiene	San Francisco Port Authority	Bureau of Investigations
Department of Corrections	California State Police	Department of Motor Vehicles	Harbor Police	License Bureau
Department of Youth Authority	Department of Industrial Welfare	Department of Professional and Vocational Standards	Department of Social Work	
California Disaster Office	Fair Employment Practice Commission	Department of Public Health	State Fire Marshal	
Department of California Highway Patrol	Department of Insurance	Department of Parks and Recreation	Office of Consumer Council	
Department of Education	Department of Investments	Department of Conservation	Department of Business Taxes	

Source: James Stinchcomb, *Opportunities in Law Enforcement and Criminal Justice Careers* (Chicago: VGM Career Books, 2003).

Local, County, and State Salaries

The median annual salary for police and sheriff's patrol officers was about $58,320 in 2015, the last year for which these figures were available. Detectives make more than patrol officers. In 2015, the median annual income for detectives and criminal investigators was approximately $77,210.[44] Police officers also receive paid vacation, sick leave, and medical and life insurance—benefits that many other employers do not provide to their employees. Because police officers are usually covered by pension plans, many retire at half-pay after 20 or 25 years of service.[45]

Opportunities in Federal Law Enforcement

There are also ample opportunities for individuals aspiring to a career in federal law enforcement, particularly since the creation of the Department of Homeland Security. Similar to the variation within state law enforcement agencies, there are a number of federal agencies that fulfill numerous roles—those that are responsible for criminal investigations, intelligence gathering, and law enforcement, as well as those that perform compliance and security functions.[46]

Most of these agencies require that an applicant have an undergraduate degree. Those agencies that perform investigative functions often require specialized skills, such as legal training or knowledge about taxes and finance. Today, for example, the Drug Enforcement Agency is seeking persons with a background in pharmacy, and the Border Patrol is looking for persons who speak Spanish.[47]

Persons interested in a career in federal law enforcement should expect to move to a different geographic area of the country. First, if a person is hired by a federal law enforcement agency, he or she will most likely be sent to the Federal Law Enforcement Training Center in Glynco, Georgia. Second, although most agencies try to relocate recruits to a geographic area of their interest, the city or state in which they will live and work is not guaranteed. About 50 percent of all federal law enforcement officers were assigned to the five locations listed in Exhibit 15–4.[48]

Federal Salaries

The salaries of about 75 percent of federal law enforcement officers are determined by the General Schedule (GS) pay system. The GS system comprises 15 grades—

EXHIBIT 15–4

Top Five Jurisdictions Employing Federal Officers

Jurisdiction	Number of Federal Officers
California	10,469
Texas	8,836
New York	6,556
District of Columbia	6,508
Florida	4,980

Source: Law Enforcement Career Starter, www.netlibrary.com/nlreader.dll?bookid=28378&filename=page_3.html.

GS-1 through GS-15. There is also a salary range of 10 steps within each grade. The entry-level pay that a federal law enforcement officer receives varies by agency. However, some federal agents and inspectors receive law enforcement availability pay (LEAP), which increases the pay of these agents by 25 percent because of the substantial amount of overtime they are expected to work.

Individuals working for the FBI begin with a salary of about $61,100 a year depending on where they are stationed. Agents who are not promoted to a supervisory position can earn as much as $145,929 a year after several years. As with other law enforcement jobs, federal agents receive excellent benefits, including paid vacation and sick time, medical coverage, and life insurance.[49]

The Future of Police Research

A generation ago, we knew very little about policing. We did not know what patrol officers did during a typical eight-hour shift. We did not know who they arrested, or why they did not arrest some people. Everyone assumed that patrol deterred crime, but there was no scientific evidence to support that belief. We did not know if some tactics were more effective than others in preventing crime.

Today, we have a lot of information related to those questions. Since the late 1960s, a "research revolution" in policing has enormously expanded our knowledge base. The National Academy of Sciences concluded that "no other country has made a more concerted effort to harness the rigor of social science to the study of policing."[50] As previous chapters of this book have described in detail, we can make some informed statements about what works and what does not work in policing. But knowledge does not come easily or cheaply. The research revolution in policing is the product of a large investment of funds in scientific research. The primary source of that funding is the federal government, though some additional research funds come from private foundations such as the Ford Foundation. Significant federal funding of research in criminal justice began in 1968 with the creation of the Law Enforcement Assistance Administration. Today, the federal government supports criminal justice research primarily through the National Institute of Justice. Additional research is supported by the National Science Foundation, the COPS Office of the U.S. Justice Department, and the U.S. Department of Homeland Security.

Does Research Do Any Good?

Many people ask whether research does any good. Does anyone actually read all of those studies—other than the professors who wrote them and the students who are assigned to read them in class? Does research have any impact on policy? Is social science research on policing worth the investment of our money?

The answer to these questions is a qualified yes. People do read research reports, and there are a number of examples of how research has influenced police policy. But the impact is neither automatic nor direct. Some research has no impact at all. In some cases, the impact of the research is delayed for many years. And in some cases, flawed research has a significant impact.[51]

One of the best examples of the impact of research on policy is the development of community policing. Often characterized as a "new paradigm" for policing, community policing emerged after research discredited the assumptions of the traditional professional model of policing. Specifically,

- The Kansas City Preventive Patrol Experiment found that increasing the level of patrol did not deter crime more effectively than the normal level of patrol.
- Several studies found that faster response time to calls for service did not result in more arrests.
- The RAND Corporation study of the criminal investigation process found that traditional detective work did not increase the number of crimes solved.

Along with other research, these studies forced policymakers to rethink the role of the police and the goals of basic police operations. In this effort, they built on some other important research findings:

- The Newark Foot Patrol Study found that increasing the number of foot patrol officers reduced citizen fear of crime (even though crime did not actually go down) and that citizens also had more positive feelings about the police.
- Several studies found that the police are heavily dependent on citizens for reporting crime and providing information about crime and other problems.

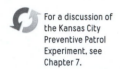

For a discussion of the Kansas City Preventive Patrol Experiment, see Chapter 7.

It took several years for these studies to have an impact, as police experts considered the implications of the important findings. Synthesizing these findings, a combination of researchers and policymakers eventually developed the idea of community policing based on research that suggested that (1) traditional police operations have not proven effective and (2) the police cannot effectively respond to crime and disorder by themselves but need good relations and close cooperation with citizens.

Politics and Research

Political factors have a major effect on the impact of research. This is particularly true with subjects that arouse intense public and political feelings. The best examples come from outside the field of policing. There is much dispute over whether the death penalty deters crime, whether "right to carry" gun laws increase or decrease crime, and whether tougher sentencing laws deter crime. On all three subjects, there is research supporting both sides. These three subjects are hotly debated political issues, and politics affects both the research (particularly the chosen methodology) and the response to particular studies.

Police Practitioner—Researcher Relationships

Since the 1990s various experts and policymakers have called for enhancing the relationship between police practitioners and researchers. They argue that transmission of knowledge between the two groups will increase each group's capacity to more effectively perform its job. For example, police agencies that partner with researchers increase their access to state-of-the-art information and have the opportunity to work with those who can help them understand criminological problems and who can evaluate their responses to these problems. Similarly, researchers gain the opportunity to become more socially embedded in their community, gain access to data for their research, and gain the chance to have an impact on crime and the response to crime.

A recent Department of Justice survey examined the prevalence and characteristics of police practitioner–researcher partnerships. About 50 percent of large

---

EXHIBIT 15–5

Agency Reasons for Not Participating in a Partnership (n = 591)

Do not have the funding/resources to engage in a partnership (staffing, etc.).	56%
Have not been approached by a researcher.	27
Do not think partnering with a researcher would be of much use to my agency.	15
Do not trust the motives or intent of researchers wanting to partner with my agency.	2
Heard of other agencies having a negative experience in partnerships with researchers.	2
Other	16

Note: Agencies could report more than one reason.
Source: Jeff Rojek, Hayden P. Smith, and Geoffrey P. Alpert, "The Prevalence and Characteristics of Police Practitioner—Researcher Relationships," *Police Quarterly,* published online 11 April 2012, DOI: 10.1177/1098611112440698.

agencies reported that they had collaborated with a research partner in the past five years, compared with less than 25 percent of smaller-sized agencies. More than 80 percent of the agencies that had worked with a research partner indicated that the partnership was successful or somewhat successful. As seen in Exhibit 15–5, most of the agencies that had not participated in a research partnership over the past five years indicated that they had not done so because they did not have the funding, they had not been approached by a researcher, or they did not think that partnering with the researcher would be of much use.[52]

The authors of the Department of Justice study concluded that police practitioner–researcher partnerships are fairly common but maintained that lack of funding is a major barrier for police agencies to partner with researchers. They also acknowledged that there are too few qualified researchers to work with every agency, particularly for small to medium-sized agencies. Several leading police researchers have called for enhancing the practitioner–researcher relationship by creating regional research centers that would collaborate with local police agencies.[53]

The Future of Federal Support for Research

Given the enormous contributions of social science research to our understanding of policing and the reliance of research on federal funds, it is important to consider the future of federal support for police research. The future of federal support for research is uncertain, however. The National Academy of Sciences found that even in the past, the level of research support has varied considerably from year to year. This has made it difficult to develop a stable and focused research agenda. Even more serious, because of the federal government's budget problems, support for research through the National Institute of Justice has been reduced and may be reduced even further. Given the important contributions of research in the past, this is a potentially serious problem for the future of the American police.

Impact of the War on Terrorism

The terrorist attacks on the World Trade Center and the Pentagon on September 11, 2001, have had a radical impact on American society. We are all subject to new security measures in airports, government buildings, and other places. The federal government has declared a war on terrorism that has changed our foreign policy. The war on terrorism is also having a profound effect on domestic policy in ways that directly affect state and local police agencies.

Role Expansion

Along with the federal government, state and local law enforcement agencies are increasingly concerned about possible terrorist activities. This includes such efforts as (1) investigating suspected terrorists; (2) preparing for and responding to specific terrorist acts such as the bombing of a building; and (3) preparing for possible terrorist acts involving weapons of mass destruction (WMD), including chemical and biological weapons.

These activities involve a major expansion of the role of state and local police agencies. There is the danger that adding these new roles and responsibilities will divert personnel and effort from current responsibilities. These new responsibilities are also costly. Training for possible terrorist acts is expensive—just as all forms of training are expensive. Maintaining a special unit or command officer responsible for coordinating antiterrorist efforts means that additional officers will have to be hired or diverted from current assignments.[54]

Racial and Ethnic Profiling

For further discussion of racial profiling, see Chapter 12.

The war on terrorism has resulted in an increase in stereotypes about Arab Americans in the minds of some people. The Arab American Anti-Discrimination Association has reported an increase in acts of discrimination against Arab people. Some of these acts are similar to the racial profiling experienced by African Americans. The Leadership Conference on Civil and Human Rights issued a report, *Wrong Then, Wrong Now,* on the illegal profiling of Arab Americans.[55] To address some of these issues, the Department of Justice created a four-hour cultural competency course to educate local and federal law enforcement officers about Arab and Muslim cultures and customs.

Personnel Challenges

Following 9/11, local police agencies have faced several personnel challenges. First, invasions of Afghanistan and Iraq have resulted in the mobilization of the National Guard and the military reserves. As a result, almost every police department has lost some personnel to military duty. This creates personnel shortages for large departments, but in small agencies, it can create a critical situation. A small rural department with only three or four officers cannot afford to lose one of its officers. In some cases, the chief of police has been mobilized for military duty.

Second, local police agencies are faced with increasing demands to fulfill needs related to homeland security. For example, personnel in many jurisdictions have been diverted away from traditional patrol and investigative activities and are being used to guard critical infrastructures, such as public buildings, nuclear facilities, dams, and bridges. Additionally, they are fulfilling roles in intelligence task forces and supporting federal agencies in providing security to seaports and airports. RAND Corporation conducted a study of how the Long Beach Police Department adapted to the changing service demands placed on it after 9/11 and reported that the changes were significant. Examples of the study's findings are presented in Exhibit 15–6.

EXHIBIT 15–6

Examples of How the Long Beach Police Department Has Adapted to Post-9/11 Service Demands

- Created counterterrorism unit.
- Created terrorist liaison officers.
- Reassigned officers to assess and protect critical infrastructures, such as the port, airport, and water treatment facilities.
- Sent officers to train in new skills, such as WMD response and signs of terrorism.
- Established port police equipped with small boats.
- Redistributed officers to respond to areas with high population growth.
- Increased visibility and response times by switching most officers from two- to one-person patrol cars.
- Reduced staffing on lower-priority programs such as Drug Abuse Resistance Education (D.A.R.E.) and Community Reactions Division.
- Reduced staffing on narcotics division.
- Reduced foot patrols.
- Requested additional resources to cover additional demand, both from the city for local needs, and from the government for national needs.

Source: Barbara Raymond, Laura J. Hickman, Laura Miller, and Jennifer S. Wong, *Police Personnel Challenges After September 11: Anticipating Expanded Duties and a Changing Labor Pool,* RAND Corporation Occasional Paper (Santa Monica, CA: RAND Corporation, 2005).

Role Change

Some policymakers and academics have argued that as a consequence of 9/11, a new era of policing has emerged—referred to as intelligence-led policing (ILP) or predictive policing. Developed in England, ILP is based on the belief that some problems cannot be addressed through community policing alone and that enhanced intelligence capacity is needed to respond to crime and security threats.[56] As such, ILP emphasizes data collection and analysis for the purpose of increasing the probability that problem individuals will be identified and apprehended. At its core, ILP narrows the mission of the police to law enforcement, and the preferred activity is arrest and incapacitation. Interventions are driven by intelligence and focus on persons of interest. For ILP to be effective, police organizations are to be highly structured and maintain a top-down management style.[57]

Today, the prevalence of ILP in police agencies in the United States is unknown. Recently, the Department of Justice provided some seed money to several police agencies so that they could serve as demonstration sites to test the effectiveness of the strategy. The sites included the Los Angeles Police Department; the Washington, D.C., Metropolitan Police Department; the Chicago Police Department; the New York City Police Department; the Boston Police Department; the Shreveport, Louisiana, Police Department; and the Maryland State Police.[58] At least two of the sites—Shreveport and Chicago—released their evaluation results and both reported that the implementation of ILP had no effect on crime.[59] Although it is unclear whether ILP will emerge as a powerful force in policing in the future, it is clear that if it going to play a role in policing, police agencies will be required to increase their capacity to collect, maintain, and disseminate intelligence.

CASE STUDY

Evaluating the Impact of Officer-Worn Body Cameras in Phoenix, Arizona, Project Focus

The Phoenix Police Department (PPD) is a large municipal police agency, with more than 3,000 authorized sworn personnel, and it serves a community of more than 1.5 million people. One of PPD's precincts, the Maryvale Precinct, has historically been a location for a high-volume of police activity and violent crime, relative to other areas in the city. In 2010, the violent crime rate for Maryvale was approximately 85 crimes per 10,000 residents, compared to 55 per 10,000 for the rest of the city. Domestic violence is also a recurring problem. In 2010, there were more than 3,300 calls for service that were initially dispatched as domestic violence incidents in Maryvale Precinct. The Phoenix SPI (Smart Policing Initiative) project focuses on evaluating the implementation of body-worn cameras in this precinct of the city.

Objectives

The Phoenix SPI body-worn camera project focused on two primary objectives: (1) increase police accountability (e.g., deter officers' and citizens' inappropriate behavior, or record police misconduct); and (2) increase the effectiveness of the police in their response to crime in general and domestic violence specifically (e.g., improve officer reporting, court proceedings, or public cooperation). The study also sought to examine the potential impact on officer performance, both in the adoption of, and adaptation to the body-worn camera technology, and to assess the impact of cameras on officer job performance and satisfaction. The Phoenix SPI project thus examined the effect of the body-worn camera technology in six principal areas: (1) officer compliance with camera activation policies; (2) utility and use of body-worn cameras; (3) impact on officers' job performance; (4) impact on public compliance and cooperation; (5) impact on officer accountability; and (6) impact on domestic violence case processing and outcomes.

Implementation

In 2011, the Bureau of Justice Assistance (BJA) awarded PPD an SPI grant to purchase, deploy, and evaluate police body-worn cameras. The design and implementation of the Phoenix SPI project included the purchase of 56 body-worn camera systems (VIEVU) and deploying them in the Maryvale Precinct, which is operationally and geographically divided into two similarly sized patrol areas. The implementation of the cameras occurred in one of the two Maryvale Precinct squad areas, Area 82 (the target area). All officers assigned to the target area were issued the equipment and were provided training in its use, maintenance, and related departmental policy.

Arizona State University, Phoenix SPI research partner, conducted the evaluation of this project, examining the effect of implementing police-worn body cameras on complaints against the police and domestic violence case processing and outcomes. Data analysis relied on a pre-post comparison between the target and comparison area.

Outcomes

Frequency and Use of Cameras

Analysis of the camera metadata indicated a decrease in incidents recorded by a camera during the implementation period (with a high of 42.2 percent in May 2013 and a low of 13.2 percent in March 2014). Domestic violence incidents were the most likely to be recorded (47.5%), followed by violent offenses (38.7%), backup (37%), status offenses (32.9%), and subject/vehicle stops (30.9%). Other offense types were recorded less often.

Officer Perceptions of Cameras

Officer surveys revealed that officers found the technology comfortable and easy to use, but were dissatisfied with long download times, increased amount of time that it took to complete reports, and the possibility that video recordings might be used against them by the department. They also found that video submitted to the court was difficult to process because of logistical problems associated with chain of custody and the time that it took the prosecutors to review video files.

Impact of Cameras

The cameras were found to be beneficial in a number of ways. First, officer productivity as measured through the number of arrests increased significantly. For instance, the number of arrests increased by about 17 percent among the target area, compared to 9 percent in the comparison area. Second, complaints against the police declined significantly. Complaints against officers who wore the cameras declined by 23 percent, compared to a 10.6 percent increase among comparison-area officers and a 45.1 percent increase among patrol officers in other precincts. Third, officers who wore cameras and received a complaint were significantly less likely to have the complaint sustained when compared to the comparison area and other PPD patrol officers. Fourth, the officer self-report data suggested that a significant number of complaints were not pursued because of video recordings. Lastly, analysis of the data indicated that following the implementation of body-worn cameras, cases involving domestic violence were significantly more likely to be initiated, result in charges filed, and result in a guilty plea or verdict.

Lessons Learned

As part of the Phoenix SPI final evaluation, the project team identified a variety of lessons learned, including: developing a city-wide strategic plan with key stakeholders, increasing attention on the needs of city prosecutors, developing and deploying camera training, and increasing officer compliance with camera activation.

Source: Excerpt from Assistant Chief Michael Kurtenbach (Phoenix SPI Team), Charles Katz (Phoenix SPI Research Partner), and Vivian Elliott (SPI Project Manager), *SMART Policing Initiative Quarterly Newsletter* 15 (Spring 2015).

SUMMARY

The American police face many challenges in the immediate future. Technology, crime analysis, the state of the economy, and the war on terrorism will force many changes on the police. How the police will respond to these challenges and external changes is not clear. The only thing that is certain is that 10 years from now—if not sooner—American policing will be different from what it is today.

KEY TERMS

computer-aided dispatch, 546
records management systems, 546
Taser, 553

tactical crime analysis, 554
strategic crime analysis, 555
administrative crime analysis, 555

crime mapping, 555

FOR DISCUSSION

1. Get into groups and discuss the pros and cons of technology in policing today. Think about the impact of technology on police officers, police agencies, and citizens.
2. As a class, discuss whether you think police officers are paid too little or too much. Are police officers paid more or less than similar occupations? Should police officers be paid more, and if so, why?
3. As a class, discuss what role, if any, researchers should have in police organizations.

INTERNET EXERCISES

Exercise 1 Visit your favorite social media site and try to identify how your local police agency uses the application. Is it useful? Are their some ways that the agency could improve its presence on the social media site? What recommendation would you provide to the agency about its use of social media, based on what you have reviewed?

Exercise 2 Visit your local police department's website and look for the page describing the qualifications for becoming a police officer. Look at each of the qualifications to determine whether you fit the criteria to become a police officer in that department.

Exercise 3 Visit www.officer.com to learn about various jobs available in police agencies across the country. Think about whether you would be interested in working for a police agency located in another part of the country. What factors would influence your decision?

Exercise 4 Visit the International Association of Crime Analysts website (www.iaca.net). The site will provide you with information on how to become a crime analyst.

Exercise 5 As a class, watch and discuss the presentation "How Collaboration between Researchers and Police Chiefs Can Improve the Quality of Sexual Assault Investigations: A Look at Los Angeles" (available at www.nij.gov/multimedia/presenter/presenter-nijconf2011-collaboration/).

NOTES

1. Edward Maguire and William King, "Trends in Policing," unpublished manuscript, Manassas, VA, 2004.
2. As quoted in Jim Chu, *Law Enforcement Information Technology* (New York: CRC Press, 2001), 3.
3. Ibid.
4. Ibid.
5. Ibid.
6. Ibid.
7. James J. Willis, Stephen D. Mastrofski, and David Weisburd, "Compstat and Bureaucracy: A Case Study of Challenges and Opportunities for Change," *Justice Quarterly* 21 (September 2004): 463–496.
8. Samuel Walker, *Early Intervention Systems for Law Enforcement Agencies: A Planning and Management Guide* (Washington, DC: U.S. Department of Justice, 2003).

9. Samuel Walker, Stacy Osnick Milligan, and Anna Berke, *Strategies for Intervening with Officers through Early Intervention Systems: A Guide for Front-Line Supervisors* (Washington, DC: Police Executive Research Forum, 2006).

10. Mary Beth Sheridan, "License Plate Readers to Be Used in D.C. Area," *Washington Post,* August 17, 2008, C1.

11. International Association of Chiefs of Police, *Law Enforcement Information Management Section, Issue Identification: Privacy Issues Concerning the Utilization of Automated License Plate Readers,* Draft (Washington DC: Author, March 2009).

12. Bruce Taylor, Christopher Koper, and Daniel Woods, "Combating Vehicle Theft in Arizona," *Criminal Justice Review* 37, no. 1 (2012): 24–50.

13. American Civil Liberties Union, "You Are Being Tracked: How License Plate Readers Are Being Used to Record Americans' Movements," 2013, https://www.aclu.org/technology-and-liberty/you-arebeing-tracked-how-license-plate-readers-are-being-usedrecord.

14. International Association of Chiefs of Police, *Law Enforcement Information Management Section, Issue Identification.*

15. Charles M. Katz, "Monitoring and Evaluation Plan for the PPD On-Officer Video Camera Project," unpublished document, Arizona State University, Phoenix, AZ.

16. Ibid.

17. Barak Ariel, William A. Farrar, and Alex Sutherland, "The Effect of Police Body-Worn Cameras on Use of Force and Citizens' Complaints against the Police: A Randomized Controlled Trial," *Journal of Quantitative Criminology* 31, no. 3 (2015): 509–535.

18. Weston Morrow, Charles M. Katz, and David E. Choate, "Assessing the Impact of Police Body-Worn Cameras on Arresting, Prosecuting, and Convicting Suspects of Intimate Partner Violence," *Police Quarterly*, in press.

19. City of Wichita, "Police Body Worn Cameras," December 2014, https://lintvksnw.files.wordpress.com/2014/12/police-body-worn-camera-report.pdf.

20. Department of Justice, "Office of Justice Programs Comprehensive Body-Worn Camera Program," May 1, 2015, https://www.justice.gov/sites/default/files/opa/press-releases/attachments/2015/05/01/body-worn_camera_fact_sheet_.pdf.

21. International Association of Chiefs of Police, "2015 Social Media Survey Results," http://www.iacpsocialmedia.org/Portals/1/documents/FULL%202015%20Social%20Media%20Survey%20Results.pdf.

22. Edward F. Davis, Alejandro A. Alves, and David Alan Sklansky, "Social Media and Police Leadership: Lessons from Boston," *New Perspectives in Policing* (March 2014): 10.

23. Joel D. Lieberman, Deborah Koetzle, and Mari Sakiyama, "Police Departments' Use of Facebook: Patterns and Policy Issues," *Police Quarterly* (2013). doi:1098611113495049.

24. Michael T. Pettry, "Social Media: Legal Challenges and Pitfalls for Law Enforcement Agencies," *FBI Law Enforcement Bulletin* (December 2014), https://leb.fbi.gov/2014/december/legal-digest-social-media-legal-challenges-and-pitfalls-for-law-enforcement.

25. Accessed at https://www.fbi.gov/services/cjis/ncic

26. M. Chau, H. Atabakhsh, D. Zeng, and H. Chen, "Building an Infrastructure for Law Enforcement Information Sharing and Collaboration: Design Issues and Challenges," presented at the National Conference on Digital Government, Los Angeles, May 21–23, 2001.

27. Martin J. Zaworski, "Assessing an Automated, Information Sharing Technology in the Post '9–11' Era—Do Local Law Enforcement Officers Think It Meets Their Needs?," February 2005, www.ncjrs.gov/pdffiles1/nij/grants/208757.pdf.

28. C. Uchida, "Outcomes of Police Use of Force: Evaluating the Use of Tasers in the U.S.," unpublished manuscript (Silver Springs, MD: Justice & Security Strategies, 2005), 2; Jim Weiss and Mickey Davis, "The Latest TASER Technology," *Law and Order* magazine (September 2003): 1–5.

29. National Institute of Justice, *Study of Deaths Following Electro Muscular Disruption,* NIJ Special Report (Washington, DC: National Institute of Justice, 2011).

30. Ibid.

31. C. Moss, "Less Than Lethal Weapons," www.iejs.com/TechnologyandCrime/Law_Enforcement_Technology/less_than_lethal_ weapons.htm.

32. Cheryl W. Thompson and Mark Berman, "Improper Techniques, Increased Risk," *Washington Post*, November 26, 2015, http://www.washingtonpost.com/sf/investigative/2015/11/26/improper-techniques-increased-risks/.

33. William Bozeman, William E. Hauda, Joseph J. Heck, Derrel D. Graham, Brian P. Martin, and James E. Winslow, "Safety and Injury Profile of Conducted Electrical Weapons Used by Law Enforcement Officers Against Criminal Suspects," *Annals of Emergency Medicine* 53, no. 4 (2009): 480–489.

34. Timothy O'Shea and Keith Nicholls, *Crime Analysis in America* (Mobile, AL: Center for Public Policy at the University of South Alabama, March 2002).

35. See International Association of Crime Analysts' website at www.iaca.net.

36. O'Shea and Nicholls, *Crime Analysis in America.*

37. Deborah Osborne and Susan Wernicke, *Introduction to Crime Analysis* (New York: Hayworth Press, 2003).

38. Arizona Criminal Justice Commission, *Crime Mapping in Arizona Report* (Phoenix, AZ: Statistical Analysis Center, 2002).

39. See the National Institute of Justice's MAPS program at www.ojp.usdoj.gov/nij/maps.

40. Arizona Criminal Justice Commission, *Crime Mapping in Arizona Report.*

41. Jenni Bergal, "Touting Prevention, Police Put Crime Info Online," Pew Charitable Trust. STATELINE, January 20, 2015, Access at: http://www.pewtrusts.org/en/research-ad-analysis/blogs/stateline/2015/1/20/touting-prevention-police-put-crime-info-online.

42. Cynthia Mamalian and Nancy La Vigne, *The Use of Computerized Crime Mapping by Law Enforcement: Survey Results* (Washington, DC: National Institute of Justice, 1999).

43. U.S. Department of Labor, Bureau of Labor Statistics, "Police and Detectives," www.bls.gov//ooh/protective-service/print/police-and-detectives.htm.

44. U.S. Department of Labor, Bureau of Labor Statistics, "Occupational Employment and Wages," May 2015 , http://www.bls.gov/oes/current/oes333051.htm

45. Ibid.

46. Thomas Ackerman, *Guide to Careers in Federal Law Enforcement* (Traverse City, MI: Sage Creek Press, 1999).

47. James Stinchcomb, *Opportunities in Law Enforcement and Criminal Justice Careers* (Chicago: VGM Career Books, 2003).

48. Law Enforcement Career Starter, www.netlibrary.com/nlreader.dll?bookid528378&filename5page_3.html.

49. Office of Personnel Management, "Salary Table 2016-CHI (LEO)," https://www.opm.gov/policy-data-oversight/pay-leave/salaries-wages/salary-tables/pdf/2016/CHI%20(LEO).pdf.

50. National Academy of Sciences, *Fairness and Effectiveness in Policing: The Evidence* (Washington, DC: National Academies Press, 2004), 34.

51. This issue is discussed in Samuel Walker, "Science and Politics in Police Research: Reflections on Their Tangled Relationship," *Annals of the American Academy of Political and Social Science* V, 593 (May 2004): 1–20.

52. Jeff Rojek, Hayden P. Smith, and Geoffrey P. Alpert, "The Prevalence and Characteristics of Police Practitioner–Researcher Relationships," *Police Quarterly* 15, no. 3 (2012): 241–261.

53. Ibid.

54. U.S. Department of Justice, *Office of Community Oriented Policing Services, Local Law Enforcement Responds to Terrorism: Lessons in Prevention and Preparedness* (Washington, DC: U.S. Justice Department, 2003), available at www.cops.usdoj.gov.

55. Leadership Conference on Civil Rights, *Wrong Then, Wrong Now: Racial Profiling before and after September 11* (Washington, DC: Leadership Conference of Civil Rights, 2003).

56. Gregory Treverton, Matt Williams, Elizabeth Wilke, and Deborah Lai, *Moving toward the Future of Policing* (Santa Monica, CA: RAND Corporation, 2011).

57. Ibid.

58. National Institute of Justice, Predictive Policing. http://www.nij.gov/topics/law-enforcement/strategies/predictive-policing/Pages/welcome.aspx

59. Priscillia Hunt, Jessica Saunders and John S. Hollywood. "Evaluation of the Shreveport Predictive Policing Experiment." Santa Monica, CA: RAND Corporation, 2014. http://www.rand.org/pubs/research_reports/RR531.html. Jessica Saunders, Priscillia Hunt, and John S. Hollywood. "Predictions put into practice: a quasi-experimental evaluation of Chicago's predictive policing pilot:" *Journal of Experimental Criminology,* September 2016, Volume 12, Issue 3, pp 347–371

Glossary

287(g) agreements A Memorandum of Understanding between Immigration, Customs and Enforcement (ICE) and a local law enforcement agency that allows the local law enforcement agency to enforce immigration laws within its jurisdiction on behalf of ICE.

911 communications center Receives incoming calls from citizens, makes a series of discretionary decisions about how to handle those calls, and in some cases dispatches police cars to the scene of the incident.

A

abuse of authority Actions by a police officer, under the guise of his or her authority, that tend to injure or insult a citizen, trespass on human dignity, and/or violate a citizen's inherent civil rights.

accountability Having to answer for one's conduct. Both police organizations and individual officers are distinctly accountable to the public, elected officials, and the courts for how well they control crime, maintain order, and perform these tasks while remaining in compliance with the law.

accreditation The process of voluntary professional self-regulation that serves as an approach to establishing minimum national standards in policing.

active officers Officers who initiate more citizen contacts, back up officers on other calls, assert control in situations with citizens, and make more arrests.

actual caseload Those cases actually worked by detectives.

administrative crime analysis Focuses on providing summary statistics and data to police managers to better understand crime and disorder problems.

administrative rulemaking A legal concept for the process of controlling discretion through written departmental policies.

affirmative action Originating in 1965, a program to establish specific goals and timetables for the employment of minorities and women for any private employer or government agency receiving federal funds.

analysis The second stage of the SARA model of problem-oriented policing, in which the police collect information about a problem to help identify its scope, nature, and cause.

assessment The fourth stage of the SARA model of problem-oriented policing, in which the effectiveness of the response is evaluated through rigorous feedback that allows for revision if the response is not successful.

assessment center A technique used in police departments to evaluate the ability of an applicant to handle the job being sought through promotion.

authorized strength The maximum number of sworn officers any given law enforcement agency is authorized to employ.

B

backbone of policing The backbone of policing is patrol, the central feature of police operations.

background investigations Examine the applicants previous employment, criminal record, educational attainment, and financial status to determine their eligibility for employment.

bar girl A prostitute who works out of bars or other entertainment establishments.

behaviorally arrested Occurs when taking a suspect into custody and involves a number of different actions, such as a stop (in which the officer tells the individual not to leave), a verbal statement that the person is "under arrest," or physical restraint of a person.

benchmark The measure that is used to determine whether or not a pattern or practice exists.

blue curtain of silence A code of silence among police officers whereby officers refuse to testify against corrupt officers, creating a veil of secrecy around police actions.

blue-ribbon commissions Commissions serving as a form of external accountability for police conduct that address a full range of police issues and bring together leading experts to help improve local departments.

body-worn cameras Small digital cameras worn by police officers which record officer encounters with citizens.

bona fide occupational qualifications (BFOQs) Established qualifications that are reasonably necessary to the normal operation of that particular job.

Boston police strike Occurred in 1919 when 1,117 officers went on strike and formed a police union after having received no pay raise in nearly twenty years. After violence and disorder erupted throughout Boston, the strike quickly collapsed and the striking officers were fired.

bribe   Something offered or given to a person in the hope of influencing that individual's views or conduct. Police bribes can include monetary payoffs to protect illegal activity, provide information on criminal investigations, remove criminal files, or alter testimony in court.

broken windows   A theory developed by James Q. Wilson and George L. Kelling, argues that police should focus their resources on disorder problems that create fear of crime and lead to neighborhood decay.

brothel prostitutes   Prostitutes who work for legal brothels, illegal message parlors, and escort services.

bureaucracy   A pyramidal model of government administration in which tasks are grouped into separate bureaus or departments and information flows up and down according to the hierarchical structure. Marked by diffuse authority, visible divisions of labor, and inflexible rules of operation, each employee answers to one supervisor, creating a uniform and clear chain of command.

C

call girls   Sex workers who represent the upper end of the economic scale of prostitution.

career development   Involves opportunities to use one's talents and develop expertise in a particular area.

career perspective   Helps understand how police officers interact with law enforcement organizations.

case solvability factors   Factors that have been shown in the past to be related to the probability that a crime will be solved.

Christopher Commission   An independent commission, named after the former U.S. Secretary of State Warren Christopher, who led an investigation examining the patterns and practices of the Los Angeles Police Department in the wake of the Rodney King incident.

citizen complaint   A formal complaint by a citizen about the conduct of a police officer.

citizen oversight   An approach designed to provide independent citizen input for complaints filed against the police through agencies that independently review citizens' complaints, monitor the complaint process, scrutinize general police practices, review department policy and recommend policy changes, and audit the quality of complaint investigations.

civil service system   A nearly universal set of formal and legally binding procedures governing personnel decisions in police organizations, ensuring that such decisions are based on objective criteria and not on favoritism, bias, or political influence.

civil suits   Legal actions used when an individual or organization believes that a police agency has engaged in misconduct and seeks civil redress.

civilian review boards   External or citizen oversight agencies that handle citizen complaints.

civilians   Those who follow the pursuits of civil life and are not employed as sworn officers or officials.

clearance rate   The traditional measure of success in criminal investigations for a police agency based on the percentage of crimes solved by arrest.

code of silence   Also known as the "blue curtain," a code of honor among police officers whereby officers refuse to testify against corrupt colleagues, creating a veil of secrecy around police actions.

coercive force   Includes the power to take someone's life (deadly force), the use of physical force, and the power to deprive people of their liberty through arrest.

cohort effects   Officers hired in one decade will have different ideas and lifestyles than officers hired in later decades.

collaborative reform   The Department of Justice partners with a local law enforcement agency to provide it with technical assistance to address significant civil rights issues.

collective bargaining   A method of determining conditions of employment through bilateral negotiations according to the following principles: employees have a legal right to form unions; employers must recognize employee unions; employees have a right to participate in negotiations over working conditions; and employers are required to negotiate with the union's designated representatives.

communications center operators   Information brokers who receive citizen calls and translate them into official bureaucratic responses.

community cooperation model   Holds that effective responses to non-crime calls can help the police establish greater credibility with the public.

community outreach   Reaching out to segments of the population who might not otherwise have ready access to the police in their community.

community partnership   A collaborative partnership that stresses increased interaction between the police and the public to make the police more responsive to the community's needs and reduce community decay and disorder.

community policing   A model of policing that stresses a two-way working relationship between the community and the police, in which the police become more integrated into the local community and citizens assume an active role in crime control and prevention.

COMPSTAT   (Computerized Statistics) An organizational model, first used by the New York City Police in 1994, that allows police departments to blend timely intelligence, effective tactics, rapid deployment of personnel, and vigorous follow-up and assessment.

computer-aided dispatch   Also known as CAD, this a more effective and efficient technology that allows agencies to manage calls for service from the public.

confining discretion   Fixing the boundaries of rules.

consent decree   Police reforms that are ordered by the federal government and supervised by a federal judge who can punish the police department if it does not implement the required reforms.

constable   A peace officer who is empowered to serve writs and warrants but has a smaller jurisdiction than a sheriff.

containment   A strategy used by police to confine the homeless problem to one area of a community to both minimize disorder and keep homeless people out of public view.

contingency theory   A theoretical framework for understanding the structures and practices of police organizations based on the underlying premise that these organizations are created and structured to achieve specific goals, such as crime control, and will ultimately fail if unable to adjust to environmental contingencies.

consolidation   When two or more law enforcement agencies combine into one law enforcement agency.

consultation   Meetings that take place between the police and the community that allow citizens and the police to share information with one another.

contract services   When one unit of government pays another unit of government for police services.

convicted offender index   One of two types of data collected by the FBI as part of their National DNA Indexing System (NDIS). The convicted offender index contains genetic information on offenders who have been required to provide blood samples for genetic typing.

coproducers of crime control   A two-way working relationship between the community and the police in which the police become more integrated into the local community and citizens assume an active role in crime control and prevention.

coroner   A medical examiner responsible for aiding criminal investigations by probing deaths not thought to be of natural causes.

corruption   A form of misconduct or deviant behavior by police officers that involves the misuse of authority in a manner designed to produce personal gain for themselves or for others.

counterpunching   Occurs when someone calls the police about another person to divert attention from his or her own behavior.

county police   Police agencies that operate on a countywide basis and lack the non-law-enforcement roles of the county sheriff. About 1 percent of local departments are county police.

"coveted" assignments   Assignments that are regarded as highly desirable by rank-and-file officers.

crime-fighter image   The idea of the police as the "thin blue line," fighting a war on crime.

crime mapping   Crime analysis that allows analysts to identify spatial patterns and hot spots of different types of crimes.

crime prevention   A utilitarian idea that it is better to prevent crime than to respond after the fact.

crime prophylactic model   Holds that police intervention can defuse potentially violent situations and prevent them from escalating into criminal violence.

crime rate   Number of offenses per 100,000 population.

crimes of vice   Activities associated with public morality such as prostitution, pornography, liquor laws, and other sexually oriented businesses.

criminal justice system insiders   Professionals who regularly make important decisions about criminal cases such as police, prosecutors, defense attorneys, and judges.

cultural competence   The ability to understand and respond appropriately to differences in languages and traditions.

D

damage awards   Money or other benefits that are provided to a person as compensation for an injury or other harm they experienced.

D.A.R.E.   The most popular demand reduction strategy is the drug education program known as Drug Abuse Residence Education.

deadly force   The legal right of police officers to use force with the intent to kill if placed in a defense-of-life situation.

decentralize   To place greater decision-making responsibility on rank-and-file officers at the neighborhood level and to become more responsive to neighborhood residents.

decertification   The process of revoking a police officer's license to work in a given state; addresses the problem of an officer who is fired from one department for misconduct and is then hired by another, but does not prevent the fired officer from being hired in another state.

de-escalation   A technique for resolving police-citizen encounters without the use of force.

defense-of-life standard   States that police officers are allowed to use deadly force only in situations where their own lives or the life of another person is in danger.

deformalize   To eliminate many of the rules and policies that stifle creativity and discourage problem solving within police organizations.

delayerize   To decrease the amount of social and administrative distance between the beat officer and the chief of police.

demand reduction strategy   Attempting to reduce the demand for drugs on the part of potential users.

demeanor of the suspect   Includes the physical and verbal language used by a suspect including but not limited to hostility and disrespect.

despecialize   To replace specialized police units with neighborhood officers who are more knowledgeable about the problems their neighborhoods face.

differential response   The screening of 911 calls by the police to provide responses appropriate to the nature and severity of the calls.

digital revolution in communications   The impact of digital technology on policing, particularly in the form of cell phone cameras and police body-worn cameras.

directed patrol   Instruction to patrol to look for specific persons or types of crimes, or to patrol certain areas intensively.

discipline matrix   A formal schedule for disciplinary actions, specifying both the presumptive action to be taken for each type of misconduct and any adjustment to be made based on an officer's previous disciplinary record.

discovery time   The interval between the commission of a crime and its discovery.

discretion   The freedom to act on one's own judgment.

discrimination   Differential treatment based on some extralegal category such as race, ethnicity, or gender.

disparity   Differences or inequalities that are not necessarily caused by differential treatment.

domestic disturbance   A dispute, requiring police response, that involves two or more people engaged in an intimate relationship (married or divorced couples, live-in lovers, people on a first date, problems between adults and children, or adults and elderly parents).

domestic terrorism   Terrorism planned and carried out by Americans on American soil.

domestic violence   A disturbance between two or more people engaged in an intimate relationship that has escalated to a degree involving actual or threatened violence.

driving while black   The allegation that the police single out African American or Hispanic drivers for traffic stops on the basis of their race or ethnicity rather than suspected criminal conduct.

E

early intervention system   A management information system that systematically compiles and analyzes data on problematic police officer behavior, citizen complaints, police officer use-of-force reports, and other indicators to identify officers with recurring performance problems.

education generation gap   The difference between the younger, better-educated officers and the veteran officers with less education.

employee assistance program   A program through which officers can receive professional counseling related to a specific problem.

employment discrimination   Making employment related decisions that are based on traits, which are forbidden by agency regulations or state or federal laws.

English heritage   Brought by colonists and included English common law, high value on individual rights, the court systems, forms of punishment, and different forms of law enforcement.

equal employment opportunity (EEO) index   Measures the extent to which a police department reflects the community that it serves.

ethnicity   Cultural traits such as language, religion, and family patterns that characterize a group of people.

exclusionary rule   Holds that all evidence obtained by searches and seizures in violation of the Constitution is, by that same authority, inadmissible in a state court.

external mechanisms of accountability   Accountability procedures by persons, organizations, and branches of government outside the police agency.

F

field training   A supplement to classroom training that allows for practical experience under the supervision of a training officer in on-the-job type situations.

field training officer (FTO)   An experienced police officer assigned to supervise recruits during field training.

fleeing-felon rule   Declared unconstitutional by the Supreme Court in 1985 (*Tennessee v. Garner*), this ruling allowed police the legal right to use deadly force in apprehending a felon attempting to escape.

focused deterrence strategies   A form of problem-oriented policing that threatens high risk offenders with sanctions and communicates the threat for the purpose of deterring high risk offenders from committing crime in the near future.

foot patrol   Officers within a department who make neighborhood rounds on foot. While extremely expensive and able to cover only limited ground, foot patrol allows for enhanced police–community relations.

force factor   A framework for examining a police officer's use of force in relation to the actions of a citizen to help determine if the officer's actions were reasonable.

foreign terrorism   Terrorism coordinated and perpetuated by foreign persons or countries against the United States.

forensic index   One of two types of data collected by the FBI as part of their National DNA Indexing System (NDIS). Forensic index data contain DNA profiles from genetic evidence gathered from crime scenes.

four systems of justice   Refers to enforcement patterns that varied based on the racial components of the offender/victim relationship.

Fourteenth Amendment   Guarantees of equal protection under the law by stating that all persons born or naturalized in the United States are citizens therein, and no state shall make or enforce laws that deprive citizens of life, liberty, or property, without due process of law, or deny to any person within its jurisdiction the equal protection of the laws.

Fourth Amendment   The constitutional guarantee of protection against unreasonable searches and seizure.

fragmented   Broken down into separate, decentralized parts.

functional specialization   A form of organizational structure in which employees are assigned specific duties based on their areas of expertise, thereby allowing less critical tasks to be delegated to paraprofessionals.

functions of patrol   Patrol is used to deter crime, enhance feelings of public safety, and to make officers available for service.

G

Garrity **ruling**   The Garrity ruling, based on Garrity v. State of New Jersey states that a police officer can be disciplined and even dismissed for refusing to answer questions by internal affairs, but the information disclosed cannot then be used against him or her in a criminal prosecution.

general service law enforcement agencies   Those that are regularly engaged in (1) preventing crime, (2) investigating crimes and apprehending criminals, (3) maintaining order, and (4) providing other miscellaneous services.

grass eater   A police officer who passively accepts gratuities offered to him or her.

gratuities   The most common form of police corruption; gifts or favors given to police officers, sometimes out of a sincere effort to thank the officers but often out of self-interest with an expectation of better police service.

G.R.E.A.T.   The most popular police-led gang prevention program is called Gang Resistance Education and Training (GREAT).

group solidarity   A strong sense of fellowship between officers derived from a common work environment.

H

hammered informants   Those individuals who agree to be an informant because of the stress associated with their arrest.

hate crime   A criminal offense against a person or property motivated in whole or in part by the offender's bias against a race, religion, disability, ethnic/national origin, or sexual orientation.

Herman Goldstein   The originator of the concept of problem-oriented policing.

Herman Goldstein Award   Presented at a police executive conference to recognize the most innovative and successful problem-oriented policing project implemented by a police agency.

high-speed pursuit   A situation where a police officer attempts to stop a vehicle and the suspect knowingly flees and is pursued at a high rate of speed.

highway patrol   Agencies having statewide authority to enforce traffic regulations and arrest non-traffic violators under their jurisdiction.

honest law enforcement   An approach representative of low expectations for law enforcement that states police would continue to patrol neighborhoods, answer calls for service, intervene in problem situations, and try to apprehend offenders, but would not make unjustified claims that they are preventing crime.

Hoover, J. Edgar   Director of the Federal Bureau of Investigation from 1924 to 1972. Although Hoover increased the size and scope of the bureau's capabilities, he is best known for systematically misusing his power and exaggerating the bureau's effectiveness.

horizontal cliques   Informal networks formed between similarly ranked officers.

hot spot   An area that receives a disproportionate number of calls for police service and/or has a very high crime rate.

hostility from citizens   Can result in changes in officers' attitudes.

I

independent monitor   Appointed by the court as a consequence of a consent decree; oversees implementation of court ordered reforms; assists the department in implementing the reforms; and issues public reports on the progress of implementation.

informal organizational culture   The values and traditions communicated informally among officers.

injunctions   Court orders that prohibit a specified group from a specific course of action.

In-service training   Training provided to employees to enhance their professional skills.

insiders   Police officers who get to see firsthand how the system works.

institutional theory   A theoretical framework for understanding the structures and practices of police organizations based on the premise that police organizations are social institutions that operate in relation to their external social and political environment.

intelligence led policing   A policing model that believes that enhanced intelligence capacity is needed to decrease crime and other problem behavior and to increase the probability that problem individuals will be identified and apprehended.

internal affairs unit   Also known as the office of professional standards, this unit is responsible for investigating alleged misconduct by police officers.

internal benchmarking   Compares the performance of individual officers with peer officers.

internal mechanisms of accountability   Accountability procedures within the police department.

investigatory stops   When an police officer briefly detains an individual based on reasonable suspicion of criminal activity.

J

job satisfaction   Feelings among police officers of pride, enjoyment, and happiness about their work.

job security   Civil service rules and police union contracts make it very difficult to fire an officer, except for criminal conduct.

job stress   Conditions associated with one's work environment that are mentally or physically disruptive; the major cause of job dissatisfaction.

job stress coping mechanisms   Confidential assistance programs that utilize health professionals and/or peer support groups to help employees cope with personal or work-related problems.

K

Kansas City Gun Experiment   Designed to reduce gun-related crimes by removing guns from the streets of a high-crime precinct in Kansas City; represented a combination of problem-oriented policing (by focusing on a particular problem) and "hot spots" (by concentrating on particular areas of high criminal activity).

Kansas City Preventive Patrol Experiment   Conducted from 1972 to 1973, the experiment measured the impact of different levels of patrol on criminal activity, community perceptions, police officer behavior, and police department practices, while being the first independent and objective experiment (that met the minimum standards of scientific research) to test the effectiveness of patrol.

Kerner Commission   Created in 1967 to study issues of race relations; found that hostility between the police and ghetto communities was a major cause for disorder. Officially known as the National Advisory Commission on Civil Disorders.

L

language barriers   Arise when the citizen speaks a language other than English that the responding officer does not speak.

lateral entry   Moving from one police department to another at either the same rank or a higher rank.

Lautenberg Amendment   A federal law passed in 1996 prohibiting anyone with a conviction for domestic violence from owning a firearm.

Law of Equal Employment Opportunity   Designed to eliminate employment discrimination by making it illegal to refuse employment to, discharge, or deny benefits and compensation to anyone on the basis of race, ethnicity, color, religion, or sex.

legalistic style   An organizational style used in police departments that emphasizes aggressive crime fighting and attempts to control officer behavior through a rule-bound, "by-the-book" administrative approach.

legally arrested   Occurs when an individual is deprived of his or her liberty by legal authority and is under arrest or simply taken into custody. A police officer must have the intent to arrest, must communicate that intent to the person, and must actually take the person into custody.

legitimacy   In policing, legitimacy is the belief of citizens that the police have a right to exercise their authority.

local merger/consolidation   Two or more law enforcement agencies combine into one law enforcement agency.

local political control   A tradition, inherited from England during the colonial period, that places primary responsibility for public protection with local governments, both city and county.

local political culture   Values and traditions, communicated informally in a particular department, town, or community, that influence the organizational structure of policing and officer discretion in that area.

London Metropolitan Police   Created in 1829, the LMP represents the first example of an efficient, proactive police force. The LMP introduced three important elements of policing: the mission of crime prevention, the strategy of preventive patrol, and an organizational structure similar to the military.

low-visibility work   Officers generally work alone or in pairs with no direct supervision.

M

Mapp v. Ohio   A controversial Supreme Court decision that established Fourth Amendment protection against unreasonable searches and seizures by the police.

meat eater   A police officer who actively and aggressively demands gratuities.

mercenary informants   Those individuals who provide information to the police in exchange for money.

mercy booking   Arresting a mentally ill person for a minor offense so that he or she will be booked into the county jail and receive needed mental health care.

minimum age level   Twenty-one is the minimum age to become a police officer in most communities.

Minneapolis Domestic Violence Experiment   A study conducted from 1981 to 1982 to determine the relative deterrent effect of arrest, mediation, and separation in misdemeanor domestic violence incidents; it found that arrests produced lower rates of repeat violence than separation or mediation.

Miranda v. Arizona   A Supreme Court case that requires the police to advise citizens of their rights.

mixed approach to police accountability   A blend of internal and external accountability procedures.

mobilization   Communities are mobilized under such programs as Neighborhood Watch and Crime Stoppers to help prevent crime and disorder.

moderates   Male police officers who accepted the idea of policewomen in principle but were unhappy about women on patrol duty.

moderns   Male police officers who accepted policewomen relatively easily, recognized that police work rarely calls for physical strength, and accepted the idea that job opportunities should be open to everyone on the basis of individual merit.

"moral career" of a police officer   A process involving a series of stages that move from lesser to greater tolerance of and/or involvement in corrupt activities.

municipal police   Also known as *city police,* the municipal police make up the most important component of American law enforcement. Representing the majority of all law enforcement agencies and sworn officers, municipal police are responsible for dealing with serious crime, difficult order maintenance problems, and a wide range of emergency services.

myth of full enforcement   The notion or idea that police officers do not use discretion and enforce all laws.

N

Newark Foot Patrol Experiment   Conducted from 1978 to 1979 to test the effect of foot patrol on crime and public perception; the Newark experiment concluded that added foot patrol did not affect serious crime, but did have a positive impact on public perception of the police.

Newport News   The city in Virginia where the first experiment in problem-oriented policing occurred in the 1980s.

nominal caseload   All cases assigned to an officer.

O

occupational deviance   Criminal and improper noncriminal behavior committed during the course of normal work activities or under the guise of a police officer's authority.

officer-initiated activity   Includes stopping, questioning, and frisking suspicious citizens, making informal contacts with law abiding citizens; stopping vehicles for possible violations, writing traffic tickets, checking suspicious events; and making arrests.

officially arrested   Occurs only once the police make an official arrest report.

oral interviews   Conducted by most police departments as part of the police officer application process to detect those who might be incompatible with good police work.

order maintenance   Includes such activity as minor fights and disturbances, domestic incidents, public nuisances.

order maintenance calls   Include such incidents as minor fights and disturbances, domestic incidents, and public nuisances.

organizational culture   Values and traditions, communicated informally, that influence the organizational style of policing within a police department.

outside employment   A significant number of police officers supplement their income with work outside the law enforcement agency.

P

passive officers   Include those officers who initiate few contacts with citizens, respond only to calls to which they are dispatched, and make few traffic stops and arrests.

patronage   When local politicians used jobs on the police force to reward their friends.

pattern or practice suits   Lawsuits that allege the regular practice of police misconduct by a local law enforcement agency.

peace officer   A status granted to individuals who have certain powers not available to ordinary citizens and who provide certain legal protections. A peace officer can be a police, probation, parole, or corrections officer.

Peel, Robert   Credited as the father of modern policing; fought to improve the basic structure of law enforcement and persuaded the English Parliament to establish the London Metropolitan Police in 1829.

performance evaluations   An employment review designed to provide feedback to the officer so that he or she has an opportunity to improve.

performance review   A formal discussion with an employee about their performance and actions that should be taken by the employee to improve their performance.

personnel standards   Policies that define expectations of employee workplace performance.

pervasive organized corruption   The most serious form of corruption; exists at an organized level that penetrates the higher levels of the department.

pervasive unorganized corruption   When a majority of personnel in an agency are corrupt, but who have little relationship to each other.

physical disorder   A form of societal neglect resulting from physical decay within a neighborhood; examples include vandalism, dilapidation, and abandonment of buildings, and trash buildup.

physical force   The use of coercive force by a police officer to control a person and bring a situation under control.

police academy   A training facility where recruits learn to become police officers.

police aides   Nonsworn personnel used by police departments to handle low-priority calls and routine assignments, freeing sworn officers for more critical tasks.

police auditor or inspector general   A professional who is independent of the police and who provides policymakers with an objective review of police misconduct.

police brutality   The use of excessive physical force by the police.

police buffs   People who are supportive of the police and serve as informants because of their unique access to information.

police corruption   Acts involving the misuse of authority by a police officer in a manner designed to produce personal gain for himself or for others.

police–community relations   Relations between the police and racial and ethnic minority communities.

police–community relations crisis   Occurred in the 1960s and stimulated a series of national reports on the police that greatly enhanced knowledge about policing and made recommendations for improving policing.

police–community relations (PCR) units   Programs designed to improve relations with minority communities.

police knowledge model   Holds that non-crime calls give officers a broader exposure to the community with the result they have more knowledge that will help them solve crimes.

police legal advisor   A lawyer or team of lawyers employed by the police department.

police officer   A nonmilitary person who is employed by a government agency and has the legal status of a peace officer.

Police Officer Bill of Rights   State laws that provide for First Amendment and due process rights of police officers.

police–population ratio   The traditional measure of the level of police protection in a community; usually calculated as the number of officers per 1,000 population.

police professionalism   Often took on such principles as specialization, hierarchy, clear lines of authority, and written rules of policy.

police subculture   The major social norms that govern police conduct.

police union   An organization legally authorized to represent police officers in collective bargaining with the employer. Police unions spread rapidly in the 1960s after officers were angry and alienated over Supreme Court rulings, criticisms by civil rights groups, poor salaries, and benefits.

policy review   The practice of reviewing policies and procedures and making recommendations for change.

political era   A period in US history when the police derived much of their legitimacy and authority through political patronage.

political patronage   The practice of politicians appointing governmental or political positions based on friendship instead of merit.

positive use of discretion   Used by an officer to promote effective and efficient police work.

preference of the victim   Actions taken by the police are often a reflection of the complainant.

preliminary investigation   The first stage of investigating a crime, consisting of five steps: identifying and arresting any suspects, providing aid to any victims in need of medical attention, securing the crime scene to prevent loss of evidence, collecting all relevant physical evidence, and preparing a preliminary report.

preservice training   Required prior to beginning work as a police officer and includes attendance at a police academy and completion of field training.

President's Crime Commission   A comprehensive study of the entire criminal justice system conducted from 1965 through 1967.

President's Task Force on 21st Century Policing   A task force created in 2014 by President Obama to understand and recommend changes to address problems between the police and the public.

proactive crime strategies   Anticrime strategies initiated by the police themselves, as opposed to occurring in response to a citizen request for service.

probationary period   Typically a one year period following preservice training when an officer can be dismissed without cause.

problem-oriented policing   A model of policing that stresses planned responses to crime and disorder problems.

problem solving   Identifying the underlying causes of problems rather than responding to the problems themselves.

procedural justice   The extent to which the police exercise their authority fairly.

professionalization movement   Developed a specific agenda of reform defining policing as a profession which has an obligation to serve the entire community on a nonpartisan basis; sought to remove the influence of politics on policing.

profiling (see racial profiling)

promotion   Advancement in rank or responsibility usually based on merit, but sometimes the result of personal favoritism.

psychiatric first aid   Application of immediate informal, field-based counseling by a police officer.

public interest organization   Private, nonprofit organizations that serve the public.

public safety consolidation   Consolidation of public safety services such as police, fire, and emergency medical services within the same jurisdiction.

Q

quasi-military style   Suggests that the police are organized similar to the military by wearing a uniform, possessing a military rank and command structure, adopting an authoritarian organizational style, carrying weapons, and possessing the legal authority to use deadly force, physical force, and arrest.

R

race   Traditionally defined as referring to the major biological divisions of the people of the world.

"racial divide"   Differences in opinions between races about public policy.

racial profiling   The practice of making police stops solely on the basis of one's race or ethnicity and not because of criminal activity.

rank hierarchy   Hierarchy based on the officer's rank.

reactive crime strategies   Anticrime strategies used by police when responding to a civilian's request for service.

reality shock   The astonishment a new police officer experiences when encountering the unpleasant aspects of dealing with the public, the criminal justice system, and the department during the first weeks and months on the job.

records management systems   Used to input and organize information from different types of reports in one easy to access format.

regionalization   When several jurisdictionally based agencies combine their efforts to provide services in a geographic area.

residency requirements   A requirement in some police departments that their officers live within the city or county where they are employed.

residual deterrence   Also called the *phantom effect*, involves assuming that the police are patrolling an area from their having been seen in the area or nearby at another time, leading to the presumption that the police are present when there is no patrol in the area.

resource dependency theory   A theoretical framework for understanding the structures and practices of police organizations based on the premise that such organizations must obtain resources to survive, and that to obtain these resources they must engage in exchanges with other organizations in their environment.

response   The third stage of the SARA model of problem-oriented policing, in which data collected during the analysis stage are used to develop a strategy to address the problem and, ultimately, implement a response.

response time   The total amount of time between the commission of a crime and the moment a police officer arrives on the scene.

reverse discrimination   Discrimination focused on whites and/or males; in violation of the 1964 Civil Rights Act and the equal protection clause of the Fourteenth Amendment.

rewards hierarchy   Typically corresponds with an officer's rank and seniority within the department.

ride-along programs   Allow citizens to spend a few hours riding in a patrol car.

risk management   A process used to reduce costs associated with lawsuits against the organization.

Roosevelt, Theodore   Served as police commissioner of New York City between 1895 and 1897 and later as president of the United States.

rotten apple   A theory that describes a situation where an officer is independently engaged in corrupt acts.

rotten pocket   Exists when several corrupt officers cooperate with one another.

routine supervision   One of the central tasks of police management; this responsibility primarily falls on sergeants.

S

SARA   Problem-oriented policing is typically implemented through a four stage process known as SARA: scanning, analysis, response, and assessment.

scanning   The first stage of the SARA model of problem-oriented policing, in which officers take steps to identify possible problems and expose their underlying causes.

scenario-based training   A method of training that relies on a description of an unfolding event where students use their class room training to solve potentially real events that could take place in the field.

selection tests   Exams that are designed to reduce the number of applicants to those who are most qualified.

selective contact   A lack of cross-sectional contact and communication between police officers and a community that leads to misperceptions about public attitudes toward the police.

selective perception and memory   The likelihood that police officers will remember traumatic or unpleasant incidents with citizens, even though only 2 to 5 percent of contacts involve hostility or conflict.

seniority hierarchy   A form of hierarchy based on the number of years of service the officer has been employed as an officer with an agency.

seniority system   A personnel process in which officers with more years on the job have first priority in requesting assignments.

service calls   Responds to incidents including medical emergencies, welfare checks, and general assistance.

service style   A style of policing that emphasizes responsiveness to community expectations and typically found in suburban communities.

sex trafficking   The recruitment, harboring, transportation, provision or obtaining a person for the purpose of a commercial sex act that is induced by force, fraud, or coercion, or when the person who is forced to perform the commercial sex act is under 18 years old.

sexual harassment   Unwanted sexual advances, offensive sexually-related behavior, or discrimination in assignments or promotion.

sexual misconduct   Any behavior by an officer that takes advantage of the officer's position in law enforcement to misuse authority and power (including force) in order to commit a sexual act, initiate sexual contact with another person, or respond to a perceived sexually motivated cue (from a subtle suggestion to an overt action) from another person.

shared services   When two or more agencies combine resources to accomplish certain activities or goals.

sheriff   An elected county official who is responsible for all three components of the criminal justice system: law enforcement, courts, and corrections. Usually is directly involved in partisan politics in ways that municipal police chiefs are not.

situational factors   Circumstances and factors that possibly influence officer behavior at the time of the incident.

skeezers   A woman who trades sex for crack cocaine.

Smith, Bruce   An early police scholar who led efforts to establish the Uniform Crime Reporting (UCR) system and whose research shaped the transition of policing into the reform era.

social control   An organized and planned response to deviance and socially problematic behavior.

social disorder   A form of societal neglect resulting from the disorderly actions of individuals in a neighborhood; examples include public drinking, street corner gangs, street harassment, street-level drug sale and use, noisy neighbors, and commercial sex.

social work model   Holds that the latent coercive power of the police can help to steer potential lawbreakers into law-abiding behavior.

span of control   The theory of span of control assumes that any supervisor can effectively supervise a limited number of people, and is typically measured as the ratio of sergeants to officers.

special district police   Police agencies designed to serve only specific government agencies. Examples include the Los Angeles School District Police Force and the Metropolitan Transit Police Force in the Washington, D.C., subway system.

standard operation procedure manual Written rules and policies that are codified in a department.

state police Agencies that have statewide police powers for both traffic regulation and criminal investigations.

status hierarchy Hierarchy based on officers' assignments or jobs within the police agency.

stereotypes about cops Heavily influence the public image of who the police are, what they believe, and how they act.

stereotyping Beliefs and perceptions developed through training, experience, culture, and policies that allows officers to develop a visual shorthand for suspects based on visual cues.

Stop Question and Frisk A tactic where police stop a pedestrian for a minor infraction, or based on reasonable suspicion, question them, and frisk them for weapons for the purpose of identifying and arresting wanted criminals, those involved in disorder, and confiscating guns.

strategic crime analysis Focuses on long term crime trends to develop strategic plans to address particular problems.

street cop culture Values street experience and a tough, personalized way of dealing with people on the street.

street-level bureaucrats A name given to patrol officers because they make decisions that produce actual police policy as it affects citizens.

streetwalker One who represents the lower end of the social and economic scale of prostitution by soliciting on the streets, thus being highly visible to both the police and the general public.

subjectively arrested Occurs when someone having an encounter with the police believes he or she is not free to go, leading to the perception of having been arrested.

supervison The continuous review and monitoring of a subordinate employee.

supply reduction strategy Attempting to reduce the supply of drugs available to potential sellers and users.

systemic bias A pervasive pattern of discrimination against members of a particular group within an organization.

T

tactical crime analysis Typically involves the identification of specific crime problems in particular geographic areas.

Taser Thomas A. Swift Electric Rifle (TASER) is a battery powered electro-muscular device that fires two metal prongs, attached to a wire that delivers electricity, immobilizing the suspect.

task forces An organizational unit within a police agency that consists of officers from different ranks who are selected based on their talents rather than their rank.

team policing A radical innovation in the 1970s involving restructuring police operations along neighborhood lines and decentralizing decision-making authority.

terrorism The unlawful use of force or violence against persons or property to intimidate or coerce a government, the civilian population, or any segments thereof in furtherance of political or social objectives.

Title VII of the 1964 Civil Rights Act Makes it illegal to refuse to hire or to discharge any individual, or to otherwise discriminate against any individual with respect to employment on the basis of race, color, religion, sex, or national origin.

traditionals Male officers who were committed to the image of policing as dangerous work involving aggressive action and requiring physical strength.

transparency The concept that police organizations should be more open with the public about their operations.

tribal police Agencies whose primary responsibility is to provide general law enforcement services for Indian Nations.

turnover The number of employees hired by a company or department to replace workers who have left their jobs in a given period of time.

U

unconscious or implicit bias A form of bias or prejudice that is rooted in assumptions about race or ethnicity that are below the level of consciousness.

unfounding a crime Failure of a police officer to complete an official crime report when a citizen reports a crime.

use of force review board Reviews and provides findings and recommendations to the Chief of Police about police use-of-force incidents.

V

vengeful informants Serve as a source of information to the police for the purpose of exacting revenge on someone.

verbal abuse The use of inappropriate language, particularly racial and ethnic slurs, by police officers.

vertical cliques Informal networks formed between lower and higher ranking officers.

vice   Victimless crimes with no complaining party and involving prostitution, gambling, or narcotics.

victimless crime   A crime that has no complaining party and often involves behavior that many people regard as legitimate, resulting in conflicting public attitudes about how vigorously the laws should be enforced.

victim–suspect relationship   The social distance between the suspect and victim.

Vollmer, August   Chief of police in Berkeley, California, from 1905 to 1932, known as the father of police professionalism for advocating higher education for police officers and promoting organizational reform within departments.

W

war on crime   A term used to describe criminal justice policies that emphasize strict law enforcement and harsh punishments.

war on drugs   A term used to describe criminal justice policies that emphasize strict enforcement of drug laws and punishment of persons arrested for drug offenses.

the watch   A group that patrolled the city in Colonial America to guard against fires, crime, and disorder.

watchman style   An organizational style used in police departments that emphasizes peacekeeping without aggressive law enforcement and few controls over rank-and-file officers.

Wells, Alice Stebbins   A leader of the policewomen's movement. Wells organized the International Association of Policewomen in 1915.

Wickersham Commission   Created in 1929 by President Herbert Hoover as the first national study of the American criminal justice system. Officially known as the National Commission on Law Observance and Enforcement.

Wilson, O. W.   Leader of the police professionalization movement from the late 1930s through the end of the 1960s. Developed a formula for efficient management of personnel by assigning patrol officers on the basis of a workload formula that reflected reported crime and calls for service.

workable caseload   Includes those cases that have sufficient leads and therefore are worth attempting to solve.

work environment of policing   Includes such factors as the organizational culture, public behaviors, public attitudes and job responsibilities that a police officer encounters that contributes to the exercise of discretion.

Z

zero-tolerance policing   Based on the belief that aggressive enforcement of laws directed at combating disorder will motivate residents to better care for their community, a policy that calls for the police to focus primarily on disorder, minor crime, and the appearance of crime through interventions that vigorously enforce criminal and civil laws and are conducted for the purpose of restoring order to communities.

Name Index

A

Abdulmutallab, Umar Farouk, 314
Ahmed, Ramzi, 314
Alex, Nicholas, 140
Alexander, Michelle, 427
Alpert, Geoffrey, 232, 381, 382, 384, 392, 413, 424, 428, 446
Anechiarico, Frank, 482–483
Antunes, George, 223
Archbold, Carol, 180, 192, 395, 512

B

Barker, Thomas, 455, 468, 472
Barton, Gina, 482
Bayley, David, 29–31, 190, 194–196, 215, 221, 225, 252, 329–331, 342, 427, 530
Berk, Richard, 267
Bittner, Egon, 13, 252
Black, Donald, 52, 258, 274, 275, 288, 369, 380, 418, 427, 527
Blumberg, Abraham, 415
Bobb, Merrick, 496, 498, 507, 510, 512
Bonner, Heidi, 352
Bordua, David, 295–296
Bouza, Anthony, 142
Bowen, Kenneth, 477
Braga, Anthony, 218, 359
Brandl, Steven, 297
Bratton, William, 113, 267, 355, 532
Briar, Scott, 275
Brissette, James, 477
Brody, David, 199
Brown, Lee, 81
Brown, Michael, 9, 63, 405–406, 420, 489, 523, 528
Buerger, Michael, 344
Burge, Jon, 477
Burnham, David, 457, 459, 482, 528
Bush, George W., 86, 310, 314
Butler, Smedley, 41

C

Campbell, D., 105
Campbell, K., 105
Campos, Pamela, 504
Caracappa, Stephen, 477
Carter, David, 455, 472

Cassell, Paul, 515, 517
Castellano, Thomas, 305
Chaiken, Jan, 143
Chaiyavej, Somvadee, 182
Chambliss, William, 466, 467
Chitwood, Michael, 149
Chu, Jim, 545
Clinton, Bill, 344
Cochrane, Charles Jr., 184
Cohen, Bernard, 143
Compass, Edwin P., 483
Coolidge, Calvin, 43
Cordner, AnnMarie, 180
Cordner, Gary, 79, 180, 231, 297, 336, 351
Cowper, Thomas, 104
Crank, John, 109, 304
Cumming, Elain, 228
Curtis, Edwin U., 43

D

Dabney, D., 114
Daley, Richard M., 341
Daley, Robert, 459
Davis, Goliath, 334–335
Davis, Kenneth C., 370, 371, 385, 386, 390, 391, 395
de Blasio, Bill, 57
DeLone, Miriam, 433
Doerner, William G., 141, 202
Dowd, Michael, 194, 474
Dunham, Roger, 232, 381, 382, 413, 428
Durk, David, 482
Duvall, Lucie, 146

E

Eck, Emily, 218
Eck, John, 218, 297, 328, 333, 345, 347
Eigenberg, H. M., 158
Emanuel, Rahm, 342, 505
Engel, Robin, 497
Epp, Charles, 406, 431, 517
Eppolito, Louis, 477
Escobar, Gipsy, 132
Eterno, John, 288

F

Fagan, Jeffrey, 357, 407
Fajardo, R., 94

Falcone, David N., 71
Faulcon, Robert, 477
Flavin, Jeanne, 271
Fogelson, Robert, 34
Forst, Brian, 90
Fradella, Henry F., 356, 392, 396, 426, 525
Frank, James, 297
Fridell, Lorie, 155, 422
Furstenburg, Frank, 231, 420
Fyfe, James J., 12, 24, 54, 56, 183, 216–217, 383, 384, 392, 397

G

Gardiner, John, 480
Garner, Edward, 421
Garner, Eric, 63, 406, 489, 517
Garofalo, James, 190, 195–196, 221, 225, 252
Geller, Amanda, 357
Geller, William A., 500
Gelles, Richard, 257, 258
Gill, Charlotte, 344
Gilsinan, James, 225
Gisevius, Robert, 477
Giuliani, Rudolph, 355
Glick, Barry, 492
Goldman, Roger, 203
Goldstein, Herman, 21, 59, 290, 345, 371, 385, 386, 391, 395, 455, 469, 471, 476, 495, 506
Goldstein, Joseph, 386
Grant, J. Douglas, 143
Grant, Joan, 143
Gray, Freddie, 63, 406
Green, Jack, 353
Guyot, Dorothy, 108

H

Haarr, Robin, 179, 185, 336, 469
Haller, Mark, 37
Hamilton, Alexander, 88
Harcourt, Bernard, 328, 358
Harrington, Penny, 56, 175
Hartnett, Susan, 8, 188, 339
Heaphy, John, 297
Herbert, Steve, 178, 179, 189, 384
Hirschel, David, 262

Holliday, George, 414, 528
Hoover, Herbert, 47
Hoover, J. Edgar, 45, 48–49, 89

I

Irlbeck, Dawn, 183
Ivkovich, Sanja, 416, 479

J

Jacobs, James B., 482–483
Joh, Elizabeth, 90
Johnson, Lyndon, 51
Jurik, Nancy, 180, 195

K

Kaminski, Robert, 140
Kane, Robert, 464–465, 468
Kappler, V. E., 158
Katz, Charles, 123, 124
Kelley, Clarence, 234, 472
Kelling, George L., 58, 326–327, 343, 356, 391, 397
Kelly, Raymond W., 13, 315
Kennedy, David, 140, 175, 406, 428–429
Key, V. O., 467
King, Martin Luther Jr., 49
King, Rodney, 53, 414, 506, 518, 523, 528, 532, 552
King, William, 13, 111–112, 115, 545
Klein, Malcolm, 308
Klinger, David, 275, 381, 383
Klockars, Carl, 469
Kochel, Tammy Rinehart, 427
Kornblum, Allan, 482
Krantz, Sheldon, 515
Kraska, Peter, 104

L

LaFave, Wayne, 370
LaFree, Gary, 382
Langworthy, Robert, 304
Lanier, Cathy, 153
Larson, Richard, 236
Leo, Richard, 515–517
Leuci, Robert, 475
Lichtenburg, Illya, 254
Lincoln, Abraham, 33
Littlejohn, Edward, 517
Loftus, Elizabeth, 298
Lopez, Christy, 152, 427
Lovrich, Nicholas, 120, 124
Lundman, Richard J., 275
Lurigio, Arthur, 188

M

MacDonald, Heather, 435
MacDonald, John, 267, 357
Macdonald, Morgan, 62, 521
Mack, David, 477
Maguire, Edward, 13, 111, 124, 328, 333, 345, 545
Malee, Kathryn, 480
Manning, Peter, 223, 224, 304, 395
Mapp, Dolree, 514
Marshall, Thurgood, 48
Martin, Margaret, 262
Martin, Susan, 149, 158, 180, 185, 202, 312
Martin, Susan Ehrlich, 180, 195
Marx, Gary, 303
Mastrofski, Stephen D., 94, 251, 253, 258, 327–328, 336, 382, 427
McCabe, K., 94
McCarthy, Garry, 124
McCorkle, Richard, 263
McDonald, Laquan, 179, 420, 439, 505
McGinniskin, Barney, 35, 38
McGuffee, K., 158
McKinley, William, 40
McMullen, M., 468
McNamara, John H., 168
Meehan, Albert, 435
Messner, Steven, 309
Meyer, John C., 252
Miedzianowski, Joseph, 477
Miethe, Terance, 263
Miller, Batya, 39
Miller, J. Mitchell, 302
Miller, Susan, 184
Miller, Walter, 306–308
Miller, Wilbur, 37
Miranda, Ernesto, 49–50
Morash, Merry, 182
Murphy, Patrick V., 333, 472–474, 501, 528
Myrdal, Gunnar, 373, 419

N

Najim, Eyad Mahmoud Ismail, 314
Nicholls, Keith, 554
Niederhoffer, Arthur, 134, 415

O

Obama, Barack, 63, 406, 551
Orfield, Myron, 516
Osborne, Deborah, 554
O'Shea, Timothy, 554
Outlaw, Danielle, 154

P

Packer, Herbert, 177, 530
Parker, William, 52–53, 472, 473
Parkhurst, Charles H., 39, 40
Peel, Robert, 24, 31, 53, 103, 214, 220
Pepinsky, Harold, 292
Perez, Rafael, 475, 477
Petersilia, Joan, 298
Phillips, P. W., 113
Piliavin, Irving, 275
Plunkitt, George W., 37
Pogrebin, Mark, 268
Ponder, Michael, 435
Pontillo, Matthew, 152
Powell, James, 51

R

Rahr, Susan, 7, 131, 150, 172, 175, 199
Ramsey, Charles, 55, 59, 521
Ratcliffe, Jerry, 242
Raudenbush, Stephen, 328
Reiss, Albert, 52, 183, 189, 214, 274, 275, 295–296, 388, 424, 527
Reuss-Ianni, Elizabeth, 187
Riccio, Lucius, 297
Rice, Stephen K., 131, 150, 172, 175, 199
Riis, Jacob, 40
Rinehart-Kochel, Tammy, 291
Roncek, D., 124
Roosevelt, Franklin D., 49
Roosevelt, Theodore, 36, 39, 40, 44
Rosenbaum, Dennis, 188
Rosenfeld, Richard, 309, 356
Rubinstein, Jonathan, 302
Ruiz, Jim, 459

S

Sampson, Robert, 328
Sanders, William B., 290, 296
Schiesl, Martin, 53
Schimmel, Gertrude, 55
Schlosser, Eric, 467
Schmidt, Wayne, 396
Schoolcraft, Adrian, 289
Schulenberg, Jennifer, 371, 385
Schulz, Dorothy, 56, 180, 192
Schwartz, Joanna, 518
Scott, Eric, 223
Scott, Walter, 63, 406, 527
Serpico, Frank, 482, 501, 528
Shelley, Louise, 490
Sherman, Lawrence, 60, 261, 283, 333, 358, 455, 468, 471–472, 482, 492
Shpritzer, Felicia, 55
Silver, Allan, 31

Sklansky, David, 55, 144, 178
Skogan, Wesley, 7, 8, 59, 150, 188, 327,
    328, 333, 339, 438, 443
Skolnick, Jerome, 54, 173, 175,
    177–179, 187, 302, 378, 429, 490
Smith, Alisa, 254
Smith, Bruce, 106
Smith, Douglas, 383
Smith, Sean, 314
Snipes, Jeffrey B., 258
Spelman, William, 347
Spillar, Kathy, 181
Spohn, Cassia, 433
Steele, Tom, 545
Stephens, Darrel, 497, 502, 504
Stevens, Christopher, 314
Stewart, James, 343
Stinson, Philip, 461
Stoutland, Sara E., 411, 419, 437
Straus, Murray, 257, 258
Supina, Anne E., 258

T

Teplin, Linda, 268, 369
Thale, Christopher, 36
Thurman, Quint, 344
Tracy, Robert, 124–125

Tuch, Steven, 414–415, 419, 445, 457
Tyler, Tom, 7, 407, 425

U

Uchida, Craig, 305

V

Vernon, Wyman, 472
Villavaso, Anthony, 477
Visher, Christy, 382
Vollmer, August, 41, 42, 47, 106

W

Wakeman, Stillman S., 36
Walker, Samuel, 62, 121, 395, 430, 433,
    506, 514, 521, 530
Warren, Earl, 48
Wasby, Stephen, 517
Watson, Elizabeth, 56
Webb, Jack, 53
Websdale, Neil, 344
Wechter, Jayson, 502
Weisburd, David, 114, 273, 352, 470
Weitzer, Ronald, 413, 414–415, 419,
    445, 457

Wellford, Charles, 231, 420
Wells, Alice Stebbins, 42, 55
Wells, L. Edward, 71
Wernicke, Susan, 554
Werthman, Carl, 275
Westley, William, 54, 172, 178, 179,
    219, 417, 470, 505
White, Karletta M., 423
White, Michael D., 132, 134, 267, 356,
    392, 396, 426, 464–465, 525
Wilkins, Robert, 60–61
Williams, Hubert, 333
Wilson, Darren, 63, 343
Wilson, James Q., 58, 255, 326–327,
    387, 417
Wilson, O. W., 42, 47, 106, 110,
    214, 473
Woods, Arthur, 41
Worden, Robert, 238

Z

Zansberg, Steven, 504
Zaworski, Martin, 553
Zhao, Jihong, 120, 124, 335, 344
Zhao, Solomon, 122

Subject Index

A

Abuse of authority, 455, 518–519
Accountability, 4, 5
  accreditation of agencies, 512–513
  alternative measures to crime rate, 492–493
  bias prevention training, 15–16
  blue-ribbon commissions, 527
  body-worn cameras and, 564
  citizen oversight, 16–17
  collaborative reform and, 522–523
  command-level review, 499–500
  corrective action, 500
  crime control and, 530
  criminal prosecution of police, 523
  defined, 12
  digital technology and, 527–528
  discipline process, 502–504
  early intervention systems, 506–512
  external mechanisms of, 513–529
  goals and methods, 12
  historical perspective on, 490–491
  internal, 494–501
  internal affairs/professional standards units, 501–506
  meaning of, 489–491
  measuring police effectiveness, 491–492
  mixed approach to, 531
  news media as mechanism of, 528–529
  organizational culture and, 498–499
  performance evaluations, 500–501
  police conduct and, 494
  police legal advisors, 512
  public interest groups and, 529
  risk management, 511–512
  on routine police-public contacts, 15
  technology and, 552
  on use of force, 12–14
Accreditation, 94, 194
  nature of, 512–513
  procedures, 50
  pros and cons of, 513
ACLU, 53
Active officers, 189–190
Active supervisors, 222
Actual caseload, 292
Addressing Sexual Offenses and Misconduct by Law Enforcement, 182

Administration
  new directions in, 1930-1960, 47–49
  professionalization movement and, 43–44
  unions and, 57
Administrative crime analysis, 555
Administrative rulemaking, 50, 388
  combating racial profiling through, 61
  ensuring compliance, 392–394
  impact of, 392
  limits of, 396–397
  police discretion control and, 56–57
  principles of, 390
  standard operating procedure manual, 394–395
Adventure/machismo culture, 178
Advisory committees, 440
Affirmative action, 147
African American officers
  earliest, 35
  on the job, 183
  as percentage of officers, 55, 145
  in police subculture, 182–183, 186
African Americans
  civil rights and, 51
  college credits and, 149
  drug possession and, 138
  drug use/disparities in arrests for, 304–305
  "hassled" by police, 412
  hiring quotas, 148
  hiring requirements and, 137
  imprisonment rate disparities, 426
  lynching of, 33
  obstacles to recruitment of, 140–141
  race riots and, 44, 48
  racial divide in policing neighborhoods of, 428–429
  racial profiling and, 60–61
  stop and frisk programs and discrimination, 21, 154, 178, 356, 425, 529, 530
Age, and attitudes toward police, 413
Agencies
  basic sources on, 72
  consolidation of, 77–79
  government, 72
Agency accreditation, 50
Age qualification, 135

Aggressive preventative patrol, 63
Akron (Ohio) Crisis Intervention Team (CIT), 270
Albuquerque Police Department, 300
Alcohol use, 37–38
American Bar Association, on rule making, 388–389
American Bar Foundation, 52, 53
  patrol survey (1956-1957), 227
American Civil Liberties Union (ACLU), 53, 138, 529, 550
American political system, 513–514
Americans with Disabilities Act, 144
Animal Liberation Front (ALF), 313–314
Anti-immigration bills, 121
Applicants
  age, 135
  background investigations, 142
  criminal record, 138, 478
  drug-testing of, 478
  education, 136–137, 148–149
  height and weight, 136
  motivations of, 139–140
  predicting performance of, 142–143
  residency requirements, 138–139
  selection tests, 141–142
Arab American Anti-Discrimination Association, 562
Arab Americans, 410–411
Arbitration, 118
Arizona Gang and Immigration Intelligence Team Enforcement Mission (GIITEM), 113
Arizona State University, 564
Arrest reports, 492
Arrests
  defining, 294–295
  discretion in, 291
  drug-related, 304, 427
  factors influencing, 426–427
  interaction of demeanor, race and, 427–428
  unconscious bias, stereotyping and, 429
Asians and Asian Americans, 409
Assigning officers, on basis of race or ethnicity, 444–445
Attitudes of police
  behavior and, 189
  hostility from citizens and, 168

organizational effects on, 187–188
toward citizens, 417–418
toward community policing, 188–189
Attitudes toward police
accusations of being "hassled," 412
age and, 413
gender and, 414
impact of controversial incidents on, 414–415
intercity variations, 414
neighborhood quality of life and, 413–414
other occupations compared, 415–416
race and ethnicity and, 411–412
social class and, 413
Attorney, right to, 5
Attrition, 202
Austin, Texas, 15
Authority, challenges to, 198
Authorized strength, 74
Automated Regional Justice Information System (ARJIS), 553

B

Background investigations, of applicants, 142
Bakke decision (1978), 149
Baltimore County Police Department hate crime unit, 312–313
Baltimore Police Department
experimental 311 system, 238–239
officer use of patrol time, 232
police misconduct, 514
police-population ratio, 215
Bank robberies, 49
Bar girls, 264
Battle dress uniforms (BDUs), 104
Beech Grove, Indiana, 239
Behaviorally arrested, 295
Behavior on the job
attitudes and, 189
conflicting work demands, 177–178
factors shaping, 178–179
Benchmarks for traffic stop data, 433–434
Bias
prevention training, 15–16
systematic, 15
unconscious or implicit, 16, 155, 422, 429
Bilingualism, 443
Bill of Rights (Florida Police Officers'), 119–120
Bill of Rights (U.S.), limited police authority and, 30
Black Lives Matter, 63

Blue curtain of silence, 475, 505
"Blue flu," 120
Blue-ribbon commissions, 527
Body-worn cameras (BWCs), 528, 550–551, 564–565
Bona fide occupational qualifications (BFOQs) standard, 144
Border protection, 87
Boston, Massachusetts
colonial watchmen, 32
early police departments, 34
first Irish-born police officer in, 38–39
police strike of 1919, 43
riots of the 1830s, 33
Boston Police Department Gun Project, 351–352
Boulder County Police Department, 259
Breaking the Silence on Law Enforcement Suicides, 199
Bribes, 458–460
Broad scope of the criminal law, 375
"Broken Windows" essay (Wilson and Kelling), 58, 326, 391
Broken windows hypothesis, 326–328
Brothel prostitutes, 264
Bruno v. Codd (1978), 260
Brutality. *See* Police brutality
Buenos Aires Metropolitan Police, 170
Buffalo Valley Police Department (Pennsylvania), 78
Bureaucracies
characteristics of, 105–106
police departments as, 105–106
police professionalism and, 110
positive contributions of, 108
problems with, 108
Bureau of Alcohol, Tobacco, Firearms, and Explosives (ATF), 89–90
Bureau of Indian Affairs, 83
Bureau of Investigation. *See* Federal Bureau of Investigation (FBI)
Bureau of Justice Assistance (BJA), 93, 307, 564
Burglary
investigations, 290, 292
by police officers, 460–461
Burn-out, 197

C

Cadets, 240–241
California. *See also* specific city
police training in, 47
POST system, 156
state agencies with police power, 557
California Highway Patrol, 85

Call boxes, 35, 547
Call girls, 264
Calling the police. *See* Order maintenance
Call service workload, 228, 230
Campus police, 83, 84
Capacity to use force, 174
CAPS (Chicago Alternative Policing Strategy), 8, 59, 60
in action, 339–340
evaluation of, 340–342
obstacles to change, 338–339
personal background and awareness of, 341
planning, 337–338
setbacks, 341
top problems at beat meetings, 339
Career as an officer
beginning police work, 168–170
career development, 191
hypothetical life events, 167
lateral entry, 193
outside employment, 193–194
promotion, 191–192
salaries and benefits, 190–191
special unit assignments, 192–193
starting out on the job, 170–172
Career criminals, 308–309
Case attrition, 298
Case screening, 292
Case solvability factors, 295
Case studies
"Broken Windows" and police discretion, 397–398
COMPSTAT in Chicago, 124–125
de-escalating police-citizen encounters, 63–64
domestic violence response training, 158–159
electroconductive weapons policy, 393
Fraser/Winter Park (CO) Police Department, 94–95
Philadelphia foot patrol experiment, 242
police corruption after Hurricane Katrina, 483
police reform in Los Angeles, 532–533
responding to chronically inebriated individuals, 276
social media as Neighborhood Watch, 360
untested evidence, 316–317
Cato Institute's police misconduct report, 461
Cell phones, 547

Center for Constitutional Rights, 529
Center for Problem-Oriented Policing,
    21, 60
Centers for Disease Control and
    Prevention (CDC), 82, 271
Central tendency phenomenon, 195
*The Challenge of Crime in a Free
    Society,* 52
Chandler, Arizona, 357, 359
Charleston (South Carolina) slave patrol, 32
Charlotte-Mecklenburg Police
    Department, 240, 502, 512
Checking discretion, 390
Chemerinsky report, 499
Chicago, Illinois
    Citizen's Police Data Project, 528–529
    Mayor's Office of Inquiry and
        Information, 340
    race riots and, 44, 48
    reform efforts, 42
Chicago Alternative Policing Strategy
    program. *See* CAPS (Chicago
    Alternative Policing Strategy)
Chicago Police Department, 80
    Accountability Task Force, 201, 479, 527
    CAPS (*See* CAPS (Chicago
        Alternative Policing Strategy))
    code of silence in, 173, 505
    COMPSTAT case study, 124–125
    corruption in, 477
    permanent beat assignments, 335
    racism and, 439
    Ramsey and, 59
    stops and searches policy, 530
Chicago Riot Commission, 44
Child abuse, 168–169
Christopher Commission, 143, 194, 479,
    505, 527
Church trials, 33
Cincinnati, Ohio
    early police academy, 35
    police reform, 39
    race riot (2001), 61–62
Cincinnati Collaborative Agreement,
    520, 521
Cincinnati Initiative to Reduce Violence
    (CIRV), 21
Cincinnati Police Department
    Chief's Scholars Program, 191
    "pattern or practice" suit against,
        61–62
    Risk Management System (EIS), 507
Citizen/civilian oversight, 5, 16–17, 444,
    524–527
    goals and objectives of, 526
    models of, 524

pros and cons of, 526–527
    spread of, 57–58
Citizen complaints, 168
    difficulty in investigating, 502
    as measure of department
        performance, 492
    pattern or practice case reforms, 519
    response studies, 52
    standards for investigating, 504–505
Citizen disrespect, 198
Citizen review boards, 51, 444, 524, 525
City of Canton, Ohio v. Harris (1989), 154
Civilian Complaint Review Board
    (NYC), 51
Civilianization, 76
Civil litigation, 492–493
Civil rights, 51
    demand for citizen review boards, 51
    hostility toward, 49
    racial profiling and, 61
Civil Rights Act (1964), 5, 55, 93
    employment discrimination outlawed
        by, 146
    Title VII of, 144
Civil service, 115–116, 134
Civil suits, 517–518
Clearance rates, 293–294, 492
Cleared by exception, 294
Cleveland, Ohio, 9
Cleveland Division of Police, DOJ
    investigation of, 480
Cleveland Police Department, 498, 508
Cliques, 109
Code of silence, 173, 174, 505–506
Cohort effects, 187
Collaborative reform, 522
Collaborative Reform Program, 522
Collective bargaining, 117
College campus police, 83, 85
College degree, as hiring
    requirement, 137
Colonial American law enforcement,
    32–33
Combined DNA Index System (CODIS),
    316–317
Command-level reviews, 499
Commission on Accreditation for Law
    Enforcement Agencies (CALEA),
    50, 94, 143, 302, 303, 423, 444,
    512–513
Communication
    bureaucracy and, 108
    call boxes, 35
    devices, 547
    digital revolution in, 527–528
    information technology and, 545

911 operators and, 10
    telephone, 45, 46–47
    two-way radio, 45, 46
Communications center, 223–226
    911 systems, 223
    operators, 224, 226
    processing calls for service, 224–225
Community-based crime prevention
    programs, 285
Community cooperation model, 251
Community Oriented Policing Services
    (COPS Office), 58, 199–200, 344,
    522–523
Community outreach, 526
Community partnerships, 22, 329–332
    consultation, 330–331
    effectiveness of, 332–333
    mobilization, 331–332
    types of, 330
Community policing, 52, 58–59,
    110–111, 490
    attitudes toward, 188–189
    broken windows hypothesis, 326–327
    characteristics of, 327–337
    in collapsed communities, 332–333
    community partnerships, 329–332
    compared to other policing forms, 354
    conflicting community interests, 344
    decentralization and accountability, 343
    at departmental level, 337–342
    effectiveness of, 344
    foot patrols, 332
    impact on poor and minority
        communities, 344
    impetus for change, 325–326
    job satisfaction and, 199–200
    organizational change, 333–335
    police role in, 342
    politics and, 342–343
    problems and prospects, 342–344
    problem solving, 336–337
    as research-based policy, 54
    types of disorder, 327
Community Policing Consortium, 195
Community service officer (CSO), 240
Compensation, 120
    federal salaries, 558–559
    fringe benefits, 140
    incentive pay to bilingual officers, 443
    local, county, and state, 558
    overtime, 191
Complex responsibilities of the police,
    17–21
COMPSTAT, 60, 113–114, 548
    as accountability measure, 494
    in Chicago (case study), 124–125

Computer-aided dispatch, 546
Confidence (public)
    in American institutions, 416
    international percentages of, 417
    in the police, 412
Confining discretion, 390
Conflicts of interest, 194
Consent decrees, 6, 188, 518, 520–522
Consolidation, of agencies, 77–79
Constables, 32–33, 82
Consultation, 330–331
Contextual discrimination, 433
Contingency theory, 122
Contracting, 79
Controlling discretion era, 371
Convicted offender index, 300
COPLINK, 552
Coproducers of crime control, 329
Coroner, 82–83
Corrective action, 500
Corruption. *See* Police corruption
Cost, of police protection, 75–76
Counterpunching, 252
County police, 80, 557
County sheriff, 81–82
Coveted assignments, 193
"Craigslist killer," 264
Crime. *See also* Gangs and gang-related
        crime; Terrorism
    career criminals, 308–309
    case structural factors, 295–296
    downgrading seriousness of, 491
    environmental factors, 297
    guns and gun crimes, 309–311
    hate crimes, 311–313
    not reported, 286–287
    organizational factors in solving,
        296–297
    in poorer neighborhoods, 217
    prevention, 31, 285–286
    rapid police response to, 54
    reporting, to police (percentages), 286
    reporting and unfounding, 288–289
    solved, 18, 21
Crime analysis, 554–556
    administrative, 555
    strategic, 555
    tactical, 554–555
Crime-attack model, 353
Crime control
    accountability and, 530
    assumptions, 284–285
    avoiding aggressive tactics, 376
    strategies, 283–284
Crime-fighter image, 18–19
Crime mapping, 555–556

Crime prophylactic model, 251
Crime rate, 491
Criminal apprehension, 286–289
    citizen reporting of crime, 286–287
    reporting and unfounding crimes,
        288–289
Criminal intent, 523
Criminal investigation
    case attrition, 298
    case screening, 292
    clearance rate, 293–294
    defining an arrest, 294–295
    detective myths, 289–290
    DNA and, 299–300
    eyewitness identification, 298
    follow-up investigations, 291–292
    improving, 300–301
    informants and, 302–303
    measuring effectiveness of, 293–295
    officer productivity and, 297
    organization of detective work,
        290–291
    process, 291–292
    reality of detective work, 292
    undercover police work, 301–302
Criminalistics, 299
Criminal justice programs, 41, 53, 56
Criminal justice system
    comprehensive study of, 52
    corruption and, 456
    encountering, as an officer, 169
    insiders, 169
Criminal law, police corruption and, 467
Criminal prosecution, of corrupt
        officers, 479–480, 523
Criminal records, police applicants
        and, 138
Criminals, apprehending, 286–289
Criminology, as academic discipline, 53
Crises, in police organizations, 112
Crisis intervention (CIT) programs,
        23, 270
Critical Incident program, 522
Critical Response Program, 522
Critical thinking skills, 135, 153
Cultural competence, 442
Cultural conflict, police corruption and,
        467–468
Customs and Border Protection, 86, 87
Cynicism, 169, 383, 469

D

Dallas, Texas, 15
Dallas Police Department, 138
Damage awards, 492–493, 517–518

Dangerous police tasks
    domestic disturbances, 259
    potential *vs.* actual, 175–177
    traffic enforcement, 254
D.A.R.E. (Drug Abuse Resistance
        Education), 274, 276, 306
Data
    personnel, 74–75
    on use of force, 14–15
Database technology, 545–546
Data-driven policing, 60
Davis v. City of Dallas, 144
Dayton, Ohio, 255
Deadly force
    administrative rulemaking and, 50, 57
    African Americans and, 51
    defense-of-life standard, 12, 24, 384,
        388, 421, 444
    discretion and, 370
    policies, 12
    by race/ethnicity, 420–422
    restrictive policies for, 54
    study of, in NYC, 54
    unconscious bias and police
        use of, 422
"Death investigators," 82
Death of officers
    by felonious assaults, 175–176
    historical data on, 177
    suicide, 198–199
Decentralize, 110
Decertification, 56, 203
Decision-making, tactical, 153
Decline, of organizations, 112
De-escalation, 14, 152–153, 371
    as alternative to use of force, 152–153
    training in tactics of, 132, 522
Defense-of-life principle, 12, 24, 384,
        388, 421, 441
Deformalize, 110–111
Delayerize, 111
Demand reduction strategy, 303
Demeanor of suspect, 381, 427–428
Democracies, 490
Democracy and the police, 5
Department of Homeland Security,
        87–88, 315
    Customs and Border protection, 86, 87
    Federal Emergency Management
        Agency (FEMA), 88
    Immigration and Customs
        Enforcement, 87
    Transportation Security
        Administration (TSA), 88
    U.S. Coast Guard, 88
    U.S. Secret Service, 88

Department of Justice, 88–90
  Bureau of Alcohol, Tobacco,
    Firearms, and Explosives (ATF),
    89–90
  Civil Rights Division, 479
  Drug Enforcement Administration
    (DEA), 89
  Federal Bureau of Investigation (FBI),
    89, 91
  investigations of police agencies,
    480–481
  U.S. Marshals Service, 90
Departments of Public Safety. *See* State
  police
Despecialize, 111
Detectives
  discretion and, 375
  myths regarding, 289–290
  reality of detective work, 292
  work organization, 290–291
Detroit, Michigan
  police-population ratio, 75, 215
  riots and, 34, 48, 51
Differential response to calls, 237–238
Digital revolution in communications,
  527–528
Dimensions of trust and confidence,
  436–438
Directed integrity tests, 475
Directed patrol, 241
Disbanding, of police organizations, 112
Discipline
  appropriate levels of, 503–504
  openness/transparency and, 504
  process of, 502–503
  records and personnel decisions, 505
Discipline matrix, 503
"Discovery" of discretion era, 370
Discovery time, 231
Discretion
  administrative rulemaking and, 56–57,
    390, 392–394
  argument for abolishing, 386–387
  conflicting public expectations and,
    376–377
  control of, 385–388
  definition of, 370
  demeanor of the suspect, 381
  enhancing professional judgment
    with, 387
  examples of, 369–370
  factors limiting, 379–380
  informal bureaucratic controls of,
    387–388
  legal and extralegal factors, 382
  limited police resources and, 378–379

nature of criminal law and, 375–376
  organizational culture factors and, 380
  positive use of, 373–374
  potential abuse of, 372
  preference of the victim, 381
  social and medical issues, 377
  study of, 370–371
  systematic rulemaking and, 395–396
  underlying sources of, 375–379
  work environment of policing, 377–378
  written policies guiding, 50, 388–398
Discretionary arrest decisions
  organizational factors and, 384–385
  situational factors and, 380–384
  social and political factors, 385
Discrimination, 93
  acknowledging, 10
  African American juveniles and, 275
  coveted assignments and, 193
  in disciplinary actions against
    minority officers, 503
  discrimination-disparity continuum, 433
  employment, 147–149, 443–444
  of gay and lesbian officers, 185
  against Jewish businessmen, 39
  misuse of discretion and, 372
  police corruption and, 38–39
  racial profiling and, 60–61
  racial segregation, 51
  reverse discrimination, 148
  stop, question and frisk (SQF)
    programs, 359
Discrimination *versus* disparities, 432
Discriminatory assignments, 146
Disorder, 327
Displacement, 244
Dissatisfaction, 169–170
Disturbance calls, 176
Diversity
  achieving, in police employment,
    143–149
  Equal Employment Opportunity
    and, 144
  goals of, 143
  impact of, 149, 179–189
  intersection of gender, race, ethnicity,
    and sexual identity, 185
  legitimacy of police force and, 9–10
  reflecting the community served,
    144–145
  representative police forces, 9–10
Divorce, 198
DNA evidence, 299–300
Domestic terrorism, 313–314
Domestic violence, 369
  in academy curricula, 56

administrative rulemaking and, 50
  calling the police, 257–258
  defining terms, 256–257
  factors influencing arrest decision,
    259–260
  future of policy toward, 263
  impact of arrest on, 260–262
  improving response training for,
    158–159
  mandatory arrest policy, 260, 389
  by police officers, 263
  police policy changes on, 57
  police response to, 258–263
  prevalence of, 257
  special training for response to, 262–263
Donde esta la justicia?, 442
Don't Shoot (Kennedy), 140
Dragnet (television show), 53
"Driving while black," 383, 430, 529
Drug Enforcement Agency (DEA),
  4, 86, 89
Drug enforcement strategies, 303–304
Drug offenses, police applicants and, 138
Drug policing, 303–306
Drugs
  demand reduction, 303, 306
  marijuana, 305–306
  minorities and the war on drugs,
    304–305
Drug testing, 478
Drug trafficking, police corruption
  and, 456
Drunk-driving, 255–256
Due process, 5, 372
Duplication of services, 76

E

Early founding effects, 111
Early intervention system (EIS), 6, 60,
  548–549
  in Cleveland PD, 508
  components of, 509
  effectiveness of, 511
  forms of interventions, 509–510
  multiple goals of, 510
  nature and purpose of, 507
  pattern or practice case reforms, 519
  patterns of officer behavior and, 507
  performance indicators/thresholds,
    507–509
Earth Liberation Front (ELF), 313–314
East St. Louis race riots, 44
Education, 41
  criminology, 53
  FBI academy, 49
  hiring requirements, 136–137

law enforcement programs, 47
rising levels of, 186–187
Educational incentive programs, 191
Education generation gap, 186
Effectiveness, 17–24
complex responsibilities of the police,
17–21
in dealing with juveniles, 23–24
in dealing with the mentally ill, 22–23
evidence-based programs, 24
ineffective strategies, 21
partnerships with the public, 22
problem-oriented, 21–22
Electroconductive weapons (TASERS),
393, 553
Employee assistance programs (EAPs),
200, 498
Employee Polygraphy Protection Act, 202
Employment discrimination, 147–149,
443–444
Employment outlook, 556–559
Enforcement and Removal Operations
(ERO), 87
Enforcement of federal immigration
laws, 441
England's police departments, 73
English heritage, American policing and,
30–31
Entry-level hiring requirements, 50
Equal Employment Opportunity Act, 144
Equal employment opportunity (EEO)
index, 145
Equal Protection of the Law, 5
Era of denial, 370
Ethical standards, public perception
of, 416
Ethics, 56, 138
Ethnic groups
Arabs and Arab Americans, 410–411
Asians and Asian Americans, 409
Hispanics, 409
Native Americans, 410
riots and, 34, 48
tensions with police, 36–37
Ethnicity
assigning officers on basis of, 444–445
definition of, 408
legitimate use of, in police work, 436
official data on, 408–409
public opinion about police and,
411–412
traffic stop outcomes by, 431
training on, 445–446
Ethnic profiling, 562
Ethnic slurs, by police, 430
Evidence-based programs, 24

Excessive force, 10, 59, 423–424, 552.
See also Deadly force; Use of force
Exclusionary rule, 397, 515, 530
Executive Order 11246 (affirmative
action), 147
Eyewitness identification, 298

F

Facebook, 551
Fair and Impartial Policing, 16, 155, 174
Family connections, and law
enforcement careers, 140
Federal Bureau of Investigation (FBI), 4,
44–45, 86, 89, 91
crime lab, 49
Hoover and war on crime, 48–49
Intelligence Branch, 315
National Academy, 49
Uniform Crime Reports, 72
Federal Emergency Management
Agency (FEMA), 88
Federal government, role of, 93
Federal law enforcement agencies,
86–90, 558
after September 11, 2001, 86
Department of Homeland Security,
87–88
Department of Justice, 88–90
employment opportunities, 558
Federal Law Enforcement Training
Center (Georgia), 558
Federal Mediation and Conciliation
Service, 118
Felonious assaults, 175–176
Female officers. *See* Women police
officers
Ferguson, Missouri
city use of police to raise revenue, 385
traffic ticket quotas, 9
Ferguson Police Department
DOJ investigation of, 480–481, 514
killing of Michael Brown, 63,
405–406, 489, 523
Field internal affairs units (FIAUs), 474
Field observations, 52
Field training, 56, 155–156, 478–479
Field training officer (FTO), 16, 155–156
Fifth Amendment right, 202
Firearms, 37
Firearms and firearm training, 56
Firefighters, 199
First Amendment rights, 201
Fisher v. Texas (2016), 149
Fleeing-felon rule, 421
Florida State Law Enforcement Training
Academy, 141

Floyd v. the City of New York (2013), 359
Focused-deterrence programs, 21, 54, 352
Foot patrol, 219, 332
Force, use of, 42, 424–425
accountability and, 12–14
collecting and analyzing data on, 14–15
command-level review of, 499–500
Los Angeles Police Department and, 53
policies on, 13
Force factor framework, 424–425
Force investigation team (FIT), 499
Ford Foundation, 54
Foreign terrorism, 314
Forensic index, 300
Formal corrective action, 500
Fort Worth, Texas COMPSTAT
evaluation, 114
Four systems of justice, 419
Fourteenth Amendment, 5, 15, 425, 529
Fragmentation, of American law
enforcement, 72–73, 76–80
alternatives to, 77–79
reconsidering, 79–80
Fraser, Colorado, 78, 94–95
Fraternal Order of Police, 116
Friendship patterns, 109

G

Gambling, 377
Gangs and gang-related crime, 306–308
gang suppression, 307–308
G.R.E.A.T. program, 308
Gang units, 113, 122, 123
Garrity ruling, 202, 474
Gay and lesbian officers, 184–185
Gay and lesbian persons, police abuse
of, 429
The Gay Officers Action League
(GOAL), 184
General Schedule (GS) pay system,
558–559
G4S (security firm), 90, 92
Glass ceiling, 180
Global Justice XML Data Model
(GJXDM), 552
Global Terrorism Database, 313
Gossip, 109
Government agencies, 72
Grade inflation, 195
Grass eaters, 458, 471
Gratuities, 458, 471
G.R.E.A.T. (Gang Resistance Education
and Training), 273, 276, 308
Greensboro, North Carolina, 51, 238
Grievance procedures (unions and),
117, 118

Group solidarity, 173
Growth periods, in organizations, 111–112
Guardian mentality, 7, 131–132
Guided discretion, 386
Guns and gun crimes
    buy-back programs, 311
    gun suppression, 309–311

H

Hammered informants, 302
Hate crimes, 311–313
    police response to, 312–313
    scope and nature of, 311–312
Hate Crime Statistics Act (1990), 311
Height requirement, 136
Hierarchical command, 110
High-speed pursuits, 232–234, 384, 389
Highway patrols, 44, 85–86
Hiring
    entry-level requirements, 50
    minimum qualifications, 135
    minorities, 55
    outlook for police employment, 556–559
    personnel process, 132–133
Hiring quotas, 148
Hispanic American officers, 55,
        183–184, 186
    college credits and, 149
    hiring quotas, 148
    hiring requirements and, 137
    obstacles to recruitment of, 140
    as percentage of officers, 145
Hispanic communities, 409–410
    language barriers in policing, 443
    racial profiling and, 61
    Spanish-speaking officers and, 11
    stop and frisk programs, 21
History, 29–64
    community policing, 58–59
    creation of modern police, 31
    crises of the 1960s, 49–54
    data-driven policing, 60
    English heritage, 30–31
    federal investigations of police
        misconduct, 61–62
    first American police officer, 29
    first modern American police forces,
        33–40
    impact of police on crime and
        disorder, 40
    law enforcement in colonial America,
        32–33
    national crisis over policing
        (2014-2016), 63
    new developments, 1970-2016, 55–64
    police unions, 57

"political era" of 1830s-1900, 34–36
President's Crime Commission, 52
problem-oriented policing, 58–60
professional era, 1900-1960, 40–45
    purpose of studying, 29–30
    reform agenda, 41–42
    research revolution, 53–54
    Supreme Court decisions, 49–50
    technology and, 45–47
HIV-infected persons, 271–272
Homeland security
    role of local police in, 13
    terrorism, 62
    training programs and, 132
Homeland Security Act (2002), 87
Homeless persons, 266–267
Homicide investigations, 290
Honesty, public perception of, 416, 457
Honolulu Police Department "coffee
        with a cop" program, 330
Hookers, 263
Horizontal cliques, 109
Hostility, from citizens, 168
Hot lists, 549
Hot spots, 60, 218, 241
Houston, Texas, 10, 15, 56
Houston Police Department, 332
Human immunodeficiency virus (HIV),
        271–272
Hurricane Katrina, 483

I

Immigrants
    cultural barriers in policing, 442
    engaging immigrant communities,
        441–442
    language barriers in policing, 442–443
    neighborhood saloons and, 38
    non-English 911 call services, 239
    Palmer Raids and, 45
    police brutality and, 36–37, 39
Immigration
    anti-immigration bills, 121
    enforcement of federal laws on, 441
    police corruption and, 38–39
Immigration and Customs Enforcement
        (ICE), 4, 87
Impasse settlement, 117–118
Implicit bias, 155
In-custody deaths, 16
Independent monitor, 520
Indian Self-Determination and Education
        Assistance Act of 1975, 84
Individual acts of discrimination, 433
Informal corrective action, 500
Informal organizational culture, 384

Informants, 302–303
Information technology, 545–546
Inglewood, California, 122
Injustice, acknowledging, 10
Innovation, 122
Innovative supervisors, 222, 497
Inspector general, 58, 444, 524, 525–526
Intelligence-led policing (ILP), 563
Interagency task forces, 112–113
Internal affairs
    accountability and, 501–506
    investigations, 16–17, 473–474
    training, 502
Internal benchmarking, 434
International Association of Chiefs of
        Police, 182, 461
International Association of
        Policewomen, 42
International Union of Police
        Associations, 116
Interventions, 509–510
Interviews (of police applicants), 141
Intimate terrorism, 158
Investigative tactics, on corruption,
        474–475
Investigatory traffic stops, 431–432
Invisible Institute, 413, 528
Irish Catholic officers, 36–38

J

Japan's police system, 73
Jewish immigrants, Sunday Closing Law
        and, 38–39
Job actions, 120
Job satisfaction
    community policing and, 199–200
    sources of, 196–197
Job security, 140, 191
Job stress, 168–170, 197–198
    coping with, 200
    gender-related, 198
    sources of, 168–170, 197–198
    suicide and, 198–199
    work shifts and personal life, 170–171
Justice Department
    Civil Rights Division, 6
    investigations into local police
        departments, 6
    Special Litigation Section, 6
Justice Without Trial (Skolnick), 173,
        177, 490
Juvenile crime hot spots, 273
Juveniles, 23–24, 272–276
    controversy over policing role, 273
    crime prevention programs, 275–276
    on-the-street encounters, 274

race discrimination and, 275
special juvenile units, 273–274

K

Kansas City, Missouri, 506
Kansas City Gun Experiment, 309–310
Kansas City Preventive Patrol
    Experiment, 24, 31, 53, 54, 58,
    234–236, 255, 325, 560
Kerner Commission, 9, 21, 51, 52, 55,
    143, 419, 439, 527
Knapp Commission, 301, 419, 458, 463,
    466, 475, 479, 482
Kolts Commission, 518

L

Labor unions, police suppression of, 40
Language barriers, in policing, 442–443
Larceny investigations, 290
Las Vegas Metropolitan Police
    Advanced Officer Skills
        Training, 157
    Collaborative Reform program, 522
    training of recruits, 154
    use-of-force review board, 494
Lateral entry, 193
Lautenberg Amendment, 263
Law enforcement
    agencies, 72, 73–74
    basic features of, 71–73
    components, 72
    discretion and, 375
    employment outlook, 556–559
    federal agencies, 86–90
    "industry" perspective, 71–72
    international perspective, 72–73
    personnel, 74
    size and scope of, 73–76
Law Enforcement Assistance
    Administration (LEAA), 54, 559
Law enforcement officer's bill of rights
    (LEOBR) laws, 200
Law enforcement career motivations,
    139–140
Law Enforcement Management and
    Administrative Statistics, 72, 116
Lawlessness in Law Enforcement
    (Wickersham Commission), 47
Legalistic style, 221
Legally arrested, 294–295
Legitimacy, 6–10, 405
    building, 8, 436–446
    crisis of, 325
    defined, 6
    diversity and, 9–10

procedural justice, 7–8, 406–407
    public interactions and, 8–9
License plate readers, 549–550
Lie detectors, 202
Lincoln (Nebraska) Police Department,
    191, 242
Litigation
    civil suits, 517–518
    pattern or practice suits, 518–522
Local police departments, 73–74
    employment outlook, 557
    federal investigations into, 6
Local political control, 71
Local political culture, 385
London Metropolitan Police, 31, 37
    influence of, on American policing, 34
Long Beach Police Department, 563
"Long hot summers," 51
Los Angeles, California, 48
Los Angeles County Sheriff's
    Department, 79, 142, 503, 518
Los Angeles Police Department
    application process, 134, 135
    blue curtain in, 475
    calls for service/units dispatched
        (2010), 225
    Chemerinsky report, 499
    Christopher Commission report on,
        505, 506
    consent decree and, 188, 521, 530
    corruption in, 455, 464, 477, 478
    detainee surveys of police
        conduct, 493
    employment discrimination
        settlements, 157
    general training updates
        after OIS, 157
    lateral entry program, 193
    performance review, 509
    personnel evaluations, 498–499
    police-community relations and,
        52–53
    reform in, 472
    Rodney King assault and, 414–415
    women police officers, 42
Lowell, Massachusetts, 114, 494
Low-visibility work, 469
Lynching, 33

M

Madison Police Department, 498
"Making Good Cops in the Twenty-First
    Century," 132
Management Awareness and Personnel
    Performance System (MAPPS),
    507, 510

Management principles,
    professionalization and, 42
Mapp v. Ohio (1961), 5, 50, 93, 379,
    514–517, 529, 530
Maricopa County Sheriff's Office, 240,
    293, 481
Marijuana, 305–306
Marine Advisory Support Team
    (MAST), 330
Maryland State Police, 60–61
Meat eaters, 458, 471
Mediation, 259
Medical examiner, 82–83
Memorandum of Agreement (MOA), 59,
    518–519
Memphis CIT Model, 270
Mental-health-based specialized mental
    health response, 271
Mental health commitment, 369
Mental health issues, 200
Mentally ill persons, 22–23, 267–271
    crisis intervention, 270
    police response to, 268–269
Mercenary informants, 302
Mercy booking, 268
Mesa Police Department, 301,
    306–307, 549
Mexican Americans. *See* Hispanic
    American officers; Hispanic
    communities
Miami-Dade Police Department,
    232–233, 330
Miami Police Department,
    460–461, 478
Michigan State University, 48
Military style, 131. *See also* Quasi-
    military style
Milwaukee Police Department, 482
Mine Resistant Ambush Protected
    (MRAP) vehicles, 62
Minimum standards, 93–95
    accreditation, 94
    role of federal government, 93
    role of state governments, 93–94
Minneapolis, Minnesota immigrant
    population, 442
Minneapolis Domestic Violence
    Experiment, 260–261
Minneapolis Police Department, 274, 389
Minnesota Multiphasic Personality
    Inventory (MMPI), 143
Minorities. *See also* specific group
    affirmative action and, 148
    inappropriateness of term, 408
Miranda v. Arizona (1966), 5, 49–50, 93,
    379, 515, 529, 530

Misconduct
    civil suits, 517–518
    decertification for, 56, 203
    federal investigations of, 61–62
    female *vs.* male officers, 181
    injunctions to stop patterns of, 523
    pattern or practice of, 518–522
    reforms, 440–441
Mixed approach to police
        accountability, 531
Mobile computing, 546, 547–548
Mobile radios, 547
Mobilization, 331–332
Moderns, 180
Mollen Commission investigations, 194,
        455, 457, 461, 465, 523
"Moral career" of a police officer, 471
Morale, 108
Multiagency task forces, 113
Municipal police, 80
Municipal Police Administration
        (Wilson), 47
Myth of full enforcement, 386

N

NAACP, 53
Nassau County (New York) Police
        Department, 80
National Academy of Sciences report on
        policing, 137
National Advisory Commission on
        Criminal Justice Standards and
        Goals, 77–78, 213
National Association for Civilian
        Oversight of the Police (NACOLE),
        17, 57, 524
National Association for the
        Advancement of Colored People
        (NAACP), 53, 529
National Black Police Association
        (NBPA), 182–183
National Center for the Analysis of
        Violent Crime (NCAVC), 91
National Center for Women and
        Policing, 134, 179
National Consortium for the Study of
        Terrorism and Responses to
        Terrorism (START), 313
National Crime Information Center,
        292, 552
National Crime Victimization Survey
        (NCVS), 217, 491
National crisis over policing, 63
National Information Exchange Model
        (NIEM), 552

National Institute for Occupational
        Safety and Health, 199
National Institute of Ethics, 506
National Institute of Justice, 54, 316, 559
National Labor Relations Act (1935), 117
National Organization of Black
        Law Enforcement Executives
        (NOBLE), 183
National police crisis, 2014-2015, 405–406
National Police Research Platform, 200
Native Americans, 410
Neighborhoods
    crime prevalence in poorer
        neighborhoods, 217
    levels of police protection in, 419–420
    police corruption and, 468
    racial divide in policing, 428–429
Neighborhood Watch programs, 332
Newark, New Jersey, 51
Newark Foot Patrol Experiment,
        58, 219, 560
New Jersey, citizen complaints in, 504–505
New Jersey Department of Public
        Safety, 85
New Jersey State Police, 507, 510, 520
New Orleans Police Department
    corruption in, 477, 479, 483
    DOJ investigation of, 481
    Public Integrity Division, 476
Newport News, Virginia, 59–60, 349–351
News media, 169
New York City Bias Incident
        Investigation Unit (BIIU), 312
New York City Police Department
        (NYPD), 80
    Civilian Complaint Review Board, 51
    code of silence in, 506
    Community Police Officer on Patrol
        (C-POP), 343
    COMPSTAT and, 60, 113–114
    corruption in, 455, 458–459, 464–466,
        468, 472, 475, 477, 501
    creation of police force in 1845, 34
    damage awards, 492–493
    early history of, 36–37
    early police training, 35
    gay and lesbian officers, 184
    inspector general, 58
    integrity tests in, 475–476
    internal affairs division, 474
    manipulation of crime statistics,
        288, 289
    officer dissatisfaction, 169
    patrol experiment, 233
    police-population ratio, 215
    scenario-based training, 154

    stop and frisk program, 154, 178, 356,
        425, 529, 530
    zero-tolerance policing, 355–357
    Zone Enforcement Unit, 315–316
New York City Special Investigative
        Unit, 301
New York Civilian Complaint Review
        Board, 525
New York State Police, 85
Nextdoor network application, 360
911 communications center, 223
    non-English 911 services, 239
911 incident-based policing, 345
Nominal caseload, 292
North Carolina State Crime
        Lab, 299

O

Oakland Police Department
    reform in, 472, 482
    supervisor training, 157
Occupational deviance, 455
Offensive language, 9
Officer-initiated activity, 220
Officer-involved shootings, 16, 157,
        420–422, 522, 528
Officer-worn cameras. *See* Body-worn
        cameras (BWCs)
Officially arrested, 295
Omaha, Nebraska, 216, 423
One-officer *versus* two-officer patrols,
        219–220
Openness and transparency, 10–12
Oral interviews, 141
Order maintenance, 4, 228, 251. *See also*
        Traffic enforcement
    domestic disputes, 256–263
    homeless persons, 266–267
    mentally ill persons, 267–271
    police response, 252–253
    public expectations, 253
Order maintenance policing. *See*
        Zero-tolerance policing
Organizational birth, 111
Organizational change
    community policing and,
        333–335
    evidence of, 335–336
Organizational culture, 334
    accountability and, 498–499
    officers' attitudes shaped by, 54
Organizational structure, 334
Organized crime, 456, 467
Outside employment,
        193–194
Overtime, 191

P

Palmer Raids, 45
Paramilitary units, 104
Partnerships with the public, 22
Passive officers, 189–190
Patrol
  aggressive preventative patrol, 63–64
  assignment to, 216, 218
  as backbone of policing, 213
  call service workload, 228, 230
  central role of, 213–214
  communications center, 223–226
  computers/video cameras and, 239–240
  crime/noncrime incidents and their distribution, 229
  customer feedback, 242
  discretion and, 374–375
  distribution of officers, 216–217
  effectiveness of, 54, 233–237
  evading duty, 232
  foot patrols, 332
  functions of, 214
  high-speed pursuits, 232–234
  history of, 31
  hot spots, 218
  impact on crime rate with increase in, 24
  improving traditional, 237–244
  Kansas City Preventive Patrol experiment, 234
  management of, 47–48
  motorization of police, 64
  Newark Foot Patrol Experiment, 236–237
  officer use of patrol time, 231–232
  organizational styles, 221–222
  organization and delivery of, 214–220
  in the political era, 35–36
  response time, 230–231
  routine supervision of, 495–498
  sergeant's supervisory role, 222–223
  staffing patrol beats, 220
  stress and, 197
  styles of, 220–222
  systematic study of, 226–228
  types of, 218–219
  women officers on, 181
Patrol car, 45–46
Patronage, 35
Pattern or practice suits
  case reforms, 519–520
  court-appointed monitors and, 520
  impact of consent decrees, 520–522
  settlement of, 518–519
Peer pressure, 470
Pennsylvania State Constabulary, 44

Pennsylvania State Police, 85
Pentagon attack (2001), 561
Performance
  cohort effects on, 187
  organizational effects on, 187–188
Performance evaluations, 500–501
  problems with, 195–196
  traditional, 194–195
  writing skills and, 192
Performance review, 509
"Perishable skills," 156
Personnel data, 74–75
Personnel process, 134
Personnel standards, 49, 52
Perspectives on Policing, 333
Pervasive organized corruption, 465–466
Pervasive unorganized corruption, 465
Philadelphia, Pennsylvania
  beat boundaries, 217
  early law enforcement in, 34
  foot patrols and crime reduction, 332
  reform efforts, 42
Philadelphia Foot Patrol experiment
  results of, 243–244
  target area selection, 242–243
Philadelphia Integrity and Accountability Office, 503
Philadelphia Police Advisory Board, 51
Philadelphia Police Department, 158
  academy training and, 151
  corruption in, 455
  foot patrol experiment, 242–244
  Ramsey and, 59
Phoenix, Arizona, 264
Phoenix Law Enforcement Association, 121
Phoenix Police Department
  body-worn cameras case study, 564–565
  community environment/case solvability study, 297
  gifts/rewards, rules and regulations on, 456
  G.R.E.A.T. program, 308
  organizational chart, 106, 107
  TASERS and, 553
Physical disorder, 327
Physical force, 423–424. *See also* Police brutality
Pittsburgh Police Department, 62, 195, 518
Police
  applicants (*See* Applicants)
  career perspective, 133
  federal government and, 93
  history (*See* History)
  purpose of having, 3–4
  roles and responsibilities of, 18

state governments and, 93–94
  stereotypes of, 133–134
Police academy, 151–152, 336
Police Administration (Wilson), 42–43, 47, 106
Police aides or cadets, 240–241
Police auditor, 58, 444, 524, 525–526
Police-based specialized mental health response, 271
Police-based specialized response, 271
Police brutality, 423–424
  corruption and, 463–464
  immigrants and, 36–37, 39
  National Black Police Association on, 182–183
  Wickersham Commission report on, 47
Police buffs, 302
Police-citizen interactions, 418–436.
    See also Public interactions
  complexity of, 371–372
  de-escalating, 63–64
  delay in responding to 911 calls, 420
  discretion and, 371–372
  neighborhood police protection levels, 419–420
  use of deadly force, 420–422
Police commission, NYC, 39
Police-community relations, 406
  building legitimacy in, 436–446
  cultural barriers, 442–443
  different communities of color, 407–411
  dimensions of trust/confidence and, 436–438
  engaging immigrant communities, 441–442
  engaging the community, 438–439
  gender and sexual preference issues, 410
  language barriers, 442–443
  public participation in policy making, 439
  respectful treatment and, 437–438
Police-community relations (PCR) units, 51, 439–440
Police corruption
  becoming corrupt, 470–471
  bribes, 458–460
  brutality and, 463–464
  case study, 483
  code of silence and, 174
  controlling (*See* Police corruption control strategies)
  costs of, 456–457, 459, 463
  defined, 455–456
  in early American policing, 33
  five most corrupt officers, 477
  gratuities, 458

Police corruption—(*cont.*)
immigration, discrimination and, 38–39
levels of, 464–466
managing anticorruption
    investigations, 473–474
pervasiveness of, 465–466
police subculture and, 469–470
politics and, 37–38
sexual misconduct, 461–462
theft and burglary, 460–461
theories of, 466–470
types of, 458–464
underlining professionalism, 456–457
Police corruption control strategies
attitude of chief, 472
external, 479–483
internal, 463, 472–479
limits of, 482–483
rules and regulations, 472–473
Police departments. *See also* Local
    police departments; specific
    department
as bureaucracies, 105–106, 108, 110
changes in, 110–114
civil service procedures, 115–116
community policing, 110–111
contingency theory, 122
dominant style of, 105
informal aspects of, 108–109
institutional theory, 122–123
life-course perspective of, 111–112
as organizations, 105–109
police unions, 116–121
resource dependency theory, 123–124
six largest, 71, 80
task forces, 112–113
Police Discipline: A Case for Change
    (Stephens), 502
Police Discretion (Davis), 370
Police Executive Research Forum (PERF),
    10, 14, 54, 56, 131–132, 174
education levels of officers, 148–149
on homelessness, 266
hot spots study, 241
model policy on use of race/ethnicity, 61
performance evaluation report, 501
The Police for the Future (Bayley), 329
Police Foundation, 54, 234
Police knowledge model, 251
Police management, 334–335
Police officers
African American, 55
changing profile of, 55–56
determining police-population ratio,
    214–216
Hispanic, 55

predicting performance of, 142–143
rewarding honesty of, 476
rights of, 200–202
women as (*see* Women police officers)
Police-population ratio, 76, 214–216
Police professionalism, bureaucracy
    and, 110
Police-Public Contact Survey, 423,
    430–431
Police reform
failure of, in 1890s, 39–40
professionalization movement and,
    41–42
Police responsibilities. *See* Complex
    responsibilities of the police
Police science courses, 41
Police service aides, 241
Police Services Study, 79, 227, 229
Police subculture, 172–178
African American officers and, 182–183
corruption and, 469–470
discretion and, 380
diversification and, 186
impact of women officers on, 179–181
new perspectives on, 178–179
original concept of, 172–174
Police training
changes in, 149–157
consequences of inadequate, 154–155
de-escalation, 152–153
field training, 155–156
fragmented and inconsistent, 154
inadequacy of, 56, 462
innovations in, 152
preservice training, 151
probationary period, 157–159
on procedural justice, 155
return-to-duty training, 157
scenario-based, 153–154
of supervisors, 157
tactical decision-making, 153
on unconscious bias, 155
Police union contracts, 200, 201
Police unions, 43, 57, 116–121
as advocates for state legislation, 121
aspects of, 116
collective bargaining, 117
grievance procedures, 117
impact of, 120–121
impasse settlement and strikes, 117–120
Policewomen. *See* Women police officers
Policies and procedures
citizen oversight and, 396
standard operating procedure manual,
    394–395
systematic rulemaking, 395

Policies on the use of force, 13
Policing
capacity to use force as defining
    feature of, 174–175
dangers, potential *vs.* actual, 175–177
data-driven, 60
framework for understanding, 4–6
hot-spots, 60
as low-visibility work, 378
racial divide, 428–429
technology and, 45–47
Policing a Free Society (Goldstein), 345
Policy and procedure manual, 394
Policy manual, 394
Policy review, 396, 525
Political culture, police corruption
    and, 468
Political system, 513–514
Politicians, lack of support from, 169
Politics, corruption and, 37–38
Portland, Oregon community surveys, 493
Portland (Oregon) Police Department,
    56, 175, 331, 377
Predictive policing, 563
Preference of the victim, 381
Preliminary investigation, 291
Preservice training, 56, 93–94, 151
President's Crime Commission, 52, 73,
    227, 370, 419, 527
President's Task Force on 21st Century
    Policing, 3, 4, 55, 63, 131, 325
community policing and, 325, 329
on diversity, 143
on internal police management
    issues, 170
on policies and policy manuals, 392
Ramsey and, 59
on residency requirements, 138
Preventing Crime (Sherman), 333
Private security, 72, 90, 92
Proactive crime strategies, 283
Proactive integrity tests, 475–476
Probationary period, 157–159
Problem-oriented policing (POP), 21–22,
    58–60, 345–347, 490
compared to other policing forms, 354
effectiveness of, 349–353
future of, 352–353
in Newport News, 349–351
problem-solving process, 347–349
as research-based policy, 54
in San Diego, 351
traditional *versus,* 346
Problem solving
community policing and, 336–337
COMPSTAT and, 494

Procedural justice, 7–8, 155, 406–407
Professionalization movement, 40–45
  achievements of, 42–43
  administration and, 43–44
  community policing and, 58
  continuation of, 47–48
  military ethos, 43
  new law enforcement agencies, 44–45
  police unions, 43
  race relations and, 44
  reform agenda, 41–42
Professional standards units, 501–506
Prohibition of the 1920s, 467
Project on Policing Neighborhoods
    (1996-1997), 227, 232, 385
Project Safe Neighborhood, 310
Property crime investigations, 290
Prostitution, 263–266
Psychiatric emergency service
    referrals, 269
Psychiatric first aid, 268
Psychological tests and evaluations, 143
PTSR framework, 495
Public confidence, undermined by
    corruption, 457
Public interactions. See also
    Police-citizen interactions
  in the political era (1830s-1900),
    36–37
  respectful policing, 9
Public interest groups, accountability
    and, 529
Public Law 93-638, 84
Public opinion, 411–415
  factors affecting, 411–414
  impact of controversial incidents on,
    414–415
  mobilizing, against corruption, 482
  perspectives on American society
    and, 415
  surveys, 493
Public safety consolidation, 78
Pulled Over (Epp et al), 432
Pulling levers, 352

Q

Quasi-military style
  criticisms of, 103–105
  military model myth, 104
Quotas, 9, 178

R

Race
  assigning officers on basis
    of, 444–445

definition of, 408
  legitimate use of, in police work, 436
  major groups, 409–411
  official data on, 408–409
  public opinion about police and,
    411–412
  traffic stop outcomes by, 431
Race relations, 48
  in academy curricula, 56
  during professionalization
    movement, 44
  training, 445–446
Racial profiling, 15, 60–61, 562
  different contexts of, 434–435
  traffic enforcement and, 430–436
Racial segregation, 33, 51
Radio, two-way, 45, 46
Rampart scandal, 53, 80, 194, 464, 477,
    498–499, 501
RAND Corporation studies, 54, 292,
    296, 314, 560
Randomized integrity tests, 475
Rank hierarchy, 115
Reactive crime strategies, 283
Reality-based training, 132
Records management systems (RMSs),
    546–547
Recruitment, 132, 134–139
  of college students, 56
  effective screening of, 476, 478
  elements of process, 134–135
  military recruits, 146
  obstacles to, 140–141
  open recruitment efforts, 139
  RAND report on, 139
Re-Engineering Training on Police Use
    of Force, 522
Reform. See Police reform
Regents of the University of California v.
    Bakke (1978), 149
Relational databases, 546
Religious tensions, 36–37
Reno, Nevada, 458
Repeat offenders, 284, 308–309
Replacement effect (drug dealers), 303
Report on Police (Wickersham
    Commission), 41
Representative police forces, 443–444
Research
  federal support for, 561
  future of, 559–561
  importance of, 559–560
  police-researcher relationships, 560–561
  politics and, 560
Research and Best Practices program, 522
Research revolution, 53

Residency requirements, 138–139
Residual deterrence, 236
Resource dependency theory, 123–124
Respectful language, 390
Respectful policing, 9
Response time, 230–231
Return-to-duty training, 157
Reverse discrimination, 148
Reverse 911, 239
Rewards hierarchy, 115
Rialto, California, 551
Ride-along programs, 440
Rights of police officers, 200–202
The Rights of Police Officers (ACLU), 529
Riots
  civil rights movement and
    (1964-1968), 51
  in the 1800s, 33–34
  Kerner Commission and, 51
  race-related, 44, 61–62
  Watts district of Los Angeles (1965), 51
  Zoot Suit Riot, 48
Risk. See Dangerous police tasks
Rivalries, 109
Rizzo v. Goode (1976), 523
Robbery investigations, 290
Rockford, Michigan, 78
Rotten apple theory, 465, 466
Rotten pocket, 465
Routine supervision, 496
Roving task forces, 63–64

S

Sacramento, California virtual
    Neighborhood Watch, 360
St. Petersburg Police Department, 473
Salaries. See Compensation
San Antonio, Texas, 215
San Diego Police Department
  "Job Dimensions for Police Officers,"
    135, 136–137
  misconduct report policy, 506
  Pre-Investigation Questionnaire, 142
  sexual abuse scandals, 501–502
San Diego police-population ratio, 75, 215
San Francisco Office of Citizen
    Complaints, 525
San Jose, California police-population
    ratio, 215
San Jose Independent Police Auditor,
    194, 502–503
San Jose Police Department, 61
  EEO index and, 145, 146
  traffic stop patterns, 435
San Jose State College law enforcement
    program, 47

Santa Barbara (California) Police
    Department, 219
SARA Problem-Solving model, 347–349
    analysis, 349
    assessment, 349
    response, 349
    scanning, 348, 350
Scandals
    media-generated, 482
    Rampart scandal, 53, 80, 164, 194,
        464, 477, 498–499, 501
    sexual abuse, 501–502
Scenario-based training, 132, 153–154
Schenectady, New York, 242
School-based crime prevention
    programs, 285
Scottsdale Police Department Crime
    Analysis Unit, 555
Scott v. Hart (1979), 260
Search and seizure, 5, 514–515
    Fourth Amendment and, 154
    Mapp v. Ohio (1961), 50
    searches without arrests, 15
Sears, Roebuck, 90
Seattle, Washington, 276
Seattle Police Department
    community service officers, 241
    homeless-related situations and, 266
    policy on use of force, 152
    use of force policy, 519–520
Secret Service, 88
Securitas, 90
Segregation, 51
Selection tests, 141–142
Selective contact, 417–418
Senate Church Committee
    (1975-1976), 49
Seniority hierarchy, 115
Seniority system, impact of, 170–172
Sentencing Project, 426
Sergeants
    approaches to supervision by, 497
    failures in supervision, 497–498
    as patrol supervisors, 222–223
    performance evaluations and, 196,
        500–501
Service calls, 228
Service Employees International Union
    (SEIU), 90
Service style, 221
Settlement agreement, 6
Sexism, 180–181
Sex trafficking, 265
Sexual assault investigations, 290
Sexual harassment, 146, 182, 461
Sexual minorities, abuse of, 429

Sexual misconduct, by police officers,
    461–462
Shadow economy, 467
Sheriff
    in colonial America, 32–33
    department models, 81
    role of, 81–82
Shootings
    officer-involved, 16, 24, 157,
        420–422, 522, 528
    restrictive police policies and, 54
Sit-ins, 51
Situational couple violence, 158
Skeezers, 264
Skin tone, as factor in being stopped/
    arrested, 423
Slave patrol, 32
SMART Policing Initiative (SPI), 93
Social class, and attitude toward
    police, 413
Social control, 31, 33
Social disorder, 327
Social media, 551
    as a virtual Neighborhood Watch, 360
Social work model, 251
Sovereigns, 122
Span of control, 196, 222, 496–497
Special Counsel to the Los Angeles
    Sheriff's Department, 58
Special district police, 83
Special investigation commissions, 479
Specialization, 42, 106
Special Litigation Section, U.S. Justice
    Department, 6
Special unit assignments, 192–193
Spokane County Sheriff's Office, 301
Spouse abuse, 260. See also Domestic
    violence
Spying, by FBI, 49, 89
Standard operating procedure
    manual, 394
Standard operating procedure
    (SOP), 106
Standards. See also Minimum standards
    fragmentation and inconsistency
    of, 76
Standards and Guidelines for Internal
    Affairs, 501
Standards for Law Enforcement
    (CALEA), 94
Standards Relating to the Urban Police
    Function (American Bar Assoc.), 53
State governments, role of,
    93–94
State police, 44, 85–86, 557
Status hierarchy, 115

Stereotypes/stereotyping
    about cops, 133–134, 168
    arrests and, 429
    unconscious, 422
Stop, question and frisk (SQF), 356, 359
Stop and frisk programs, 21, 154, 356,
    376, 425–426
Strategic crime analysis, 555
Street cop culture, 187
Street gangs. See Gangs and gang-related
    crime
Street level bureaucrats, 378
Streetwalkers, 263–264
Stress. See Job stress
Strikes, police unions and, 117–120
Structuring discretion, 390
Subculture. See Police subculture
Subjectively arrested, 295
Suffolk County (New York) Police
    Department, 80, 495–496
Suicide, 198–199
Sunday Closing Law, 38–39
Supervision
    discretion and, 373
    elements of close/effective, 495–496
Supervisors
    as coaches/mentors/leaders, 498
    effectiveness of, and reducing
        corruption, 476
    failures of, 497–498
    innovative, 497
    of patrol officers, 495–498
    supportive, 222
    training of, 157
Supply reduction strategy, 303
Supreme Court
    impact of decisions on police,
        515–517
    Mapp v. Ohio (1961), 50
    Miranda decision, 49–50
    on search and seizure, 514–515
Surveys of public opinion, 493
Syracuse, New York, 242
Systematic bias, 15
Systematic discrimination, 433
Systematic rulemaking, 395
Systematic social observation, 226–228
Systematic under-enforcement of the
    law, 372–373

T

Tactical crime analysis, 554–555
Tactical decision-making, 153
Tactics refresher, 157
Tag readers, 549
Take-down techniques, 152

Tallahassee, Florida police recruits, 143
Tammany Hall, 37, 39
TASERS, 393, 553
Task Force Report: The Police
    (1967), 52
Task forces, 112–113
Teamsters Law Enforcement
    League, 116
Technological revolution
    patrol car, 45–46
    telephone, 45, 46–47
    two-way radio, 45, 46
Technology, 545–553
    in the field, 548–552
    future of, 552–553
    major applications of, 545–548
Telephone reporting units (TRUs), 238
Ten Most Wanted List, 49
Tennessee v. Garner (1985), 93,
    389, 421
1033 program, 62
Terrorism, 62
    domestic, 313–314
    foreign, 314
    responding to, 314–316
    scope and nature of, 313
Terrorist attacks of September 11, 2001,
    88, 89, 313, 314, 561
Terry v. Ohio, 177, 425
"Testilying," 506
Texas Department of Public Safety, 85
Texas Rangers, 44
Theft, by police officers, 460–461
The watch, 32–33
"Third degree," 527
Thomas A. Swift Electric Rifle
    (TASER), 393, 553
311 nonemergency numbers, 238–239
Title VII of the 1964
    Civil Rights Act, 144
Totalitarian societies, 490
Traditional supervisors, 222
Traffic enforcement, 253–256
    danger of, to police, 254
    demographics, 254
    discretion and, 369
    discrimination *versus* disparity, 432
    drunk-driving crackdowns, 255–256
    interpreting traffic stop data, 432–434
    investigatory stops, 431–432
    police justification for disparities in,
        435–436
    policies, 255
    racial profiling and, 430–436
    traffic stop outcomes, by race/
        ethnicity, 431

Traffic ticket quotas, 9
Training and training programs
    bias prevention, 15–16
    crisis intervention (CIT) programs, 23
    in discretion, 371
    reality-based, 132
    scenario-based, 132
    use of force policies and, 519
Transparency. *See* Openness and
    transparency
Transportation Security Administration
    (TSA), 88
Tribal police, 83–85, 410
Turnover, 202
Two dimensions, 490
287(g) agreements, 441
"Two Models of the Criminal Process"
    (Packer), 530

U

Unconscious bias, 16
    arrests and, 429
    use of deadly force and, 422
Unconscious stereotypes, 422
Undercover police work, 301–302
Underutilization, 148
Unfounding a crime, 288–289, 373
Uniform Crime Reporting (UCR) system,
    49, 72, 83, 233, 293, 345, 491
Uniforms, 104
Union contracts, 140
Union-organizing. *See also* Police unions
    emergence of police unions, 57
    police suppression of, 40
University campus police, 83, 84
U.S. Advisory Commission on
    Intergovernmental Relations, 82
U.S. Coast Guard, 88
U.S. Customs and Border
    Protection, 86, 87
U.S. Fish and Wildlife Service, 86
U.S. Forest Service, 86
U.S. Marshals Service, 90
U.S. Secret Service, 88
U.S. v. Dickerson (2000), 515
Use of force, 173, 480. *See also* Deadly
    force
    accountability on, 12–14
    capacity to use, as defining feature of
        policing, 174–175
    command-level review of, 499–500
    compliance with policies on, 393–394
    data on, 14–15
    excessive, 423–424
    independent investigations and, 16–17

officers with performance problems,
    506–507
pattern or practice case reforms, 519
patterns in, 424–425
police academy training shortcomings
    and, 151
training on, 152–153
waiting period following, 201
Use of Force Review Board, 14,
    499–500

V

Varieties of Police Behavior
    (Wilson), 384
Vengeful informants, 302
Vera Institute, 358
Verbal discourtesy, 9, 430
Vertical cliques, 109
Vigilantism, 33
Violence against citizens, 173. *See also*
    Officer-involved shootings; Police
    brutality; Use of force
Violent Crime Control Act (1994),
    61–62, 480–481, 518, 519
Violent resistance, 158

W

Wackenhut, 90, 92
Waiting periods, after use-of-force
    incident, 201
War on drugs, 304–305, 427
War on terrorism, 62
    changing roles in, 563
    expanding role of police in, 562
    impact of, on policing, 561–563
    personnel challenges, 562
    profiling as result of, 562
Warrior mindset, 7, 18, 131, 172,
    175–176
Washington, D.C.
    Metro Transit Police Department, 83
    Office of Police Complaints, 525
    police-population ratio, 215
    Repeat Offender Program (ROP), 309
Washington, D.C. Police Department,
    142, 170
    affirmative action and, 149
    corruption in, 478
    MOA and reform, 520
    police-population ratio, 75
    Ramsey and, 59
Watchman style, 221
The watch, 32–34
Weapons, technologically advanced,
    553. *See also* Guns and gun crimes

Websites, with SOP manuals, 394
Weeks v. United States (1914), 515
Weight requirement, 136
White Americans
    college credits and, 149
    reverse discrimination argument, 148
"Whorehouse riots," 34
Wichita, Kansas, 551
Wickersham Commission, 41, 47, 527
Wilkins v. Maryland, 61
Winter Park, Colorado, 78
Witness Protection Program, 90
Women police officers, 55–56, 146–147
    affirmative action and, 148
    attrition, 202
    Charlotte-Mecklenburg (North
        Carolina) and, 147

domestic violence and, 256–258
gender-related job stress, 198
hiring quotas, 148
impact of, on police subculture,
    179–181
limitations on, 42
misconduct and, 181
obstacles to recruitment of, 140
on patrol duty, 181
patrol officers, 181
as percentage of officers, 145
sexual harassment of, 182
stereotypes and, 134
Worcester (Massachusetts) police service
    aides, 241
Workable caseload, 292
Work shifts, 171

Work styles, 189–190
World Trade Center attacks, 62, 561
Wrong Then, Wrong Now, 562

Z
Zero-tolerance policing
    characteristics of, 353–355
    compared to other policing forms, 354
    effectiveness of, 355–360
    impact on poor and minority
        communities, 358–359
    potential problems with, 357
    social influence of, 353
Zoot Suit Riot, 48

Globalization and
Business Practice

To William Nichols with boundless thanks for your enthusiasm and encouragement

Globalization and Business Practice

Managing Across Boundaries

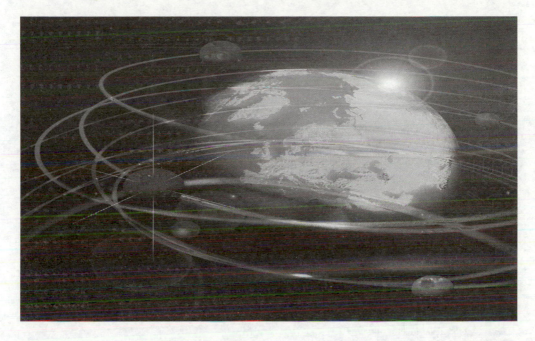

Barbara Parker

SAGE Publications

London · Thousand Oaks · New Delhi

SAGE Publications Ltd
6 Bonhill Street
London EC2A 4PU

SAGE Publications Inc
2455 Teller Road
Thousand Oaks, California 91320

SAGE Publications India Pvt Ltd
32, M-Block Market
Greater Kailash - I
New Delhi 110 048

British Library Cataloguing in Publication data

A catalogue record for this book is available from the British Library
ISBN 0 7619 5693 X
ISBN 0 7619 5694 8 (pbk)

Library of Congress catalog card number 98-60535

Typeset by Type Study, Scarborough, North Yorkshire
Printed in Great Britain by Butler & Tanner Ltd, Frome and London

Contents

List of Tables and Figures   vi
Preface   x
Acknowledgements   xiii

1   Introduction   2

2   Global Enterprises   46

3   The Global Role of Business   98

4   Global Culture   160

5   The Global Economy: Trade, FDI, Capital   234

6   The Global Economy: Labor   306

7   Global Political and Legal Environments   388

8   Global Industries and Tasks   456

9   Globalization of Technologies   516

10   Globalization of the Natural Environment   590

Index   648

List of Tables and Figures

Tables

1.1	Asian GDPs	14
1.2	Sample acquisitions for 1996 and 1997	17
1.3	World's top 10 branded goods, 1996	22
1.4	Blurring boundaries	26
2.1	Stateless organizations, 1997	53
2.2	Success characteristics for global start-ups	57
2.3	Size and ownership of global enterprises	58
2.4	Dimensions of paradox	66
2.5	Internal focus of managerial attention	76
2.6	A comparison of domestic and global mindsets	89
3.1	The top 50 companies from the *Business Week* 100	105
3.2	World's top 100 economies, 1995	107
3.3	Asia's billionaires in the $5 billion club	108
3.4	Confucian values evident in China and Japan	126
3.5	US, Japanese, and Western European models of business	128
3.6	Women in positions of corporate authority, 1997 and 1998	132
3.7	Levels of strategy defined	141
3.8	CEO roles and behaviors	147
3.9	Transnationally competent managers	149
4.1	Cultural contrasts	170
4.2	Scores on four national cultural dimensions for 53 countries or regions	172
4.3	Country comparisons on six dimensions of culture	176
4.4	Globalization of popular music	186
4.5	Global demographic groups	197
4.6	Cultural barriers vs winning shared values	205

4.7	What you see is (not) what you get	212
4.8	Sources of workplace diversity	216
4.9	Corporate diversity initiatives	218
4.10	Characteristics of successful global team leaders	221
5.1	Index of Economic Freedom, selected 1997 rankings	241
5.2	Global price comparison of selected goods and services (dollars)	247
5.3	How they stack up	251
5.4	The hamburger standard	252
5.5	Real GDP growth, in annual average (%)	253
5.6	Hidden champions	258
5.7	World direct investment flows (billions of dollars)	263
5.8	Approaches to decision-making	285
5.9	Activities across borders	288
6.1	Normal working time in the manufacturing sector, 1992	319
6.2	Hourly compensation worldwide	321
6.3	Engineering compensation	323
6.4	Hourly wage comparisons in the international clothing industry, 1992	324
6.5	Unemployment rates	333
6.6	High unemployment forecasts (%)	334
6.7	Changes in international human rights regimes, 1945–1985	348
6.8	Staffing philosophy	364
6.9	Principles behind the new vs old career paradigms	370
7.1	Tax freedom day in selected countries, 1995	394
7.2	Privatization, by industry, 1994	398
7.3	Acts of aggression, 1996	407
7.4	A sample of trading groups	411
7.5	Pacific Rim trade: statistics on APEC members	419
7.6	Nongovernmental organizations: a sample	426
7.7	Conflict diagnostic model	447
8.1	Intrafirm activities by industry, 1982	467
8.2	Global industries and participants	468
8.3	Global industry leaders, 1997	471
8.4	The hidden champions' both/and philosophy	474
8.5	*Les Hénokiens* 22	479
8.6	Restructuring industrial economies	480
8.7	National competitiveness rankings, 1995–1997	483
8.8	Fostering fit: matching global demands with business competencies	490
8.9	Global presence and strategy combine to influence the relationship between a business and its industry	496
8.10	Who is where? Globalization at the top	500
8.11	Sixteen characteristics for achieving sustainable advantage through people	500

8.12 Strategy, structure, and cultural behaviors appropriate to firm presence abroad   502
9.1   Historical innovations and breakthroughs   522
9.2   The effects of television technology   528
9.3   Information Age change   533
9.4   Internet hosts per person, 1996   549
9.5   World Wide Web domains, 1998   551
9.6   Internet use and national priorities   556
9.7   Northern Telecom's transformation, 1985–1995   565
10.1 Labor productivity in OECD nations, 1960, 1985, 1995, measured by value added per hour worked   594
10.2 Highest six estimated populations for 2050 (millions)   612
10.3 By the millions   619
10.4 DFD applications   631

Figures

2.1   Managing globalization of business   74
3.1   The corporate business model and the corporate community model of business   123
3.2   The process ends where it begins   127
3.3   Latin American values as illustrated in layers   130
3.4   Where the overseas (nonresident) Indians live   130
3.5   Evolution of organizational structures   139
3.6   The self-renewal process in Japanese firms   144
4.1   Culture: what you see doesn't tell you why   165
4.2   Maslow's hierarchy of needs   168
4.3   Schwartz's two-dimensional model of motivational values   178
4.4   Traditional influences of culture on business organizations   180
4.5   Business activities in a global context   182
4.6   Identify the icon   213
5.1   A closed national economic system   242
5.2   An open system view of national economies   244
5.3   Floating away   248
5.4   Human Development Index: country ranking, 1994 (selected countries)   255
5.5   Expanding calculus of self-interest   257
5.6   Service industries   260
5.7   Changes in ratio of real trade to real GDP, 1960–1994 (%)   262
5.8   Latin America looks inward   265
5.9   Performance of the Dow Jones World Stock Market Indexes   267

5.10	Dollar/yen fluctuations, 1990–1998	271
5.11	Global functional structure	289
5.12	Global divisional structure	290
5.13	Global matrix structure	291
6.1	The world's labor force by sector and country income level	313
6.2	Comparative compensation	322
6.3	By how much does education raise wages?	327
6.4	The immigrant waves reaching Europe: origins of asylum-seekers in Europe in 1988 before the Berlin Wall collapsed, and in 1991	336
6.5	Two scenarios: wage convergence/wage divergence	344
6.6	Spider's web organizations	358
6.7	Japanese- and Western-style organizational knowledge creation	361
7.1	Indonesia's Agency for Strategic Industries	401
7.2	Gangs and global crime	409
7.3	Who are we?	415
7.4	ISO 9000 leadership process	431
7.5	Corruption perception index, 1997	444
7.6	The stress curve	445
8.1	Five forces of industry competition	464
8.2	The shamrock organization	504
8.3	Structural orientations	505
8.4	Examples of interlinkages for N.V. Philips	508
9.1	Growth of scientific knowledge	538
9.2	Nolan's stage theory of computer use in business	541
9.3	Personal computer shipments in millions	545
9.4	The shape of the Internet	547
9.5	International connectivity	548
9.6	The pace of change: the market for global telecommunications services	558
9.7	Industry power shift	564
9.8	Some technology hot spots	567
9.9	Business software piracy rates, 1994–1996	572
10.1	Population growth	614
10.2	The issue wheel	618
10.3	Gassing up the world: the world's biggest emitters of carbon dioxide (in millions of metric tons)	627

Preface

MANAGING ACROSS BOUNDARIES

The world increasingly resembles a global marketplace where integration across 'traditional' borders is evident in almost every dimension of life. The daily news demonstrates growing worldwide integration across boundaries like time or national borders that once seemed immutable, and in academic fields the boundaries between disciplines like management, finance, marketing and other fields also have become more fluid. These and other global shifts described in this book have resulted in re-evaluation of business academics and also of business practice. Increasingly, a world with fewer boundaries calls for organizations able to transcend vertical and horizontal boundaries and create hybrids that are both cost effective and responsible to local, regional, domestic, international, and global communities of interest. Unlike other books that purport to map the 'one best way' to approach a topic of study, this book argues that globalization requires thoughtful combinations of management tradition with emerging business practices. Further, it raises many questions about globalization to be answered as today's students make business decisions.

TEXT FEATURES

This text is unique because it presents national, business, and human opportunities and challenges in the context of growing globalization in six spheres: culture, economics, politics, industries, technology, and the natural environment, to pose important questions about life, work, and management in an interdependent world. This is the first book to look at all of these environments at the global level, and one of a handful of books to link global activities with business management practices. Following the first three introductory chapters, each chapter provides an intensive examination of one of the six global environments listed above; each raises important questions about globalization; and each describes ways business managers operate in global environments. For example, Chapter 4 (a) examines the topic of cultural globalization, (b) raises issues associated with worldwide cultural globalization, and (c) describes how business managers develop globally competent people, processes, and structures. The wide range of global and managerial topics covered in chapter descriptions of people, processes, and structures offers great teaching and learning flexibility. Those most interested in strategic management can concentrate their reading on processes like strategy and structural issues associated with globalization in each chapter, whereas teachers and students of organizational behavior may devote their energies to understanding how globalizaation affects people in terms of hiring, development, training, teamwork, and leadership. Additionally, chapters subsequent to the first need not be read in sequence, although the first three chapters help to set the context for consideration of global environments in Chapters 4–10.

The text draws from tradition and current research generated by academicians and practitioners in multiple fields within and outside schools of business, and in doing so crosses disciplinary boundaries. The multidisciplinary scope of the book not only reinforces the global nature of the text, it also provides many ways to show how diversity of worldwide business extends far beyond activities of firms from postindustrial and developed economies. The introductory case for each chapter outlines concepts reinforced throughout the chapter, and each chapter contains examples and cases based on the experiences of firms other than those based in the US and other advanced economies, including the experiences of small- to medium-sized firms in the global arena. Finally, each chapter concludes with a summary of key chapter concepts and a set of discussion questions.

TEACHING AND LEARNING AIDS

Evidence of global integration surrounds us, but confirmatory data can be elusive or contradictory. When the latter occurred, I relied most often on data produced by nongovernmental agencies, particularly those with an established reputation. Most of the latter provide periodic electronic updates, and can be reached at websites accessible through my homepage.

Internet resources, particularly the World Wide Web, provide a particularly rich source of data on globally active businesses and research. At the same time, printed library resources should not be overlooked in the search for insight into the theory and management of global business activities. Valuable print and electronic resources have been collected and appear in a comprehensive students' web page developed in support of this text.

The author wishes to refer readers to her students' homepage at http://www.seattleu.edu/~parker where she makes regularly updated material available. All material contained in that site is the author's, and has no connection whatever with Sage Publications, who disclaim all responsibility for the site and its contents.

Acknowledgements

The global scope of this book produced challenges made less daunting by opportunities to field test content with Seattle University students from around the world. First and foremost they earned my gratitude and thanks for their patience, encouragement, and helpful insights. Tom Thompson particularly helped by drafting Chapter 9. Colleagues and friends at Seattle University and the University of Auckland also contributed ideas and personal support for which I am very grateful, and I particularly applaud James Tallerico, Barbara Di Ferrante, and David Ackerman for their efforts. The Executive Committee at the Albers School of Business and Economics and the Seattle University Summer Faculty Fellowship Committee provided summer grant funds that helped immeasurably.

Many thanks also to the people at Sage Publications who worked so hard with me on this project, including: Sue Jones who originally committed to the text; Rosemary Nixon and Hans Lock, Commissioning Editors; Vanessa Harwood, Production Editor; Justin Dyer, Copyeditor; Andy Esson, Designer.

Thanks also go to the following reviewers who provided wonderful ideas and helpful feedback: Peggy Golden, Florida Atlantic University; Robert Moran, American Graduate School of International Management (Thunderbird); Cynthia Hardy, McGill University and the University of Melbourne; and Nancy Napier, Boise State University.

Finally, I thank my family. The contents of this book span multiple boundaries and transcend more than one academic tradition to describe globalization. My desire to forge new connections surely comes from my parents Robert N. and Charlotte Bush who long ago confounded the boundaries of local tradition by raising their three little daughters abroad. Thank you. Thanks also to my husband and partner William Nichols whose patience is astounding. My children Katherine Parker and Gabriel Parker are among the many seeking world justice and to them I offer encouragement and say 'good on ya'.

PERMISSIONS

The author and publishers wish to thank the following for permission to use copyright material:

Academy of Management for **Figure 6.6** from Quinn et al. (1996) 'Leveraging intellect', *Academy of Management Executive*, 10: 3, p. 21; **Table 2.2** from Oviatt & McDougall (1995) 'Global start-ups: Entrepreneurs on a worldwide stage', *Academy of Management Executive*, 9: 2, pp. 30–43; **Box 10.1** from Gladwin et al. (1995) 'Shifting paradigms for sustainable development: Implications for management theory and research', *Academy of Management Review*, 20: 4, p. 877; **Figure 8.4** from Ghoshal and Bartlett (1990) 'The multinational corporation as an interorganizational network', *Academy of Management Review*, 15:4, p. 605.

Brigham Young University, The David M. Kennedy Center for International Studies, for **Figure 3.3** from Spencer (1991) *Understanding Latin American Underdevelopment and Tension with the United States: A Question of Applying the Right Paradigm*. Copyright (c) 1991.

Business Horizons for **Figure 7.6** adapted from Kreitner (1982) 'Personal wellness: It's just good business', *Business Horizons*, 25, Figure 2 p. 32. Copyright (c) 1982 by the Foundation for the School of Business at Indiana University.

Business Week for **Table 4.9** from 'Diversity, making the business case', *Business Week*, 9.12.96, Special Advertising Section, Exhibit 6.

The Economist for **Table 6.2** from 'Sliding scales', *The Economist*, 2.11.96, p. 17; **Figure 5.4** from *The Economist*, 21.6.97, p. 108; **Figure 7.3** from 'More-or-less European Union', *The Economist*, 26.8.95, p. 46; and **Table 5.4** from *The Economist*, 12.4.97, p. 71. Copyright (c) *The Economist*, 1996, 1997, 1995, 1997.

Elsevier Science Ltd for **Table 9.1** from Makridakis (1989) 'Management in the Twenty First Century', *Long Range Planning*, 22: 2, 37–53.

The Free Press, a Division of Simon & Schuster, for **Figure 8.1** from Porter (1980) *Competitive Strategy: Techniques for Analyzing Industries and Competitors*, Fig. 1.1, p. 4. Copyright (c) 1980 by The Free Press.

Richard H. Hall for **Table 3.4** for Hall and Xu, 'Research Note: Run silent, run deep – cultural influences on organizations in the Far East', *Organization Studies*, 569–576.

The Haworth Press, Inc. for **Table 4.5** from Hassan and Katsanis (1994), 'Global market segment strategies and trends' in Hassan and Kaynak, eds. *Globalization of Consumer Markets: Structures and Strategies*, p. 58.

Hazel Henderson for **Figure 5.5** from Henderson (1996, 1997) *Building a Win-Win World: Life Beyond Global Economic Warfare*, Berrett-Koehler Publishers, p. 154 (original appeared in Henderson (1981, 1988) *The Politics of the Solar Age: Alternatives to Economics*, Anchor/Doubleday).

Jossey-Bass Publishers for **Table 4.10** from O'Hara-Devereaux and Johansen (1994) *Globalwork*, p. 106.

The New York Times for **Table 8.5** from Tagliabue, 'This business club is the real old boys' network', *The New York Times*, 30.10.94, p. 4; and **Figure 5.8** from Brooke, 'South America's big trade strides', *The New York Times*, 10.12.94.

Nortel plc for **Figure 9.7** and **Table 9.7** from Monty (1997) 'Northern Telecom: The anatomy of a transformation', pp. 4, 24.

Oxford University Press, Inc. for **Figure 6.7** from Nonaka and Takeuchi (1995) *The Knowledge-Creating Company: How Japanese Companies Create the Dynamics of Innovation*. Copyright (c) 1995 by Oxford University Press, Inc.; and **Figure 6.1** from World Bank (1995) *World Development Report 1995: Workers in an Integrating World*. Copyright (c) by The International Bank for Reconstruction and Development/The World Bank.

Routledge for **Figure 8.3** from White and Poynter (1990) 'Organizing for world-wide advantage', p. 97 and **Figure 3.6** from Nonaka (1990) 'Managing globalization as a self-renewing process', p. 70, in Bartlett, Doz and Hedlund, eds. *Managing the Global Firm*.

Sage Publications, Inc. for **Figure 10.2** from Stead and Stead (1996) *Management for a Small Planet*, 2nd ed., p. 22.

Seattle Times Co. for **Figure 6.4** from *The Seattle Times*, 26.11.92.

Sloan Management Review for **Table 7.7** from Greenhalgh (1986) 'Managing conflict' *Sloan Management Review*, 27: 4, pp. 45–51.

Sandra Thiedemann for **Table 4.1** adapted from Thiedemann (1991) *Bridging Cultural Barriers for Corporate Success*, Lexington Books.

Time Inc. for **Table 10.4** from Bylinsky, 'Manufacturing for reuse', *Fortune*, 6.2.95, pp. 103–12. Copyright (c) 1995 Time Inc.; **Table 8.2** from 'Global 500 list', *Fortune*, July 1996. Copyright (c) 1996 Time Inc.; Merrifield, 'Wharton School', *Fortune*, 4.4.94, p. 75. Copyright (c) 1994 Time Inc.; **Table 8.3** for data from 'Global 500', *Fortune*, 4.8.97. Copyright (c) 1997 Time Inc.; and **Figure 9.3** and **Table 9.4** for data from Martin, 'When info worlds collide', *Fortune*, 28.10.96, pp. 130–33. Copyright (c) 1996 Time Inc.

UNCTAD for **Tables 5.7** and **6.4** for data from (1994) *World Investment Report 1994*, Sales No. E94.II.A.14.

John Wiley & Sons Ltd for **Table 5.9** from Melin (1992) 'Internationalization as a strategy process', *Strategic Management Journal*, 13, p. 100; and **Table 8.1** from Kobrin (1991) *Strategic Management Journal*. Copyright (c) John Wiley & Sons Ltd.

John Wiley & Sons, Inc. for **Figure** 7.4 from Badiru (1995) *Industry's Guide to ISO 9000*; and **Table 4.2** from Bangert and Pirzadas (1992) 'Culture and negotiation', *The International Executive*, 34: 1, pp. 43–64.

The World Bank for **Figure 6.5** from (1995) *World Development Report 1995*; **Table 3.2** from (1996) *World Development Report 1996*; and **Figures** 5.7 and 6.1 from (1996) *World Bank Policy and Research Bulletin*, Aug.–Oct. 1995, April–June 1996.

Every effort has been made to trace the copyright holders, but if any have been inadvertently overlooked the publishers will be pleased to make the necessary arrangement and acknowledgement at the first opportunity.

Chapter 1

Introduction

CHANGES IN CHINA SHAPE WORLDWIDE OPPORTUNITIES AND THREATS   4

Globalization variously defined   6
Definitions affect business responses   6
Permeable borders of globalization   6
Organizations shape globalization and its definition   7

Organization of the text   7
A brief review of chapter contents   9

Sources of globalization   12
Technology   12
Economy   13
Politics   17
Culture   19
Natural environment   20
Business activities in global industries   21

The changing landscape of management   25

A second look at 'changes in China'   28

Examining business traditions   31

Perspectives on globalization   32
Globalization: nothing new?   32
The New World Order and neo-colonialism   33

Transformative social forces   36
Businesses as countervailing forces   36

Key chapter concepts   37

Review and discussion questions   39

References   41

CHANGES IN CHINA SHAPE WORLDWIDE OPPORTUNITIES AND THREATS

China's industrial output between 1990 and 1995 grew at an average annual rate of 22.8%, attracting interest from foreign investors and native Chinese alike. Many of the latter abandoned traditional agricultural work to search for jobs in urban areas, and perhaps, like busy city-dwellers everywhere, they found it easier and more desirable to substitute more meat, eggs, and milk for their traditional grain-based diet of the past.

Urbanization and economic development as well as changes in diet provided new opportunities for business. Dietary change, for example, has yielded business opportunities both within and outside China. For example, farmers in China are shifting their production from grain by building ponds for farm-raised fish or grain-fed livestock. Additionally, with migration from the country to China's cities, there is growing need for urban housing and business services such as telecommunications and freight delivery. Importers of grain see an opportunity to enter China's still large market for rice. To date, China's demand for grain imports has made Vietnam the third largest exporter of rice in the world. Increased imports of grain from Vietnam, as well as increased industrial production throughout China, have provided entrepreneurs all over Asia with business opportunities that make them more interdependent with business activities throughout the world. Within the agricultural industry, Chinese and Vietnamese farmers now find their prices are closely linked to world commodity prices rather than to the Communist world alone. Further, firms like Motorola, Siemens, and General Motors are providing foreign direct investment (FDI) amounting to billions of dollars fueling economic growth in manufacturing as well as agricultural and service sectors, creating jobs and further stimulating exodus from rural to urban areas. One example of a foreign direct investor is the Anglo-Dutch firm Unilever, which committed £100 million to seven joint